BOOKBINDING
AND THE CONSERVATION
OF BOOKS

BOOKBINDING
AND THE CONSERVATION
OF BOOKS

A DICTIONARY OF
DESCRIPTIVE TERMINOLOGY

Matt T. Roberts

and

Don Etherington

Drawings by Margaret R. Brown

LIBRARY OF CONGRESS

Washington
1982

A NATIONAL PRESERVATION
PROGRAM PUBLICATION

Library of Congress Cataloging in Publication Data:

Roberts, Matt, 1929-
    Bookbinding and the conservation of books;
    A dictionary of descriptive terminology.
    Bibliography: p. 289
    Supt. of Docs. no.: LC 1.2:B64/3
    1. Bookbinding—Dictionaries. 2. Books—
Conservation and restoration—Dictionaries.
I. Etherington, Don. II. Title.
Z266.7.R62   686.3'03   81-607974
ISBN O-8444-0366-O   AACR2

For sale by
the Superintendent of Documents, U.S. Government Printing Office
Washington, D.C. 20402

TABLE OF CONTENTS

v

The old saw that you can't judge a book by its cover is not precisely true. Actually, it cannot be applied to the earliest known form of the book, the Codex. Many surviving Codices possess bindings which are almost an integral part of the text. Their fundamental designs and the frequent sumptuous embellishment of the covers with gold and silver mounts encrusted with jewels or semi-precious gems or enamels offer compelling insight into the contents of the books they protect. These magnificent survivors of many centuries of use and adoration are among the great bibliophilic treasures of those fortunate libraries and museums who possess them. It is a matter of great regret that in many instances the bindings have been stripped, stolen, or otherwise removed from the texts they encased, for such bindings frequently offer valid evidence of their places of execution. What would we not give to know what kind of binding originally was placed on the noble *Book of Kells,* since it might well have provided the missing clues to the earliest history and provenance of this great manuscript of the Gospels.

In many instances certain book covers artistically admired for their craftsmanship in the use of ivory, silver, and, at a later date, leather remain as single objects, and we can only speculate about the texts they encased. We owe a great debt to the Egyptian Christians, the Copts, who most probably were the first to use leather as covers for their scriptural texts. Once introduced it became the most common material used for bookbinding throughout Europe; it was not supplanted essentially until the nineteenth century when cloth bindings became common. Velvet had, of course, been used much earlier for embroidered bindings.

Early on binding developed as a craft, and it became a highly skilled craft, one which has endured to this day. Over the years as books proliferated the need for bookbinding increased; the invention of printing provided a new impetus to the craft and probably revolutionized it. The earliest printed books were issued by their printers in unbound sheets; those who purchased them arranged to have them bound according to their individual requirements. That is one of the reasons why the study and investigation of fifteenth-century bindings can reveal such interesting details about the early history of these original covers. We know, for example, that a number of copies of Johann Gutenberg's famous Bible of 1455 were bound not at Mainz, where this Bible was printed, but at Erfurt; and we also know that one of the binders in that community was named Johannes Fogel, since one of the blind stamps used to embellish the leather stretched over the original wooden boards contained his own name. Other bindings of a slightly later period carry on their leather covers a stamp which is a recognizable portrait of an early printer, Johann de Westphalia; another group reveals the arms of the city of Cologne, providing valid evidence of the place of binding. Indeed, the study of the basic designs of early bindings and the blind stamps used to decorate them has become the object of intensive bibliographic research. The late Ernst Kyriss devoted many years of productive scholarship to documenting the sources of innumerable early German bindings carrying blind stamps. For the early years of the sixteenth century, Konrad Haebler performed a similar service by categorizing and classifying the numerous rolls used on German bindings of that period. The bindings of other countries have also received careful attention, but much more work remains to be done.

It is not surprising to find early German books in contemporary Italian bindings, and early Italian printed books in German or French bindings, indicating that the book trade was quite mobile. Stylistically, it is often possible to identify early and also later bindings by their country and even their city of origin. It is also true that rich and affluent bibliophiles such as Matthias Corvinus (King of Hungary), the King of Naples, and later Jean Grolier of Lyons and Paris, one of the greatest of all bibliophiles, took great pains to have their libraries appropriately and sumptuously bound. Books from these and other great collections are easily recognized and highly prized by their present-day owners. England and, especially, France have produced countless royal bindings of extraordinary interest and variety.

The art of fine bookbinding is well represented in France, where it continues to flourish. One must not lose sight of the lacquered bindings from Islam (a separate chapter in themselves), the embroidered covers executed by English needleworkers in the seventeenth century, or the beautiful silk bindings found on Chinese and Japanese books of all periods. There is infinite variety to be found in the study of this historic craft.

There is also much to be said about early binding in this country and much more to be written. Although in its earliest period it was frankly derivative and with certain exceptions can hardly be regarded as distinguished, there were attempts at refinement.

There has been a tremendous interest in the history of bookbinding in this country in recent years, stimulated in part by the late Dorothy Miner's monumental exhibition of bindings, principally from American collections, which was handsomely mounted at the Baltimore Museum of Art in 1957. Over seven hundred exceptional bindings, covering more than fourteen centuries, were on display. It was a delight for all those who shared in it or saw it, and its impact is still being felt today. Another stimulant to this heightening of interest is the emphasis that has been placed recently on the preservation and restoration of all aspects of the book, including papyrus, vellum, and paper. Modern scientific approaches have introduced a new vocabulary, much of which is not readily comprehended by those whose interests are most intimately concerned with the books of all ages.

The purpose of a foreword is to inform the reader, if he cares to peruse it, about the contents of the text it introduces. The text of the present book is not a history of bookbinding—although there is a great deal of history about the craft contained herein, and it also discusses the materials used, the notable binders whose names illuminate it, and other useful information. It is rather an up-to-date dictionary.

The succinct definitions and explanations, as well as the biographical vignettes, contained in this dictionary will be a boon to those who seek this kind of information. Those concerned, whether they are practicing binders, technicians, rare book librarians, collectors, or simply laymen, will find this a welcome source of answers to their questions. Not the least of these is the one frequently asked of me during my long service in the Library of Congress as Chief of the Rare Book Division. How can I best treat the leather bindings in my personal library? But this is only one of the thousands of questions to which this dictionary provides the ready answers. The text speaks accurately and helpfully to all those who will seek it out and profit from the immense amount of information it presents in a lucid and comprehensible form.

FREDERICK R. GOFF
Honorary Consultant in
Early Printed Books
Library of Congress

Although numerous books, both theoretical and practical, have been published on the subject of bookbinding and the conservation of archival materials, there would seem to be a need for one that approaches the subject by examining the meaning and usage of the many terms, expressions, and names pertaining to the various subjects. The nomenclature of bookbinding, its offshoots and more recent progeny, has not, at least insofar as the present writers have been able to determine, been presented in a comprehensive dictionary, although various aspects of the book and its production have been explored in dictionary form, sometimes superlatively, as in the American Paper and Pulp Association's *Dictionary of Paper* and John Carter's *A B C for Book Collectors*. The authors of this volume hope that it will help fill a considerable gap in the literature of conservation, one that has for some time been all too evident.

Although this dictionary is intended first and foremost for those actively involved in one or more aspects of the overall field of bookbinding and book conservation, including bookbinders, conservators of library and archival materials, and the like, it is perhaps no less intended for those working in related fields, such as bibliography and librarianship, where the many terms and expressions relating to the overall field may be less familiar and even more confusing.

The compilers accept full responsibility for the selection of terms for inclusion, as well as for the even more difficult task of rejection. The definitions themselves, although herein the responsibility of the same persons, were, whenever possible, drawn from the most authoritative sources available (as indicated by the number in parentheses at the end of a definition, which refers to the Sources and Bibliography section) and supplemented by the experience of the authors. Even though the bibliography and sources cited represent but a relatively small segment of the extensive corpus of literature in the field of conservation, we believe they provide a reasonably good sampling and may benefit the reader by offering an authoritative source for the terms and sometimes providing a source for further investigation. Definitions that do not cite a source are entirely the responsibility of the authors.

Where a term has more than one definition, each is numbered and arranged in its descending order of significance in relation to bookbinding.

The arrangement of the dictionary is letter-by-letter, rather than word-by-word, which means that, while the placement of terms such as **C-stage,** or **m. m. system,** etc., will be within the body of the respective letters of the alphabet, and not at the beginning, there should be no problem with locating hyphenated or one- or two-word structures, such as **springback,** or the more accepted **spring-back,** as long as the spelling of the term is known. The same is true of **fore edge** (correct), as opposed to **foreedge** (sometimes used but awkward). (Foredge would be incorrect.) Fore edge, it should be noted, is only hyphenated when used as a modifier, e.g., **fore-edge painting.** The arrangement of the dictionary, then, is:

head	**head box**
headband	**headcap**
headbanding	**headed outline tool**
headbolt	**head trim**

The most common (sometimes simply the most commonly encountered) form or spelling of a term has been used, e.g., **myrabolans,** not myrabalans, **gauffered edges,** not **gauffred, gaufré,** or **goffered,** with the variations in spelling being included with the bold-faced heading. Where a term is also called by another name the synonym is given at the end of the definition, e.g.:

abaca. Also called "manila hemp."
adhesive binding. Also called "perfect binding" or "unsewn binding."

See references have been used extensively, as have *see also* references, which refer the reader to other terms closely, or sometimes only indirectly, related to the term being discussed. *See also* references and cross references to the terms defined in this dictionary which are cited within the definition itself are set in small capitals, e.g.:

forel. A grade of PARCHMENT made from split sheepskin and dressed in imitation of VELLUM.

There is always the problem of the extent to which one wishes to go in defining any one term. While there may be relatively little one can say, or would want to say, about a material such as **Armenian bole,** or a procedure such as **lengthwise lettering,** one could offer quite a lengthy discourse on the finer considerations of **break** or the molecular structure of **glue.** But this is a dictionary, not an encyclopedia, a guide to the vocabulary of a field, not a compendium on a specific subject.

A number of persons, both near and far, have generously contributed both their time and expertise in evaluating and criticizing this work. George Kelly, Research Scientist, Research and Testing Office of the Library's Preservation Office, read and commented on the chemical terms. Harold Tribolet, retired, formerly Manager, Graphic Conservation Department, R. R. Donnelly & Sons, Chicago, Illinois, read and offered comments on an earlier version of the work. Bernard Middleton, of London, bookbinder and historian of bookbinding and its related subjects, read and offered extensive comments on the manuscript, especially those terms relating to hand bookbinding and bookbinding history. John Chalmers, bibliophile and former Librarian of the Washington Cathedral Library, Mount Saint Alban, Washington, D.C., read the final version and wrote many pages of comments and criticism. Betty Roberts read and reread several manuscripts and proofread still others. Margaret Schaffer typed the final manuscript and also read the galleys and page proof. Our deep and heartfelt thanks to all.

A DICTIONARY
OF DESCRIPTIVE
TERMINOLOGY

a. The front or recto side of a leaf of a book. It is called "a" when the leaves rather than the pages are numbered. The back or verso side is referred to as "b." *See also:* FOLIATION (2).

aa pattern. The code designation for a book cloth embossed with a watered silk pattern over the T PATTERN, producing a MOIRÉ EFFECT. *See also:* MOIRÉ BOOK CLOTH.

abaca. A type of plantain or banana (*Musa textilis*), native to the Philippine Islands. The outer sheaths of its leaf stems yield a fiber used extensively in the manufacture of certain papers, e.g., saturating papers, where great strength is required. The fibers range in length from 3 to 12 mm, the average being 6 mm, and vary in thickness from 0.016 to 0.032 mm, averaging 0.024 mm. They taper very gradually towards the ends; the central canal is large, and the fine cross-hatchings are numerous. Also called "Manila hemp." (17, 323)

aberrant copy. A copy of a book that has unmistakable binding and/or printing errors and not merely simple defects. (156)

abhesive. A material having the capability of resisting ADHESION. Surfaces are coated with abhesive substances to reduce sticking, heat sealing, and the like. Silicone paper is an example of an abhesive material. (222)

abrasion. The rubbing or wearing away of a material due to contact with another material. Some very large books, manuscripts, etc., may be damaged by abrasion because of the large surface area of the leaves rubbing over one another (particularly when the publication is being opened or closed), as may the leather coverings of books when they are removed from the shelves. Dust, also, is a significant cause of abrasion of book papers and covers.

abrasion resistance. The ability of materials, such as paper, board, cloth, leather, etc., to withstand the abrading action of the same or another material, e.g., other paper, dust, a book shelf, etc. The property is usually measured in terms of rate of loss of material by weight when abraded under specified conditions and length of time. *See also:* RESISTANCE TO WEAR. (17, 58, 72)

abrasives. Substances used to wear down or clean other substances. Abrasives may occur naturally (e.g., diamond, corundum, pumice, etc.), or be manufactured (e.g., silicon carbide, fused alumina, metallic abrasives, and the like). The hardness of an abrasive is measured by MOH'S SCALE, which is arbitrary. For numerous grinding and buffering purposes, the graded grains of abrasive are bonded together in a vitreous rubber or metallic matrix to produce grinding wheels; for hand use, the grains are bonded to paper or cloth by means of a suitable adhesive.

absolute humidity. The actual quantity of water vapor present in a given volume of air. Absolute humidity is expressed either in grams per cubic meter, or in grams per cubic foot. *See also:* HUMIDITY; RELATIVE HUMIDITY.

absorbency. The degree of receptivity of a material to liquids, either in liquid or gaseous form. Measures of absorbency include: 1) the time a material requires to absorb a specific volume of liquid; 2) the rate of rise of a liquid along a vertical strip of a material, the end of which is immersed in the liquid; 3) the total area of a specimen wetted by the liquid within a specified time period; and 4) the total absorptive capacity of a material expressed as the quantity of liquid absorbed by a completely saturated specimen. Absorbency is of importance because paper, for example, generally has the ability to absorb or give up moisture depending upon the wetness, i.e., RELATIVE HUMIDITY, of the atmosphere around it, and, because the effect is not uniform in all directions. Because of the latter, the MACHINE DIRECTION of the paper used in producing books becomes an important factor in both

printing and bookbinding. *See also:* COCKLE (1); WARPING. (17, 72, 144)

absorbent papers. A group of soft, unsized papers used to soak up water and other liquids. Although not sized, the papers may be treated with synthetic resins as a method of enhancing their wet strength. Absorbent papers include blotting papers, as well as the base papers used in the manufacture of IMITATION LEATHER, VEGETABLE PARCHMENT PAPER, WET-STRENGTH PAPER, and the like. (17, 290, 324)

absorption. A term used in the adhesive industry to indicate the capillary or cellular attraction of a surface to draw off a liquid adhesive into the substrate.

acacia. A genus of woody plants of the family *Leguminosae*. The sap and pods of certain species, notable *Acacia arabica* and *A. senegal,* are used in the manufacture of GUM ARABIC. *Acacia mimoa, A. mollisima* and *A. catechu* (also called Borneo cutch) are also used in the tanning of leather. *See also:* VEGETABLE TANNINS. (130, 175)

acacia gum. *See:* GUM ARABIC.

acanthus. The name given a leaf of the acanthus plant (*Acanthus spinosus*) introduced as ornamentation in ancient Greek architecture. It has been applied in various modified forms in succeeding styles of architecture. In bookbinding, the acanthus ornamentation is a typical impression of the finishing tool cut to represent two such leaves pointing in different directions. The acanthus decoration was also used as a decorative motif by illuminators of manuscripts, especially Carolingian artists of the 9th century. (250)

accelerated aging test. A procedure which is designed to indicate in a relatively short period of time what will happen to materials, such as paper, ink, etc., over a period of years in storage. It commonly involves heating the specimen in an oven under specified controlled conditions. Under ideal circumstances, the material is exposed to an environment which increases the *rate* of its degradation without changing its *nature.* It is generally accepted, for example, that heating paper for three days in an oven at 100° C is equivalent in its effect to approximately 25 years under normal library storage conditions.

Although sound in theory, accelerated aging tests are, at this time, of limited usefulness. The reason is that conditions of storage, which vary widely, have a considerable influence on the degree of permanence; also, it is difficult to verify empirically the accuracy of such tests except by experiments conducted over a number of years. Such tests have actually been made, although to a limited extent. It is known, for example, that the strength of paper tends to diminish in storage, and experiments have indicated that the FOLDING ENDURANCE declines to a significantly greater extent than such other properties as tensile, or tearing, strength; consequently, folding endurance tests conducted subsequent to accelerated aging may well provide a good indication of a general loss of strength. In addition, as to the *rate* of deterioration, the effect of heat is very much like that of natural aging under *average* conditions; therefore, it is probably reasonable to assume that heat affords a practical means of accomplishing accelerated aging. (18, 62, 144)

accordian fold. *See:* CONCERTINA FOLD.

accordian-pleated fold. A method of folding endpapers so that the pleat provides a hinge at the inner joint of the cover. The pleat also provides for expansion to allow the covers to swing open freely and not exert strain on the first and last leaves of the book. In certain cases, however, it can also create a sharp, knife-like fold which, if wide enough, may cause a brittle leaf to bend sharply and crack at that point. (81)

account book. *See:* BLANKBOOK.

account-book binding. *See:* BLANKBOOK BINDING.

account-book paper. *See:* LEDGER PAPER.

acetate. The salt or ester of ACETIC ACID. *See also:* CALCIUM ACETATE, CELLULOSE ACETATE, POLYVINYL ACETATE.

acetate envelopes. Envelopes, usually made of transparent cellulose acetate, used for the temporary protection of documents, letters, prints, photographs, maps, etc. They are superior to paper envelopes in that they substantially reduce the danger of acid transfer. Their use, however, is declining in favor of polyester envelopes. *See also:* CELLULOSE ACETATE; POLYESTER FIBERS.

acetate ink. An ink with special adhering qualities intended for drawing or printing on such materials as films and acetates.

acetic acid. A volatile, colorless acid (CH_3COOH), prepared by the oxidation of acetaldehyde, by oxidation of ethyl alcohol, or by the distillation of wood. It is used extensively in the manufacture of CELLULOSE ACETATE, and has been used for washing leather bindings to remove grease prior to tooling. Being a relatively weak organic acid, as well as volatile, it is not considered to be particularly harmful to paper or leather, and is to be preferred to ordinary vinegar in preparing leather or book edges for tooling or gilding, as vinegar is likely to contain traces of sulfuric acid. (198)

acetic ether. *See:* ETHYL ACETATE.

acetone. A colorless, volatile, flammable ketone (CH_3COCH_3), having a pleasing odor, that occurs in pyroligneous acid and can be prepared by dehydrogenation of isopropyl alcohol, by bacterial fermentation of corn mash, and by other means. It is miscible with water, alcohol and ether. Acetone is effective as a solvent in removing pressure sensitive tape from paper because it dissolves not only the adhesive but (in some cases) the tape itself. Its use is limited, however, because of its tendency to dissolve ink, and its highly flammable nature. In leather manufacture, it is used as a solvent for finishes. It is also used to prepare other solvents, such as methyl isobutyl ketone and mesityl alcohol, and as a solvent for paints, varnishes, lacquers, and cellulose acetate. Acetone decomposes photochemically to produce ethane, carbon monoxide and small amounts of diacetyl and methane. (173, 306)

acid. A substance capable of forming hydrogen ions when dissolved in water. The majority of inorganic acids may be regarded as compounds of an acidic oxide and water; where the oxide involved is that of a metal, it may exhibit amphoteric characteristics, i.e., act sometimes as an acid and sometimes as a base, depending upon the other materials present. Typical organic acids contain the COOH group, but other acid groupings, e.g., the sulfonic—SO_3H, give acidic properties to organic compounds.

Aqueous solutions of acids have a sharp taste, turn litmus red, liberate CO_2, form a metallic carbonate, and evolve hydrogen in reaction with certain metals, e.g., iron.

The 'strength' of an acid is measured by the value of its dissociation constant, a strong acid such as hydrochloric being substantially fully ionized in solution, and a weak acid such as formic being predominantly un-ionized.

Acids, and particularly the inorganic acids (because of their corrosiveness and low volatility), are harmful to paper and bookbinding materials. Their presence weakens the holding power of the individual links of the cellulose chains of paper, causing brittleness; results in corrosive effects in some inks; and weakens the fibers of leather.

The source of acids in archival materials may be intrinsic or extrinsic. They may be present in the materials used in the manufacture of paper, adhesives, leather, etc., and may be left in intentionally, e.g., alum-rosin sizing; they may be introduced during manufacture and not sufficiently removed, e g., acids used in clearing and/or dyeing leather; or they may gain access during storage, e.g., sulfuric acid in paper or leather, resulting from the atmospheric pollutant, sulfur dioxide (SO_2). *See also:* ACID GASES. (72, 195, 198, 306)

acid dyes. A very large class of dyes containing acidic groups, such as the sodium salts of sulfonic acids or phenolic groups. They are more soluble and have less tinctorial value than BASIC DYES but they also have greater light fastness. *See:* FAST COLORS. They do not form lakes with tannin. Acid dyes are used in dyeing leather, paper, etc., and their particular value lies in their ability to produce brighter, more uniform colors. They are normally applied from an acid dye liquor (acetic, formic, or sulfuric acid); however, unless applied from a neutral or only slightly acid dyebath, i.e., pH of 6.0 to 7.0, their use is likely to result in acid degradation of the material dyed. *See also:* FUGITIVE COLORS; LAKE. (17, 67, 72, 363)

acid-free leather. Ostensibly, leather manufactured without the use of acids, but interpreted by most producers to mean leather from which as much acid as possible has been removed. The removal of acid used in producing leather is a costly and time-consuming process, and calls for repeated washing of the stock. Tanning agents which contain a relatively high amount of salts of weak acids, of which MYRABOLANS is one, are said to protect leather against acids used in manufacture or those absorbed from the atmosphere. (175, 306)

acid-free paper. In principle, papers which contain no free acid and have a pH value of 7.0 or greater. In practice, papermakers consider a paper having a pH value of 6.0 or greater to be acid free. Such papers may be produced from cotton fibers, rags, esparto, jute, chemical wood pulps, or virtually any other fiber, with special precautions being taken during manufacture to eliminate any active acid that might be present in the paper pulp. However free of acid the paper may be immediately after manufacture, the presence of residual chlorine from bleaching operations, aluminum sulfate (alum) from sizing, or sulfur dioxide in the atmosphere, may lead to the formation of hydrochloric or sulfuric acid unless the paper has been buffered with a substance capable of neutralizing acids. *See also:* ALKALINE RESERVE. (144, 198)

acid gases. Gases which may form destructive acids in paper, board, leather, and other book materials. Sulfur dioxide (SO_2), present in the air as a pollutant, is one such gas; it can form highly destructive sulfuric acid (H_2SO_4), either by oxidizing to form sulfur trioxide (SO_3), which in the presence of water vapor, is transformed into H_2SO_4, or by combining directly with water vapor to form sulfurous acid (H_2SO_3), which, while a weak acid itself, reacts with oxygen to form H_2SO_4. It is suspected that the rate of conversion is increased by the presence in the paper of metallic catalysts, such as iron or copper, which may enter the paper during manufacture, but as yet there is no proof of this. (193, 265)

acidity. A condition or state in which the concentration of hydrogen ions in an aqueous solution exceeds that of hydroxyl ions. Acidity is probably the most important single factor affecting the permanence of archival materials. Acidity alone, however, does not necessarily connote destructiveness; the nature of the acid, i.e., the strength of its acidic properties, is of more importance than its quantity; e.g., a relatively small amount of sulfuric acid may have a greater destructive effect than a larger quantity of lactic acid. Because of this, both pH value and titration are necessary to achieve adequate evaluation of the potentially destructive effect of an acid. *See also:* HYDROGEN-ION CONCENTRATION. (144)

acid migration. The transfer of acid from a material containing acid to one containing less or no acid. This may occur either when the two materials are in contact with each other, or by vapor transfer from one material to nearby materials not actually in contact with it. Boards, endpapers, and protective tissues, as well as the paper covers of

books and pamphlets, may contain acid and transfer it to otherwise low-acid or acid-free paper of the text. Also called "acid transfer." *See also:* BARRIER SHEET.

acid size. A ROSIN SIZE that contains an appreciable part of unsaponified but emulsified free rosin. If, when diluted, the rosin size produces a milky emulsion, it is then known as "white size."

acid transfer. *See:* ACID MIGRATION.

acid wash. A solution consisting of hydrochloric acid diluted in water. At one time it was used to clean grease and other foreign material from the edges of books prior to gilding. It was usually applied after the initial scraping and sanding, and before the final light sanding.

acme seal. The now obsolete name given a SEALSKIN, dyed and having a plain, dull finish and a natural grain.

acrylic resin (acrylic coating; acrylic plastic). A thermoplastic resin prepared by polymerizing acrylic acid ($C_3H_4O_2$) or methacrylic acid ($C_4H_6O_2$), or a derivative of either, especially an ester, e.g., methyl methacrylate. One such acrylic resin, polymethyl acrylate, which is a tough rubbery material, is used, usually as manufactured in emulsion form, for textile and leather finishes, lacquers, and pressure sensitive adhesives, and as a mixture with clay to coat papers used in high gloss printing. (42, 364)

additives. 1. Substances added in small proportions to products to improve their performance, or to enhance their attractiveness or value. Additives are also used to prevent bacterial action, drying, staling, as well as to inhibit corrosion, oxidation, decomposition, etc. 2. All of the nonfibrous raw materials used in making paper. They may be added at any point during the papermaking process or after the paper has been manufactured. Treatment of the entire sheet (internal treatment) entails mixing the additives with the paper pulp, in which case they are known as wet-end additives. If only the surface of the sheet is to be treated, the additives are applied directly to the surface of the paper, and are known as external additives. Paper additives are used to color and size paper, control pH, improve physical properties, and increase wet strength. They are also used as defoamers, dispersants, plasticizers, preservatives, retention aids, and the like. (58, 98)

adherend. A material that is held to another material by means of an ADHESIVE.

adhesion. A term indicating that two surfaces are held together by interfacial forces, which may consist of valence forces (chemical adhesion), interlocking action (mechanical adhesion), VAN DER WAALS FORCES, or combinations thereof. (309)

adhesive. A general term for any of several substances capable of bonding materials to each other by chemical or mechanical action, or both, and which may be activated by water, nonaqueous solvents, pressure, heat, cold, or other means.

Adhesives may be classified by temperature (hot-, cold-, intermediate-, room-temperature setting, etc.); by type of solvent (water, alcohol, etc.); by type of application (brush, roller, spray, etc.); or by origin (animal, vegetable, or synthetic). They may be further classified as natural or synthetic (resin). The natural adhesives are primarily of animal or vegetable origin (sodium silicate (water glass) being virtually the only inorganic natural product important as an adhesive) and include animal glue, casein, blood albumen (which is unimportant as an adhesive in archival work), and vegetable adhesives. The synthetic resin adhesives include the thermoplastic resins, the thermosetting resins, and the elastomeric adhesives.

The adhesives used in archival work must exhibit three properties: 1) they must wet the surfaces to be joined but not so much as to cause the adhered materials to cockle; 2) they must have sufficient flexibility so as not to crack when the joint is flexed; and 3) they must be strong but not as strong as the materials they bond, so that stress to the point of failure of the joint will not damage the archival material but will result only in the failure of the adhesive. *See also:* ALBUMEN; CASEIN; CEMENT (2); COLD GLUE; DEXTRIN; FISH GLUE; FLEXIBLE GLUE; GLAIR; GLUCOSE-GLYCOL PASTE; GLUE; HARD GLUE; HOT-MELT ADHESIVE; ISINGLASS; MICROENCAPSULATED ADHESIVE; MUCILAGE; PADDING COMPOUND; PASTE; POLYVINYL ACETATE; RABBIT SKIN GLUE; RESINOUS ADHESIVES; RICE GLUE; RUBBER ADHESIVES; VEGETABLE GLUE; WOOD PASTE. (48, 89, 102, 149, 186, 198, 222, 309)

adhesive binding. A method of securing loose leaves into a solid text block by means of an adhesive rather than by means of sewing, stitching, etc. In general, there are four techniques of adhesive binding in use today: 1) PADDING (2); 2) manual adhesive binding, which is still practiced by hand binders and some library binders; 3) semi-automatic adhesive binding, which is the usual method in library binderies and some paperback edition binderies; and 4) fully automatic adhesive binding, which is the usual method in edition binding.

Two basic methods are used to secure the leaves in adhesive binding: 1) application of the adhesive to the edges of the collected and clamped leaves, without fanning, in which case there is little if any penetration of adhesive between the sheets; and 2) fanning the clamped leaves, either in one direction or both (in the latter case 180°), so that the adhesive is applied a slight distance onto the leaves, thus forming a more secure bond. A HOT-MELT ADHESIVE is usually employed in the first method, whereas a cold RESINOUS ADHESIVE, e.g., POLYVINYL ACETATE, is typical in the latter method. It is not unusual, however, to use a combination of the two adhesives. The resinous adhesives are generally used alone, but hot melts may be used in either a one-shot operation (hot melt alone), or in a two-shot application (a primer of polyvinyl adhesive, followed by the hot melt, in which case the leaves are usually fanned upon application of the cold adhesive).

Adhesive binding generally results in a book that opens easily and lies flat. It is also a relatively economical form of binding, especially when long runs of the same edition are being bound. The method lends itself well to the mass production of low-priced paperbacks, catalogs, telephone directories, and the like. It is also finding greater use in library binding for books that are not in sections and have relatively narrow margins, as well as for rebinding books printed on paper that is deteriorating. Adhesive binding, however, is not a satisfactory method of binding coated and similar papers.

Adhesive binding, in one form or another, is not a new concept; in fact, it dates back to the 1830s when William Hancock invented the so-called CAOUTCHOUC BINDING in England. Overall, however, even though the method is very practical for books that are to receive heavy use over a relatively short period, (e.g., telephone directories), adhesive binding is generally considered to be inferior to the sewn binding and its permanence has yet to be demonstrated. Also called "perfect binding," or "unsewn binding." *See also:* ADHESIVE BINDING MA-CHINE; ONE-SHOT METHOD; TWO-SHOT METHOD. (15, 16, 81, 89, 294, 320)

adhesive binding machine. A machine that applies an adhesive, and sometimes a cloth lining, to the edges of the leaves or sections of a book. Adhesive binding machines may be classified as: 1) intermittent, with all operations being performed while the book is stopped; and 2) continuous, with all operations being performed while the book is in motion. In addition, they may be classified as: 1) in-line, with the books being carried in one direction at a constant elevation; 2) rotary or circular, with books being carried in a circular path; and 3) oval, with books being carried over an extended oval path. There are variations within all of these categories. Adhesive binding machines used in library binderies are generally in-line machines which operate intermittently or continuously, with the books being inserted and removed from the machine by hand.

Adhesive binding machines date back to the latter part of the 19th century, but their greatest period of development was following World War II. (89, 320)

adhesive dope. A chemical solvent used as a wash for the turn-in areas of imitation-leather book cloths and other impervious materials to facilitate adhesion of the board papers. It has very limited use today.

adhesive glassine tape. A gummed glassine paper, generally of BASIS WEIGHT of 25 pounds (24 × 36 — 500). It is sometimes used in mending the leaves of books, as well as for hinges, for which purposes it is supplied in rolls of narrow width. Its use for the repair of archival materials is not recommended, as it has a tendency to stain the paper and is difficult to remove. *See also:* HEAT-SET TISSUE. (17)

adhesive paper. A paper coated with a water-activated, heat-activated, or pressure-activated adhesive. *See:* GUMMED PAPER; HEAT-SET TISSUE; PRESSURE-SENSITIVE TAPE; SE-LIN LABELING SYSTEM.

adjusted. A MARBLING SIZE that has been put into proper condition to receive the colors by the addition of OX-GALL, so that when the colors are dropped on they will spread evenly. The correct amount of gall will cause a drop of marbling color to expand to its maximum without thinning. *See also:* MARBLING. (335)

advance sheets. 1. A copy of a book, in sheets or gatherings, for preliminary notices, simultaneous publication in two or more places, or for early cataloging. Advance sheets for review or early cataloging are usually in unbound gatherings. 2. Generally, sheets of a publication e.g., some serial publications or other documents, printed separately for use before they are issued collectively. In a stricter sense these are more appropriately called "preprints." (69, 140)

advertisements bound-in. A statement to the effect that advertisements have been included in the binding of a volume bound from parts or issues, or in the rebinding of a volume, usually a serial publication. Some libraries instruct the binder to remove all advertisements not containing subject matter (on either side of the leaf), or those that are paginated separately. This is done to save shelf space; it is questionable, however, whether sufficient space is saved to warrant the effort. In addition, the presence of advertisements can be of value to scholars and is of value to collectors.

aerosol. A dispersion in which a material is dissolved or suspended in a liquid which volatilizes to produce a fine spray when pressure is released. The spray carries the active material. In archival work, aerosols are used for dispersing deacidification solutions; in this case the propellant, which must be inert and nonflammable, is frequently a chlorofluorocarbon, e.g., freon 12, dichlorodifluoromethane (CCl_2F_2).

against the grain. Paper which has been folded at right angles to the direction in which the fibers tend to lie, i.e., the MACHINE DIRECTION. A well-produced book always has the grain or machine direction running from head to tail so that the back or binding fold of the paper is not against the grain. Correct grain direction means that the leaves of the book will be more inclined to lie flat when the book is open. The term applies specifically to machine-made paper, as HANDMADE PAPER has no definite grain direction.

agalite. A natural fibrous form of talc, gray in color and consisting principally of hydrated magnesium silicate. It gives paper a greasy or soapy feel, and enables it to take a high finish. It is little used today. (62)

agar (agar-agar). The polysaccharides agarose and agropectin, occurring as cell-wall constituents of red marine algae (genera *Gelidium, Gracilaria*, etc.), from which it is extracted by hot water. It is available as a dry powder, flakes, or strips. Agar is the metallic (usually calcium) salt of a sulfuric acid ester of a complex polysaccharide of gelactose, but its exact structure is not understood. It dissolves in hot water and, upon cooling, sets to a jelly at concentrations as low as 0.5%. It is used as a gelling and stabilizing agent, as a misciformis sizing for silk, and as an adhesive emulsifying agent. (72)

agate (agate burnisher). A natural stone, consisting of a form of silica, similar to chalcedony, with colored bands of purple or brown, shaped and polished for use as a burnishing tool, particularly in edge gilding. *See also:* BURNISHER (2).

agatine. A marble pattern consisting of black in large spots, green in rivers, scarlet in sprinkles, and blue in small spots. Various designs are made from this combination of colors. (152)

"agenda" format. A narrow book format, i.e., one where the height of the book is disproportionately greater than its width, to the extent of 3:1 or greater, as compared with the usual ratio of 2:1 or 3:2. The "agenda" format proportions are similar to those of the consular diptych. The diptych was often adapted in the middle ages for use as covers of ceremonial lists and processional music, which had to be written in a format to conform with these constrictions; the "agenda" possibly stems from that format. (347)

aggressive tack. *See:* DRY TACK.

aging. A general term describing the natural degradation of paper, adhesives, leather, and other archival materials, while in storage. With some textiles, aging denotes oxidation by exposure to air. Aging is greatly influenced by the environment in which the materials are stored. *See also:* ACCELERATED AGING TEST; ENVIRONMENT; PERMANENT MATERIALS; PERMANENT PAPER; YELLOWING.

air-dried. Handmade- and the better machine-made papers dried in a current of air, either at normal or elevated temperatures, as distinguished from paper which is dried by contact with heated rolls. This method of drying reduces stresses, including DRIED-IN STRAIN, which are imposed on paper while drying, because the sheet is allowed to dry, and therefore contract, at a slower rate. *See also:* ANISOTROPIC BEHAVIOR. (98)

air dry. A condition usually associated with paper (and paper pulp) and leather. Paper is said to be air dry when its moisture content (usually 3 to 9%)

is in equilibrium with the atmospheric conditions to which it is exposed. Leather is considered to be air dry when its moisture content is approximately 14% of the weight of the leather. Their different moisture contents in the air dry state makes it difficult to regulate the conditions of storage of a leather bound book. (17, 363)

airmail paper. A lightweight paper made for printing publications such as newspapers that are to be sent by airmail. It usually contains fillers to improve opacity, and is generally made in a basis weight of 10 pounds (17 × 22 — 500). Airmail paper is also used at times for guarding sections, mending tears, etc. For these purposes, it is preferable that the paper have a high rag content and an alkaline reserve of about 3%. (17, 58)

air permeability. The property which permits the passage of air when a difference in pressure exists across the boundaries of the material. Air permeability is one indication of a substance's porosity. *See also:* VAPOR PERMEABILITY. (17)

Aitken, Robert (1735–1802). One of a group of Scottish craftsmen in the bookbinding trade who immigrated to America in the years immediately before the Revolutionary War. Aitken appeared in Philadelphia in 1769, as a bookseller. He returned to Scotland that same year, apparently to learn bookbinding, because upon his return two years later he advertised himself as both bookbinder and bookseller. After 1773 he began to print books as well, and, in 1782, published the "Aitken Bible," the first complete Bible in English to be published on the North American continent.

Aitken produced hundreds of bookbindings ranging in style from paper wrappers (both blue and marbled) to more or less richly gilt leather bindings. His work included blue paper boards, raised cords as well as flat spines, both plain and marbled endpapers, and bindings in full calf- or sheepskin with red title labels and gilt bands across the spines. Although Aitken produced scores of "plain" bindings, he was also capable of a binding style that was rich and luxurious in its gold tooling, especially for American bookbinding of that time. He was, in general, an imaginative and diverse bookbinder, although he was not known for his exactness and polish in finishing, nor was he particularly artistic. Because Aitkin was also an engraver, it has been suggested that

he may have cut his own finishing tools, possible in imitation of Scottish designs. (45, 200, 347)

ajoure bindings. A style of bookbinding executed during the last third of the 15th century in Venice. Ajoure bindings were embellished with pierced or translucent patterns, in a manner referred to as "letting in the daylight." They generally featured openwork designs of foliage, angels' heads, satyrmasks, birds, baskets of fruits, etc. (156, 347)

à la cathédral. *See:* ARCHITECTURAL STYLE.

album. 1. A book of envelopes or jackets, usually with a decorative cover and often with descriptive notes. It is intended to contain phonograph records. 2. A book of blank leaves designed to contain written records, clippings, postage stamps, and the like.

albumen. A class of protein found in egg whites. A mixture of egg white and vinegar (GLAIR) is used in book finishing; its purpose is to secure the gold leaf to the covering material prior to the impression of the heated tool. Albumen is also used as an adhesive in edge gilding.

album paper. A type of cover paper used for photograph albums. It is manufactured in gray and black in basis weights of 50 to 80 pounds (20 × 26 — 500). A basic requirement of this paper is that it not cockle when wetted with adhesives, while another essential requirement is that it contain no impurities which might alter or damage the photographs. (17, 324)

alchemic gold. A gold ink composition developed early in the 20th century as a substitute for imitation gold leaf. It was said to be "free from acid," as well as non-tarnishing. Its principal virtue seems to have been that it eliminated the necessity of sizing, laying-on, and rubbing off. (164, 264)

aldehyde tanning. Essentially a formaldehyde tannage. Several aldehydes react with hide protein to prevent putrefaction, but only FORMALDEHYDE has been used to any extent in the manufacture of leather. Formaldehyde is soluble in water, the resultant solution generally being known as FORMALIN. Aldehyde tanning is used principally in tanning white, washable leathers, usually sheep- or lambskins, with the grain split or shaved off. Such leathers are seldom used in bookbinding. *See also:* ZIRCONIUM TANNING. (291, 306, 363)

alder (bark). The bark of the common alder tree (*Alnus glutinosa*), used to some extent in small tanneries in southeastern Europe and Turkey for tanning leather. The bark contains 9 to 16% or more tannin, while the dried fruit yields about 16% tannin. The use of alder bark is not extensive—mainly because, when used alone, it imparts an objectionable reddish-brown color to the leather, and also tends to make the leather brittle. Other alder barks have also been used in tanning, including *Alnus incana* (in Europe and North America), *A. nepalesis* and *A. nitida* (in India), and *A. cordata* (in Italy). (175)

Aldine leaves. Small finishing stamps bearing a leaf and stem design. It was employed by the binders of Aldus Manutius, and also extensively by 19th century bookbinders on monastic bindings. *See also:* ALDINE (ITALIAN) STYLE. (334)

Aldine (Italian) style. A style of bookbinding originated by Aldus Manutius but not restricted to the books printed by Aldus or his family. Aldine bindings, which were produced during the late 15th and early 16th centuries, were characterized by the use of brown or red morocco; by solid-faced ornaments with no shading (which were similar to those used in printing the text); and by title or author in simple panels in the center of the upper cover, which could be read while the book lay on a shelf or table. Early examples of the Aldine style were tooled in blind with an outer frame and a center ornament.

Possibly because of the Greek binders Aldus employed, as well as the fact that gold tooling (probably) originated in the Near East, Aldine tools display definite signs of Eastern origin. Early Italian bindings convey a consistent feeling of the shape and proportion of the book, which is demonstrated by: 1) the use of border and panel as schemes of design; 2) a remarkable sense of the value accorded ornamentation; 3) the areas of leather left undecorated; and 4) restraint in the decorative detail with the result that it was always in proper subordination to the overall effect of the embellishment. *See* PLATE IV. (124, 172, 280, 334)

algarobilla. The dry pods of a shrub native to Chile (*Caesalpinia brevifolia*), from which a tannin is extracted. As a tanning material, algarobilla somewhat resembles DIVI-DIVI; however, it is less prone to discolor the leather. It also produces a better weight and imparts greater firmness to leather. Algarobilla gives a light-colored tan liquor which before fermentation colors leather slightly to a light reddish yellow; however, after fermentation it produces a very bright color. It is usually blended with other tannins. Although algarobilla is one of the pyrogallol class of tannins, it penetrates the hide substance very rapidly, and has a fairly low natural pH and salts content and a relatively high acids content. The tannin content of the pods is generally in the range of 45-50%. *See also:* VEGETABLE TANNINS. (175)

alkali. A substance which has the properties of a base, especially a hydroxide or carbonate of an alkali metal, e.g., calcium. Since all of these substances, when dissolved, increase the hydroxyl ion concentration, the term alkali is synonymous with base. An aqueous alkaline solution is one with a pH value greater than 7.0. Alkalies are used in conservation work principally in adhesives, and in deacidifying and buffering paper. *See also:* ALKALINE RESERVE; HYDROGEN-ION CONCENTRATION.

alkaline buffer. *See:* ALKALINE RESERVE.

alkaline filler. A FILLER (2) used in the manufacture of paper. Calcium carbonate ($CaCO_3$) is the most commonly used alkaline filler.

alkaline process. A method of treating fibrous raw materials with alkaline solutions to liberate fibers or to purify paper pulps. Lime, sodium carbonate, sodium hydroxide, sodium sulfate, and sodium sulfide are used in this process, with sodium hydroxide being used most often. It may be used in both the sulfate and sulfite processes. (17, 144)

alkaline reserve. A buffer, or reserve, of an alkaline substance added to a paper for the purpose of counteracting any acid which may be introduced into it subsequent to DEACIDIFICATION. Soaking paper in a solution of calcium bicarbonate or magnesium bicarbonate adds a small amount of calcium or magnesium carbonate which neutralizes any acid present and also provides a reserve to counteract acid which may enter the paper at some future time. (The bicarbonates are converted to the carbonates during the drying of the paper, with the liberation of carbon dioxide.) The treatment is effective only as long as free alkali remains. Papers which are to remain acid free for long periods of time, e.g., 500 years, should have approximately 3% precipiated carbonate by weight of paper. (198)

all along (all across; all on). A method of sewing a book, usually by hand and generally on cords or tapes. The thread goes "all along," inside the fold of the section—that is, from kettle stitch to kettle stitch of each successive section, one complete length of thread for each section. "All along" is traditionally associated with the best method of sewing a book by hand, although books were sewn TWO-ON and even THREE-ON when the sections were very thin or when an economical method was required. The term is also used, somewhat incorrectly, to describe machine book sewing when each section is sewn with the full number of threads. Also called "one on" and "one sheet on." (236, 335)

alligator grained leather. A grain effect embossed on various types of leathers, such as calf, sheep, or cow, in imitation of the genuine reptilian leather. *See:* ALLIGATOR LEATHER.

alligator leather. A leather produced from the skin of any member of the reptilian order *Crocodilla*. Generally, only the belly area of the animal is used, the heavily scaled back being too course and horny. The beauty of alligator leather stems in part from the fact that the scales have a natural "enamel," which, originally, was usually destroyed by crude tanning methods. Later it was preserved, and even enhanced, by "plating" the skin with heated metal plates which gave it its high glaze. Alligator leather is very durable and also very expensive. This term is largely confined to the United States; in Europe it is generally called "crocodile leather." (351, 363)

all on. *See:* ALL ALONG.

all-over style. 1. A style of finishing in which the entire cover, as distinct from the corners, center or borders, is decorated by a single motif, multiple motifs, or a decorative roll. 2. Any pattern in a book cloth which runs both across and down the roll. (130, 156)

alpha cellulose. That part of a cellulosic material that is insoluble in a 17.5% solution of sodium hydroxide at 20° C. under specified conditions. While alpha cellulose consists principally of cellulose, it does include other components that are insoluble under the test conditions. Because the permanence of paper depends to some extent on the absence of non-cellulosic impurities, the determination of true cellulose (alpha cellulose) gives an indication of the stability of the paper, and therefore its permanence. *See also:* BETA CELLULOSE; CELLULOSE; GAMMA CELLULOSE. (17, 72, 144)

alpha grass. *See:* ESPARTO (GRASS).

alpha protein. A soy bean protein used in the manufacture of adhesives that are to be combined with casein glues, or used for coating paper.

alum. A salt used in papermaking and in the TAWING of skins. True (potash) alum is chemically a double salt of aluminum, or potassium aluminum sulfate ($K_2SO_4 \cdot Al_2(SO_4)_3 \cdot 24H_2O$). The papermaker's alum in use today is not true alum, but either aluminum sulfate ($Al_2(SO_4)_3 \cdot 14H_2O$), ($Al_2(SO_4)_3 \cdot 18H_2O$), or a mixture of these hydrates, and is manufactured by treating pulverized bauxite with sulfuric acid. It is soluble in water, and, while slightly alkaline in the dry form, it is decidedly acidic when dissolved in water. Alum has two major functions in papermaking: 1) to control pH; and 2) because of its floculating ability, to retain other additives in the paper, notably the sizing agent.

ROSIN is a basic material used in sizing paper today. As a sizing agent it imparts water (ink) resistance to paper; however, in order for the rosin to be able to impart water resistance it must be rendered insoluble, which is the function if alum.

Although the full role of alum in the sizing of paper is not completely understood, one of its functions is to make rosin come out of solution (precipitate) while it is in close contact with the fibers of the paper-making slurry. The fibers are thus coated and impregnated with a solid and water-resistant mixture of rosin and what is probably a compound of rosin and aluminum oxide.

Although the excessive use of alum is considered detrimental to the permanence of paper, the papermaker tends to overdose with alum rather than underdose, so as to avoid soft-sizing. In addition, alum is considered by some papermakers to be a panacea for other troubles, such as frothing, sticking of the paper web to the wet presses of the papermaking machine, etc. Overdosing with alum leads to excessive acidity and, under certain circumstances, may lead to severe deterioration of the paper. While alum is not a particularly strong acid, in the presence of certain other substances it can assume a greater strength. Chlorides, which may be present in the paper as a result of bleaching processes, or natural to the water itself, can be particularly harmful. Excessive alum, in the form of aluminum sulfate, may react with chlorides present to form aluminum chloride ($AlCl_3$), which in the presence of moisture and heat, will form hydrochloric acid (HCl)—one of the most powerful of all acids in its effect on cellulose.

Alum is sometimes used in solution to wash the leaves of books; in the past it was added to paste to act as a preservative, or as a hardener to render the dry paste less water soluble. It is also used at times as a mordant for marbling colors. *See also:* ALUM WATER. (32, 43, 72, 195, 236)

aluminum leaf. A bright leaf or foil made of aluminum and often substituted for silver in blocking edition bindings. While it tarnishes less rapidly than silver, it lacks the appearance of richness and depth of silver leaf. It is also less expensive. (83, 140)

aluminum sulfate. A salt of aluminum ($Al_2(SO_4)_3$), occurring naturally in considerable quantities in alumstone (alumite) and feather alum. It is manufactured by treating bauxite with 80% sulfuric acid at 110° C., the resulting solution being purified, concentrated, and allowed to solidify. *See also:* ALUM.

alum-size bath. A size bath consisting of ALUM dissolved in water and used by some restorers to remove coffee, tea, blood and some ink stains from paper. (335)

alum-tawed skin (alum "tanning"; alum-tawed "leather"). *See:* TAWING.

alum water. ALUM dissolved in water and used to sponge paper and the edges of books before laying on the marbling colors. The alum acts as a binding medium, attracting and securing the ox-gall and colors to the paper. It also acts as a mordant and is also useful in counteracting excessive gall. (161, 264, 335)

American leather. An obsolete term for one of the varieties of enameled cloth made to imitate leather. *See also:* IMITATION LEATHER. (256)

American marble. A drawn marble pattern usually used on the edges of stationery bindings, and consisting of black, blue surrounding the black, yellow on the blue, and red on the yellow. The marble is drawn in the same manner as the comb NONPAREIL MARBLE, with an additional drawing of the comb the width of the trough. (264, 339)

American Russia. An imitation RUSSIA LEATHER produced from cowhide or the hide of the American buffalo (bison). It is usually a straight-grained leather. Also called "Russia cowhide."

amorphous. A term applied to adhesives, with reference to their non-crystalline structure.

amylaceous. Pertaining to, or of the nature of STARCH; starchy. *See also:* PASTE.

amyl acetate. A colorless, volatile liquid ester ($C_7H_{14}O_2$), that is very slightly soluble in water, but miscible in alcohol and ether. It is used as a solvent for CELLULOSE ACETATE. Although at one time it was believed to have a preservative effect when applied to leather, it is much too volatile to have afforded lasting protection, even if initially effective.

anchoring. *See:* TYING DOWN. *See also:* HEADBAND.

anglos. An imitation RUSSIA LEATHER made in Great Britain from cowhide. *See also:* AMERICAN RUSSIA. (343)

anhydrous. A term normally used with reference to the chemical salts and solvents, lanolin, etc., meaning that they are free of water.

anhydrous lanolin. *See:* LANOLIN.

aniline. An aromatic primary amine ($C_6H_5NH_2$). It is a derivative of ammonia in which one hydrogen atom is replaced by the phenyl group. It is manufactured by the reduction of nitrobenzene with iron filings and either hydrochloric acid or ferrous chloride, and subsequent steam distillation after the addition of lime. Aniline is an oily, colorless, toxic liquid, which darkens upon exposure to air. It is soluble in water, alcohol, and ether, and forms a number of salts. It is the base from which a great number of intermediates for dyes are prepared, including dimethylaniline and diethylaniline, which in turn yield many so-called BASIC DYES, such as methyl violet, methyline blue and malachite green. (195)

aniline dyed. A leather that has been dyed by immersion in a dyebath and has not received any coating or pigment finish. (61)

analine dyes. A class of synthetic, organic dyes originally obtained from analine (coal tars), which were, in fact, the first synthetic dyes. Today the term is used with reference to any synthetic organic dyes and pigments, regardless of source, in contrast to animal or vegetable coloring materials, natural earth pigments, and synthetic inorganic pigments. Analine dyes are classified according to their degree of brightness, or their light fastness. Basic dyes are known for their extreme brightness, as well as for their lack of COLOR FASTNESS. Aniline dyes are used to impart color to paper, cloth, leather, etc. Also called "coal tar dyes." *See also:* ACID DYES; BASIC DYES; DIRECT DYES; DYE; LAKE. (17, 164, 343)

aniline ink. An inexpensive volatile printing ink consisting of a dyestuff dissolved in a methylated spirit and bound with a resin. It is considered to be a very fast drying ink. Aniline inks are considerably inferior in permanence to many other types of ink, and are also subject to smudging by water. Although all colors are available, they are lacking in COLOR FASTNESS. (144)

aniline leather. A hide or skin that has been tanned with a vegetable material and then colored either by immersion in a dyebath or by staining, and has not been coated or pigmented. Leather so colored has a depth of coloring said to be superior to pigment coloration. (351)

aniline stained. A leather that has been colored by brushing, padding, or spraying, but which has not received any coating or pigmented finish.

animal glue. *See:* GLUE.

animals-in-foliage panel. A form of decoration consisting of a PANEL (1) divided in half vertically, each half containing curving foliage with an animal within each curve. (250)

animal size. *See:* SIZE. (2, 3)

animal sized. A paper sized with a gelatin or glue (and sometimes alum, which acts as an insolubilizer). The gelatin or glue-and-alum solution acts as a preservative and enhances the water resistance of the paper. Generally, only high-grade writing papers, bonds, ledgers, and handmade paper are animal sized. *See also:* SURFACED SIZED; TUB SIZED. (17, 82, 316)

anionic (substances). Substances, such as dyes, tannins, oils, etc., that dissolve in water and ionize so that the characteristic ion (dye, tannin, oil, etc.) is the anion and carries a negative charge. They tend to precipitate with CATIONIC (positive charge) SUBSTANCES. (98, 306)

aniseed. The seed of anise (*Pimpinella anisum*), which produces a pungent oil once used as a preservative for paste.

anisotropic behavior. A material, e.g., paper, that exhibits different properties when tested along axes of different direction. Because paper is hygroscopic, a change in the dimension of its fibers takes place when the relative humidity around it changes; the change is transmitted to the entire sheet, with the result that its length and width are increased or decreased. As the majority of the fibers in machine-made paper lie in the direction of the moving wire of the papermaking machine, i.e., the MACHINE DIRECTION, by far the greater expansion or contraction of dimension of such a paper is in the CROSS DIRECTION, sometimes being on the order of

1.5 to 4.0 times that in the machine direction.

Paper exhibits anisotropic behavior basically because of two factors: 1) as stated above, the orientation of the fibers in the machine direction causes them, and therefore the sheet, to expand or contract preferentially in the cross direction. In fact, at one time it was thought that this was the major reason for anisotropic behavior in paper; 2) more recently, however, although orientation of the fibers is still thought to play a role in the behavior, the major reason is considered to be built-in strain, also known as dried-in strain. The matting of fibers formed from the wet slurry on the wire of the machine moves into the dry end of the papermaking machine and is dried rapidly in the drier sections. Because it is wet, the web will contract during drying. Because the tension of the web is in the plane of the machine direction, the paper is able to contract considerably in the cross direction but not in the machine direction, which results in a built- or dried-in strain. The drying is actually so rapid that relaxation of the strain is impossible on the machine, nor does it occur after the web of paper leaves the machine as the dried paper does not have sufficient plasticity for this to happen. Consequently, a machine-made paper has an inherent dried-in strain. Actually, there is some dried-in strain in the cross direction also, as the felts of the machine reduce shrinkage somewhat in that direction. This characteristic results in an anisotropic sheet, one which will expand more in the cross direction than in the machine direction when exposed to an increase in the relative humidity of the surrounding atmosphere. If, at some time in the future, the paper is wetted in water, the dried-in strains will be released and, if the sheet is then allowed to dry freely and without restraint, its anisotropic characteristics will be largely lost. Anisotropic characteristics in paper are of great importance in printing, especially in printing processes which involve wetting the paper.

annatto. A yellowish-red coloring material obtained from the pulp surrounding the seeds of the annatto tree (*Bixa orellana*), and sometimes used in coloring leather and cloth. It is soluble in both alcohol and oil. Its lack of COLOR FASTNESS makes it unsuitable for archival use.

antelope-finish suede. A fine, soft leather having a velvety, lustrous nap. It is produced from lamb-, goat-, or calfskin,

sueded on the flesh side and finished to resemble antelope leather. (61)

antiblocking agent. A substance used in either a coating mixture or as an overcoating to prevent one sheet of paper from adhering to another, or to any other object, within a specified range of temperature and humidity. Antiblocking agents are usually waxes or synthetic polymers; a light dusting of talcum powder is sometimes used for the same purpose.

antichlor. A substance used in removing the remaining traces of free chlorine or hypochlorite not removed from a paper pulp by washing. Typical antichlors include sodium bisulfite ($NaHSO_3$) and sodium thiosulfite ($Na_2S_2O_3$). The antichlor is usually added to the pulp stock near the end of the bleaching stage, and is allowed to react until no blue coloration is obtained with a potassium-starch indicator. This removes the last traces of hypochlorous acid, hypochlorite ion, and free chlorine. The reaction products are then washed out. Antichlors are seldom used in multistage bleaching operations, as they are considered to be wasteful of bleaching agents. (72)

antifoam agents. *See:* DEFOAMERS.

antimony. A metalloid element (Sb) that is usually a metallic silvery white, but is also found in the black amorphous form. It has been used since at least the late 17th century to blacken the edges of books, especially Bibles, prayer books, and the like. *See also:* BLACK EDGES.

antique. A term used to describe: 1) BLIND TOOLING; 2) a marble pattern (*See:* ANTIQUE MARBLE); 3) a form of edge decoration (*See:* ANTIQUE EDGES); 4) leather finished with an old or natural grain; and 5) a paper with a natural rough surface or finish. *See:* ANTIQUE BOOK PAPER.

antique binding. 1. A modern binding executed in the style of some earlier period, but generally with no intent to deceive. *See also:* CONTEMPORARY BINDING (2). 2. *See:* ECCLESIASTICAL BINDINGS.

antique book paper. A book paper generally produced in the United States from bleached chemical wood pulp with a large amount of short-fibered pulp and given a soft, relatively rough finish. In Great Britain it is produced largely from ESPARTO (GRASS) pulp. Antique book paper varies from lightweight to relatively heavy weight; 60-pound, basis weight antique bulks approximately 330 pages to the inch. Many books, and particularly novels, are printed on this type of paper, especially those containing only textual matter and/or bold line drawings. Antique papers generally are not suitable for fine line drawings or half-tone illustrations. (17, 72)

antique cover paper. A cover paper with an antique finish.

antique edges (antique style). A further embellishment of the edges of a book following gilding. It involves applying gold of a different hue, e.g., LEMON gold, over the gilded edge, with the design being worked into the overlaid gold; the untouched (new) gold then is rubbed off. Sometimes the effect of antique edges is produced without the designs if the original gold is left unburnished, or is burnished and then washed with water. The technique is seldom employed today. *See also:* GAUFFERED EDGES. (241, 343)

antique grain. A surface pattern on leather consisting of markings or creases, usually irregular, in which the hollows or valleys are given a contrasting color to produce a two-tone or two-color effect. The creases are produced either by EMBOSSING (1) or BOARDING (1). (61)

antique marble. A series of marble patterns executed by dropping red, black and yellow, or red, blue and yellow, on the marbling size, and raking once up and down; this is followed by an application of green coloring and, if the pattern is to be an antique spot, pink or green spots. Finally, there is a sprinkling of white. Other colors are also used. The antique marble is produced in a variety of patterns, including spots, straight, and curled. (369)

antique tooling. *See:* BLIND TOOLING.

a pattern. A cloth pattern with a long, narrow grain. *Cf:* J PATTERN; L PATTERN.

apparent density. The weight per unit volume of a sheet of paper. It is calculated by dividing the BASIS WEIGHT of the paper by its caliper. The value so derived depends upon the definition of a ream, i.e., whether 480, 500, 516, etc., sheets. *See also:* DENSITY; SPECIFIC GRAVITY. (17)

apparent specific gravity. The weight of a given volume of leather divided by the weight of an equal volume of water, making no allowance for voids or air spaces in the volume of leather measured. *See also:* SPECIFIC GRAVITY. (363)

appliqué work. A design on EMBROIDERED BINDINGS consisting of spirals in gold and silver which, when flattened, give the appearance of a series of rings. They were sometimes used as a border.

When the appliqué was not very large, a variation was to make a series of small stitches along all edges, masking the stitches with an overlaid gold cord. (111)

apron. 1. The lower cloth on a ruling machine that carries the ruled sheets from the lower cords to the lay-boy or receiving box. 2. The extra amount of unprinted paper left to serve as the binding edge of a leaf that folds out. *See also:* FULL APRON.

aqua regia. A mixture of nitric acid (HNO_3) and hydrochloric acid (HCl), in a solution of one part of the former to three parts of the latter. Aqua regia was used in making so-called "killed spirits," largely in the 18th century, to impart a wine-like tint to red marbling color. The "killed spirits" were produced by adding a block of tin to the acid solution, which resulted in the formation of tin chloride ($HNO_3 + HCl + Sn = SnCl + NO_2 + H_2O$). (152)

aqueous. Containing water, or water based. Adhesive systems such as starch, dextrin, natural gums, animal glue, etc., as well as some inks, certain de-acidification systems, leather tannins, bleaching solutions, and the like that use water as the carrier are aqueous systems.

arabesque. A relatively old form of book decoration, revived by French gilders and reintroduced into England in about 1829. It consists of interlaced lines and convoluted curves arranged in a more or less geometrical pattern. The name derives from the fact that it was brought to its highest perfection by Near Eastern artists. The term is also used to describe a style of ornamentation in relief, consisting of fanciful human or animal figures combined with floral forms. Arabesque is also sometimes inappropriately applied to the embossed designs on book covers. (181, 241, 342)

arabesque plates. Solid brass plates cut, usually in intaglio, with a design and imprinted on a leather cover by means of a blocking press, or large fly embossing press. (152, 181)

arabic gum. *See:* GUM ARABIC.

arabic numerals. The numerical symbols 0, 1, 2, 3, 4, 5, 6, 7, 8, 9, as distinguished from the Roman I, X, L, etc., so called because of their origin in the Near East. They have been used in the foliation of books since the late 15th century. Arabic numerals first appeared in European manuscripts in the 12th century, although they probably came to the Near East by way of India

in the 8th century. Arabic numerals are commonly used for paginating the text of a book, although Roman numerals are still often used for preliminary and end matter, despite the obvious affectation. (156)

archil. A dye obtained from certain lichens of the genera *Roccella* and *Lecanora* by means of fermentation. Its hue varies from moderate red to dark purplish-red, depending on whether the dye bath is acid or alkaline. It was used in the past in the manufacture of purple marbling color. It has only moderate COLOR FASTNESS. (97, 152)

architectural motif. A form of decoration consisting of a pattern of straight lines running almost the length of the cover and connected alternately at head and tail by heavier horizontal lines. (130)

architectural style. A 16th century style of finishing consisting of architectural motifs—porticoes, moldings, columns, pediments, arches, and the like. The central feature was a pair of columns supporting an arch under which there was a panel for lettering of the title. This style, of which only a relatively few examples have survived, generally emphasized straight and curved fillets, interspaced with shaped tools. The 19th century French bookbinder JOSEPH THOUVENIN revived the style as "à la cathédral." *See:* CATHEDRAL BINDINGS. The contents of the books bound in the architectural style seldom related to architecture. (140, 347)

Argentina, Conradus de. *See:* CONRADUS DE ARGENTINA

Armenian bole. A friable, earthy clay, usually of a red color due to the presence of iron oxide; it consists essentially of hydrous silicates of aluminum and (sometimes) magnesium. It is used as a coloring material and is also applied to the edges of books during gilding. In the latter use it serves both to provide a base for the gold leaf and to impart to it a greater depth and luster. When mixed with paste and a small amount of oil, it may be used to sprinkle the edges of books. (335)

arming press. A small hand BLOCKING PRESS, at one time used for impressing ARMORIAL BEARINGS on the covers of books, but now used for blocking short runs of edition bindings, as well as in miscellaneous binding work. (203, 278)

armorial bearings. Solid plates of brass, engraved in relief with family heraldic insignia, and used to block insignia on the covers of books belonging to prominent and/or royal families. Armorial bearings have been seldom used in the decoration of bookbindings since the middle of the 19th century. (128, 262, 347)

armorial bindings (armorial panels). Leather or cloth bindings embossed with armorial seals or plaques, frequently in a panel, or embroidered bindings in which the arms were raised in relief and worked in thread. (69, 342)

art binding. A term sometimes used to describe a book that has been bound by a master craftsman in the "best manner," using only the finest materials available. The term is applied only to books bound by hand and covered in leather or vellum, and usually only to those bindings that are unique or at least distinctive in design. (373)

art canvas. A relatively heavy book cloth, usually impregnated, which may be a single or double WARP and is sometimes lined with tissue paper to prevent penetration of adhesives. It has been used for covering large, heavy books, as well as library bindings. (264)

artificial gold. *See:* IMITATION GOLD.

artificial grain. A grain pattern embossed or rolled into a leather, usually in an attempt to imitate a superior type of leather. *See also:* BASIL; GRAINED UP. (335)

artificial leather. *See:* IMITATION LEATHER.

art linen. A relatively heavy cloth of a generally flat and uneven color, and usually impregnated. When art linens are produced with a design, the patterns are usually florid and ornate. (204)

art paper. 1. A good quality paper used by artists and conservators. It has a highly finished, smooth surface produced by supercalendering or by coating. Its principal characteristic is its close formation. In Great Britain, "art paper" is considered to be a body paper or board coated with a mineral substance, such as barium sulfate or china clay, which gives it a smoothness that is suitable for the printing of fine halftones, and the like. In the United States, art paper is generally made from chemical wood pulp, while in Great Britain the best art paper is made from 90 to 95% esparto and 5 to 10% chemical wood pulp. Esparto is good because it is less likely to stretch and has a natural affinity for coating materials, which gives it a superior surface for halftone reproductions.

Heavily coated art papers are prone to cracking, flaking, and pulling away of the coating. The binding of books produced on such papers can be difficult because of the tendency of the paper to crack when folded. *Cf:* IMITATION ART PAPER.

2. A fancy figured paper used for endpapers in edition binding. (17, 58, 182, 287)

art parchment. A thick, heavy, hard-sized paper manufactured from cotton fiber and/or chemical wood pulps. To some extent it has the natural appearance of PARCHMENT. It is used for documents, or in other applications where a heavy paper is required; in the latter half of the 19th century it was used as a cover paper. *See also:* DOCUMENT PARCHMENT (1). (17)

art vellum. A relatively thin book cloth, which, although impregnated, has only moderately good wearing qualities. It is a smooth cloth with a textured pattern printed on a white base fabric. Art vellums were used extensively for the sides of half- and quarter-bindings. (105, 205)

asbestine. A mineral compound of almost pure fibrous magnesium silicate, which possesses physical characteristics between those of talc and asbestos. It is used as a LOADING (1) agent in paper manufacture, particularly for blotting papers and board. (17)

ash (ash content). The inorganic residue remaining after a sample of paper is burned, driving off combustible and volatile compounds. The "ash content" is defined as the percentage the residue is of the original weight of the sample. (17, 98)

"as is." *See:* BIND "AS IS."

assembly time. A term used in the adhesive industry to indicate the time lapse between the application of an adhesive and the application of heat, pressure, or both. *See also:* CLOSED ASSEMBLY TIME; OPEN ASSEMBLY TIME. (309)

assiette. A compound consisting of bole, bloodstone, and gelena (lead sulfide, PbS), used to prepare the edges of books for gilding. *See also:* GLAIR.

A-stage. An initial stage in the reaction of some thermosetting resins wherein the resin continues to be soluble and fusible. "A-stage" is characterized by an initial lowering of viscosity. Also called "Resol." *See also:* B-STAGE; C-STAGE. (309)

asterisk. The symbol (*) used to mark a corrected page (CANCEL) supplied to the binder to replace an incorrect leaf (CANCELLAND).

atlas. A volume consisting of maps, with or without descriptive material, which is issued to supplement or accompany a text, or is issued independently. An "atlas" is also defined as a volume of plates, engravings, etc., illustrating any field of knowledge. Atlases are sometimes difficult to bind because of narrow margins, stiff and/or heavy paper, or foldouts.

atlas folio. The largest of the folios, with dimensions of approximately 25 or 26 x 17 inches. *See also:* ELEPHANT FOLIO.

atlas paper. A large size of drawing paper similar to map paper except that it is usually coated and made in a basis weight that is heavier so as to minimize SHOW THROUGH. Originally, the term referred to a paper suitable for printing maps and atlases; today, however, MAP PAPER is the more commonly used term. (17)

attaching boards. The process of gluing the tapes and spine-lining material to the inside of single boards or between SPLIT BOARDS, or the LACING-IN of the cords through holes drilled or punched in boards. In general, it is the binding process of joining the boards to the text block; it is not to be confused with CASING-IN. In edition and library binding, the term has no meaning other than gluing the boards to the covering material, either by hand or by means of a CASE-MAKING MACHINE. (236, 335)

attapulgite clay. A fibrous claylike material, essentially $((OH_2)_4 \ Mg_5Si_8O_{20} (OH)_2) - 4H_2O)$, rich in magnesium, and used as a filling material in papermaking, usually in coatings for reproduction papers. The clay is also called "fuller's earth," from its ability to remove dirt and grease from wool, a process called "fulling." (17)

aureole. A light or luminous area surrounding the blind impressions of a book cover; it is caused by the leather not being wetted all over, but only on the areas being tooled.

author's binding. A copy of a book to be presented by an author. Such bindings were normally produced in a superior manner; gilt vellum bindings were common in the 16th century, and panelled morocco in the 17th and 18th. The term has little meaning today. (69)

automatic clamping. A term used with reference to the clamp of a cutting machine, which descends upon any height pile to be cut and exerts approximately the same clamping pressure for all heights and types of material. (145)

automatic spacing. The BACK GAUGE of a cutting machine that moves forward a pre-determined distance following each cut. It is most effective in cutting long-run, large-sized sheets requiring many cuts. (320)

automatic stitcher-feeder machine. A bookbinding machine that gathers and inserts a number of folded sheets and stitches them through the folds. The sheets are either fed by operators to the carrier saddle at various stations, or are fed automatically. As each folio is carried along the saddle, another is fed over it at each station until the section or book is complete. When the section reaches the end of the machine it is automatically knocked even, saddle stitched and delivered to a receiving trough. (179)

aux petits fers. *See:* PETITS FERS.

available chlorine. The amount of chlorine (usually about 35%) in the bleaching powder used by papermakers in bleaching paper pulp, that can be relied upon for bleaching purposes. (197)

avaram (bark). A tree (*Cassia auriculata*) found in India, the bark of which is one of the most important sources of indigenous tannin of the Indian Sub-continent. The bark usually has a tannin content of approximately 18%, along with about 10% soluble non-tans. Avaram has long been used extensively by Indian tanners, and it is because of it that the extensive Madras export trade in light-tanned or half-tanned leathers was established. Although WATTLE (BARK) has largely superseded it in the tannage of cattle hides, avaram is still in great demand for the tannage of goat- and sheep-skins, i.e., "East India kips." Avaram is self-bating and penetrates the skin rapidly, producing a pale colored, tough, elastic leather. Used alone, the leather is likely to develop a reddish color when exposed to sunlight; however completion of the tannage with MYRABOLANS prevents this from happening. Avaram is considered to be an ideal tannin for the preparation of half-tanned skins or kips that are to be shipped elsewhere for finishing. *See also:* VEGETABLE TANNINS. (175)

awl. A pointed tool used in bookbinding for piercing holes in paper for fold sewing, side sewing, or for punching holes in boards preparatory to lacing-in. Awls are available with different points and shapes for different uses; a straight, relatively blunt awl is used for punching holes in boards, while a curved and relatively sharp one is used in sewing. (183)

azured tool. A finishing tool with closely spaced parallel lines cut diagonally across its surface—so called from the use of heraldic illustrations of thin horizontal lines to indicate the color blue. The tool appears to have been introduced in France in about 1545. (59)

b.a. An obsolete designation for a pattern in book cloth resembling linen weaving.

babul (bark). A tree (*Acacia arabica*) found in India and Africa, the bark of which yields one of the most important indigenous tanning materials in the Northern areas of India and Pakistan. The average tannin content of the bark is about 12%, along with about 8% soluble non-tans. Babul is one of the condensed class of tannins, and, when used alone, tans very slowly and produces a leather that is somewhat harsh and dark in color, but firm and durable. It is usually used along with MYRABOLANS to improve color and reduce other undesirable characteristics resulting from the use of babul alone. In recent years the use of babul bark has declined in favor of WATTLE (BARK). *See also:* VEGETABLE TANNINS. (175)

baby calf. A CALFSKIN leather produced from small, lightweight skins of calves that have not been weaned. It has a smooth or fine-boarded grain surface and is free of any artificial surface pattern. The finish is glossy and is produced by ironing, glazing, or plating. Baby calf is fairly tough leather with a dermal network of fine, even texture. *See also:* VEAL. (61)

back. 1. *See:* SPINE. 2. To shape a ridge or shoulder on the sides of the spine of a text block after sewing. *See:* BACKING. 3. The main portion of a HIDE (1), obtained by cutting off both sides of the belly and the head. 4. Boards composed of plies of different stock, the side of superior quality being called the "top" and the other side the "back."

back boarding. The process of BOARDING (1) leather with the flesh side in for the sole purpose of softening it.

backbone. The SPINE (2) of a book.

back cornering. The process in bookbinding of cutting away a small triangular piece of the head and tail edges of the boards of a book at the joints. The cut is made at two angles, one to the board edge and the other to the thickness of the board. The amount removed and the angle of the cut are determined by the width of the leather turn-ins and their thickness where they meet the edge of the board. The purpose of back cornering is to relieve the strain on the joints of the book when the covers are

B

opened; otherwise, a strain would occur because of the additional thickness of the leather caused by the turn-ins. Back cornering also facilitates setting and shaping the headcaps.

Back cornering was at first done on the inside of the boards, allowing for "laced-in" headband cores or tabs. By the late Middle Ages, back cornering was a standard procedure for books with folded-down or stubbed cores. The modern method of cornering on the outside surfaces of the boards facilitates the current method of headcapping and probably stems from the 18th century. (237, 335)

back cover. 1. *See:* LOWER COVER. 2. The outside surface of the lower cover of a publication, such as a periodical issue. The term is used here with reference to publications that contain printed or illustrative matter on the outside of the cover.

backed. 1. A book that has had its spine shaped to create the shoulders to receive the boards. *See:* BACKING. 2. A damaged leaf of a book, either text or plate, that has been "laid down on" or adhered to silk, paper, linen, plastic film, adhesive film, etc., for reinforcement. *See also:* NYLON. 3. *See:* RE-BACKED.

back edge. The left-hand or gutter of a RECTO (1), corresponding to the right-hand edge of a VERSO (1). The opposite edge is the back edge of publications that read from right to left.

backed-filled finish. A type of finish used on cotton cloth. The filling material is applied to the "back" side of the cloth to supply the required body and finish, and does not appear on the "top" or exposed side. (269)

backer (backing machine). A hand- or power-operated machine used for BACKING books. The backer stems from the days when a book was rounded by hand and then placed in the backer to quickly form the shoulders for the boards. Today, in both edition and library binding, the most common method is to round and back books in two consecutive operations in a ROUNDING AND BACKING MACHINE. Unusually large books, which will not fit in a machine, are generally backed by hand or in a hand-operated backer. *See also:* JOB BACKER. (256, 264)

back folds. The folds of the sections of a book, through which they are sewn, or

BACK CORNERING

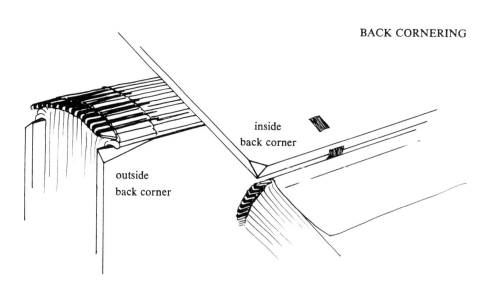

outside
back corner

inside
back corner

otherwise fastened to one another. In context, they are sometimes referred to simply as folds. *See also:* SECTION (1). (237)

back gauge. A movable device on a cutting machine against which the pile of paper or board is placed when measuring the line at which the material is to be cut.

back gluing machine. An edition binding machine used to glue up the spines of books and automatically convey them along a drying section which quickly sets and hardens the glue. The maximum size book that can usually be processed in such a machine is 12 by 9 inches, and the minimum 3 by 2 inches, with a thickness up to 2½ inches. A fully automatic back gluing machine can process up to 2,400 books an hour. *See also:* TRIPLE LINING AND HEADBANDING MACHINE. (343)

backing. The process of shaping a ridge or shoulder on each side of the spine of a text block prior to the application of the spine lining material. The backs of the sewn sections or leaves are bent over from the center to the left and right until shoulders are formed against which the boards will fit. The dimension of the shoulders is determined by the thickness of the boards to be used, which, in turn, is determined by the size and bulk of the book. In addition to providing for the boards, backing also: 1) allows for the swell of the spine caused by the thread used in sewing, or by excessive guarding; 2) helps maintain the round of the book by the fact that each leaf from the center outward is folded over the leaf next to it so that it cannot work its way forward and thus cause the book to

BACKING

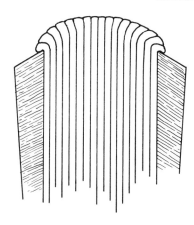

cave in (*See:* START); 3) helps impart more flexibility to the book by creating a slight crease in each leaf near the spine, to the extent that backing has something of a scoring effect which makes the book easier to open and facilitates turning the leaves (*See:* SCORE); and 4) makes a better joint for the cover, one which opens easier and is stronger, since the point of strain during opening is spread over a strip of the covering material, e.g., a FRENCH JOINT. Furthermore, the angle of conformation of the spine caused by backing probably provides for better vertical standing support of the text block.

Backing may be accomplished by hand with the use of a BACKING HAMMER or, in the case of edition and library binding, by means of a ROUNDING AND BACKING MACHINE. In some cases—e.g., very large books—backing may be done in a BACKER as a separate operation.

Some authorities consider the backing of a book to be the most important and difficult of all the processes in the craft of hand bookbinding, and poor or inadequate backing is certainly one of the major sources of problems in the processes of edition and library bookbinding.

Although books dating from at least as early as the beginning of the second half of the 15th century were often rounded, backing for the purpose of forming shoulders seems not to have been an established procedure before 1500, or perhaps somewhat later. It is uncertain when bookbinders discovered that rounding and backing was a superior bookbinding technique. The swell caused by sewing sometimes causes books to assume a slight round with no effort on the part of the bookbinder, and, over a long period of time, the pressure of the boards perhaps even results in the effect of backing. (209, 236, 335, 339)

backing boards. The boards used in hand binding to assist in BACKING a book. Backing boards are generally made of a very hard wood and are frequently faced with strips of metal. The upper edge of the board is beveled at an angle of approximately 80°, over which the outer sections or leaves on both sides of the text block are bent. The board is also thicker at this edge than at the lower, so that when it is placed on the side of the text block near the spine and secured in the LYING PRESS, the force of the press is concentrated nearest the spine. (92, 183, 335)

backing flannel. A heavy cloth material

used at times to line the spines of larger books. A more common technique today is to use two linings, usually a first lining of cloth over which is applied a paper lining *See also:* SPINE LINING FABRIC. (27, 196)

backing hammer. A heavy iron hammer with a short handle, heavy face, and wedge-shaped head, used in rounding and backing books. It is sometimes referred to as a "collet hammer" or "bumping hammer" *See also:* BACKING; ROUNDING AND BACKING MACHINE. (335)

backing iron. *See:* BACK-MOLDING IRON.

backing paper. *See:* INLAY (1); SPINE LINING PAPER.

backing press. A vertically oriented press with steel plates brought together by means of a single screw. The top edge of each plate is beveled to an angle of approximately 80°, so that when the plates are closed on the text block, the press serves the same function as BACKING BOARDS. (25)

back lining. *See:* SPINE LINING.

back margin. The INNER MARGIN, or the margin between the point where the sections or leaves are joined and the edge of the print. In books that read from left to right it is the left-hand margin of a printed recto, corresponding to the right-hand margin of the verso. Also called "gutter margin." (102)

back mark. The disfiguring ridge or "mark" in a sheet of paper which has been dried on a pole or line. Also called "pole mark," or "stick mark."

back-molding iron. An implement, usually made of iron, approximately 20 inches long, 6 inches wide and 2½ inches thick, and used in forming the

BACK-MOLDING IRON

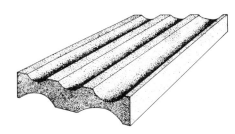

millboard for the SPRING-BACK of a book. The iron is made with several grooves of various widths on both sides. (264)

back saw. A short, fine-toothed hand saw

stiffened by means of a metal rib along its back edge. It is used to saw-in the kettle kerfs and the grooves for sawn-in cords. Although almost any small saw will suffice in lieu of the back saw, it has the advantages of being short, stiff and easy to hold. It must be very sharp to avoid tearing the paper. Also called "tenon saw."

backstrip. 1. A term used incorrectly with reference to the SPINE of a book. *See also:* REBACKED. 2. *See:* GUARD (1). 3. *See:* INLAY (1).

back to fore edge. The distance from the spine to the fore edge of a book. The term is probably used mainly to indicate that a book is of uniform thickness across its width, i.e., that the boards are parallel. The implication is that there has been proper compensation for any swelling of the spine caused by sewing or excessive guarding. *See also:* BACKING; CONVEX COVERS. (335)

bacterial resistance. The resistance of a material to the growth of bacteria and/ or mold. This property represents one of the more significant advantages of resinous adhesives over the conventional adhesives. (258)

bactericide. A material used in small concentrations, e.g., 0.1% by weight of the material being treated, to kill, or inhibit the growth of, bacteria that may occur in liquid or solid adhesives, or may attack carbohydrate or proteinaceous adhesive films. (222)

Badier, Florimond (fl 1645-1660). A Parisian bookbinder, apprenticed to Jean Thomas in 1630, who became a master bookbinder in 1645. His name is associated with the art of POINTILLÉ (1) and sumptuous doublures. Badier also used a distinctive finishing stamp cut in the shape of a man's head. Only three signed bindings of his are known; many bindings attributed to him may be the work of imitators. At one time, Badier was considered by some authorities to be the legendary LE GASCON; this was largely because of his pointillé style. (73, 347)

bagasse pulp. A paper pulp obtained from the crushed stalks of sugar cane (usually considered to be *Saccharum officinarum*), following the extraction of the juices. The pulp is prepared for use by mechanical disintegration in water, either with or without chemical treatment. The pulp produced is coarse, bulky, and of low strength, and is used principally in the manufacture of boards. (72)

bag binding. An additional protective covering provided a book. It is usually made of leather. *See also:* GIRDLE BOOK. (104)

Bagguley, Thomas. An English bookbinder, of Newcastle under Lyme, who, in the late 19th century, devised a method of tooling vellum and similar materials in permanent colors. Bagguley limited his technique to vellum, as he considered leather to be too lacking in purity of color to offer a satisfactory ground for unrestricted color decoration. Because of the delicate nature of his work, he further restricted his technique to vellum doublures. *See also:* "SUTHERLAND" DECORATION. (94)

BAND NIPPERS

ball tool. A small finishing tool cut in the shape of a ball.

bamboo. A giant grass of the tribe *Bambusseae*, located in the tropical areas of the Eastern Hemisphere, and cultivated successfully in some parts of the southern United States. The fibers are not unlike those of straw in many aspects. Bamboo fibers have an average length of 2.4mm., which puts them between the softwood and hardwood fibers. It is used extensively in India for the manufacture of all grades of chemical pulp and paper. Paper made from it is relatively soft and bulky, with a high tearing resistance but relatively low burst and tensile strength. Although writing and printing papers are produced from 100% bamboo pulp, superior results are realized when the bamboo is blended with other pulps that increase burst and tensile strength.

Bamboo is also the traditional material used in making molds and other devices used in the manufacture of handmade paper. (17, 143)

band board. A wooden block about 9 by 12 inches, 6 inches thick at the head and 5 at the foot, on which headbanders in library binderies used to lay their zinc boards with dampened headbands, prior to attaching them to the text blocks. (256).

band driver. A blunt, chisel-shaped tool, usually made of wood, and used in hand binding to attain uniformity and also to correct any irregularities of the bands on which the book is sewn. *See also:* BAND NIPPERS. (94, 261)

banding. *See:* BANDS (2).

band nippers. Pincers which have broad, flat jaws, used for straightening the bands of a book sewn on raised cords, and also for nipping up the leather during covering. The better nippers are nickleplated or made of stainless steel to avoid discoloring the leather, and are equipped with a spring to keep the jaws open when in use. (161)

band pallet. A type of PALLET (1) used to impress a complete design on the spine of a book between the raised bands. Sometimes called a "butterstamp." (97)

band pattern. A device, generally made of brass, with holes drilled indicating the position of the bands of books to be sewn on raised cords. (264)

bands. 1. The cords or thongs on which the sections of books are sewn. They may be raised for FLEXIBLE SEWING, sawn-in for RECESSED-CORD sewing, or FLEXIBLE NOT TO SHOW. Early bands (or thongs, as they were originally called) were made of leather, which was not very durable, or tawed skin, which was very durable. Leather thongs began to be replaced by cords during the latter years of the 16th century. Hemp and linen cords are commonly used today.

Sewing on raised bands came into use in England sometime between the 12th and 13th centuries, although the technique had been introduced into northern Europe centuries earlier. The first raised band sewing was on double bands, ranging in number from two to five. The bands were positioned so that there was a greater space between the bands themselves than between the top and bottom bands and the head and tail of the book. Single bands began to replace double ones and, by the mid-16th century, had become predominant in the more economical styles of binding.

2. Strips of reinforcing material (usually leather) which extend across the spine, or spring-back, and onto the sides of a book, usually a stationery binding. The bands may be placed on the boards before covering, in which case they are called "underbands," or

BANDS

over the covering material, where they are known as "overbands." Bands are used to strengthen large blankbooks in the area of the joints, and to provide additional leather at areas of heavy surface abrasion. They also protect, to some extent, the lettering on the spine of the book. When overbands are used, they are generally decorated in some manner, usually in the design of their lacing or riveting; this step is needed because adhesive alone will not keep the overbands attached to the book. In the case of underbands, the decoration of the covering leather is often concentrated around the area of the bands.

The size and position of the bands, both over and under, are based on definite proportions of the cover of the book. Bands may be single, double, or double straight. When single bands are used, the cover is divided into 19 equal parts. Each band is 3/19 the length of the cover, and there are 3/19 the cover

length between the bands. The top and bottom bands are each 2/19 from the head and tail edges of the cover, respectively. All three bands extend into the cover 2/5 of its width. Double bands, in addition to providing additional strength across the spine, also provide an additional thickness of leather along the edges of the boards. These bands are more complicated than single bands, as the bands at head and tail are equal to 5/19 of the length of the cover, with 2 of the 5/19 bands extending the full width of the cover, while the other 3/19 extend only the customary 2/5. The center band also extends 2/5 the width. With double band there is no space between the bands and the head and tail of the boards.

A variation of the double band is the double straight. In this technique, the length of the cover is divided into five equal segments. Each band is 1/5 the length of the cover. The head and tail bands extend the full width of the cover, while the middle one extends the customary 2/5.

Bands were also used to some extent

BANDSTICKS

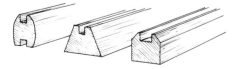

in limp vellum binding, in which case the bands were sewn through the sections of the book.

The use of bands as a technique for strengthening bindings has been practiced since at least the 14th century. At one time they were commonly referred to as "Russia bands" because of the use of RUSSIA LEATHER in making them.

3. Lines in gold or in blind impressed by means of a pallet across the spine of a book sewn on recessed cords in the same positions as would be occupied by the raised bands used in flexible sewing. 4. False bands attached to a HOLLOW BACK book or a TIGHT BACK book sewn on recessed cords, in imitation of flexible sewing. 5. The strips of brass attached to the tail edges of the covers of large blankbooks, for the purpose of protecting the leather covering from wear. 6. A form of decoration consisting of wide parallel lines with ornaments impressed between them. (83, 123, 152, 236, 241, 256, 264, 343)

bands frayed. The cords (bands) of a book which have been separated (frayed out) into individual threads. The frayed out cords, which extend out from the text block 1 to 2½ inches, are glued between split boards, and are frayed out so as to avoid bulging of the boards. *Cf:* LACING-IN. (25)

bandstick. 1. A hard, smooth length of wood, frequently beechwood, used in pressing and smoothing the leather over the bands on the spine. The bandstick may consist of a narrow strip having a smooth sharpened edge on one side, in which case it is used to work one side of a band at a time, or it may be grooved so that the stick fits over the band. The latter type may have graduated grooves on both sides to accomodate bands of varying widths. 2. A tapering length of hard, smooth wood, used in pressing and smoothing the leather on the spine between the raised bands. Also called "rubbing-up stick." (232, 264)

barium carbonate. A white compound ($BaCO_3$), insoluble in water. The use of BARIUM HYDROXIDE in the deacidification of paper results in the formation of barium carbonate as the alkaline reserve in the paper, due to the action of atmospheric carbon dioxide on the barium hydroxide.

barium hydroxide. A white, toxic alkali ($Ba(OH)_2$), formed by the reaction of barium monoxide with water, or by the action of sodium hydroxide on soluble barium salts. It is one of the agents used in the non-aqueous deacidification of paper.

barium sulfate. A white, soluble, heavy compound ($BaSO_4$), obtained either from the natural mineral barytes, or by chemical treatment of barium with sulfuric acid, and used both as a filler and coating pigment in paper manufacture, particularly photographic papers. It is used alone or in combination with other pigments. It has good affinity for ink, a bright color, and good opacity. It does not, however, produce a high finish. It is also used to form the pigment LITHOPONE. The artificial compound is also known as "blanc fixe." (72)

bark. 1. The outer surfaces of trees and other woody plants. The inner side of the bark of certain trees, e.g., birch, has been used in the past as a surface for writing. Bark books were rather common in Central Asia and the Far East until comparatively recent times. Bark is vulnerable to dampness and curling in climates of high relative humidity and to cracking in dry areas. 2. *See:* VEGETABLE TANNINS. (102)

barkometer. An instrument used to measure the weight of a vegetable tannin liquor per unit volume.

bark skiver. A vegetable (oak bark) tanned sheepskin, light tan in color, and used extensively in the 19th century as a covering material for law books. It is not considered to be either permanent or durable. *See also:* LAW SHEEP.

bark tanned. A general term used to indicate a leather that has been vegetable tanned mainly by means of tannins derived from the bark of trees, as distinguished from mixed tannages. *See also:* VEGETABLE TANNINS.

barm skin. The name given a leather apron sometimes worn by bookbinders.

barrier sheet. A leaf inserted in a book to prevent the transfer of ink (and possibly acid substances) from a plate or illustration to a facing page, as well at times to elucidate the plate or illustration it accompanies. The sheet may be a highly sized paper, so called acid-free paper, or, more often, glassine paper. It may be loose in the book, sewn in with the binding, or, in the usual case, tipped to the leaf it protects. Barrier sheets are frequently made of an inferior quality of paper, one which will eventually develop acidity that can in turn be transferred to the facing text leaves, weakening them. For this reason, they should be removed, or, if they bear letterpress and therefore must be retained, deacidified

and buffered, strengthened (if necessary), and reinserted in the volume. *See also:* ACID MIGRATION. (173)

bar roll. A ROLL (1) cut with a series of parallel raised lines at right angles to its sides.

Barrow, William J. (1904-1967). An American document restorer and former director of the W. J. Barrow Research Laboratory, located in Richmond, Virginia, at one time considered by many authorities to be the leading independent scientific center for research into paper and the deterioration of paper. Barrow developed a process for laminating brittle documents between tissue and cellulose acetate film, as well as a highly effective means of deacidifying paper. He demonstrated the actual facts of paper stability over the past four centuries and developed a durable paper having a high degree of permanence. Barrow was also involved in other investigations connected with paper and ink for a period of more than 30 years, and was probably the most important single contributor to the knowledge of methods of achieving permanence and durability of archival materials. The Barrow laboratory ceased operations in 1977. *See also:* DEACIDIFICATION; LAMINATION. (7)

Bartlett, Roger (c 1633-1712). An English bookbinder who was apprenticed to Samuel Satterthwaite in 1647, and was set up in his own business in London in 1654. He subsequently left London and set up business in Oxford some time after the great fire of 1666 and began producing the excellent gold-tooled presentation books for which he is well known. His bindings include certain distinctive features, including rows of floral volutes along cottage roofs, as well as swags hanging from the eves. Bartlett retired to his birthplace (Watlington in Oxfordshire) in 1711 or 1712, apparently having sold his bindery. The latest important binding executed by Bartlett is dated 1685, but records indicate that he continued binding thereafter. (50, 205, 253)

barytes. *See:* BARIUM SULFATE.

base. 1. *See:* ALKALI. 2. A metal block on which a die or electro for stamping or embossing is mounted. 3. A prepared bed in a blocking press over which cases are fed, and which provides a solid foundation for producing sharp impressions.

base coat. The first of a multiple system of coatings. The base coat is frequently a relatively inexpensive filling material designed to prevent excessive penetra-

tion of subsequent and often more expensive coatings.

base fabric. In general, the basic cloth used for covering books, regardless of the final form it may take, i.e., coated, impregnated, or filled. Base cloths are usually of cotton, thoroughly cleaned, free from waste, evenly woven, with the warp yarns woven in pairs. (209)

basic dyes. A class of dyes, usually synthetic, that act as bases, and which are actually ANILINE DYES. Their color base is not water soluble but can be made so by converting the base into a salt. The basic dyes, while possessing great tinctorial strength and brightness, are not generally light-fast; therefore their use in the dyeing of archival materials is largely restricted to those materials not requiring this characteristic. Basic dyes were at one time used extensively in dyeing leather, mainly because they are capable of combining directly with vegetable-tanned leather without the use of a mordant. *See also:* DYE. (17, 62, 72)

basic size. The sheet size of paper, determined by trade custom, as that agreed upon for calculating the BASIS WEIGHT of the paper. Initially it was the size which could be printed, folded and trimmed with the greatest economy. Some of the specifications for basic sizes in use in the United States are:

Type of paper	Size (in inches)
Bible	25 X 38
Blanks	22 X 38
Blotting	19 X 24
Bond	17 X 22
Book	25 X 38
Cover	20 X 26
Glassine	24 X 36
Gummed	25 X 38
Index	25½ X 30½
Ledger	17 X 22
Manifold	17 X 22
Manuscript	18 X 31
Mimeograph	17 X 22
Newsprint	24 X 36
Offset	25 X 38
Onionskin	17 X 22
Opaque	25 X 38
Poster	24 X 36
Tag	22½ X 28½
or	24 X 36
Text	25 X 38
Tissues	24 X 36
Vellum bristol	22½ X 28½
Writing	17 X 22

All are based on a ream of 500 sheets. (17, 316, 324)

basil. A vegetable-tanned, sheep- or lambskin, producing a soft, smooth leather but with only moderately good wearing qualities. Its smooth surface lends itself well to graining in imitation of other skins, such as goat. There are several types of basil, including E. I. (East India), N. Z. (New Zealand) and Aus. (Australia), all of which are generally tanned with native or mimosa bark. Crust basils are tanned loose in pits and sold dry as taken from the drying sheds; strained basils are tanned as *crust,* but wet down, set out with a slicker, stretched and allowed to dry; tawed basils are sheepskins dressed with alum and salt and finished in a white or nut brown color; and organ basils are also tawed but with the salt removed. Diced basils are skins which have been dyed red, glazed, and embossed with a diced cross line. Because of their relatively poor wearing characteristics, basils are not often used today in bookbinding, although in the first half of the 20th century they were employed fairly extensively in binding cheaper blankbooks, and the like. (61, 69, 343)

basis weight. The actual weight of a ream of paper (normally 500 sheets, but at times 480 or 516), cut to its BASIC SIZE. The standard, or basic, size ream of paper varies with different grades of paper. Some papers and boards are produced to a specified caliper (thickness), rather than to a specific weight; an example of this is heavy cover paper. The United States Government Printing Office uses a unit of 1,000 sheets, which is also used in the M. M. SYSTEM. In most foreign countries, as well as in certain domestic test procedures, the standard size is a square meter, with the weight being expressed in grams per square meter. The basis weight of board is commonly expressed in pounds per 1,000 square feet. Book paper basis weights are based on the 25 by 38 inch sheet size, while cover paper weights are calculated on a size of 20 by 26 inches. (17, 72, 334)

basket cloth. A fancy weave of cloth, usually a better grade of buckram with a pattern similar to the wicker work in baskets. In the first decades of the 20th century it was used to some extent in edition binding. (256, 264)

bast fibers. Strong woody fibers obtained from both the phloem and pericycle of various plants, and used in the manufacture of paper. Bast fibers, which include those of hemp, jute, mitsumata, and ramie, among others, are generally thinner than cotton fibers but their tubes have thicker walls than does cotton. Bast fibers are also generally

stiffer and stronger than cotton fibers. (17, 42, 198)

bathbrick. Powdered brick used in dusting the GOLD CUSHION before laying on the GOLD LEAF for cutting. Its purpose is to prevent the leaf from sticking to the cushion. (130, 335)

batik. A cloth consisting of a dyed fabric of which parts which are not intended to be colored are protected by wax, which is later removed. Batik is used for covering books, particularly in the area of Indonesia where the technique originated, and also as a novelty in other areas. (332)

bating. A process which is usually defined as "reducing" or "removing." The basic purposes of DELIMING and bating are to remove calcium hydroxide (or other alkali) from the skin, to lower pH, and, of great importance, to treat the skin substance with proteolytic enzymes so as to obtain desired grain appearance in the finished leather. Bating also serves to impart softness, stretch, and flexibility to the leather, while at the same time providing the basis for a clean, smooth grain by loosening scud consisting of hair roots, pigment materials and grease. It also eliminates all traces of the firm, plumped, and swollen state of the skin induced by the alkaline unhairing liquors by bringing the skin into a soft, fallen condition. Today bating is employed mainly in tanning light leathers, such as those used in bookbinding, where drape, flexibility, and softness of handle are of primary importance.

The origin of bating is somewhat obscure but probably dates back to the time when LIMING was not a common practice. It may have been originated by a tanner who noticed that skins badly soiled with dung often produced a softer, stretchier, silkier leather.

As recently as the early years of the present century, the process of bating consisted of immersing the delimed skins in water at a temperature of 35-40° C., and then adding a liquid paste of pigeon or hen dung. The skins were run in this liquor until they acquired a particularly soft, flaccid and silky handle. The finished leather was found to have a very smooth, clean, flat, flexible grain and was very soft and stretchy. Considerable variations in time, temperature and quantities were used for various types of leather. The effect of bating was produced by enzymes, which, under appropriate conditions of temperature and pH, are capable of dissolving and digesting some of the protein constituents of the

skin. In a properly controlled process they are given only sufficient time for further removal of undesirable inter-fibrillary proteins, or to modify or weaken those fiber structures which, by binding the collagen fibers tightly together, would cause the grain to be wrinkled and the resultant leather to have no stretch.

Today bating is accomplished by the the use of enzymes extracted from animal tissue, e.g., the pancreas of swine or sheep, or from microorganisms such as molds and bacteria, called respectively pancreatic and bacterial bates. (248, 275, 291, 306, 363)

batwing skiver. A bookbinder's expression for the thinnest SKIVER produced. It is made from the flesh split of sheepskin, and was at one time used for linings and title labels for law and similar books. (91, 274)

Baumé (hydrometer). A hydrometer for measuring the density of liquid and gum solutions, named after its inventor, Antoine Baumé. The Baumé scale is either of two arbitrary hydrometer scales, one for liquids heavier than water and the other for liquids lighter than water, that indicate specific gravity in degrees. The calculation (in the United States) for liquids heavier than water is:

$$\text{Specific gravity at } \frac{60°}{60°} \text{ F} = \frac{145}{145 - °\text{Baumé}}$$

and for liquids lighter than water:

$$\text{Specific gravity at } \frac{60°}{60°} \text{ F} = \frac{140}{130 + °\text{Baumé}}$$

Slightly different conversions are used in other countries or in specific industries. (179, 362)

bead. 1. An old American term for HEAD-BAND. 2. A small twist formed when twisting the silk or cotton in head-banding. 3. A fore-edge clasp made of cat gut and beads, used to keep vellum bindings tightly closed. *See also:* CLASPS. (83, 250, 261)

beamhouse operations. The processes in leather manufacture that take place following curing and preceding the actual tannage of the skin. These processes include some or all of the following: SOAKING (1), LIMING, UN-HAIRING, SCUDDING, FLESHING, DELIMING, BATING (or PUERING), DRENCHING, AND PICKLING, not necessarily always in the order given. The skin may also be split before tanning. The principal objectives of beamhouse operations are to rid the stock of substances not wanted in the finished leather, notably the class of proteins known as keratin, and to put the skins into the proper chemical and physical condition for subsequent processing. To produce satisfactory leather, beamhouse operations must be carried out in such a manner that no damage is done to the fibrous (collagen) part of the skin that is converted into leather, nor to its internal structure.

The term derives from the "beam," a convex wooden slab sloping upward from the floor, over which the raw stock is placed for trimming, fleshing, unhairing, or scudding by hand. (248, 363)

beater. A machine used in papermaking. It consists essentially of a tank, usually provided with a partition or "midfeather," that contains a heavy roll designed to revolve against a bedplate. Both roll and bedplate can be fitted with horizontal metal bars set on edge. In operation, the pulp material in a water slurry circulates between the roll and bedplate and is rubbed, cut, macerated, and separated into a fibrous mass for further processing into paper. Sometimes fillers, loadings, dyes, etc., are added to the stock in the beater. Some authorities contend that the beater, introduced in 1670, was partially responsible for the decline in quality of paper, as miniscule iron particles, breaking away from the sides or working parts of the machine, entered the paper and caused it to deteriorate. *See also:* REFINER. (17, 58)

beater sized. A paper which has been sized by means of materials added to the BEATER, or if not the beater, to the pulp before sheet formation, as contrasted to paper that has been SURFACE SIZED, or TUB SIZED. (17)

beating. 1. A hand operation of flattening the leaves or sections of a book before sewing, the purpose of which is to compress or, in the process of rebinding, to remove the backing shoulders. *See:* KNOCKING OUT THE GROOVE. Books are seldom beaten today. *See:* BUNDLING (1); NIPPING (1); SMASHING. 2. The process of swelling and separating the fibers and fibrils of rags, wood pulp, etc., either batchwise or in a BEATER, or by passage through a REFINER. (261, 350)

beating hammer. A heavy, short-handled hammer, with a bell-shaped face, used in beating the leaves and sections of a book so as to flatten and compress them. Such hammers generally weigh 10 to 14 pounds, and sometimes even up to 16 pounds. The introduction of the ROLLING MACHINE (1827) made the beating hammer virtually obsolete. (172, 236)

beating stone. A marble or litho stone, or a flat plate of iron, set in a frame filled with sand, on which the leaves or sections of books are beaten. (261)

bed. The base of a standing (or similar) press, on which books are placed and toward which the PLATEN descends.

Bedford, Francis (1800-1884). An English bookbinder whose work was considered to be unsurpassed by any of his contemporaries. Bedford worked for Charles Lewis until the latter's death in 1836, and then with John Clarke until 1850 when he started his own business. Bedford copied earlier Venetian bindings, with twisted or Saracenic ornaments, as well as later Veneto-Lyonese bindings common in England during the reign of Elizabeth I. He also produced many imitations of the mosaics of ANTOINE MICHEL PADELOUP. (347)

Bedford style. Hand-stained bindings produced from a leather sometimes referred to as "fair calf" (a bark tanned calfskin), washed over frequently with a weak solution of potassium carbonate (K_2CO_3), and exposed to light. The staining process took as long as 6 months. In addition to the potassium carbonate, copperas (ferrous sulfate— $FeSO_4$), also known as "green vitriol," was used to produce a particular effect. The carbonate gave a warm brown-toned sprinkle, the sulfate gave a gray, and the two together gave a black. *Cf:* ETRUSCAN CALF. (94, 154, 236, 347)

beeswax. A wax obtained from the hives of bees, i.e., an animal wax. Beeswax is a complex substance secreted by the worker bees for the purpose of constructing honeycombs. The wax is obtained by melting the honeycomb structure, and then filtering the wax before it is allowed to set. Beeswax usually contains a number of mineral wax adulterants. The wax, which is often bleached by shredding it into thin flakes and setting it out in the sun, has a softening range of 62-66° C. It is used: 1) to lubricate the thread used in sewing books by hand; 2) with LANOLIN and other substances for LEATHER DRESSINGS. In the latter use it is considered valuable by some conservationists because, as it is harder than most other waxes, it supplies body to the dressing at a reasonably low softening temperature, and also provides a polished or glossy finish which some find desirable; its use, however, as well as that of any wax on leather,

is considered by a number of authorities to be detrimental to the permanence of leather; 3) as a base for the colors used in MARBLING; and 4) to provide a suitable surface for burnishing the gilt edges of books, although it is generally considered to be inferior to CARNAUBA WAX in this application, as carnauba is less likely to streak. (29, 291, 335)

beeswing. *See:* HIDE BUFFING.

Belgian hare. A long-legged breed of rabbit found in Belgium, the hind leg of which was the traditional implement used by gold beaters to apply finely powered gypsum (BRIME) to the goldbeater's skins. This was done to eliminate as much roughness as possible to allow the gold to expand freely and evenly over the skin. (29)

belly. The extreme left or right side of a complete hide, removed by cutting the hide along a line parallel to the spine and at such a distance from it as to remove approximately 23% of the total area of the hide for the two bellies. The belly includes the front and hind shank. The line of cutting is determined more accurately for any individual hide by noting the change in feel from the denser structure of the crop to the looser structure of the belly. (61, 363)

belly grain. The tanned, outer grain side split from a BELLY.

benched. An obsolete term referring to a book prepared for sewing or some other forwarding operation. It was also applied to the process of flattening the backing ridge of a section. *See:* KNOCKING OUT THE GROOVE. (164, 256)

bench knife. Two blades, the upper of which is curved and fitted with a handle, while the lower is drilled and countersunk so that it can be bolted to the bench. Bench knives are made in various sizes to cut from 16 to 42 inches. They are useful for cutting lightweight board, but are not as heavy or efficient as the BOARD CUTTER. (66)

bench sewing. An obsolete term applied to sewing a book through the folds, the significance being that the sewing was done on a SEWING FRAME, or bench.

Bentonite. A claylike mineral consisting largely of montmorillonite, and characterized by its high absorptive power and active colloidal properties. It is usually dark, dull, and powdery, but waxy on freshly cut surfaces. Its color varies from yellowish-green to nearly black. Bentonites are products of the change of volcanic ash, and are characterized by an alkaline oxide and alkaline earth content of 5 to 11%. They are used as a filler in paper, for deinking paper pulp, for decreasing pitch problems in papermaking, and the like. The name derives from its discovery in Benton, Wyoming. (17)

benzene. A colorless, aromatic hydrocarbon (C_6H_6), usually obtained by the carbonization of coal, or from petroleum fractions by means of catalytic dehydrogenation. It is used to remove excess glair or grease from leather bindings. Although used extensively in the past, it is seldom used today because of its high flammability and extremely toxic nature. It is not to be confused with benzine (also used for the same purposes), which is a petroleum product obtained by distillation.

bergamot. A pear-shaped fruit (*Citris bergamia*), the rind of which yields a pungent oil, used at one time as a preservative for paste. (371)

beta cellulose. That part of a cellulosic material which will dissolve in an alkaline solution under the conditions of the ALPHA CELLULOSE test, but which will reprecipitate if the alkaline solution is acidified. *See also:* GAMMA CELLULOSE. (17)

between bands. The spaces on the spine of a book between the raised bands, either the ones on which the book is sewn or the false bands attached to give the outward appearance of genuine bands. For purposes of decoration, the spaces are referred to as panels. (94)

bevel. 1. The angle of the bevel of BEVELED BOARDS. 2. The angle of cut of the edges of a panel or of an INLAY (4) or ONLAY.

beveled boards (beveled edges). The boards of a book, and especially the large, thick boards of heavy books, which have been cut or sanded on the outside or inside edge along the head, tail, and fore edge. The purpose of beveling is to remove the clumsy effect of thick boards and create a pleasing, tactile quality.

The outside edges of boards usually were square until the 13th century; after that time, they were often beveled, sometimes steeply, or, in the case of decorated bindings, on a more gentle slope. The inside edges were also frequently beveled during the 15th century, particularly in Germany.

When the outer edges of boards are beveled the edge along the spine is also often beveled on the inside, so that it follows the swelling of the spine. (58, 236)

bhabar. *See:* SABAI GRASS.

bibelot. An unusually small book. *See also:* MINIATURE BOOK.

Bible paper. A very lightweight, highly opaque paper, used primarily for low bulk books, such as Bibles, dictionaries, etc. Its basis weight generally ranges from 14 to 30 pounds ($25 \times 38 - 500$). Bible paper of a basis weight of 20 pounds bulks up to 1,100 sheets per inch. The paper is generally produced from bleached chemical wood pulps, often with the addition of mixes of linen and/or cotton fiber, along with rag pulps, flax, and the like. Bible paper is heavily loaded with titanium oxide or other high grade pigments to improve opacity. Other important characteristics, other than printability, include strength, good folding endurance, and permanence. The term "Bible paper" is sometimes used with reference to any book paper having a basis weight of 30 pounds or less. *See also:* INDIA PAPER. (17, 58, 365)

Bible style. A style of binding at one time applied to all flexible, round-cornered, leather bookbindings. *See also:* YAPP STYLE. (256)

bibliogenesis. Of or relating to the production of books.

bibliogony. Of or relating to the production of books. Also called "bibliogenesis."

bibliology. The scientific description of books from the earliest times to the present, including all of the materials and processes involved in their production.

bibliopedist. The craftsman or worker who binds books; a bookbinder. The term is most appropriately applied to one who binds books by hand.

bibliopegic. Of or relating to the binding of books.

bibliopegistic. Of, or relating to, a bookbinder, especially one who binds books by hand.

bibliopegy. The art or craft of binding books. The term is more appropriately applied to the craft of binding books by hand.

bid. A written, usually legally binding, offer of a bookbinder, generally the owner of a bindery, but sometimes an individual bookbinder, to bind the books of another for a certain price, either by the individual book or by lot. A bid may be negotiated in any of several manners, usually according to the wishes of the customer. The binder may quote a flat price for all materials submitted for binding, regardless of style or format; he may quote two prices, one for serial publications or serial-format materials and

another price, usually lower, for monographs and similar materials; he may bid on all work according to the height of the trimmed and cased work, e.g., up to and including 8 inches, over 8 inches and including 10 inches, etc., usually with an additional charge for extra thickness, e.g., greater than 2½ inches; he may quote a flat rate for materials according to type, i.e., textbooks, fiction, reference books, theses, etc.; or, he may quote according to both height and format, e.g., 8, 10, 12 inches, etc., serials, 8, 10, 12 inches, etc., monographs, and so on. A bid may also include a stipulation (and a quote) of extra charges, as for example, hand sewing, pockets, stubbing, scoring, guarding, etc.

In extra (hand) binding, on the other hand, the binder will generally quote an estimated price for the individual book, or for a specified group of books, with the understanding that the final price (which to a great degree will depend on the amount of time spent on each book) may be higher or lower.

Assuming there is no decrease in the quality of the binding provided, and that the binder adheres faithfully to the specifications, the advantage of a bid situation is that the library may enjoy lower prices for its binding. The disadvantages, however, probably outweigh any monetary saving. Bookbinding, whether by a company or an individual, is essentially a service and not a commodity, and a successful binding program, i.e., one that is designed to preserve a collection over the long run, depends more on mutual cooperation and recognition as to the purpose of the library, as well as what the binder can and cannot do, than on any possible savings resulting from a low bid.

bight. The length of a single stitch in a machine-sewn book.

bind. *See:* BIND ALL; BIND "AS IS;" BIND FROM SHEETS; BIND IN; BOOKBINDING.

bind all. An instruction to the binder to bind a volume, usually a serial publication, with title page, index, advertisements, or any other material attached.

bind "as is." An instruction to the binder to bind material in the order, or in the condition, in which it is received from the library, regardless of any seeming imperfections, e.g., a missing issue of a serial, a missing title leaf, etc.

binder. 1. One who binds a book; a bibliopegist, or bookbinder. 2. A looseleaf binder (or notebook). 3. A material used to cause other materials to bond, or adhere, or, in papermaking, to cause fibers to bond, coatings to adhere, etc. 4. An adhesive substance, usually of liquid or molten form, used to create adhesion between aggregates, globules, etc. It is distinguished from an ADHESIVE in that it performs an internal adhesive function rather than a surface adhesive function. (17, 142, 309)

binder's block. *See:* BINDER'S BRASS.

binder's board. The wood, pasted paper, single- or multiple-ply sheets, or other base stock, for the covers of any bound or cased book, i.e., any book in hard covers. Boards, in one form or another, have been used to cover and thereby protect the leaves of codices since the earliest times of bookbinding.

Although PASTEBOARD (1) was used very early in the Near East, in Europe, until about 1500, boards were nearly always made of wood (usually oak), hence the name. These wooden boards varied greatly in thickness, even up to one inch, although it is entirely possible that very thick boards were designed to contain relics, as well as to cover the book. The use of wooden boards began to decline in favor of pasteboards during the first quarter of the 16th century, and in time paper "boards" virtually replaced wood entirely, except in certain novelty or specialty uses.

Boards made of tarred rope, sailcloth, netting, and the like, came into use in England for more expensive bindings sometime around the beginning of the 18th century, and continued to be employed extensively until World War II, or for sometime thereafter, when they became very expensive and difficult to procure. These so-called tar, semi-tar, and rope boards, which are generally referred to as MILLBOARD (1), are very hard and stiff.

The binder's boards of today are usually made of paper and are available in many weights and thicknesses. Machine-made boards are generally available in four qualities: 1) machine boards, including a wide range of boards made from paper on a cylinder or Fourdrinier machine. These are usually single-ply, solid boards made to full thickness in one operation. They generally range in thickness from 0.030 to 0.300 inch; 2) STRAWBOARD, which originally was the yellowish board from Holland (and was sometimes called Holland board), but which now represents a generic board made from straw or similar material; 3) CHIPBOARD,

made from waste paper, wood chips, and other inexpensive materials; and 4) RAG BOARD, made from rag stock.

In terms of permanence, the various types of boards used today are probably of equal quality. Even old strawboard, which would appear to be the least permanent of all, shows little deterioration with age, even after a hundred years. Its characteristic brittleness is a physical property of this type of board and has little to do with deterioration. That boards in general deteriorate very little may be due largely to the fact that the boards of a book are generally, though not always, completely covered over and are thus largely protected from atmosphere, light, and other potentially damaging effects. It is perhaps interesting to note that, in terms of permanence (as the term is generally understood), strawboard and pasteboard, possibly due to the absence of metallic impurities, are probably more "permanent" than the hard and tough millboard.

The weight (thickness) of the boards used in bookbinding should be appropriate to the size and weight of the volume being bound, and will generally range in thickness between 0.060 inch and, in the case of very large volumes, 0.205 inch in thickness. *See also:* LAMINATED BOARD. (143, 162, 180, 198, 230, 236)

binder's brass. A brass block engraved in relief with letters or a design, and used for blocking the covers of books, by means of either a hand-operated press or an automatic blocking machine. *Cf:* ZINCO. (307)

binder's cloth. A cloth binding of any age, which is not the product of EDITION BINDING. The term was most commonly used to indicate collections of pamphlets, French novels, etc., which the collector did not have bound in leather. Such bindings are almost always blocked from type or standard dies, and, if decorated at all, usually in an ordinary manner. Exceptions date from the earliest years of edition binding in cloth, when materials and style were still in the early stages of development. (69)

binder's record. The record kept by a binder, for the purposes of maintaining an accurate record of the various materials received from different customers. Such records generally include instructions for binding or special attention, including the manner in which similar materials were bound in the past, color of covering material, type of covering material, recorded size,

lettering format, style and size of type, and the like. (24, 259)

binder's stamp. 1. The stamp or label applied to a book indicating the bindery that bound the book, and sometimes the month and year in which the book was bound. It is generally located on the inside tail edge of the lower cover. This method of signing a bookbinding first became fashionable in the 20th century. 2. *See:* BINDER'S BRASS. (261)

binder's ticket. A small engraved or printed label, usually found on the upper outside corner of one of the front flyleaves, giving the name (and usually the address) of the bookbinder. Tickets were used from the early 18th century until about 1825, but were not often seen in England until about 1780. The use of the ticket gave way to the practice by binders of lettering their names in gilt, blind, or ink, usually on the bottom turn-in of either upper or lower board. This record was sometimes referred to as a "name pallet." A variation of the ticket, usually printed, was used by some edition binders during the 19th century, and was usually located on the inside tail edge of the lower cover. (69)

binder's title. The form in which the title of a book appears on the spine or cover, the implication being that the title on the outside may differ, usually by being abbreviated, from the title as it appears on the title page.

binder's waste. 1. *See:* WASTE SHEET (1). 2. Scraps of cloth, leather, board, etc., too small to be classed by themselves. 3. The scrap paper resulting from the trimming of books, and which, being clean, white, and unprinted, commands a premium price in the waste paper market.

bindery tapes. The tapes used to cover the binding edge of checkbooks, composition books, pads or tablets of writing paper, scrapbooks, and the like. They are also used as gussets for file folders, and as reinforcements for the punched edges of loose-leaf notebook paper. Bindery tapes make use of a variety of backing materials, ranging from Holland, cambric, and gusset cloths, through strong latex-impregnated materials to embossed, coated kraft papers. The tapes are made in a variety of colors, and most are applied automatically on stripping machines. The adhesive used on these tapes must be of reasonably high quality and strength, must have a moderate amount of working life after wetting, and must be capable of bonding quickly after application. Also called "gum stripping tapes." (309)

bindery warehouse. The unit or division, usually in an edition bindery, where the simpler forms of binding, i.e., pamphlets, single periodical issues, as well as other miscellaneous operations, such as cutting, folding, stapling, etc., take place, as contrasted with the main bindery, where the more elaborate styles of binding occur, generally those involving sewing. Many finishing operations, e.g., blocking, are common to both. The term is more prevalent in Great Britain than in the United States. (58)

bind from sheets. Bookbinding which originates from the flat or folded sheets, usually the former, as received from the printer. Binding from sheets is carried out principally in edition binderies, although pamphlet binding, as well as blankbook binding, might also be considered as such. A book to be bound by hand will generally be in better binding condition if received in sheets (or gatherings), but this occurs only in rare instances today. (83)

bind in. An instruction to the bookbinder to bind into the book separate supplementary material, as designated by the customer.

binding. 1. The style in which a book is bound, e.g., edition binding, library binding, etc. 2. The covers of a bound book. 3. The finished work resulting from the processes involved in binding a book. 4. The concept of securing the leaves or sections of a publication so as to keep them in proper order and to protect them. 5. The style in which a book is decorated, e.g., fanfare style, cottage style, etc.

binding agent. An intermediary between a bookbinding establishment, usually a library bindery, and the customer, although not directly employed by either. The binding agent is a more-or-less independent salesman who solicits business for a commission.

binding before purchase. A term generally considered to mean the purchase of books by a library in sheets, to be bound according to the library's specifications before they receive any wear, and while the paper is still fresh, clean and unwrinkled. Binding before purchase is rare today, except for PRE-LIBRARY BOUND publications, which is not strictly the same thing. (25)

binding book. A book used by a library, in which the particulars of materials sent out for binding or rebinding are entered. It may vary in the information recorded, from a simple list of

titles to full bibliographical information and binding instructions. The binding book has been largely superseded by the BINDING SLIP. (94)

binding edge. The edge of the gathered leaves or sections that is sewn, or otherwise secured. The binding edge of books published in the Western world is traditionally the left edge of a recto, corresponding to the right edge of a verso, but it may be any edge, the most common variant being the head.

binding margin. *See:* INNER MARGIN.

binding post. A metal post, generally threaded, used to secure pre-punched loose leaves between stiff or semi-flexible covers. Binding posts, which may be adaptable to expansion, are frequently considered a permanent form of binding. *See also:* POST BINDER (256, 274)

binding priorities. The ranking or ordering of different types of library materials to be bound or rebound. Priorities may be based on a variety of factors, including historical or research value, age, condition, use, monetary value, special or local interest, format, or combinations thereof. The establishment of priorities frequently, if not usually, implies that the library: 1) does not have sufficient funds to bind everything it acquires; or 2) does not consider it necessary to bind or rebind everything. An example of a system of priorities would be: 1) books of value, or of special interest to the library, that should be bound or rebound without regard to cost; 2) books of permanent interest but of no special monetary value, that should be library bound, but for which the best work would be too expensive; and 3) books of temporary interest that need to be held together and kept in readable condition for occasional reference or short-term hard usage. (84, 208, 326)

binding process. The two major divisions of BOOKBINDING, which are FORWARD-ING and FINISHING (1). Forwarding entails the binding operations, which are the work of the bookbinder; finishing includes decoration and embellishment of the outside (and sometimes the insides of the boards) surfaces of the covers (including the creation of the design), and is the work of the artist. Both operations may be, and frequently are, especially in the United States and Great Britain, performed by the same person.

binding program. The policies and procedures of a library relating to the care and preservation of its book collection, insofar as such procedures relate to

library binding. A sound binding program is based on four fundamental factors: 1) a set of defined procedures within the library, with assignment of authority and responsibility, preferably to one person; 2) a binding budget adequate not only for the binding of new acquisitions but for rebinding in a systematic manner; 3) written binding specifications designed to provide for the preservation of the book collection, based on the purposes and goals of the library; and 4) an agreement or contract with a library binder of recognized competence. (208)

binding quirewise. A method of sewing a book, in which the sections are placed one inside another and then sewn or saddle stitched through the combined back folds. (179)

binding (bindery) record. A record of books sent to the binder. This may consist of circulation cards, duplicate binding slips, or special records kept in a book.

binding schedules. The times of pick-up and delivery by the binder from and to the library. Aside from the method of transportation, which should be by means of the binder's own truck, or at least on a non-commingled basis on contract, and not by common carrier, the binding schedule depends largely on five factors: 1) when the volume can best be spared from the library; 2) the most convenient time for preparing books for binding; 3) when the binder can bind books with the least delay; 4) when the library can accumulate a sufficient number of volumes to make up a shipment of reasonable size; and 5) when the library is in the best position to pay for the work done. 131)

binding schemes. A term at one time used to describe an organized scheme carried through an individual's or library's book collection, in which, for example, all books on history were bound in red, technical books in black, fiction in brown, poetry in buff, books relating to the sea in blue, books on travel in orange, and so on. Such schemes have declined in popularity since the turn of the century, and particularly since the development of systematic classification schemes. *See also:* BRIGHTER BINDING. (310)

binding slip. A card, slip, sheet, or other form of written instructions sent to the bindery with each volume, or set of volumes, specifying the binding requirements for that volume or set. The typical binding slip generally specifies the author (if any), title (sometimes abbreviated), classification number, other bibliographical information, binding style (unless previously agreed upon), color of covering material, as well as any pecularities of the book that should be brought to the attention of the binder, such as margins, condition of the paper, foldouts, loose material (for pockets), etc. A multiple form provides identical copies for the binder, as well as the library, and serves as verification for the work specified.

binding specifications. The description of the materials, manufacturing processes, and standards of workmanship to be employed in binding books for a library or similar institution. Material specifications include the quality and weight (or size) of thread, paper, cloth (or leather), adhesives, mending tissues, gold, foil, inks, etc., of such things as endpapers, guards, stubs, hinges, inlays, linings, tapes, sewing thread, covering materials, and the like. Manufacturing specifications include collation, preparation for sewing, special checking, reinforcing, removing back folds, scoring, construction and attachment of endpapers, trimming, gluing-up, blocking, casing-in, inspection, etc. Workmanship specifications include sewing, rounding and backing, adhesion of materials, turn-ins, squares, corners, trimming and the like. Specifications, it should be noted, are not intended to instruct the binder in how to bind a book, but only to insure an acceptable end product. (16, 25, 83)

binding variations. Differences in the bindings of books issued in the same edition by a publisher. The differences might include color or type of cloth, blocking, etc. Such variations may stem from a number of manufacturing causes, especially if all copies printed are not bound at the same time, or some are rebound, as in REMAINDER BINDING. Variations may also result from unsatisfactory storage conditions. (69, 156)

birch (bark). The bark of the common European birch *(Betula verrucosa)* or *(B. pubescens)*, used in leather manufacture, particularly in Russia, for hundreds of years. The outer bark, which peels off easily, is not used; it is the inner bark from which the tannin, in the amount of 10 to 15%, and 11% soluble non-tans, is extracted. Older trees, those 50 to 60 years of age, yield the richest tannin. Used alone, birch produces a pliable, leather of a yellowish-brown color; it is, however, more often mixed with some other

tannin, often willow bark. In addition to tannin, the oil obtained from the bark is used to dress the leather, imparting to RUSSIA LEATHER its characteristic odor. Other species of birch have been used to a limited extent in North America and India. *See also:* VEGETABLE TANNINS. (175)

birch broom. A "broom" made of strips of birch wood and used for stirring the MARBLING SIZE. A birch broom has been the traditional implement for this operation, but whether it was because of the quantities of water used, the screening action of the birch strips, or some other reason, is not clear. (97, 335)

bite. 1. The ability of an adhesive to penetrate or dissolve the uppermost layer of the adherends. 2. That quality in paper which causes it to take ink, pencil, or printing impressions readily. 3) In engraving, the corrosion of the metal by acid, i.e., the action of acid dissolving away superfluous metal. (138, 139)

bites. An informal expression sometimes used to indicate pieces of paper torn from the margin of a leaf, so-called because of their occasional resemblance to "bites."

black book. An obsolete term applied to any of the various books, usually of a devotional nature, so-called from the style of their type, the color of their bindings, the nature of their contents, or combinations thereof. They also frequently had BLACK EDGES. (274)

black edges. The edges of a book that have been blackened by sponging them with ink, followed by ivory black, lampblack, or antimony mixed with paste. Although used extensively in the 19th century on devotional and funereal publications, they are uncommon today. (152, 241)

blacking the squares. The process of coloring the edges and squares of the boards of a book, as well as the headcaps, with a black pigment, such as vinegar-black mixed with gum arabic, so as to enhance the effect of tooling in blind. The technique is uncommon today. (152, 241)

black lead. Commercial powdered graphite, which, when mixed with water, glair, and (sometimes) Armenian bole, is applied to the edges of books before gilding. *See also:* GILT EDGES. (335, 371)

blacks. 1. An obsolete term for a grade of book cloth of a "common" quality, dyed throughout. 2. A general term applied to black papers used for covers, photograph albums, and the like. (256)

black step. A heavy line, 6 points thick and about 24 points long, which appears on the back of a folded section of a book after the printed sheet is folded. The collective black steps run from the head to the tail of the gathered sections, generally about 24 points below each other. When the book is gathered the black steps appear as a diagonal line running from head to tail across the back of the text block, and any missing or misplaced section immediately becomes obvious because the black step is broken. Also called "back mark," "collating mark," and "quad mark." (156)

blanc fixe. *See:* BARIUM SULFATE.

blankbook. Originally, a book in which the printing was limited to page headings or divisions. The page was generally blank or ruled and was intended to receive writing. Today, blankbooks include a variety of items, including account books, albums, scrapbooks, exercise and manuscript books, etc. Blankbooks intended for the accounting of court records, etc., are generally ruled, horizontally and/or vertically, to facilitate writing. Since in most cases the information recorded is considered to be of permanent value, the paper and binding of the book must be of superior quality. Called "account book" in Great Britain. *See also:* BLANKBOOK BINDING. (227, 274)

blankbook binding. A style of binding for books meant to be written in and which, therefore, must lie flat at any place the book is open. Blankbook binding is one of the principal subdivisions of STATIONERY BINDING and differs greatly from the other major unit of binding, LETTERPRESS BINDING. One of the major differences is that blankbooks, or account books, as they are also called, are rounded but not backed, having instead a SPRING-BACK, which, in conjunction with the LEVERS, causes the spine of the book to "spring" up when the book is opened, thus giving full access to the gutter of the opposing pages. The best blankbook binding is very durable, with sewing on wide bands of webbing, rather than tapes, the ends of which are secured between split boards. The books also have heavy linings and strongly reinforced endpapers, called "joints" in a blankbook. In addition, it is not unusual for the folios to be sewn first to heavy cloth guards before being sewn to the webbings. Additional strength is sometimes imparted by hubs on the spine (which also protect the lettering) and bands either over or under the covering material. Although formerly always covered in leather, many blankbooks are now covered in heavy duck or canvas. Called "account-book binding" in Great Britain. (58, 320, 339, 343)

blankbook frame. An obsolete term for a sewing frame designed to be used when tapes instead of cords are used in sewing. *See also:* SEWING FRAME. (115)

blankbook paper. *See:* LEDGER PAPER.

blank cover. A term sometimes applied to the covers of a bound book that are not blocked or ornamented in any manner.

blanking. 1. The process of blocking book cloths that are patterned, i.e., grained. Before the use of hot dies and foils eliminated the need for blanking, the cloth was struck with the uninked die, which flattened out the pattern or grain of the cloth, leaving a smooth surface to take the ink on the subsequent strike. 2. A term sometimes used incorrectly with reference to blinding. *See:* BLIND TOOLING. (91, 365)

blank leaves. The unprinted leaves at the front and back of a book. They may be an integral part of the book as received from the publisher (printer's flyleaves), or they may be added by the bookbinder (binder's flyleaves). They are not necessarily part of the endpapers. (69)

blank rolling. A method of sprinkling a FLESHER, in which an iron solution is applied to the leather and rolled in. The nap is then restored by brushing.

blank tooling. *See:* BLIND TOOLING.

bleach. 1. A chemical, usually an oxidizing or reducing agent, used to whiten or increase the brightness of a material, e.g., paper or paper pulp. *See also:* BLEACHING (1) 2. A solution of chlorine or a similar chemical. 3. To whiten or increase the brightness of a material, or to remove stains from paper. *See:* BLEACHING (2).

bleached groundwood paper. A paper manufactured from groundwood pulp which has been bleached by means of a suitable chemical, e.g., sodium peroxide, zinc hydrosulfite, etc, or a combination of chemicals. It is substantially brighter than unbleached groundwood paper and is not significantly less bright than paper produced from bleached sulfate or sulfite pulps. (17, 72)

bleached sulfate paper. A class of paper generally used in grades of white, as well as for boards requiring strength. The pulp is fully bleached with chlorine dioxide, or the dioxide plus peroxide, with or without hypochlorite, in multistage bleaching operations. Its high brightness is attainable with strength characteristics not substantially lower than that of an unbleached chemical pulp. (17, 72)

bleached sulfite paper. A paper which has been bleached in one stage by means of peroxide or hypochlorite, or in a multistage operation using peroxide and/or chlorine dioxide. The paper has high brightness with good stability. (17, 72)

bleaching. 1. The process of treating pulps used in papermaking with chemicals to alter their color so that the pulp and the resulting paper will have greater brightness. Such bleaching is usually accompanied by partial removal of noncellulosic materials, e.g., LIGNIN. 2. The process of chemically treating archival materials in order to remove stains, discoloration, foxing, etc., and/or to restore brightness. Both oxidizing—i.e., chemicals which take up electrons—and reducing—i.e., chemicals which give up electrons— chemicals are used, the former much more extensively than the latter. Chemicals which are, or have been, used include CALCIUM HYPOCHLORITE, CHLORAMINE T., CHLORINE DIOXIDE, FORMALDEHYDE, HYDROGEN PEROXIDE, POTASSIUM METABISULFITE, SODIUM CHLORATE, SODIUM CHLORITE, SODIUM HYPOCHLORITE, and SODIUM PEROXIDE. 3. The process of lightening the color of a vegetable-tanned leather by means of the removal of the oxidized tannins and insoluble matter from the outer surfaces of the skin, usually by treatment with a solution of sodium carbonate, washing, and then treatment with diluted acid. Chrome-tanned leathers are usually bleached by treating the skin with acid solutions of syntans and at times by precipitating white pigments in the grain layer of the leather to impart a bleached appearance. 4. The destructive effects of chemical agents on water colors, inks, fugitive colors, etc. 5. The generally undesirable and destructive effect of natural and artificial light on archival materials, especially cloth and leather bookbindings. (62, 77, 218, 320, 323)

bleaching powder. *See:* CALCIUM HYPOCHLORITE.

bled. The printed image, plates, or illustrations of a book that have been cut into during trimming, e.g., BLEED BORDER, BLEED ILLUSTRATION.

bleed. 1. To trim the edges of a book to the extent that part of the letterpress is removed. 2. A printed image which runs off the edge of a page. 3. The process of deliberately trimming so as to "bleed" a page. *See also:* BLEED BORDER; BLEED ILLUSTRATION. (82, 365)

bleed border. A heavy border on a printed page or sheet, especially on the cover of a pamphlet or booklet, printed in such a position that part of it is cut away in trimming.

bleed illustration. An illustration that runs to one or more edges of the page, leaving no margin. If the bleeding is to be accomplished by means of cropping, the illustration must be designed so that nothing of importance is removed by trimming. When an illustration occupies an entire page, it is said to bleed on three sides, i.e., head, tail, and fore edge, and run flush to the gutter. *See also:* CENTER SPREAD. (131)

bleeding. 1. *See:* BLEED. 2. The removal of color from a paper or paper pulp due to the action of water or another liquid, which dissolves the coloring matter. 3. Discoloration of the surface of a paper due to the migration of residual oils. 4. The tendency of colored papers to stain contiguous leaves, usually due to the presence of water or moisture of some kind. 5. The diffusion of uncombined materials from the interior of leather to the grain surface where they may contaminate other materials or mar the appearance of the leather. This usually occurs at elevated temperatures and is commonly designated as staining. (17, 72, 325, 363)

blesbock. A South African antelope, *Damaliscus albifrons*, the skin of which has been used to produce a bold-grained leather, in imitation of SEALSKIN.

blind blocking. The process of lettering or decorating a book with BINDER'S BRASS or ZINCO only, i.e., without gold leaf, ink, or foil. (307)

blind finishing. Any of the several techniques of decorating a binding by tooling without the use of gold, or other leaf metals, or coloring materials. Blind finishing includes: 1) impressing the surface of the covering material with a heated tool (*See:* BLIND TOOLING); 2) embossing leather from the flesh side while wet, with the pattern being outlined by an indented line; and 3) cutting the leather so as to create a design in relief. *See:* CUIR-CISELÉ.

blind impressions. Virtually the same process as BLIND BLOCKING, except that it generally applies to hand tooling. In blind impressions, there are generally two impressions of the tool or letter, the first made through the design or lettering on paper with a warm tool and a second done directly on the impression. This second step assures an evenness and straightness of the impression, and, because the impression through the paper is larger, the second makes the final impression the correct size. (161)

blind lines. 1. The impressed lines on the spine of a leather binding along each side of the raised bands. Such lines are usually impressed with a two-line PALLET (1). 2. The blind lines made by a FILLET (1) without the use of leaf metal or foil. (335)

blind-stamped panel (blind-stamped binding). A form of decoration on the covers of a binding impressed by means of an engraved stamp (bearing a *complete* design) on the dampened leather. Virtually all early plates were cut intaglio (with a three dimensional effect and not as a two dimensional printing block), the resulting image on the cover being in relief. Panels were still being used in (German) bookbinding until well into the 18th century.

The art originated in the Low Countries, and was practiced there from the 14th century on. Characteristic designs consisted of animals in circles or loops of foliage. The art flourished in France from about 1488 to 1528; in Germany, extensive use was made of blind-stamped panels on covers of pigskin bindings, mainly after 1550. The blind-stamped panel was in use in England from about 1480 to 1580, but it was not really popular until about 1500. The most used motifs included the royal arms and heraldic devices. Rectangular panels made with a single stamp continued in use until about 1623.

Because of the great pressure required to impress a complete design, a standing press of some kind must have been used.

The most commonly used leathers for these bindings were calfskin and pigskin. (140, 166, 236)

blind stamping. A term originally used with reference to stamping a leather cover with small, unheated tools that were cut intaglio so that the impression was in relief. *See also:* BLIND TOOLING. (236)

blind tooling. A method of decorating a book in which impressions are made in the covering material, usually leather or tawed skin, by means of heated tools, pallets, rolls, fillets, or combinations of one or more of these. As the name implies, blind tooling does not entail the use of leaf metal, foil, or any other coloring material, with the possible exception of carbon, which is sometimes used to darken the impressions.

The effect of blind tooling rests largely on the depth and uniformity of the impressions (which makes it unsuitable for use with hard covering materials) and the ability of the heated tool to produce a darkened color (see above)—factors which make leather, especially in the lighter shades, an ideal medium for this method of decoration.

The critical aspects of the technique are the temperature of the tool and the degree of dampness of the leather. In general, the damper the leather the cooler the tool should be, and vice versa. In tooling leather blind, the surface is given a quick initial strike to "set" the leather in the impression. The tool is then impressed again and rocked slightly, which polishes and darkens the impression. When blind lines run across the spine of the book, polishing is accomplished by sliding a pallet along the lines; on the covers, where a fillet is used for long lines, it is fixed so that instead of rolling, it slides along the impression.

Blind tooling has been used as a means of decorating books since the early days of bookbinding, and can be traced back to COPTIC BINDINGS of the 7th or 8th centuries, and even earlier. There is reason to believe that the technique was brought to Europe from the Mediterranean area about the same time as other Coptic techniques being used, possibly by imported craftsmen; however, little is known of blind-tooled bindings until the 12th century and early part of the 13th. In one form or another, the technique has been used continuously up to the present day, but during the 16th to 18th centuries, its use was more or less limited to inferior calf- and sheepskin bindings. Near the end of the 18th and during the early years of the 19th centuries blind tooling was often used on fine bindings in conjunction with gold. Also called "antique tooling." (94, 123, 130, 236, 335)

blind warbles. *See:* WARBLES.

blisters. 1. Bubbles or pockets of air, water vapor, solvent vapor, etc., trapped between the board and PASTE-DOWN of a book, causing the board paper to bulge, forming a blister. A blister effect may also be caused by a small mass of adhesive, which stretches the covering material, or by failure of the covering material to adhere properly, causing a protuberance or "blister" between board and covering material. 2. Defects in paper resulting from too rapid drying of the web or poor condition of the drying felts which allows air between the felt and web. Blisters are also defects in coated papers caused by too rapid expansion of moisture in the interior of the sheet when subjected to the high drying temperatures of web presses. (5, 17)

block. A piece of metal, without a handle, bearing an engraved or etched design and used in decorating the covers of a book. It is intended to be used in a press. *See also:* BLOCKING (1); BLOCKING PRESS. (82, 234)

block book. A book printed from cut blocks of wood. Although it is presumed that block books preceded the invention of printing from movable metal type, most of the extant examples of block books are from the period 1460 to 1480, i.e., subsequent to printing from metal types. Each block was cut for an entire page, and, in the earliest examples, each leaf was printed only on one side, usually with a thin, brownish ink. The spread of printing virtually eliminated the demand for this type of book but they continued to be printed until at least the end of the 15th century. These later examples were printed on both sides of the leaf with ordinary printing ink. Block books are essentially picture books, sometimes with a small amount of text, also cut in wood. (69, 140, 156)

blocking. 1. The process or technique of impressing a design into the covering material of a book by means of a stamp or BLOCK having an engraved or etched surface. The term applies to the impressing of type, blocks, etc., with foil, leaf, etc., or without (BLIND BLOCKING). Since the area that can be blocked by hand is relatively small (about one square inch, or less), large areas are blocked using a BLOCKING PRESS. The permanency of the blocking, particularly when gold leaf is used, depends largely on the pressure applied by the craftsman, or the force of the blocking press, which drives the raised surfaces of the block or die into the covering material. Hand blocking may be done on curved or flat surfaces, while blocking by means of a press is generally done on flat surfaces only. 2. The surface tackiness that book cloths sometimes develop as they age. 3. An undesirable condition in which a dry adhesive film is reactivated by heat, pressure, moisture, etc., and adheres to a material in contact with it. (94, 179, 236, 276, 309)

blocking foil. A thin plastic film with a

high vacuum deposit of gold or other metal and backed by a pressure-sensitive adhesive. White and colored pigments are also available. They are used in the same way as gold leaf, the impression being obtained by means of a heated die, block, type, etc. Blocking foils are used extensively in library and edition binding. (81, 92, 161)

blocking powder. A finely ground resin used in dusting over the impressions in silk and velvet before gold tooling. Such resins are used in lieu of GLAIR because moisture would stain the silk or velvet. The powder has the advantage of requiring only a moderately hot tool, whereas glair requires considerably more heat to make the gold adhere. Blocking powder, however, does not provide the solidity of adhesion to gold leaf that is obtainable with a liquid size; therefore, it is generally used only when a liquid size is impractical. (154)

blocking press. A press which heats blocks and impresses lettering, designs, etc., into the covers of books. In edition binding this is done automatically, gold or pigment foils being fed through the machine on a thin plastic BLOCKING FOIL. The blocking press is used for BLIND BLOCKING or ink blocking; heat is not required for the latter process. When gold leaf is used it is laid directly on the book cover. The blocking press first came into use in England in the period 1830-32 for gold blocking on book cloths. Before this time books were blocked with a block that was heated off the press and then laid on the cover and pressed. Also called "embossing press" and, in the United States, "stamping press." (107, 203, 236)

block printing. The process of printing from hand-carved blocks of wood or linoleum. Modern blocks, which are made up of relatively heavy lines and solid areas, are cut for relief printing, and are inked or colored only on the uncut surfaces. If printing in two or more colors is required, the colors can be applied and printed in one impression, printed in two or more impressions, or two or more blocks can be cut. In the early days of block printing, it was a common practice to print the outline of the design and then apply the colors by hand. The relatively soft surfaces of blocks of wood or linoleum limit the number of impressions that can be made. (234)

bloodstone burnisher. *See:* BURNISHER(S) (1).

bloom. 1. A deposit of ellagic acid formed in and on leathers tanned with vegetable tannins of the pyrogallol class, probably as a result of the action of enzymes native to the original source, i.e., bark, acorns, etc. Although bloom affects the physical properties of leather in that it increases weight yield, firmness, and water resistance, it is deposited in insoluble form and is not chemically combined with the fibers of the leather. Its presence at times gives an unsightly appearance to the leather. 2. A misty surface appearance in an illustration, caused by an excess of acid or too much drier in the ink. 3. The dulling film that sometimes appears on varnish and glossy paint films, particularly in industrial atmospheres. It usually consists of minute crystals of ammonium sulfate produced by the reaction betwen sulfur dioxide, ammonia, and oxygen in condensed moisture on the film. Bloom can appear on a freshly lacquered surface when rapid evaporation of the solvents causes the temperature of the surface to fall below the dew point. Moisture is deposited on the film, causing a limited precipitation of cellulose nitrate and giving the film a permanent cloudy appearance. (175, 195, 306, 363)

blotting paper. A completely unsized sheet of paper, generally used to take up excess ink from hand-written documents, letters, etc. It is also used to absorb moisture from freshly washed or deacidified book and manuscript papers, prints, maps, etc. It is often made from high grade rag or cotton linters, and also from chemical or mechanical wood pulps, or mixtures thereof. The paper is porous, bulky, and has a low finish and little strength. Basis weights generally range from 60 to 140 pounds (19 × 24 − 500). Aside from its use as an absorbent paper, it can be ground up, mixed with size, and used to fill in worm and other small holes in paper. (17, 316)

blue (blue sort). Hides and skins that have been chrome tanned but not finished. Such skins are usually called "in the blue," or "blue sort." (325)

blue agate marble. A cover marble, consisting of black coloring in large (united) drops, with blue streams down the boards uniting with the black. *See also:* GREEN AGATE MARBLE. (97, 152)

blue-and-gold edition. A format for volumes of poetry, essays, etc., popular in the United States in the 1870s. The covering cloth was blue and the edges were gilt. The books were small, measuring about 6 by 3½ inches. (169)

blueprint paper. A paper produced from cotton fiber pulp, bleached chemical wood pulp, or combinations thereof, in basis weights of 12 to 30 pounds (17 × 22 − 500). It has a well-formed, fairly smooth surface, good wet tensile strength, and, although well-sized, uniform absorbency. Blueprint paper must not contain chemicals which might have an adverse effect on its sensitizing materials. The paper is sensitized by treating the base paper with chemicals, including potassium ferrocyanide, as well as with iron salts, such as the oxalates and tartrates. (17)

blue stormont marble. A marble pattern used for both endpapers and edges, consisting of a red vein with indigo fillers dotted with numerous small interstices in the form of a fine network. This pattern was popular during the first half of the 19th century, but was also used in the 18th. *See also:* STORMONT MARBLE. (97, 236)

board. A generic term for a stiff and thick "paper." The distinction between board and paper is somewhat vague; however, in general, board is heavier in basis weight, thicker, and stiffer than paper. Most sheets 0.012 or more inches in thickness are considered to be boards, while nearly all less than 0.006 inch are termed paper; most of those in between these dimensions are also classed as paper. Blotting paper, in excess of 0.012 inch, however, is still classed as paper, and liner board, although sometimes less than 0.012 inch thick, is classed as board. *See also:* BINDER'S BOARD. (17, 19, 42)

board cutter. A lever type of cutter mounted on a flat bed and used for cutting hard millboard, and similar materials. The bed is equipped with a movable gauge against which the stock is placed for accurate cutting, and a foot-operated clamp which secures the material for cutting. The blade usually has one or more counterweights at the end opposite the handle to help prevent the knife from falling accidently, and also to reduce the effort required to raise the blade. *See also:* BENCH KNIFE; ROTARY BOARD CUTTER. (66)

boarded leather. A leather which has been softened and the grain side of which has been lightly creased by the process of BOARDING (1).

boarding. 1. A method of producing a design on the grain side of leather, as well as softening it, by means of a series of creases produced on the surface of the skin. Boarding is accomplished by folding the leather, grain side to grain side, and working the fold across its surface. A straight or "willow" grain results when the skin is boarded on one direction, and a box or "cross" grain when it is also boarded at right angles to the first. Boarding a third time in a direction diagonal to the first two produces a pebbled-grain pattern. Boarding may be done by hand, using a cork-surfaced board called a GRAINING BOARD, the fold of the leather being rolled under the board, or, as is the usual case today, by means of a boarding machine, in which the leather is rolled between two cylinders, one covered with cork or rubber and the other with felt or rubber. 2. *See:* GRAINED UP. (306, 363)

board knife. 1. A knife of eliptical shape attached to the arm of a hand-operated BENCH KNIFE. 2. One of the circular knives of a ROTARY BOARD CUTTER. (66)

board machine. *See:* CYLINDER MACHINE.

board paper. *See:* PASTEDOWN.

boards. 1. A generic term for the pieces of wood, metal, or metal-edged wood used to assist in gripping books while in process of being bound. Such boards are used in pressing, backing, bundling, gilding, trimming, and other operations. 2. The state or condition of being IN BOARDS or OUT OF BOARDS. 3. *See:* BINDER'S BOARD.

bock. A leather made from the skin of a so-called Persian sheep, which is a sheep that has coarse hair instead of wool. It was used in the latter part of the 19th and early part of the 20th centuries as a substitute for goatskin. When finished and grained (usually embossed) in imitation of MOROCCO, it was referred to as "bock morocco." (91, 256)

body paper (board). The foundation paper or board for finished papers, such as art, chromo, coated, gummed, and others, which are made by coating or treating with composition. (82)

bolt. The folded edge at the head, tail, or fore edge of a section of an unopened book. Depending on location, it is known as a head bolt, tail bolt, or fore-edge bolt. Bolts are generally located at the head and fore edge, but cannot be located at all three edges in any one section. The folded edge opposite the fore edge is not a "bolt," but a spine fold, or "last fold." Bolts are often opened quickly and with little care, resulting in ragged edges that are difficult to handle when turning leaves. A dull knife used carefully will result in a clean cut, while a knife that is too sharp is difficult to control and often

cuts away from the bolt and into one or more leaves.

bolt knife. One of the two types of knives that can be used for cutting the edges of books with the PLOW. The bolt knife is fastened to the shoe of the plow, consequently its position cannot be changed, as can that of the SLIDING KNIFE. The sliding type is less expensive and easier to attach, and has almost completely superceded the bolt type.

bond. 1. In adhesives, the process of joining two structures together, i.e., to create an assembly by means of adhesive linkage. 2. A form of insurance agreement under which a bonding company guarantees to pay a library within stated limits for any financial loss, or for failure of the binder to perform in accordance with the terms of the contract, i.e., to follow specifications, to charge the agreed-upon price, to return materials within the time specified in the contract, or to otherwise be found in default of the contract. 3. *See:* BOND PAPER. (309)

bonding strength. The resistance of paper, either coated or uncoated, to splitting or to the picking or lifting of its surface while being printed. (17)

bond paper. A grade of writing or printing paper, now only vaguely associated with bonds, legal documents, etc., i.e., where durability and permanence are required. Bond paper today is widely used for forms, invoices, etc., and is a strong, tough paper that can take stiff, hard ink that dries by oxidation rather than by penetration. Bonds are produced from cotton fiber pulp, bleached chemical wood pulps, or combinations thereof. Although a bond is a typical writing paper, almost all of it is printed, e.g., letterheads; therefore it must have good printability, as well as good writing and erasing qualities. It must also possess cleanliness, formation, color, finish, and freedom from fuzz. It is usually made in basis weights ranging from 13 to 24 pounds (17 X 22— 500). (17, 287, 316)

bond strength. The unit load, applied in tension, compression, flexure, peel, cleavage, or sheer, required to break two adherend materials, with failure occurring in or near the plane of the bond. The bond strength of adhesives used in archival work should be such that stress to the point of failure will result in failure of the adhesive, rather than either adherend. (309)

bone cutting. A colloquial term used with reference to the slitting operation performed when an insert must be tipped-

in a section, rather than onto the first or last leaf. (339)

bone dust. An abrasive composed of crushed and ground bones, which, when mixed with powdered chalk and pumice, is used to clean vellum bindings.

bone glue. A GLUE processed from the collagen content of bones, mainly from "green" or fresh bones of bovine animals. Bone glue prepared from solvent-extracted, degreased bones is called "extracted bone glue." (184)

Bonet, Paul (1899–1972). An artisan and bibliophile who turned to the art of creating designs, Bonet was probably the most influential French designer of bookbindings of his day. He was at first influenced by the bindings of PIERRE LE GRAIN. While his early work was in purely geometrical gold fillet design, his later creations were related more closely to the spirit and theme of the book being decorated. Bonet had available to him the best bookbinders and gilders in Paris, and with them he concentrated on the contrasting textures of leathers, wood, and even metals, with surfaces sceulptured and pierced, achieving nearly mathematical repetition of linear forms and even surrealist effects produced by collage and photography. *See* PLATE IX. (104, 347)

bonnet board. A very hard-rolled, thin, smooth-surfaced board similar to file indices; sometimes used for notebook covers.

book. 1. A collection of written, printed, illustrated, or blank leaves of paper, parchment (or vellum), papyrus, or other flexible or semi-flexible material, strung or bound together. Today, in its most familiar form, a book is considered to be one or more folded and gathered sheets of paper, fastened together at one edge, and trimmed on one or more of the remaining three edges to form a continuous series of uniform leaves. Specifically, a book is a collection of single sheets or folded leaves, bearing printing or writing, that have been folded, stitched, sewn, or secured by adhesive along the binding edge, generally rounded and backed, and usually secured between boards that have been covered in cloth, paper, or like material, or which have been bound in leather. *See:* CODEX. 2. A collection of tablets of wood, ivory, or other rigid material, containing writing, drawings, etc., and sometimes covered with blank covers of the same or different materials. 3. A continuous roll of parchment, or similar material, or a strip of parchment creased between columns and folded in the manner of a CONCERTINA FOLD, and containing writing, etc. *See also:* SCROLL (1). (102, 123, 156, 161)

book and job folding machine. A type of buckle folding machine having four folding levels, each at right angles to the preceding and following levels, which permit up to four right angle folds, resulting in 16 leaves (32 pages) from one sheet. This type of machine also has one and sometimes two parallel sections, which enables it to produce a section of up to 64 leaves from one sheet. Book and job folding machines are also sometimes equipped for cutting, padding, and trimming. *See also:* FOLDING MACHINES. (320)

book basis. The BASIC SIZE of the sheet of paper most often used in book printing in the United States—25 by 38 inches.

bookbinder. A craftsman who binds book; a binder; a bibliopegist. The term is also applied to one who creates the designs for the finishing of a book, but who may or may not actually execute the design. Although usually assumed to mean a hand bookbinder, the term is frequently applied to the owner or manager of a bookbinding establishment, e.g., a library bookbinder.

bookbinder's type. Individual letters and number of ordinary type, without handles, designed to be set in a LETTERING PALLET or BLOCKING PRESS, and used to letter books. The use of the pallet or press gives uniformity to the lettering

BOOK

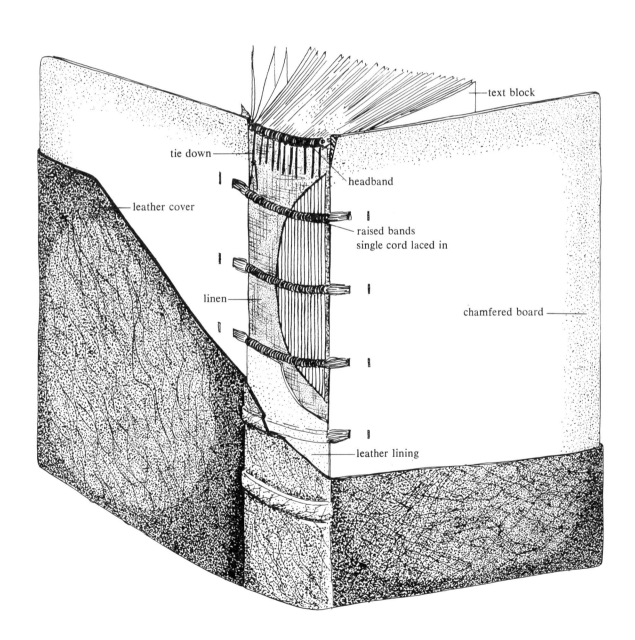

and saves time, but it does not give the freedom and individuality that is available with the use of HAND LETTERS. Type, on the other hand, is extremely useful when lettering a number of copies of the same title. (339)

bookbindery. A place where books are bound, such as a library or edition bindery, etc. Also, as generally understood, a place where various operations connected with printing, but not always with bookbinding, are carried out, such as ruling, perforating, numbering, folding, gathering, padding, etc. *See also:* BLANKBOOK BINDING; BOOKBINDING; EDITION BINDING; GENERAL JOB BINDING; GENERAL OFFICE STATIONERY BINDING; LIBRARY BINDING; MANIFOLD BINDING; MECHANICAL BINDING; PAMPHLET BINDING.

bookbinding. The hand and/or machine processes by which leaves or sections (usually paper, but also parchment (or vellum), papyrus, etc.) are secured within covers to form a codex or book, as opposed to a roll.

Historically, bookbinding did not exist in the manner of today until the codex began to replace the scroll, or roughly 2,000 years ago, when parchment notebooks came into use. Leaves of a quadrangular shape were found to be more convenient than scrolls but they had to be secured and covered for protection. Although classical texts and ecclesiastical works did exist in codex form before the 1st century A.D., the codex did not become common for other works before the 4th century.

The earliest extant decorated bookbindings were altar Bibles, which were often elaborately bound and ornamented with jewels, gold, and ivory. Bookbinding in leather, however, was an art believed to have been practiced by the Copts in Egypt. Surviving examples of Coptic bindings, in red and brown leather, from the 8th and 9th centuries, represent a maturity of style and a variety of techniques which would indicate experience in bookbinding that probably developed over hundreds of years. Unlike European bindings of later times, they appear to have been executed by specialists in diverse forms of leather decoration and display a wide range of artistry, including tooling, piercing, and working with a stylus.

The earliest known Islamic bindings were influenced by Coptic methods and techniques. The format they used for these early books was what we sometimes refer to today as OBLONG, or "landscape." At first the Islamic binders tooled only in blind, and in a formal style, but by the 11th century the characteristic Islamic design consisted of an oval center design with triangular cornerpieces, and, by the 13th century, the present day book format had been adopted and gold was being used in finishing. *See:* GOLD TOOLING. Two hundred years later floral designs were replacing geometric patterns and some pictorial bindings were being executed by means of embossing. Vivid coloring and delicate filigree tooling were used with considerable effect on the DOUBLURE (1), and, by the 16th century, lacquered bindings of excellent quality were being produced. By the 16th century, however, Islamic binding began to deteriorate, and the decline has persisted to this day.

In Europe, the earliest known example of a decorated leather bookbinding is that of the Gospel according to St. John, found in the tomb of St. Cuthbert (d. 687); it is almost certainly an English binding of the 7th or 8th century. Although this remarkable binding shows the influence of Coptic and Islamic binding, European binding took on its own characteristics and by the 10th century had progressed along totally different lines from that of the Levant. One of the principal differences was in the manner of sewing, which was on raised bands; embellishment, too, developed along different lines, almost always being in the form of blind tooling executed with individual tools.

Gothic bindings of the second half of the 15th century were mainly decorated with blind lines and individual tools, but the ROLL (1) which was first used in Germany, was also developed during this period (in about 1470), while the PANEL STAMP was being used in the Netherlands as early as the 13th century. The art of CUIR-CISELÉ was also practiced in German speaking countries. Gothic bindings continued to be produced in Germany and Eastern Europe until after the 16th century; however, by about 1470 or so, gold tooling was introduced into northern Italy (probably Venice), with the influence of the Near East being seen in the designs, the pattern of individual tools, as well as the superior delicacy of the workmanship.

Until about the middle of the 16th century the gold tooled bindings produced in Italy were the best in Europe; other countries, especially France, imitated the Italian style. By 1538, however, morocco leather was being used in France, replacing calfskin, and from that time onward the Parisian crafts-men have produced bindings that have seldom been exceeded in beauty and craftsmanship. The tools used in this great era of French bookbinding were derived by way of pattern books for embroidery or metalwork from Oriental or arabesque models; most of the designs incorporated interlacing strapwork. Elaborations of this strapwork were seen in the FANFARE STYLE.

The most characteristic early 16th century English bindings were those blocked in blind with panel stamps of the royal arms (which represented only a form of decoration and not royal ownership), while the earliest recorded use of gold tooling in England dates from 1519. Gold tooling did not become common in England until about 1530.

Fine binding declined in France in the 17th century despite the artistry of the fanfare patterns and tools having POINTILLÉ outlines. One notable binder of that time was FLORIMOND BADIER, who also worked in pointillé tooling. In England, where variegated colors and delicate tooling became standard, the golden age of English bookbinding was during the period of the Restoration. Some of the tools in use at that time were of the pointillé style, while others, including small floral volutes, were more English in character. A common feature of many English bindings of this time was the broken pediment associated with the COTTAGE STYLE.

The early 18th century witnessed a revival of French bookbinding, including the mosaics of AUGUSTIN DU SEUIL and ANTOINE MICHEL PADELOUP. High standards were also displayed in DENTELLE bindings with their lacy gold tooled borders, some being the work of the Derome family. *See:* DEROME STYLE. English binding deteriorated in the first half of the 18th century, partly because English craftsmen hung on to the cottage style after it had lost its effectiveness, and partly because they then began working with the uninspiring HARLEIAN STYLE. And yet, the 18th century produced ROGER PAYNE, a bookbinder who has been called England's greatest, and one of the few English binders the French thought worthy of copying. In addition, the 18th century produced another of England's great bookbinders, EDWARDS OF HALIFAX, who produced some remarkable TRANSPARENT VELLUM BINDINGS.

The use of onlays and inlays increased during the 19th century, the bindings often being tooled in the cathedral style. *See:* CATHEDRAL BINDINGS. From about 1840 to 1880 there was little innovation in leather binding in any country, the emphasis being on delicacy and precision in tooling in the manner of previous times. The 19th century witnessed three major factors which have had an enormous effect on bookbinding to this day: 1) the rise of edition binding with its rapid development of a great variety of machines designed to produce books by the millions; 2) a severe decline in the quality of both paper and leather produced for the manufacture of books; and 3) the introduction of cloth as a book covering material. *See:* BOOK CLOTH. In the latter part of the last century new vigor was infused into fine binding largely through the efforts of MARIUS MICHEL in France and THOMAS J. COBDEN-SANDERSON in England.

In France, following World War I, the origins of contemporary binding are to be found in the work of PIERRE LEGRAIN during his brief career as a bookbinder in the 1920s. His influence was enormous and is still being felt, and, in turn, those he influenced, including PAUL BONET, have had considerable influence upon their successors.

The influence of Cobden-Sanderson was also felt well into the 20th century. The fact that he was an amateur bookbinder and not apprenticed to the trade of bookbinding seemed, in part, anyway, to have freed him from the deleterious influences that held sway during a great part of the 19th century, as manifested in the generally poor workmanship and even poorer materials plus a mania for retrospective binding. Cobden-Sanderson founded an amateur school of binding, which proceeded to flourish under DOUGLAS COCKERELL, who was Cobden-Sanderson's apprentice at the Doves Bindery. Cockerell, also, through his writings as well as his bindings, has had a considerable influence on the craft.

English bookbinding fell on hard times between 1920 and the Second World War, not in small part because of book collectors' desire to have their books in original mint condition (including book jacket), a desire which persists to this day. The fine binder had but little opportunity to apply modern concepts of design to modern books.

Bookbinding following the war was given considerable impetus by the efforts of EDGAR MANSFIELD in design and ROGER POWELL in construction. The teaching of Mansfield, which commenced at the (then) London School

of Printing in 1948, has influenced, at least to some degree, the concepts of design of virtually all contemporary English and American bookbinders. (71, 89, 94, 157, 200, 202, 225, 236, 242, 243, 252, 270, 271)

Operations. There is a reasonably well-marked distinction between that part of the bookbinding trade dealing with books meant to be read, known as letterpress (from the time when all books were printed by letterpress), and those intended to be written in, called stationery binding. Each of these may again be divided into four groups, according to the particular class of binding involved:

Letterpress binding
1. Extra leather binding, i.e., hand binding
2. Library binding
3. Edition (or publisher's) binding
4. Miscellaneous binding, e.g., pamphlet binding

Stationery binding
1. Blankbook (account-book) binding
2. Manifold binding
3. Exercise and notebook binding
4. General office and stationery binding, e.g., checkbook binding.

The operations of bookbinding begin with the folding of the sheets into sections (or signatures) and conclude, in library and edition binding, with casing-in; and in hand binding, with the pasting down of the board papers. The finishing of a hand-bound book, while also a part of bookbinding, is generally considered to be artistic work. In a very general sense, the operations may be divided into three very broad categories: the steps involved in preparation for binding, FORWARDING, and finally, FINISHING (1). Preparation includes all the operations up to and including folding, most of which are actually the work of the printer and not the bookbinder. (*See:* BINDERY WAREHOUSE.) Forwarding, as the name connotes, carries the book up to covering and pasting down (or casing-in), as well as edge gilding, marbling, etc. Finishing includes lettering and any decoration. Since edition and library bindings are blocked (lettered and/or decorated) before being cased, forwarding and finishing are somewhat intermingled. The sequence of operations followed by the bookbinder or bindery from the time the sheets (in edition binding and occasionally hand binding) or books and/or

periodical issues (library binding and hand binding) are received to final inspection are as follows:

NOTE: B refers to blankbook binding, E to edition binding, H to hand binding, and L to library binding.

B	E	H	L	
				Entering record
	x		x	Entering record
x	x	x		Folding (only occasionally in hand binding)
x				Sorting to remove incorrectly or poorly ruled sheets
x	x	x		Gathering (only in hand binding if sheets have to be folded; in edition binding, gathering sometimes follows the tipping on of endpapers)
		x	x	Collating
			x	Removing spine folds (for oversewing or adhesive binding)
		x	x	Pulling (in preparation for resewing through the folds)
		x	x	Knocking out the old backing ridge (if required)
		x	x	Mending, guarding, general repairs, etc.
		x	x	Guarding plates, refolding maps, making stubs, etc.
	x	x	x	Pressing (bundling)
x	x	x	x	Making joints for blankbooks, or endpapers for others
x				Guarding first and last three folios (sections)
x		x	x	Marking and preparing for sewing
x	x	x	x	Sewing and attaching endpapers or joints
x				Nipping or smashing
		x		Fraying cords
x	x	x	x	Gluing up the spine
x	x	x	x	Trimming (See alternative hand binding method, below)
		x		Cutting fore edge out of boards
x	x	x	x	Rounding
x		x	x	Backing
		x		Cleaning off spine and drying
x				Clothings
x				Making tongue
	x		x	Lining spine
		x		Cutting head and tail out of boards
x		x		Cutting and preparing boards
x				Paring and slotting tongue
	x		x	Case-making
x		x		Cutting leather

B	E	H	L	
x				Making spring-back (may be done in batches in advance)
x				Attaching spring-back (and levers)
	x		x	Making plate or casting type for blocking
	x		x	Blocking case
x	x			Attaching boards
x				Trimming ends of spring-back
x	x			Paring leather
x	x			Covering
x	x			Trimming margin of turn-ins
x				Siding
	x		x	Casing-in and/or building-in
x	x			Pasting down board papers
x	x			Pressing
x				Cutting index
x				Numbering (occasionally follows folding)
x	x			Decorating and/or lettering
x	x			Cleaning off
	x			Jacketing

There are four basic characteristics of a well-bound (modern) book: flexibility, durability, solidity, and accuracy. Flexibility is a characteristic of the spine of the book which allows the book to open freely with minimum strain on the structure. The factors affecting flexibility include the method of sewing (or otherwise joining the leaves or sections), the grain direction of the paper, the presence of tipped-in plates, the characteristics of the paper, the lining of the spine, rounding and backing, and finally, the materials and techniques used in covering the book. *See:* FLEXIBLE SEWING; OVERSEWING; ADHESIVE BINDING; MACHINE DIRECTION; PAPER; SPINE LINING; HOLLOW BACK; TIGHT BACK. Durability is a characteristic of a binding which enables it to withstand flexing, abrasion, impact, tearing, and staining or soiling. It is built into a binding in certain places, but particularly in the sewing, attachment of the endpapers, rounding and backing, the lining of the spine, and the attachment of the boards (in hand binding), or casing-in or building-in (in edition and library binding). Inferior materials, and especially inferior adhesives, spine linings, endpapers and covering materials will adversely affect durability. *See:* ROUNDING; BACKING; ENDPAPERS; LACING-IN; CASING-IN. Solidity is a characteristic a book displays when it has the appearance of a compact entity, lies flat when closed, and is loosely jointed at the spine. Good pressing (or casing-in), gluing, and especially good rounding and backing, are essential, as also is the use of boards of a suitable weight. Accuracy is a somewhat vague term, but is manifest in the ability of the book to stand vertically without leaning or falling over. This is accomplished by square trimming, proper attachment of the boards (or case-making and casing-in), and square cutting of the boards. (56, 57, 89, 92, 100, 115, 126, 135, 152, 170, 236, 279, 280, 320, 335, 343, 371, 372)

book blocks. Flat, smooth boards of varying lengths and thicknesses, with one end shaped to fit the spine of a rounded book, and used to support the cover while pasting down the board paper or leather joint, and also when tooling the turn-ins or doublure. The block prevents strain at the joint of the book.

book cloth. A generic term for the woven fabrics used in covering books. They are usually, but by no means always, woven cotton fabrics, which may be bleached or mercerized, dyed, filled with pigment colors, gelatinized, starched, coated or impregnated, calendered, and embossed (grained). They are divided into classes according to type and quality. Specifications for the fabrics used for book cloths are:

Book Cloths
(starch-filled and impregnated)

Group	Weight
A	Light
B	Medium
C	Heavy
C-1	Heavy

Buckrams
(starch-filled and impregnated)

Group	Weight
D	Light
E	Medium
F	Heavy

The specific (minimum) requirements for these fabrics are as follows below:

The breaking strength sum for embossed cloths has been established as 25% less than the figure for cloths that are not embossed.

Pyroxylin treated fabrics, which were introduced in about 1910, represented a major breakthrough in book cloth. The term "pyroxylin treated," as applied to book cloths, means either pyroxylin coated or pyroxylin impregnated cotton fabrics. The difference between the two is the quantity of protective coating applied and the manner of application, as well as the type of material treated. The pyroxylin composition consists of gelatinized nitrocellulose, a plasticizer to impart softness and flexibility, coloring matter, and a solvent. The fabrics used for impregnation are lightweight muslins, while those used for coating are heavier drills, twills, and sheeting. Coated fabrics are sometimes embossed in imitation of leather. The surface of impregnated fabrics retain the texture of the base materials. Pyroxylin impregnated fabrics are superior to starch-filled fabrics because their surfaces are more water resistant, they are more resistant to insects and fungi, and are generally stronger. They wear well and are particularly suitable for use in library binding. Pyroxylin coated fabrics are used extensively in edition binding because of the decorative effects obtainable. They, too, are water repellant and immune to insect attack and fungi, but they do not wear as well as impregnated cloths because of cracking at the joints and occasional peeling of the coating.

Book cloths for cheaper editions are closely woven, lightweight, starch-filled cotton fabrics, sometimes lightly embossed to conceal the weave of the fabric. They are generally attractive but have little strength or durability. They are also vulnerable to water spotting and soiling, and cannot be wiped clean. In addition, they are generally unsuit-

Group	Stripped-cloth weight—not less than:	Warp plus filling threads per inch— not less than:	Breaking strength sum (warp plus filling)—not less than: Pounds	Breaking strength— not less than: Pounds	
	Ounces/square yard			Warp	Filling
A	1.7	92	60	38	15
B	2.1	104	77	50	20
C	3.4	104	105	55	42
C-1	4.2	94	120	64	48
D	4.7	58	110	65	35
E	6.0	106	165	100	55
F	7.9	110	200	120	70

able for printing by offset lithography.

The book cloth used in library binding is generally of two types, pyroxylin impregnated and starch filled. The Library Binding Institute specifications for impregnated cloth, i.e., buckram, call for a base fabric of cotton, the warp yarns of which are to be woven in pairs, and with specifications the same as for group F, above. In addition, the Institute requires that the dye used must penetrate through the fabric so that both sides will be covered equally prior to the application of the impregnating compound (except in the case of "linen" type finishes). The impregnating compound must be uniform and homogeneous and be of either the nitrocellulose or cellulose acetate type. The weight of the impregnating compound must constitute at least 10% of the total weight of the finished fabric and must contain no oxidizable oils. The plasticizer, including oil (if any), must not exceed 20% by weight of the impregnating compound, nor must the weight of the pigment exceed 25% of the compound. Residual solvents, if any, are not to exceed 0.01% by weight of the finished fabric, and the pH of the cloth, as measured by standard methods, is not to be less than 6.5 nor more than 7.5, except in the case of the use of acid dyes, in which case the pH must not be less than 6.0. Cloth specifications state that the finished cloth shall be sufficiently water resistant to permit no penetration of water within a period of ten minutes, as determined by the ring test. The finished cloth is to be sufficiently grease resistant to permit no penetration of oleic acid within a period of five minutes, as determined by the ring test. The finished cloth must be capable of adhering permanently to boards and board papers under normal processing using either an animal glue or a resinous adhesive, and must resist rub-off to the degree that loss by abrasion shall not exceed 8% by weight of the fabric, when subjected to abrasion for 10 minutes by flint paper (2/0), on a disc 2 inches in diameter rotating at 1,250 rpm under 3 pounds of pressure. The finished cloth is to be free of marked odor, and its fastness to light shall be such that it will not lose color or fade when subjected to fadeometer exposure for 15 hours.

Cloth as a covering material for books is said to have been introduced, in England, by William Pickering, possibly as early as 1821-23, although books bound in burlap go back to the 1760s. Pickering's cloth was calico, a

soft clothing material which disintegrated in the presence of glue unless it was lined with paper. ARCHIBALD LEIGHTON is generally credited with being the first to introduce a really durable cloth for covering books. The first true book cloth was a dyed and glazed calico, prepared with a starch filler to make it resistant to the moisture in glue.

The first cloth had little character and was aesthetically unpleasant. It was also without natural texture and the threads gave it a somewhat raw and unfinished appearance. What was needed was some sort of decoration which would make the threads less obvious. When this came about, it took the form of embossed grains worked on the material, either in the roll or piece. One of the earliest designs, introduced in 1831, was a water finish, which may have been an outgrowth of the watered silk patterns that were introduced in 1828; it was used only for a short period because of its high cost and poor durability. *See also:* CLOTH GRAINING.

For several years following the introduction of cloth, it was the usual practice of binders to buy the cloth in its basic white color, and then have it dyed, filled, and otherwise prepared for use, or to dye and finish it themselves. Embossing was done at first by means of ribbon embossers, but this was expensive, and the larger binderies did their own embossing by means of manually operated, heated rollers. By the 1840s, however, the complete manufacture of finished book cloth had become a separate business.

Notwithstanding its obvious advantages, it was not until the middle of the 19th century that cloth largely replaced paper in regular edition binding. The rapid increase in the use of cloth was largely due to the successful methods that were developed of blocking in gold on cloth-covered cases. It was then possible to give cloth bindings a finished appearance which enabled them to be compared favorably with hand-tooled leather and, therefore, acceptable as a permanent binding. (71, 89, 147, 187, 188, 209, 236, 264, 286, 326, 341)

book conservation. *See:* CONSERVATION; RESTORATION.

book corners. Protective caps for the corners of book covers, sometimes made of leather, but also of metal or the same material that covers the book. Also called "corners." *See also:* BOSSES.

book covers. A protective cover or

CHEMISE of soft leather, such as DOE SKIN (1), or, in the case of blankbooks, a material such as canvas, sewn or slipped over a leather-covered book for protection against abrasion, moisture, light, etc. Soft leather covers were common in the Middle Ages and early Renaissance, and canvas or cloth slip-on covers are still being used for blankbooks. (115)

book crafts. The operations that are carried out in the production of books, including papermaking, printing, design of books, design and production of illustrations, and bookbinding. (335)

book-drill. 1. A linen cloth used to reinforce endpapers. This type of reinforcement is sometimes required because opening the cover, particularly in the case of side sewn books which have little flexibility, strains the sewing and will eventually cause the endpaper to break away unless it is reinforced. 2. A high-speed electric drill used for producing holes of a very small diameter through the paper of books to be overcast but not resewn. A similar drill, usually in a press, is used to drill holes completely through the leaves of a book that is to be side sewn.

book forming and pressing machine. A machine used in edition binding which applies heat and pressure by means of "creasers" to shape the spine of the text block. Such a machine is generally designed to be used in conjunction with a CASING-IN MACHINE. *See also:* BUILDING-IN MACHINE. (320, 433)

book jacket. A wrapper originally used to protect the covering material of the book from soiling or other damage, but now also used for promotional purposes. It may be plain, printed, or illustrated, and is flush with the covers of the book at head and tail, but folded over the fore edge of both covers. It is usually detachable. Modern book jackets are often very elaborately designed and are frequently printed in color. The book jacket, in one form or another, can be traced back to the 16th century. Also called "book wrapper," "dust cover," "dust jacket," "dust wrapper," "jacket," and "wrapper." (12, 156, 252)

book jacketing machine. A machine which automatically places jackets on newly bound edition bindings. The majority of such machines can jacket books up to a maximum of 10 by 8 by 2 inches, generally at speeds up to 35 books or more per minute. (343)

book label. A simple printed or engraved name ticket (usually paper but sometimes leather), stuck to the inside of the upper cover or one of the front flyleaves of a book, generally for purposes of identification or ownership. A more elaborate label is known as a BOOKPLATE. (69)

booklet. A small book. The term "booklet," like PAMPHLET, has been defined in a number of ways, including: 1) an affected term for a short book or pamphlet; 2) a small book, commonly bound in paper and generally used for advertising purposes; 3) a small book containing up to but not more than 24 pages, which is sufficient for classification as larger than a pamphlet; 4) a stitched pamphlet of eight or more pages, usually with a cover, and small enough to be carried in one's pocket; 5) a publication containing more pages than a pamphlet but fewer than a book and which may have a paper, limp, or stiff cover; (6) any pamphlet that is sewn or stitched but not permanently bound; and 7) a paper-covered publication in book format ranging in size from a few pages to a small-scale edition of a book. (139, 142, 256, 316)

book lice. Very small wingless insects of the order Corredentia, usually of the family Atropidae, that will attack paper and book materials, and appear capable of living on mold and mildew. Also called "deathwatch." *See also:* BOOKWORMS.

bookmark. 1. *See:* REGISTER. 2. Any printed or woven paper or other material, an inch or 2 wide and usually 4 or more inches in length, used in marking a place in a closed book for future reference. Bookmarks are frequently decorative, carrying advertisements or commemorative illustrations.

book papers. A class or group of cultural papers which have in common characteristics that, in general, make them suitable for the graphic arts. The various characteristics are designed to meet the requirements of the method of printing and the end use of the publication produced. Book papers are produced from rag pulps, mechanical and chemical wood pulps, esparto pulp, cotton fiber pulps, reclaimed paper stock, or combinations of different pulps. Mineral fillers, sizing, coloring matter, or other materials are added to the pulp in whatever combination is needed to give the appearance, strength, opacity, brightness, printability, permanence, etc., to fit the immediate or end use of the paper. The bulk of this type of paper is produced on a conventional FOURDRINIER MACHINE and is machine dried; however,

some book papers are made on cylinder and hand molds.

Uncoated book papers are used in the printing of periodicals, books, pamphlets, and the like, and are converted into other products such as tablets, ledger paper, etc. They are generally made on a Fourdrinier machine and may or may not be surfaced sized. They are made to various bulk specifications and in a variety of finishes, including antique, eggshell, machine, English, and super-calendered, as well as in special or fancy finishes. Uncoated papers are made in basis weights 30 to 150 pounds (25 × 38 — 500), the most common weights being 30 to 70 pounds.

Coated papers are used in the printing of periodicals, books, pamphlets, etc., where the use of fine halftone illustrations may be required. They are well sized and possess good tearing strength. The base papers are coated with white mineral pigments mixed with adhesives such as casein, starch, latex, resin, or glue, either on the papermaking machine as part of the manufacturing process or as a separate operation subsequent to the manufacture of the base paper. Waxes or soaps may also be added to the coating mixtures to add to the finish and feel of the paper. The mineral pigments employed include clay, satin white, barium sulfate, calcium carbonate, calcium sulfite, and titanium oxide, which may be applied as such or in mixtures, the selection of the combination used being determined by the effect required. The adhesives and the amounts used are selected according to the surface strength of the coating and its resistance to moisture and vehicles used in the printing inks. Coated papers may be coated on one or both sides with a single or double coating. Virtually all are supercalendered, with finishes ranging from a dull matte to a high gloss. The basis weights for these papers range from 30 to 150 pounds (25 × 38 — 500), with 40 to 80 pounds being most common. Coated papers usually have a brighter color, greater opacity, and a higher finish than uncoated book papers. (17, 36, 40, 63, 78, 323, 346, 366)

bookplate. A label, usually printed or engraved, frequently with a distinctive design, identifying the owner of a book, and usually pasted or tipped to the inside of the upper cover. Bookplates may be simple to the point of giving only the name of the library or other owner (sometimes with the ex-

pression "ex libris" included), or very elaborately designed, frequently with heraldic emblems or insignia.

The use of the bookplate can be dated back to at least as early as 1516, but in England, France, and Germany they did not become popular until the 18th century. There was a tremendous revival in their use and study in the 1890s, and again since about 1965. During both periods collectors have formed societies, produced journals and publications, and actually commissioned many bookplates for their own sake, that is, not necessarily intended for use in books, but rather for exchange with other collectors.

Over the years many eminent engravers have designed bookplates, and among the examples still extant are a great number which were executed with considerable skill. Because of the relative scarcity of engravers in America before 1800, bookplates were rare before that time; however, since about 1840, they have been fairly common in this country.

Their use in libraries is quite common today, but in some institutions, largely for reasons of economy, the bookplate has been replaced by a rubber stamp. (69, 200)

book pocket. A receptacle of stiff paper, cloth, buckram, leather, or an ordinary envelope, pasted on the inside of a book usually the lower cover to hold loose material, maps, charts, user cards, etc. Some book pockets, such as those found in many English (as well as Continental) almanacs from the late 17th to the early 18th centuries, have concertina (expansion) folds at head and tail and open at the fore edge. Sometimes a COMPENSATION GUARD is required to provide for the thickness of the material in the pocket. The opening of the typical pocket is at the head, or less often, at the binding edge. (12)

book repairer. The so-called one man bookbinder or repairer, an itinerant bookbinder who offers to bind, rebind, restore and/or clean books in a library, generally quickly and at low cost. Book repairers are not nearly so numerous as they were in the past; however, they still exist, and probably many thousands of books have been "restored," some well and some poorly, by these itinerant bookbinders. (131)

book rest. A device designed to hold a book in position during the tooling of the area where the spine curves around onto the sides. Its advantage is that it provides a better angle at which to

35

work, as well as better sighting. The sloping sides of a FINISHING PRESS are also used for the same purpose. (130)

book sander. A machine used in library binderies to remove the spine folds of a book having binding margins so narrow that the folds cannot be trimmed away in a cutting machine. Modern sanders can be adjusted to remove as little as 1/32 inch. The sander is also preferred by many library binders because it is faster than a cutting machine. (164)

books in sheets. "Books" as received by the binder in flat (unfolded) sheets, which must be folded, gathered and collated, and which must then have any maps, illustrations, etc., inserted before the actual binding processes. The sheets are sometimes identified by a SIGNATURE (1), which may be either a letter and/or number, and in the case of sets may include the volume number, printed at the tail margin (in the direction line) of the first, and occasionally on succeeding pages of each. Before the rise of edition binding most publications were delivered to the bookseller in sheets, to be bound to the customer's order. "Books in sheets" today is almost exclusively a term restricted to edition binding. (83, 335)

book sizes. The dimensions of books, as measured, in inches, centimeters, or millimeters, from head to tail and from spine to fore edges of the cover. The descriptions given to book sizes are based on a still currently used system that involves using the size of a leaf as a fraction of the folded sheet on which it was printed. With reference to the printing of books, an even number of leaves always results when a sheet is folded, i.e., 2, 4, 8, 16, etc., resulting in printed pages on each side of the leaf, i.e., 4, 8, 16, 32, etc. Except for the largest size, the FOLIO (1), the name of the size indicates the fractional part of the sheet one leaf occupies, e.g., quarto (2 folds, 4 leaves, 8 pages), ¼ of the sheet; octavo (3 folds, 8 leaves, 16 pages), ⅛ of the sheet, etc. In this system, since books are printed from different sizes of sheets (See: BOOK BASIS), the fractional designation by itself cannot denote an exact size; therefore it is a common practice to give the name of the sheet before the fractional name, e.g., *royal octavo,* which is an octavo ⅛ the size of a sheet 20 × 25 inches or, excluding the SQUARES, a book 10 × 6¼ inches (before trimming). Paper is cut to so many sizes, however, that the terms *crown, royal, post,* etc., unless qualified, are practically meaningless. *See:* SIZES OF PAPER. Untrimmed sizes for three commonly used sheet sizes are given below. The customary trim of ⅛ inch at head and tail will reduce the height of the text block by ¼ inch; however, the size of the bound book, assuming ⅛ inch squares will make the height of the book the same as the sizes given. It should be mentioned that not all sheet sizes given are folded to produce

Book sizes

Size (in inches)	Name	Times Folded	Leaves per Sheet	Pages per Sheet	Size of Untrimmed Page (leaf)
25 by 38	folio	1	2	4	25 by 19
25 by 38	quarto	2	4	8	19 by 12½
25 by 38	octavo	3	8	16	12½ by 9½
25 by 38	sixteenmo	4	16	32	9½ by 6¼
25 by 38	thirty-twomo	5	32	64	6¼ by 4¾
25 by 38	sixty-fourmo	6	64	128	4¾ by 3⅛
20 by 25	folio	1	2	4	20 by 12½
20 by 25	quarto	2	4	8	12½ by 10
20 by 25	octavo	3	8	16	10 by 6¼
20 by 25	sixteenmo	4	16	32	6¼ by 5
20 by 25	thirty-twomo	5	32	64	2½ by 3⅛
20 by 25	sixty-fourmo	6	64	128	3⅛ by 2½
18 by 23	folio	1	2	4	18 by 11½
18 by 23	quarto	2	4	8	11½ by 9
18 by 23	octavo	3	8	16	9 by 5¾
18 by 23	sixteenmo	4	16	32	5¾ by 4½
18 by 23	thirty-twomo	5	32	64	4½ by 2⅞
18 by 23	sixty-fourmo	6	64	128	2⅞ by 2¼

Size names and their equivalents

Old Name	Modern Name	Abbreviation	Symbol
folio	folio	fo or f	
quarto	quarto	4to	4°
sexto	sixmo	6to or 6mo	6°
octavo	octavo	8mo or 8vo	8°
duodecimo	twelvemo	12mo	12°
sextodecimo	sixteenmo	16mo	16°
octodecimo	eighteenmo	18mo	18°
vincestmo-quarto	twenty-fourmo	24mo	24°
vegisemo-quarto	twenty-fourmo	24mo	24°
trigesimo-decundo	thirty-twomo	32mo	32°
quadragesimo-octavo	forty-eightmo	48mo	48°
sexagesimo-quarto	sixty-fourmo	64mo	64°

British book sizes

Size Name	Octavo Size	Quarto Size
pott	6¼ by 4	8 by 6¼
foolscap	6¾ by 4¼	8¼ by 6¾
crown	7½ by 5	10 by 7½
large crown	8 by 5¼	10½ by 8
large post	8¼ by 5¼	10¼ by 8¼
demy	8¾ by 5⅝	11¼ by 8¾
post	8 by 5	10 by 8
small demy	8½ by 5⅝	11¼ by 8½
medium	9 by 5¾	11½ by 9
small royal	9¼ by 6⅛	12¼ by 9¼
royal	10 by 6¼	12½ by 10
super royal	10¼ by 6¾	13½ by 10¼
imperial	11 by 7½	15 by 11

books of the very small size indicated. All folds, following the first, are right-angle folds.

The common book-trade designation of sizes was originally related to a sheet of handmade paper measuring 19 × 25 inches, which was the common size of the papermaking mold. When folded to 8 leaves, or 16 pages, and trimmed, each was 6½ × 9¼ inches, approximately, and was the standard dimension of an 8vo. When folded to make 16 leaves, or 32 pages, it was a 16 mo. With the present great variety of paper sizes, all dimensions are by necessity only approximate. (52, 69, 140, 156, 169)

books of permanent interest. A category established by Douglas Cockerell shortly after the turn of the century in an effort to categorize the time, effort and funds to be expended in binding books of an "intermediate" nature—i.e., books of permanent scholarly, historical, etc., interest, but of relatively little monetary or esthetic interest, which should be solidly and well bound, but for which the most expensive work would be inappropriate. In Cockerell's day, this category of books was bound by hand, sewn with linen thread around cotton or linen tapes, which were secured between split boards (when the books were large and heavy), and covered with strong cloth or the most durable leather, or a combination of the two, e.g., quarter or half bindings. In greatly modified form, the Library Binding Institute has continued to define this category of books. *See:* PERMANENT MATERIALS. *See also:* BOOKS OF TEMPORARY INTEREST; BOOKS OF VALUE. (83)

books of temporary interest. Books that must be bound and kept clean and usable for only occasional use. This category assumes that the handling such books receive and the storage area of the library will suffice for less than a full and "permanent" binding, which is often not the case. *See also:* BOOKS OF PERMANENT INTEREST.

books of value. Books that are valuable and/or rare, which may or may not have any special scholarly value, or books of special interest to a particular library, and which are bound in the best manner and with the best materials. *See also:* BOOKS OF PERMANENT INTEREST.

book support. A wood or metal device generally placed to the right side of a row of books on a shelf to support and maintain them in a vertical posi-

tion. Book supports are available in several forms: 1) the spring type, which hangs from the ribbed shelf above (but which sometimes does not reach down to the smaller books); 2) the metal support, with a stamped-out metal tongue that slips under the first few books; it rests on the same shelf as the books to be supported, and should be flanged to prevent it from "spearing" or otherwise damaging the books; 3) the type that locks into the ribbed shelf on which the books rest, and which can be difficult to slide if the locking key becomes twisted; 4) the magnetic support, which is usable only on ferrous metal shelves; and 5) wooden supports, some of which are very elaborate and are generally used to support more valuable books, or books in specially designated areas. The better book supports have a felt- or cork-covered base, especially for use on wooden shelves, and, for valuable books, a felt- or cork-covered face. The typical metal support is generally available in two sizes—regular, about 6 inches tall, and oversize, about 9 inches tall.

book wall. The arrangement in a double-sided case of one or more sets of books displaying the upper and lower covers of craft bookbindings where comprehensive designs flow across adjacent surfaces to create a unified image. The book wall is the creation of the contemporary English bookbinder PHILIP SMITH. (311)

bookworms. The larva of any of some 160 species of beetles. The mature female insect lays her eggs on the edges of books, or in the crevices of bookshelves, and the larvae, when hatched, burrow into the books, or shelves, riddling them with tiny tunnels. Various bookworms, as they are mistakenly called, have been identified, or supposedly identified, among which are: *Anobium domesticum, A. eruditus, A. Paniceum, A. pertinax, A. punctatum,* and *A. striatum; Acarus cheyletus* and *A. eruditus; Dermestes lardarius; Aecophora pseudospretella; Sitodrepa paniceum; Attagenus pellio; Lepisma saccharina; Ptinus fur; Antherenus varius; Lyctus brunneus; Catorama mexicana;* and *Rhizopertha dominica.* Of the types, the most notorius and destructive are: *Sitodrepa paniceum,* the drugstore beetle, the female of which is capable of producing as many as 800,000 descendants in a year; *Lyctus brunneus,* the powder-post beetle, which consumes wooden bookshelves and cases, packing the holes with a

flourlike debris, so that nothing substantial remains of the shelf; *Ptinus fur,* the spider beetle, first mentioned by Linnaeus in 1766, which can cause severe damage to books, papers, and leather if left undisturbed for long periods of time; *Anobium punctatum,* the common furniture beetle, the larvae of which bore long cylindrical holes in books and bookshelves; *Catorama mexicana,* the Mexican book beetle; *Dermestes lardarius,* the larder beetle, which prefers cheese, ham, etc., but which will devour leather if nothing else is available; and *Rhizopertha dominica,* which has caused extensive damage in libraries.

Most of these so-called bookworms are small and dark- or reddish-brown. They enter libraries through windows, poorly fitting doors, etc., and seem to proliferate in libraries where dust, dirt, heat, darkness, and poor ventilation are prevalent.

The measures used over the years for the control or elimination of bookworms are virtually legion, including numerous remedies to be rubbed into leather, added to paste, sprinkled on bookshelves and books, etc. Among the many remedies used are: alum and thymol, alum and vitriol (sulfuric acid), (oil of) anis, beeswax, benzene, bitumen, borax, buckbean, cajeput oil, camphor, chili, chloropicrin, cinchona, cinnamon, cloves and oil of cloves, colcynth, copal varnish, copper, cresote, derris, (oil of) eucalyptus, formalin (formaldehyde), kerosine, khuskhus, lac varnish, lavender, margosia, mercuric chloride, mirbane oil, nitrobenzene, muriatic (hydrochloric) acid, musk, myrrh, napthalene, nicotine, orrisroot oil, ozone, pennyroyal, pepper, petroleum, phenol, porpoise oil, pyrethrum powder, Russia leather shavings, sandalwood, sassasfras, shellac, snuff, thyme, thymol, turpentine, vermouth, and wormwood. Some of these remedies were totally ineffective; some were temporarily effective; and some were as destructive as, or even more so than, the pests themselves.

Any preparation or process used to destroy the larvae or beetles must have sufficient residual effect not only to destroy existing larvae but also larvae which will hatch subsequent to the initial treatment. Treatment should be applied in conjunction with proper ventilation, temperature and humidity control, and cleanliness, so as to discourage future infestation.

Fumigation is frequently used to rid libraries of beetle and larvae infestation. Four general methods are used: 1) fumigation of the entire library with hydrogen cyanide, carbon disulfide, or methyl bromide, which, of course, necessitates closing the library for several days; 2) fumigation of batches of books in specially designed vacuum chambers, with a combination (1:9 by weight) of ethylene oxide and carbon dioxide, which is a method well suited to the fumigation of new acquisitions; 3) routine fumigation of the entire collection, carried out batchwise in a chamber, using methyl bromide; and 4) fumigation of one or more books in a small air-tight box, using paradichloro-benzene crystals, which is a method suitable for use by the private collector. Although the first method is potentially dangerous and causes considerable inconvenience, it is the only one which will destroy beetles or larvae which are on the bookshelves. *See also:* BOOK LICE; SILVERFISH. (47, 143, 247, 335)

book wrapper. *See:* BOOK JACKET

boomer press. A now obsolete modified form of the STANDING PRESS. The power of the boomer press was obtained by a combination of four levers working on toggle joints, through which passed a right and left hand screw. The rotation of these screws caused the pressing surfaces to approach or move apart with a uniform motion, according to the direction of the rotation. This press had several advantages over the regular standing press, including: 1) once the pressure was applied it did not release slightly as the ordinary press is likely to do, so that the material under pressure remained under full pressure, and could, therefore, be pressed in somewhat less time; and 2) the enormous pressure it was capable of exerting. (8, 97)

border. 1. An ornamental design in a repeat pattern in blind or gold around the edges of the covers of a book, frequently enclosing one or more center pieces of a different design. 2. An ornamental design along one or more sides of a page of an illuminated manuscript or of the body of printed matter, or surrounding an illuminated miniature.

boric acid. A weak, volatile acid (H_3BO_3), obtained naturally, or by treating borax with a mineral acid. It is used to thicken and preserve adhesives made of GUM ARABIC. (142)

Borneo cutch. *See:* ACACIA.

bosses. Brass or other metal knobs, studs, SHOES, or ornamentation fastened to the cover of a book for ornamental value or to prevent the leather from being scratched or otherwise marred. Bosses originally were attached to books that were meant to lie on a lectern and not stand on bookshelves. Not all books were provided with them, and they were more common in Germany than elsewhere. There was usually one boss at each corner of both covers and another in the middle of each cover, or ten in all, although the center bosses were sometimes left off. It is commonly assumed that the use of bosses declined with the advent of printing from movable metal type, the proliferation of books, and vertical shelving in cupboards and book stacks. In addition, the relative increase in the use of pasteboard instead of wooden boards also reduced the use of bosses, although in Germany, where wooden boards were still common in the 16th century, they continued to be used more often than elsewhere. Today, books with bosses are frequently kept in boxes so as to prevent damage to adjacent books on the shelves. *See also:* ROLLER SHOES. *See* PLATE I. (69, 83, 236)

bottle rubber. *See:* GOLD RUBBER.

bottom color. The base color applied to a leather and then corrected to the desired shade by the application of succeeding colors during the finishing process. In SUEDE LEATHER, however, the bottom color is the final shade. (164, 248)

bottom combs. *See:* MARBLING COMBS.

bottom edge. *See:* LOWER EDGE.

bottom split. The innermost layer of a split cowhide. Because they are relatively thick, cowhides are generally split into at least two layers (and sometimes three) if they are to be used as a "light" leather. If split once, the two layers are the grain and flesh splits; if split twice, the layers are the grain, middle, and bottom split. When processed into leather the bottom split is called a BUFFING (1). (363)

bouilly. *See:* CUIR-BOUILLI.

bound flexible. A term sometimes used to indicate a book that has been sewn on single or double raised cords, the slips of which have been laced into the boards. *See also:* FLEXIBLE SEWING; LACING-IN. (115)

bound in. An insert which has been sewn in with the sections of a book. *See also:* BIND IN. (131)

bouquet marble. A drawn marble pattern formed in the manner of small flowers side by side and used mainly for marbled endpapers. The bouquet is generally produced from two or three shades of brown and one throwing of black. After the colors have been dropped on, drawn with a stylus and combed in the usual manner, a rake is drawn through the colors right and left across the entire surface of the size in such a manner that the teeth of the second row trace exactly through the pattern left by the teeth of the first row. A somewhat different pattern is produced by treating the colors in the same manner but omitting the marbling comb and spreading the drops of color only with a stylus into very narrow cross lines followed by raking. (151, 327)

box. 1. A container for maps, bundles of loose sheets, samples of materials, disintegrating books, etc., that may be open at one end or completely closed in. *See also:* CUT CORNER PAMPHLET FILE; PAMPHLET BOX; PRINCETON FILE; PULLOFF BOX; SLIPCASE; SOLANDER BOX. 2. A leather "marble" consisting of marbling water thrown on in small drops, followed by small spots of brown and black. Additional marbling water is then thrown on in large drops, followed by small spots of blue sprinkled on. When all is dry, scarlet and two or three coats of orange are sprinkled on. The leather is bent and twisted in several places during the course of applying the colors and water to form veins. 3. A surface pattern in leather, usually black calfskin, consisting of fine, box-shaped creases formed by BOARDING (1) the skin in two directions, head to tail and belly to belly. *See also:* WILLOW (2) 4. The trough-like receptacles on a folding machine into which the folded sections drop. 5. One of the magazines of a gathering machine. (66, 152, 339, 363)

box pocket. A stiffened three-dimensional BOOK POCKET.

box side. A cowhide cut in half down the backbone, full chrome, semi-chrome, or vegetable tanned, and usually colored black. It has a grain pattern of fine box-shaped creases formed by BOARDING (1) in two directions, head to tail and belly to belly. When colored it is usually called WILLOW SIDE. (61)

bradawl. An AWL with a chisel edge used for piercing holes in boards in preparation for LACING-IN. (133)

Bradel binding. A type of binding having a hollow back, and not unlike a library binding, except that it is considered to be temporary. The style was originated in Germany by Alexis Pierre Bradel, also known as Bradel l'aîné, and also as Bradel-Derôme, son-in-law and successor to Nicholas-Denis Derôme. The style was taken to France sometime between 1772 and 1809. Bradel bindings generally have split boards into which are attached the extensions of the spine lining cloth. The edges are uncut, sometimes with the head edge being gilt. They generally have a leather or linen spine. In France the style was known as "Cartonnage à la Bradel," or as "en gist." *See also:* LESNÉ, FRANÇOIS A. D. (347)

Braille book (Braille binding). A book printed by the Braille process, i.e., the dampened paper is embossed with codes of raised dots. Braille books are bound much like other books except that they are generally liberally stubbed and they are not pressed after casing-in, as the pressure would flatten the raised characters.

Braille printing paper. Paper used in the Braille printing process. It is usually produced from a high quality chemical wood pulp in basis weights of 32 to 36 pounds (17 X 22 - 500). Significant properties required include a smooth surface, good elongation, and high tensile strength. (17)

branding. 1. A method of marking a book with hot irons that burn letters or symbols into one or more edges, generally for purposes of indicating ownership. Branding was most often employed in Mexico, and was initiated in the early 17th century by the monks in charge of convent libraries. Brands of iron or bronze were used, usually on the head edge, although it was sometimes done on the fore edge and occasionally on both head and tail edges. Unfortunately, the process often damaged the covers, title pages, and endpapers; however, as a mark of ownership, it was effective in deterring the theft of books, as the brand could only be removed by trimming deep into the margins. 2. The process of rolling a FLESHER or SHEEPSKIN with hot rolls for the purpose of smoothing the skin. (115, 264, 274)

brashiness. The relative inflexibility of the cast film of a dry animal glue. The term also refers to brittleness of an adhesive resulting from drying, plasticizer migration, and the like. (222)

brass boarded. A leather, usually a cowhide BUFFING (1), that has been boarded by hand or grained with a faint parallel line effect. (256)

brass boards (brass bound bounds). *See:* BACKING BOARDS; CASING-IN BOARDS.

brayer. 1. An old term for a pestle with which ink was spread before being applied to a printing surface. Made of wood, it was round, flat at one end, and had a handle at the other end. 2. A printer's hand inking roller, also used in making BRAYER PRINTS.

brayer prints. Decorative endpapers and cover prints produced by rolling an inked brayer over paper under which flat objects, such as leaves, ferns, etc., have been placed. Alternative methods are to ink the objects and press the paper on them with a clean brayer, or to roll the inked brayer over the paper and then place objects underneath and roll with an ink of a different color. (183)

Brazil wood. The heavy wood of any of the tropical trees, family Leguminosae, which yield a red, water-soluble dye, brazilin ($C_{16}H_{14}O_5$), which at one time was used to produced coloring materials used both in marbling and in dyeing leather. Brazil wood dyes have been largely superceded by the synthetic dyestuffs.

bread crumbs. The particles of ordinary crustless bread, used by some restorers to remove loose dust from maps, charts, etc., and for dry cleaning the leaves of books. (173)

break. 1. The parting of adjacent sections of a book due to failure of the sewing. *See also:* START. 2. A crack in the gold or foil BLOCKING or tooling of a book. 3. In papermaking, a complete separation of the web of paper, either on or off the machine. 4. In leather manufacture, the minute wrinkles formed when the grain surface of leather is bent so that its grain side is sharply concave. If the wrinkles formed are very fine, and there are many of them to the linear inch, the leather is said to have a *fine break*, whereas if they are large and there are relatively few to the linear inch, the leather is said to have a *coarse break*. A very important aspect of the "break" in leather is that when the leather is flexed to cause the break to appear, it should disappear once the leather is again flattened. Since a fine break is considered to be one of the more important characteristics of leather, tanners attempt to obtain as fine a break as possible. In order to achieve this, it is necessary to prevent excessive cohesion of the fibers in the grain surface of the leather, which is one of the major purposes of FAT-LIQUORING leather. Break is influenced to a great extent by the amount of oil in the grain layer and increases in fineness with an increase of oil.

The butt area of a skin usually has a finer break than the belly; tighter skins have finer breaks than looser ones, and a leather like calfskin will have a much finer break than cowhide.

Improper methods of finishing may cause an otherwise fine break to become coarse, but the kind of tannage has little effect on break. (102, 248, 363)

breaking length. The length of a strip of paper, cut either in the machine or cross direction, or a strip of cloth, cut either in the warp or filling direction, which would break of its own weight when suspended vertically. It is a value calculated from the tensile strength of the material. Under normal circumstances paper will have a greater breaking length in the machine direction than in the cross direction, and cloth a greater breaking length in the warp direction than in the filling. (42, 98, 341)

breaking strength. 1. *See:* BURSTING STRENGTH. 2. The breaking load or force, expressed in pounds per inch, required to rupture a material, such as cloth or paper.

breathing. A property of leather, characterized by a resistance to water in the liquid form but having the ability to allow the passage of water vapor. "Breathing" is considered important in maintaining the suppleness and handle of leather, and is one reason why some conservationists oppose the use of hard waxes in leather dressings.

Brethren of the Common Life. *See:* BROTHERS OF THE COMMON LIFE.

(Le) Bretons, Pere et Fils. Two renowned producers of marbled papers of 17th century France. They produced finely veined papers, some of which, with fine veins of gold and silver, were very equisite. The Bretons also made excellent papers stenciled with flowers on paper with a highly calendered surface. (217)

brick guard. A type of COMPENSATION GUARD, but specifically one side stitched to the text block to compensate for pocket material. (339)

brightening agents. Chemical agents at one time used extensively in leather dye batches to brighten the color of the finished leather. One such agent was sulfuric acid, which is not only destructive but virtually impossible to remove from leather effectively and completely. Another was formic acid, which, being weaker and more volatile, was less destructive. *See also:* P.I.R.A. TESTED. (298)

brighter binding. A movement initiated in about 1910 in Great Britain by Alexander Philip to encourage libraries to have their books bound in bright, colorful cloth, so as to enliven the appearance of the then drab and colorless bookstacks in the libraries of that time. The belief was that bright bindings meant bright cheerful libraries, whereas a library filled with dark blue and black bindings had the opposite effect. *See also:* BINDING SCHEMES. (261)

brightness. Originally, a judgement of the amount of light reflected to the eye from the surface of a material, regardless of hue or color saturation. Brightness is now measured by optical comparators. Many factors affect the brightness of a material such as paper, including the degree of bleaching of the pulp, as well as the addition of chemicals. Chemically treated high-grade text and book papers have a brightness in the range of about 96 (on a scale of 100), coated papers range from about 70 to 85, while mechanical wood machine-coated papers are in the range of about 60 to 75. Newsprint is generally below 60. (17, 72)

brightness reversion. A paper pulp, and particularly a bleached paper pulp, which has lost BRIGHTNESS because of natural or artificial aging. (17)

brime. A finely powdered burnt GYPSUM. Brime is dusted on GOLDBEATERS' SKIN in order to eliminate as much friction as possible during the MOLD (2) stage in the manufacture of gold leaf. (29)

brining. A method generally used in the larger abattoirs for curing hides and skins for transportation to tanneries. After flaying, the hides are washed thoroughly to remove blood and soluble protein matter and the hair is scraped under a spray of water. The flesh side is brushed vigorously to remove surplus flesh. The hides are then hung in pits or run in large paddles in a very strong solution of sodium chloride, using 30 pounds of salt to every 10 gallons of water. This gives a very good and uniform salt penetration for heavy hides in 12 to 14 hours. The hides are then drained and piled, and treated with salt in the WET-SALTING process. The purity and strength of the brine must be checked before it is reused, as it may become contaminated with halophilic bacteria. The use of a salt solution as a preliminary treatment for preserving cowhides has been standard practice in South America for many years, and has been in commercial use in the United States since about 1935. Brining, followed by wet-salting, is a more expensive method of cure than salting alone; however, it reduces putrefactive

damage to the hides to a considerable extent over simple salting. (248, 306)

bristol board. A lightweight board that can be made on either a Fourdrinier or cylinder papermaking machine. There are three types of bristols: 1) index, 2) mill, and 3) wedding. They range in thickness from 0.006 inch and greater. The original bristol board, made in Bristol, England, was a pasted board made of rag content paper, but very little bristol today is of this character. Bristols are sometimes filled, but are more commonly pasted or plied, the thicker sheets being made by pasting sheets of the same stock together until the desired thickness is attained. They are designated as 2-ply, 3-ply, etc., according to the number of sheets used. The highest grade of bristol is wedding, followed by index and mill. (17, 234, 320)

British marble. A marble pattern, with or without veins, which somewhat resembles the SPANISH MARBLE. It is usually executed entirely in varying shades of black, although colors are sometimes used. (241, 369)

brittleness. The property or condition of a material, such as, paper, board, adhesives, etc., that causes failure of the material when it is deformed by bending. As virtually any material will fail if bent or folded a sufficient number of times, brittleness is of practical interest only when deformation producing failure is small or the number of folds is relatively small in number.

Over the course of many years, high acidity in paper, and particularly acidity resulting from inorganic acids of low volatility, has been suspected of being the chief cause of brittleness in paper. This acidity can be attributed to several sources: 1) papermaking procedures, e.g., excessive ALUM in sizing or excessive chlorine in BLEACHING (1), which may lead to the formation of acid; 2) ink; and 3) conditions of storage, which may allow acid gasses such as SULFUR DIOXIDE to gain access to the paper, which, in the presence of heat and other conditions, may lead to the formation of acid. *See also:* ACID; ACID GASES; ACIDITY; ACID SIZE; DE-ACIDIFICATION; DURABILITY (OF PAPER); FOLDING ENDURANCE. (17, 34, 41, 348)

broad (broad fold). 1. A sheet of paper which, after being folded, has the grain direction running with the shorter dimension of the paper. 2. A sheet of paper folded in such a manner that the resulting pages are wider than they are deep, i.e., an OBLONG fold or page, as

distinguished from an upright page or "deep fold."

brocade. 1. A book cloth, generally made from silk or cotton, woven in jacquard construction and characterized by all-over formal design of slightly raised floral and figure designs introduced by additional threads in the filling. 2. In papermaking, a heavily embossed cover paper. 3. A marbled paper with a brocadelike pattern. (183)

brochure. A "stitched work" (from the French "brocher," to stitch). It is a short printed work, with or without a paper or self-cover, and sewn or stitched. (139)

broken (broken back). 1. The tendency of a book to open readily at a place or places where the binding has been forced or strained, causing the book to lose its shape. This may be caused by: 1) improper opening of a new book that is tightly bound; 2) improper backing, which flattens the spine and affects its contour; 3) using paper with the grain running at right angles to the spine, resulting in leverage and causing THROW OUT of one or more sections; 4) sections, either with or without plates, that are too bulky, and are forced apart during backing, leaving ridges; and 5) the use of animal glue, during the gluing process before rounding and backing, that is too cold or is not sufficiently flexible. In a TIGHT BACK leather binding, it may result in ridges appearing on the spine where the leather has been forced away from the paper. 2. A book broken completely through so that it is in two or more pieces. This generally occurs in relatively old books, particularly those of the 19th century, in which the paper and glue have become so embrittled and inflexible that when the book is opened, it breaks apart. (83, 102)

broken line. 1. A blocked or finished line or rule intentionally "broken" by uniformly spaced openings. 2. A blocked line that is not solid as a result of breaks in the gold leaf. (256)

brokers. Binding agents, who were go-betweens or self-appointed salesmen of publishers or library binders, and who solicited binding business and then let out the work to the lowest-priced bidder on their list. Mason Locke Weems ("Parson Weems"), the creator of the George Washington cherry tree myth, seems to have been one such agent, working between binders and the publisher, Matthew Carey. Binding brokers, who flourished in the United States well into the 20th century, are rare today. (131, 308)

bronzed edges. A decorative edge pattern on a book produced by impressing bronze leaf on the edges by means of an engraved roller. The leaf is first pressed into the gravure and then rolled on the edge. This technique was generally executed over colored edges, with albumen or gum arabic being used to secure the leaf to the paper. Bronzed edges were employed mainly in the latter part of the 19th century.

bronze leaf. *See:* DUTCH GOLD.

bronze powder. A metallic powder made from various bronze or brass alloys and used principally in lacquer or varnish vehicles, or with bronzing liquid, as the so-called gold paint. The powder can be prepared to duplicate every shade of gold from a pale or lemon color to a deep coppery hue. Bronze powder darkens or discolors after a relatively short time, and this, plus the fact that the paint made from it has a lackluster, grainy quality, makes it unsuitable for use in bookbinding. (236)

Brothers of the Common Life. Associations of clerics and laymen that originated in the Netherlands in the 14th century. The reformers, Gerhard Groote and Florent Radewyns, inspired a small group of men at Deventer (Holland) to join together in community life in pursuit of holiness. The movement spread throughout the Netherlands and Germany and was influential until the time of the Reformation.

One of the principal occupations of the Brothers was the production of books, but, unlike the monastery scribes, they established their book trade specifically for the purpose of supporting their organization, using the profits derived from the sale of books in their missionary work. In addition, instead of offering their works in Latin, they issued them in the vernacular of the area in which they were produced.

At the Convent of St. Jerome at Ghent, the Brothers were noted for the excellence of the manuscripts and bindings they produced. Two examples of their work are embellished with a panel representing their patron, St. Jerome, kneeling before a crucifix. In the background, beyond the mountains, is a view of the belfry of Ghent, surmounted by the dragon, and the spires of three churches.

Their first book was issued in 1476 from the Nazareth Monastery in Brussels. (141)

brush. An implement used for the application of paste, glue, or other adhesive liquid, powder, glair, etc., to the surface of paper, board, cloth, leather, or other material. A brush is composed of a gathering of hair or bristles (natural brushes), or some synthetic material, secured in a plastic compound and held in a metal ferrule which is crimped around a handle. A high quality brush always has the natural tips of the hairs or bristles. The various shapes of brushes are achieved by cutting, trimming, and fashioning the root (butt) ends of the hairs. A pointed brush, for example, is shaped by inserting the hairs, tips downward, in a brass "cannon," in the size and shape made for the purpose, and trimming them at the root end. Very superior brushes have a considerable hold of hair within the ferrule, sometimes as much as is seen beyond the ferrule, while cheaper brushes have but little hold. (66, 233)

brushing. The process of developing a mild luster on the finished surface of a leather by the action of a rotary brush. The term is also used with reference to freeing the surface of leather of the fine fibrous dust created by buffing—i.e., by drawing the skins between a pair of long rotary brushes. (363)

brushing out. *See:* FIBRILLATION.

B-stage. A secondary stage in the reaction of some thermosetting resins, characterized by softening of the resin when heated and swelling when in the presence of certain liquids, but without complete fusing or dissolving. The "b-stage" is also characterized by a progressive increase in viscosity. The resin portion of an uncured thermosetting adhesive is usually in this stage. Also called "resitol." *See also:* A-STAGE; C-STAGE. (309)

buckle. 1. The wrinkling near the head and binding edge of a section, which may be caused by paper that is too thick, or by too many folds in forming the section, and which may be accentuated by the grain direction of the paper being incorrect—i.e., running from spine to fore edge rather than head to tail. 2. Book covers or cover boards that have been warped and twisted in several directions. *See also:* COCKLE (1-3). (131)

buckle folding. *See:* FOLDING

buckram. A BOOK CLOTH made from cotton or linen, usually the former, and closely woven, occasionally with a double warp. It is filled or coated and calendered to give it a smooth finish which blocks well and is reasonably durable. Originally, the term applied only to a starch-filled fabric; today, however, it applies also to coated and impregnated fabrics having a heavy base. The material used to fill the interstices and/or cover the base fabric is usually pyroxylin, but it may be starch, china clay, clay, or other nonfibrous material.

buckskin. A leather produced from the hides of male deer or elk. It usually has a suede finish and is oil tanned or alum tawed. It has a soft texture, and is pliable and reasonably strong. Examples of its use (in England) can be traced back to the 16th century. Imitation buckskin is sometimes made from sheepskin. *See also:* DEERSKIN. (278, 325)

buds. A decorative ornament filling a small panel on a ROLL (1), usually in the conventionalized form of a spray bearing buds. (250)

buffalo. A leather produced in imitation of RUSSIA LEATHER, but of far greater strength than the genuine leather. It is made from the hide of the large, shaggy-maned North American ox, *Bison bison,* and was used extensively in covering books in the United States in the latter half of the 19th century.

buffed leather. A leather from which the top surface of the grain has been removed. *See also:* BUFFING (2); CORRECTED GRAIN. (61)

buffing. 1. A very thin innermost split of a hide, usually a cowhide, which is colored and grained to give the appearance of the outer surface of the hide. A buffing is created when a hide is split into three layers. At one time it was used extensively for linings, as well as for covering trade books. It was never used in fine bookbinding. 2. The process of producing a fine nap on the grain surface of leather by means of carborundum paper or on the flesh sides of small skins by the action of an emery wheel. In sandpapering the grain surface of leather, the sharp edges of the carborundum, or other abrasive material, cut the miscroscopic fibrils in the grain surface and produce a fine nap on the surface. Many of the grain defects in a leather do not penetrate into the leather nearly to the depth of the grain layer, and can be entirely removed by buffing. When a leather is buffed to a measurable depth, as it may have to be if the grain defect is very deep, it is said to be *buffed;* when it is buffed to a lesser depth, it is said to be *snuffed.* When a leather is buffed so lightly as not to impair the grain pattern, the leather is said to have a CORRECTED GRAIN. 3. The process of polishing the leather covers of a book with a soft fabric wheel. (264, 278, 325, 358, 363)

buffingnette. A water-resistant cloth made in imitation of leather. While it is adequate for the sides of books that receive considerable use, as it is stain and water resistant, it is not adequate for full covering, as it does not wear well in the areas of the joints. It is also difficult to block, and labels do not adhere to it well unless the surface is abraded and coated with shellac. (105)

buff leather. A leather which has a yellowish, cream or white surface and is finished with a soft, velvet nap. It is produced from cowhide from which the grain layer has been removed by FRIZING. It is an oil-tanned leather. (351)

build in (building in). The process of placing newly cased-in library books between smooth or brass-bound boards and applying pressure in a standing press or hydraulic press, or applying dry heat and (considerable) pressure for a brief time (usually 8 to 15 seconds) in a hydro-press or BUILDING-IN MACHINE. Building in forms the joints, compresses the book, secures it firmly in its case and reduces substantially any possibility of board warpage. *See also:* CASING-IN. (139)

building-in machine. A machine used to BUILD IN the text block of a book into its case or covers. Building-in machines substitute heat and great pressure for the element of time required to set and cure the adhesive and form the joints. For intermittent or relatively small production, a single-clamp machine, such as the type often found in library binderies, is often adequate. It can build in books up to 12 by 14 by 4 inches in size, and can process up to five books per minute, depending upon the skill of the operator and the CLAMP DWELL setting of the machine. In general, the longer the dwell time, the more solid the binding, which is essentially the reason why a book built in by this type of machine is not as solid as one left in a press for a longer period of time. In edition binding, multiple-clamp machines are usually used, and can process up to 36 books per minute. In edition machines, books may be manually inserted, or fed in automatically after CASING-IN. *See also:* CASING-IN MACHINE. (320)

built-up lettering. Multilined decorative lettering, "built up" by forming the letters with pallets and gouges rather than by the use of hand letters. (335)

built-up patterns. Decorative patterns in blind or gold built up from individual line and solid tools. (310)

bulk. 1. The thickness of the gathered leaves or sections of a book before sewing, or the thickness of the bound book before its covers are attached, or before casing-in. 2. The thickness of a sheet of paper in relation to its weight. With two papers of equal weight per ream, the one which "handles" the thicker is said to "bulk" the better. 3. The thickness of a specified number of sheets of paper or board under a specified pressure. Bulk here is important in gauging the thickness of a proposed book. 4. In papermaking in its most correct meaning, "bulk" is the ratio of fiber volume of a sheet to total volume, including air spaces which may be void or filled with loading or sizing materials. *See also:* BULK EQUIVALENTS. (17, 234, 261, 264)

bulked up. A deliberate attempt to make a book thicker and, therefore, of a more substantial appearance. Books, and especially novels, are sometimes "bulked up," i.e., printed on BULKING BOOK PAPER so that a higher price may be charged. Such paper, however, is often inferior in both strength and printing quality to a more compact paper. (256)

bulk equivalents. The number of pages per inch of a paper of a given caliper (thousandths of an inch):

Caliper/ 4 Sheets	Pages per Inch
5.5	1,454
6.0	1,332
6.5	1,230
7.0	1,142
7.5	1,066
8.0	1,000
8.5	942
9.0	888
9.5	842
10.0	800
10.5	762
11.0	726
11.5	696
12.0	666
12.5	640
13.0	614
13.5	592
14.0	570
14.5	552
15.0	532
15.5	516
16.0	500
16.5	484
17.0	470
17.5	456
18.0	444
18.5	432

Caliper/ 4 Sheets	Pages per Inch
19.0	420
19.5	410
20.0	400
20.5	390
21.0	380
21.5	372
22.0	364
22.5	356
23.0	348
23.5	340
24.0	332
24.5	326
25.0	320
25.5	314
26.0	308
26.5	302
27.0	296
27.5	290
28.0	286
28.5	280
29.0	276
29.5	272
30.0	266
30.5	262
31.0	258
31.5	254
32.0	250
32.5	246
33.0	242
33.5	238
34.0	234
34.5	232
35.0	228
35.5	224
36.0	222
36.5	218
37.0	216
37.5	212
38.0	210
38.5	208
39.0	204
39.5	202
40.0	200
40.5	198
41.0	194
41.5	192
42.0	190
42.5	188
43.0	186
43.5	184
44.0	182
44.5	180
45.0	178
45.5	176
46.0	174
46.5	172
47.0	170
47.5	168
48.0	166
48.5	164
49.0	162
49.5	162
50.0	160

(52)

bulking book paper. A paper produced to give maximum bulk per unit ream weight. It is produced from a number of paper furnishes designed to impart this property, including cotton linters, rag pulp, esparto, and chemical wood pulps. Some grades contain a large percentage of mechanical wood pulp mixed with other pulps. The paper furnish is provided with little or no fillers. This paper is usually made to specifications of finish, caliper, or both. Bulking book paper picks easily and often causes difficulties in printing. *See also:* BULKED-UP; NOVEL PAPER. (17)

bumping hammer. *See:* BACKING HAMMER.

bundle. 1. A seldom used term applied to a printed sheet that has been folded to make a section. 2. A unit of board measure, generally of weight of 50 pounds. The actual number of boards in a bundle will depend on area and caliper of the boards. 3. At one time, a package of paper containing 2 perfect reams, or 1,000 sheets, but in today's usage, a package of paper weighing about 125 pounds and containing any number of sheets, depending on the size, caliper, and type of paper. (17, 316)

bundling. 1. The process of tying up the sections of a book under pressure before GATHERING (1), for the purpose of keeping them clean, flat, and ready for gathering, while at the same time compressing them into a compact and solid state. 2. The process of gathering together a number of skins of leather, usually 12, of the same kind, weight, and grade. The total area of leather is indicated on the bundle. (179, 236, 320)

bundling press (bundling machine). A type of press used to compress the newly folded sections of a book or group of books, usually of the same title. Bundling presses are usually of three types: 1) the hand-bundling press, which consists of a floor stand on which two jaws are mounted horizontally. One of the jaws is stationary

BUNDLING PRESS

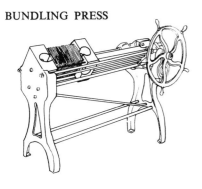

and the other movable. The group of sections with strings around it is placed between the jaws and compressed by forcing the movable jaw towards the stationary one. The jaws are designed so as to allow for the tying of the bundles while under pressure; 2) the power-bundling press, which is either vertically or horizontally oriented, and in which a movable bed is driven toward a stationary head by power supplied by an electric motor through a system of gears and racks; and 3) the pneumatic bundling press, which may also be vertically or horizontally oriented, in which the movable jaw is driven by a piston to which power is supplied by compressed air. In all three types, when the sections of several books are to be bundled together, the groups are placed between boards, bundled, and the entire group, including boards, is tied before being removed from the press. (142, 320, 339)

buried cords. *See:* SAWING IN.

burnish. 1. The glossiness or brilliance produced by rubbing the gilt edges or leather cover of a book with a burnishing or polishing tool. *See also:* BURNISHER(S) (2). 2. In papermaking, to burnish or polish the surface of a paper. *See also:* GLAZED (1). (94)

burnished edges. The colored or gilt edges of a book which have been polished, usually by means of a bloodstone or agate implement called a BURNISHER (2). *See also:* BURNISHERS(S) (2).

burnisher(s). 1. One who burnishes the edges of a book. 2. The tools used to burnish the edges of a book. They are made of metal, agate (quartz), or bloodstone set in handles. The bloodstone type is the best and also the most expensive. Burnishers are generally available in two basic shapes—flat and toothed. They are relatively delicate tools and chip easily if handled roughly; they may be kept smooth and in good condition by rubbing them on the flesh side of a piece of leather coated with whiting, or, if too rough to be smoothed in this manner, by rubbing them on a zinc-lined board coated with a small amount of flour or emery mixed with machine oil. (66, 99, 278)

burnishing brushes. A black lead or shoe brush, having stiff but not harsh bristles, and used, after coating the edges of a book with black lead, to burnish the edges before glairing for edge-gilding. (66)

burnt gypsum. *See:* BRIME.

burnt sugar. One of the coloring materials which, when dissolved in water,

can be used to restore the proper tone or shade to the leaves of a book that have been washed. The burnt sugar is added to the resizing bath, and the paper is "toned" at the same time it is sized. (154)

burnt umber. A dark brown pigment produced by calcining raw umber, and used in a mixture of red ochre, oil, and water, as a sprinkle for the edges of books. *See also:* SPRINKLED EDGES; UMBER. (371)

burst factor. The BURSTING STRENGTH of paper in grams per square centimeter divided by the BASIS WEIGHT of the

BURNISHERS

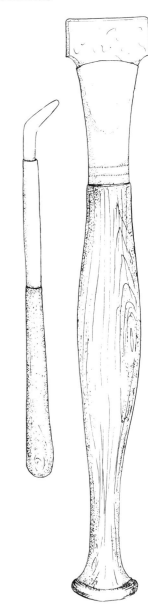

paper in grams per square meter, which gives the burst factor as a numerical value. *See also:* BURST RATIO. (17, 72)

bursting strength. The combined tensile strength and stretch of a material as measured by the ability of the material to resist rupture when pressure is applied under specified conditions to one of its sides by an instrument used for testing the property. Testing for the bursting strength of paper is a very common procedure, although its value in determining the potential permanence or durability of paper is suspect. *See also:* BURST FACTOR; POINTS PER POUND. (17, 72)

burst ratio. The BURSTING STRENGTH of a material in points per pound. *See also:* BURST FACTOR.

butcher cuts. Damage to hides and skins caused by improper and/or unskilled flaying, and usually seen in the form of cuts or furrows on the flesh side. In extreme cases, the cuts may go completely through the skin, thus reducing its value greatly. Butcher cuts are sometimes particularly noticeable on parchment and vellum. (363)

butt. 1. That part of a hide or skin corresponding to the animal's back and sides after cutting away the shoulder and belly, and consisting of the thickest and strongest part of the skin. *See also:* SHELL. 2. Any type of hinge or joint used for reinforcement, or for fastening a bulky insert into a binding. (256, 261, 325)

butterstamp. *See:* BAND PALLET.

buttonhole stitch. An embroidery stitch used in making a HEADBAND, and executed by drawing the needle and thread from the upper through the lower edge of the core, and out over the lower thread of the preceding stitch. The stitches are repeated, sometimes in alternate colors, e.g., blue and green, to form a firm line of adjacent loops around the core. (83, 111)

C. The Roman equivalent of 100. *See also:* ROMAN NUMERALS.

cabinet size. *See:* OBLONG.

cable pattern. *See:* ROPE PATTERN.

cabretta leather. A leather produced from the skins of sheep which have hair instead of wool, i.e., straight-haired sheepskins. The leather is produced in India, China, South America, and Africa, the best grades coming from the latter two areas. In the United States, the term is generally considered to indicate specifically a Brazilian sheepskin. Cabretta is generally chrome tanned and has a very fine grain and a strong fiber network. (61, 325)

cahier. A number of loose sheets assembled for binding, or bound loosely together to form a notebook or pamphlet. 2. The French expression for the signature of a bound book.

cake glue. Generally, an animal GLUE supplied in large slabs up to 3 inches in thickness. The slabs are broken into small pieces, soaked in cold water until they absorb as much water as possible, and then heated to useable consistency. Flexible (internally plasticized) glue does not have to be soaked.

calcium acetate. A chemical $(Ca(C_2H_3O_2)_2 \cdot 2H_2O)$, prepared by neutralizing acetic acid with lime or calcium carbonate, and used in the preparation of other acetates and in the deacidification of paper.

calcium bicarbonate. A salt obtained by replacing only one of the two hydrogen atoms in carbonic acid (H_2CO_3) by the metallic atom calcium, giving $(Ca(HCO_3)_2)$. It is employed in a 0.2% solution to carbonate excess calcium hydroxide used in deacidifying paper, and also to precipitate calcium carbonate into the fibers of the paper being treated. The precipitated calcium carbonate acts as a buffer to neutralize any acid that forms in the paper subsequent to treatment. (31)

calcium carbonate. A salt $(CaCO_3)$, occurring naturally, usually in sea deposition, and prepared commercially by passing carbon dioxide either through cold lime water, which precipitates the calcite crystalline type, or hot lime water, which gives the aragonite crystalline type. The calcite is the thermodynamically stable form. Calcium carbonate is sometimes precipitated into

paper by suitable chemical reactions to deacidify the paper, and is also used both as a filler and a coating pigment in the manufacture of paper. (31, 67, 143)

calcium hydroxide. A strong alkali $(Ca(OH)_2)$, which can be formed by the reaction of calcium oxide (CaO) with water. If the oxide is treated with only sufficient water to make it crumble to a fine, white, dry powder, slaked lime is produced. By slaking the paste formed from the oxide with an excess of water, a suspension called "milk of lime" is formed. A clear solution of the hydroxide in water is known as lime water. Calcium hydroxide is used extensively in a very strong solution (pH of approximately 11.4) in the LIMING and UNHAIRING of hides and skins in leather manufacture, and in the deacidification of paper. In the latter use, the resulting pH is approximately 11.0, and paper so treated is easily oxidized unless the pH is reduced by exposure to carbon dioxide or the paper is treated subsequently with a solution of calcium bicarbonate. (31, 363)

calcium hypochlorite. Any hypochlorite of calcium, e.g., the normal anhydrous salt $(Ca(ClO)_2)$, that is generally found in commercial products containing 70 to 75% available chlorine. Calcium hypochlorite is used by many paper conservationists to bleach archival papers, and it is also used as an oxidizing agent to reduce the effects of FOXING. Its use is potentially harmful, as the chlorine is difficult to remove. Also known as "bleaching powder."

calcium sulfate. A salt $(CaSO_4 \cdot H_2O)$, very slightly soluble in water. In its natural form, it may exist as anhydrite $(CaSO_4)$ or gypsum $(CaSO_4 \cdot H_2O)$.

It is used as a filler pigment in the manufacture of paper. Precipitated calcium sulfate is known as "crown filler," or "pearl filler." *See also:* BRIME.

calcium sulfite. A salt $(CaSO_3)$, prepared by reacting sulfurous acid with calcium hydroxide, and used as a filler coating pigment in paper manufacture.

calender. Horizontal cast iron rolls with hardened, chilled surfaces resting one on another in a vertical bank at the dry end of the papermaking machine. The paper web is passed between all or part of the calender rolls to increase the smoothness and gloss of its surface. *See also:* SUPERCALENDER. (17, 80)

calendered. A paper or cloth that has been given a smooth surface by passing it through a CALENDER one or more times. Paper which receives a minimum of calendering is said to have an antique finish. With more calendering it acquires a machine finish, then an English finish, and, finally a supercalendered (highly glazed) finish. *See also:* CALENDERED CLOTH. (143, 276)

calendered cloth. A cloth that has had a filler of starch, usually soybean flour, impregnated into the weave of the base cloth by means of iron or steel rollers exerting a great pressure. If the rolls are heated, a high gloss is also imparted. The cloth may also be embossed during the calendering process. (341)

calf finish. Originally, the smooth, ungrained finish of any animal skin tanned for use in bookbinding, and later used to designate CALFSKIN finished in a variety of grains in imitation of alligator, lizard, snakeskin, etc. (256)

calf lined. A lining on the innerside of a limp cover, consisting of CALFSKIN in lieu of the board paper. This type of lining was thin and glued to the leather cover only at the outer edges. This left the covers pliable so that the book could be rolled up. Calf linings have been used at various times, and, although they are still used to some extent today, their most extensive use was in the years immediately before and after 1900. (105)

calf paper. A colored and embossed paper somewhat resembling leather and used occasionally for covering books.

calfskin. In its broadest sense, a leather made from the skin of an immature bovine animal. In a more limited sense, however, it is considered to be leather made from the skin of a bovine animal that has not been weaned, or at least has been fed only milk, and whose skin does not exceed a certain weight (15 pounds or slightly more) in the green salted state. The heavier skins of immature milk-fed animals, i.e., those up to 25 or 30 pounds in the green state, are often referred to as "veals" rather than calfskin.

The best calfskins for bookbinding purposes are prepared by tanning in oak bark or sumac tanning liquors. Its freedom from grain defects makes calfskin suitable for finishing in delicate shades of color. It may be finished rough or smooth, the latter being more common, and, as it may be without any noticeable grain pattern, it may be tooled with very little preliminary blinding in.

Books which are full bound in calfskin may be described as being diced, grained, marbled, mottled, scored, sprinkled, stained, or tree, according to the form of decoration used. In addition, special styles are known as divinity, antique, law, reverse, or rough calf.

Calfskin has been used as a covering material for books since 1450, or even earlier, and, up to the end of the 18th century, it was a common bookbinding leather. Thereafter, various forms of sheepskin, and later cloth, replaced calfskin as the most commonly used bookbinding material.

There are two distinct views concerning the durability of calfskin. Some contend that because the skin is from an immature animal, the leather made from it cannot be durable, even when carefully selected and tanned, because the fibers of the skin are not fully developed. Furthermore, there is the argument that, since the skin is very soft, it shows scratches and mars too easily, and, when used, the book must then be varnished or kept in a box. Others, however, argue that if the skins are selected carefully and tanned very slowly in oak bark or sumac, calfskin makes a quite durable leather capable of withstanding considerable wear.

Physiologically, calfskin is not nearly as weak as its detractors maintain. Although the fiber network is indeed lacking the depth of cowhide, the fiber bundles are reasonably stout and contain numerous finer fibers which are long, highly ramified, and of high tensile strength. This is because, in any young animal, the connective tissue, i.e., skin, develops more rapidly than some other parts of the body, such as the muscles. The dermal network of calfskin is therefore reasonably well developed and exhibits remarkable strength and toughness. In addition, there is no denying the fact that there are calfskin bookbindings that have come down to us in their original bindings; many are several hundred years old. In as much as the durability of calfskin before the 18th century was not in doubt, it may be that it was the lowering of tanning standards that resulted in less durable calfskin. Furthermore, the bleaching methods employed to produce light-colored skins, as well as the techniques of decorating calf bindings with acid and other chemicals to produce mottled-, sprinkled-, and tree-calf effects were probably the major reasons for its reputation of insufficient durability. *See also:* SLUNK; TREE CALF. (207, 291, 351, 363)

calf split. A flesh split of a calfskin, sometimes embossed so as to make it resemble the grain side of the skin. The split lacks the necessary strength to be used for anything other than linings and labels.

calico. A plain white cotton fabric that is heavier than muslin. As early as the first quarter of the 19th century calico was dyed in various colors and used for covering publishers' bindings; it was in fact one of the first cloths to be used for covering books. It is still used to some extent for lining the spines of edition bindings, although for this purpose it is inferior to several other fabrics. *See:* SPINE LINING FABRIC. (71, 236)

caliper. 1. The thickness of a material measured under specified conditions. Caliper is usually measured in thousandths of an inch (mills or points), or, under the metric system, in millimeters. 2. The instrument used to measure the thickness of a material. *See also:* THICKNESS.

cambric. 1. A fine linen thread used in lieu of silk for working headbands. 2. A fine, closely woven white linen fabric, used in library binding for hinges, spine linings, extensions, etc.

Cambridge calf (Cambridge sheep). A method of decorating a calf- or sheepskin binding by sprinkling on two tints, leaving a rectangular "pane" (panel) in the center of each cover. This technique was used extensively from the 1670s and again during the early decades of the 18th century. It was revived and used to a considerable extent during the second half of the 19th century. (371)

Cambridge style. An English style of bookbinding practiced largely on theological works and in university libraries. Although used elsewhere, the style was so highly favored by binders in Cambridge in the early years of the 18th century that it became recognized as their speciality, which probably accounts for the name. Books bound in this style were sewn on raised cords, covered in calfskin that was masked and sprinkled in such a manner as to leave a stained central rectangular panel, a plain rectangular frame, which, in turn, was surrounded by a stained outside frame. The books had Dutch marble endpapers and red edges. The spine was pieced with red russia leather labels and had double blind lines at head and tail on each side of the raised bands. The covers were decorated with a two-line fillet close to the edges and on each side of the panel, and with a narrow flower roll worked on each side of the panel close to the lines. There were many variations of this style, including some books tooled in gold, and some with marbled covers and sprinkled panels. (69, 154)

cameo bindings. A style of Italian binding of the first half of the 16th century, which was imitated by French binders and also by ROGER PAYNE at a later date. The style consisted of designs in relief made from dies cut intaglio, somewhat in imitation of gems or metals. Leather was the medium most often used, although vellum was also used, being pressed while wet on the die, and with the cavities being filled with a composition of lacquered paste to preserve the shape of the figures. After being attached to the center of the leather cover, they were sometimes gilt and painted. Cameo bindings were a development of the antiquarian interest in classical coins and gems, actual examples of which at first provided the sources of the molds. French examples executed for Henri II and Jean Grolier bore a central medallion stamped with an intaglio cut die. The design was embossed on a gilded and colored background. *See also:* CANEVARI BINDINGS. (110, 141, 279, 347)

camlet. To marble. *See:* MARBLING.

camphor. A crystalline terpenoid ketone ($C_{10}H_{16}O$), occurring naturally in the $(+)-$, $(-)-$ and $(\pm)$ forms. Ordinary commercial camphor is the $(+)-$ type, obtained from the wood of the camphor tree (*Cinnamomum camphora*), mainly from Formosa. It can also be manufactured, using pinene ($C_{10}H_{16}$) as the raw material. It is sometimes used in an effort to rid books and bookcases of BOOKWORMS, and as a plasticizer in cellulose nitrate plastics.

cancel(s) (cancellans). 1. A replacement leaf or leaves, printed because of a mistake in the original printing, an imperfect page, etc., that is to replace the corresponding faulty section before the book is actually published. Cancels have been common since the beginning of printing from metal type; however, with the development of high speed printing presses, it has become more economical simply to reprint an entire signature rather than go to the expense of inserting a cancel by hand.

The substitution of the cancel by either the printer or binder depends on when the mistake is discovered. If the binder is to make the substitution, the printer may mark the incorrect leaf with an asterisk to indicate to the binder that he is to cut out that leaf and tip the replacement to the stub. If the replacement leaf bears a signature mark the asterisk should precede the signature letter.

2. In bookbinding, in a broad sense, all leaves that are not to be bound in. This applies specifically to the waste sheets. (69, 131, 234)

cancelland (cancellandum). The incorrect, inaccurate, or otherwise disposal leaf that is to be cut out and replaced by a CANCEL. (140)

cancellation. The removal of a leaf, leaves, or an entire section of a publication because of an error, or for some other reason. When a leaf is removed, the remaining stub is termed a disjunct leaf. *See also:* CANCEL; CANCELLANDUM. (12, 343)

cancel title. A replacement title page substituted for the original. *See also:* CANCEL; CANCELLANDUM. (234)

candelilla wax. A WAX found as an exudate on the leaves and stems of a plant (*Euphorbia antisyphilitica*), found in northern Mexico and the southwestern United States, and obtained by boiling the leaves and stems with water and sulfuric acid. It is yellowish-brown in color and is opaque to translucent. It is classed as hard wax and has a softening range at 64 to 68° C. It is used in making varnish and as a substitute for CARNAUBA WAX to impart a high gloss to leathers that are not glazed. (291)

Canevari bindings. *See:* GRIMALDI, GIOVANNI BATTISTA.

canton flannel. A soft cotton fabric, napped on one side, and sometimes used as a spine lining fabric, usually in library binding. The nap side is placed next to the spine. (102)

canvas. A firm, closely woven fabric, usually made of cotton, hemp, or linen, in plain weave, and produced in various weights. Canvas has been used as a covering material for books for centuries, and was one of the principal fabrics used for embroidered bindings. Its greatest use historically, however, has been for rough job bindings, certain varieties of chapbooks, textbooks published between 1770 and about 1830 in England, and some types of reference books. Today its use is virtually limited to the covering of very large books, newspapers, etc., and as a CHEMISE for leather-bound county record books and other large stationery bindings. *See also:* ART CANVAS; DUCK. (69, 82, 111, 264)

canvas finish paper. A heavy, durable cover paper, made with a textured finish in imitation of canvas. It is used mainly for semi-stiff covers for brochures, pamphlets, etc. (86)

caoutchouc binding. A particular (and probably first) form of ADHESIVE BINDING, invented by William Hancock, and patented in 1836, in which the single sheets were secured with a rubber solution obtained from the latex of certain tropical plants, especially of the genera *Hevea* and *Ficus*. According to Hancock's specifications, the edges of the assembled leaves were roughened and then coated with the caoutchouc, which, when dry, was followed by one to five coatings of a stronger rubber solution. When the last coating was applied, a strip of cloth coated with the caoutchouc was applied in a warm, sticky condition and rubbed down firmly.

Great numbers of these bindings were produced both in England and the United States from about 1840, and the process was used for many of the illustrated "table books" of the 1860s, as well as for many large folios printed on very thick paper. The process afforded both openability and durability, or so for the latter it was believed at the time. Both characteristics depended to a large extent on the purity of the rubber solution, and the degree to which it remained flexible. That it did not remain very flexible has been demonstrated by the fact most caoutchouc bindings have fallen apart. Also called "guttapercha binding," although incorrectly, because gutta percha, which is also obtained from tropical trees, was tried and found to be unsuitable. (89, 236)

caoutchouc polish. A caout-rubber base varnish, used occasionally in the 19th century for varnishing the leather covers of books. *See also:* CAOUTCHOUC BINDING. (97)

cape. Originally, a leather made from South African hair sheep. Today it is considered to be any leather made from a hair sheep, except East Indian native vegetable tanned sheep. (325)

capping up (capping). 1. *See:* HEADCAP. 2. The process of placing a paper covering or "cap" over the edges of a book following headbanding, so as to prevent the edges from becoming soiled or damaged during the subsequent operations. (237, 261)

capstan. A decorative ornament, often found on English and French head-in medallion rolls, the principal feature of which roughly resembled a vertical spindle-mounted drum. (250)

caput mortuum. *See:* VENETIAN RED.

carbolic acid. *See:* PHENOL.

carbonaceous inks. A general term used in describing a group of inks produced from finely ground carbon or a similar substance, e.g., soot or lampblack, and which are jet black and very stable. A glutinuous substance is used as a binder. Such inks are the simplest of all inks to produce, and have been known from the earliest times. They have no destructive influences on paper but they do present difficulties to restorers because they are so easily affected by water. The carbonaceous inks may be subdivided into CARBON INK, CHINESE INK, and the SEPIA INKS. (143)

carbon disulfide. A colorless, highly refractive liquid (CS_2). It is prepared by heating sulfur and wood charcoal, or by reacting methane with sulfur vapor over a catalyst. It is used in the manufacture of carbon tetrachloride, and for fumigating books. Its customary disagreeable odor results from the presence of small amounts of other sulfur compounds. Carbon disulfide is both toxic and flammable.

carbon ink. A modified form of CHINESE INK. Carbon ink is a mixture of finely divided carbon carried in a vehicle of glue or a gum. It is extremely stable, as evidenced by the characters on manuscripts of the 7th to 10th centuries, and even Egyptian papyri, which are darker and more distinct than those of the 16th century, when IRON-GALL INK came into use. Carbon ink has no destructive effects on paper, but it does present problems to restorers because it is so easily affected by water. (143)

carbon lettering. Carbon in powdered form, used in lieu of gold leaf or other metal or foil for lettering books, particularly when the covering material is canvas, or a similar fabric. The pallet and type are heated as for gold blocking, but the type is coated with carbon and then pressed firmly into the covering material. ART VELLUM is also a suitable material for carbon lettering. In very humid climates, this type of lettering may require several days to dry sufficiently for the books to be handled. At times, carbon ink is used in lieu of carbon. (358)

carbon paper. A thin paper coated with carbon black or some other coloring matter in a vehicle of wax or an oil-soluble substance and used for making duplicate copies. It is sometimes used by bookbinders to produce a dark color on a bookbinding approximating blind tooling. Carbon paper is also used for making paper pattern layouts prior to lettering, and when the leather does not darken uniformly with water. Size must first be applied, otherwise the carbon will rub off.

carbon tetrachloride. A colorless, mobile, nonflammable, liquid (CCl_4), used as a solvent and grease remover, and as a fumigant for books. It is both toxic and volatile. It also gives off chlorine, which, in the presence of glowing charcoal, e.g., a lighted cigarette, becomes phosgene, which is even more toxic.

carboxymethylcellulose. An aqueous adhesive prepared by reacting chloracetic acid ($ClCH_2COOH$) with alkali cellulose, and used in the SUNDEX PROCESS. (198)

cardboard. A board 0.006 inch or more in thickness. It is stiffer than paper. Although the generic term "board" is used in lieu of the term "cardboard" in bookbinding parlance, the covers of many pamphlets, brochures, etc., as well as the card used to line prints, posters, etc., and also used in FILLING IN (1), are of a thickness that would fit them into the definition of cardboard. (17, 234, 264)

cardboard prints. Printed cover-, end-, and other decorative papers, produced by gluing artistically shaped cuts of cardboard to a sheet of cardboard, inking with an oil-base printing ink and pressing on the paper to be decorated. (183)

carnauba wax. A yellowish-white or green, sticky exudation on the leaves, berries and stalks of the carnauba palm (*Copernicia cerifera*), found in South America, and especially Brazil. It is believed to consist largely of myricyl ceretate and myricyl alcohol ($C_{29}H_{59} \cdot CH_2 \cdot OH$). It is used to impart a high gloss to leathers that are not to be glazed, and by bookbinders to polish the edges of books after gilding and burnishing through paper. The wax imparts a high gloss to the edges and is preferred to beeswax by some as it is less likely to streak. Carnauba wax has a softening range of 83 to 84° C., which makes it especially suitable for use in very hot climates. (195, 291)

carragheen moss. A dark purple, branching cartilaginous seaweed (*Chondrus crispus*), found on the coasts of Northern Europe and North America. The moss is used in the preparation of MARBLING SIZE, about 4 ounces of the moss being sufficient to make 9 or 10 quarts of size. Carragheen moss was first used in making marbling size sometime after the middle of the 19th century. The extract of the moss is also used as a thickening agent and viscosity stabilizer in some adhesives. (217, 237, 335)

cartonnage à la Bradel. *See:* BRADEL BINDING.

cartouche. 1. An elaborate style of decoration popular in Italy about the middle of the 16th century. The decoration consists of elaborately interlaced fillets filling the entire field of the covers, and sometimes accompanied by arabesques, worked in a single line with tools cut in the shapes of flowers. 2. A term meaning literally a scroll or paper with the ends rolled up, bearing the title, and sometimes other information, pertaining to a book. 3. A frame, either plain or decorative, or a scroll, in which the title, name of the cartographer, and other particulars of a map are placed. The cartouche usually appears in a corner of the map, and in old maps it was frequently decorated with scenes, animals, armorial designs, etc. 4. A small rectangular ornament usually found on a ROLL (1), formed by one or more lines, generally with a plain center. (94, 234, 250)

cartridge paper. A paper similar in appearance to hard antique paper. It is tough, closely formed, and is usually produced from chemical wood pulps, esparto, or a combination of the two. The degree of sizing depends on the purpose for which it is to be used, and its surface may be rough, semi-rough or smooth. Cartridge paper is generally unbleached or only slightly bleached, and is made in basis weights ranging from 60 to 80 pounds. It is used for endpapers, linings, and compensation guards. The term "cartridge paper" is not generally used in the United States. The name derives from its original use in forming the tube section of shotgun shells. (17, 58, 182)

case. 1. The covering material, boards and inlay of a book, i.e., a book cover ready to be attached to the text block. Edition and library bindings have cases and are said to be case bindings. 2. A box or cover made to protect a book. *See:* PORTFOLIO (1); PULL-OFF BOX; SLIPCASE; SOLANDER BOX.

case binding. A general term for a method of bookbinding, introduced in Great Britain in the 1820s, in which the case (covers) of the book is made separately (and, in edition binding, usually in large numbers) from the book (the text block and endpapers), and later attached to it by gluing the board papers of the text block to the inside of the boards of the case. This operation is known as CASING-IN. Case binding is distinguished from those methods of binding in which the covers are not made separately, as in craft bookbinding IN BOARDS (1). Case binding is the principal method employed in both edition and library binding. (203, 276, 355)

case-hardening. An irregular, distorted (drawn) grain in a leather, usually accompanied by hardness and thinness of the leather itself. It is caused primarily by over-tanning. *See:* OVER-TANNED. (306)

case hide. An expression used in Great Britain to describe a stained or otherwise colored leather, generally having a smooth, more or less glossy surface finish. It is sometimes embossed with an artificial grain. Case hide is produced from a full grain or buffed cow hide and is vegetable tanned. (61)

casein. An acid-coagulable protein, occurring as a suspension of calcium caseinate in skim milk. It is possible to isolate it as an alkali-solution white powder by treating cow's milk with either mineral acid or rennet. The acid casein is used in the sizing of paper, as a simple adhesive, in the manufacture of coated papers, and as a plastic in leather finishes. Casein adhesives are little used in bookbinding as they can only be made workable by the addition of rather strong alkalies, which makes them unsuitable for use with paper or vellum. (52, 198, 309)

case-making. A general term usually applied to the production of cases for edition bindings, generally by means of semi-automatic or automatic machines. The term may also be applied to library binding, in which case-making is carried out by hand. *See also:* CASE-MAKING GAUGE; CASE-MAKING

MACHINE; CASING-IN. (102, 179, 183)

case-making gauge (case gauge). A gauge used in the production of identical book cases in relatively small quantities. The case is made by hand, the gauge being used to indicate where the boards and INLAY (1) are to be placed on the covering material which has been cut to size and glued. Case-making gauges are adjustable for different sizes of cases, turn-ins, and widths of inlay. (259, 261)

case-making machine. A hand- or machine-fed machine used to assemble the covering material, boards, and inlays of case-bound edition books. Case-making machines are of two general types: sheet fed, either by hand or machine, and roll fed, by machine. Roll fed machines require two additional steps in their operation as compared with sheet-fed machines, namely, corner cutting and separation of the individual cases. The covering material, however, does not have to be pre-cut. Sheet fed machines receive the covering material in the correct size for the individual case with the corners already cut.

Case-making machines may be modified for use of paper as the covering material, to make round-cornered cases, to use light board instead of paper for the inlays, and to make album covers which have one narrow and one wide board, with a hinge. Modern case-making machines can produce up to 21 cases per minute with dimensions of 5½ by 7½ inches to 9½ by 15½ inches, with extended capabilities using accessory equipment.

The case-making machine dates back to the latter years of the 19th century; its greatest period of development was 1891-95. (89, 196, 203, 320)

casing-in. The process of securing the text block and attached endpapers into a case that was produced as a separate operation, lettered and (especially in edition binding) sometimes decorated. In library binding, casing-in generally takes place in a BUILDING-IN MACHINE, or equivalent, while in edition binding, it is generally done in a CASING-IN MACHINE. (179)

casing-in boards. Wooden boards cut square at the edge and lined on one edge with a brass strip that extends beyond one or both sides of the board about ⅛ inch. The brass extension creates the joints of the book during the CASING-IN operation. Such boards are used when the book is cased by hand and pressed in a standing- or

hydraulic press. The BUILDING-IN MACHINE has metal flanges at the edges of the jaws which accomplish the same result. *See also:* PRESSING BOARDS. (264)

casing-in machine. A semi- or fully-automatic machine which fits books into their pre-made cases and completes the binding operation.

Semi-automatic machines require an operator to hang the books in their centers over a metal "wing." The machine then automatically clamps the book, coats the board papers with adhesive, fits the case on the text block and completes the operation. Three-wing casing-in machines are capable of processing books up to 3 inches in thickness (including covers), and, lying open, 14 inches high and 22 inches wide, at speeds up to 25 books per minute.

A fully automatic machine does not require timed feeding or removal of books. It can process books measuring not less than 3⅜ inches in height, 2½ to 7½ inches in width and between ¼ and 1⅝ inches thick, at speeds up to 35 books per minute.

The casing-in machine came into existence in the latter years of the 19th century, and its principal period of development occurred during the early years of the 20th century. (89, 320)

castor oil. A colorless to pale yellow or greenish, viscous, non-drying fatty oil of high viscosity, extracted from beans of the castor oil plant (*Ricinus communis*). It consists almost entirely of the glyceryl esters of ricinoleic acid. At low temperatures it thickens; it solidifies at approximately -10 to $-18°$ C. It is used in leather finishing processes, and, in the sulfated form, as a preservative for leather bindings. Sulfating the oil, by reacting it with sulfuric acid, allows it to react with water. This is beneficial for books stored under hot, dry conditions, as it helps keep the leather soft and pliable under conditions of low relative humidity. (173)

catalog paper. A lightweight paper, either coated or with an English finish, usually made with a considerable proportion of mechanical pulp, and used for mail-order catalogs, telephone directories, and the like. Uniformity of weight, opacity, finish, formation, and sufficient strength to get through high-speed printing presses are desired characteristics. Basis weights usually range from 19 to 28 pounds (24 X 36— 500). (17, 324)

catalyst. 1. A substance that changes the rate of a chemical reaction without

itself being changed. A catalyst may increase the rate (positive catalyst), or decrease the rate (negative catalyst). The final state or equilibrium of the reaction is not changed by the catalyst, only the rate of approaching the final state is changed. Examples of catalytic action in the field of archival preservation include the impurities in paper, such as iron or copper, minute particles of which may inadvertently be introduced into the paper pulp in the beater operation. According to some authorities, these can act as catalysts in the formation of sulfuric or hydrochloric acid in paper, by assisting in the conversion of sulfur dioxide to sulfuric acid, or the chlorine frequently used in bleaching paper pulp, into hydrochloric acid. Leather, also, may contain minute particles of metals which may speed up the formation of sulfuric acid. 2. A chemical substance added to thermosetting resinous adhesives to speed up the cure time of such adhesives, to increase the cross linkage of a synthetic polymer, or to accelerate adhesive drying. (221, 235, 309)

catch. A metal plate secured to the fore edge, and at times to the head and tail edges, of a book cover, and fixed with a bar, over which the clasp fits. Sometimes a pin is used in lieu of a bar. *See also:* CLASPS. (250)

catch stitch. 1. Any type of locking stitch, such as KETTLE STITCH. 2. A stitch used to gather or "catch up" the sewing threads which pass around the tapes of a book. The purpose of this stitch is to prevent undue looseness of the sewing thread. Also called "link sewing." (83, 119)

catchword. The word appearing at the bottom of the page following the bottom line of print. It is also the first word of the following page. Catchwords originally appeared on the last page of a quire or manuscript, and were intended to be used by the bookbinder in gathering. Later, they appeared at the foot of every verso or even every page; however, their use in the printed books of Europe was never very consistent. In Italian books of the period 1470-1500 they first appeared at the end of each signature (section), and later at the end of every page. In the 19th century, their use in conjunction with signature marks was redundant and they were discontinued. (12, 156, 234, 365)

catechol (pyrocatechin; pyrocatechol). A colorless crystal ($C_6H_6O_2$), soluble in water, alcohol, ether, benzene, and alkalis. An alkaline solution gives a coloration with ferric chloride, which turns brown on standing in air. It can be obtained from CATECHU, a natural dye, or prepared by fusing orthobenzenedisulfonic acid with caustic soda. Catechol is the principal constituent of the condensed (catechol) tannins. *See also:* VEGETABLE TANNINS. (235, 306)

catechol tannins. *See:* VEGETABLE TANNINS.

catechu (black catechu; cutch). An extract obtained from the wood of *Acacia catechu,* a tree grown in Eastern India, and other areas, and used in tanning leather. It contains catechin and catechutannic acid. *See also:* CATECHOL; VEGETABLE TANNINS. (175)

catenati. *See* CHAINED BOOKS.

catgut. A tough cord made from the intestines of animals, such as sheep and other herbivores, and used at times for the core of the HEADBAND, especially when a round band is desired, and also for TACKETING, where additional strength is required for large stationery bindings. (172)

cathedral bindings. Bookbindings executed between about 1810 and approximately 1840 in England and France. The name derives from the motifs of the embellishment, e.g., Gothic architecture, rose windows, and the like. The design was either blocked on the cover, as in France, or built up by means of separate tools, as in England. The cathedral style was a revival of the 16th century ARCHITECTURAL STYLE by the 19th century binder JOSEPH THOUVENIN. (69, 347)

cationic (substances). Substances, such as dyes, tannins, oils, etc., which ionize when dissolved in water, so that the characteristic ion—dye, tannin, oil, etc.—is the cation and has a positive charge. *Cf:* ANIONIC (SUBSTANCES) (305)

cat's paw calf. An acid-stain pattern on a calfskin binding, somewhat resembling the paw marks of a cat. *See also:* TREE CALF.

cat's tooth decoration. A form of decoration consisting of a serrated line resembling a row of teeth. It is usually impressed with a ROLL (1), and is generally used as a border decoration.

caustic. A term used with reference to the hydroxides of alkali and alkaline earth metals, such as sodium, potassium, calcium, barium, etc., so called because they possess corrosive properties. In very dilute solutions, caustics are used to neutralize acidity in paper, to control pH in the bleaching of paper fur-

nishes, etc., and in very strong solutions in leather manufacture to lime and unhair hides and skins.

caustic soda. *See:* SODIUM HYDROXIDE.

Caxton, William (c 1416-1491). The English linguist, editor, printer, and publisher, who was the first to print books in the English language. Caxton was born in Kent, possibly in the village of Tenterton, traveled to London in 1438 and became apprenticed to the merchant Robert Large, who was also Lord Mayor of London. Three years later Large died, leaving the young Caxton some 20 marks, a not inconsiderable sum in those days. Possibly as early as 1441 Caxton moved to Bruges and by not later than 1446 had established himself in business there. While in Flanders (1446-76) he became a very successful merchant in the Anglo-Flemish cloth trade, and was made governor of the English Nation at Bruges in 1462.

It was in Bruges that Caxton entered the service of Margaret, Duchess of Burgundy and sister of Edward IV of England. It is believed that he functioned as secretary, librarian, translator, or all three, to Margaret, and it has also been suggested that it may have been her keen desire to have books in her native language that prompted Caxton to take up the trade of translating and publishing books in English. It may have been during a visit to Cologne in 1471-72 that he first encountered the craft of printing, and it is reasonably certain that he learned the craft from Johann Veldener.

Caxton returned to Bruges in 1472 and there published the first printed book in the English language, Raoul le Fevre's *Le Recueil des Histories de Troyes,* which he had translated in about 1473-74. It is supposed that Caxton financed the publication but that it was actually printed by Veldener at Louvain. Caxton returned to England in 1476, where he lived for the next 15 years, dying in London in 1491.

Regardless of what some critics may say of Caxton's lack of scholarship and education, his place in history is deserved more because of his ability as a linguist and editor, than as a printer and publisher. Even so, he printed some 18,000 pages, most in folio size, and almost 80 separate books. He did most of the administrative work of the press through his three main assistants, Wynkyn de Worde, Richard Pynson, and Robert Copland. In all, Caxton translated at least 22 books; he may

well have translated others that were never published.

It is thought that Caxton probably brought his bookbinding tools from Bruges upon his return to England, because two of his stamps are very similar to those used on books found contemporaneously in the city. Caxton's stamps were used after his death by his successor, Wynkyn de Worde, and some, thereafter, by Henry Jacobi. (50, 140)

C clamp. A C-shaped, general purpose clamp that grips between the open ends of the "C" by means of a long, flat-ended screw that threads through one end and presses the clamped material against the other end. It is used mainly for holding leather or book boards while using the SPOKESHAVE. It is called a "G-clamp" in Great Britain. (183)

cedar marble. A cover marble executed by sprinkling black and brown coloring on the covers, followed by orange in various places to give a cloudlike effect. This is followed by red placed near the orange. When this is dry, the covers are coated two or three times with yellow, which is allowed to penetrate evenly into the leather. (97, 152)

cedar oil. A colorless to pale yellow essential oil distilled from the wood of various cedars (*Juniperus virginiana, J. procera,* and others), and used by some restorers in a mixture of anhydrous lanolin, beeswax, and hexane, as a leather dressing. The cedarwood oil is said to act both as a preservative and as an agent which aids in forming a bond between the lanolin and wax in leather. *See also:* LEATHER DRESSINGS. (130, 291)

cellulose. The chief constituent of the cell walls of all plants and of many fibrous products, including paper and cloth. Cellulose is by far the most abundant organic substance found in nature. It is a complex polymeric carbohydrate $(C_6H_{10}O_5)_n$, having the same percentage composition as starch, i.e., 44.4% carbon, 6.2% hydrogen, and 49.4% oxygen, and it also yields only glucose on complete hydrolysis by acid. The portion of a cellulosic material that does not dissolve in a 17.5% solution of sodium hydroxide is termed ALPHA CELLULOSE; the portion that dissolves in an alkaline solution and precipitates upon acidification is known as BETA CELLULOSE; and the portion that dissolves in an alkaline solution but does not precipitate upon acidification is called GAMMA CELLULOSE. *See also:* CELLULOSE ACETATE;

CELLULOSE CHAIN; CELLULOSE FIBERS; CELLULOSE NITRATE; COTTON LINTERS; HEMICELLULOSES; LIGNIN; PAPER. (72, 198)

cellulose acetate. An acetate salt of cellulose, produced from COTTON LINTERS and used in archival work: 1) as a photographic film base (often called "safety film" since it is not readily combustible); and 2) in conjunction with an adhesive, such as one of the polyvinyl resins, in laminating, heat sealing, etc. Cellulose acetate is manufactured in a wide variety of thicknesses, ranging from 0.001 to 0.005 inch, and is clear, hard and glossy. It has little tear strength and has almost the same HYGROSCOPICITY as cellulose itself; however, when moist, it does not stretch as much as paper. (31, 34, 81, 303)

cellulose chain (cellulose molecule). A term used to describe the cellulose molecule, which appears to be built up of between 150 and 1,500 very simple units, in the form of a long, thin structure, not unlike a chain. Each link of the chain consists of a slightly modified form of the common sugar, glucose; the strength of paper depends to a large extent on the continuity of these linkages. Destructive agents, which can weaken and open the individual links of the chain, cause it to break into smaller lengths, resulting in what is generally considered to be BRITTLE-NESS in the paper. The mechanical strength of any aggregate of cellulose fibers, such as paper, decreases in response to the reduction in chain length, the process continuing ultimately to the point where only glucose remains. (198)

cellulose ester. An ester of cellulose, such as CELLULOSE ACETATE or CELLULOSE NITRATE.

cellulose fibers. The basic raw material used in the manufacture of paper and other cellulose products. Cellulose usually exists in association with substantial amounts of other substances that are removed insofar as possible in the papermaking process. An exception to this is the seed hair fibers, or COTTON LINTERS, which exist as almost pure cellulose. The approximate cellulose content of some of the materials used in making papers are:

Material	% Cellulose
Cotton	98
Ramie	86
Hemp	65
Jute	58
Deciduous woods	41-42
Coniferous woods	41-44
Cornstalks	43
Wheat straw	42

The cellulose fibers used in making paper have certain inherent properties which enable them to form a web, i e., a sheet of paper, including: 1) hydrophilicity, which permits them to be readily dispersed in water; 2) a fine structure which perimts FIBRILLA-TION; 3) sufficient fiber length to form a highly entangled web of considerable strength; and 4) the ability to form hydrogen bonds between fibers as the web dries, thus providing additional strength in the sheet of paper. (144)

cellulose film. A transparent film produced from cellulose fibers by a process that involves steeping, shredding, and converting the fibers into a viscose solution, or cellulose xanthate, which is subquently extruded to convert it into a film. It is made in a limited range of thicknesses, between 0.00085 and 0.0016 inch, and, when rendered moisture resistant, may be used to seal documents, book leaves, etc., for protection. It is a fairly flexible film of considerable strength. (81)

cellulose nitrate. A film made from cotton waste, wood, or waste cellulose film. It is produced by the nitration of cellulose, usually with a mixture of nitric and sulfuric acids. It has been used as a film base for photographic purposes, as well as to encase documents, book leaves, etc.; however, its flammability, the fact that it causes severe deterioration of the materials it supposedly protects (because of the generation of oxides of nitrogen which yield nitric acid in the presence of water), and the fact that it cannot be manufactured in thickness down to 0.001 inch, has precluded its use in preservation work. (34, 81)

cellulose varnish. A cellulose-base varnish (usually cellulose nitrate), available in an aerosol dispenser, and useful as a protective sealing film over the lettering on a book cover, if used in moderation. It is flammable. (92)

cement. 1. A term meaning to bond together or to adhere with a liquid adhesive. 2. A liquid adhesive having a solvent base composed of a synthetic elastomer resin. 3. An inorganic paste. (222, 309)

center and corner piece style. A common style of decoration, essentially Eastern in origin, featuring a center ornament, circular or (occasionally) oval in shape, and often ARABESQUE, in com-

bination with corner pieces generally made up of a quarter segment of the center ornament. The style was common on the Continent and especially in England from about 1580 to 1620. *See also:* CENTERPIECE. (243, 347)

center fold. *See:* CENTER SPREAD.

center-fold sewing. A generic term sometimes used with reference to the sewing of a book through the folds of the sections. *See:* FLEXIBLE SEWING; MACHINE SEWING; RECESSED-CORD SEWING; TAPE SEWING.

centerpiece. 1. A finishing stamp, usually ARABESQUE, blocked in the center of the cover and generally used in combination with center pieces or corner stamps. It was a popular form of decoration in the late 16th and early 17th centuries. Also called "centerstamp." 2. A piece of metal, usually embossed and engraved, and fastened to the cover of a book. (236, 259)

center spread. The two center pages of a section or, more specifically, the two center pages of a periodical issue, printed side by side on a continuous sheet so that there is no margin between them. Such a publication must be sewn through the center fold to avoid obscuring part of the printed matter. Also called "center fold." (316)

centerstamp. *See:* CENTERPIECE.

center-to-center. 1. The distance from the center of one punched hole (punched through the paper for side sewing or fold sewing) to the center of the next hole. 2. The distance between holes punched through loose-leaf papers, or the covers of a post binding, etc. (83)

center tools. The ornamental stamps on the spine of a volume between the raised bands. Of the customary six spaces, the title is normally in space two (from the top), the author in space four, the year of publication in space six, with "center tools" in spaces one, three, five and six (just above the date). (94, 261, 371)

centipoise. One hundredth of a poise. It is a unit for measuring the viscosity of an adhesive. The viscosity of water at 20°C. is approximately one centipoise. (222)

ceramic paper fibers. Noncellulosic paper fibers produced from inorganic materials. Ceramic fibers include all refractory fibers made of alumina, zirconia, thoria, magnesia, fused silica, hafnia, berylia, titanium oxide, potassium titanate, and their mixtures, with or without silica. By definition, monooxide ceramics, such as alumina ceramics, are composed of at least

80% oxides. More often they contain 90% or more base oxides, while special products may contain 99% and sometimes 100%. The main group of ceramic fibers is composed of silica in admixture with special oxides, such as aluminum and magnesium oxides, barium, and calcium.

Ceramic fibers may be produced in numerous ways, including, blowing methods, spinning methods, continuous-spinning methods, colloidal evaporation processes, vapor deposition, single-crystal and whisker methods, oxidation, crystallization, pseudomorphic alteration, etc. Ceramic paper fiber is not used in book production because of the very high cost of the fibers as compared with wood and other organic fibers; however, such papers do print and fold well and are considerably more durable. (42)

certification plan. A proposal for library binding drawn up in the 1930s by the Joint Committee of the American Library Association and the Library Binding Institute, to enable library binders to apply for certification by agreeing to meet certain requirements, including:

1. Submitting samples of their work so as to demonstrate the bindery's capability of producing so called Class "A" work (the samples being reviewed by a board appointed by the Joint Committee);
2. Proving responsibility and reliability by means of sworn answers to questions, and permitting the investigation of replies;
3. Providing satisfactory references;
4. Carrying sufficient insurance;
5. Pledging to conduct the business of the bindery fairly, treat customers honestly, and maintain minimum standards and good labor conditions; and
6. Becoming a member of the Library Binding Institute

The certification of library binders is now solely under the jurisdiction of the Library Binding Institute. (131)

certified library bindery. A bookbinding establishment in the United States or Canada that specializes in library binding and meets the minimum specifications of the Library Binding Institute, as outlined in the CERTIFICATION PLAN. A certified library binder is defined as one who produces binding which will achieve two objectives: 1) meet the requirements of libraries for an end product capable of withstanding the rigors of normal library circulation or use; and 2) provide maximum reader usability. A certified

library binder is required to warrant that the binding covered by his invoice is Library Binding and complies with all requirements of the Library Binding Institute Standards for Library Binding, except as noted in the invoice. Certified library binders are also required to adhere to the Trade Practice Regulation for the Library Binding Industry, maintain compulsory insurance to protect the customer's property in their custody, and participate in the industry quality control program. (131, 208)

cessing. A technique used to allow excess tan liquor to drain from hides and skins, particularly the former. The hides are piled up flat on a wooden stillage or pallet and covered to prevent overdrying the surface and edges of the pile. Cessing is also used in place of HORSING UP when it is necessary to have a flat leather with no creases. Also called "piling." (306)

chained books. Books that in the past were attached to shelves, reading desks, pulpits, pews, etc., by means of chains. From the 15th to the early 18th century, books were secured in this manner to prevent them from being stolen. The chains used for this purpose varied in length from nearly 3 feet to almost 5 feet, while the links ranged in size from 1½ to almost 3 inches in length, with a width of about ½ inch. The problem of the chains breaking when twisted was partially overcome by the inclusion of a swivel in the middle or at one end.

When the books were meant to be stood on end the chains were usually attached to the fore edge of the upper cover (and occasionally the lower) by means of a ring held to the board by a length of thin brass which was bent around the edge of the cover and riveted in place. Often, however, the ring was not used, the chain being attached directly to the clip on the cover. This required that the book be shelved fore edge out, a method of shelving that endured well into the 17th century, even when chains were not used. Books meant to lie permanently on lecterns, or the like, often had the chains attached to the bottom or top edge of the lower cover.

Chains were used, it has been said, because "The thievish disposition of some that enter into libraries to learn no good there, hath made it necessary to secure the innocent books, even the Sacred volumes themselves, with chains—which were better deserved by those persons, who have too much

learning to be hanged, and too little to be honest."

The practice of chaining books began to die out by the middle of the 17th century when it became a more common practice to shelve books with their spines out. See PLATE I. (46, 236)

chain lines (chain marks). The widely spaced watermark lines, about 25 mm apart, parallel to the shorter sides of a sheet of laid paper, caused by the "chain wires," i.e., the wires to which the finer laid wires of the MOLD (1) are attached for support. They usually correspond to the position of the bars or ribs of the mold to which they are often fastened. Occasionally, the shadow of the rib can be seen on either side of the chain line. Generally the chain lines run vertically in the leaves of a folio, horizontally in a quarto, and again vertically in an octavo. Sometimes, in the late 17th and early 18th centuries, this rule is reversed because of the use of a split sheet, or the use of a double mold, resulting in "turned chains." (69, 136, 225)

chain stitch. 1. See KETTLE STITCH. 2. An ornamental stitch in an embroidered binding that resembles the links of a chain, and is used in working in silver and other colored threads into the binding. (111)

chain wires. See: CHAIN LINES.

chalk. See: CALCIUM CARBONATE.

chalking. 1. The process of applying pumice, brick dust, red earth, or a similar material, to the GOLD CUSHION prior to laying the gold leaf on it for cutting. Chalking helps prevent the leaf from sticking to the cushion. 2. A printing defect caused by the use of an ink that has been over-reduced, or an ink that is not suitable for the paper, causing the ink vehicle to soak into the paper leaving the pigment on the surface where it can easily be smudged or rubbed off. 3. A condition encountered in some papers where fine particles of pigment break off the sheet during finishing, converting, printing, or subsequent use.

chalky appearance. The surface of a coated paper that is lacking in gloss. The condition is probably due more to the type of coating material used, as well as to the coating process, than to the degree of calendering which the paper undergoes. (17)

chamfered edges. See: BEVELED BOARDS.

chamois. Originally, a soft, pliable leather made from the skin of the chamois (*Rupicapra rupicapra*), a small goatlike antelope found in the high mountainous areas of Europe and the Caucasus. Chamois was at one time used to some extent in bookbinding, but is seldom, if ever, used today because it is hygroscopic, and, if kept dry by artificial means, tends to become hard and prone to cracking. The original chamois was a vegetable-tanned leather. Today, the leather called "chamois" is a suede-finished leather made from the FLESH SPLIT of a sheep- or lambskin, or from sheep or lamb from which the grain has been removed by FRIZING (3), and tanned by processes involving the oxidation of fish or marine animal oils in the skin, using either only the oils, in which case it is a full-oil tannage, or, in a first stage using formaldehyde and then the oils, in which case it is a combination tannage. In the United States, the term "chamois" without qualification, is restricted to the flesh split of a sheepskin tanned solely with oils. The old term for the full oil process was "chamoising." Also sometimes called "shammy." (170, 306, 325, 363)

chamoletting. An old term for MARBLING.

champlevé bindings. Bindings produced between the 11th and 13th centuries. The process involved cutting designs into a thin sheet of gold or copper, which formed the cover, with cavities filled with enamel. Sometimes the enamel was limited to the decoration of borders and corners. Champlevé can be distinguished from CLOISONNE BINDINGS by the irregular widths of the metal enclosing the enameled areas. (124, 280, 357)

charcoal drawing paper. A drawing paper produced in such a manner as to be suitable for use with charcoal or pencils. It generally has a high cotton fiber content. It is made in basis weights of 60 to 75 pounds. (17)

chased edges. *See:* GAUFFERED EDGES.

check binding. A general term for the style of binding in which the sheets are wire stabbed or stitched, and then covered with lightweight strawboards, or checkbook cover boards, which are lined with plain paper, marbled paper, or cloth, and cut flush. Some have round corners. This style of binding is not rounded and backed and has a tight back. Books under ¾ inch in thickness are generally side stitched, while those over that thickness are nailed or studded. The term derives from the method of binding checkbooks for banks. (256, 300)

check pile. A procedure for obtaining the desired number of sheets in a PAD without having to count each group. The exact number of sheets is counted for one (check) pad, and, using this pile as a "check pile," the approximate number of sheets is placed in an adjacent pile. Sheets are added or removed from the second pile until the heights of the piles are the same, at which time the second pile supposedly has the same number of sheets as the "check pile." A better method is to use a PAD COUNTER (2). (74)

cheeking. The process of reducing the thickness of the head areas of unhaired skins by means of splitting.

cheesecloth. A lightweight, unsized cotton fabric, loosely woven and used to a limited extent in edition binding as a spine lining fabric. (120)

chemical wood pulp. A paper pulp prepared from both coniferous and deciduous trees, in which the LIGNIN and other undesirable materials are removed by cooking the wood with an alkaline sodium sulfide solution, or a sodium sulfite solution, leaving the cellulose fibers in an aqueous suspension of the dissolved lignins, etc. The fibers are washed and are then used "as is" to produce unbleached paper or are bleached to produce white paper.

The fibers from coniferous trees are ribbonlike and have thin walls. Generally, two distinct types of fibers can be distinguished: 1) a broad fiber of a width of about 0.05 mm and a length of about 2.5 to 4 mm, and 2) a narrower fiber about 0.02 mm wide and 1.5 to 5 mm long. The fibers of deciduous trees are shorter than those of the conifers, being between 1 and 1.5 mm long, but they are usually thicker.

In chemical tests to determine the presence of chemical wood pulp in paper, an iodine-zinc chloride solution gives a pale violet, pale blue, or reddish blue, depending upon the type of chemical pulp. (93, 98, 143)

chemise. 1. A cover of SILK or CHEVROTAIN, used in the 15th century to protect leather bookbindings. The chemise was sometimes used in the Middle Ages in lieu of binding. 2. A loose cover for a book with pockets into which the boards are inserted. 3. Broadly, the canvas covering used to protect leather-bound stationery bindings. (140)

chestnut. The wood of the European chestnut *(Castanea sativa)* and the American chestnut *(C. dentata),* from which tannin is extracted. Chestnut tannin extract was used extensively in France and other European countries, as well as in the United States, in the latter part of the 19th century and early 20th century. In the United States its use has declined sharply since the introduction of the Oriental chestnut blight *(Endothia parasitica),* which has virtually destroyed the American chestnut. Today Italy is the largest producer of chestnut wood extract for tanning.

The bark of the chestnut is not used because it imparts a dark color to the tannin, and its high sugar content would result in a higher percentage of soluble non-tans in the extract. The usual tannin content of the southern European chestnut is 10 to 13%, or higher, which is considerably higher than that obtained from trees in northern climates. The wood does not seem to reach its highest tannin content until the trees are at least 30 years old.

Chestnut extract tans rapidly and produces a firm leather. If used alone, however, it may impart a reddish color to the leather that is not desirable; therefore, it is used in combination with quebracho, mimosa, myrabolans, and valonia.

Chestnut is one of the pyrogallol class of tannins, and has a naturally low pH value. It also has a relatively low salts content and a high acids content. *See also:* VEGETABLE TANNINS. (175, 306, 363)

cheverell. A goatskin PARCHMENT that has been converted into a supple and strong leather with the characteristic bold grain pattern. It proved to be an exceptionally durable bookbinding leather. The conversion was effected by a simultaneous tannage using alum and oil, followed by intensive fatliquoring and staking. Cheverell was used in England, France, and Italy during the 13th to 15th centuries. (291)

chevrette. A leather produced from the skin of a young goat which is being, or has recently been, weaned, or the skin of an immature goat. Sometimes, any lightweight goatskin or kidskin is referred to as "chevrette." (61)

chevrotain. A leather produced from the skin of any of several very small deerlike mammals of Asia and West Africa, and used in England, principally in the Middle Ages, for chemises. Like the skins of does, lambs and other very young animals, it is soft and supple. It is sometimes inaccurately referred to as CHEVRETTE. (115)

Chicago posts. Metal screw posts having two heads, one fastened to a full length post, which is drilled and tapped with a thread, the other attached to a shorter post, which is threaded to be inserted in the main post. The purpose of such posts is to allow additional sheets to be added to the book. (256)

chicory. An herb *(Cichorium intybus),* at one time added to size solutions to adjust the tone of newly washed book leaves so as to make them match the shade of the unwashed leaves. (83)

chiffon silk (chiffon lining). A sheer, very lightweight fabric in plain weave, made of hand-twisted single yarns of silk and used at one time to repair and reinforce torn leaves, documents, etc. Although its weight and sheerness permit even the finest print to be legible, it is little used now because of its lack of permanence. (81, 120)

China clay. A white, powdery material arising from the decomposition of granite feldspar. The term originally applied to the beneficiated KAOLIN mined in Europe, but is now applied to all beneficiated kaolin. *See also:* CLAY. (143)

China paper. A soft, very thin WATER-LEAF (1) paper, produced in China, and elsewhere, from bamboo fibers. It has a pale yellow color and a very fine texture. The usual sheet size is 57 by 27 inches. Is is used for proofs of woodcuts, for woodcuts to be mounted on a stronger paper, and, now and then, for superior editions of books. It is also called "Chinese paper," or "Indian proof paper." (17, 69)

"Chinese" Chippendale bindings. A class of CHIPPENDALE BINDINGS. These bindings were generally covered in red morocco, and were tooled in gold with designs representing "Chinese" motifs and symbols, following the vogue represented in the decorative arts of the mid-18th century. The bindings often featured rococo frames made up of recurving and serrated motifs forming irregular compartments and perches for beehives with bees in flight, boats, Chinese archers and spearmen, columns and pilasters, doves, flowers, grapes and other fruit, horses rising from the sea, lions supporting shields, phoenixes, etc. (347)

Chinese ink. An INK of considerable antiquity, made from lampblack or soot obtained by burning vegetable oils, such as sesame or wood (tung oil). The quality of the oil is of major importance in this type of ink. The collected soot is sifted; heated along with white, transparent oxhide, or fish glue; and pounded in a mortar until it is soft and pliable and can be molded into sticks. This type of ink, having a base of carbon, is very stable when properly prepared, and, not having

acidity, has no harmful effects on paper; however, it is easily affected by water. (130, 143)

Chinese marble. A type of cover marble, consisting of solid dark brown over the entire leather cover, with whiting in spots or streaks, over which blue and then large spots of red are thrown. The whiting not covered by color is washed off when the covers are dry. (95)

Chinese paper. *See:* CHINA PAPER (1).

Chinese wax. A white or yellowish crystalline WAX, formed on the branches of the ash tree *(Fraxinus chinensis)* from the secretion of the coccus insect *(Coccus ceriferus).* It resembles SPERMACETI WAX, but is harder, more friable and has a higher melting point (80 to 83° C.). It is used in polishing leather, sizing paper, etc. (291)

Chinese white. A dense form of zinc white—zinc oxide (ZnO)—sometimes used as a bonding agent when coloring the edges of books. (335)

chipboard. A thin, hard-surfaced, grayish board, normally produced from paper stock, including waste papers. It has a relatively low density, and is available in the thicknesses of 0.006 inch and up. It is sometimes used in edition binding for covering boards; in library binding and craft binding, however, it is never used for anything but lining board. (256, 277)

Chippendale bindings. A style of book decoration, where the books were generally covered in red morocco, and were tooled in gold with elaborate rococo borders of swirls and acanthus leaves enclosing areas dispersed with meshes of dotted lines. Incorporated in all this were various figured tools, including dancing angels, trumpeters, doves, fruit, musicians, swooping phoenixes, etc. *See also:* "CHINESE" CHIPPENDALE BINDINGS. (347)

chiseled leather. *See:* CUIR-CISELÉ.

Chivers, Cedric (c 1853-1929). A British bookbinder sometimes referred to as the dean of library binders. Chivers developed a method of hand oversewing, in which the stitches pass diagonally through the paper; it is still in use today and is called the "Chivers method." One of the major disadvantages of the usual method of overcasting, or oversewing, groups of individual leaves which are subsequently to be sewn on tapes or cords in the usual manner of hand sewing, is that the book often has a tendency to open up and become strained between the groups; this occurs only when the paper is unusually thick. Chivers' solu-

tion was a method by which three holes are punched in each of the sections in such a manner that their positioning alternates from section to section; they are also punched obliquely through the paper to eliminate strain due to side pull. Thread passes through and returns in such a manner that every section is sewn to the next two sections on each side.

Chivers was also famous for his DURO-FLEXIBLE BINDING, as well as his VELLUCENT BINDINGS. (94, 236)

chloramine t (sodium p-toluenesulphon-chloramide ($C_7H_7ClNNaO_2S \cdot 3H_2O$)). White crystals prepared from p-toluene-sulphonamide and sodium hypochlorite, and used in a 2% aqueous solution to remove fox marks and stains from paper, and also for general bleaching purposes. It is applied directly to the paper by means of a soft brush or by soaking. It is very difficult to wash out and failure to rid the paper of it may result in the formation of highly destructive hydrochloric acid. (102, 265)

chlorine. A commonly occurring, nonmetallic, univalent and polyvalent element (Cl), belonging to the halogens, and used, generally in the form of chlorine dioxide (ClO_2), or hypochlorite ($Ca(ClO)_2$), as a bleach to whiten paper pulp, usually in one or more of the final stages in a multistage sequence. Its use as a bleaching agent in paper manufacture began in 1774 but its deleterious effects, while noticed almost immediately, were largely misunderstood or ignored. Chlorine residues are extremely difficult and expensive to remove, and many chlorine compounds break down slowly forming highly destructive hydrochloric acid in the process. Chlorine is also used as a disinfectant in leather manufacture. (198, 235)

chlorine bath. A dilute solution of CHLORINE and water (or the commercial product, Chlorox, diluted with water), used to remove stains from paper, as well as for general bleaching purposes. For the disadvantages of using chlorine solutions for bleaching purposes, see CHLORINE.

chlorine dioxide. A heavy, explosive gas, (ClO_2), produced by the action of chlorine or sodium chlorite, and used in bleaching paper pulp from a water solution, usually in one or more of the final stages of multi-stage sequence. *See also:* CHLORINE.

chlorine number. The amount in grams of chlorine gas, or its equivalent in bleaching powder, that can be absorbed by 100 grams of oven dry paper pulp in a specified period of time and under specified conditions. (17)

chlorine water. *See:* CHLORINE BATH.

chloropicrin. A colorless liquid (CCl_3NO_2), having a very toxic vapor. It is prepared by treating sodium picrate with chlorine, or calcium picrate with bleaching power, and is used at times in fumigating books.

chop cut. A method of trimming newly printed sheets before folding, in which the large sheet is trimmed on all four sides but the individual leaves are trimmed in the process of separation, after which no further trim is required. This procedure is largely restricted to economy printing. The normal procedure is to trim all four sides of the large sheet, cut it apart to separate the sections, and then trim each individual section. "Chop cut" cannot be used if the individual sheet or section bleeds. (329)

chrome glue. A light-colored, easily worked glue made from scraps of chrome-tanned leather. It is said to be inferior in strength to regular hide glue. (81)

chrome liquor. A solution of basic chromic salt used in CHROME TANNING leather. It is prepared by treating a strong solution of sodium dichromate ($Na_2Cr_2O_7 \cdot 2H_2O$) with a reducing agent, such as sulfur dioxide (SO_2), or a mixture of glucose and sulfuric acid. (305)

chrome oxide (chromic oxide). A green, insoluble powder (Cr_2O_3), which is the basis for many salts of chromium used in tanning leather by the chrome process. It is also used as a light- and heat-fast green pigment. (305)

chrome retan. A process in leather manufacture in which the skins are tanned throughout their thickness by the chrome process and, subsequently, are further treated with vegetable and/or synthetic agents. The retanning agents penetrate the skin deeply, but do not necessarily penetrate throughout the skin. *See also:* SEMI-CHROME TANNAGE. (61)

chrome tanning. A method of tannage stemming back to the discovery, in 1858, that leather could be produced by treating skins with basic chromium sulfate ($Cr(OH)SO_4$). The two basic methods employed today are the one bath and two bath methods, the former being most often used. The most widely used chemical in chrome tanning is sodium dichromate (sodium bichromate) ($Na_2Cr_2O_7 \cdot 2H_2O$), from which chromium sulfate is produced.

As in vegetable tanned leather, the degree of control exercised in the tanning process has great influence on the nature of the leather produced. If, for example, the final pH of a chrome-tanned leather is too low, the leather will be flat, hard, and wet, and may show grease spots on the surface; if it is too high, the leather will probably be plump, loose, dry, and may have a drawn grain or be too soft in the BLUE SORT. It is, therefore, imperative in chrome tanning to obtain the optimum pH, i.e., 3.4 to 3.5 in the one bath method, or 3.2 to 3.4 in the combination single and double bath method, and to maintain it.

The two bath method has almost been completely superseded by the one bath tannage, except in certain cases where the older two bath process is thought to give a particularly uniform tannage and a deposit of colloidal sulfur in the leather.

The major characteristics of chrome-tanned leather are its blue-green color and absence of filling power, i.e., an empty tannage. Chrome-tanned leather tends to be softer and stretchier than vegetable-tanned leather, and is very stable in water. Unlike vegetable-tanned or alum-tawed skins, chrome-tanned leather can withstand boiling water and has a shrinkage temperature higher at times than 100° C.; however, it does not resist perspiration or organic acids well and is difficult to emboss. In addition, it does not take gold tooling well and is difficult to fabricate in such operations as turning-in, etc. It is, on the other hand, a very durable leather. (101, 164, 248, 306, 363)

chromium sulfate (chromic sulfate). A salt of chromium ($Cr_2(OH)SO_4$), in the form of green crystals that are soluble in water and form an acid solution. It is used in CHROME TANNING. (304)

chromo paper. A heavily coated paper suitable for color printing. Surface characteristics said to enhance color printing include smoothness, uniformity of ink receptivity, high total reflectance, and neutrality of shade, which means the paper is truly white rather than tinted. The term is not generally used in the United States. *See also:* COATED ART PAPER. (17, 156, 324)

circles. Finishing tools in the shape of ⅓, ½, ¾, and full circles, in sizes generally ranging from ¼ to 2½ inches in diameter. *See also:* GOUGE. (97, 137)

circuit edges. The projecting flexible covers of limp bindings turned over to protect the leaves and edges of books,

usually of a devotional nature. The circuit edge differs from the yapp edge in that the overlap of the cover is not continuous. The covering leather is turned over at head and tail, with an independent flap at the fore edge. The corners are square. This technique allows the flaps to fold flat onto the edges. Sometimes called "divinity circuit," or "divinity edges." *See also:* YAPP STYLE. (66, 94, 264)

citric acid. A colorless, crystalline or white powdery tricarboxylic acid ($C_6H_8O_7$). Citric acid is used to remove ink, and similar stains from paper, and is particularly useful in removing iron stains. Its advantage over chlorine solutions is that, being a weak and volatile organic acid, it is much less damaging to the paper.

cl. Abbreviation for CLOTH.

clamp. A device designed to bind, constrict, or press two or more parts together so as to hold them firmly in their relative positions for some subsequent operation, to allow adhesives to set, or for trimming, printing, and the like. They may be operated by hand, mechanically, by air pressure, or hydraulically. (145)

clamp dwell. The time interval of the holding action of a CLAMP. Although "dwell time" may be controlled manually, as with the clamp of a hand-operated board chopper, the term relates more accurately to the automatic release of a clamp, such as in a BUILDING-IN MACHINE, which holds the pressure for a pre-set length of time. When a clamp does not release immediately upon completion of an operation, it is said to have a "long" dwell. The typical GUILLOTINE cutting machine has such a dwell; the clamp remains on the pile being cut until the knife has risen to a safe height, which prevents the knife from rippling the sheets on its return motion and thus disturbing the pile. (145, 320)

clam shell coverer. A machine used in edition binding to apply paper covers to side stitched books that are not rounded and backed. The machine glues the spine, rolls or presses the cover onto it, and carries the book to the cover breaker where the back and both sides along the spine are pressed by formers. Book sizes handled range from a minimum of 7 by 5 inches to a maximum of 12 by 9 inches, and up to 1⅛ inches in thickness (with a special attachment for books up to 2 inches thick), at speeds up to 160 books per minute. (320)

clasps. The hinged fasteners of brass, precious metals, iron, etc., often elaborately chased, and intended to secure the covers of books, ledgers, albums, etc. They are sometimes provided with a lock, and are designed to hold the covers of a book closed, or when provided with a lock, to prevent opening by unauthorized persons. Clasps are attached after forwarding is completed except for the board papers, because by that time the final thickness of the book is known and any rivets on the inside of the boards will be covered by the board papers. Because a single

CLASPS

clasp has a tendency to distort the boards, two are generally used, and are usually placed opposite the centers of the second and fifth panels of the spine. All metal-hinged clasps have to be made to fit the individual book, as a perfect fit is necessary; however, where the hinge consists of a leather strap, adjustments can easily be made. Stretching of the leather with use, thus causing looseness, can be overcome by making the strap of leather over vellum, which also provides additional strength.

The use of clasps appears to be as

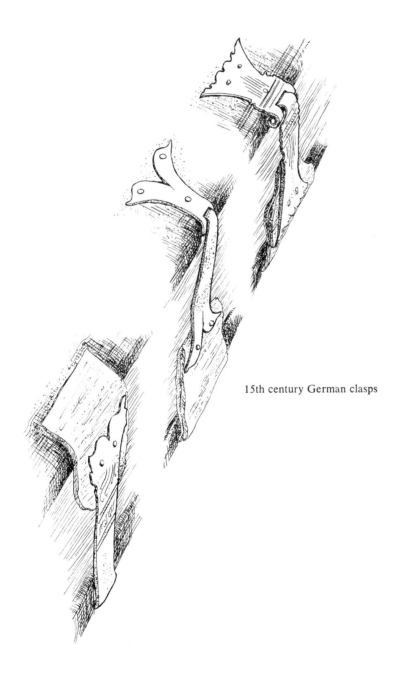

15th century German clasps

old as the codex itself. In its earliest form, which was Coptic bindings, the clasp consisted of a strap attached to the fore edge of the upper cover and wound around the book over the fore edge several times, the bone attached to the end of the strap being tucked between the strap and the lower cover. Another method, which may actually have been used more often than the strap, consisted of the plaited thong with loops which fit over bone pegs at the edge of the lower cover. A clasp of this type seems to have been used in England at least as early as the 12th century. The strap was fastened to the fore edge of the upper cover, and the end, which had a metal-rimmed hole, was taken around to the middle of the lower cover and was attached to a metal pin.

English bookbinders of the 14th century began using two straps instead of just one, something which had been done earlier and more often on the Continent of Europe. The hole and pin type was more or less abandoned early in the 14th century and replaced by clasps and catches attached to the fore edge. Initially, each clasp consisted of a strip of leather having a metal hook on one end. Later, the metal part of the clasp was the full thickness of the book and was sometimes attached to the board by means of a metal hinge. In bindings of the 15th and 16th centuries, and probably earlier, the location of the clasp is a reasonably accurate indication of the country of origin. English and French bindings usually had them attached to the upper cover with the catch on the lower, while bindings of the Netherlands and Germany had the catch on the upper cover. Italian binders often attached the clasp to the upper covers and often used as many as four clasps.

The velvet-covered books of the royal collection in England in the 15th and 16th centuries often had ornamental gilt clasps, which were often combined with elaborately ornamented gilt cornerpieces and centerpieces which helped prevent abrasion of the velvet.

The use of metal clasps began to decline early in the 16th century, probably because they could not be securely attached to the pasteboards which were replacing boards made of wood. The weight, size, and material of the books being published at that time did not require clasps, and clasps were no longer economically feasible for the normal run of books. In most cases they were replaced by TIES (1). Clasps made of brass were still used in the 16th century for some books which were bound with boards of wood, and silver clasps and cornerpieces were often used on small Bibles and other devotional works as late as the late 17th and early 18th centuries. In certain German bindings, however, e.g., Bibles, clasps were used continuously until the end of the 18th century. This was notably true in America, for example, where almost all German-American bindings, e.g., the Saur Bibles, were issued in calfskin over wood with two heavy claps attached to the lower cover. Brass clasps were revived during the latter part of the 19th century, mainly for Bibles and prayer books, but also for photograph albums, diaries, and the like. They were often attached to metal frames which protected the edges of boards. (83, 105, 236)

Class "A" library binding. Library binding that meets the standards set forth in the minimum specifications promulgated by the Joint Committee of the American Library Association and the Library Binding Institute. The qualification for Class "A" binding, as accepted today, is set forth, defined and regulated exclusively by the Library Binding Institute, as detailed in its *Standard for Library Binding.*

clay. A colloidal, lusterless, fine-grained, earthy substance which generally develops plasticity when wetted but is permanently hard when fired. Chemically clays are aluminosilicates, which do not form large crystals. The finely divided aluminosilicates, which are responsible for the properties associated with clays, are called "clay minerals." Clays with a preponderance of the clay mineral "kaolinite" are used both as fillers and as coating pigments in the manufacture of paper. Other clays are used in small amounts. Used in excess, as it is in some art papers, clay becomes an adulterant to the detriment of the strength and durability of paper. *See also:* ATTAPULGITE CLAY; BENTONITE; KAOLIN; PAPER CLAY. (17, 235, 343)

clay-finished paper. A paper, such as imitation art paper, coated with finely pulverized clay to impart a smooth finish suitable for halftone illustrations. Such papers present difficulty in binding, as they are difficult to sew (especially to oversew), and there is often the tendency for the clay to separate from the base paper, especially under humid circumstances or if the paper becomes wet. In addition, they are unusually stiff and frequently must be scored. (52, 278)

clay tablets. The earliest form of the "book." Clay tablets were generally used for records and were inscribed in cuneiform writing on wet clay, which when hardened was usually protected by a cover (outer shell), also of clay, which was inscribed with a copy, abstract, or title of the contents. (12, 156)

cleaning. A general term used to describe the removal of mud, dirt, dust, grease, stains, etc., from the covers or leaves of a book, map, print, etc. Cleaning is done in a variety of manners, depending on the nature of the soiling, the material soiled, and the facilities available. It may range from gentle rubbing with bread crumbs to complete washing and restoration. (173, 335)

cleaning off. A term descriptive of a more or less obsolete process of removing excess adhesive from the spine of a book subsequent to lacing-in. Cleaning off is generally done by applying paste to the spine, and, when the glue has softened, scraping off both paste and excess glue with a CLEANING-OFF STICK or plow trimmings. Once a book has been rounded and backed and its shape has been set, the glue on the spine, other than that between the sections, is not required, and, in fact, should be removed to permit greater openability of the book and also to clear the sections of excess glue as a consideration of the binder of the future who may have to rebind the book. Cleaning off also helps in setting the shape of the spine and makes for a cleaner, smoother spine—factors which are very important in the case of a tight back binding.

The increasing use of resinous adhesives in hand binding, such as the polyvinyl group, in lieu of hot glues, has meant that cleaning off has become more difficult, if not impossible, even though the use of these adhesives makes shaping the spine of even greater importance. The plasticized polyvinyls are neither softened by paste nor are they soluble in water; furthermore, they do not seem to affect openability adversely. If, however, removal is necessary, they are alcohol soluble. (83, 236, 261)

cleaning-off stick. A long, thin stick with a rounded but not pointed end, used to clean off excess animal glue from the spine of a book. *See also:* CLEANING OFF. (172)

clearing. The process of lightening the color and removing metallic stains from the grain surface of newly tanned leather. Clearing is done by drumming the leather in a cold solution of weak acid, e.g., a .25 or 1% solution of oxalic ($H_2C_2O_4$) or sulfuric (H_2SO_4) acid; if heavy STRIPPING (1) or clearing is required, or if the original tannage was not satisfactory for the leather required, it is not uncommon to retan the leather at this time. (306)

cleat. *See:* KERF.

cloisonné bindings. Enamelled bindings produced during the 11th century, mainly by Greek and Italian craftsmen. Cloisonné is a technique of surface decoration in porcelain enamel on metal, in which each color area is surrounded by a thin line of metal, flush with the surface of the enamel. Thin fillets of flattened wire are set on edge and soldered to the metallic base in the desired pattern. The cloisons, or cells, are then filled with a colored vitreous composition, fired, ground smooth, and polished. Cloisonné can be distinguished from CHAMPLEVE BINDINGS by the uniform thinness of the metallic lines. (124, 280, 347)

closed assembly time. The time interval between the completion of assembly of the parts to be adhered and the application of heat, pressure, or both. *See also:* ASSEMBLY TIME; OPEN ASSEMBLY TIME. (309)

closed bolts (closed folds; closed sections). Any fold in a section that is not perforated or cut during the process of folding, or before the binding process is completed. *See also:* BOLT. (256)

closed joint. That type of JOINT (1) which is formed when the covering boards are laced on, i.e., where the boards are right up to the backing shoulders. Also called "tight joint." *See also:* FRENCH JOINT; LACING-IN; SUPPORTED FRENCH JOINT. (12)

close formation. The closeness of texture and FORMATION of a sheet of paper, i.e., a sheet in which the formation is uniform and free from a WILD (1) or porous appearance when viewed by transmitted light. It is frequently the sizing or loading agents that "close" the sheet by filling the interstices between fibers. A well-closed sheet has more RATTLE and hardness, and generally greater opacity. (42)

cloth. A generic term for all of the fabrics employed in bookbinding and conservation. Cloth is made by weaving, felting, knitting, knotting, bonding, or crocheting natural or synthetic fibers and filaments, in various textures, finishes, and weights. It may be plain, filled, coated, or impregnated. Woven cloths, with the exceptions of certain "double warp" cloths, have a warp (the threads that run the length of the cloth over and under the filling), and a filling, also called the weft, running across the grain at right angles to the warp. Both are generally expressed in number of yarns per inch. Since the number of threads in the warp is generally greater than the filling, the strength of a cloth is greater in the direction of the warp (or "grain" of the cloth).

Cloth is made from a wide variety of animal, vegetable, and synthetic fibers. Animal fibers include those obtained from animal hair—e.g., wool— and those obtained from insects, such as silk. Vegetable fibers include vegetable hairs, e.g., cotton; bast fibers from the stems of plants, such as flax, hemp, jute, etc.; and fiber bundles, such as sisal, esparto, straw, etc. The fibers most often used in bookbinding are cotton, flax, and silk. *See also:* BOOK CLOTH. (52, 102, 341)

cloth boards. 1. An old term for PRESS-ING BOARDS used to create the joints of a case binding during the casing-in operation. 2. An obsolete term for the boards of a book. 3. A term sometimes used to indicate a book bound in cloth. 4. *See:* CLOTH-LINED BOARD. (256)

clothbound. A book bound in full cloth with stiff boards.

cloth-cased book. A case binding having cloth as the covering material. The term is usually restricted to an edition or library binding, particularly the former. (154, 339)

cloth-centered. A term applied to a type of duplex paper or board, one having a cloth core (or center), usually canvas, linen, muslin, etc., with paper laminates on both sides. It is used where great strength, resistance to wear, and folding endurances are required, as with large maps. (58, 156)

cloth graining. The all-over patterns imparted to cloth to achieve a certain effect. Cloth is grained or embossed, as it is also called, by means of heated flat embossing plates, when done by the piece, or by heated engraved rollers when done by the roll. Grain patterns include rib, wave, ripple, dotted line, diaper, patterned sand, morocco, sand, pebble, crackle, frond, and numerous others. (69, 341)

cloth hinges. 1. Cloth joints extending from the spine of the text block to the insides of the boards of the book, or between split boards. Such hinges are simply an extension of the spine lining fabric. 2. Any cloth or muslin rein-

forcement of the first and last sections which joins the endpapers to those sections. 3. The board-stiffened, cloth covered "lips" fastened into loose-leaf covers for use in conjunction with metal fasteners or posts. 4. Any cloth jointing used to bind in heavy inserts. (256)

clothings. The strips of leather, cloth or parchment (or vellum) which are glued to the spine of a stationery binding between the webbings, both to strengthen the spine and help maintain its shape. Also called "strappings." (82)

clothing up. *See:* CLOTHINGS; FIRST LIN-ING; SECOND LINING; SPINE LINING (1); TRIPLE LINING.

cloth-jointed endpaper. An endpaper that is reinforced at the fold by means of a strip of cloth. The cloth joint is used where reinforcement or extra strength is required and the appearance of the cloth strip is not objectionable. For maximum effectiveness the sewing to the text block should be through the cloth. The sewing may be concealed by inserting the cloth joint into a zig-zag; however, as this type of endpaper is utilitarian and used mainly for large account books, this is seldom done. *See also:* LIBRARY STYLE ENDPAPER. (343)

cloth-lined board. A board backed with linen or linen canvas. Such boards are used where additional strength is required but additional thickness is not desirable. *See also:* CLOTH-CENTERED. (58)

cloth printing. Book cloths decorated by letterpress, offset, or gravure printing. In the latter two processes, even full color photographs and artwork can be printed on a suitable cloth. The picture-cover bindings used by library binders are an example of cloth printing. (234)

cloth stiffened cover. A style of binding consisting of a cloth cover secured to the spine of a book and stiffened on the sides with thick paper or board inserted between the cover and the endpapers. *See also:* PAPER-STIFFENED COVER. (343)

cloth stubs. Linen or muslin strips bound into a book, usually during sewing, as a strengthening medium for heavy inserts.

cloth tooling. The process of tooling in gold on a cloth binding. As with leather, glair is required, and, in addition, greater pressure is required because the surface of cloth is harder, especially the surface of a filled cloth. Pyroxylin impregnated cloth or imitation leather sometimes has to be washed with methylated spirits before being tooled. (54)

cloth weight. The weight of a given cloth,

measured in ounces per square yard, or ounces per linear yard, depending on the cloth. Starch-filled book cloths range from 1.7 to 7.0 ounces per square yard, vinyl coated fabrics from 14 to 31 ounces per linear yard (with a per linear yard allowance of minus 1 ounce to plus 2 ounces), and proxylin-coated cotton fabrics from 5.0 to 28.5 ounces per linear yard. The Library Binding Institute specifications for pyroxylin-impregnated buckram call for a cloth of not less than 7.9 ounces per square yard. (209, 341)

cloudy (cloud effect). *See:* WILD (1).

club bindery. A fine hand bindery founded in 1895 by Edwin Holden, Robert Hoe, and other wealthy American bibliophiles, most of whom were members of the Grolier Club. The purpose of the Club Bindery was to provide American bibliophiles with bookbindings of a quality equal to those available in Europe, thus avoiding the delays and other inconveniences of having to send books to Europe to have them bound. William Matthews was given the responsibility of organizing the shop, and he proceeded to hire the Clubs' first craftsmen, Frank Mansell, finisher, and R. W. Smith, forwarder. Other craftsmen employed by the bindery included Henri Hardy and Leon and Paul Maillard, French finishers; Adolf Dehertog and Charles Micolci, a coverer and assistant finisher, respectively; Mary Neill, sewer; Anna Berger, mender, repairer, etc.; and others.

The Club Bindery exerted a considerable influence on fine binding in America; unfortunately, however, not even the wealthiest of the stockholders had the resources to supply sufficient work to keep the bindery going. Efforts to transfer ownership of the club to the employees failed and the Club Bindery went out of existence in April of 1909. (331)

c m pattern. The code name for a small pebbled pattern in a book cloth.

coal tar dyes. *See:* ANILINE DYES.

coated. Paper or board which has had its surface modified by the application of clay or other pigment and adhesive materials, or other suitable material, with the intent of improving its finish in terms of printability, color, smoothness, opacity, etc. The term is also applied to lacquered or varnished papers and book cloth, as well as other covering materials.

coated art paper. A coated paper particularly suitable for printing, especially halftones where definition and detail in shading and highlights are an essential consideration. It is usually a paper of good quality, with a high brightness and a glossy, highly uniform printing surface. (17)

coated cover paper. A paper made in heavy weights and used for the covers of pamphlets, catalogs, etc. It is usually coated on both sides and is available in white and colors, with a dull or high finish. Good folding strength is an essential property. (17)

coated one side. *See:* SINGLE COATED PAPER.

coating. The mineral substances used to cover the surface of a paper or cloth for the purposes of creating a new surface having certain desirable properties. This property in paper is usually that of printability, but may also be for purposes of decoration. In cloth it is usually used to increase strength and water resistance, but its decorative effect may actually sometimes be of greater importance. The coating material fills the interstices of the cloth or the minute "hills and valleys" which are present in the surface of even highly calendered paper. (143, 323)

coating clay. A CLAY used to coat paper. Coating clays are of a smaller particle size and higher brightness than filler clays. It is a refined clay, usually KAOLIN, that meets specifications. Freedom from grit, correct particles, good color and brightness, low viscosity, and purity of mineral type are among the requirements. (17)

"Cobb" paper. A paper named after Thomas Cobb, an English papermaker, who introduced it about 1800. The paper is thin, finely textured, wove, and generally somewhat drab in color, and subject to considerable stretching when wet. During the first half of the 19th century it was used extensively for the covers of "boarded" books, and large quantities were used for the endpapers of economy leather bindings in the last half of the 19th century. (94, 236, 371)

Cobden-Sanderson, Thomas J. (1840–1922). An English lawyer who left the legal profession to take up bookbinding, working for six months under Roger de Coverley before opening his own shop. Cobden-Sanderson produced some 100 bindings, and his work was generally considered to be superior to that of his contemporaries. His forwarding was excellent, and his finishing was skillfully designed and executed, and noted as much for its restraint as for its elaboration. He produced these bindings with the use of only a relatively few simple tools worked in intricate combinations. He designed his own tools, and, with the exception of sewing and edge gilding, did all of his own forwarding. Cobden-Sanderson signed his bindings with the initials C S and the date, usually on the doublure, a practice widely imitated since by craft binders.

Cobden-Sanderson's binding had a highly beneficial influence on the binding of his day. To a certain extent, he started bookbinding on a path away from the situation in which the vast majority of bookbinders seem unable or unwilling to consider new approaches, except within the narrow limits of accepted methods. His influence on his contemporaries was considerable, and it is not unreasonable to maintain that his influence is being felt to this day.

Cobden-Sanderson gave up his own bindery in 1893 to establish the Doves Bindery, originally for the purpose of binding the publications of William Morris' Kelmscott Press. He did no more binding from this time, but restricted his activities to creating the designs and supervising the work of the bindery. (2, 94, 236, 281, 347)

cochineal. A red dyestuff obtained from the dried bodies of the female of the insect *Dactylopius coccus.* The deep red color of the dye stems from carminic acid $(C_{22}H_{22}O_{13})$. Cochineal was used extensively in the 19th century in the production of red marbling colors and scarlet lakes. It is also used in the dyeing of wool and silk. (97, 235)

Cockerell, Douglas Bennett (1870–1945). An English bookbinder, first apprentice to THOMAS J. COBDEN-SANDERSON. Many of Cockerell's bindings are elaborately tooled with symmetrical arrangements of conventionalized flowers and leaves, sometimes within compartments formed by interlaced lines which often flow from the raised bands. This style, which he apparently originated, gives spine and covers unity, and shows that the designs were conceived essentially in terms of a book cover. His interlacing patterns usually have no loose ends, and his plant forms appear to expand. Small spaces are filled in with gold dots, and butting lines are strengthened by a thorn, often with a dot at each side.

Cockerell was not only a fine bookbinder but also performed a service in his teaching and writing, pointing out some of the destructive methods then being used by binders, such as excessive paring of leather and thinning of slips, headbanding with inadequate tying down, the use of acids on leather to create decorative effects, etc. He also called for sound principles in construction and the use of chemically and mechanically sound materials. He encouraged the use of native-dyed goatskins for covering, and did much to establish the use of the ZIG-ZAG ENDPAPER, which until recently was used extensively by craft binders. He also was aware of the merits of alum-tawed skin, and his use of it in rebinding manuscripts, and particularly his use of tawed goatskin on the *Codex Sinaiticus,* helped establish the reputation of durability which this type of skin enjoys today. He also promoted the use of rough edge gilding (*See:* ROUGH GILT).

Cockerell's publications included *Bookbinding and the care of books, Some notes on bookbinding,* and *Bookbinding as a school subject.* (94, 217, 236, 347)

Cockerell, Sydney (1906–). A British bookbinder and senior partner of Douglas Cockerell & Son, a firm established by his father DOUGLAS COCKERELL.

Cockerell has designed and fabricated marbling equipment, and has been largely responsible for the revival of the art of marbling paper. He is also the inventor of the pneumatic ram used in tooling, the ball bearing fillet, and the tract-guided fillet. In addition, he has contributed to the knowledge of book structure, e.g., the idea of using a free guard around the first and last sections of the text block and also the use of free guards around the folds of vellum sections.

He assisted with the repair and binding of the *Codex Sinaiticus,* and has repaired and bound several early manuscripts, including the *Codex Bezae.*

Cockerell is an honorary member of the Society of Scribes and Illuminators, a Fellow of the International Institute for Conservation of Historic and Artistic Works, and a Master of the Art Workers Guild. His publications include *Marbling paper,* the appendix to *Bookbinding and the care of books,* and *The repairing of books.* He has also contributed to several handbooks and encyclopedias.

cockle (cockled). 1. A wrinkled or puckered condition in a sheet of paper or board (or vellum) caused, in the case of paper or board, by nonuniform drying and shrinkage, or from heat and humidity, and, in the case of vellum, by humidity. 2. A condition of the paper in books caused by excessive humidity and wetting. Cockling in books is

An 1892 binding by Thomas J. Cobden-Sanderson on an 1841 copy of J. R. Lowell's
A Year's Life. Reproduced from *Bookbindings by T. J. Cobden-Sanderson,*
printed by the Spiral Press, 1969, for the Pierpont Morgan Library.
(18.3 cm. by 11.5 cm. by 1.5 cm.)

magnified significantly if the grain direction of the paper is not parallel to the binding edge. 3. A term also applied to book covers (boards) rising, pulling, waving or curling, and caused by incorrect grain direction of the covering cloth, board paper, or the board itself, or by the use of the wrong type of adhesive or too much adhesive. 4. A warty growth in sheepskin. (98, 139, 156, 335)

coconut oil. A nearly colorless, fatty oil extracted from coconuts of the palm (*Cocus nucifera*), or from copra, and used to make gold leaf adhere to the surface of the covering material before impressing the heated tool or die.

codex (pl. **codices**) **(caudex).** An ancient book composed of leaves of writing material fastened together so as to open like a modern book, as distinct from a SCROLL (1) or VOLUMEN, which it superseded. It was introduced originally in the 1st century A.D. The English word derives from the Latin *caudex* or *codex*, meaning a tree trunk or stem stripped of bark. Originally, the name was applied to two or more tablets of wood, metal, or ivory, hinged together with rings, the inner sides of which were covered with wax which could be inscribed with a stylus. Later on the term was applied to books of this format made of papyrus. vellum, or parchment. Although papyrus usually appeared in the form of a scroll, and parchment and vellum in the form of the codex, there was a brief intermediate stage, the papyrus codex. This came at a time when parchment was not yet fully accepted, partly because it was thought to be a somewhat vulgar material, and partly because, when the codex was new, it was not realized that papyrus was not really suitable to that format.

Scribes and bookbinders have long attempted to match the sides of materials forming the leaves of books. The early scribes were concerned with the arrangement of the sides of papyrus, which were different because of the placement of the strips, and therefore the orientation of the fibers, during manufacture. When the number of sheets of papyrus were placed one upon another with each one the same way up, and were then folded down the middle to make a section, the first half of the section had the horizontal lines uppermost, while the second half had the vertical lines uppermost. This method was sometimes adopted, whereas in other cases the sheets were alternated so that horizontal faced horizontal, and vertical faced vertical. In the case of vellum, the practice is to arrange the leaves so that flesh-side faces flesh-side and grain-side faces grain-side, in much the same manner as such papers as azure are faced light side to light side and dark side to dark side. Even modern day book papers have sides, a felt side on the machine-made papers and a wire side on hand-made papers. (94, 123, 192, 236, 365)

coffee. The common beverage obtained from the plant, genus *Coffea*, and used by some restorers to tint the leaves of books that have been washed and/or bleached, so as to tone them to the shade of those leaves that were not treated. (335)

cohesion. The union of the particles of one substance by meanes of primary and secondary valence forces. As applied to an adhesive, cohesion exists when the particles of an adhesive (or the adherend) are held together. *Cf:* ADHESION. (309)

coil binding (coiled binding). *See:* SPIRAL BINDING.

cold flow. *See:* CREEP.

cold glue. Synthetic adhesives that do not require heating and which effect adhesion simply by drying. Cold glues are being used more and more in bookbinding, particularly in library and hand binding. *See also:* RESINOUS ADHESIVES; FISH GLUE.

cold gold. *See:* GOLDMARK.

cold pressing. A bonding operation in which the parts to be joined are subjected to pressure without the application of heat. In hand binding, virtually all pressing comes under this definition, whereas in edition and library binding, some pressing operations require the application of heat. (309)

cold-setting adhesive. An adhesive that sets at a temperature below 20° C. (68° F.). Most of the adhesives used in bookbinding fall into this category.

collagen. The principal constituent of the fiber-network layer of hides and skins used in producing leather. Collagen is organized in long, wavy bundles which vary in diameter from about one to twenty microns. These bundles branch in a complex and random manner to form a three dimensional network upon which many of the qualities of leather depend, and it is this complex network of fibers which provides leather with its unique character.

Collagen is a protein of the sclero-protein class, which is the most important constituent of the connective tissue of an animal. The molecules (14 × 2900 Å) appear to comprise a triple helix of linear polypeptide strands, composed of glycine, proline, and hydroxyproline. When collagen is boiled in water, the strands separate and undergo partial hydrolysis, yielding gelatin. (291, 363)

collate. To put the leaves, issues, or sections of a serial publication or book in the correct order; to make certain that no maps, charts, illustrations, etc., are missing; to determine if margins are adequate for the desired type of sewing, as well as for trimming; to note tears, or other damage to leaves in need of repair; and to determine the general condition of the publication, including the paper on which it is printed, the grain direction of the paper, the presence of bled illustrations, and the need for pocket material, stubs, guards, etc., for the purpose of selecting the most appropriate binding style.

collating mark. *See:* BLACK STEP.

collation. 1. That part of the description of a book, other than its contents, as a physical object. Collation gives the number of volumes, pages, columns, leaves, illustrations, photographs, maps, etc., as well as the size and format. 2. The process of comparing minutely, page by page, line by line, or even symbol by symbol, either visually, or by means of electro, electro-mechanical, or chemical means, in order to determine whether or not two books are (more or less) identical copies or variants. (69, 156)

collet hammer. *See:* BACKING HAMMER.

color. 1. The multiple phenomena of light, manifest in the appearance of objects and light sources that are specified and described totally in terms of a viewer's perceptions pertaining to hue, lightness, and saturation for physical objects, and hue, brightness, and saturation for sources of light. The normal human eye is sensitive to a range of wavelengths from approximately 3.8/10,000 to 7.6/10,000 mm., with the longest wavelength being perceived as red, followed in descending order by orange, yellow, green, blue, indigo and violet. These are called Newton's *spectral colors*, i.e., they are seen when a beam of sunlight is split into its component parts, as it passes through a prism. Notwithstanding this separation, however, a precise limit for any single color cannot be made because the spectrum undergoes a continuous transition throughout the series. If the human eye perceives all seven kinds of light in the spectrum, and in the same proportions, the "color" seen is white.

The color of a particular object is usually contingent on the white light striking the surface of the object and being completely or at least partially absorbed in the surface of the material, with the remaining light being reflected from it. Consequently, when a person sees the color "red," for example, it means that all of the incoming wavelengths (white light) have been absorbed by the surface of the object viewed *except* those wavelengths which constitute the color we have designated as red. If the light reflected from the surface of the object is allowed to pass through a further colored layer before reaching the eye, such as, for example, a transparent yellow film, more light will be absorbed, and the result will be a mixed color, i.e., orange. This process is called "substractive color mixture," or color obtained by successively eliminating light of different wavelengths from white light.

Pigments, as well as dyes and inks, are mixed with one another to create new hues according to the subtractive system. In theory, any chromatic hue may be obtained by a mixture of the three primary colors. In practice, however, many hues can only be approximated by mixing primaries.

See also: COOL COLORS; FAST COLORS; FUGITIVE COLORS; WARM COLORS.

2. Pigment or aniline colors used on the edges of books or on endpapers for tinting or coloring purposes. 3. The suspension or slurry of the materials for use in the pigment coating of paper. (17, 140, 233, 234, 350)

colored brushed top. The decoration of the head edge of a book by means of coloring and brushing with a stiff brush. (343)

colored burnished top. The decoration of the head edge of a book by means of coloring followed by burnishing. (58)

colored edges. The edge or edges of a book that have been decorated with water colors or dyes applied to the edge or edges and usually burnished. The colors are generally mixed with thin glue and edge gilding size. The most commonly used colors are red, yellow, green, and blue; brown, black and pink have also been employed. If only one edge is colored, it is usually at the head.

Coloring the edges of books appears to be virtually as old as the codex itself, the earliest known example being purple edges on a 4th century book. Red, ochre, and yellow were often used in the 15th to 17th centuries, while solid red edges sprinkled with yellow were popular in the first half of the 16th century. Colored edges have been common to the present day in miscellaneous binding and from the late 19th century on edition bindings.

Although the coloring of edges appears to be purely for decorative effect, its actual function has always been to protect the edges from dust, dirt, and handling. *See also:* ANTIQUE EDGES; FORE-EDGE PAINTING; GILT EDGES; MARBLED EDGES; RED UNDER GOLD EDGES; ROUGH GILT; SPRINKLED EDGES. (161, 236, 335, 343)

colored endpapers. Generally, tinted endpapers made from handmade paper. Colored or tinted endpapers appear to have been first used sometime near the end of the 16th century. Some of the earliest examples were printed with small repeated patterns that sometimes require up to three woodblocks for their execution. Of these papers, probably the greater number are of Dutch or German origin, although many are

English. The Italian colored endpapers are generally very well done, often bearing small patterns devised on a geometrical scale. In the execution of these papers, the color was used in a very liquid form, producing a kind of blotted effect. In the 18th century these papers were also used for covering inexpensive trade bindings. (172)

colored inks. Inks of various colors used for both printing and writing. Numerous dyes and pigments have been used in the manufacture of these inks. Those made from pigment and vegetable colors were used for hundreds of years, but are rarely used today. Inks made from minium (red lead), red ochre (rubrica) or vermillion were used by the Romans, while in the middle ages verdigris or metallic inks (powdered gold or silver in a gum) were often used. From about 1600 to the time the first use was made of inks produced from alizarin or aniline dyestuffs (1861), natural indigo, logwood, cochineal, and similar vegetable pigments were commonly used ingredients in colored inks.

Inks made from synthetic dyestuffs, while inert in solutions of the dye and water, and therefore not harmful to paper, are not nearly as permanent as iron-gall or carbon inks, although they are more permanent than the early synthetic dyestuffs. (143)

colored paper. Paper colored on one or both sides during manufacture by means of coloring pigments. When its use is to be for cover papers, endpapers, etc., the shade may range from light to very dark; for printing purposes, however, the usual colors are the light shades, since a dark ink is not very legible on too dark a paper, and printing very light inks on dark paper is not generally practical as two impressions are usually required to obtain adequate opacity. Duplex papers are those with different colors on the two sides of the sheet. (204, 234)

colored paste-papers. Decorative endpapers produced by mixing color with paste and soap and spreading the mixture over two sheets of paper, which, while still wet, are pressed together. When separated, the transfer of color from the sheets produces a mottled effect on each. Colored paste-papers are sometimes used for covering books, although they have little water resistance unless waxed. Green, red, and blue are among the most commonly used colors. *See also:* COLORED ENDPAPERS; PASTE PAPERS. (172, 371)

Primary colors are: red, yellow, and blue. Secondary colors, derived from primary colors, are:

Primary Colors	Secondary Colors
red and yellow	orange
yellow and blue	green
red and blue	purple

Tertiary colors, derived by combining primary and secondary colors, are:

Primary Colors	Secondary Colors	Tertiary Colors
red and yellow	orange	
yellow and blue	green	citrine
red and yellow	orange	
red and blue	purple	russet
yellow and blue	green	
red and blue	purple	olive

colored printings. The name of an inferior quality of paper, containing a considerable percentage of mechanical wood pulp and used for the covers of pamphlets and similar publications. (156)

colored under gilt. The edge or edges of a book gilded over a coloring (usually red) of dye or water color. Pigment colors are generally unsuitable for this decoration. Colored under gilt is used extensively for Bibles and devotional works. (343)

color fastness. That property of a pigment or dye, or the leather, cloth, paper, ink, etc., containing the coloring matter, to retain its original hue, especially without fading, running, or changing when wetted, washed, cleaned; or stored under normal conditions when exposed to light, heat, or other influences. Color fastness in paper is measured with a fadeometer, and in cloth by a launderometer. *See also:* FAST COLORS; FUGITIVE COLORS. (17, 209)

colorimeter. An instrument for measuring or specifying color by means of comparison with synthesized colors, i.e., by reference either to other colors or to complex stimuli, not in general identical with the actual color stimulus, and giving results not independent of abnormalities in the color vision of the observer. The typical colorimeter has a built-in standard light source, three colored filters, photoelectric cells or phototubes, a standard reflecting surface, and, in modern instruments, photoelectric cells and electronic circuits to replace the human eye as the receptor. The results of a colorimeter examination are expressed as "chromaticity coordinates." (197, 233)

color lake. *See:* LAKE.

color reversion. *See:* YELLOWING.

comb binding. A form of MECHANICAL BINDING consisting of a plastic strip on the spine from which curved prongs extend. They are inserted into holes punched into the leaves to be held. The name derives from the resulting "comb" appearance of the binding. This type of mechanical binding provides a more-or-less solid spine on which the title of the publication may be printed. Its disadvantages, however, are many: leaves may be removed quite easily by unauthorized persons, and groups of leaves often slip from the grasp of the flexible prongs. In addition, leaves tend to tear from the binding because the large, usually rectangular, slots leave relatively little

paper along the line of the punched holes. (316)

combed edges. The edges of a book decorated with black, red, blue, and yellow colors, in the ratio of 1:2:3:4 respectively, in a combed, figure-eight effect.

combination oil tannage. A type of tannage, or process of tannage, in which the skin is first tanned with formaldehyde and is subsequently treated by the OIL TANNING process. Some CHAMOIS leathers are tanned by this method. (61)

combination press. A particular type of press, either manufactured commercially or homemade, frequently the latter, that serves more than one purpose, e.g., as a LYING PRESS that can be turned on its side and used as a NIPPING PRESS, or a press that serves as a STANDING PRESS, BACKING PRESS, or as a press for CASING-IN, having brass-edged boards built into both cheeks. (173, 231)

combination style. An old term used in America for a binding in which the forwarding was done as though for a hand-bound book, i.e., boards to be laced-in, followed by covering, but then having the cover (case) made separately. The case was then "hung on" the text block, the cloth joints were glued down and a lining paper was glued to the insides of the cover boards. (256)

combination tanned. A general term sometimes applied to a leather tanned by two or more tanning processes. Combination processes include CHROME TANNING followed by VEGETABLE TANNING, i.e., CHROME RETAN; vegetable tanning followed by chrome tanning, or SEMI-CHROME TANNAGE; tanning with formaldehyde followed by treatment with oil, or COMBINATION OIL TANNAGE. (61)

combined tannin in leather. Tannin that has combined so vigorously with the hide or skin protein that it cannot readily be removed by washing. (363)

combined water-soluble matter in leather. That material present in leather in a state of loose chemical combination with the hide protein and which can be removed from finely ground leather only by prolonged washing. (363)

comb marble. *See:* NONPAREIL MARBLE.

come away. The ability of a heated finishing tool to separate or "come away" cleanly during blind tooling without sticking to the dampened leather and thus damaging the grain surface. Rubbing the tool over the flesh side of a piece of scrap leather which has been

rubbed with a mixture of white wax and lard (1.25 parts wax to 1.0 part lard) facilitates clean removal of a tool. (97)

commercial binding. A term understood to mean the binding of both short and long runs of identical books largely by machinery, i.e., edition binding, but not including blankbook binding, pamphlet binding, or padding, in distinction from the binding of single books of dissimilar nature, such as craft binding and library binding. (81, 115, 320)

common binding. An English term for a quality of binding that includes sewing on tapes by machine, cloth joints, a canvas or sheepskin spine lining, strawboards, and a covering of sheepskin or buckram.

common calf (common sheep). A very simple style of leather binding, often not headbanded or backed, and without pastedowns or lettering on the spine. They were produced for the inexpensive edition or retail trade, particularly during the 17th and 18th centuries. The vast majority of the 17th century bindings were in full leather, as were those of the first half of the 18th; thereafter they were also bound in half leather. (237)

common carrier. An individual or firm that undertakes to transport books to or from a bindery or library on a commercial basis, and who is responsible for losses as prescribed by law. The majority of the library binders today either own and operate their own vehicles or arrange for transportation on a NON-COMMINGLED contract basis.

common marble. A type of thrown marble, applied to leather covers, and consisting of black and brown streaks applied by throwing or sprinkling. The black is generally applied first. (97, 152)

common red. A red marbling color prepared from a mixture of Brazil wood, nut galls, and sal amoniac (ammonium chloride) boiled in water. (97)

commons (common color). An obsolete English term for a grade of book cloth intermediate in quality between the cheaper linens and more expensive extra cloths and buckram. Commons were dyed before receiving the final coat of color. The thready appearance noticeable on linen-finished cloth was less apparent on commons because of the dye and additional coating. (256, 276)

compensation guard. A thickness of linen or paper, usually the latter, bound into a volume to compensate for the thickness of folded maps, charts or other bulky material within the text block, or pocket material, so as to incorporate such material without distorting the shape of the book. They are sometimes made by binding in a full section of blank leaves placed ahead of the bulky material, and then cutting out all except a narrow portion after binding. The more common method, however, is to bind in folded strips of guard paper when the book is to be sewn through the folds, or strips of paper when the book is to be oversewn or otherwise sewn through the sides of the leaves. (102)

compensation pad. A pad of waste paper, slightly thicker than the difference in thickness from the spine to fore edge of a sewn book (the difference in thickness being the result of sewing swell). The pad makes the book the same thickness from spine to fore edge and overcomes the problem of distortion when the guillotine clamp is applied during trimming of the head and tail edges of the book. (276)

complementary color. One of a pair of colors usually considered to be in extreme contrast to each other. Red and green, yellow and violet, and blue and orange are pairs of complementary colors. The complementary of a primary color is produced by mixing the other two primary colors, e.g., green (which is a mixture of yellow and blue) is the complementary of red. (233)

composition leaf. *See:* DUTCH GOLD.

compressibility. The decrease in caliper of a sheet of paper, expressed as a percentage, resulting from an arbitrary specified increase in load. The conditions under which the determinations are made must be fully specified. Compressibility of paper is of considerable importance in both printing and bookbinding. *See also:* BUNDLING (1). (17)

concealed binding. A term sometimes used to indicate a MECHANICAL BINDING concealed within a wraparound cover. (54)

concealed joint. *See:* INVISIBLE JOINT.

concertina fold. A method of folding a sheet of paper, first to the right and then to the left, so that the sheet opens and closes in the manner of a concertina. Also called "accordian fold," or "zig-zag fold." *See also:* ZIG-ZAG END-PAPER. (58, 278)

concertina guard. A type of GUARD (1) used in conservation binding. It is made of good quality paper (generally Japanese copying paper) and is used so that the adhesive applied to

the spine does not come into direct contact with the sections. The depth of each fold does not normally exceed ⅛ to 3/16 inch. The use of the concertina guard makes pulling of the book easier in the event that rebinding is necessary, and also reduces the possibility of damage to the folds of the sections. A forerunner of this technique consisted of loose individual guards around each section of vellum books. This type of guard is used only in the best conservation binding because it is difficult and time consuming (therefore expensive) to sew a book when using the concertina guard.

condensation. 1. A chemical reaction in which two or more molecules, e.g., of an adhesive, combine upon the separation of water or some other simple substance. If a polymer is formed, the process is known as polycondensation. *See also:* POLYMERIZATION. 2. The process of changing from a vapor into a liquid, as when steam condenses into water.

conditioning. A term which has virtually the same meaning as SEASONING, but, unlike that term, is generally considered to refer to the exposure of paper to an accurately controlled and specified environment for the purpose of bringing the moisture content of the paper into equilibrium with the surrounding atmosphere. Standard atmospheric conditions in North America are considered to be 50% relative humidity and 73° F. In other countries the standard calls for a relative humidity of 65% (±2%) and a temperature of 68° F. ±3° F.). Conditioning is of considerable importance for papers which must lie flat in sheet form, or which must give good register when printed. Unequal internal strains are set up when paper is dried on the papermaking machine, because the tension in the direction of the web travel, i.e., the MACHINE DIRECTION, produced by drying, is greater in the cross di-

rection. *See:* ANISOTROPIC BEHAVIOR. Since most papers are dried to a moisture content of about 3% (by weight of the paper), they tend subsequently to absorb moisture until the moisture content amounts to approximately 5 to 9% (depending upon the humidity of the atmosphere in which they are stored). This tendency is increased once the paper is cut, because cut edges are able to absorb atmospheric moisture faster than the surface of the sheet itself, especially when the paper is stacked in piles. When a stack of paper absorbs moisture, the edges, particularly those corresponding to the cross direction, will expand more rapidly than the center, which causes cockling. In like manner, a "spongy" effect may occur, due to absorption of moisture by the top surface of the upper sheets in the pile. This expansion may take place between the printings of a multi-color printing sequence, or when the paper is dampened as in the offset-litho printing process, with the result that the colors used will overlap in some places and leave gaps in others. Moisture absorption, particularly when the grain direction of the paper does not run parallel to the spine of the book, can cause cockling along the binding edge and waviness in the leaves, resulting in a book that will not close properly. The latter problem can sometimes be overcome, at least to a degree, by pressing the book in an atmosphere of low relative humidity, but the problem of cockling along the binding edge can only be overcome by a method of IMPOSITION which results in the grain direction of the paper running parallel to the binding edge. (17, 42, 144, 156, 276)

conditioning time. The time interval between the removal of the adherends from the conditions of heat, pressure, or both, used in accomplishing bonding, and the attainment of approximately maximum bond strength. (309)

CONCERTINA GUARD

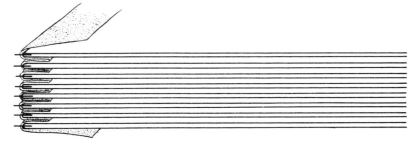

conjugate leaves. The leaves of a section which form one continuous piece of paper, i.e., leaves which are said to belong to one another. The form in which the sheet is imposed and folded determines which leaves are conjugate. In a sixteen-page section, for example, the first and sixteenth, second and fifteenth, etc., leaves will be conjugate. (69)

Conradus de Argentina. A 15th century German bookbinder, who produced bindings characterized by compartments adorned with well-designed stamps representing roses, fleur-de-lis, etc. Conrad also produced several of the ERFURT BINDINGS of that time. (94)

conservation. 1. The conscious, deliberate and planned supervision, care and preservation of the total resources of a library, archives, or similar institution, from the injurious effect of age, use (or misuse), as well as external or internal influences of all types, but especially light, heat, humidity and atmospheric influences. 2. A field of knowledge concerned with the coordination and planning for the practical application of the techniques of binding, restoration, paper chemistry, and other material technology, as well as other knowledge pertinent to the preservation of archival resources. Cf. RESTORATION.

consistency. 1. That property of a liquid adhesive that enables it to resist deformation. The property is not considered to be fundamental to adhesives; it is, however, manifest in the viscosity, plasticity, as well as other properties of the adhesive. See also: VISCOSITY COEFFICIENT. 2. The air-dry (or oven-dry) percentage by weight of fibrous material in a paper stock or suspension. (17, 98, 309)

contact bonding. An adhesive assembly process which utilizes adhesives that are dried to the condition where they display very little adhesive attraction to each other but still possess considerable cohesive attraction and strength properties. When two surfaces, for example, are coated with an adhesive and allowed to dry to the point where they no longer display TACK, they can be conveniently handled; when the two surfaces are then joined, however, they immediately attract each other and cohere, instantly forming a strong bond. If the two surfaces are allowed to dry for too great a time, however, the ability to cohere is destroyed, unless the adhesive is dampened with a solvent and then allowed to dry once again to the stage of non-tackiness. This type of adhesive is used extensively in attaching plastic laminates to surfaces and is convenient to use in other applications where immediate bonding is important. Such contact adhesives are usually based on synthetic elastomers.

contemporary binding. 1. A bookbinding produced immediately following the printing of the book; or, before 1700, a binding in the style of the decade or even the quarter century. 2. A new binding of an old book done in such a manner as to appear contemporaneous, to a greater or lesser degree, with the original binding, or one of the binding styles of the time when the book was published. Contemporary bindings of this type, while not creative or imaginative, are not unethical provided no attempt is made to disguise the fact that they are new bindings of older books. (373)

continuous guard. A type of guard to which the folios of blankbooks are frequently sewn, the purpose being to allow the book to lie very flat when open. The folds of the guard, which are about ½ inch deep, are double the number of the folios of the book. Unlike the CONCERTINA GUARD, the folios (sections) do not fit into the folds of the guard, but rest against the edges of the folds of the guard, with the results that the opposite edges of the guard become the spine of the book, much in the manner of the REVERSED-V GUARD. The continuous guard is usually made of linen.

continuous trimmer. A trimming machine which does not have to be stopped and started for each cut, as is the usual case with the typical guillotine cutter. It has a revolving cutting bed equipped with four faces, each of which has its own clamp. When one clamp is filled with books, it closes and the bed makes a quarter revolution carrying the books under the fore-edge knife. While the fore edges are being trimmed, the operator fills the next clamp, the bed makes another quarter turn, and the heads and tails of the books in clamp one are trimmed at the same time the fore edges of the books in clamp two are being trimmed. Another quarter turn brings the books in clamp one over a conveyor where they are released. (339)

conventional foliage. A form of bookbinding ornamentation, usually structured by means of individual tools, which is generally unrealistic but still clearly suggestive of foliage. (156, 250)

convex covers. Book covers that are convex in shape because the book is thicker in the middle than at the spine and fore edge. Very old books sometimes had covers that were made convex intentionally, apparently in the belief that they could hold and support the leaves better by conforming to the shape of the text block. The text block was curved because the early printers produced books that were somewhat swollen in the middle, the swelling being due to the sheets being dampened before printing so as to obtain a better impression. This resulted in the fibers of the paper in the center part of the sheet being stretched and separated by the force of the type. The fibers did not return to their original conformation following printing, resulting in a slight additional thickness of the paper in the print area.

cool colors. Colors which are situated in the green-violet half of the color circle, i.e., colors in which blue is dominant. Bluish grays are referred to as cool colors. See also: WARM COLORS. (233)

copal. A resinous substance obtained from the exudations of living trees in areas of the tropics, or from fossils, rendered soluble in alcohol or other organic solvents, and used in the manufacture of printing inks and certain varnishes. In its dry form, it is also used in the manufacture of gilding powders. (156, 264)

copolymer. A complex polymer, resulting from the polymerizing together of two or more different monomers or monomer combinations. A copolymer is a true compound and often has properties distinct from those expected of a physical mixture of the separately polymerized component monomers. An example of an important copolymer used in archival work is the vinyl chloride-vinyl acetate copolymer.

copperas. See: FERROUS SULFATE.

copper naphthenate. A green cupric salt of naphthenic acid and copper, with the combined fungicidal properties of naphthenic acid and copper. It is practically non-volatile and is used in a 0.1% concentration to control the growth of molds and fungi. There is some risk involved in its use because its presence in paper increases the liability of the paper to damage in a polluted atmosphere, possibly due to the catalytic action of the copper with regard to sulfur dioxide, resulting in the formation of sulfuric acid. (198)

copper number. A number expressing the

amount of copper reduced from the cupric to the cuprous state by a given amount of cellulosic material. It is useful as a measure of purity, particularly in relation to the strength and resistance to chemical degradation of paper and board. The copper number gives the degraded celluloses, and particularly those that result from bleaching. Although the copper number test is subject to reservations, it is generally agreed that a lower copper number enhances the chances of longevity of the paper. The test does not, however, apply to lignified fibers, and must be corrected for noncellulosic constituents. (72, 143)

Coptic bindings. Bindings produced by the Copts, or Egyptian Christians. The Coptic style of sewing is not unlike that of present-day machine edition sewing, in that it is also in the form of chain stitch linkings appearing as so many braids across the spine of the book. In addition, the covers of Coptic bindings were frequently sewn or laced to the text block by a number of hinging loops. Some Coptic bindings had wooden boards (from about the 4th century to the Middle Ages), but the majority had boards built up by layers of waste papyrus. They also had lined spines with flanges, as well as headbands. They were covered in leather as early as the 4th century and were tooled in blind, or by blind blocking, although decoration with inked and painted ornaments, as well as cut-out openwork backed with pieces of painted or gilded parchment were also used. Decoration consisting of openwork with parchment backing was executed before the leather (which was already cut to size) was attached, as was blind tooling or stamping when the fragile papyrus boards were employed. The tooling was in all likelihood done with unheated tools on moistened leather. Coptic bindings make up the oldest surviving "family" of leather bookbindings, and represent the ultimate source of all decorated leather bindings. (104, 158, 236, 347)

copy. 1. A single example of a written or printed work. 2. One of the theoretically identical specimens of a work which together comprise an edition, impression, or issue. Different copies may also be printed on different qualities of paper. When printed in a different format, they constitute different editions, e.g., a paperback edition, and generally follow the original issue. 3. An imitation or reproduction of an original work. 4. To imitate or repro-

duce an original work by printing, or some other means. 5. Subject matter, either manuscript or printed, that is to be put into type or plates. 6. The material to be reproduced by photographic or other means, as well as the result of some process of reproduction. (12, 274)

cording. The process of inserting and tying string or cord on hanging cards, calendars, catalogs, and other items, the material being either pre-punched or pierced with an awl. Cording is done either by hand or on semi-automatic or automatic machines. (58, 82)

cord marker. An old term applied to the marks made across the spine of a gathered book to indicate the positions of the cords, tapes or bands on which the book was to be sewn, and, in the case of sewing on recessed cords, where the sawing-in was to be done. (256)

Cordoban leather. Originally, a "leather" that was basically alum-tawed hair sheepskin, usually of a naturally white color but also dyed red. It was first produced in Córdoba, Spain, by a combination of Arab and Spanish craftsmen following the Moorish invasion of the 8th century. Sometime during the 14th or 15th century the method of producing Cordoban changed from tawing to vegetable tannage. Within Spain the name for all these materials, including CORDOVAN LEATHER, was *guadameci*. The terms "Cordoban," "Cordovan," and "Spanish leather" have been used in England for centuries to denote indiscriminately several kinds of leather, some imported from Spain, others from France and Holland, as well as some actually produced in England and called "cordwain," which is probably a corruption of the French *cordouan*. (351)

Cordovan leather. A soft, fine-grained, colored leather produced mainly from the SHELL of a horse butt, but now also produced from goat- and pigskin. It is a vegetable tanned and curried leather. The name derives from Córdoba, Spain, where the leather was first produced. Cordovan is well known for its non-porosity, density, and good wearing characteristics. At one time it was used fairly extensively in bookbinding, particularly in Spain. *See also:* MUDÉJAR STYLE. (291, 363)

cords. The cotton, hemp, linen, or silk cords or bands, of varying thicknesses, which extend across the backs of the gathered sections and are used in sewing books through the folds. They are either sunk into saw cuts in the sec-

tions, as in RECESSED-CORD SEWING, or rest against the sections to form the raised cords or bands used in FLEXIBLE SEWING. *See also:* BANDS (1); TAPES; THONGS (2); WEBBING(S) (1). (198, 236)

cord sewing. *See:* FLEXIBLE SEWING; RECESSED-CORD SEWING.

corduroy. A durable, cut-pile fabric having vertical ribs, made of cotton or plain and twill weaves, and made in various weights and colors. Corduroy was used to some extent in the early part of the 20th century as a covering material for blankbooks and other large volumes. (264)

cordwain. An English term for CORDOBAN LEATHER, or CORDOVAN LEATHER.

corium. *See:* DERMIS.

cork back. An imitation leather having a reverse surface of ground cork, producing the appearance of the flesh side of a leather.

corner(s). (1). The juncture of the two edges of a book cover at the fore edge and head and tail. Types of corners include the LIBRARY CORNER, ROUND CORNER, and SQUARE CORNER. 2. The cloth, leather, or other material on the corners of half bindings. 3. A CORNERPIECE (2). 4. *See:* BOOK CORNERS.

cornered (cornering). The corners of boards that have been rounded, or the covering material which has been formed around the rounded corner. Boards are generally round-cornered on a cornering machine, or with a curved chisel. (58, 139, 259)

cornering machine. A foot- or power-operated machine used for cutting the round (or other shape) corners, of paper, cards, book boards, etc. The machine employs a curved chisel for this purpose. (264)

corner knife. A type of knife used for cutting leather at the corners of a book in the process of covering. (115)

corner mitering. The process or operation of accurately joining the edges of the covering material of a book that has been turned-in at the edges of the board. The purpose is to have a minimum of overlapping of cloth, or a pared overlapping of leather or vellum.

Corner mitering has been altered considerably down through the history of bookbinding. One particular method, which was used well into the 16th century, involved cutting the leather so as to leave a tongue, with the cutting usually being done after the leather had been turned-in. In other methods, the leather was turned-in and then cut so that the vertical edges of the leather butted, or nearly so. An opposite technique was to cut the leather before turning it in, with the result that it overlapped a great deal more than is usual today, and left a small gap at the corners. This technique appears to have been in general use from the second half of the 16th century to the end of the 18th or early years of the 19th. Toward the end of this period the leather was pared thinner and the gap at the corner was considerably neater. During the last three-quarters of the 19th century the most common method of corner mitering of full leather bindings was to pare them diagonally and on a bevel before turning-in, so that the two edges overlapped to the extent of the bevel, coming together at an angle of 45° from the corner. (236)

cornerpiece (cornerstamp). 1. A bookbinding finishing tool, usually ARABESQUE, designed to be used at the corners of a leather binding, usually for the purpose of matching a centerpiece or other form of decoration. 2. Metal corners attached to a binding to protect the corners of the covers from damage. Removable pasteboard cornerpieces are sometimes used to protect the corners of books during shipment. (156, 310)

corner pull test. A test similar to the PAGE PULL TEST, except that the leaf clamping device is limited to gripping only the upper or lower corner of the leaf. This test is designed to determine if a leaf will tear before it can be pulled from the binding, and is used mainly in testing the strength of adhesive bindings.

corners. *See:* BOOK CORNERS.

corner tool. A bookbinding finishing tool used to make corner designs on a binding. It can also be used to make the center design, four impressions of the same tool resulting in a center pattern. *See also:* CORNERPIECE (1). (97, 261)

corrected grain. A leather from which the surface of the grain has been partially removed by BUFFING (2) to a depth governed by the condition of the stock, and upon which a new surface has been built by means of various finishes. *See also:* BUFFED LEATHER. (61)

corrected white. *See:* DYED WHITE.

correct pattern. The contour of a hide flayed so as to permit the tanner to produce the maximum amount of good leather. It is a standard pattern adopted by packers and tanners. (363)

corrugations. Wrinkles across the middle of sheets of handmade paper, caused by the paper being wetted during printing and not drying evenly thereafter. The sheet is stretched in the printing area by the force of the press, resulting in uneven tension between the printed and unprinted areas. *See also:* CONVEX COVERS. (154)

Corvinus bindings. Bindings belonging to Matthias Corvinus, King of Hungary (1458–1490) and famous as a patron of the arts. The magnificent library which he gathered together at the royal palace of Budapest contained manuscripts celebrated as the most marvel-ous masterpieces of Italian miniature painting of the Renaissance. They were executed by the greatest Florentine miniaturists of the day. These manuscripts, embellished with gold and colors on the inside, were adorned with equally superb bindings, many of which are in red velvet or morocco leather, decorated with gold tooling, inlays of leather of a different color, enamel, and cameos. Some were strongly reminiscent of Oriental motifs, while others were more Italian in character. Many manuscripts were also bound in brocade with bosses and clasps of silver.

In 1526 the king's library, which was estimated at anywhere from 1,500 to 3,000 volumes, was sacked by the Turks. (347)

Cosway bindings. Leather bookbindings produced in the usual manner, except that they have miniature paintings inset into their covers. They are named after Richard Cosway (c 1742-1821), the English miniaturist. Cosway actually had nothing to do with the execution of these bindings, as they were not introduced until early in the 20th century. They were probably the invention of the firm of Henry Sotheran, booksellers, or their manager, J. Harrison Stonehouse. The books were bound by Robert Rivière, in good quality Levant morocco, with morocco joints, watered-silk linings, and the miniatures painted on ivory, glazed, and insetted in the covers. (236)

cottage style. (cottage roof). A style of book decoration in which the top and bottom of a center rectangular panel slope away from a broken center, producing a kind of gabled effect. The spaces are filled in, at times, with French sprays and branches in combination with lacework, and sometimes with the same small tools used in the fan ornament. Although this style of decoration may have originated in France, perhaps as early as 1630, it is most characteristic of English binding of the late 17th century (c 1660) to about 1710. The style was still being used on pocket almanacs and devotional books as late as, or even later than, 1822. (124, 158, 172, 281)

cotton. A soft, fibrous, usually white organic substance that clothes the seeds of various plants, especially of the genus *Gossypium*. The cotton fiber resembles a flat, twisted tube, having a thin wall and a wide central canal, known as the lumen. Because of this wide lumen, the cylindrical fiber collapses upon drying to the form of a

CORNER MITERING

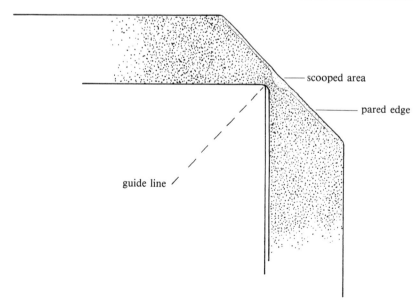

scooped area

pared edge

guide line

flat, twisted tube, somewhat in the shape of a corkscrew. The fiber length may be as much as 30 mm. and the width between approximately 0.01 and 0.03 mm., giving a ratio of length to width of more than 1,000 to 1. Cotton consists of more than 90% cellulose, exclusive of COTTON LINTERS. Since it is almost pure cellulose, cotton fibers are readily affected by acids and moderately strong oxidizing agents. Alkali compounds in moderate amounts and at normal temperatures, however, have little effect on them.

Cotton is used extensively in the manufacture of sewing thread, spine lining cloth, book cloth (including buckram), as well as higher grade papers and other products used in archival work. (143, 198)

cotton bating. A soft, fluffy cotton fiber, having a sized surface to hold the fibers together, and used as a padding medium for album covers, gold cushions, etc. (256)

cotton content. *See:* COTTON FIBER CONTENT PAPER.

cotton drill. *See:* DRILL (1).

cotton fiber content paper. Papers which are made from cellulose fibers derived from COTTON LINTERS, cotton or linen cuttings, and lint cotton. Flax is also sometimes included in this definition. Also called "rag content paper" and "cotton content paper." (17, 93)

cotton linters. The fine, silky fibers which remain adhered to the seeds of the cotton plant after ginning, including parts of the longer textile fibers, or "lint," as well as coarse, short fuzz fibers in most upland species of the plant. When purified, linters are used in the manufacture of paper. They can be used to replace from 5 to 35% of the rag content of fine papers with little or no loss of strength. Linters improve uniformity and the color properties of paper, and also provide a cleaner, bulkier sheet. Although linters do find use in papermaking, their principal use is as a raw material in the manufacture of cellulose derivatives. (17, 42, 72)

cotton parchment. A parchmentlike material produced by soaking cotton fibers in a solution of sulfuric acid and then rolling the fibers into sheets. *See also:* IMITATION PARCHMENT. (197)

cotton thread. *See:* SEWING THREAD.

cotton wool. A raw cotton wadding, usually referred to as absorbent cotton, and used as an applicator for stains, dyes, and other bindery operations. (237, 335)

couch. 1. The operation of transferring or laying sheets of handmade paper from the mold to the felts for pressing. 2. To press the newly made sheets of paper on the felts. 3. To press a sheet on the wire of a cylinder papermaking machine and transfer it onto the felt for pressing and drying. 4. To press water from a sheet on a couch roll of a FOURDRINIER MACHINE, or extra water by means of a suction couch preparatory to transferring it to a felt. (140, 197)

coucher. 1. An obsolete term for a large book meant to rest on a table or stand, especially a cartulary, register, or antiphonary. 2. The workman who lifts the newly formed sheets of handmade paper from the mold in which they are formed, and transfers them to the couch board on which he builds up a POST (1). (140)

couching. 1. *See:* COUCH. 2. A method of embroidering a binding consisting of gold threads laid on the surface of the cloth and held down by threads of bright red silk coming from the back of the material. Ancient methods of couching were numerous, with zig-zags, wave patterns, and all manners of diapers being produced by the position and arrangement of the stitches that controlled the gold thread. (115)

couch roll. A roll or cylinder on a papermaking machine the purpose of which is to press, i.e., de-water, or COUCH (4) the newly formed web of paper from the wire, and to transfer the web to the wet press for further de-watering. Couch rolls are of two basic types: the suction couch roll and the pressure couch roll. The suction couch roll is a heavy metal shell drilled with numerous small holes through which a high vacuum exists for the rapid removal of water from the web as it travels over the roll. The pressure couch roll consists of two rolls which apply pressure to the web to remove water. (17)

counter. 1. An automatic device for recording the output or activity of a machine or device. 2. The bed or base of a blocking press. 3. The interior white area of a type letter.

counterbalance. A device on a board cutter, or similar device, consisting of a bar or rod with a weight or weights that are adjustable so that they can increase or decrease the countebalancing effect on the blade. The rod or bar is an extension of the knife, and, by the action of gravity, works to prevent the knife from dropping and also assists in raising the knife following the cut. Although originally intended to enhance the usability of the blade, the counterbalance today is considered to be more of a safety device than a functional part of the cutting operation. (145)

counterchange. A decorative binding motif consisting of a cover broken into divisions in which there is a reversal of dark and light shading. If the cover is divided in half vertically, the left half of the background may be of a dark shade, and the right a light shade, while the panel in the center, also divided vertically, would have a light left and a dark right side. (94, 183)

countermark. A smaller and subsidiary WATERMARK found in antique papers, usually in the opposite half of the sheet to the watermark. It usually consists of the name or initial of the papermaker, the date, and the place of manufacture, although small devices such as a small post-horn or cabalistic signs have been used. The countermark was introduced in the 17th century. (69, 156)

countersunk. 1. A bookbinding having a panel sunk or depressed below the surface of the covering material, and designed to take an inlay, label, or the like. 2. A type of WATERMARK produced by pressing down the woven cover or face of either a mold or dandy roll. Also called "intaglio" (2). (12, 156)

cover. 1. The outer covering of a book placed on a text block to protect it both in use and storage, and, in many cases, to serve as a medium of decoration. A cover may be limp, e.g., a LIMP BINDING, which has no boards and the covering (usually vellum) is turned-in on itself and covered with the board papers; semi-limp (or semi-flexible), in which the boards are thin and flexible and are covered with leather or cloth and drummed on. *See:* DRUMMING ON. 2. A SELF COVER, as of a pamphlet; or a stiff cover, e.g., more or less rigid boards covered with leather, vellum, cloth, paper, or combination thereof. Stiff covers are usually glued down all over, turned in and covered with board papers. In edition and library binding, the term CASE (1) is more appropriate. 3. The outside leaf of a periodical issue. (131, 236 256)

cover boards. An obsolete term applied to two thicknesses of board glued together to give greater thickness (and strength) to the boards used for large blankbooks. *See also:* SPLIT BOARDS.

covering. 1. The material, such as leather, vellum, cloth, paper, or combinations thereof, which cover the spine and usually the sides of a book. 2. The process of pasting or gluing the cloth, leather, etc., to a book, drawing it over the spine and boards, and turning it over the edges of the boards at the fore edge, head, and tail of the book. (161, 172)

covering folder. A FOLDER (1) of bone, ivory, or wood, shaped generally like an ordinary folder, except for a slight arc cut from one edge, leaving a more tapered end with a narrow rounded tip. (115)

cover papers. A class of papers used for the covers of pamphlets (other than self covers), catalogs, brochures, or any other stitched publication, to provide protection during handling and (sometimes) to enhance appearance. They are made in white and a wide range of colors. The majority have plain edges; however, they are also available with deckle edges. Cover papers generally have good folding characteristics, and have rough finishes or are embossed with fancy designs. They are usually produced from chemical wood pulps, sometimes in mixtures with mechanical wood pulp, and, although many are made from pulps containing varying amounts of cotton fiber pulps, they have but little permanence. Various coated papers, including plain, heavy, plastic-coated, cast-coated, metallic, and cloth-lined papers are also used. Common basis weights of uncoated cover papers are 50, 65, 80, and 2/65 pounds (20 × 26 - 500), while weights of coated papers are 60, 80, and 100 pounds (20 × 26 - 500). Aside from folding endurance, desired characteristics include dimensional stability, uniformity of printing surface, and durability. (17, 86, 139, 234)

covers bound in. 1. A term used to indicate that the original covers of a book are used in the rebinding of the book. It may include the entire covers (including the spine), the boards and their covering only, or simply the covering of the boards. Sometimes this is called "rebuilding old corners." 2. The paper covers of a periodical issue, pamphlet, booklet, etc., included in the original binding because of their bibliographical or illustrative content. In this sense, the term applies mainly to library binding. (12, 156, 261)

cover title. 1. The title blocked on the original covers of a book or pamphlet, or a publisher's binding, as distinguished from the title blocked on the spine of a book by a bookbinder. *Cf:* BINDER'S TITLE 2. In terms of collation, a cover title is one printed on the paper cover of a work issued without a title

page. The paper is usually, although not necessarily, of a different stock and color than that used for the text. *See also:* SELF-COVER. (140)

cover (cloth) turned-in. The covering material of a book that is turned over the edges and onto the inside surfaces of the boards, the (uneven) edges of which are covered by the PASTEDOWN. Although the term is generally applied to edition and library bindings, books bound by hand are also usually turned-in. In library binding the customary turn-in is ⅝ inch, while in edition binding it is seldom more than ½ inch, and frequently less. (58, 209)

cowhide. In a strict sense, a leather made from the unsplit hide or the grain split of the hide of a cow; however, the term is sometimes used to indicate leather made from the hide of *any* bovine animal. The term is not applied to leather made from the flesh split of a cow or any other bovine animal. Cowhide has a slight grain or corrugation, and is a tough and strong leather, takes gold tooling well, and, when properly prepared, wears well. In addition, if it is of the best quality (and handled frequently), it is usually very durable.

Cowhide is not often used for covering books, except possibly very large volumes, such as blankbooks. Even the usual grain split is far too thick for the usual book, and, if pared to a thickness suitable for such a book, it loses a considerable part of its strength. *See also:* AMERICAN RUSSIA; IMITATION RUSSIA; RUSSIA LEATHER. (102, 129, 164, 343, 363)

c-pattern. The code name for a pattern in a book cloth formed by covering the surface of the cloth with small raised dots. Also called "crêpe." (256)

cracking. 1. A defect in a coated paper caused by the formation of fissures in the coating layer which then lifts from the base paper during printing, folding, or some other converting operation. Cracking is a bothersome and frequently encountered defect in art papers. 2. Fissures in the crease of a sheet of paper when it is folded or scored. (17)

craft bookbinding. A general term used since the 1890s to indicate the binding of individual books for specific customers. Such work included rebinding, the restoration and/or rebinding of rare books, and (sometimes) the restoration of works of art on paper. *See also:* EXTRA BINDING. (140)

crash. 1. A course, open weave, starched cotton material, sometimes napped on

one side, and used in edition binding for lining the spines of books. It is not used in library and hand binding because it is too lightweight and flimsy. *See also:* SPINE LINING FABRIC. 2. A cloth pattern peculiar to the buckram grades of book cloth, of a coarse, pebbled effect. (131, 173)

crayon-resist papers. Endpapers and other decorative papers produced by rubbing the paper with crayon over some roughened surface, and then covering the rubbings with a water color wash. The wash does not adhere to the areas that are waxed. (183)

crazing. 1. Fine cracks in an adhesive which may extend in a network on or under the surface or through a layer. It is caused by excessive shrinkage characteristics of the adhesive film, too rapid drying of the adhesive, or by flexing of a brittle adhesive. 2. The process by which yellow or transparent parchments often become whiter and more opaque when folded, producing irregular and disfiguring effects at the joints of vellum bindings. (291, 309)

cream split. A leather produced from a split sheepskin that is heavily glazed.

creasability. The ability of a sheet of paper or board to be folded without any cracks appearing in the area where the crease occurs. Creasability differs from BRITTLENESS, as the latter property involves a small degree of bending and is generally a manifestation of chemical changes within the paper. (17)

crease. 1. The impression made on a cover by the use of a heated finishing tool, of single or double blind lines. In full leather bindings, they are usually placed near the edges of the covers, while on half-or three-quarter bindings they are usually at the intersection of the leather spine and corners and the cloth or paper sides. 2. To make the band impressions distinct on the spine of a book. 3. The wrinkle, fold, or crimp in paper caused by folding. 4. *See:* SCORE. (42, 204)

creaser. 1. *See:* FOLDER (1). 2. A curved finishing tool having lines cut on its face, and used to impress an ornamental blind line or lines on a leather binding. 3. A machine used in edition and library binding for creasing the endpapers even with the back edge of the text block and sealing them down by means of heat. For this purpose, the cloth joint of the endpaper is coated with a heat-sealing adhesive. 4. A device employed in some folding machines for creasing coated papers. (94, 264, 322)

crease retention. The ability of a paper,

e.g., a GUARD, to remain folded after being creased mechanically. The term assumes that no adhesive is used. Crease retention and CREASABILITY are not the same. (17)

creasing strength. That characteristic of a sheet of paper or board which causes it to retain its tensile strength after it is folded or creased. Creasing strength is of particular importance in the papers used for endpapers. (17)

creep. A change in the dimensions of a material which takes place with time when the material is under constant load, following the initial "instantaneous" elastic rapid deformation. Creep at room temperature is sometimes called "cold flow." (42, 309)

crêpe. See: C-PATTERN.

crêpeline. See: SILK GAUZE.

cresting roll. A type of finishing tool, consisting of a ROLL (1) having two undulating and intersecting lines below and a series of tufts above. See also: HERALDIC CRESTING. (250)

crimping. The process of applying a series of fine creases or bender marks to the hinges of leaves of loose-leaf books, the purpose of which is to enable the leaves to be turned over easily and to lie flat. The lines of the creasing prevent undue bulking at the area of crimping. A sufficient series of creases closely spaced imparts a rolling effect ensuring a flexibility that is difficult to obtain by any other means. Cf: SCORE. (264, 316)

crinoline. A stiffened, open weave fabric, generally made of cotton, and sometimes used in edition binding as a substitute for CRASH (1) in lining the spines of books. (81, 196)

crocketed cresting. A binding decoration consisting of rectangular stamps ornamented with crockets, which are small curved designs, or with (roughly) triangular stamps, which, when placed together pointing outwards, present a cresting effect. (250)

crocking. The removal of a dye or pigment from the surface of paper, the coloring or finishing materials from the surface of leather, or the transfer of coloring matter from the surface of one cloth to another by the action of rubbing. (341)

crocodile leather. See: ALLIGATOR LEATHER.

cropped. 1. A book that has had too much of its margins trimmed, especially at the head edge, although not so much that the leaves are BLED. 2 A book that has had its edges cut beyond the shortest, or PROOF (1) leaf. 3. A photograph of which part of the top, bottom or

sides is omitted during reproduction, in order to focus attention on a central theme, to bring it into proper proportions for the space it must occupy, or to bleed it deliberately. (156, 234, 365)

cross direction. The direction of a machine-made paper, which is at right angles to the MACHINE DIRECTION, i.e., the direction across the direction in which the web travels. The cross direction of paper generally has less strength and folding endurance than the machine direction, although, in some papers, after aging, the opposite may be true. The cross direction has greater tearing resistance, and paper also expands more in the cross than in the machine direction when the moisture content of the paper increases. See also: AGAINST THE GRAIN; ANISOTROPIC BEHAVIOR.

cross laminated. A board or other laminate having one or more layers oriented at right angles to other layers with respect to the grain direction of the layers. Alternating grain directions of the laminate outward from the center layer is generally assumed. The built-up boards used in the binding of very large books are frequently cross laminated to provide additional strength and also to reduce the possibility of warping. See also: PARALLEL LAMINATED. (17)

crown filler. See: CALCIUM SULFATE.

crushed. 1. A leather which has been heavily pressed, causing the grain to be flattened, or crushed, thereby leaving a smooth, glazed, yet grained effect. Such leather has an unnatural appearance and is now seldom used in craft bookbinding. 2. A defect in a machine-made paper, having the appearance of a paper with a broken, mottled, or cloudy formation. It may be caused by: 1) running the paper web under the dandy roll while it is too wet; 2) running the web through the presses while too wet; or 3) running the web through the calender or supercalender while still containing too much moisture. Paper crushed at the dandy roll or in the presses results in coarse mottling, while paper crushed in either of the calenders has a finer mottling, often accompanied by blackening. (17, 83, 94)

crushed levant. A term sometimes applied to a large-grained LEVANT leather bookbinding having a more-or-less smooth polished surface. See: CRUSHED MOROCCO. See also: CRUSHED (1). (156, 264)

crushed morocco. A MOROCCO leather that has had its grain surface crushed to the extent that it is smooth. Crushing of this nature is done before the leather

is attached to the book. The characteristic high polish is applied subsequent to binding. Although a certain effect is attained by this process, to a great extent it defeats the original purpose of using morocco leather, i.e., its beautiful grain pattern. (12)

crushing machine. An early form of the NIPPING PRESS.

crushing plates. See: POLISHING PLATES.

crusting. The process of storing dry leather for conditioning or aging, during which time it absorbs water from the atmosphere until it reaches equilibrium with the relative humidity of its environment. During this period some of its constituents become more uniformly distributed throughout the thickness of the leather. In addition, greater fixation of the tanning materials may occur. (363)

crust splits. A type of leather which, after tannage, has not been further processed but has simply been dried. The term "crust" is used in this sense mainly in association with a leather such as sheepskin, while the term ROUGH TANNED is similarly employed with reference to cowhide. (61)

crust stock. Tanned skins awaiting final coloring or finishing. "Crust stock" is a relatively common form in which to ship tanned skins from the country of origin to another country for final processing. (306)

crusty break. A BREAK (4) of leather characterized by coarse, sharp wrinkles that are generally displeasing to the eye. (363)

crystalline cellulose. A segment of the molecular structure of CELLULOSE, in which all of the included parts of the individual chain molecules are arranged in a regular, three-dimensional spatial arrangement, as in a crystalline lattice, so that a definite x-ray diffraction is produced. (17)

C-stage. The third and final stage in the reaction of some thermosetting resins, characterized by the relatively insoluble and infusible state of the resin. Some thermosetting resins in this stage are fully cured. Also called "resite." See also: A-STAGE; B-STAGE. (309)

cuir-bouilli. A method of decorating a book utilizing the capability of a vegetable tanned leather to be molded when wet. After being thoroughly softened in water the leather can be formed or molded into various shapes, which, on drying, retain those shapes with a remarkable degree of permanence. The wet-mold leather can be more permanently set by drying it under moderate heat, the degree of rigidity obtained being determined by the drying temperature. A faster method, and one that produces extremely hard and rigid shapes, is to dip the molded leather into boiling water for anywhere from 20 to 120 seconds. This is the process that gave rise to the name "cuir-bouilli." Such a process involves the partial melting of the fixed tannin aggregates in the leather. At a temperature approaching 100°C. these aggregates become plastic and can be made to flow and redistribute themselves throughout the fiber network of the leather. On cooling, the fibers become embedded in what can best be called a tough, three-dimensional, polymer network or resin, somewhat similar to the materials made by condensing formaldehyde with substances such as phenol, urea or melamine. The leather actually sets so hard that some books bound in this manner required no boards. The decoration itself was executed by cutting the leather lightly while damp, after which the design was hammered in relief. The shaped leather was then immersed in boiling water, and dried, and the depressions were filled with molten wax so as to preserve the designs.

The molding of leather was known in Saxon times in England, and was widely practiced during the middle ages in both England and on the Continent. The motifs used were generally mythological animals and interlaced foliage. In the late 19th century interest in the molding of leather was revived and used extensively for many objects, including bookbindings. (94, 236, 291)

cuir-ciselé. A method of decorating a bookbinding in which the design is cut into dampened leather instead of being tooled or blocked. The design is first outlined with a pointed tool and then dampened. It is then brought into relief by depressing the background, usually by stamping a succession of dots into the leather very close together by means of a pointed tool. Certain parts of the design are sometimes embossed from the flesh side of the leather, and in such cases the decorating must be done before covering.

This technique of embellishment, which may well have been the highest manifestation of the medieval bookbinder's art, was widely practiced only during the 15th century and only in certain areas, principally southeastern Germany and in Spain. No English and Flemish and practically no Italian examples are known.

The finest cuir-cisélé bindings have been identified as the work of MAIR JAFFÉ. More recent (and excellent) examples were produced in France by MARIUS MICHEL, c 1866. (141, 236, 291, 347)

cumdach. A rectangular box, usually constructed of bronze, brass, or wood, often plated with ornamentation of silver or gold, and used for the storage of valuable and/or sacred works. (156)

cuprammonium hydroxide. A solution of cupric hydroxide in aqueous ammonium hydroxide ($Cu(NH_3)_4 \cdot (OH)_2$), which is capable of dissolving cellulose if the concentration of copper and ammonia are within given limits. The VISCOSITY (2) of a cellulosic solution in cuprammonium hydroxide is often used in quality control in the manufacture of paper. (17)

cuprammonium viscosity. The VISCOSITY (2) of a cellulosic solution, or a paper pulp in cuprammonium hydroxide under specified conditions, especially those of temperature, cellulose concentration, and solvent composition. Cuprammonium viscosity is used to determine the average molecular weight of the dissolved cellulose. (17)

cupriethylenediamine hydroxide. A solution of cupric hydroxide in aqueous ethylenediamine ($Cu(OH)_2 + xNH_2 CH_2CH_2NH_2 \rightarrow ([NH_2CH_2CH_2NH_2]_2 Cu (OH)_2)$. The solution will dissolve cellulose when the concentration of copper and ethylenediamine are within certain limits. The VISCOSITY (2) of a cellulosic solution in cupriethylenediamine is used in quality control in the manufacture of paper. (17)

cupriethylenediamine viscosity. The VISCOSITY (2) of a cellulosic solution or a paper pulp in cupriethylenediamine hydroxide under specified conditions, especially those of temperature, cellulose concentration, and solvent composition. It is used to determine the average molecular weight of the dissolved cellulose. (17)

curing. 1. The process of changing the physical properties of a resin or adhesive by chemical reaction, which may be in the form of condensation, polymerization, or vulcanization, and which is usually accomplished by the action of heat and catalytic action, alone or in combination, with or without pressure. 2. Methods such as BRINING, DRY-SALTING, PASTE DRYING, and WET-SALTING, used to prevent putrefactive or other damage to hides or skins before tanning. *See also:* DRYING (1).

curing temperature. The temperature to which an adhesive, or the adhesive and adherends, is subjected to effect curing of the adhesive. The temperature which the adhesive reaches in the curing process—i.e., the adhesive curing temperature—may differ from the temperature of the surrounding atmosphere—i.e., the assembly curing temperature. *See also:* DRYING TEMPERATURE; SETTING TEMPERATURE. (309)

curing time. The period of time during which a joint is subjected to heat, pressure, or both, in curing the adhesive. Further curing may take place subsequent to this time period. (309)

curl. A defect in paper or board, appearing as a curvature in the sheet, caused by "two-sidedness" of the sheet, which results in unequal shrinkage between the felt and wire sides when the paper or board is subjected to changes in relative humidity. In addition, fiber orientation has an influence on the direction and magnitude of curl. The result of curl is the tendency of the paper or board to form a tube (curl) at the edges, the axis of which is parallel to the machine direction of the material. (17, 42, 98)

curling. A warping or other distortion of an adhesive joint due to the penetration of moisture or solvents into the adherend surface, causing an unequal contraction and expansion of the adherends. *See also:* WARPING; WAVY EDGES. (222)

curl marble. A marble pattern consisting of red, blue, green, and yellow (or orange), laid down on the marbling size in that order, or, alternately, brown or red only for one-color curls, and curled by means of a frame which contains as many pegs as the required number of curls, turned two or three times in a circular direction. The curl pattern was in common use from about 1660 to 1870, especially in France, where it was much used for endpapers, but rarely on the edges of books. (217, 369)

curried leather. A leather which has been subjected to the process of CURRYING. CORDOVAN LEATHER is an example of curried leather.

currying. A process used in tanning heavy leathers, in which oils and greases are incorporated into the tanned hide in order to increase tensile strength, pliability, and water repellency. Currying also affects the finish and grain of the leather. The process is usually carried out in a drum (drum stuffing) using mechanical action. The oils used include mixtures of raw cod oil, paraffin, and beef (or mutton) tallow. *See also:* FATLIQUORING. (291, 363)

cusped edge stamp. A finishing tool used to produce an indented outline having the appearance of an oak leaf. The leaf effect is generally reinforced by impressing curved lines from the center outwards. Also called "headed outline tool." (141)

custom-bound. An obsolete term for a book which is bound according to specific instructions, rather than in accordance with general specifications. It was a term used principally in the library binding. *See also:* CRAFT BOOKBINDING; EXTRA BINDING. (12)

customer work. An obsolete term for work produced by the bookbinder for individuals, in distinction from work done for libraries. The term referred principally to library binding. *See also:* CRAFT BOOKBINDING; EXTRA BINDING. (241)

cut (cutting). 1. To trim the edges of books. *See:* BLED; CROPPED; CUT AT THE HEAD; CUT DOWN (1); CUT FLUSH; CUT SOLID (1); OPENED; OUT OF BOARDS; PROOF (1); TRIMMING (1). 2. A term sometimes applied to a book which has had its edges cut. 3. To cut the cloth, leather, vellum, or paper covering for a book. 4. Cutting so as to enable other operations to be carried out, e.g., a sheet imposed work and turn has to be cut in half before it can be folded. *See:* IMPOSITION. 5. The incision made in opening bolts of sections to facilitate tipping-in inserts. 6. The cut made in separating lifts (piles) of sheets for binding. (82, 154, 196, 256)

cut at the head. A book which has had its head edge trimmed, the usual interpretation being that the fore edge and tail have not been trimmed. (335)

cut away. Any part of a section that is removed and not replaced by a CANCEL. *See also:* CANCELLANDUM. (343)

cutch. 1. A packet of leaves in which thinly rolled and cut gold is first beaten in the manufacture of gold leaf. After the gold is rolled to a thickness of 0.001 inch and 1¼ inches wide, it is then cut into 1¼ inch squares. Two hundred ninety of these sheets are interleaved with 4½ inch squares of vellum or paper, forming the "cutch," which is secured with leavy bands of parchment. The name derives from the Latin *calcare*, to tread. *See also:* GOLD LEAF; MOLD (2); SHODER. 2. A vegetable tannin obtained from the heartwood of *Acacia catechu*, a tree distributed widely throughout the Indian Subcontinent and adjoining areas. Cutch consists principally of catechutannic acid (25-35%), catechin (2-10%), quercetin, and catechu red. When used alone, it produces a harsh leather, which often has an undesirable

yellow color. Although it has been used as a tanning material to some extent, particularly in England and Italy, the term "cutch" is better known as a tannin prepared from the bark of MANGROVE trees. *See also:* VEGETABLE TANNINS. (29, 175)

cut corner pamphlet file. A free-standing type of box, the upper rear corners of the sides of which are cut away to half its height, leaving the upper half of the back and the top open. It is generally used to house pamphlets and other such materials in the book stack. *See also:* PRINCETON FILE. (156)

cut down. 1. A term applied to a book trimmed to a size less than given in specifications. *See also:* CROPPED (1, 2). 2. The slipping or dipping of the plow knife when cutting the edges of a book, resulting in an irregular edge. 3. The bands, cords, or tapes on which a book is sewn "cut down" to the correct length for lacing-in or insertion between split boards. (256, 261)

cut flush (cut flush binding). A book that has no SQUARES, meaning that the leaves and covers are cut even, or "flush." In most cut flush work, trimming is done after the covers (which are usually, but by no means always, paper, limp, or the self covers of a pamphlet) have been attached. The trimming is generally done in a guillotine cutter. As a (very) general rule, no book with any degree of pretension is cut flush. (335, 339, 343)

cut flush, turned in. A book having the covering material on the spine cut flush at the head and tail edges but the cloth or paper covering on the sides turned over the edges of the boards. This technique necessitates the book being trimmed before covering. (343)

cut in boards. *See:* IN BOARDS.

cut-in index. *See:* THUMB INDEX.

cut on the quarter. A technique of cutting the wooden boards used in bookbinding. They are cut on the line of the medullary rays, thus reducing the danger of warping. (236)

cut open. A finishing tool having the design on its face defined by lines. (115)

cut out. A term sometimes used in edition and library binding meaning: 1) to cut the bolts of sections and remove blank leaves; 2) to die cut folded maps and inserts to allow for folding free of the binding edge; 3) to die cut board patterns to be used in protecting embossed covers when pressing; 4) to die cut panels to size for inserting; 5) to trim the turn-ins of covers; and 6) to cut out compensation material leaving stubs (compensation guards). (256)

cut out of boards. *See:* OUT OF BOARDS.

cut-out shapes (cut outs). 1. Decorative patterns, generally of a geometric shape, made of cloth, leather, paper, etc., and pasted to the covers of a book. *See also:* INLAY (4); ONLAY. 2. Special shapes of irregular pieces of paper or board cut out from printed matter by means of steel dies. (139, 183)

cuts for index. Thumb cut apertures made by hand or by a thumb cutter on the fore edge of a book. *See:* THUMB INDEX. (256)

cut size. A sheet of paper cut in the guillotine or rotary trimmer to dimensions of 16 by 21 inches or less. Size 8½ by 11 inches is the most common "cut size." (17)

cut solid. 1. The edges of a book which have been cut smooth and even, particularly at the head and fore edge. Library and edition bindings are almost always cut solid, usually by means of a guillotine cutter or three-knife trimmer. When edition bindings do have rough (deckle) edges, it is usually an affectation. Books bound by hand also generally have edges cut solid, but this was by no means true in the past. Edges cut solid make it easier to turn the leaves and also reduce the incursion of dust. 2. The faces of finishing tools that are solid metal, sometimes with line veinings, in distinction from tools CUT OPEN. (343)

cut stock. Materials, such as board, cloth, inlays, etc., which have been pre-cut to the proper size for a run of books. The term applies specifically to edition bindings. (269)

cutter-out. An obsolete term for the bindery worker who cut the leather covers for books. The job called for an experienced workman, one with a good knowledge of leather, and the ability to detect flaws and shades of color in the skins. (372)

cutter-perforating machine. A multi-purpose machine that can be used for slitting, both large- and pin-hole perforating, punching, tab cutting, index cutting, cutting and creasing, label punching, round corner and thumb-hole cutting, trimming, strip cutting, scoring, slitting, embossing, nipping, and blocking, by means of standard attachments and interchangeable tools. Such machines are generally hydraulically powered. (343)

cut through index. An INDEX used in stationery binding, e.g., a blankbook, that has all of the leaves of the book allotted to the letters of the alphabet in proportion to the frequency of their use. (276)

cutting board. 1. A wedge-shaped board of beech or other hard, fine-grained wood, similar to a backing board but with a square top edge. Cutting boards are available in various lengths, the most common being 8, 12, and 15 inches. The top edge is generally about ⅝ inch thick and the bottom edge about ¼ inch. They are used in the LYING PRESS when trimming edges with the PLOW, and also for edge gilding. 2. A specially constructed block about 3 feet square, composed of small blocks of hard wood set on end and glued together. The top is treated with oil to help keep the surface smooth. It is used as a block for cutting leather. (161, 183)

cutting machine. *See:* GUILLOTINE; THREE-KNIFE TRIMMER.

cutting plates. Millboard, zinc, or glass surfaces on which endpapers, guards, and similar materials are cut. Millboards are superior for such cutting as they do not dull the edge of the knife as quickly; however, they must be replaced more often. (133)

cutting stick. A length of wood, plastic, or soft metal, inserted in the table of a GUILLOTINE, against which the knife edge strikes. It is usually square, but in some machines it is round and can be rotated by hand or power so as to present a fresh surface after a certain number of cuts. A worn stick will cause the knife to chew the paper rather than cut it cleanly. (145, 338)

cuttlebone (cuttlefish bone). A piece of shell or bone from a cuttlefish, used to smooth and polish the mended edges of a torn leaf by removing the excess fibers of the paper used for the repair. (83)

cut to register. A watermarked paper cut in such a manner that the WATERMARK appears in the same position in each sheet. (17)

cylinder machine. A papermaking machine which utilizes a wire curved around one or more cylinders or molds that are partially immersed and rotated in vats containing a dilute stock suspension. The pulp fibers cling to the wire and are formed into sheets on the cylinders as the water drains through and passes out at the ends of the cylinders. The wet sheet is couched off the cylinder onto a felt held against the cylinder by a couch roll. Cylinder machines consist of one of more cylinders, each of which forms a sheet composed of the same or different stocks. The multi-cylinder machine forms webs which are successively couched one upon the other before they enter the press section. This allows for considerable variation in thickness and weight of the finished sheet, as well as for the formation of bristols. The press section and the dry end of the cylinder machine are essentially the same as those of the FOURDRINIER MACHINE. The cylinder machine was invented in 1805 by the Englishman Joseph Bramah, and was improved considerably in 1808 by John Dickinson. In England it is called a "board machine," or "vat machine." (17, 60, 180, 320)

D. The Roman equivalent of 500, although the symbol probably was not used by the Romans themselves. The Roman symbol for 1,000 was CIƆ, and early printers designated 500 as IƆ, which later became D. *See also:* ROMAN NUMERALS.

damask. 1. A decorative design of variegated patterns or crocheted compartments on a book cover. 2. A firm, lustrous fabric made with flat, conventional patterns in satin weave on a plain-woven ground on one side and a plain-woven pattern on a satin ground on the reverse side. It is usually made of cotton, silk, rayon, or combinations thereof. It has been used as a book cloth.

dammar (gum). Any of several semifossil or recent resins, principally of East Indian origin, but especially a soft, clear to yellow recent resin obtained mainly in Malaysia and Indonesia from trees of the family Dipterocarpacae (especially of the genera *Shorea, Balanocarpus* and *Hopea*) and used in the manufacture of PRINTING INKS.

damping stretch. The alteration in the dimensions of a sheet of paper when it becomes wet. Since paper fibers increase more in diameter than in length when moistened, the dimensions of the sheet will increase more in the cross direction than in the machine direction. This is one reason why it is essential that the "grain" or machine direction of book papers be parallel to the binding edge of the book. Handmade papers, when moistened, generally expand more or less equally in all directions, as these papers have no definite grain direction. (17)

d & f. In RULING, the abbreviation for downs and feints. *See also:* **f.**

dandy roll. A light skeleton roll or cylinder, covered with wire gauze, which exerts light pressure on the wet web of paper at a point near the first suction box. Its purpose is to mark the sheet (web) with a design carried on the surface of the roll, either to produce a wove or laid effect in the web, or, when letters, figures, or other devices are worked in wires on the surface of the roll, a WATERMARK. In the latter case, the roll is known as a watermarking dandy. Originally, the dandy roll was driven by the Fourdrinier wire, but

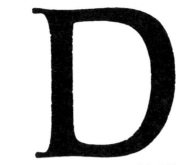

with the development of higher speed papermaking machines, it became the practice to drive the dandy roll separately in order to eliminate drag which would result in distortion of the watermark. Plain dandy rolls are now used extensively to level the surface of the web and improve or assist in sheet formation. *See also:* LAID MOLD. (17, 98, 189, 365)

dates, translation of. The conversion of dates, usually from the Roman into Arabic. Other than Arabic, the most common imprint date (or date of publication) to be found in books, at least those publication of the Western world, are the Roman numeral dates. They are translated:

Roman	Arabic
I, i or j	1
II or ii	2
III or iii	3
IV or iv	4
V or v	5
VI or vi	6
VII or vii	7
VIII or viii	8
IX or ix	9
X or x	10
XI or xi	11
XII or xii etc.	12
XX or xx	20
XXX or xxx	30
XL or xl also XXXX	40
L or l	50
LX or lx	60
LXX or lxx	70
LXXX or lxxx, also XXC	80
XC or xc also LXXXX	90
C or c	100

CL or cl	150
CC or cc	200
CCC or ccc	300
CD or cd, also CCCC	400
D or d, also IƆ	500
DC or dc, also I C	600
CM or cm	900
M or m also CIƆ	1,000

Hebrew dates found in imprints may be converted to the Christian date by consulting the Jewish encyclopedia under Calendar, Table I. Islamic dates may be converted by consulting the tables found in John J. Bond's *Handy Book of rules and tables for verifying dates with the Christian era,* 4th ed. London, 1889, pp. 228-250. The French Revolution calendar is given below:

Year

1	Sept. 22	1792
		-1
2	Sept. 22	1793
		-2
3	Sept. 22	1794
		-3
4	Sept. 23	1795
		-4
5	Sept. 22	1796
		-5
6	Sept. 22	1797
		-6
7	Sept. 22	1798
		-7
8	Sept. 23	1799
		-8
9	Sept. 23	1800
		-9
10	Sept. 23	1801
		-10
11	Sept. 23	1802
		-11
12	Sept. 24	1803
		-12
13	Sept. 23	1804
		-13
14	Sept. 23	1805
		-14
	Dec. 31	1805
		end

Months (12 of 30 days each, with five additional days)

Vendémaiaire	(vintage)
Brumaire	(fog)
Frimaire	(sleet)
Nivôse	(snow)
Pluvôise	(rain)
Venlôse	(wind)
Germinal	(seed)
Floréal	(blossom)
Prairial	(pasture)
Thermidor or Fervidor	(heat)
Fructidor	(fruit)

daylight. The maximum distance between the platen and the bed of a press when it is opened fully. Daylight is also defined as, or is an indication of, the maximum number of books, or books and pressing boards, that can be placed in the press at any one time.

deacidification. A term generally considered to mean the removal of acid from, or the reduction of the acidity in, a material, such as paper. The usual process of deacidification is to treat the paper with a mild alkali which initially neutralizes any acid present and is then converted into a compound that remains in the fibers of the paper to act as a buffer to neutralize any further acidity that may develop (usually as a result of exposure of the paper to atmospheric SULFUR DIOXIDE). High concentrations of strong alkalies are to be avoided because if the pH of the paper is allowed to rise to a very high level, i.e., 10.0 or above, and to remain there for any length of time, there is risk of oxidization of the cellulose under such alkaline conditions. In the usual case, however, even if the pH, immediately subsequent to acidification, is as high as 10.0, reaction with atmospheric carbon dioxide usually reduces it below that point.

The weakness of most deacidification methods is that slightly alkaline papers are immune to acid attack only for as long as the free alkali remains, and when this is neutralized the paper is again vulnerable. In order to prevent this, the amount of residual alkali remaining in the paper following treatment should be equivalent to at least 3% calcium carbonate by weight of the paper. *See also:* ALKALINE RESERVE; DOUBLE DECOMPOSITION; NON-AQUEOUS DEACIDIFICATION; VAPOR-PHASE DEACIDIFICATION. (31, 33, 39, 198, 265)

dead spots. The low-finished areas in an otherwise highly finished paper.

dead white. A neutral white, such as that of a paper having no perceptible tint.

deakins. Very small calfskins.

deckle. 1. The removable, rectangular, wooden frame forming the raised edge of the wire cloth of the mold used in making paper by hand; it confines the paper stock suspension on the wire cloth. 2. On the Fourdrinier papermaking machine, the arrangements along the side of the wire on which the papermaking stock flows, which prevent the stock from flowing over the edge of the wire. This type of deckle may be moving or stationary. (17)

deckle edge. The feather edge or edges of a sheet of paper formed where the stock flows against the deckle, or, in handmade papers, by the stock flowing between the frame and the deckle of the mold. A simulated deckle edge may also be formed by means of a jet of water or air. Handmade paper usually has four deckle edges and machine-made paper, two; however, a machine-made paper can be manufactured with four simulated deckle edges. An "imitation" deckle edge is one produced on a *dry* sheet of paper by such means as tearing, cutting with a special type of knife that gives a deckle edge effect, sand blasting, sawing, etc.

Early printers looked upon the deckle edge as a defect, and almost invariably trimmed most of it off before binding; however, collectors wanted to see traces of the "deckle" as proof that the book had not been trimmed excessively, or CROPPED (1, 2), as deep trimming was a notorious practice particularly in the 17th century (and even to this day). In the latter part of the 19th century, it became the fashion to admire the deckle edge for its own sake, and to leave books printed on handmade paper untrimmed. This left the book with ragged edges that collected dust, were unsightly (to some), and difficult to turn. In modern books, deckle edges are largely an affectation, and entirely so if the book is printed on machine-made paper. (17, 82, 94, 102)

decorated covers. 1. *See:* FINISHING (1). 2. In library binding, an illustration, design, or special lettering on the upper cover of a book. A decorated cover would also include books, such as paperbacks with illustrated covers when the original cover is attached to the cloth cover, with or without coating. 3. In edition binding, a design, illustration, or special lettering blocked or printed by offset on the book cloth. (131, 183)

decorated papers. Papers used for covers, endpapers, linings, portfolios, etc., and decorated in some manner. *See:* BRAYER PRINTS; CARDBOARD PRINTS; CRAYON-RESIST PAPERS; CUT-OUT SHAPES; FOLD AND DYE PAPERS; INK AND FOLD PAPERS; PARAFFIN PRINTS; PASTE PAPERS; PATTERNED PAPERS; PRINTED PAPERS; STENCIL PRINTS; STRING PRINTS.

decorative roll. Any patterned FILLET (1) that deviates from a plain straight line.

deerskin. A leather with a loose, open structure, made from the skin of deer, or other animals of the family Cervidae. It was used for bookbinding purposes as long ago as the 8th century. In the Middle Ages it was largely superseded by calfskin, sheepskin, and goatskin. (140, 291)

defective binding. Any imperfections in the paper, sections, plates, printing, cloth, leather, etc., that make up a bookbinding. (256)

defective sheets. Sheets of printed paper discarded in the process of binding because of paper or printing defects and/or binding spoilage. (256)

defoamers. Agents which inhibit the build up of foam, or which reduce foam or entrapped air by causing the bubbles to burst, thus releasing the air. Most commercial defoamers are mixtures of surface-active agents, hydro-carbons, alcohols, polymers, etc., to increase their effectiveness in multiple applications. Defoamers are used in papermaking operations. Also called "anti-foam agents." (17)

degrain. 1. To remove the grain from a leather, generally by pressing or rolling the hide or skin under pressure. *See:* CRUSHED (1). 2. SUEDE LEATHER finished on the flesh side, the grain layer having been entirely or partially removed, following tannage, by splitting or abrasion. (61)

degreasing. The removal of excess natural grease from skins, mainly sheepskins, but also other skins which may happen to be particularly greasy. Degreasing may be necessary because excessive amounts of grease in a skin may interfere with uniform penetration of tannins or dyes, cause difficulties in finishing processes, and/or show as dark, greasy patches in the finished leather.

A typical method of degreasing is with the use of paraffin. The well-drained, but still damp, pickled skins are drummed vigorously with about half their weight of paraffin oil (or kerosine, water, and salt), which loosens the grease. To aid penetration of the paraffin into the wet skin, a small amount of a wetting agent, e.g., 5% of a non-ionic wetting agent, may be added. The loosening of the grease is hastened by heating the paraffin beforehand. At the conclusion of the paraffin drumming, the now greasy paraffin is drained off. A considerable amount of greasy paraffin may still be held in the skins and can be removed by squeezing processes, such as SETTING OUT, or by centrifuging. However, as these processes are difficult and expensive to carry out, it is more usual to wash the skins in a 5% salt solution. Salt must be used as water alone would result in acid swelling. (306, 363)

degree of tannage. The number of pounds of tannin that are combined with 100 pounds of hide protein. (363)

delamination. 1. The splitting apart of one or more of the layers of a laminate due to failure of the adhesive, or cohesive failure of the laminate. 2. The removal of the laminating material from a document. Delamination of cellulose acetate film may be accomplished by soaking the sandwiched document in a solution of acetone, assuming proper tests have indicated that the ink on the document will not be affected by the solvent. Delamination is difficult to accomplish and generally more than one treatment is required to remove all traces of the laminate. *See also:* LAMINATION; SUNDEX PROCESS. (218, 309)

delignification. The process by which LIGNIN is removed from cellulosic materials by means of chemical treatment. The residue that remains consists of cellulose, hemicelluloses, and other carbohydrate materials. (17)

deliming. The process of neutralizing the alkali, e.g., calcium hydroxide, used in liming and unhairing hides and skins. Deliming, which usually takes place in conjunction with BATING, is accomplished by running the hides or skins in a drum or paddle to which has been added water and a proprietary compound consisting of a mixture of an ammonium salt (preferably ammonium sulfate) and proteolytic enzymes at a water temperature of 80 to 90° F. For more efficient control, and to produce a particularly fine grain in the leather, the ammonium sulfate (or boric acid), in the amount necessary to neutralize the lime, is added before the addition of the bating enzymes. (291, 363)

delivered flat. Printed sheets delivered to the binder unfolded, as they come from the press. The term relates largely to edition binding, but is also applicable in many cases to pamphlet and stationery binding.

deluxe binding. A somewhat abused term originally indicating a book bound by hand in leather, the implication being that superior materials and methods were used throughout. The term is also used by edition binders (or publishers) to indicate a book covered in a superior grade of cloth (or imitation leather), or a book supplied with a box or case. *See also:* EXTRA BINDING. (12, 264, 365)

deluxe edition. An edition of a work produced on a grade of paper superior to that of the standard edition, more-or-less expensively bound, sometimes printed with special type, and often limited in number. At times, however, the term is used merely as a selling term with little or no justification. (12, 140)

dendritic growths. Minute to relatively large discolorations in a sheet of paper due to oxidization of minute particles of metal present in the paper. The presence of the metal is generally believed to be due to the use of metal beaters. etc., in the manufacture of the paper. With the passage of time, irregular fern-shaped designs radiate from the particles. *See also:* FOXING. (140)

denier. A unit of fineness of silk, rayon, or nylon yarn, equal to the fineness of a yarn weighing 1 gram for each 9,000 meters. Denier increases with the square of the fiber diameter. (42)

denim. A firm, durable, twilled fabric, usually cotton, woven with colored warp and white filling threads and sometimes used in bookbinding for covering large books, e.g., blankbooks, where additional strength and durability are required. (183, 196)

density. In general, the ratio of the weight of a material to its volume, or the mass of the material per unit volume. Density should not be confused with POROSITY. *See also:* APPARENT DENSITY.

dentelle (dentelle border). An 18th century style of book decoration, usually in gold, consisting of a combination of elliptical scrolls of slightly shaded leafy character joined to clusters and borders of great richness, resembling lace, and pointing toward the center of the cover. ANTOINE MICHEL PADELOUP has often been credited with the introduction of the dentelle style, which actually took its inspiration from embroidery and the decorative arts rather than lace. Of the many binders who used this technique, the most notable were the Deromes and PIERRE-PAUL DUBUISSON. (69, 172, 279, 363)

dentelle à l'oisseau. DENTELLE decoration which includes birds in the design of the borders. The principal bindings featuring this motif were done by Nicolas Derome. *See also:* DEROME STYLE. (156)

dermis. That part of a hide or skin below the epidermal-dermal junction, consisting of a condensation of fibrous connective tissue which supports blood and lymph vessels, sebaceous and sudoriferous glands, hair follicles and their associated muscles, etc. In the grain layer of the dermis these fibers become very thin and tightly woven, and are so interlaced that there are no loose ends on the surface beneath the epidermis. Consequently, when the epidermis is carefully removed, a smooth layer is revealed, sometimes known as the hyaline layer, which gives the characteristic grain surface of leather. Toward the center of the dermis (or corium) the fibers are coarser and stronger, and the predominant angle at which they are woven can indicate the properties the resultant leather will display. If the fibers are more upright and tightly woven, a firm, hard leather with little stretch can be expected, while if they are more horizontal and loosely woven, a soft, stretchier leather can be anticipated. The interior of the dermis is generally the strongest part of the skin. (291, 306, 363)

Derome style. A style of book decoration practiced by the Derome family of France in the 18th century. The most famous of the family was Nicolas Denis Derome (active 1761-c 1789)—Derome le juene—who was also known the the "great cropper" because of his tendency to trim excessively. Nicolas Derome also used sawn-in cords in order to obtain the HOLLOW BACK, which prevents the spine of the book from flexing and thus possibly cracking the gold. He also achieved great fame by his use of the DENTELLE border, taking the dentelles of Padeloup as models. His also are made up of dentelle tools in combination, rather than in repetition, and are represented by symmetrical corner tooling of a very richly engraved floriated scroll work. An essential feature in Nicolas Derome's finest dantelles is a small bird with outstretched wings. *See also:* DENTELLE À L'OISSEAU. (154, 342, 363, 373)

designation mark. The letters which correspond to the initial letters of a title of a book, and any volume number, sometimes printed along side the SIGNATURE MARK to assist the binder in gathering. (156)

designer bookbinders. A British society of bookbinders founded in 1951 as "The Hampstead Guild of Scribes and Bookbinders." In spirit it succeeded the Hampstead bindery, which, about 1900, operated with the "Guild of Women Binders." While originally centered in Hampstead, London, the present society reached the point where no member lived there, and, as the calligraphic elements also declined, the name "Guild of Contemporary Bookbinders" was adopted. In 1968 the present name was assumed. One of the goals of the society is "to exert a progressive influence on the design and technique of bookbinding," (2(b) of the Constitution). Full membership is open by election to any amateur or professional bookbinder who has attained the required standard. Candidates submit samples of their work on which a vote is taken by the Executive Committee. Many outstanding bookbinders, including Edgar Mansfield (the first president), Ivor Robinson, and Bernard Middleton, have served as president of the society.

developed dyes. Dyes whose colors are developed after application by treatment with sodium nitrite ($NaNo_2$). Developed dyes are used on suede leathers so as to prevent CROCKING.

devil. A stick fitted with short quills set at a downward angle. The devil is the traditional implement used for frothing GLAIR. (261)

dew point. The temperature at which a vapor, especially in the atmosphere, begins to condense. *See also:* RELATIVE HUMIDITY.

dextrin. An intermediate product formed during the hydrolysis of starch to sugars. There are three classes of dextrin: 1) amylodextrin, which gives a blue color with iodine and is soluble in 25% alcohol; 2) erythrodextrin, which gives a red color with iodine and is soluble in 55% alcohol; and 3) achrodextrin, which gives no color with iodine and is soluble in 70% alcohol. All are soluble in water but are precipitated by strong alcohol. They are used as adhesives in the manufacture of gummed tapes and paper. (17, 198, 235)

dhawa (country sumac; Indian sumac). A tree (*Anogeissus latifolia*) common to many parts of India, the leaves of which yield a tannin used in that country. The tannin content of the leaves varies considerably, ranging from less than 30% to more than 50%, depending on the age of the trees when the leaves are gathered. The proportion of soluble non-tans is 10 to 13%. Dhawa is considered to be well suited for the tanning of light leathers, giving a soft

leather of a light color and firm texture. Dhawa is also the source of GHATTI GUM. *See also:* VEGETABLE TANNINS. (175)

diacritical marks. Marks over, under, after, or through various letters in the alphabets of several languages, designed to indicate the nature or stress of the sounds they represent. While lower-case letters having accent marks are cast as units, in display printing it is sometimes necessary to cast accent marks separately, i.e., the so-called floating accents. In library binding, diacritical marks are generally added by hand after the case has been blocked. Commonly used marks include:

acute	/
cedilla	ç
circumflex	∧
Umlaut (or diseresis)	..
grave	\
tilde	~

diaper pattern. 1. A gold- or blind-tooled decorative pattern, consisting of a motif constantly repeated in geometric form. The pattern may consist of figures such as diamonds, lozenges, or flowers, separated only by background, or by constantly repeating compartments, each filled with designs. 2. A publisher's cloth with a cross-hatched effect of minute lozenges or squares. Diaper cloths were popular in the late 1830s and 1840s, and have remained standard patterns on fabrics in one form or another ever since. 3. The uniformly patterned background for pictorial scenes in illuminated manuscripts. Its extensive use dates from the latter part of the 13th century. (83, 94, 156, 347)

diatomaceous silica (diatomite; diatomaceous earth). The siliceous remains of microscopic diatoms, which are aquatic plants. Diatomaceous silica is used as a dulling or flattening agent in coating and as a filler in paper. Also known as "infusorial earth" and "kieselguhr." (17)

diced pattern (diced binding; diced leather). 1. The decorated cover of a book tooled with cubes or diamonds. RUSSIA LEATHER is often "diced" and diced calf has been used frequently since the first quarter of the 19th century. 2. A pattern ruled or embossed in leather in the form of diamond squares. 3. A pattern in publishers' book cloth, in the form of a bold diamond, popular between 1835 and 1845. (140, 159, 261)

die. An engraved stamp used in embossing a design or letter in leather, or on cloth

or paper. *See also:* HAND LETTERS; STAMP (1) (139)

die cutting. 1. The process of cutting special shapes (cutouts) in leather, cloth or paper. The cutouts are used for labels, inlays, onlays, etc. 2. The process of lowering the background leather, leaving the cut out area, or counter, undisturbed and raised above the impression. (189, 316, 320)

Diehl, Edith (1876–1953). One of the foremost American women bookbinders. Diehl studied the craft in France, Belgium, and England—in the last named country under T. J. Cobden-Sanderson at the Doves bindery—and also with Sangorski and Sutcliffe's bindery. She opened her own shop in 1906, in New York City, and achieved her principal fame through her teaching. Diehl was at one time associated with the bindery of William E. Rudge. She is also the author of *Bookbinding; its background and technique* (1946). (347)

die sunk. A depression produced by the application of a die or block, either heated or cold. *See also:* BLIND TOOLING; BLOCKING (1).

diethylene glycol. A colorless and almost odorless chemical ($C_4H_{10}O_3$), miscible with water, alcohol, and chloroform, but insoluble in benzene and carbon tetrachloride. It is a solvent for cellulose nitrate, but not for the acetate. It is used as a softening agent for textile fibers, as a moistening agent for glues and paper, as a solvent for certain dyes, and as a plasticizer in some leather finishes.

diethyl zinc. An organometallic compound ($Zn(C_2H_5)_2$), that is readily volatile (B.P. 123° C. at one atmosphere). It has been proposed as a vapor-phase deacidifying agent, and gives promise of being effective; it leaves an alkaline reserve of zinc oxide in the paper, which not only protects against acid but is an effective fungicide as well. Treatment must be carried out in the absence of air or moisture, as diethyl zinc ignites on contact with air and explodes on contact with moisture. This requires that the books be absolutely dry before treatment; therefore they must be treated with the gas in a vacuum chamber and the excess diethyl zinc must be removed or neutralized before the chamber is opened. Treatment with diethyl zinc leaves the paper with a pH of approximately 7.5 and does not appear to have any adverse effect on leather or other book materials.

digester. A vessel in which pulpwood, straw, esparto, rags, or other cellulosic

Front Leaf   Back Leaf

The consular diptych of Philoxenus in ivory. Constantinople (?), A.D. 525.
From the Dumbarton Oaks Collection.
(33.3 cm. by 12.8 cm.)

materials are treated with chemicals and heat to produce the pulp used in the manufacture of paper. A digester is usually constructed to withstand elevated pressures and is made of materials designed to resist the chemicals used in pulp preparation. Digesters may be cylindrical, spherical, horizontal, vertical, stationary, rotating or designed to tumble. Most are stationary. A digester may be designed for batch operation, in which it discharges its pulp at the conclusion of a fixed cycle, or it may be designed for continuous operation, in which case it moves the raw material and chemicals at a fixed

rate from the charging end to the discharging end. (17)

diluent. A substance added to another, e.g., an adhesive, to reduce its concentration, or to an ink, to reduce its viscosity, and so on. Water is the principal diluent used in archival work. *See also:* EXTENDER (1); THINNER. (309)

dimensional changes in leather. The increase or decrease in the thickness and area of a leather due to increasing or decreasing relative humidity of the surrounding atmosphere. (363)

dimensional stability. That property of a paper, board, etc., which relates to the

consistency of its dimensions. The property is associated with changes occurring in a material due to changes in moisture content, the application of load, or simply with the passage of time. Dimensional stability of paper is important in printing, especially in multi-color processes, since papers with poor dimensional stability may give misregister. This is because, when they are run through the press, the dimensions change from one color run to the next. *See also:* CREEP; HYGROEXPANSIVITY. (17, 139)

dip. A term sometimes applied to a batch of books, which have been trimmed, jogged and clamped, and are then ready to be "dipped" for marbling the edges. (256)

diptych. An ancient hinged writing tablet consisting of two tablets of wood, ivory or metal, having wax in the hollowed inner surfaces, on which writing could be done with a stylus. The hinges were generally metal rings or thongs threaded through the holes. Near the outer edge on the inside of one tablet as a small trench designed to hold the stylus, which was a small bone or metal instrument pointed at one end for writing and flat at the other end for removing writing in the wax. In the middle of each inner side a small knob protruded to keep the wax surfaces apart. Ordinary diptychs were generally made of beech, fir, or citron wood, but those made for ceremonial use, or for important recipients, were often made of ivory, sometimes beautifully carved, and fitted with gold or jewels. The most lavishly embellished specimens belong to the Byzantine period, 530 to 560. Because they were small enough to hold in one hand, in Latin they were sometimes called "pugillaria." The diptych is interesting because it is both a manuscript and a binding. (12, 109, 373)

direct dyes. A class of ANILINE DYES, so called because they have such great affinity for cellulose fibers, i.e., paper and some cloths. While both these and ACID DYES are sodium salts of dye acids, direct dyes do not require the use of a MORDANT. Their shades are duller than those of either acid or BASIC DYES and they tend to have less tinctorial value than the basic dyes; however, they have the very important advantages of being much more lightfast than the basic dyes, and in certain instances, more so than even the acid dyes. (17)

directional ventilating power. The ventilating power of leather, which is greater in one direction than in the other, in that it allows water to migrate more freely from the flesh side to the grain side than vice versa. (363)

direction line. The line of printed characters in a publication when the abbreviated title of the book, i.e., the DESIGNATION MARK, follows the signature mark, or letter, printed at the foot of the first page of each sheet. It is intended to serve as a guide to the binder when gathering. Until the end of the 18th century the direction line, printed below the text of the page, and often between the text and the footnotes, contained the CATCHWORD, signature, press figures, and occasionally the volume number or part number. *See also:* SIGNATURE AND CATCHWORD LINE. (140, 156)

direction word. *See:* CATCHWORD.

directory paper. A lightweight printing paper made with a substantial proportion of mechanical wood pulp. The balance of the pulp is usually unbleached sulfite or semi-bleached sulfate pulp, although the paper is also made from deinked paper stock plus chemical wood pulp. Its essential characteristics are uniformity of basis weight, opacity, strength, and a finish suitable for high speed printing. Permanence is not considered to be an essential property. Usual basis weights are 18 to 28 pounds (24 × 36 − 500). It is used mainly for printing telephone directories, city directories, and the like. (17)

disc refiner. A type of REFINER consisting of one or more matched pairs of discs lined with a pattern of ribs. One disc rotates, while the other is stationary or rotates in the opposite direction. The paper stock flows from the center outward, or vice versa, and is macerated, rubbed, and cut (refined). The degree and extent of the refining depends upon several factors, including the pressure between the discs, the type of ribbing on the faces of the discs, and the consistency of the pulp suspension. (17)

disc ruling machine. *See:* RULING MACHINES.

disodium pyrophosphate. A chemical ($Na_2P_2O_7$) used as a mold inhibitor in paper. It is used in an aqueous solution of 1½ ounces of disodium pyrophosphate, ⅙ ounce of potassium ferrocyanide, and ½ ounce of soda crystals in 1 gallon of water. The purpose of the soda crystals is to prevent the paper from turning a greenish hue after treatment. The inhibitor solution may be made up with an addition of gelatin or glue, or other sizing material, if the

paper to be treated must be also sized. (198)

dividers. 1. The draftsman's instrument used in bookbinding for a variety of purposes, including measuring the distance between bands or webbings and cutting stock, patterns, etc. 2. The heavy sheets of cardboard or paper, frequently of cover-paper weight or heavier, used to divide the sections of a book when two or more sections, parts, or issues are bound together. (264, 274)

dividing into sections. A term applied to the process of dividing the leaves of a book to be oversewn into "sections" following the removal of the back folds. The normal thickness of each section is 0.055 inch; however, books printed on paper that is unusually thick or bulky are sometimes divided into sections 0.065 inch in thickness. (209)

divi-divi. The tannin-rich pods of a large genus of trees and woody climbers (*Caesalpinia*) native to the tropics and sub-tropics The most important is *Caesalpinia coriaria*. Divi-divi pods contain a high percentage of tannin (40-45%) which is easily leached out. It is one of the pyrogallol class of tannins and produces a light-colored leather. It is usually used along with other tannins, because when used alone it produces a leather that is soft and spongy in a damp atmosphere and which lacks pliability in dry weather. In addition, the amount of sugary matter present in the pods results in too rapid fermentation of the tan liquor. This may produce reddish stains in the leather, which can, however, be controlled to some extent by the use of appropriate antiseptics. Divi-divi is also used in leather manufacture as a dye. *See also:* VEGETABLE TANNINS. (175)

divinity bindings. *See:* ECCLESIASTICAL BINDINGS.

divinity calf. 1. A plain, drab, khaki-colored calfskin binding, popular in the mid-19th century for theological and devotional books. The style was particularly popular in the rebinding of books of an earlier time. The bindings were tooled in blind with single lines terminating in OXFORD CORNERS. The style sometimes also featured beveled boards and red edges. Sometimes called "Oxford style." 2. A leather used principally for the inside cover linings of limp leather prayer books and small Bibles. (69, 156, 371)

document parchment. 1. A paper made to replace the more expensive genuine PARCHMENT, and used for legislative acts, treaties, and the like. It is pro-

duced from selected linen and cotton fibers, and is almost always surfaced-sized with high quality animal glue or with special tub sizings. Document parchment is produced in basis weights of 48, 56, 72, and 88 pounds (17 × 22 - 1,000). The paper should be manufactured in such a manner as to insure maximum permanency and durability. 2. A vegetable parchment paper used for diplomas and documents. (17)

doeskin. 1. A soft, supple leather made from the skin of an adult female deer and used in England as early as the 16th century for covering books. 2. A soft, supple leather, usually white or cream colored but sometimes dyed, having a fine suede finish, produced from lambskin or sheepskin split and and tanned by a combination tannage, e.g., formaldehyde and oil, or formaldehyde and alum. *See also:* BUCKSKIN. (172, 278)

dog ear. 1. An oversize, unfolded corner in a publication caused when a sheet in a pile of paper having a corner turned under is trimmed in the guillotine. After trimming, the corner of the defective sheet extends beyond the trim size of the sheet when the folded corner is then unfolded. The dog ear is often useful in early books in determining the size of the leaf and the sheet because it reveals the size of the untrimmed leaf. 2. The turned-down corner of a leaf. *See:* DOG EARED.

dog eared. A book or other publication having one or more corners of the leaves turned down, generally by readers.

domestic goat. GOATSKIN, and, in general, virtually any skin imported in the cured state, i.e., dry-salted or wet-salted, and then converted into leather in the importing country. (363)

dominotiers. The name given to the earliest known "marblers" of historical importance—the dominotiers of France. The name derives from the Italian *domino*, a word which refers to the little cloak or hood, which was part of the working apparel of the early marblers. The dominotiers apparently were highly successful, as they were shortly granted royal permission to form a guild, along with the wood engravers. Those specializing in the making of marbled papers were called *marbreurs*. Unfortunately, because of its highly perishable nature, very little of this early marbling has come down to us. (217)

dongola. A term sometimes applied to leathers such as goatskin, sheepskin, or calfskin tanned and finished to resemble KIDSKIN.

dope. A solution of a cellulose ester, such as cellulose acetate or nitrate, or a cellulose ether, such as ethyl cellulose or benzyl cellulose, in a volatile solvent, such as acetone, amyl acetate, etc., and used as a coating for paper. *See also:* LACQUER. (17)

dos à dos binding. A form of bookbinding in which two books, usually small and frequently of a complementary nature, e.g., a Psalter and New Testament, are bound back to back so that they open in opposite directions, one of the three boards being the common lower board of both volumes. The spines and fore edges are opposed. Their upper boards are usually either embroidered or covered with gold-tooled leather. However the dos à dos binding is picked up, it opens at the beginning of one of the two books. (69, 156, 347)

dotted line style. *See:* PINHEAD STYLE; POINTILLÉ (1).

double coated paper. 1. A paper or board which has received two coatings on the same side with either the same or different coating materials. A paper or board coated on both sides is not double coated but is *coated two sides.* 2. A paper or board heavily coated, but not necessarily with two coatings. (17, 52)

double cord sewing. A book sewn on double raised cords, i.e., two cords set adjacent and almost touching, the sewing thread leaving and re-entering the section through one hole. Double cord sewing is substantially stronger than sewing on single cords and the sections are better supported against the pull of the thread where required most, i.e., at the point where the thread leaves and re-enters the section. *See also:* FLEXIBLE SEWING.

double covers. A term used in pamphlet binding to indicate two covers, the inner one of which is of the same type and color paper as the outer, but of a lighter basis weight.

doubled. An impression in leather, such as in blind tooling, which is said to be doubled when the tool has been twisted in the impression, or when a repeat impression does not fall exactly over the first.

double decomposition. A chemical reaction that takes place between two compounds, in which the first and second parts of one compound unite with the second and first parts, respectively, of the other compound. One of the compounds is usually insoluble. The principle of double decomposition has been used in deacidifying paper, as, for example, when a soluble calcium or magnesium salt is dissolved in water and the paper is immersed in it. After the paper has been dried it is then impregnated with a soluble carbonate, such as that of ammonium or sodium. Sodium carbonate and calcium chloride, for example, react to form insoluble calcium carbonate and soluble sodium chloride: $CaCl_2 + Na_2CO_3 \rightarrow CaCO_3\downarrow + 2NaCl$;

or, using calcium chloride and ammonium carbonate: $CaCl_2 + (NH_4)_2CO_3 \rightarrow CaCO_3\downarrow + 2NH_4Cl$.

The soluble sodium or ammonium chloride is removed by washing the paper with water, and it is important that the chloride be removed as completely as possible, as its presence in the paper is potentially harmful. The advantage of the double decomposition method is its simplicity, plus the fact that a much greater alkaline reserve can be deposited in the paper than is generally possible with most other methods.

double gold. 1. GOLD LEAF that is twice the customary thickness, or approximately 1/100,000 to 1/125,000 inch in thickness. 2. Regular gold leaf that is doubled upon itself before laying down. Double gold leaf, of this form, or as described above, is easier to handle and gives a brighter and more solid appearance. It is used mainly in edge gilding. (130, 335)

double headbands. Headbands for very large volumes worked on two lengths of thong, or other core. This type of HEADBAND usually appears in the form of a thicker band with a thinner band in front or above. (83, 152)

double kettle stitch. A KETTLE STITCH tied twice so as to provide additional strength. (335)

double mounting. The process of attaching one label over a larger one of a different color. It gives the effect of a colored border around the smaller label. (86)

double plate. 1. *See:* DOUBLE SPREAD (1). 2. A single unit of illustration extending across two contiguous pages, often printed on a folio so imposed that it becomes a CENTER SPREAD.

double register. Two registers in one book. *See:* REGISTER. (1)

double scored. Paper that has been scored along two distinct, closely spaced lines. Double scoring allows for a partial rolling effect of the leaf and thereby improves turning. *Cf:* CRIMPING. *See also:* SCORE.

double-shear stroke. The multiple movement of the descending knife of a guillotine. First, there is the downward motion through the pile being cut; second, the single-shear motion across the face of the pile; and third, the double-shear motion where the cutting edge of the knife starts to cut higher at one side of the pile and by a rocking motion becomes approximately parallel when it reaches the bottom of the cut at the table. The double-shear stroke thus cuts more like a scissors, with the knife edge entering each sheet in the pile at its side and gradually cutting across it. The advantages of the double-shear stroke are: 1) less power required to cut; 2) less strain on the machine and the knife; 3) a more perfectly cut edge; and 4) a smoother face to the pile. *Cf:* SINGLE-SHEAR STROKE. (145)

double-sixteen folder. A particular folding machine capable of folding two 16-page sections or one 32-page section. This folder can also be equipped to produce two 32-page sections, though of a smaller page size. Double 16s have three folding levels and four sets of folding rollers. The sheet is slit in half at the first folding level and each half is folded individually at right angles at the second level. It is folded once again at the third level, which has only one set of folding rollers; in this level, if the sections are to be outserts, each of the two folded sheets is folded in succession, whereas if the sections are inserts, both sheets are combined and folded together. A fourth folding level may be added to make the machine capable of producing two 32-page sections. *See also:* FOLDING MACHINES. (320)

double skin. *See:* PIPING. (1)

double slipcase. 1. A SLIPCASE in two parts, one of which fits into the other. 2. A single slipcase fitted inside with a divider which enables it to accommodate two books while keeping their covers from touching.

double spread (double page spread; double truck). 1. Two facing pages on which printed matter is spread across as if they were one page. When an illustration is printed this way two blocks are used unless the spread is in the center of the section, in which case it is a CENTER SPREAD. Also called "two page spread." *See also:* CONJUGATE LEAVES. 2. The application of an adhesive to both adherends of an assembly. (139, 309)

double-stitched binder. A commercial type of "binder" sometimes used for in-house repair of books. It consists of two lengths of heavy cloth sewn together along two parallel lines, the distance between them being approximately the thickness of the book to be recased. Each layer is gummed on the outside surface. The spine of the book is attached to one layer of cloth along with the new endpapers, while the other side is attached to the inlay and boards. The standard widths (between rows of sewing) ranges between ¼ inch and 3 inches. (138)

double thick cover paper. Two thicknesses of cover paper laminated together with adhesive to produce a very stiff cover paper. The more common basis weights are 100 pounds (two 50-pound sheets) and 130 pounds (two 65-pound sheets).

double-tone ink. A printing ink consisting of a mixture of an oil-soluble dye, a stable body pigment of a different color, and a medium. Such inks are used for the printing of halftones when a gravure effect is desired. The halftone is actually printed in the usual manner; however, sometime later overtones appear on the print, due to the dye of the ink spreading as a halo around the printed dots forming the image. Paper finish and tone also affect the result. (140)

double two sheets on. A method of sewing a book on tapes that is reputed to give still greater strength than the ALL ALONG method. Each section is sewn "two sheets on" with the preceding section, resulting in each section being sewn to the sections both above and below it. This gives greater holding power because two threads pass through each section; consequently, if one thread breaks the other still holds the section. Unless the first and last sections are sewn all along, however, the weakness of this method is that these sections, which receive the greatest strain when the book is being used —particularly the first section—are not held very securely. In addition, not all of the sections are held by the kettle stitches. (196)

doubling. The unintentional printing of a repeat image from a single form that is out of register. Doubling is particularly troublesome in halftone work because it adversely affects both tone and color values. It may be caused by several things, including rippling of the paper or premature contact with the form or offset blanket. It may also occur if sheets slip in the gripper or if the paper stretches during printing. Play in the press cylinders resulting in printback of ink picked up from the paper by the blanket can also cause doubling, as can the succeeding print-

ing unit being slightly out of register with the original print. (17)

doublure. 1. An ornamental inside lining of a book cover, which takes the place of the regular pastedown and fly leaf. It is usually of leather or (watered) silk, generally with a leather hinge and is often very elaborately decorated. The typical doublure consists of a silk fly leaf and a leather board covering, but sometimes both board covering and fly leaf are of silk; rarely, both are of leather. In a strict sense, however, the term refers only to leather linings.

The doublure was known in Turkey at least as early as the 14th century, but the earliest known European doublures are a binding of about 1550, in the British Museum. Their use was revived in the reign of Louis XIV (1643-1715), but they were not used very extensively until about 1750, after which they became very popular. Doublures have been used continuously since that time—more so in France, where they have always been more popular than elsewhere. The word itself is French, meaning "lining" or "doubling of material." Also called "ornamental inside lining."

2. In a very general sense, an ornamental endpaper. *See* PLATE X. (172, 236, 335, 343)

doublure margin. In a strict sense, the space on the inside of a book cover between the DOUBLURE (1) and the edges of the board, which, when there is no doublure, are simply the TURN-INS (1). (173)

do up. An old term of English origin for the processes of folding, stitching and wrapping, or binding books in cloth.

down at the head. 1. Sections which have not been fed properly to the head gauge of the cutting machine, causing an "up and down" appearance in the heads of the sections of a book. 2. Plates or maps that have not been placed up to the top edge of the leaf. (256)

downtime. The time during which a machine, department, or entire bindery is inactive during normal working hours, because of repairs, setting-up, lack of material, etc. Downtime becomes extremely costly in certain plants, such as paper mills, edition binderies, or binderies specializing in adhesive binding, because of the very high cost of the equipment used, as well as the cost of idle labor. (316)

drag. The pulling effect on the first and last sections (or leaves) of a book, caused by endpapers that have been attached directly to the sections (or

leaves), rather than being sewn to the tapes or to a guard which is attached to the sections or leaves.

draw. 1. The displacement of the cut sheets by the thickness of the guillotine cutting knife. Draw is a common cause of imperfectly cut paper. 2. The dragging action of the knife of a cutting machine, which tends to draw a book or pile of sheets out from under the clamp when cutting papers are heavily coated with clay. 3. The tension applied to paper between the sections of a papermaking machine, such as the press or drier sections. (17, 145)

drawer-handle tool. A finishing tool often used in England and the Netherlands during the second half of the 17th century. It was generally used in groups or sequences, and is so named because of its similarity to the handle of a drawer. (156, 347)

drawing color. The darkening of the impressions made in leather during blind tooling. This is done by means of a hot tool, a smoked tool (soot or lampblack [carbon] or carbon paper), or by wetting the leather with water or vinegar. (115)

drawing on (drawing around; drawing over). A term sometimes applied to the process of drawing the leather covering over the spine of a book, preparatory to turning and setting the head.

drawn flanks. The flank area of hides and skins that have shrunk and display furrowed lines on the grain surface over the underlying blood vessels.

drawn grain. A grain in a leather which shows an irregular pattern of creases or narrow grooves, produced by tanning the skin in such a manner that the main thickness has contracted relative to the grain layer, which is then fixed in a puckered or "drawn together condition." (61)

drawn-in (drawing in). *See:* LACING-IN.

drawn marble. A general term applied to a type of edge marble consisting of multi-colored scales. The colors used are black, blue, or green, yellow and red, put on the size in that order. The black is dropped on in such a manner that the first drop comes into contact with the edge of the second, the second with that of the third, and so on, so that a color ribbon is formed. The blue (or green) is placed on the size in unconnected drops on both sides of the black. The yellow is dropped on both sides of the black so that each drop of blue has a yellow center and the red is placed so that each drop of yellow has a red center. The colors are then drawn by a stylus in wavy lines through each

other past the black, producing white
lines between the colors. The comb is
then drawn across producing the
scales. Variations of drawn marbles, in
addition to comb edges, include the
"American," "bouquet," "peacock,"
and "snail." (264)

drawn-on covers (drawn-on solid). A term
applied to the binding of square-backed
periodical issues, pamphlets, and paperbacks, in which the cover is attached
by gluing it to the spine. When the endpapers are pasted down, it is said to be
"drawn-on solid." (156, 307)

drenching. An old method of deliming
and acidifying unhaired skins, in lieu
of BATING or PICKLING, by means of
immersion in a water infusion of fermented barley, sour dough, flour, or
the husks of cereals. The organic acids
(lactic and acetic) in the solution neutralized any remaining lime in the stock
and the particles of barley, etc., exerted
a cleansing action of the skins, absorbing dirt and greases, etc. The cleansing
action was very effective because the
enzymes produced by the bacterial cells
not only broke down the carbohydrates
in the plant materials to produce acids
but also digested the mucopolysaccha-
rides of the ground substance.

Drenching was often difficult to control, as the enzymes did not restrict
their attack to the carbohydrates either
in the solution or the skins, but often
degraded the fibers of the dermal network as well. In addition, too much
acid swelling was produced with resulting impairment of the skin structure and, therefore, of the quality of
the leather produced.

When drenching is used today, as in
certain vegetable tannages calling for
specific acid conditioning during the
early stages of tanning, weak solutions
of organic acids, such as lactic, acetic
and formic, are used in lieu of fermented cereal solutions.

Because of the gas bubbles of carbon
dioxide produced by fermentation,
which caused the skins to rise to the
surface of the paddle, the process was
also called "raising." (291, 363)

dressing. A general term applied to the
series of processes involved in converting rough tanned hides and/or
crust leather into finished leather. *See
also:* CURRYING; LEATHER DRESSINGS;
PURE DRESSED. (61)

dried-in strain (dried-in stress). That part
of potential strain or stress remaining
in machine-made paper subsequent to
manufacture. The property is caused
by tension or restriction of shrinkage
during drying as the web moves

through the papermaking machine.
Dried-in strain diminishes with time
and can be reduced rapidly in the
presence of high humidity or if the
paper is wetted. *See also:* ANISOTROPIC
BEHAVIOR. (17)

drill. 1. A strong, heavy, durable cotton
fabric in twill weave, used as a base
for certain grades of imitation leather,
and sometimes finished for use as a
covering material for very large books,
e.g., blankbooks. 2. To make a round
hole in paper for the purpose of overcasting or side sewing, usually by
means of a high-speed drill. The term
also applies to making holes in paper
for loose-leaf, spiral, or similar type of
binding. 3. A hand- or power-drill for
making holes in book paper, binder's
board, etc. (183, 256).

drive punch. A hollow steel punch used
for making holes in leather, paper, etc.,
for eyelets and snap fasteners.

dropping colors. The placement of MAR-
BLING colors on the size in the marbling
trough. Also called "throwing colors."
(327)

drum. A revolving cylindrical container
used in leather manufacture for such
operations as washing, tanning, dyeing,
fatliquoring, etc. It is usually equipped
with pegs inside for lifting and agitat-
ing the stock. The operation of tumbling the stock is known as "drumming."

drumming on. The process employed in
attaching silk doublures. A special
technique is required because adhesives
cannot be applied directly to silk as
they would penetrate the material. A
piece of silk larger than the space enclosed by the turn-ins and leather joint
is laid on a piece of paper the exact size
of the enclosure. The edges of the silk
are turned over the paper and glued
to the back. The paper is then glued to
the board. The silk is secured only at
the edges and is otherwise free (like a
drum), being drawn taut but not glued
down. If the DOUBLURE extends to the
very edge of the board, the enclosure is
filled in with thin board to bring the
board surface up to the level of the
turn-ins and joint.

dry. To change the physical state of an
adhesive applied to an adherend by the
loss of solvent constituents by evaporation, absorption, or both.

drying. 1. A method of preparing hides
and skins for storage and/or transportation so as to prevent PUTREFACTIVE
DAMAGE. Drying is employed principally in situations where insufficient
salt is available for WET-SALTING, or

where the cost of salt is too high to be
economical.

As bacteria must have a certain
amount of moisture or free water if
they are to attack a hide or skin, putrefaction can be effectively stopped or
prevented by removal of the water to
the point where the skin contains only
10 to 14% moisture. At this point the
activity of the bacteria ceases, and
some types are killed, while the others
dry up into spore form, in which they
can remain for long periods or until
there is enough water for them to again
become active.

Curing by drying requires considerable care, especially with thick hides,
because: 1) if drying is too slow, as
may be the case in relatively wet, cold
climates, putrefaction may occur before the moisture content is low enough
to inhibit bacteria; and 2) if drying is
too rapid and the temperature is too
high, part of the wet skin will begin to
gelatinize, which will show as holes in
the hide when it is subsequently brought
back to its normal moisture content.
Too rapid drying also makes the hide
hard and brittle and prevents drying of
the inner layers.

Drying as a means of curing is usually practiced in countries with hot, dry
climates. The skins may be: 1) ground
dried—by simply spreading them out
on the ground, sometimes on a bed of
twigs or stones. This is potentially dangerous because of poor ventilation on
the ground side and too high a temperature on the exposed side, plus contami-
nation with dirt; 2) sun dried—in
which the skins are hung or laid over
poles or wires in the sun. This method
affords better ventilation and quicker
drying, but may result in heat damage
or pole or wire marks, showing as hard
creases down the skin; 3) frame dried
—in which the skins are loosely
stretched out on frames, which are arranged so that they do not receive the
direct rays of the mid-day sun. This
results in less danger of heat damage
and a superior, flatter shape; however,
a skin shrinks on drying, and if it is
stretched too tightly on the frame, over-
straining may cause thinness and weakness; and 4) shade dried—where the
skins are dried in an open-sided, covered shed, designed to avoid the direct
heat of the sun but to allow good ventilation. *See also:* DRY-SALTING.

2. The process of allowing books to
be "set" after each operation, involving
the use of adhesives and/or seasoning
a book in a press after casing-in or
covering. (256, 291, 306, 363)

drying cracks. Fissures in the surface of a paper coating caused by an unduly rapid evaporation of the moisture in the coating.

drying memory. A characteristic of certain hot-melt adhesives which causes them to attempt to return to the shape or configuration they had when they set. When a hot-melt adhesive is applied to the flat spine of a book, and the book is subsequently rounded and backed, the "memory" of the adhesive tends to cause it to revert to the original flat configuration it had when it set, thus also flattening the spine of the book. This loss of round will eventually cause the binding to fail, i.e., the book will become loose in its case because of the strain of the backing shoulders caused by the loss of round.

drying temperature. The temperature to which an adhesive, the adherends, or both, is subjected in order to dry the adhesive. The temperature of the adhesive in process of drying may differ from the temperature of the surrounding atmosphere. *See also:* CURING TEMPERATURE; SETTING TEMPERATURE. (309)

drying time. The length of time during which an adhesive, the adherends, or both, is allowed to dry, during which time no heat, pressure, or both is applied. *See also:* CURING TIME; SETTING TIME. (309)

drying tunnel. A tunnel in which damp leather is placed for drying in a current of air, often under carefully controlled conditions of temperature and humidity.

dry open. A method used on combination case bindings that involves hanging the book in its case, gluing down the cloth joints with the cover boards held open, and allowing the book to dry in that position before completing the binding process. (256)

dry pressing. An obsolete term applied to the operation of pressing out the indentations made in paper by the type during printing, so as to make the printed sheet smooth. Pressing of this nature was done in a standing- or hydraulic press, the printed sheets being placed between sheets of hard-rolled boards. (138)

dry-rub resistance. The resistance offered by the coated or uncoated surface of a material to wear resulting from mechanical action on the surface of the material. *See also:* WET-RUB RESISTANCE. (17)

dry-salting. A method of preserving hides and skins for storage and/or transportation before tanning, so as to prevent PUTREFACTIVE DAMAGE, by curing them in a very strong solution of brine—i.e., about 30 pounds of salt for every 10 gallons of cold water, followed by drying, or by WET-SALTING, followed by drying. In both methods, the hides are subject to a thorough and uniform salt penetration and are then hung up to dry. Dry-salting substantially reduces the weight of the hides and therefore the cost of transportation that is incurred in wet-salting; it also reduces or eliminates many of the dangers involved in simple DRYING (1). Large numbers of hides, however, require great quantities of salt. In dry-salting, care must be taken that: 1) drying is carried out gradually and evenly; otherwise the hides may become too hot and partially gelatinize, which not only prevents drying of the inner layer and causes the hides to become hard and brittle, but also results in the gelatinized parts leaving holes when the stock is later returned to its normal wet condition; and 2) when the hides are to be tanned, they must be soaked in water until they have taken up as much water as they had before curing; dry-salted hides require more time and more careful soaking than does wet-salted stock.

Sodium chloride (NaCl) is the most commonly used salt for this process, but a salt "earth" known as KHARI, is actually to be preferred because it contains about 60% sodium sulfate ($Na_2 SO_4$), 20% magnesium sulfate ($Mg SO_4$) and 5% sodium chloride, and is less hygroscopic than common salt. It is more suitable for the hot, humid areas during the rainy seasons, from which most dry-salted hides are prepared. (248, 291, 363)

dry size. A powdered size used in gold-tooling suede leathers, velvet, silk, and also cameo papers. *See also:* ALBUMEN; BLOCKING POWDER.

dry stamping. A technique used in the production of multi-colored paste patterns for end- and other decorative papers. Colored paste is first brushed over the surface of the paper, the paste brush then being drawn from top to bottom of the sheet in regular strokes, leaving a uniform layer of color on which parallel brush marks are faintly discernible. While the surface is still wet, a dry printing implement is pressed on the wet color. When it is removed, some of the color adheres to it, leaving a faint unit on the paper of a lighter color than the remaining background. An engraved brayer is also used at times to create a continuous design. (86)

dry strength. The resistance to failure of an adhesive joint measured immediately after drying under specified conditions. *See also:* WET STRENGTH. (309)

dry tack. That characteristic of some adhesives, and especially nonvulcanizing rubber adhesives, to adhere to themselves during the period in which volatile constituents are evaporating, even though they may appear to be dry. Also called "aggressive tack." (309)

dubbin. A paste prepared from cod oil and tallow, the proportions of which vary according to the time of year—in winter generally two parts oil to one of tallow, and the reverse in the summer. There are two types of tallow in general use, one of which is mutton (melting point 40-45° C.), and the other beef (melting point 35-40° C.). Dubbin is used to incorporate oil into some tanned leathers in the STUFFING (2) or CURRYING processes. (306)

Dubuisson, Pierre-Paul (fl 1746–1762). An 18th century French bookbinder, who succeeded ANTOINE MICHEL PADELOUP as royal binder. Dubuisson excelled in the creation of dentelles similar to those of the Deromes, and was an accomplished heraldic designer as well as bookbinder and gilder. He, and his father, René, specialized in the binding of almanacs, devising the shortcut of decorating their covers with well-designed engraved plaques designed to be used in a press, instead of working with individual tools. (94, 347)

duck. A plain, closely woven, durable fabric, now usually made from cotton. It is woven in various weights and used for covering large, heavy books, especially blankbooks, and other large stationery bindings. (264)

dull-coated. A paper having a coated surface that is low in gloss. It is usually a free sheet base stock coated two sides with calcium carbonate or blanc fixe, and finished with a flat or smooth surface offering minimum gloss or glare. It is made to standard book sizes and weight, and is suitable for printing fine halftones. (17, 156)

dull gilt. The edges of a book that have been gilt and then burnished through thin paper, producing a solid, uniformly dull metallic surface. *See also:* GILT EDGES. (154, 335)

dumb. A more-or-less obsolete term used in lieu of "blind" with reference to blind printing, blind tooling, blind perforating, etc. (256)

dummy. 1. A made-up text block, generally of blank leaves, sewn and trimmed but not cased or covered and meant to represent the bulk of a forthcoming publication. 2. The layout of a forth-coming book, including the actual arrangement of the printed matter, specifications for type, illustrations, etc. 3. A piece of leather or cloth mounted on a board to show the exact size and lettering of a publication, usually a periodical. *See also:* RUB (1). (129, 139, 156, 234)

duodecimo. *See:* TWELVEMO.

duodo bindings. Bindings executed by Parisian gilders for Pietro Duodo, Venetian ambassador to Henri IV of France, 1594–1597. The distinctive feature of his bindings (and apparently most of his library consisted of small books similarly bound) was rows of laurel wreaths enclosing various small flowers, the central wreath enclosing his arms. This style was imitated by English binders of the early 18th century and by French binders in the late 19th century. (140, 347)

duplex. 1. A term used with reference to the texture, finish, or color of a paper. A *duplex texture* refers to a paper that may be smooth on one side and rough on the other, while a *duplex finish* refers to a paper that may have a linen finish on one side and a burlap finish on the other, and so on. A *duplex color* refers to a paper that is stained on one side only, or that is colored with different colors on either side. A duplex color may also be obtained by laminating together two papers of different colors. 2. A general term applied to a paper or board with two or more plies. (17)

duplex book trimmer. A type of cutting machine having two trimming knives parallel to each other on opposite sides above a central cutting table. The table consists of a cutting block equipped to clamp the pile firmly. Two piles of books, each 5 to 6 inches high, are placed spine to spine against the gauges. This brings the fore edges of each pile on opposite sides at the table and under the knives. After cutting the fore edges, the other edges of the book are brought into position by giving the table a quarter turn. This also changes the position of the knives on the knife-bars above, drawing them closer for trimming the heads and tails of both piles simultaneously. *See also:* THREE-KNIFE TRIMMER. (142)

duplex paper. *See:* DUPLEX. (1)

durability (of paper). The degree to which a paper retains its original strength properties while at the same time being relatively heavily used, as a manuscript or book. Realistically, the expression implies a paper which has a high initial strength, e.g., a paper carefully produced from cotton fibers, rags, or a high grade chemical wood pulp, as opposed to one produced from a combination of chemical and mechanical wood pulps, for example, which has relatively little initial strength.

Some 80 years subsequent to the development of the (Fourdrinier) papermaking machine, there was the beginning of a widespread concern over the relatively rapid deterioration of paper, and in the years between 1885 and 1930, various governmental and other groups, such as the United States Department of Agriculture, the German government, the Royal Society of Arts (Great Britain), and the Library Association of Great Britain, investigated the problem. The earliest of these investigations focused attention on the *method* of paper manufacture; only much later did it become apparent that the *materials* used in making paper, the *care* taken in stock preparation, and the *sizing* and *bleaching* agents utilized also had to be considered.

Research into the qualities (both durability and permanence) of paper has been fairly extensive in recent decades. The overall collective results of this research would seem to indicate that the retardation of paper deterioration requires: 1) careful control of stock preparation at every stage of manufacture, and avoidance of excessive beating of the fibers, which shortens and therefore weakens the fibers and also sometimes prevents proper felting during sheet formation. In addition, impurities, inherent in the stock and/or incorporated from equipment, e.g., copper or iron, must be avoided or removed insofar as possible; 2) great care taken to remove the chemicals used in pulping, e.g., sulfates and sulfites, so as to avoid subsequent hydrolysis of the paper; 3) the removal of unbleached cellulose fibers so as to prevent possible deterioration; 4) avoidance of excessive mineral loadings, as too much loading inhibits felting of the fibers and also weakens the paper; 5) tub-sizing (preferably with gelatin) of archival and/or papers to be handled frequently, as this type of sizing not only adds a protective film to the paper but also strengthens the paper considerably; 6) that bleaching agents, e.g., chlorine compounds, be removed as completely as possible in order to avoid the possibility of the formation of hydrochloric acid in the paper; 7) that mechanical wood pulp, which con- tains a relatively high percentage of impurities, e.g., lignin, and which also has very short fibers, should be avoided in archival and heavy use papers; and 8) that the paper be manufactured in such a manner that it retains its coatings over a long period in storage.

Books, documents, and other archival materials should be housed in air-conditioned quarters having controlled temperature and relative humidity. Taking into consideration that people probably will be working in the storage (bookstack) area, a reasonable temperature might be 60 to 65° F, with a relative humidity of 50 to 60%. The area should also be as dark as practical, with time switches that turn off lights automatically. The area should be completely free from dirt, and insects and their larvae. If flourescent lighting is used, which gives off less heat than incandescent lighting, it should be filtered, as the ultraviolet light radiated from flourescent lights over a long period of time could cause deterioration of book papers. (32, 36, 40, 143, 157, 198)

duro-flexible binding (duro-flexile). A style of library binding devised and patented by Cedric Chivers in the latter part of the 19th century. The duro-flexible binding was designed to give additional strength where most needed, i.e., in the hinges and first and last sections. This was done by lining the endpapers with jaconet and using a three-jointed endpaper. The books were sewn all along on linen tapes. The spines were lined with a pliable leather, and both tapes and lining were secured between split boards. They were covered with a thin, vegetable-tanned pigskin, with linen on the sides. (94, 236)

dust cover. 1. *See:* BOOK JACKET. 2. A blank leaf inserted at the end of a pamphlet or booklet having a self-cover.

dusting. The process of spreading ground, raw vegetable tanning materials over and between hides being tanned in layer vats to add to the tanning strength of the tan liquor. Dusting was a common practice before the days of concentrated tanning extracts. (363)

dust jacket (dust wrapper). *See:* BOOK JACKET.

Dutch antique marble. A modification of the NONPARIEL MARBLE.

Dutch binding. An obsolete term for a style of binding that includes a vellum or parchment spine, usually of a green color. (152)

Dutch corner. *See:* LIBRARY CORNER.

Dutch gilt papers (Dutch flowered papers).

A type of highly decorative papers that were not marbled but were printed by means of blocks of wood or metal, or by engraved rollers. They were used from about 1700, and, although known as "Dutch gilt" or "Dutch flowered," they were actually produced in Germany and Italy, the Dutch connection possibly arising from the fact that the papers were imported into Holland for reexport to France and England, although not all of them arrived in France and England by that route.

A great variety of designs was employed in these papers, many being in imitation of the brocades and demasks of the period. Some have figures of huntsmen, animals and birds, saints, mythological beasts, and Renaissance strap and scroll patterns; many are embossed, and some are printed on colored paper.

The probable method of their execution consisted of transferring gold size to the paper by means of wooden plates or engraved rollers, the former first being pressed onto a pad saturated with the size, the latter having the size painted on. When the size on the paper had dried to the correct state, the gold was dusted on, and, when the size was dry, the superfluous gold was brushed off. If it was desired to have the gold raised the size was thickened with yellow ochre or red lead. The method of coloring is unknown, but it may have been done by dabbing or stencilling. (217, 236)

Dutch gold (Dutch leaf; Dutch metal). The generic name for a blocking foil that has found considerable use as a substitute for gold leaf since the latter years of the 19th century. It was introduced in Germany and its use, in sheet form, expanded rapidly, followed by a similar foil in roll form. Although often referred to as "bronze leaf," bronze being an alloy of copper and tin, it is actually composed of brass, which is an alloy of copper and zinc. As the amount of copper is increased, the color of the leaf deepens. Unlike gold leaf, Dutch gold discolors, tarnishing more rapidly in polluted environments. When blocked on leather, the leaf or foil turns green very quickly; and even when blocked on cloth or paper, it will eventually discolor. Discoloration is due to the action of gases in the atmosphere, such as hydrogen sulfide (H_2S), plus heat and light. Great differences exist in the rate of tarnishing among the

various brass foils, however; flat foil for some reason discolors less rapidly than the rolled Dutch gold. This may be due to the high melting-point waxes used on the flat foil but not on the rolled, which coat the metallic particles after they are deposited on the material in the blocking process. This coating apparently acts as a (partial) seal against the deteriorative effect of the atmosphere. Because of the chemical action of the plasticizers in pyroxylin fabrics, the deterioration of the foil is more rapid on these fabrics than on starch-filled fabrics. (233, 236, 264, 356)

Dutch marble. A marble pattern executed by dropping a series of colors, usually yellow, and blue (in that order), which are then drawn together and intermingled by means of a comb, so that instead of shells and veins being produced, the pattern consists of a series of small, sharp scallops.

The Dutch marble is a pattern that has been used frequently in blankbook binding from the early 19th century to the present day.

Dutch metal. *See:* DUTCH GOLD.

Dutch paper. Originally, a handmade paper produced in Holland, but today any deckle-edge hand- or machine-made paper manufactured in Holland. It is a superior grade of paper used for high quality books, and, if given an antique finish, as artists' paper. Use of the expression "Dutch" may stem from the fact that in Holland handmade or *imitation* handmade paper is still called "Hollandsch papier," which does not necessarily mean paper made by hand in Holland. (17)

Dutch sewing. An obsolete (traditional) method of sewing a book, using strips of parchment or vellum in lieu of the customary bands or cords. (152)

dwell (dwell time). 1. *See:* CLAMP DWELL. 2. The period of time during which the heated finishing tool is in contact with the leather or gold leaf.

dye. A natural or synthetic coloring material, whether soluble or insoluble, which imparts its color to a material by staining or being imbibed by it, and which is employed from a solution of fine dispersion, sometimes with the aid of a MORDANT. Dyes differ from pigments, which are insoluble materials that impart color by being spread over a surface, or by being mixed in the form of an ingredient, as in the coloring of some papers and leathers.

Natural dyes, such as indigo, madder, fustic, butternut, orchil, logwood, catechu, tumeric, etc., are seldom used today. The discovery in the mid-19th century that dyes could be produced artificially from a constituent of coal tar was the first step in the decline of the use of natural dyestuffs. In large part this was because the quality and effectiveness of natural dyestuffs depended on a variety of factors, over which the user might or might not have control. These included: 1) the problem of storage; 2) the time involved in extracting color from the raw materials; 3) dependence upon a growing season; and 4) impurities. On the other hand, dyes made in the laboratory: 1) do not depend on growing seasons; 2) do not have to be ground or chipped to be made usable; 3) are, in many cases (e.g., indigo), chemically the same as the natural dyes; and 4) since they are manufactured in pure form, are unaffected by the impurities that reduce the quality or effectiveness of their natural counterparts. However, unlike synthetic dyestuffs, natural dyes produce what can be described as unique colors. They can never be duplicated exactly, and this undoubtedly adds to their appeal. No two natural dye lots are identical for the simple reason that each is going to contain impurities peculiar to the plant material from which the dye is produced; therefore, the very characteristics of natural dyes which made them obsolete also make them appealing to many craftsmen of today.

An enormous range of dyestuffs can be obtained from the manufacturers of chemical dyestuffs. They are still often referred to as "coal tar dyes" or, perhaps more commonly, "aniline dyes," because the early materials were prepared from aniline and many of the intermediates required in their manufacture are obtained by the distillation of coal tar. *See also:* ACID DYES; BASIC DYES; DIRECT DYES; LAKE; PIGMENT. (4, 72, 235)

dyed white. The neutralized or "corrected" white paper produced by the addition of blue or red coloring to the bleached pulp.

dyeing. The art or process of coloring, or altering the color of a material by the addition of another different colored material, in such a manner that the change may be considered permanent.

earth colors. Pigments manufactured by refining naturally colored clays, rocks, and earth, and also the pure iron oxide reds, such as Indian red, light red, etc. The iron oxides, although artificial counterparts, are classified with the native red earths. Earth colors are also classified as mineral pigments, along with the manufactured inorganic pigments. They are characterized by good light and heat fastness. (233, 306)

ecclesiastical bindings. A German style of bookbinding in the medieval fashion which became very popular in England following the marriage of Queen Victoria and Prince Albert in 1840. It was used especially for devotional and theological works. Its principal features included thick, heavy, bevelled boards (occasionally papier-mâché was substituted for wood), which were sometimes bevelled only in the middle of each edge, leaving the corners in full thickness. The books were covered in either calfskin of a khaki or brown color or brown morocco and were heavily tooled in blind or black, often with the medieval thin-thick-thin triple fillet. The bindings had OXFORD CORNERS, bright red edges (or gilt over red, and sometimes dull gilt edges which were then GAUFFERED), heavily rounded spines and marbled endpapers in the Dutch pattern. The books were sometimes fitted with clasps. While the bindings were generally well executed, the unusually heavy boards frequently caused the cords to break, resulting in the text block falling out of the hollow-backed "case." Also called "antique," "monastic," or "divinity" bindings. (236)

écrasé leather. A leather which has been crushed or flattened by mechanical means so as to give it a particular grained appearance. *See also:* GLACÉ. (156)

edge decoration. A general term used with reference to the application of gold leaf, color, ink, or other medium, or the tooling, painting, or other form of decoration, of one or more edges of a book. *See:* ANTIQUE EDGES; CIRCUIT EDGES; COLORED BRUSHED TOP; COLORED BURNISHED TOP; COLORED EDGES; COLORED UNDER GILT; FORE-EDGE PAINTING; GAUFFERED EDGES; GILT EDGES; GILT IN THE ROUND; GILT IN

THE SQUARE; MARBLED EDGES; RED EDGES; RED UNDER GOLD EDGES; ROUGH GILT; SPRINKLED EDGES; TOP EDGE GILT; WHITE EDGES.

edge gilding. *See:* GILT EDGES.

edge gilding machine. A machine, used mainly in edition binding, for gilding the edges of books. The books are placed in the machine and the edges are prepared for gilding in the usual manner. A sheet of gold foil is placed over the edges, and heat and pressure are applied by two heated silicone rubber rollers. The first roller, which is used in conjunction with a sheet of fiberglass, smooths the foil over the edges and insulates the foil from heat until it is under pressure. The second roller then presses directly onto the foil and seals it to the edges. Large numbers of books are edge gilded in this manner, particularly in the Bible publishing business. (229, 264)

edge index. A form of the INDEX consisting of marks on the edges of the pages of a book produced by means of printed rules that run to the edge of the sheet (bled) and can thus be seen on the fore edge of the closed book. Edge indexing has the advantage of being part of the printing process, and also allows the use of virtually unlimited headings, as well as adding nothing to the overall cost of binding. Its principal disadvantage is that the user does not know what the mark on the edge refers to while the book is closed. (234)

edge marbling machine. A machine used for decorating the edges of book in imitation of MARBLING. The principle of operation is somewhat similar to that of the platen press. The edge of the book is pressed against the printing surface which has been inked by the form rollers. Any design, color, or com-

bination of colors can be used. The machine may also be used for city directories, etc., where advertising matter is printed on the edges. (264)

edge roll. An engraved finishing tool used to impress a design on the edges of the boards of a book, usually one covered in leather. (274)

edge rolled. A method of decorating the edges of the boards of a book, usually one covered in leather, in which the edges are tooled in gold or blind by means of an engraved EDGE ROLL. (94, 261)

edges. The three outer extremities of the folded sections of book, usually trimmed and sometimes decorated in some manner. *See:* EDGE DECORATION.

edging. 1. The beveling of an edge, usually of a leather covering, but also paper, vellum, etc., by means of an EDGING KNIFE. The purpose of "edging" a leather cover is to prevent the leather turn-in from bulging, especially at the head and tail of the spine. When applied to paper, the term generally refers to the process of cutting or beveling two pieces of paper so that there is no high or low spot where they are joined. In craft bookbinding today, edging of paper is more or less obsolete, having been superceded by the use of long-fibered Japanese copying paper. 2. *See:* EDGE ROLLED.

edging knife. A knife made of hardened steel and used to pare the edges of leather on the flesh side, vellum, paper, etc. *See also:* PARING KNIFE. (133)

edition. 1. All of the copies of a work printed from the same type or plates, either issued at one time or at intervals. In the latter case, the edition may consist of a number of impressions. A statement of the edition of a book is often printed on the title page or its verso, along with the particulars of any previous editions on the verso. 2. A number of copies of a work printed at any one time, either when the text has undergone changes or the type has been partially or entirely reset, or the format of the book has been altered. The term is also applied to the copies which made up the original issue, i.e., the "first edition," as well as any subsequent editions, e.g., 2nd, revised, etc. 3. The embodiment of a work in a particular typographical form, with different editions embodying an identical text, or varying texts. 4. One of the various editions of a newspaper. *See also:* EXTRA-ILLUSTRATED; FINE PAPER COPY; FIRST EDITION; IMPRESSION (5); LARGE PAPER COPY; LIBRARY EDITION; LIMITED EDITION. (12, 69, 156, 234)

edition binding. The business of binding identical books in quantity, usually for a publisher or distributor, as opposed to binding done for an individual and LIBRARY BINDING. Edition binding usually involves the production of a type of binding known as case binding, generally in hard covers. Paperback books and other books with flexible and semi-flexible covers are produced by adhesive binderies, although adhesive binding is by no means unknown in edition binding.

The designation "case binding" or "casebound" indicates that the cover has two distinct characteristics: it is made separately from the book, and it consists of rigid or flexible boards covered with cloth, paper, leather substitutes, and, upon occasion, leather or other materials, in such a manner that the covered material surrounds the outside as well as the edges of the boards.

The major distinguishing characteristic of edition binding is the extensive use of semi-automatic and automatic equipment, some of which operates at very high speeds. This equipment is capable of processing thousands of books in a relatively short time, primarily because all of the books processed in one run are of identical size and format. Because a large, modern edition bindery uses as much automatic (and expensive) equipment as possible, edition runs smaller than about 1,500 copies are not ordinarily handled by edition binderies but by job binders and sometimes even library binders.

The equipment commonly found in a large edition bindery includes:
Blocking presses
Board cutters
Book jacketing machines
Bundling presses
Case-making machines
Casing-in machines
Cloth slitting machines
Cutter-perforating machines
Endpaper-signature stripping machines
Endpaper tipping machines
Folding machines
Gathering machines
Glueing-off machines
Nipping presses
Rounding and backing machines
Saddle-stitching machines

Sewing machines
Three-knife trimmers
Tipping machines
Triple liner and headbanding machines
Wrapping machines (book jacketing machines).

The progression of modern edition binding from purely handwork to a high degree of mechanization followed a course which may be divided into four fairly distinct phases: 1) all processes performed by hand or hand-manipulated tools—about 1780 to 1830; 2) a simplifying and speeding up of the processes while the work is still performed largely with hand tools, a change which was due largely to the pressures exerted by the increased speed of printing presses—1830 to 1870; 3) progressive introduction of machines to handle certain manipulations, e.g., folding, gathering, sewing, etc., with the balance of the processes still being done largely by hand—1870 to 1910; and 4) the present state in which the great majority of the processes are performed by machines, a phase which marks the complete breaking away of the modern industry from the parent craft of hand bookbinding —about 1950 to the present. (58, 89, 299, 314, 320, 339)

edition deluxe. 1. A "special" edition of work containing items not found in ordinary editions of the same work, such as additional plates (*See:* EXTRA ILLUSTRATED), a larger sheet size (*See:* LARGE PAPER COPY), etc. 2. A so-called superior edition of a work, characterized by a better grade of paper (sometimes handmade), superior typography, a greater or lesser degree of embellishment, sometimes a better quality of binding, and perhaps a limited number of copies (which are sometimes signed and numbered). The "edition deluxe" is as old as printing itself. In the 15th century a certain number of copies of any high quality book would usually be printed on vellum, or colored paper, such as the blue paper copies of Aldus Manitius, and "fine paper" copies, at an elevated price, were common in the 17th and 18th centuries, while large paper copies have been issued for the past three centuries. Although not necessarily considered "edition deluxe," many thousands of books have been specially (and often elaborately) bound for private collectors. 3. A cheap edition called "deluxe" or "deluxe edition," by a publisher for promotional reasons. (69, 94, 156)

Edwards of Halifax. A distinguished English (Yorkshire) family of bookbinders

and booksellers, of whom William Halifax (1723–1808) and his son James (1756–1816) were the most famous. William Halifax was known for his revival of the FORE-EDGE PAINTING and ETRUSCAN CALF bindings, the latter, which, if not evolved by William, were successfully adopted by him. He also used vellum for covering books, and decorated them with painting of portraits or scenes. In order to protect the paintings Halifax developed his own process of rendering the vellum transparent (although he was by no means the first to make TRANSPARENT VELLUM or parchment) by first soaking it in a solution of pearl ash (potassium carbonate (K_2CO_3)) and then subjecting it to high pressure. The paintings were executed on the underside of the vellum, which was then lined with white paper before being placed on the book. The patent which James Halifax was issued for this process (1785) refers to both the painting of the material, as well as the method of making the vellum transparent; however, it is not entirely clear whether the patent was granted for rendering the vellum transparent, for the paintings themselves, or both. Although it was probably for the vellum process, other techniques for rendering vellum (parchment) transparent were known more than 200 years before his time. His technique was obviously successful, as the colors remain fresh to this day. Having the painting on the underside of the vellum also allows the covers to be cleaned when soiled.

It is known that these bindings were being produced at least as early as 1781 even though the patent was not issued until 1785. There is considerable evidence to indicate that James Halifax was a businessman rather than a craftsman, and, since the books were produced in Halifax at a time when James was elsewhere, it is presumed that William invented the process.

All three specialities seem to have been carried on both in the Edwards' home town of Halifax, where Thomas (1762–1834), another son, was in business until 1826, and in London, where James and John (1785–c 1791) opened a book store in 1784, and Richard (1768–1827) another in 1792. Regardless of its place of origin, however, any binding of the period which approximates any of the three specialities in style, as well as the vellum bindings with blue lettering pieces and key-pattern gold tooling in the prevailing neo-classical style, is apt to be attributed to Edwards of Halifax. (69, 113, 140, 236)

egg albumen. The dried whites of eggs obtained usually as a yellowish powder, and used in the finishing of some leathers, as well as for making GLAIR. (259)

Egyptian marble. A cover marble executed by coloring the leather covering (before it is attached to the book) with blue, which when dry, is followed by a coating of glair, then potash water (alum). Black is then sprinkled over the leather, and when the black is nearly dry, the leather is washed with water. (95)

E. I. An abbreviation of East India, a descriptive term applied to crust, vegetable tanned cowhide (kip), buffalo hide, or skins such as goat, calf or sheep, originating in the Indian Sub-continent and tanned in India, mainly in the south, and especially around Madras. (61)

eighteen-mo. One-eighteenth of a sheet. The eighteen-mo is an unusual method of imposition resulting in a section of 18 leaves, or 36 pages. One method of producing it is to fold a sheet con-certina-wise, followed by an envelope fold, followed by a right angle fold. Although used in book production be-tween about 1770 and 1840, it is seldom, if ever, used in bookwork today. It is, however, sometimes used in advertising work, etc., where the folded sheet is to be untrimmed and remain folded in compact form until unfolded for reading. Also written 18mo. Also called "octodecimo."

elasticity. The capability of a material to recover from deformation resulting from stress. The property is determined more by the ability of the material to return to its initial shape than by its capacity to be deformed or extended. *See also:* EXTENSIBILITY; STRETCH. (17)

elastin. The yellow connective tissue of the skin which furnishes structural sup-port for the blood vessels, sebaceous and sudoriferous glands, and the like. It is woven in the collagen fibers and makes up approximately 0.3% of the structural protein of the hide composi-tion. (305, 363)

electric pen (electric stylus). An electri-cally heated instrument used over a strip of metallic foil to letter the classification number and/or other bi-bliographical information on the covers of books. (156)

elephant folio. A large FOLIO (1), ap-proximately 23 by 14 inches in size. *See also:* BOOK SIZES. (140)

ellagic acid. A crystalline phenolic dilac-tone ($C_{14}H_6O_8$), obtained from oak galls and bark and probably formed by the hydrolysis of tannin. *See also:* VEGETABLE TANNINS.

Elliott, Thomas (active 1712-1763). A London bookbinder, Elliott was ap-prenticed to Robert Steele in 1703 and finished his service in 1712. He became bookbinder to Robert Harley, and worked in the HARLEIAN STYLE, which was forced on both him and Chris-topher Chapman by either Harley, or Harley's librarian, Humfrey Wanley. The books the two produced were solidly bound in a red morocco said to be of an inferior quality. (94, 246)

Elmendorf test. A standard test for deter-mining the internal TEARING RESISTANCE of paper, named after its inventor, Armin Elmendorf. The Elmendorf test determines the average force in grams required to tear a single sheet of paper after the tear has been started. In con-ducting the test, one or more sheets are torn through a fixed distance by means of a pendulum. The effort ex-pended in tearing is measured by the loss of potential energy of the pen-dulum. The scale of the device is cali-brated to indicate the average force exerted. If multiple sheets are used, which is necessary if the reading for one sheet would fall below the scale, resistance of one sheet is determined by the formula:

$$\frac{\text{grams of force} \times 16}{\text{number of sheets}} = \text{grams required to tear one sheet,}$$

where 16 is the conversion factor, un-less an augmenting weight is added to the pendulum, in which case the con-version factor becomes 32.

The Elmendorf tester consists es-sentially of a stationary clamp, a mov-able clamp carried on a pendulum formed by a sector of a circle free to swing on a ball bearing, a knife mounted on a stationary post for start-ing the tear, means for leveling the instrument, means for holding the pendulum in a raised position and for releasing it instantaneously, and means for registering the maximum arc through which the pendulum swings when released. (72)

email en resolle. A design consisting of enamel and gold inlaid in glass or rock crystal, and which has been used to a very limited extent as a means of decorating the covers of books. The technique apparently was used by only one person, a French goldsmith, who based his patterns on the engravings

of Etienne Delaune. To produce the email en resolle the design is cut into the surface of the ground and then filled with strips of gold leaf. The de-tails of the design are then modeled by very delicate chasing on the sur-face of the leaf. Translucent colored enamels are then floated over specified areas of the gold. (347)

emblematical bindings. Appropriate orna-ments or symbolical motifs tooled on a leather binding. Some outstanding examples of emblematical bindings were produced, especially in France of the 16th century. (69)

embossed. 1. A leaf or leaves of a book which have had letters or a design raised in relief for the purpose of indi-cating ownership. The leaves most commonly treated in this manner are the title page and page 99, or descend-ing multiples of 11, i.e., page 88, 77, 66, etc. Embossing is more or less obsolete today, as most libraries have come to realize that it is not only expensive but largely ineffective as a means of deterring theft. 2. Paper, leather, cloth, etc., on which a raised or depressed design is imparted for decorative effects. *See also:* CUIR-BOUILLI. 3. A design in the covering material of a book, usually one covered in leather, but sometimes cloth or pa-per, which is in relief. 4. Lettering, or a design, which is raised above the surface of the paper of a book. *See:* EMBOSSING. 5. *See:* EMBOSSED LEATHER. (12, 58)

embossed leather. A leather which has been embossed or printed with a raised design, either in imitation of the grain pattern of some animal, or even un-related to any natural grain pattern. Cowhide is frequently embossed to give the appearance of another leather, in-cluding MOROCCO. (61)

embosser. 1. The device (usually hand-operated but sometimes operated by air pressure) used for raising letters or a design on the surface of paper, usually for purposes of establishing ownership. *See:* EMBOSSED (1). 2 The operator of such a device.

embossing. 1. The process of raising a surface pattern on leather by means of engraved cylinders or plates, gen-erally employing both heat and pres-sure. The patterns produced are often simulations of the grain patterns of some animal skins but may also be unrelated to any natural pattern. One roller or plate, in which the design is engraved, is made of steel, while the other, having a softer surface, is made of cotton or papier-mâché. The leather is embossed by passing it over a heated, steel cylinder, thermostatically controlled at a pre-set temperature, or in a press, of which there are two basic types: one in which the pressure is applied by a roller mounted on a moving carriage, and another in which pressure is applied to the platen by mechanical or hydraulic means, but without any lateral movement. In both cases the leather is pressed against a heated plate which is either smooth and polished so that the leather is ironed, or engraved to impart an artificial grain pattern. While the latter type of press is designed to employ heavier pressures, the first type is superior in that the movement of the roller causes a small amount of slip, which imparts a more lively character to the leather. On the other hand, the advantage of the mechanical or hydraulic press is that it can dwell at full pressure, which is desirable for producing deep effects in some embossing processes.

It is important that the design embossed in the leather be as permanent as possible. In this regard both the structure of the skin and the type of tannage are important. A very full and tight structure is required. Calfskin gives the ideal structure for the finer leathers and cowhide for the coarser. Vegetable tannage is far superior to chrome because it builds up the fibers to a much greater extent and makes the structure correspondingly tighter.

Embossing of leather is sometimes (and perhaps frequently) a means of simulating the grain pattern of a superior leather on an inferior and/or less expensive skin. An example of this would be a calfskin embossed in imitation of MOROCCO.

2. The process of imparting a raised or depressed design in paper: 1) by passing the paper between an engraved steel roll or plate and another roll or plate of a soft or compressible material, such as paper or cotton; 2) by pressing the paper between strong, coarse fabrics; or 3) by passing the paper between etched male and female iron or steel rolls. The operation is used to create decorative effects and is generally applied to book, blotting, or cover papers. Plate or spot embossing is a method by which individual designs, as distinguished from all-over patterns, are embossed. This technique is accomplished by means of vertical presses, the paper being embossed by placing it between the embossing die and the counter or

make-ready of the press and forcing it into the intaglio areas of the die.

3. To impress the marks of ownership into a page of a book by means of a device employing a sunken die and a raised counterpart which raises the design above the paper. *See also:* PERFORATING. (2)

4. To block the title, author, or other bibliographical information, on the cover of a book. *See also:* BLOCKING (1).

5. *See:* BLIND BLOCKING. (94, 189, 233, 234, 264)

embossing plate. A metal plate cut or etched below its surface and used to produce a design in relief on a material such as leather or paper.

embossing press. *See:* BLOCKING PRESS; EMBOSSING (1, 2); FLY EMBOSSING PRESS.

embrittlement. 1. The drying and solidification of an adhesive to the point where it exhibits fissures and stress cracks under conditions of low impact. Embrittlement may also be a condition resulting from the migration of the adhesive plasticizer into the adherend, or the solidification and stratification of a cast adhesive coating due to exposure to atmospheric conditions. 2. A loss of flexibility, primarily in paper. *See:* BRITTLENESS. (222)

embroidered bindings. Books that are covered by material embellished with needlework, following a design made specifically for the purpose of decorating a particular book. Embroidered bindings were and still are produced throughout most of the West, but the art reached its highest achievement in England, where the quality of the bindings was unsurpassed. The earliest known English example is of a 13th century manuscript Psalter owned by Anne de Felbrigge; however, the art reached its pinnacle of development in the first half of the 17th century.

The designs employed for embroidered bindings may be conveniently divided into four classes: heraldic, figure, floral, and arabesque. The heraldic designs were always used to indicate ownership, and were most often found on royal books bound in velvet, rarely on silk or satin, and almost never on canvas. Figure designs may be subdivided into three classes: scriptural, such as Solomon, David, etc.; symbolical, such as figures of faith, hope, and the like; and portraits, such as dukes, duchesses, etc. The scriptural designs were generally done on canvas, while the symbolical and portraits were mainly on satin, and

(rarely) velvet. The floral and arabesque designs were usually done on small books bound in satin, but were done occasionally on canvas and velvet.

Gold, silver, and silk threads were used for the best work, and were often protected from wear by bordering ornamentation in higher relief formed by threads of silk wound around closely or loosely with fine flat strips of silver-gilt metal. These and other materials were worked singly or twisted together in a variety of manners and worked in a great number of stitches. At times, particularly in the later periods, flat metal shapes were stitched on to save time. A more attractive APPLIQUE WORK technique was to make a spiral of metal which, when flattened, looked like a series of rings, and was sometimes used as a border.

Because canvas is generally considered to be a relatively uninteresting cloth, it was generally worked all over, while when velvet covers were used, large areas were not covered, not so much because of the beauty of the velvet, but because of the difficulties involved in sewing piled material. Appliqué decoration overcame this problem, but when the designs were actually worked directly on the velvet they were almost always in heavy gimp or gold cord.

The edges of large numbers of embroidered bindings were gilt and gauffered (sometimes with the use of color) in keeping with the ornate character of the binding. Other forwarding techniques appear to have been the same as for leather bindings, although the rounding of the spines was less pronounced. The sections were sewn on strips of vellum or thongs, and, while the latter were sometimes left raised, frequently they were filled in between so as to produce a smooth spine. Later examples were sometimes sewn on cords, which were raised, sawn-in, filled in, or flattened to avoid unevenness.

Embroidered bindings more or less went out of fashion after the 17th century. *See* PLATE III. (28, 111, 236, 280, 342, 357)

emery. A common, dark, granular corundum containing varying amounts of magnetite or hematite and used in the form of powder, grains, or larger masses, for grinding and polishing purposes.

emulsion. A disperse system in which both phases are liquids, one of which is generally water or an aqueous solution, and the other an oil or other water immiscible liquid. The droplets of the *dispersed* liquid are known as the inner phase of the emulsion because it appears to be inside the liquid medium. The surrounding liquid (the continuous phase), on the other hand, is called the external phase. The dispersion may occur naturally or it may be prepared by mechanical methods (dripping or slowly pouring one of the ingredients into the other while stirring vigorously), or developed as a result of any of several polymerization processes. The liquid in the continuous phase is usually water when the emulsion is designed for pigment coating, as of paper, for example, or for oil penetration, as in the FATLIQUORING of leather. For certain other types of application, the medium may be an organic liquid. To form a stable emulsion, a third ingredient must be present; it is called an emulsifier, or emulsifying agent, and forms absorbed films around the tiny globules of the dispersed fluid to prevent them from coalescing. A common emulsifier is soap.

A familiar, naturally occurring emulsion is whole milk, the inner phase of which consists of globules of butterfat; the external phase is a watery solution of casein, sugar, and other substances. Another natural emulsion is egg yolk, which consists of egg oil in an aqueous solution containing, among other substances, albumen and lecithin; the latter is a lipoid (fatlike) substance that is one of nature's most efficient emulsifying agents. Albumen, also, is a good emulsifier.

Milk and egg yolk are oil in water emulsions. A second type of emulsion is that of water in oil, in which the phases are reversed. An example of this type of emulsion is butter, which has aqueous constituents dispersed in tiny globules throughout the butterfat. Most manufactured emulsions are made by combining the oily ingredient with a colloidal solution, such as casein or albumen; these are not only good emulsifiers, but also confer desirable properties when the emulsion is used as an adhesive.

Emulsions are generally opaque or milky because of the refraction and dispersion of light by the minute droplets, but when dry they become transparent, or nearly so.

In addition to their use in paper and leather manufacture, emulsions are used in edge gilding, gold tooling, and other bookbinding operations. (233, 235)

enamel. 1. An opaque or semi-opaque vitreous composition applied by fusion to the surface of a metal or other substance for purposes of ornamentation and/or protection. *See also:* CHAMPLEVÉ BINDINGS; CLOISONNÉ BINDINGS. 2. A term applied to a coated paper or to the coating material on a paper.

enamelled. Originally, a supercalendered printing paper coated on both sides with a pigment such as satin white or blanc fixe; today, enamelled is considered to be any coated paper. (17)

enamelled bindings. *See:* CHAMPLEVÉ BINDINGS; CLOISONNÉ BINDINGS.

enamelled hide. A vegetable tanned cowhide with a flexible, water repellent, multi-layered coating on the grain side, built up in a manner somewhat similar to that used for patent leather, and given a grain pattern by means of embossing. At one time enamelled hide was a cowhide tanned with bark and finished with a mixture of Prussian blue (ferric ferrocyanide ($KFe(Fe(N_6))$)) and linseed oil, dried in an oven and grained. (61, 351)

enamelled seal. Originally, a Greenland sealskin, tanned with bark or sumac, and treated with a mixture of Prussian blue (ferric ferrocyanide ($KFe(Fe(N_6))$)) and linseed oil, and dried in an oven at high temperature. Today the term refers to an imitation sealskin. *See:* ENAMELLED HIDE. (61)

enclosures. Materials left or placed in a book, either accidently or deliberately, and which, unless removed, may cause damage to the paper, binding, or equipment used in binding, or which may be bound into the volume. Such items include paper clips, bookmarks, cataloging and/or binding instructions, rubber bands, newspaper clippings, leaves, flowers, letters, and the like. (173)

end board. *See:* LOWER COVER.

end leaf. *See:* FLY LEAF.

end-leaf paper. A paper manufacturer's term for the white or colored sheets of cotton fiber and/or chemical wood pulp paper in basis weights of 50 to 80 pounds ($25 \times 38 - 500$), used for the ENDPAPERS of books. It should have sufficient strength to withstand tearing, especially at the joint, high folding strength, resistance to penetration by adhesives, and a pH between 6.5 and 8.5. The sheets are often printed with ornamental patterns and special or significant designs, e.g., library motifs. (17)

end lining. *See:* PASTEDOWN.

endpapering machine. An edition binding machine that glues sheets of paper folded once only to the first and last sections of a book.

endpapers. The units of two or more leaves placed in the front and back of a book between its covers and text block. In rare instances the endpaper may consist of a single leaf. The endpaper at the front of the book is called the front endpaper, while the one at the back is called the off endpaper, or back endpaper. The leaf nearest the cover (after the WASTE SHEET (1), if any, is removed) is called the PASTEDOWN, or board paper, and, along with the recto of the leaf facing it, may be colored, marbled, ornamented; printed with maps, illustrations, scenes from the book, the motif of the library, etc.; or left blank. The leaf or leaves that are not pasted to the board are sometimes referred to as fly leaves, fly sheets, free fly leaves, or waste sheets.

In hand binding the basic purpose of the endpapers is to take up the strain of opening the covers of the book, which would otherwise be on the first and last sections or leaves. This is of particular importance in the case of the upper cover and first section or leaf. The endpapers (specifically the pastedowns) cover the raw edges of the covering material where it is turned over the boards, as well as the inside surfaces of the boards themselves. The free fly leaves protect the first and last printed leaves of the book. In addition, the board papers and fly leaves next to them have long provided a medium for decoration. *See:* DOUBLURE (1).

In library and edition binding, particularly the latter, the endpapers perform the crucial function of holding the text block in its covers, or case. In many instances, only the endpapers hold the book and case together. In library binding, on the other hand, where the spine-lining material is considerably more substantial than that used in edition binding, the lining assists considerably in this function.

The paper used for endpapers is of considerable importance—not only the quality of the paper but also the manner in which it is used. Its pH should not be less than that of the paper making up the book, and preferably higher, but it should not, in any case, be less than 6.5 or more than 8.5. The BASIS WEIGHT of the paper should be sufficient so that when the adhesive is applied, the moisture will not cause the paper to cockle, as cockling causes problems when the book is later cased-in. Furthermore, thin paper will swell excessively when moist, and then when it dries will shrink and warp the covers. There is also the danger that the adhesive will strike through and cause the board papers and adjacent leaves to stick together.

The grain or machine direction of the endpapers should be parallel to the binding margin of the book; otherwise difficulty will be experienced in casing-in. When the grain of the paper is at right angles to the binding margin, the expansion of the paper is lengthwise, and, because one edge is secured to the text block (either sewn or tipped to it), that edge cannot expand; consequently the paper will buckle along

it. If the book is cased and then pressed, these buckled areas will cause unsightly wrinkles on the board papers.

When colored endpapers are used, they should be made with fast colors so that the moisture of the adhesive will not cause the colors to offset onto the leaves of the book. When endpapers are lithographed or printed with maps or illustrations, they, too, should be printed with an ink that will not offset. (It should be noted that when a book with map, or otherwise pertinent endpapers, must be rebound, the endpapers must be carefully removed and rebound with the book, as they generally cannot be reused as endpapers; this step is expensive, and

doubly so when the front and off papers are different, which requires that both be retained.)

Marbled endpapers were at one time used extensively, but today their use is confined almost entirely to a limited number of books bound by hand. If marbled paper is used, the same precautions as to grain direction and color fastness should be observed.

The most commonly used style of endpaper construction, at least in edition binding, consists of nothing more than folded sheets tipped to the front and back of the text block. This structure is not altogether unsatisfactory if the book is to receive careful and little use, but it is entirely unsatisfactory for

ENDPAPERS

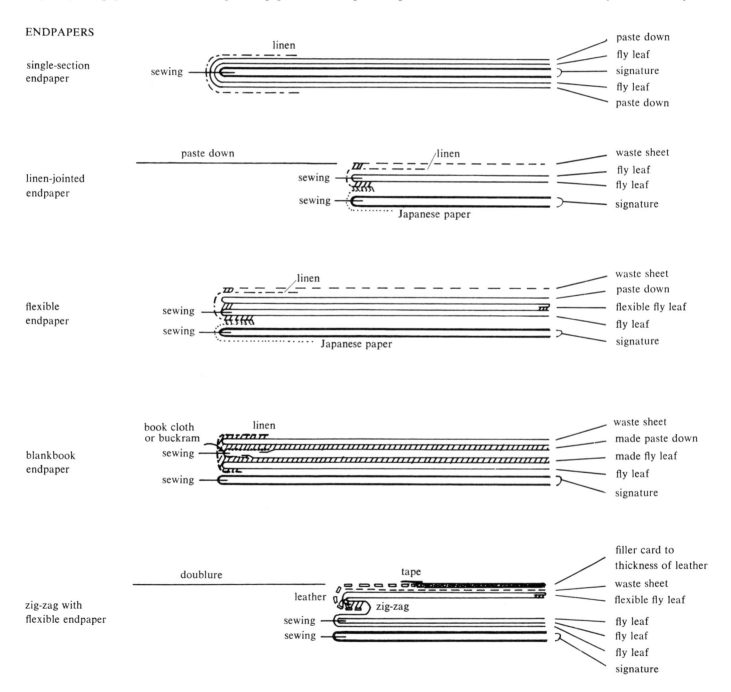

a book that is to be consulted frequently. Since the endpaper is attached to the text block only by a thin line of adhesive, it pulls loose easily leaving only a flimsy spine lining fabric made of crash or gauze holding the case to the book. There is no reinforcement of the joint; consequently, the board paper splits because of the constant bending as the book is opened and closed. These difficulties can be overcome to a certain extent by the use of a cloth joint. Occasionally the tipped-on endpapers are also sewn to the text block, as though they were additional sections. This however, just weakens them even further, because the sewing thread passes through only one layer of paper, resulting, in addition to the normal strain, in a cutting effect of the thread.

Cloth-jointed endpapers may have either concealed or exposed joints. With the concealed joint, the fold of the endpaper is reinforced by a strip of cloth which is attached on the side of the paper next to the text block and the board so that it extends about an inch onto the board paper, thus masking the cloth. The additional stiffness in the joint helps to retain its shape, but it also creates a pull on the first few leaves of the first section because it makes the cover more difficult to open.

Separate leaves of paper are used for the board paper and fly leaf in constructing the endpaper having an exposed joint. They are connected by means of a cloth strip which is visible in the joint. In edition binding, these endpapers are made on a stripping machine, and the reinforcing cloth is generally a thin, smoothly finished muslin. In library binding, on the other hand, where the visible cloth joint is used frequently in adhesive binding, the cloth joint usually consists of a strong, durable (cambric) linen. Cloth-jointed endpapers are attached to the text block in several ways. The simplest is to tip them on, which is a weak method. When the papers have a concealed joint, the folded sheet is tipped to the section and the reinforcement is folded around the endpaper and section. The cloth joint is sewn to the text block along with the section. Another method consists of sewing the cloth joint to the section. The cloth is then folded back and glued over the sewing. The endpaper is tipped on, and the cloth is carried over the endpaper and glued down. Unless the book paper is quite flexi-

ble, however, this technique will cause the end sections to open as units rather than as individual leaves.

The Library Binding Institute has promulgated standards pertaining to the construction of endpapers to be used in library binding. The endpaper consists of three fundamental parts: a pasted-down or outward endleaf which becomes the pastedown, at least two free flyleaves, and a reinforcing fabric. For monographs and ordinary periodicals, the paper used in the construction of endpaper must have a basis weight of 60 pounds ($24 \times 26 - 500$) and must meet the following requirements:

papers was done well before the coming of machine-made paper. This practice however, became more important when machine-made paper became prevalent, mainly because early machine-made paper tended to be relatively thin, and therefore weak. All of these techniques died out in the 1830s, after which time the more convenient procedure of making up the endpapers separately from the book became prevalent. Concurrently, it became the usual practice to simply tip the endpapers to the sections instead of sewing them, not only in regular commercial binding but also even in the best leather work.

	Folding Endurance (M.I.T.)* Number of folds	Tensile Strength (Testing Machines, Inc.) Pounds per 1 inch strip	Tearing Strength (Elmendorf) Pounds per 1 inch strip
With the grain**	200	40	140
Across the grain	275	25	144

  * Massachusetts Institute of Technology
** In the direction in which the majority of the fibers of a machine-made paper are oriented.

During the first several centuries of the codex, endpapers consisted of little more than two or four leaves of vellum folded and sewn along with the sections of the book. When paper became the common material for book production, it then became necessary to reinforce the folds of the endpapers. A common type of endpaper, used in the first part of the 16th century, consisted of a fold of white paper employing a strip of vellum for reinforcement. The use of printer's waste for the fly leaves of endpapers was not uncommon during the 16th century.

The practice of reinforcing endpapers began to decline at the end of the 16th ecntury, particularly in commercial binding, partly because there were more small books (where it was thought that reinforcement was not of great importance), and also because it became more and more difficult to obtain waste vellum in sufficient quantities, due to the increase production of books.

When bindings were to have plain white endpapers, it was a common practice to sew on four leaves at each end of the text block. The two outer leaves of each endpaper were often pasted together to create a stronger paste-down, while the two inner leaves were sometimes pasted together to create the "made" flyleaf, commonly associated with marbled or colored endpapers. The doubling of the board

A widely used method of endpaper construction in the 19th century consisted of pasting a folded white to a folded colored sheet, which was then folded around the free colored sheet to make a waste sheet. A white flyleaf was then tipped on followed by the made endpaper. Another 19th century technique consisted of tipping a folded white sheet to the text block and inserting the white and colored made-up leaves inside up to the fold. This provided a waste sheet, a colored board paper, a "made" leaf which opened all the way back to the fold, and eliminated the drag of the previous endpaper, and the two flyleaves. A variation of this technique used today consists of pasting the colored and white sheets together, tipping a folded white sheet to the remaining white sheet, and then swinging one of the white sheets around the assembly to serve as a waste sheet.

Cloth-joined endpapers were used as early as the 1840s but were generally not sewn in until this century. When they were sewn, the usual method was to overcast them to the first and last sections before sewing the book. Inner joints of leather were used occasionally in Europe as long ago as the 17th century, especially in France, but it was not until the second half of the 18th century that they became relatively common in the best English morocco and Russia leather bindings.

The joints of this period, few of which were sewn in, were frequently used with much wider turn-ins than would be considered appropriate today, and were usually heavily decorated with fillets and rolls, as well as small tools.

Watered silk endpapers were used frequently in fine leather binding during the second half of the 19th century and up to World War II, but are seldom used today. Watered silk has always been used in conjunction with leather joints. *See:* DRUMMING ON. *See also:* LIBRARY STYLE ENDPAPER; MADE ENDPAPER; ZIG-ZAG ENDPAPER. (13, 69, 209, 217, 236, 335, 343)

end sheet. *See:* PASTEDOWN.

engine sized. *See:* BEATER SIZED.

en gist. *See:* BRADEL BINDING.

English fibreboard. An English equivalent for that called PASTEBOARD (1) in the United States. It is suitable for small or medium-sized books; however, it has a tendency to warp if too thin a sheet is used for the covers of a large book. (204)

English linen. A highly polished linen cloth of considerable strength and durability; it is reasonably permanent if not handled excessively. Also called "legal buckram." *See also:* LAW BUCKRAM.

English opacity paper. A paper used where a lightweight paper of good opacity is required. It is made from chemical wood pulp and fillers that afford maximum opacity, and usually contains mechanical wood pulp. It has a smooth machine or English finish, and is produced in basis weights ranging from 25 to 45 pounds (25 × 38 − 500). (17)

engraved (silver) bindings. Book covers decorated with engraved precious metals, usually portraying some Biblical or other religious scene and frequently further adorned with flowers, etc. The medieval custom of enclosing important liturgical works to be used at the alter in covers of precious metals died out in Western Europe during the Renaissance, in favor of richly embroidered velvet and (later) gold-tooled leather bindings. The fashion for silver or filigree, or even enamelled gold covers, however, continued with devotional books for personal use through the 18th century, especially in German-speaking countries, Italy, and Spain. (347)

engraving. 1. The art or process of producing letters or designs on wood, metal, or other substances, by means of cutting or etching, for the purpose of printing or blocking by an intaglio process on paper or other material. 2. An engraved plate, or the impression made from such a plate. 3. An engraved inscription. 4. The process of taking an impression from an engraved plate.

entrelacs. A method of decorating borders by means of curving garlands and leaves. Their source is Muslim arabesques, with early printed specimens adorning the *Historia Romana* of Appianus, printed by Erhard Ratdolt of Augsburg in 1477. In their use in book decoration, entrelacs have been used by most French gilders since the 16th century. *See also:* COTTAGE STYLE; FANFARE STYLE. (140)

environment. The surrounding conditions or forces that influence or change books or other archival materials, and which include: 1) the entire climatic and biotic factors that act upon materials and ultimately determine their permanence, or lack of it; or 2) the aggregate of use, misuse, or nonuse that influence the permanence of materials. *See also:* DURABILITY; PERMANENT MATERIALS. (148)

enzyme. A class of complex organic substances that are capable of acting outside of living organisms and can accelerate or catalyze specific chemical transformations, such as the formation of bloom on leather, the tanning of leather (*see:* BATING), and the modification of native starches in sizing processes.

The rate of an enzymatic reaction depends upon the temperature, pH, substrate concentration, and the presence of activators, co-enzymes, and enzyme inhibitors. The reactions of enzymes usually accelerate with an increase of temperature; however, since enzymes are proteins and are denatured at elevated temperatures, reaction rates increase only to the point where denaturation overcomes the accelerating effect of increasing temperature.

Enzymes exert their influence by combining with the substrate to form an enzyme-substrate complex, which then decomposes to give the products and release the enzyme for further action. Because of this, the rate at which enzyme products are formed depends both on the concentration of the enzyme-substrate complex and the rate of its decomposition. The formation of the complex depends on mass action between the enzyme and the substrate; therefore, taking a given quantity of an enzyme, the complex increases with the quantity sufficient to convert nearly all the enzyme into the complex. (72, 195, 306, 363)

epidermis. A protective, hard-wearing layer of keratinous cells, which, although of varying thickness over the body of the animal, is very thin compared with the underlying DERMIS. It consists of a continuous mass of cells usually differentiated into the following regions: *Stratum corneum,* or the uppermost layer, containing dry, dead cells, flattened to form a relatively continuous thin outer membrane skin that is highly cornified or keratinized; *Stratum lucidum,* which is the region where dying cells are located, and which contain an oily substance that renders them translucent; *Stratum granulosum,* in which the cells contain large granules; *Stratum spinosum,* where the cells show marked spines or bridges between each other; *Stratum basale,* where the cells contain living basal cells called keratinocytes and melanocytes; and the lowest region, the epidermal-dermal junction (often called the basement membrane), which consists of a thin zone of ground substance, containing no fibers, lying between the basal cells and the dermal surface.

The epidermal-dermal layer has little resistance to bacteria and enzymes, and is easily attacked by them, as in enzyme UNHAIRING. It is also easily disintegrated by alkalis, such as caustic soda, sodium sulfide, etc., which is the basis of common commercial unhairing processes.

The term derives from the Greek "epi" (upon) and "dermis," which had its origins in the Greek "derin" (to flay). *See also:* LIMING (248, 291, 306, 363)

epithelial tissue. The cellular tissue that covers all free surfaces within and without an animal's body, and, in the case of skin, is called epidermal tissue. The epithelial tissue affords covering and general protection against light, water and other fluids, bacteria, etc. (363)

epoxy resins. A class of resins produced by the polymerization of epichlorohydrin with diphenylolpropane, and manufactured from phenol and acetone. A range of resins of widely differing molecular weights, e.g., 400 to 6,000, can be produced by varying the proportions of reactants, as well as reaction conditions. Epoxy resins possess exceptional chemical resistance and adhesion. They are usually supplied in two parts, which must be mixed before use. Such resins have limited use in conservation work; however, they are useful where exceptional strength is required, such as in corner rebuilding and box making. (235, 309)

equivalent weight. 1. The weight of a particular paper of any size expressed in terms of some other size. Equivalent weights are in direct proportion to the areas of single sheets. If the weight of a given size of paper is known, the equivalent weight of the paper of a different size can be calculated by multiplying the known weight of the paper by the area of the paper required and dividing by the known area of the paper:

$$\frac{\text{Weight of paper of which size and weight are known} \times \text{Area of paper of which weight is required}}{\text{Area of paper of known weight}} = \text{Equivalent weight}$$

Thus, the weight of a ream of paper 25 x 40 inches in the substance of 30 to 40 inches, 60 pounds per 500 sheets is:

$$\frac{60 \times (25 \times 40)}{(30 \times 40)}$$

= 50 pounds/500 sheets, 25 x 40 inches.

2. In chemistry, equivalent weight is one of the comparative weights of different compounds, elements, or radicals which possess the same chemical value for reaction when compared by reference to the same standard (usually oxygen, i.e., 8). In an acid, the equivalent weight is the quantity which would yield one gram ionic weight of hydrogen ion (1.008 g.), while in a base, it is the quantity which would yield one gram ionic weight of hydroxyl ion (17.008 g.). Thus an equivalent weight of sulfuric acid (H_2SO_4) is one-half the molecular weight, and an equivalent of aluminum hydroxide ($Al(OH)_3$) would be one-third the molecular weight. (17, 58, 139, 195)

erasibility. That property of a material relating to the ease with which writing or printing can be removed by means of mechanical abrasion, the smoothness and cleanliness of the erased surface, and the reusability of the erased surface. (17)

Erfurt bindings. A university town in Central Germany, the name of which was applied to 18th century bindings featuring a scheme of decoration in which the entire cover is divided by a double border which encloses a long, narrow panel. The outer border is narrow, with a broad inner border separated from it by several parallel lines.

Parallel lines also outline a center panel. All of the lines, both horizontal and vertical, cross near the extreme ends forming squares at the corners of the covers. The central panel is usually decorated with a pattern made up of small, almost touching, tools, and both borders are similarly decorated with a succession of tools; those of the broad inner one often are interrupted with a scroll bearing the name of the bookbinder. Many bookbinders of the latter half of the 15th century produced these so-called Erfurt bindings, including CONRADUS DE ARGENTINA and JOHANNES FOGEL. (141)

errata (sing. **erratum**). Errors or omissions in writing or printing, generally restricted to typographical errors, but sometimes including imperfections in either presswork or binding. They are usually printed on a separate slip or leaf and placed among the preliminaries, or added to an existing page of type at the beginning or end of the book. Errata sheets must frequently be tipped in by the library or the binder. (69)

esparto (grass). A coarse grass, native to Southern Spain and Northern Africa, obtained from two species, *Lygeum spartum* and *Stipa tenacissima,* and used in the manufacture of paper. Esparto fibers have thick walls and are short, normally less than 3 mm in length, with an average length of 1.5 mm. The fiber diameter varies from about 0.005 to 0.015 mm, with an average of about 0.012 mm, giving a length to diameter ratio of 125:1. The fibers also tend to be curved. One of the principal characteristics of esparto is its hairs, which are located on the inner surface of the leaf. Looking something like commas, they are commonly referred to as "comma hairs." They are also called tooth cells since they also somewhat resemble teeth. In addition to the hairs, small cells with serrated edges, appearing something like miniature concertinas, are present. Both hairs and cells have a length of less than about 0.06 mm. The best grade of esparto grass is known as Spanish, while the cheaper grade (from Africa) is called Tripoli.

Introduced in England in 1850 by T. Routledge, esparto is used extensively in Great Britain, but is seldom employed in the United States, mainly because of the cost of transporting the grass or pulp made from it. In England, it is employed principally in the production of better grades of book paper.

The presence of esparto in paper is determined by the iodine-zinc chloride test, which stains deep violet, or by boiling the specimen in a 1% solution of aniline sulfate, which turns the paper pink in the presence of the grass. Also called "alfa grass," "halfa grass," and "Spanish grass." *See also:* ESPARTO PAPER. (17, 143, 198)

esparto paper. A paper produced from ESPARTO (GRASS) pulp, usually in a mixture with a relatively small amount of chemical wood pulp. Esparto is generally used in the manufacture of better grades of printing papers (those containing 90 to 95% esparto, the balance being chemical wood). Esparto helps provide better formation and a good bulk for a given basis weight. The paper takes ink readily, presents minimum problems with regard to shrinkage and stretch, has excellent folding properties, and does not tend to dust or fluff during printing. Its major shortcoming is its low strength, which is due to its relatively short fiber length. (17, 143)

esparto wax. A yellowish-white WAX obtained from waste liquors in the preparation of ESPARTO (GRASS) pulp.

essential oil. A naturally occurring volatile liquid, formed in various parts of plant life, principally in the leaves, flowers, or fruit. The main constituents are the terpines, i.e., hydrocarbons which generally have the empirical formula $C_{10}H_{16}$, and their derivatives. They also contain alcohols, aldehydes, esters, ketones, as well as compounds containing nitrogen and sulfur. Essential oils are volatile in steam, have characteristic odors, and leave no oily marks on paper. They are virtually insoluble in water but are soluble in alcohol and ether. Many are susceptible to oxidation in the presence of air or oxygen. They are obtained by steam distillation or by extraction.

esters. Organic compounds formed by the union of an acid and an alcohol (or a phenol) with the elimination of water, and which during HYDROLYSIS break down to these component parts. An ester may also be regarded simply as an organic acid. Esters may be specified either by constituents (e.g., ethyl silicate may be considered to be the silicone ester or ethyl alcohol), or by the ethyl ester or silicic acid. Esters are sometimes used to remove fat and grease stains from paper, and, less frequently, to inhibit bookworms. (233, 235)

ether. A colorless liquid ($(C_2H_5)_2O$), with a pleasant, characteristic odor. It is highly volatile and its vapor, which is strongly narcotic, forms an explosive mixture with air. It is soluble in water to 7%, soluble in strong sulfuric and hydrochloric acids, and miscible with many organic solvents. Ether is manufactured by passing alcohol vapor into a mixture of 92% alcohol and 67% sulfuric acid at 128° C. It may also be produced as a byproduct in the manufacture of alcohol and ethylene. It is used as a solvent.

ethyl acetate. A colorless, volatile, highly flammable liquid ester ($CH_3CO_2C_2H_5$), prepared from ethyl alcohol and acetic acid. It is used as a solvent and is not dangerously toxic if handled properly. (54, 235)

ethylene dichloride. A colorless, toxic liquid ($C_2H_4Cl_2$), with an odor much like that of chloroform. It is prepared by the vapor- or liquid-phase reaction of ethylene and chlorine in the presence of a suitable catalyst. It finds some use as a solvent and is employed in the manufacture of vinyl chloride and in the fumigation of books.

Etruscan calf (Etruscan style). A method of decorating calfskin bindings by acid staining, so called because of the contrasting colors or shades of leather (light brown or terra cotta) in conjunction with dark brown or black tooling. The terra cotta shades and decoration represent Greek and Etruscan vases. Etruscan bindings usually have a rectangular panel on each cover, or, occasionally, a plain oval with a classical urn in the center. They are tooled in black, surrounded by a border of Greek palmate leaves, which are also in black, and with outer borders of classical design (Grecian key or Doric entablature) tooled in gold. The spines are also decorated with classical ornaments.

Many 19th century authorities attributed this style to John Whitaker; however, it seems more likely that it was the creation of William EDWARDS OF HALIFAX. There appears to be no very conclusive evidence as to the origin of the style, but it is known that Edwards employed it at an early date, circa 1785. It was popular during the period 1785-1820. (69, 94, 97, 158, 280)

Eucalyptus. A tree of the genus *Eucalyptus*, which has some 600 or more species, including many with bark rich in tannin. It is believed that only in Australia (to which the trees are indigenous) has the bark been exploited on a large scale, and then entirely from trees growing in the wild.

One particular bark, called Mallet (maletto) bark, obtained from *Eucalyptus astringens,* is actually one of the world's richest tannin-containing barks, having a tannin content that is often well over 40%, and even as high as 52 to 55%. Another tree, mugga, or red ironbark *(E. sideroxylon),* which is also grown commercially in Morocco, has bark containing 30 to as much as 45% tannin.

While the tanning properties of eucalyptus are good, the tannin tends to produce leather that is too darkish red in color. In addition, Mallet bark is low in soluble non-tans (8%) and therefore must be mixed with other tannins or acids to induce swelling or good plumping; mugga tannin fixes slowly giving a leather that is too soft and also dark red in color. *See also:* VEGETABLE TANNINS. (175)

Ève style (Ève bindings). A style of decoration executed by the French bookbinders, Nicholas Ève (fl 1578-1582), and his son or nephew, Clovis (fl 1584-1635). They were the Court binders and booksellers to Henri III, Henri IV, and Louis XIII during the period in which they flourished. Typical designs of their bindings included a field powdered with fleur-de-lis, and, occasionally, a center piece of the Crucifixion on the Royal Arms, and, while many bindings in the FANFARE STYLE have been attributed to them, for only a few extant fanfares can this be said with certainty. The Èves were among the first bookbinders to conceive the pattern on the covers and spine as an integrated unit. Only three extant bindings are known to be their work. All three are powdered with fleurs-de-lis. (132, 140, 154, 169)

exceptional volume. A term used by the Library Binding Institute to indicate types of books—such as music scores, certain art books, periodicals with narrow binding margins or stiff paper—which require good openability. The Institute specifies that such volumes should be sewn through the folds; when such sewing is used, any weak folds are to be reinforced with bond paper (which is too heavy for this type of guarding); loose leaves are to be hinged, and the sewing done on tapes or (sawn-in) cords. The term applies only to library binding. (209)

excitation purity. A colorimetric quantity used in designating depth of color.

expandable cloth. A type of cloth woven with a crinkled cross-thread and used for lining the spines of books, usually in edition binding. The cloth expands with the spine during rounding and backing. *See also:* STEAMSET. (140)

expanding medium. *See:* MARBLING SIZE.

expansion. A change in the dimensions of a sheet or strip of paper or board resulting from atmospheric changes. *See also:* HYGROEXPANSIVITY.

extended. 1. An addition to the inner or binding margin of a leaf of a book. This procedure is more often required for title leaves, plates, the last leaves of a book, etc., than elsewhere, as these are most likely to become detached, frayed, or otherwise damaged. Occasionally, however, if a book has to be made up from a narrower copy, the narrow leaves may be extended so that their outer edges are even with the other leaves. 2. *See:* EXTRA-ILLUSTRATED. (69)

extended cover (extension cover). A term used in pamphlet binding to indicate covers which extend beyond the trimmed edges of the leaves, as distinguished from CUT FLUSH. *See also:* SQUARES; YAPP STYLE.

extender. 1. In the adhesive industry, a substance, usually one of some adhesive capability, which is mixed into an adhesive in order to increase the amount of the adhesive, and also at times to reduce CRAZING (1). 2. A transparent or semi-transparent chemical added in powder form to a printing ink, either to alter the strength of its color or to improve working properties. (140, 309)

extensibility. The extent to which a material, e.g., rubber, leather, etc., can be stretched without breaking. *See also:* STRETCH. (17)

extension tabs. The leather, cloth or paper tabs made to extend from the fore edges of the leaves of books, usually for indexing purposes. *See also:* INDEX TAB. (264)

extra account-book binding. An English expression for a particular style of BLANKBOOK BINDING distinguished by an overall superior binding structure, including the taping of six sections at front and back, sewing by hand on webbings, made endpapers with leather joints, marbled edges, a calfskin or cowhide lining, a drawn-on SPRINGBACK (1) of millboard, split boards, and a calfskin or cowhide covering, with Russia bands. *See also:* BANDING; STATIONERY BINDING. (343)

extra binder. A somewhat archaic term for a craftsman who uses the best materials available and employs only techniques of forwarding known to be sound. An extra binder often decorates his bindings with a design created specifically for the particular book. (156)

extra binding. A term originally applied to the binding of books in full leather, usually morocco, in which the best materials and workmanship were used throughout. The term also implied extra care in finishing and extensive use of gold tooling. Today the term is used more loosely and is applied to a book or small lot of books bound with some special care, with attention not only to utility but to beauty of design and workmanship. (69, 94, 320, 343)

extra calf. An obsolete term applied to a book covered in a better grade of calfskin in lieu of morocco.

extra check binding. An obsolete term applied to a style of binding in which the leaves were wire-stitched or stabbed and bound in full canvas or cloth, or quarter-bound in leather with cloth sides. (264)

extra cloth. An obsolete term for a superior grade of book cloth, made of a base of cotton, starch-filled on the reverse side and color-filled rather than dyed. It was made in both a plain finish and in a variety of patterns, the heavy color coating concealing the weave of the fabric and giving a solid color effect. *See also:* BUCKRAM. (140)

extracted bone glue. *See:* BONE GLUE.

extra gilt. A term sometimes applied to elaborate gold tooling on the spine and covers of a leather binding.

extra high bulk book paper. A book paper which, in a basis weight of 45 pounds (25 × 38 — 500), bulks 344 pages or fewer to the inch under a pressure of 35 pounds per square inch. (17)

extra-illustrated. A book illustrated by means of engravings, variant title pages, and the like, which were not included in the book by the publisher, but added later. This additional matter may consist of original drawings, manuscripts, etc., but it may also consist of leaves taken from other books. The added material may be mounted, inlaid, or trimmed to conform to the size of the other leaves of the book. Also called "Grangerized" (a term derived from the vogue begun by the publication of James Granger's *Biographical history of England,* in 1769, in which Granger had blank leaves included so that the owner could insert desired illustrations). (69)

extra thick. A term used by library binders to indicate a book greater than a stated specified thickness, usually 2½ inches. The significance of the term is that library binders generally impose an additional charge for each inch or fraction thereof in excess of the prescribed "normal" thickness.

extra time. An hourly charge imposed by a binder or bindery, in the latter example, usually a library binder, for excessive repairs, mending, guarding, scoring, etc., beyond the extent considered "normal" for the average book. "Extra time" would normally apply to operations involved in sewing a book through the folds instead of oversewing. It may also apply to the repair and/or cleaning of water- or smoke-damaged books, or other unusual and/or time consuming work. "Extra time" is not meant to be applied in cases of regular work involved in library binding, e.g., collating.

eyelet. A fastener, made of plastic or metal, and used on looseleaf papers, stiff covers, etc. to protect apertures from tearing out where cords, thongs, or fasteners are inserted.

eyelet crusher. A hand-operated, pliers-like device used for fastening a reinforcing grommet in an eyelet.

eyelet punch. A punch and die used to make eyelets in cloth, leather or paper, generally for hanging purposes.

eyeletting. The process of reinforcing punched holes with plastic or metal grommets. This work is generally done by firms specializing in calendar work, and the like.

f. Abbreviation for *feint,* which, when applied to ruling, signifies *feint ruling,* i.e., the fine, pale horizontal lines ruled on a sheet of blankbook paper by means of a ruling machine; vertical feint lines would be indicated by d. & f. (q.v.), or *downs* and *feints.* (274)

fabric. *See:* BOOK CLOTH; CLOTH.

fabric bindings. A general term occasionally applied to a binding having a covering material consisting mainly of cloth. Specifically, the term refers to EMBROIDERED BINDINGS.

fabric book cloth. A term sometimes applied to a BOOK CLOTH that has had its reverse side surfaced with a soy-bean starch, and which is not calendered. The starch prevents adhesive penetration, while at the same time preserving the natural texture of the fabric.

fabrikoid. The trade name for a type of pyroxylin-coated BOOK CLOTH, although it is also at times used in a general sense. In the early period of its use, it was often referred to as IMITATION LEATHER. (196, 264)

face. 1. That part of a cowhide, between the ears and eyes to the nose, excluding the cheeks. It is of no use in bookbinding, and is actually generally removed before tanning. It is used in the manufacture of glue. 2. That part of a type character that appears in relief on the printing end of the type and which produces the impression in printing, blocking, etc. 3. The printing surface of a plate. 4. A particular design or style of a font of type. *See also:* TYPE FACE. (139, 156, 363)

faced. A method of folding used for books made up of DUPLEX (1) paper, in which the sheets are folded in such a manner that the same shades face each other throughout the volume. It is a term used mainly with reference to the binding of blankbooks, which are frequently made up of duplex papers. (159)

faced cloth. A cloth that is finished (coated and glazed) on one side only. As only one side of the cloth used in covering books is visible when on the book, most book cloths are "faced," in distinction to those in which the cloths are finished on both sides. (261)

facsimile binding. A bookbinding which closely resembles a binding style of

previous times. *See also:* CONTEMPORARY BINDING. (2)

facsimile leaf. A leaf (or leaves) prepared so as to closely imitate and replace that missing from a book, usually an older and generally valuable book.

facsimilist. One who restores a book or binding in such a manner that it retains its contemporary appearance. *See also:* CONTEMPORARY BINDING.

fadeometer. An accelerated aging testing device which exposes samples of colored materials or coatings to a carbon arc to determine their resistance to fading. The arc emits an intense actinic light which in a matter of hours approximates the destructive effect of a much longer period of ordinary daylight. Although it does not exactly duplicate the effect of prolonged exposure to natural light, it is still an effective indicator of the degree of light stability that can be expected of a material, and of the comparative resistance to fading of a number of samples. *See also:* ACCELERATED AGING TEST. (72, 233)

fading. The gradual loss of color of a pigment or dye that is chemically unstable. Unstable dyes or pigments become colorless (or at least less highly colored) compounds when they undergo chemical reactions upon exposure to the ultraviolet radiations of natural light, and to the oxygen, moisture, and other elements of the atmosphere. Dyes and pigments subject to these reactions are generally referred to as FUGITIVE COLORS. There is no known way of preventing the fading of unstable colors. (143, 233)

fair agate. A marble pattern consisting principally of black in small widely spaced spots, supplemented by large

drops produced by sprinkling potash on the marbling size. (153)

fair calf. *See:* LAW CALF.

fall in. The condition of a book in which the spine has collapsed inward after some use, usually because of inadequate or improper rounding, backing, lining of the spine, or combinations thereof. (335)

false back. A somewhat misleading term applied to a HOLLOW BACK. (115)

false bands. The imitation raised cords (bands) found on some books. They consist of narrow strips of leather (or other material, e.g., vellum) attached directly to the hollow of the cover, or in the case of a tight back binding, directly to the spine of the book. The false bands stand out in imitation of a book sewn on raised cords. In England, they were introduced as early as the 17th century. *Cf:* HUBS. *See also:* FLEXIBLE SEWING. (140, 172, 335)

fancy Dutch marble. A modification of the WAVE MARBLE, consisting of red, black, and any one of a variety of shades of blue. The red is dropped on first, followed by the black in the same proportion but somewhat thicker, and with more ox gall so that it spreads and produces larger spots. The blue is made still thicker so that with still more gall it spreads even more than the black. The surface is finished with more gall and water, which must be spread more than any of the colors. The surface of the size is then raked as for the "wave," and the design is finished with a double comb. (159)

fancy hand tools. *See:* UNIT TOOLS.

fancy marble. An edge marble produced by spreading a finely ground vegetable coloring matter mixed with spirits of wine (a solution of 90% ethyl alcohol in water). The alcohol causes the coloring matter to spread in a diversity of forms, which are then transferred to the edges of the book. (241)

fanfare style. An elaborate style of decoration consisting generally of geometrically formed compartments of varying sizes, each bounded by a ribbon consisting of a single fillet on one side and a double fillet on the other, each of which, with the exception of the center compartment (which is larger or otherwise distinguished), being filled with leafy spirals, branches of laurel, and other sprays, floral tools, and the like.

Fanfare was a rich and luxurious style and called for the greatest skill on the part of the bookbinder. It was imitated, with varying degrees of fidelity, throughout Europe from about 1570 until well into the 17th century, although its elements were largely imitative of previous styles of embellishment. Originally, the style was attributed exclusively to Nicholas and Clovis Éve, but it is more likely that a number of Parisian finishers executed many of these binding. The name "fanfare," which originated long after the style was first executed, derives from a binding of the 19th century binder, JOSEPH THOUVENIN, who revived the style on a volume he bound in 1829, *Les Fanfares et Corvées abbadesques. See* PLATE VI. (69, 158, 253)

fanning out (fan out; fan over). The process of working out the ends of a pile of sheets for pasting, preparatory to tipping, or for counting, folding, etc. Also called "run out," or "running out." (274)

fan style. A style of decorating a book characteristic of Italian bindings of the 17th century, and also Scottish bindings of the 18th century (usually referred to as Scottish "wheel" bindings). In this style a design in the likeness of a fan is tooled on the covers of the book making a full circle in the center of the cover, and often quarter circles in the corners. It represents a development of center and cornerpiece bindings. *See also:* SCOTTISH STYLE. (156, 334)

fascicle. Sections of a work which, for various reasons, including the economics of publishing and the convenience of printing, are issued in installments. They are frequently incomplete in themselves and do not necessarily coincide with the formal divisions of the publication. They usually consist of sections, or groups of plates, protected by temporary (sometimes printed) wrappers, and may or may not be numbered or designated as part, fascicle, etc. They present binding problems, particularly in that they do not necessarily coincide with the divisions of the work, and they must either be bound as odd units or held until publication or printing has been completed. Publication in parts, or fascicles, began in England in the early 17th century, become common in the 18th century, and has become relatively rare in the last fifty years or so. *See also:* PARTS OF A BOOK.

fast back. *See:* TIGHT BACK.

fast colors. Those colors which are resistant to the action of external influences, such as light, acids, alkalies, etc. In textile dyeing and other industrial processes, fast colors are those which will satisfactorily resist fading for the useful life of the product in which they are used. In book cloths, the term refers to nonfading over long exposure to artificial light, but not to natural light. Also called "lightfast," and, inappropriately, "sunfast." *See also:* FADING; FUGITIVE COLORS. (17, 143, 233)

fatigue failure. The failure of a material, such as an adhesive or paper, resulting from a number of repetitions of load (or strain), e.g., folding or flexing, in distinction from CREEP, which is a deformation caused by the continuous application of load over an extended period of time. (17)

fatliquoring. The process of introducing oil into a skin following tannage but before the leather is dried. In fatliquoring, which is usually applied to light leathers, the oil is introduced into the leather in such a manner that the individual fibers of the skin are uniformly coated. The actual percentage of oil on the weight of the leather is relatively small, being about 3 to 10%.

The principal function of fatliquoring is to influence the degree of fiber cohesion which takes place before drying. If there were no cohesion whatsoever, the skin would separate into its constituent fibrils, leaving no leather structure. On the other hand, if all the fibrils and fibers cohered, the skin would then take the form of a hard and horny material having no value as leather. Somewhere between these two extremes there is an ideal degree of cohesion for any given purpose for which the leather is to be used.

The fatliquoring process probably acts to control the differential shrinkage of grain versus corium (dermis) of the leather during drying, thus playing an important role in controlling the degree of tightness of BREAK of the leather. In addition, it also influences the handle, drape, flexibility, durability, stretch, and water resistance of leather, and also adds greatly to its strength. These are factors of primary importance in leather used for covering books.

Fatliquoring is usually carried out in a drum at the highest temperature practical for the type of leather, or about 45° C. for vegetable tanned leather and 60 to 65° C. for full chrome tanned leather. The skins are run in a drum for 30 to 40 minutes. After drumming, the leathers are usually struck out on the flesh side, carefully set out to smooth the grain, nailed or toggled out flat to dry, or paste dried.

To allow a small amount of oil to be spread uniformly over the very large surface area of the leather fibers, it is necessary first to dilute the oil. Although this could be done by means of a solvent, e.g., benzine, it is more economical, safer, and more convenient to emulsify the oil. In an EMULSION with water, the oil is dispersed in microscopically small droplets. It is important that the drops of oil in the water remain as an emulsion until they penetrate the leather, and not separate out as large drops or as a layer of oil, which could not penetrate the leather fiber and result in merely a greasy surface layer.

The properties of the finished leather can be varied by controlling the degree to which the emulsion penetrates before it "breaks," depositing the oil on the fibers. Relatively shallow penetration, which leaves the inner layers of the leather with comparatively little oil, gives a leather that has a tight break and is soft and resilient. On the other hand, if the oil is allowed to penetrate uniformly through the leather, the result will be a leather that is soft and stretchy, with any natural grain looseness accentuated.

The liquors incorporated into the leather are called fatliquors, of which there are several types. One of the earliest was the soap fatliquor, consisting of neatsfoot oil and common soap. When a vegetable-tanned leather is drummed in such a fatliquor, the slight acidity of the tannage neutralized the soap, causing fine drops of oil to be deposited on the fibers. The greater the acidity of the leather, the more rapidly this occurs, so that the oil may be deposited before it has penetrated sufficiently. Consequently, soap fatliquors are described as having poor emulsion stability, and are generally used where a fairly heavy surface fatliquoring is required. It is possible, however, to modify many types of oils chemically so that they become miscible with water without the use of emulsifying agents.

Sulfated oils are used frequently because they give good, fine-oil dispersions and are less sensitive to acid than soap fatliquors. This results in deeper penetration of the oils into the leather before they are deposited. Sulfated oils are prepared by treating fish, animal, or vegetable oils with sulfuric acid at a temperature of 10 to 20° C. The resultant product is washed with a strong brine solution to remove excess acid. The salt is necessary to prevent the sulfated oil from emulsifying with the water. Soda ash is then added to form the sodium salt of the sulfated oil and to neutralize the last traces of the acid. The more the oil is sulfated, which is to say, the more sulfuric acid that has been fixed, the greater will be its stability to acid and the more thorough its penetration into the leather. Conversely, the more acid the leather, the less the penetration. However, increasing the amount of sulfation or water miscibility, decreases the "oiliness" of the oil and therefore its lubricating powers.

Sulfonated oils are prepared by a similar process, usually at a higher temperature; the fatliquor contains the sulfonic group which gives greater stability and emulsions which penetrate deeper into the leather under acid conditions.

Still another method of obtaining emulsifying properties is to sulfite the oil. In this process, the oil is mixed well with a strong solution of sodium bisulfite ($NaHSO_3$), while the mixture is thoroughly aerated by means of compressed air. Sulfited oils behave in a manner similar to sulfated oils, but are usually said to be more acid stable and to afford deeper lubrication.

In addition to the emulsifying element of the fatliquor, a raw oil, such as mineral, castor, neatsfoot, cod or coconut oil is frequently included in the formulation. *See also:* CURRYING; STUFFING (2). (248, 275, 291, 306, 361, 363)

fats. The esters of fatty acids with glycerol. They are generally insoluble in water and are not very soluble in cold alcohol. They are soluble in hot alcohol, as well as ether, acetone, carbon disulfide, chloroform, carbon tetrachloride, benzene, as well as other organic solvents. Fats may be hydrolized to glycerol and fatty acids by boiling them with acids and alkalies, by superheated steam, and by the action of certain enzymes, notably the lipases. When alkalies are used for hydrolysis, the fatty acids combine with the alkali to form soap; therefore, alkaline hydrolysis is sometimes

referred to as saponification. Fats are used in the tannage of some leathers, in the FATLIQUORING of light leathers, in leather dressings, etc. *See also:* FAT TANNING; WAX.

fat tanning. A process of converting hides and skins into a stable, imputrecible material by means of treatments involving the incorporation of soft animal fats which undergo chemical changes while in contact with the fibers of the skin, leading to the fixation of fatty matter. *See also:* OIL TANNING. (61)

fatty acids. Monobasic acids which contain only carbon, hydrogen, and oxygen. They consist of an alkyl radical attached to the carboxyl group, and when saturated have the general formula ($C_nH_{2n}O_2$). Formic and acetic acids are the two lowest members of this saturated series. Unsaturated fatty acids follow several series, including: 1) the oleic acid series ($C_nH_{2n-2}O_2$); 2) the linoleic acid series ($C_nH_{2n-4}O_2$); and 3) the linolenic acid series ($C_nH_{2n-6}O_2$). There are also other naturally occurring fatty acids that are found in nature mainly as glycerides, which constitute the most important part of the fats and oils, and as esters of other alcohols and the waxes.

faulty margin. An unequal margin, one generally resulting from imperfect REGISTER (3). Such a margin may result in part of the printed matter being obscured by oversewing, or cropped unintentionally during trimming. (156)

feather edge. The finely pared edge of a piece of leather, or a thin, rough edge, such as deckle edge. *See also:* EDGING (1). (256)

feathering. 1. *See:* EDGING (1). 2. A printing fault seen as the spreading or feathering of the ink outside the printing area and generally along the direction in which the fibers lie. It may be a result of excess solvent in the ink, an unsuitable paper, or both. (156)

feather ornament. An engraved finishing tool resembling a feather. It is found mainly on clasps and catches, but also at times, in the form of a tool used in decorating leather bindings. (250)

feather stitch. An embroidery stitch consisting of a line of diagonal blanket stitches worked alternately to the left and right. (111)

featherweight. 1. Papers which are extremely light in proportion to their bulk. Pure esparto papers are the bulkiest, but are difficult to handle, as they are soft and spongy. Paper of standard bulk or above is termed

featherweight, while the same grade of paper under the standard bulk is called ANTIQUE BOOK PAPER. 2. A general term indicating lightweight book paper, thin opaque writing paper, etc. (17)

featherweight book paper. Paper used mainly for fiction, especially where bulkiness is desired for a given number of leaves. The standard basis weights range from 50 to 80 pounds ($25 \times 38 - 500$). In England, such papers are made largely from ESPARTO (GRASS). Featherweight book papers are porous and difficult to handle. (17, 140)

feather work. A style of decoration, originally used on Irish bindings of the 18th century, emphasizing curved lines probably made with a gouge, which radiate outward from a central point producing a delicate and very rich featherlike pattern. (156)

feeder. An apparatus for feeding paper into a printing press, ruling machine or folding machine, gathered sections into a sewing machine, sewn books into a casing-in machine, etc. It may also be the device on automatically fed machines performing the same function. The first feeders moved the sheet forward and adjusted it, while the sheets in the pile were still separated by hand. From this early "semi-automatic" feeder, which still exists in numerous machines, particularly in library binding, the modern completely automatic feeders were developed.

Three classes of automatic feeders are in general use: 1) the pile feeder, which operates by means of a jet of air which raises the sheet and brings it into contact with a sunction wheel which moves it forward into the feed table. As the sheets feed off the top of the pile, the entire pile is raised to keep the top sheet always at the same level. Some pile feeders separate the sheets by means of push fingers that buckle up the corners of the paper and move it forward one sheet at a time; 2) the continuous feeder, which uses bands of webbing to carry the sheets which are previously fanned out and placed on the feeder. The bands carry the sheets around a roller and up to the feed wheels where a combing wheel advances the top sheet to a guide. At the correct moment, the guide drops and another wheel drops on the edge of the paper and carries it forward. Some continuous feeders use an air jet and suction wheel to advance the sheets; 3) the friction feeder, which operates in a manner similar to the continuous, expect that the sheets are not carried around a roller; in this case each new lift of paper must be slipped under the edge of the previous lift. (278, 320, 339)

feel. The qualities or properties of texture, finish, bulk, grain, smoothness, suppleness, stretchiness, softness, etc., of leather, paper, cloth, etc., as judged by the sense of touch. Although purely subjective in nature, "feel" is nonetheless one of the properties by which leather and paper are judged. (139, 248)

felt. 1. The blanket of absorbent material, e.g., wool, placed between sheets of handmade paper that have just been removed from the mold. The purpose of the felt is to absorb water from the wet sheets. *See also:* COUCH (1, 2). 2. A continuous belt on a papermaking machine, generally made of wool, but also as a combination of wool, cotton, asbestos, and synthetic fibers. Felts perform the function of mechanical conveyors or transmission belts, provide a cushion between the press rolls, and serve as a medium for the removal of water from the wet web. 3. The blanket of a printing press used to soften the impression. 4. The inside lining found in some book boxes. 5. A cloth produced from matted fibers of wool, or wool and fur or hair, and made into a compact material by compression, usually while wet (17, 274)

felted. 1. A term sometimes applied to the characteristic of firmness or solidity of a book that has been heavily pressed several times during the course of binding, thus compacting the leaves. 2. *See:* FELTING. (343)

felted fibers. A material used in the manufacture of book-cloth substitutes, as a basis for imitation leathers, and in lieu of spine lining fabric in edition binding. It consists of synthetic fibers felted together into sheets and laminated to impart strength. One of these fiber-bonded fabrics is made from regenrated cellulose, the finished product being reasonably strong and durable. It is impregnated with appropriate fillers for use as a substitute for book cloth and leather. Untreated, the material is much cheaper than spine lining fabric and stronger than paper. Some edition binders use the parallel laid bonded fiber fabric to form the joint between the case and text block. As a book-covering material, this substitute is said to be easy to work and block, but most are aesthetically unappealing, lacking the texture and appearance of substance of cloth and buckram. They are decidedly inferior to leather in virtually every respect. They are mar-

keted under a number of trade names. (81)

felting. The process of intermingling the fibers during the manufacture of paper, either on the wire of the machine, or on the mold when making paper by hand.

felt side. The side of a sheet of paper that has not been in contact with the Fourdrinier wire, and which therefore is the smooth side of the sheet rather than the WIRE SIDE. The felt side is considered to be the "top" of the sheet. (42, 365)

fence. 1. The movable guide attachment of a card or board cutter that controls the location and extent of the cut. *See also:* BACK GAUGE. 2. The thin cards placed between the boards and fly leaves of a book to prevent marking by the turn-ins or tongue of the split boards when pressing, and also, in books having excessive swell after sewing, to facilitate smashing without "throwing out" the sections at the spine. *See also:* PRESSING TINS (2). 3. An endpaper of a blankbook. (145, 256, 276)

fenders. *See:* FENCE (2); PRESSING TINS (2).

Ferrar, Nicholas (1592-1637). One of the more interesting figures in the history of English bookbinding. Ferrar and his relative, John Collet (as well as Collet's wife and 14 children), and Ferrar's mother, established a semi-religious community called the English Protestant Nunnery, at Little Gidding, in Huntingdonshire, in about 1625. Ferrar employed a bookbinder, who taught the family the craft, as well as gilding and the so-called pasting-printing by means of a rolling press. The members of the community produced the remarkable "Harmonies" of the Scriptures, one of which was produced by Mary Collet for King Charles I. Some of their bindings were in gold-tooled leather, some were in velvet which had a considerable amount of gold tooling, and one was in red parchment with the center and corners of each cover ornamented with pieces of white parchment, pierced and gilded. Some of the embroidered bindings of this period have also been attributed to the so-called nuns of Little Gidding. (50, 205)

ferrous sulfate. An astringent salt ($FeSO_4$), usually obtained in the form of the pale green efflorescent, crystalline heptahydrate ($FeSo_4 \cdot 7H_2O$) as a byproduct, and used extensively in the 19th century in the production of SPRINKLED CALF, MOTTLED CALF, and TREE CALF bindings. Unfortunately, its

use resulted in severe deterioration of the leather in most cases. It was also used in the execution of the JAPAN MARBLE. It is sometimes used today in dyeing or finishing with dyewoods to impart a blue-black shade to leather, in the manufacture of writing inks, and in engraving and lithography. Also called "copperas," or "green vitriol." (237)

festoon drying. A method of air drying paper. The paper is hung in loops (festoons) over rods which move slowly through a drying chamber in which the temperature and humidity are controlled. This type of drying is used for paper that has been tub sized or coated. (5, 17)

fiber. 1. A small, slender tube which is the unit cell of vegetable growth and the basic unit of paper pulps. Fibers are sometimes considered to be of two classes, i.e., bast and wood, but they are more appropriately designated by reference to the tissue or region in which they occur. e.g., cortical fibers, pericyclic fibers, phloem fibers, wood fibers, leaf fibers, etc. Other types of fiber, such as mineral, animal and synthetic, are also used to a certain extent in paper manufacture.

The longest natural fibers normally encountered in papers are about one fourth of an inch in length and the shortest about one-sixteenth of an inch. Fibers are generally about 100 times longer than they are wide, although some fibers, such as cotton, have a length to diameter ratio of more than 1,000 to 1. The walls of all fibers are composed of small strands called FIBRILS. Chemically the fibrils are composed of a number of cellulose chains. Other chemical components in fibers other than cellulose include hemicelluloses and lignin.

The physical properties of length, diameter, wall thickness, and FINES content are the most significant in determining the characteristics of paper made from natural fibers. The approximate relationships between fiber characteristics and paper properties are:

Property of the Paper:	Increased by:	Decreased by:
tensile strength	long fiber	large diameter
stretch	long fiber	thick cell wall
tearing resistance	long fiber, thick cell wall	
folding endurance	long fiber	thick cell wall
opacity	thick cell wall, high fines content	long fiber
bulk	long fiber, thick cell wall	
porosity	long fiber, thick cell wall	large diameter
formation	thick cell wall, high fines, large diameter	long fiber

The chemical characteristics also have a significant effect on the properties of the paper. The length of the CELLULOSE CHAIN, for example, which is the basic unit in a fiber, contributes greatly to the strength of the fiber. If these chains are naturally short, or have been shortened either by chemical or mechanical treatment or influences, the strength of the fibers will be naturally lower or else reduced; therefore the paper will be weaker. In addition, the paper loses strength if the cellulose chains are shortened due to chemical action subsequent to manufacture of the paper.

Paper pulps that contain a high degree of hemicelluloses are easy to refine, have good bonding strength and low tearing resistance, and good RATTLE. Excessive bleaching of the fibrous stock, especially when done with strong caustic extractions, results in removal of hemicelluloses. The fibers then have greater flexibility but do not bond together effectively, resulting in a paper that is soft and absorbent.

Unbleached paper pulps tend to contain more lignin than is found in bleached pulps. The presence of lignin results in stiffer, tougher fibers which do not collapse against each other very well, resulting in fewer interfiber bonds being formed during manufacture. Bleached fibers, on the other hand, conform better and afford greater contact betwen fibers, resulting in a stronger paper. While bleached fibers conform better than unbleached, improper bleaching may result in the loss of hemicelluloses and damage to the cellulose chains.

2. The complex proteinaceous structure, composed of ropelike bundles of fibrils organized in long, wavy bundles that vary in diameter from approximately 1 to 20 microns. These pro-

teinaceous fibers make up the principal constituent of COLLAGEN. (18, 72, 323, 363)

fiber boards. 1. Pressing boards made up of laminated sheets of heavily pressed fiber. 2. Pressing boards made of hard wood that have flanges of hard pressed fiber instead of brass or other metal.

fiber composition. The various types of fibers making up a sheet of paper or board, generally expressed in percentages. Fiber physiology and various staining methods are generally used to determine fiber composition. (17)

fiberize. A process used to reduce wood chips, reclaimed paper stock, dry broke, and other papermaking fibrous materials to individual fibers. The equipment used for this includes disc mills, conical refiners, etc. Sometimes the materials are first softened with water or steam, or by chemical treatment before the mechanical action. (17, 98)

fiber orientation. The direction in which the greater proportion of the fibers of a paper have their larger dimension, which is their length. Handmade papers have the least degree of lengthwise orientation due to the multiple shaking of the mold when it is lifted from the vat, which causes the fibers to settle in various directions. Machine-made papers have the greater proportion of their fibers oriented in the longer or MACHINE DIRECTION of the paper; however, some Fourdrinier papermaking machines are equipped with shaking wires that cause more fibers to shift away from the direction of movement of the wire. (157, 320)

fibrilae. See: FIBRILS.

fibrillation. The process of loosening the threadlike elements known as FIBRILS from the wall of the fiber, thus providing greater surface area for the formation of fiber-to-fiber bonds. Also called "brushing out" (17, 98)

fibrils. The fine, threadlike elements that

make up the structure of fibers of certain natural and synthetic materials and which are considered to be made up ultimately of long-chain molecules oriented in a bundle in one direction. In vegetable fibers they are the threadlike elements of the wall of the native cellulose fiber, consisting of still finer microscopic microfibrils. In animal fibers they are the long proteinaceous filaments consisting of bundles of submicroscopic micelles, which in turn are made up of very long molecules of collagen twisted together. Fibrils are the smallest physical unit encountered in fibers; at this point the physical area ends and the chemical area begins. (17, 291, 363)

fibroblasts. Cellular structures which are thought to participate in the formation of the fibers of connective tissue in animals, i.e., FIBRILS, and which may also be responsible for the formation of ground substance. (26, 248, 291, 363)

fiddle stitching (fiddling). A term applied somewhat inaccurately to a method of lacing, rather than stitching, executed by winding thread or cord in and around v-shaped cleats of slots sawn at regular intervals in the spine of the gathered sections. See also: SMYTH-CLEAT SEWING. (12, 81)

filigree doublures. A DOUBLURE (1) consisting of ornamental openwork of an intricate design, frequently of hairlike arabesques, intricate backgrounds of flowering vines with delicate spiraling stems, cut from leather and laid over a contrasting background. See also: ONLAY. (347)

fill (fill in; filling). 1. The heavy paper pasted to the insides of the boards within the edges of the turn-ins. See also: FILLING IN (1). 2. The paper used to fill out albums bound with stubs so as to make the book of equal thickness from fore edge to spine for purposes of trimming, casing-in, etc. 3. The material used to fill a fabric. See: BOOK CLOTH; BUCKRAM 4. See: FENCE (2). 5. See: SPINE LINING (1). 6. See: LOADING (2). 7. See: WEFT. (274), 341)

filled. A BOOK CLOTH treated with a chemical compound which fills the interstices and/or covers the fibers of the fabric to give it body, color or other desirable physical or chemical characteristics. (102)

filler. 1. A material, such as acryllic, starch or pyroxylin, used to fill the interstices of a base fabric. The principal characteristics desired include cheapness, flexibility, water resistance, durability, printability, mold and fungi resistance, and resistance to insects and other vermin. *See also:* BOOK CLOTH; BUCKRAM. 2. Usually, a non-fibrous material added to the fiber furnish of paper. The major characteristics desired include cheapness, opacity, printability, color, and flatness. *See also:* LOADING (2). 3. The inner ply or plies of a board made up of multiple layers. 4. An ornamented outline or border in gold or color. 5. A relatively nonadhesive substance, such as clay, diatomaceous earth, walnut shell flour, etc., used to extend an adhesive or to provide increased bulk, and/or to improve its working properties, strength, permanence, or other characteristics. *See also:* BINDER (4); EXTENDER (1). 6. *See:* PADDING (1). (17, 42, 222, 309, 350)

filler clay. A type of CLAY incorporated into the papermaking furnish before sheet formation. Its purpose is to fill the voids between the paper fibers so as to improve printability, opacity, brightness, etc. Filler clays, such as KAOLIN, may be of a larger particle size than those clays used as COATING CLAY. (17)

fillet. 1. A wheel-shaped finishing tool having one or more raised bands on its circumference. It is used to impress a line or parallel lines on the covering material of a book, usually one bound in leather. The lines may be continuous or the fillets may have a wedge-shaped gap in the circumference to facilitate starting and stopping lines and also to enable lines to be joined evenly at corners.

It is not known when the fillet first came into use. Bindings of the 12th century, and even earlier, have impressed lines that could have been made with a fillet, but they may also have been impressed with a pallet, or similar tool, dragged across the leather rather than rolled. It is argued that it probably did not precede the roll, which was introduced in about 1470, by any great length of time, because once a wheel-type tool was introduced, it would soon be patterned. It is sometimes called a "roulette" in the United States.

2. The plain line or lines impressed on a book cover. The so-called French fillet is a triple fillet (always in gold) having unevenly spaced lines. (69, 161, 172, 236, 335)

fillet pad. A mechanical device which unwinds ribbon gold (leaf) when gilding by means of a fillet or roll. (264)

fillet rolls. Finishing tools consisting of brass rolls approximately 3½ to 4½ inches in diameter, with 1, 2, or 3 lines

on the circumference. *See also:* FILLET (1). (264)

filling. *See:* WEFT; PADDING (1).

filling in. 1. The operation of pasting heavy paper to the insides of the boards of a book within the turn-ins of the covering material. The purpose of filling in is to prevent the thickness of the turn-ins from being noticeable under the board papers. Filling in is done only in craft bookbinding. 2. A fault in blocking, printing, etc., in which the spaces in types, or the spaces between the dots of a halftone block, fill with gold, coloring, or ink. In blocking it may be caused by worn or damaged type, or by a type holder that is too hot; in printing, it may be caused by too much ink, or an ink that is unsuitable for the job, by the form being too high, the rollers being set incorrectly, or by the use of an unsuitable paper, especially one which fluffs. (92, 156, 161, 335)

film forming. That property of an adhesive which enables it to cast a continuous dimensionally stable film. Film forming also refers to the relative strength of the cast adhesive film. Adhesives with good film forming characteristics are those which tend to deposit more uniform films of high structural strength. (222)

fine paper copy. A book printed on paper of a superior quality (which often but not always is larger in size) than the

balance of the edition, which is printed on ordinary paper.

fine red. A marbling color used before the introduction of synthetic dyestuffs, and prepared by boiling Brazil dust, nutgalls, alum, sal ammoniac (ammonium chloride) and hydrochloric acid in water, or by dissolving Brazil wood in hydrochloric acid. (97)

fines. The very short fibers or fiber fragments and ray cells. Both types are very short, consequently they reduce the strength of the paper. The fines from broken fibers have thicker cell walls and larger diameters than those from ray cells, which leads to differences in the final sheet depending upon which types are present. Sometimes also called "flour" or "wood flour." (42)

finish. 1. The degree of brilliance, pliability and working qualities of cloth, leather, or paper. 2. To letter and/or decorate a book. *See:* FINISHING. 3. the surface properties of a sheet of paper as determined by its surface contour, gloss, and general appearance. It is a property which is usually determined visually. In uncoated printing papers, there are five major finishes recognized under the general terminology of machine-finish papers; in order of decreasing degree of smoothness, they are: English, machine, vellum, eggshell, and antique. For papers of higher finish, *see:* SUPERCALENDER finish. Writing papers, including bonds,

FILLET

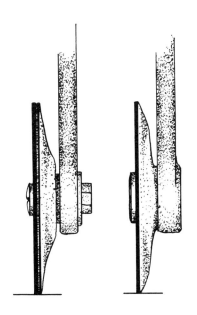

double   single

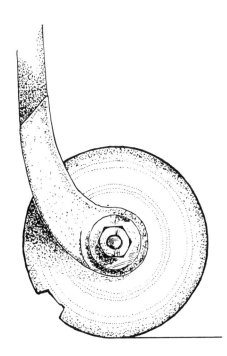

ledges, and manilas, generally have finishes called cockle, glazed, machine, supercalendered, and vellum. The finishes used for cover paper include antique, machine, plate, supercalendered, and vellum. The principal finishes for bristols are antique, egg-shell, plate, and vellum. (17, 72)

finish break. A CRUSTY BREAK of a leather —one which can be attributed to improper finishing.

finisher. 1. The bookbinder or gilder who performs the processes of polishing the leather, lettering, and embellishing, which are carried out on a hand-bound book subsequent to forwarding. In France, it is not unusual for the two operations—i.e., forwarding and finishing—to be performed by different persons; in England and the United States, on the other hand, the two are usually done by the same craftsman, except in commercial hand binding. 2. A machine used to apply varnish, lacquer, or other fluid to covering materials by means of a spray or roller, or a printing or blocking plate. 3. A term sometimes applied to flat or cylindrical polishing tools, e.g., a BURNISHER (2). (158, 173)

finishing. 1. The art or process of polishing, lettering, and embellishing the spine, covers, insides of the covers, and sometimes the edges of a book, as well as inlaying, onlaying, varnishing, and otherwise decorating and/or protecting the finished bookbinding.

The purpose of finishing is to identify (letter) and beautify the book, but, at least in the latter case, in such a manner as not to interfere with the strength of the binding. The degree of finishing depends upon the nature of the book, the craftsmanship of the binder or finisher (gilder, as he is traditionally called), whether another craftsman did the forwarding, and, at times, the wishes of the customer.

Finishing has assumed a very important role in the craft of bookbinding since the earliest times. Almost all early finishing, at least in Europe, was in blind until the latter half of the 15th century, when GOLD TOOLING was introduced into Italy. *See also:* BLIND TOOLING.

In modern finishing, all but the simplest designs are measured out and drawn or tooled on thin paper. This is then positioned on the cover and heated tools are pressed through. The paper is then removed, and the blind impressions are again blinded-in. This sharpens and deepens the impressions, and, if gold is to be used, provides a

smooth flat surface for the metal. In addition to making it possible to execute extremely difficult patterns without making errors on the leather itself, the use of a paper pattern eliminates the necessity of making basic guide lines in blind upon which the design is then built, and which almost invariably show beyond the tooling. It is uncertain when paper patterns were introduced, but they probably were not used much before 1830.

Not all leathers can be tooled successfully. Aside from the great difficulty encountered in tooling chrome-tanned leathers, only those vegetable-tanned (or tawed) leathers with surfaces firm enough to hold a line, such as goatskin, calfskin, pigskin, etc., are suitable. With the exception of sheepskin, leathers that are loose and stretchy do not retain impressions very well.

Library bindings are seldom "finished" to any greater degree than lettering of the spine, although gold lines and/or symbols are sometimes blocked on the spine. Edition bindings vary widely in the degree of their ornamentation. Whatever ornamentation they may have is usually done by means of blocking or printing. Whichever the case, they are "finished" only in the very broadest sense of the term. *See also:* BLOCKING (1); GOLD BLOCKING; INLAY (4); ONLAY; POLISHING.

2. The various operations in paper manufacture performed after it leaves the papermaking machine. Finishing operations include supercalendering, plating, slitting, rewinding, sheeting, trimming, sorting, counting, and packaging. Ruling, punching, pasting, folding and embossing are also at times considered to be paper finishing operations.

3. The processes in leather manufacture following tannage, including shaving or splitting, dyeing, fatliquoring, setting out, drying, staking, finishing or seasoning, glazing (or plating or embossing), and measuring. (118, 130, 161, 172, 194, 236, 320, 335, 343, 363)

finishing press. A small press consisting essentially of two wooden cheeks, connected by a screw at each end, with handles for turning. A press pin is not required for this type of press. The finishing press is similar to the cutting-or lying-press, but is smaller and generally has no runners. It came into use as long ago as the early 19th century, and no basic changes were made in this basic press until a completely different

type came into use in the 1880s. This new press consisted of two small cheeks, somewhat like rounded-off backing boards, which moved on joints. (161)

finishing stand. 1. A revolving stand consisting of a flat, circular board, covered with a soft, smooth material, mounted on another board. The lower board is stationary and rests on rubber knobs which are attached to its lower surface to raise it and prevent slipping. Ball bearings between the two boards allow the top one to revolve easily, thus making it possible to shift the position of the book with minimum effort. 2. A stand with a sliding shelf and an arm clamp which can be attached to the bench to hold a book while finishing. *See also:* FINISHING PRESS. (264)

finishing stove. A small stove used for heating finishing and lettering tools. Such stoves generally have a circular plate in the center which is heated, and an outer notched ring to support the handles of the tools. Modern finishing stoves are heated by gas or electricity, and some are controlled by a thermostat.

While little is known of the form of early finishing stoves, many different types were probably used, because they were frequently fabricated according to the bookbinder's own specifications. A great variety were in use during the early years of the 19th century, all of which burned charcoal or coke, as they must have done for centuries. The gas-heated stove was probably introduced in the 1830s, while the electric stove has been in use since the early part of the 20th century. (130, 161, 236, 335)

finishing tools. *See:* BAND PALLET; CIRCLES; CREASER (2); FILLET (1); GOUGE; HAND LETTERS; PALLET (1); POLISHER; ROLL (1); STAMP (1); UNIT TOOLS.

firmness of leather. That property of a leather reflected in the force required to bend a standard strip of heavy leather through an arc of given radius of curvature, so that the grain surface of the leather forms an arc of a circle of given radius. (363)

first binding. The original binding of a library book. The term is not generally used with reference to the binding of serial publications, but to the binding of pamphlets in self covers, paperback books, sewn books in temporary covers, or books in gatherings. (129)

first edition. The entire number of copies of a book or other publication printed from the same setting of type. The books may be printed at any time. A new edition does not come into being until there have been substantial changes in the type, i.e., a corrected edition, additions to the text (which is a revised edition), or until the type has been reset, which would be a new edition, 2nd edition, etc. (69, 156)

first impression. 1. The initial application of a finishing tool or hand letter to the covering material of a book. 2. All of the copies of a book printed during the first printing operation and before any alterations or additions are made. Subsequent printings following the first, producing reprints, are called "second impression," "third impression," etc. (140)

first lining. The initial strip of material attached to the spine of a book subsequent to rounding and backing. In edition and library binding, it is generally the only lining. *See also:* SECOND LINING; SPINE LINING (1). (154, 343)

firsts. 1. Hides and skins that are, or at least are designated as, perfect, i.e., free from holes, tears, putrefactive damage, etc. *See also:* GOOD SECONDS. 2. A term applied at times to the FIRST EDITION of a book. (335)

fish glue. An adhesive obtained by boiling the skins of certain fish, particularly the cod fish, and used cold mainly in the liquid form. It works easily and is used in bookbinding for tipping-in and casemaking. *See also:* ISINGLASS (191, 309)

fish grained split. A sheepskin split, dyed and finished by embossing with a small "gunpowder" grain. (97)

fish scales. A particular grain pattern in a leather resembling the scales of a fish. Leather with this type of grain was at one time used by bookbinders who wanted a leather giving the effect of being blind tooled. (97)

fixation value. The relative speed with which different vegetable tannins combine with hide substance as measured by the relative amounts which combine under specified conditions. (248)

fixative. A clear solution, such as a synthetic resin in xylene (C_8H_{10}), sprayed or coated on a work of art, a reproduction copy, etc., that "fixes" or stabilizes the image, thus making it more resistant to wear, smudging, etc. Fixatives protect and preserve, but they also at times change the refractive index and may also impart an unnatural sheen to the colors, possibly one not intended by the artist. (233)

fixed back. *See:* TIGHT BACK.

fixed tannin. *See:* COMBINED TANNIN IN LEATHER.

flag. 1. A marker, such as a small strip of colored paper, placed so as to protrude from between the leaves of a book. Its purpose is either to show the position of the book on the shelf, or to indicate that the leaf marked (or the entire book) requires special attention. 2. A slip placed in the center of each section to facilitate sewing of the headband. (139, 173)

flaking. The separating of the coating material from a coated sheet of paper or cloth, appearing in the form of flakes. Art paper and the cheaper grades of coated cloth are particularly subject to this problem. (17)

flange. The projection on either side of the spine of a text block that has been rounded and backed. It is commonly, and more accurately, referred to as the SHOULDER (1). (12, 256)

flat back binding. 1. A hand-bound book which has not been rounded and backed before the boards are attached. The term is also sometimes applied to a book which has lost its round; however FLAT SPINE is a more appropriate term for this condition. The spine of a flat back binding has a tendency to become concave. Also called "square back." *See also:* FLAT BACK CASE BINDING. 2. A leather binding which does not have bands appearing on the spine. (140, 236, 335, 343)

flat back case binding. A simple type of (library) binding which has a flat spine and is cased or has a one-piece covering. This type of binding is suitable for typescript, some pamphlets, and adhesive-bound paperbacks. (258)

flat cut index. *See:* CUT THROUGH INDEX.

flat finish. A paper having a smooth, glare-free finish.

flats. An old term applied to papers of various types which have a well closed, even formation and a high finish, and which are particularly suitable for writing purposes. The term derives from the practice of counting into quires and then folding the pack. When it became the practice to deliver writing papers unfolded, they were called "flats." Today the term is usually restricted to papers such as tablet paper, as well as to paper with a smooth, flat finish as distinguished from bond finish. (197)

flat spine. The shape given to books in the 1820s. They were not the same as the FLAT BACK BINDING because they were backed but not rounded, or had very little rounding. The flat spine and HOLLOW BACK came into use at about the same time. (236)

flax. The bast fiber from the inner bark of the flax plant (*Linun usitatissimum*), and the source of linen for thousands of years. The bast fiber is about 25 mm long and approximately 0.02 mm thick, giving it a length to diameter ratio of about 1,250:1. It is thinner than the cotton fiber and its tube has thicker walls. It is also stiffer and stronger than cotton, has a rounded section and is knotted at intervals along its length. Linen rags, cuttings, thread, etc., have long been used in the manufacture of paper. *See also:* BOOK CLOTH; SEWING THREAD. (17, 143)

flaying. The process of removing the hide or skin from an animal carcass. Flaying is normally the job of the butcher, and, in general, the methods used in flaying give first priority to producing a good quality carcass, not hide, as the animal is generally slaughtered for its meat.

The animal should be in a clean, healthy condition and the slaughter rapid and efficient. Bruising should be carefully avoided. The animal is bled after slaughter to remove blood from the carcass and also from the small veins and arteries in the skin. If this is not done rapidly, the blood will clot and putrefy, resulting in blue-black markings in the skin. The skin should also be removed immediately, while the carcass is still warm, as removal then is much easier. Subsequent to flaying, the skin cools down more quickly, giving less chance of putrefaction. Some form of curing generally follows flaying. *See also:* BRINING; DRY-SALTING; PUTREFACTIVE DAMAGE; WET-SALTING. (248, 291, 306, 363)

flea seed. A small, brown, hard seed, so called because of its resemblance to a flea. It is boiled in water to make MARBLING SIZE. It was usually used in combination with GUM TRAGACANTH in the execution of the shell and Spanish marble patterns. It was not (and apparently could not) be used for the drawn or combed marbles, as it dragged the colors and did not allow the comb to pass through smoothly. As it has no advantage over CARRAGHEEN MOSS or gum tragacanth, its use was never extensive and it is seldom if ever used at all today. (217, 236, 369)

flesher. The inside split (flesh split) of a lamb- or sheepskin, embossed and finished in imitation of grained leather, and used at times for lining the spines of cheaper blankbooks. *See also:* BUFFING (1). (61, 264)

fleshing. One of the beamhouse operations in leather manufacture. Fleshing consists of the removal of areolar tissue from the flesh side of a hide or skin. It usually precedes liming, and is generally done by means of a fleshing machine, or, in hand work, by working the skin over the beam with a sharp, two-handed knife. In European tanneries, fleshing generally takes place following liming and unhairing.

Fleshing promotes the entry of water from the flesh side, which is important as water is absorbed more readily from the flesh side than from the epidermal or grain side. Fleshing also flattens and stretches the skin, has a pronounced cleaning action, and, in the case of greasy skin, such as domestic sheep or pig, removes a quantity of surplus fat.

Good, clean fleshing is important for the success of all subsequent processes, as bits of flesh or fat on the skin can retard the penetration of tannins, fatliquors, and the like. *See also:* GREEN FLESHING. (291, 363)

flesh side. The side of a hide or skin next to the animal, or the side opposite the grain side. *See also:* BUFFING (1); REVERSE CALF; SPLIT.

flesh split. 1. The inner layer of a hide or skin separated from the main part of the skin by means of a splitting machine. 2. The leather made from such a split. *See also:* FLESHER. (61)

fleur-de-lis-lozenge. A lozenge shaped finishing tool made up of a fluer-de-lis, or a variation thereof, the three pedals and stalks of which extend to fill the four corners. (250)

fleuron. A finishing tool cut in a nondescript form, partly floral or foliage in nature, generally of a lozenge shape and generally used to fill the lozenge compartments of a panel that is divided by diagonal fillets. (250)

flexible adhesives. *See:* ADHESIVES; FLEXIBLE GLUE; INTERNALLY PLASTICIZED; RESINOUS ADHESIVES.

flexible endpaper. An endpaper designed to provide a flyleaf that is heavier than a single sheet of paper, but is still flexible enough to not interfere with the opening of the book. Developed at the workshop of British binders Roger Powell and Peter Waters between 1960 and 1965, this endpaper is constructed by tipping two folios together in two places: along the spine and along the fore edge.

flexible glue. Generally, an ordinary animal glue containing GLYCEROL or SORBITOL, the softening effect of the latter supposedly lasting longer than the former. These softening agents, or "humectants," are hygroscopic and may, under certain conditions, absorb so much moisture as to promote the growth of mold; consequently a mold

inhibitor is generally included in the plasticizer.

The origin of "flexible" animal glues is unknown, but they were certainly in use since early in the 20th century. Their use in bookbinding, however, has declined sharply in recent years in favor of INTERNALLY PLASTICIZED synthetic adhesives, such as the RESINOUS ADHESIVES. (198, 236)

flexible not to show. A method of sewing the sections of a book in which the spine of the gathered sections is sawn lightly so that the saw cuts do not penetrate completely through the folds of the sections. The sewing is then done on thin cords, encircling them as in FLEXIBLE SEWING. If the cords project above the spine after sewing they are hammered into the grooves during backing. Books sewn in this manner may have hollow or tight backs; in the case of the hollow back, the purpose of sewing not to show apparently is to prevent creasing of the leather of the spine by the cords, while attempting to retain the strength of genuine flexible sewing. In the case of the tight back, the purpose is to have a smooth spine and a book with sewing that is stronger than is possible with RECESSED-CORD SEWING; however, in this case, most of the desired benefits are negated because of the need to make the cords extremely thin. (236, 371)

flexible sewing. A method of sewing the sections of a book to cords or bands which are *above* the backs of the sections and rest against them, instead of being recessed into the paper. *See:* RECESSED-CORD SEWING. The sewing thread is looped completely around the cords, instead of passing in front of them. This type of sewing may be done on single or double cords and is one of the strongest forms of hand sewing known. The method was in use in Europe as early as the 8th century, and represents the foundation upon which hand bookbinding was built and developed for a thousand years.

The number of bands, which were always double (i.e., two cords or thongs adjacent to each other and almost touching), on which 12th and 13th century books were sewn varied from two to five (in the latter case the cords being spaced so there was a greater space between the cords than between the end bands and the head and tail of the book), although examples of books sewn on as many as fourteen cords are known. The use of double cords gradually diminished, however, and by the middle of the 16th century the technique of sew-

ing on single cords had become fairly well established, although largely for smaller books and economical bindings.

The use of flexible sewing has been dominant in fine binding until the present day; however, its use declined sharply from the end of the 18th century until the end of the 19th century, when it was revived to some extent due to the efforts of T. J. Cobden-Sanderson and Douglas Cockerell.

Flexible sewing is not suitable for books printed on very heavy paper, nor in cases where the book is made up of very thick sections. It is also unsuitable for use with coated papers. If used on small volumes, the sewing thread and, therefore, the cords, must be proportionally thinner; otherwise there will be a reduction in flexibility. (161, 172, 236, 335, 343)

flexural strength. A measure of the ability of an adhesive film to withstand repeated flexing, bending, twisting, etc. Flexural strength is of paramount importance in the adhesives used in archival work in general, and bookbinding in particular, especially in adhesives used for gluing up the spine and adhesive binding. (222)

flint hides. Hides dried without curing.

flock paper. A speciality cover paper produced by coating the sheet with size, either all over or in patterns or designs, and then applying specially dyed flock powder. Flock paper originally was intended to simulate tapestry and Italian velvet brocade. (17, 197)

flock powder. Very short or pulverized fiber, such as wool, cotton, or rayon, used in flock printing and to form velvety patterns on cloth and paper.

floriated. A border, initial letter, or book decorated with small flower or leaf ornaments. (140)

floss. Cotton or silk thread used in binding single section pamphlets, usually by side sewing tied in a bowknot. (256)

flour. *See:* FINES.

flourish style. *See:* FANFARE STYLE.

flower-headed rivet. A finishing tool cut with an ornamental head in a design resembling a daisy. (250)

fluffing. 1. The process of reducing the substance and smoothing the flesh side of a skin or hide during leather manufacture. *See also:* BUFFING (2); SNUFFING. 2. The removal of the free or loosely bonded fibers, loading material or dust from the surface of paper during impression. Fluff is a particular defect encountered in lithographic printing, and results in the printed matter showing white or gray images in paper fibers, or other material, removed from the surface of the paper. (93, 306)

flush (flush binding; flush cut). *See:* CUT FLUSH.

flush board binding. A style of binding having the boards glued to the board papers and a paper cover glued to the boards. The book is then CUT FLUSH.

fly embossing press. An early version of the BLOCKING PRESS, which was capable of exerting the enormous pressure required to block covers with engraved plates often of the same size as the cover, even quartos and folios. This type of press was probably introduced sometime in the late 1820s by JOSEPH THOUVENIN and was used extensively until the later part of the 19th century. The description "fly" may stem from the instantaneous release of pressure (the platen "flying" up). (203, 236)

flying out. A convex shape to the fore edge of a book, resulting from lack of, or improper, rounding, backing, lining of the spine, or a combination thereof.

fly leaf. A leaf or leaves at the beginning and end of a book, being the leaf or leaves not pasted to the boards, or covers, of the book. *See also:* ENDPAPERS. (69, 335)

flyswing. A very thin SKIVER used extensively for title labels on cloth- and leather-bound books, and generally lettered in gold. In library binding, the "flyswing" has been replaced by labels of paper and (occasionally) cloth. (140)

Fogel, Johannes (fl 1455-?1460). One of the most celebrated of German bookbinders, Fogel bound at least one and perhaps as many as four copies of the Gutenberg Bible, one of which bears his signature. Fogel's tools included a rope knot and a lute player stamp, as well as triple fillets accompanied by rosettes. He also worked finely made headbands in red, white, and blue silk. All of his bindings are decorated in a manner characteristic of ERFURT BINDINGS, having the long, narrow center panel enclosed in a broad border, with all lines crossing at the ends to form squares in the corners.

Little is known of Fogel after 1460. All of his extant *signed* bindings are thought to have been bound at Erfurt before 1460, and by 1461 some of his stamps were being used in conjunction with others and without his signature on the bindings, but it is not known whether he retired from binding or just stopped signing his bindings. In 1462 his lute player and rope knot finishing tools appear on a binding signed by

Paulus Lehener. It is possible, although probably unlikely, that he discarded some tools and acquired others. (141)

foil. *See:* BLOCKING FOIL.

fold and dye papers. Decorative end- and cover-papers which have been folded (in parallel folds several times or into accordian pleats) and painted with color along the edges and corners, or dipped into a dye or paint mixture. Japanese papers are usually used in this technique. (183)

fold binder. One of the simplest forms of "binding," consisting of a sheet of cover stock with a series of scores running vertically and extending outward from the center fold to allow for expansion. The grain of the cover stock should run from head to tail so as to facilitate folding and scoring. (146)

folded (folding) book. A form of book consisting of a long strip of paper folded "concertina-wise" and attached at one or both ends to stiff covers. The "folded book" is common in the Orient but much less so in other parts of the world, except in books of an unusual nature, such as books of a pictorial nature with views of places and/or panoramas. (156)

folder. 1. A thin length of wood, bone, ivory, or other material, from 6 to 12 inches long, and 1 to 1½ inches wide. The typical folder is approximately ⅛ inch thick. It is tapered to the edges, has rounded edges and ends, and is used in folding sheets by hand and cutting bolts, and also in numerous binding operations. 2. *See:* FOLDING MACHINES. 3. A publication consisting of one sheet of paper folded to make two or more leaves but not stitched or cut. 4. A large sheet of stiff paper, usually manila, folded once. It has a projection or tag for heading at the top of the rear portion. (204)

folding. The process of folding flat printed sheets into sections. The number of leaves in a single folded sheet is always a multiple of two: 4, 8, 16, 32, and 64 leaves, giving 8, 16, 32, 64, and 128 pages respectively. Sections with 6, 12, 18, etc., leaves may be obtained by the use of other than standard types of folding, or by the use of more than one sheet, e.g., an envelope fold followed by a right angle fold will give 6 leaves (12 pages), or a full sheet folded three times, plus a half sheet folded twice and insetted within the full sheet will give a section of 12 leaves (24 pages). Although a single sheet of paper can be folded nine times, in bookwork it is unusual to find a sheet folded more than four times, and most sheets are

slit or perforated if they are to be folded at right angles more than twice, so as to reduce wrinkling and buckling.

The principal folds are the parallel (or buckle) and right angle, with the latter being the most commonly used fold in bookwork. The parallel fold is generally used for very narrow books, or for those that are printed TWO UP. The third most commonly used fold, though used far less than either of the preceding, is the concertina fold, which is used for maps and folders, as well as for some book sections.

Almost all folding today is done by machine; however, in the early days of the folding machine, the work was so inaccurate that good folding could be done only by hand.

Folding is done "to the paper" or "to the print," i.e., register. *See also:* FOLD TO PAPER; FOLD TO PRINT; FOLDING MACHINES; IMPOSITION; REGISTER (4). (82, 182, 229, 234, 335, 339, 343)

folding book. *See:* FOLDED (FOLDING) BOOK.

folding endurance. The number of folds which a specimen (usually paper) will withstand before failure, under controlled conditions in a specified instrument. In the usual test, a specimen is subjected repeatedly to double folds through a wide angle while under tension.

Folding endurance is a very important indication of the durability of archival papers. The test is usually conducted in an environmental room. A decline in folding endurance is the most sensitive indicator of aging and deterioration of paper. (17, 62)

folding in gangs. A method of folding printed sheets by means of a folding machine that folds a large sheet into several sections in one operation. As the sheet passes through the machine, it is folded, cut into sections, the heads are slit and the sections are then delivered singly or inset. (140)

folding machines. Machines that fold flat printed sheets into sections. The two main features of modern folding machines are: 1) the knife which dips between two rotating rollers that form a "nip;" and 2) the plate that forms an envelope into which the sheet is propelled, bending or buckling it along a desired line as it makes its exit from the plate.

Three main types of folding machines are in use today: the knife folder, buckle (or plate) folder, and combination folders, which are machines that employ both knife and buckle folding in different stages in the same machine. All three types are designed to take standard sizes of paper and are suitable for different types and classes of work.

In the knife folder, a blunt-edged knife is set parallel with and above the slot formed by the two rollers. The rollers revolve continuously so that when a sheet is placed over them and the knife descends, the paper is caught between the rollers and carried away, a fold being made where the knife made contact. In practice the sheets are fed one at a time to stops, either by hand or by mechanical feeders, and are carried by moving tapes beneath the knife where they are precisely positioned mechanically for folding. The knife having descended, the sheet, now folded once, is carried by rollers and tapes to a second unit of knife and rollers where a second fold is made, then a third fold, etc., the folded sheets (now sections) being delivered to a stacker. If any knife is at right angles to the previous unit a fold at right angles to the previous fold is made; however, if the machine is constructed with the folding units parallel to preceding folds then parallel folds are made. If it is desired to slit the sheet into individual sections during folding, the sheet will travel through rotary slitters when passing from one folding unit to the next, and the individual sections of the sheet will be conveyed to individual folding units. In this manner, a sheet printed with 64 pages can be slit into four parts producing four individual 16-page sections. Machines are normally provided with perforators which perforate the bolts, thus preventing wrinking and buckling.

Buckle folders work on a different principle. The sheet is fed end first between a pair of continuously revolving rollers and the leading edge is guided between two closely spaced plates, the plane of the plates being at an angle of 45° to the plane of feeding. The plates are fitted with internal adjustable stops, and when the leading edge of the sheet hits these stops further forward motion is prevented. The latter half of the sheet, however, is still being propelled forward by the rollers and, being already bent at an angle of 45°, the sheet buckles at the point of entry to the plates. The buckle is gripped between the lower roller and a third roller in contact with it and the buckle passes between these rollers, thus forming a fold. The portion of the sheet between the plates is immediately withdrawn by this action, leaving the mech-

anism clear for the next sheet. The sheet continues to be propelled by rollers and the folded edge may be deflected into a second and then third plate, producing additional folds parallel to the first. Buckle folders frequently incorporate knife folding units, the knives being used to make folds at right angles to the parallel buckle fold. As with knife folding machines, perforators and slitters are incorporated for use at various stages of folding.

Buckle folders are generally run at higher speeds than knife folders, but knife folders are used in book work because they are better adapted for handling a greater diversity of papers. The largest knife folders will fold a flat sheet of 128 pages, producing four 32-page sections, each with four folds. Buckle folders, in their most complex form, can produce almost any series of folds, but, in general, they are used more for the folding of advertising matter than for book work.

The first folding machine is believed to have been introduced in about 1850 by a man named Blake. In 1856, Cyrus Chambers, Jr., patented and sold a folding machine to the Lippincott Publishing Company. Although the accuracy of early folders was poor, with hand folding still predominating for better grade work, development of the folding machine after 1862 was rapid, and in 1873 a machine was patented that would fold a 16-page section and one of 8 pages, inset the latter, and paste it in place. That same year devices to cut and slit paper as it went through the machine were introduced. Automatic feeders were also developed, one being patented in 1855.

Modern folding machines are available in many sizes, capable of folding sheets measuring 4 by 4 inches up to 26 by 60 inches and, in special cases,

even up to 50 by 74 inches. (52, 101, 179, 320, 339)

folding needle. A needle, usually of steel imbedded in a wooden handle, and used by some bookbinders in tight places for such work as mitering covers and turning-in on slipcases. It is also used at times for scoring.

foldings. A general term applied to printed sheets which have been folded in various ways to form sections. Foldings from 4 to 128 are given in the table provided below.

folding stick. A long, thin polished piece of wood, bone, plastic, or other material, used when folding paper by hand to crease the sheet without soiling or otherwise damaging it. *See also:* FOLDER (1). (173)

folding strength. *See:* FOLDING ENDURANCE.

foldouts. Inserts that are larger than the trim size of the book or other publication and which must be folded before insertion. When they are the same height as the book but wider they may be tipped in, but when they are both higher and wider, or just higher, they must be LIPPED. *See also:* FULL APRON; THROW OUT. (316, 339)

fold sewing. A general term applied to sewing a book through the folds of the sections. *See:* FLEXIBLE SEWING; FRENCH SEWING; MACHINE SEWING; RECESSED-CORD SEWING; TAPE SEWING (1).

fold to paper. An instruction to the binder to fold the printed sheets of a book so that the edges of the leaves and bolts are even. *Cf:* FOLD TO PRINT. (156)

fold to print (fold to register). An instruction to the binder to fold the printed sheets of a book to register, i.e., the edges of the printed areas are to be placed exactly over one another. *Cf:* FOLD TO PAPER. (156)

foliaged staff. A finishing stamp cut in the

		Foldings		
Section Size	*Symbol*	*Customary Number of Folds*	*Leaves*	*Pages*
Folio	fo	1	2	4
Quarto	4to	2	4	8
Sixmo	6to	varies	6	12
Octavo	8vo	3	8	16
Twelvemo	12mo	varies	12	24
Sixteenmo	16mo	4	16	32
Eighteenmo	18mo	varies	18	36
Twenty-fourmo	24mo	varies	24	48
Thirty-twomo	32mo	5	32	64
Thirty-sixmo	36mo	varies	36	72
Forty-eightmo	48mo	varies	48	96
Sixty-fourmo	64mo	varies	64	128

form of a branch entwined with foliage, sometimes intertwined with berries. A foliaged staff is usually used to form a frame. (250)

foliate. To number the leaves of a book instead of the pages. This results in the rectos and versos having the same number, as 1, 1-2, 2-3, 3-4, 4-5, etc. It is a method of numbering commonly found in blankbooks. (274)

foliation. 1. The total number of leaves, whether numbered or unnumbered, contained in a book or manuscript. 2. The numbering of the leaves of a book or manuscript. Foliation was relatively rare until the last quarter of the 15th century. It consisted originally of the word Folio, or an abbreviation, followed by a Roman numeral. Arabic figures were used in Italy between 1475 and 1500, and outside Italy after 1500. Eventually the Arabic came to be used alone. The numbering of pages (pagination), as opposed to leaves, began to replace foliation near the end of the 16th century but was not finally established until the 18th century. Reference to a page in a foliated book is generally done by using *r* and *v* for recto and verso, e.g., 1r or 1v, or by the use of *a* and *b*, e.g., 1a or 1b, the latter being preferred because manuscript v is often mistaken for r. Abbreviated ff. *See also:* PAGINATION. (140, 156)

folio. 1. The book size resulting from folding a sheet one time, giving leaves half the size of the sheet. In modern practice double-size paper folded twice, or quad-size paper folded three times would be used, thus producing the requisite folio size but in sections convenient for binding. Abbreviated Fo. or fo. 2. A leaf of parchment or paper numbered only on the recto side. 3. Loosely, the number of a page. 4. An individual leaf of a book. (234, 252, 316)

folio form. Printed sheets that have been folded and gathered, but not bound. *See also:* GATHERING (1). (322)

font (fount). The complete assortment of all letters and characters in one face and size of type. A type family includes fonts of roman, italic, semi-bold and condensed. *See also:* TYPE FACE. (12)

fonthill style. A particular style of binding in which the books were sewn on raised cords, and were top edge gilt, had marbled paper sides and endpapers, and were covered in half olive-brown morocco. Finishing consisted of lettering and the date at the tail of the spine. The name derives from Fonthill Abbey in Wiltshire, England, which was built toward the end of the 18th

century by William Beckford (1759-1844). (241)

foot. 1. The margin at the bottom of a page of type. 2. The under-surface of type. The plane parallel to the face on which the body of type rests. (12, 196)

footage. 1. The charge made by the manufacturer or supplier of leather. The method of measurement used in calculating the number of square feet of any particular skin or hide is somewhat complicated, and in practice it is usually found that a skin marked, for example, as four feet, will not give nearly that much area in cut pieces for books; particularly in the case of skins with very ragged edges, e.g., goatskin. The footage charged is usually marked on the flesh side of the skin, and is calculated to the tenth of a foot in the United States, and to a quarter of a foot in England, e.g., 4 = 4 feet, 4/1 = 4¼ foot, etc. The measuring is done either by metal pins which record the presence (or absence) of leather by touch, or by a beam of light, which indicates the absence of leather by means of a receptor element. 2. The length or area of a reel of paper expressed in linear or square measure. (335, 363)

fore edge. The edge of a book opposite the spine. Sometimes called "front edge."

fore-edge binding. A style of binding representing a degree between quarter and half-binding, in which a narrow strip of leather or cloth, usually of the same color as that covering the spine, is attached to the outer extremity of each board. The width of the strip generally varies according to the color and decoration, if any, of the material used to cover the sides. (86)

fore-edge margin. The space between the text and the outer extremity of the leaf of a book. Also called "outside margin." *See also:* BLED; MARGIN (1).

fore-edge painting. A scene painted on the fore edge of a book, either with the edge solid so that the resultant painting is visible with the book closed, or, in the more accepted use of the term, with the edge fanned out so that the painting is not visible with the book closed. When the painting is done with the leaves fanned out, the edge is generally also gilded or marbled in the usual manner, so that the closed book shows no trace whatsoever of the painting. A double fore-edge painting is one with two paintings, which can be viewed independently by fanning the leaves first one way and then the other. A triple fore-edge painting has a visible scene in addition, in which case the

edge is not gilded or marbled.

The painting of fore edges is very old, going back perhaps as early as the 10th century. These earliest fore-edge paintings consisted of symbolical designs. The art reached England in the 14th century, and among the early fore-edge paintings, such as those executed by Thomas Berthelet for King Henry VIII, consisted of treating the fore edge as a solid panel for a heraldic or other motif in gold and colors. The binder who originated the technique of painting a design on the fanned out leaves is unknown, although Samuel Mearne is thought to have employed one or more artists and binders who did this kind of painting. The first known disappearing painting dates from 1649; the art of fore-edge painting under gold reached its pinnacle in England in the latter half of the 17th century.

The art of painting landscapes on fore edges, rather than floral scrolls and armorial bearings, was pioneered by William EDWARDS OF HALIFAX, sometime around 1750. He first used monochrome (brown or gray) and later a full range of colors. Portraits were also included, often flanking a landscape. Subjects portrayed included countrysides, buildings, sports, and scenes based on the content of the book being decorated. The types of books commonly treated in this manner were Bibles and prayer books, the classics, travel books, and poetry.

Although the art of fore-edge painting is old, there is clear evidence indicating that the majority of such paintings are the work of the late 19th and 20th centuries, mainly on books dating from the early 19th century. The great number of these paintings was in response to the demand of collectors and, because there was an insufficient number of authentic examples, appropriate books of an earlier time were painted to satisfy this demand. (50, 69, 140, 236)

fore-edge tab. *See:* INDEX TAB.

fore-edge title. The title of a book written on its fore edge to identify it. This was a common practice in the 16th century when it was customary to shelve books with their fore edges outward. (156)

forel. A grade of PARCHMENT made from a split sheepskin and dressed in imitation of VELLUM. It is not a strong skin and tends to be greasy, which causes difficulties in trying to make it adhere to the boards of a book. Also called "forrel" and (rarely) "forril." (172, 343)

form. 1. A curved block placed between the endpapers of a book and its covers while the leather is being polished, so as to counteract any warpage which may have occurred due to the dampening of the leather while finishing. 2. Pages of type metal and illustrations, arranged in proper order for the printed sheet and locked in a metal frame called a "chase," ready for printing or for making an electrotype or stereotype. (12, 115)

formaldehyde. A very reactive aldehyde (HCHO), that is a colorless, pungent, irritating, combustible gas when pure, but is conveniently handled in the form of aqueous solutions or solid polymers. It is usually prepared by the oxidation of methanol or gaseous hydrocarbons. It has been used to kill, or inhibit, bookworms, and is used in the manufacture of some leathers, in the treatment of certain dyestuffs to render them fast to washing, and for bleaching archival papers. Its tanning properties stem from its ability to render gelatin insoluble in water. *See also:* ALDEHYDE TANNING; COMBINATION OIL TANNAGE; FORMALIN.

formaldehyde tanning. A process of converting hides and skins into leather by treatment with FORMALDEHYDE. *See:* ALDEHYDE TANNING. *See also:* COMBINATION OIL TANNAGE; FORMALIN. (248)

formalin. A solution of FORMALDEHYDE gas in water. A solution of 40% formalin in water, which may also contain traces of formic acid, methyl alcohol, or a white deposit of paraldehyde, is used in tanning some leathers. *See also:* ALDEYHYE TANNING. (306)

format. 1. The number of times a printed sheet has been folded to form the leaves of a section, e.g., folio (folded once to make two leaves or four pages); quarto (folded twice to make four leaves or eight pages), etc. In a broader sense, format is the general proportions and approximate size of a book or other publication which would result from such folding. *See also:* FOLDINGS. 2. In a very loose sense, the general appearance and make-up of a book, including proportions, size, quality, and style of paper and binding, typography, illustrations, and so on. *See also:* DUMMY (1). (12, 156, 234)

formation. The distribution of the solid components of a sheet of paper, with special reference to the fibers. It is usually judged by the visual appearance of the sheet when viewed by transmitted light. Formation affects not only look-through appearance but uniform-

ity in several respects, including, finish, subsequent coatings, ink receptivity, and compressibility under printing impression.

The selection of paper pulps and their subsequent refining influence formation to a great extent. Short fibers will form better than long ones, while long fibers, which give strength in terms of folding endurance and tear resistance, when used in preponderance, tend to give a cloudy or bunchy look to the formation of the sheet. Loading or fillers improve formation, permitting closer packing and greater density in the sheet, thus improving both levelness and LOOK-THROUGH. There are limits, however, to the amount of loading than can be used, as it weakens the paper because it is dead weight and contributes no strength on its own. (17, 72, 143)

formic acid. A colorless, volatile, weak organic acid (H_2CO_2). It occurs naturally, e.g., in ants, the fruit of the soaptree, etc., and is also formed as a byproduct in the atmospheric oxidation of turpentine. The principal commercial source is sodium formate, which is prepared by the reaction of carbon monoxide and sodium hydroxide under pressure and heat. Formic acid is used in leather manufacture to control pH, as well as in the acid dyeing of some leathers; in the latter case, causing the dye to fix on the leather. (306)

forming iron. *See:* BACK-MOLDING IRON.

forril. *See:* FOREL.

fortified size. A rosin acid chemically modified for use in lieu of, or together with, rosin size in improving the water resistance of paper. Most fortified sizes are reaction products of rosin with maleic anhydride.

forty-eightmo. A section consisting of 48 leaves (96 pages). In bookwork, using right angle folds, it is formed by folding a full sheet five times to form 32 leaves, and a half sheet four times to form 16 leaves, and insetting the latter. Its symbol is 48mo, or 48°. Also called "quadrigesimo-octavo." *See also:* BOOK SIZES.

forwarding. The processes or steps involved in binding a book. It has been variously defined as: 1) all of the binding processes following gathering, including covering; 2) the processes following sewing and up to covering; and 3) the processes following sewing and including covering. In edition binding, the term SHEETWORK is usually used in lieu of forwarding. (83, 123)

forwarding machine. The name some-

times given a ROUNDING AND BACKING MACHINE.

forwarding press. *See:* FINISHING PRESS.

fossil resins. *See:* RESIN.

Fourdrinier machine. A papermaking machine invented by the Frenchman, Nicolas Louis Robert in 1798, developed in England by Brian Donkin for Henry and Sealy Fourdrinier, but not placed into operation until 1804.

The Fourdrinier machine and the CYLINDER MACHINE comprise the machines normally employed in the manufacture of all grades of paper and board. The Fourdrinier machine may be considered in four sections: wet end, press section, drier section, and calender section. (The supercalender is not a part of the papermaking machine, and, in fact, not all Fourdriniers have a calender section.) In the wet end, the pulp or stock, at a consistency or concentration of 0.2 to 1.0%, depending upon the grade and weight of the paper being manufactured, flows from a headbox through a slice onto a moving endless belt of wire cloth, the FOURDRINIER WIRE. The wire runs over a breast roll, which is under or adjacent to the headbox, over a series of tubes or table rolls (or, more recently, drainage blades) which maintain the working surface of the wire in a plane and aid in water removal. The tubes or rolls create a vacuum on the downstream side of the NIP. Similarly, the drainage blades create a vacuum on the downstream side where the wire leaves the blade surface, but also perform the function of a doctor blade on the upstream side. The wire then passes over a series of suction boxes, over the bottom couch roll (or suction couch roll), which drives the wire, and then down and back over various guide rolls and a stretch roll to the breast roll.

The press section usually consists of two or more presses, whose function is to remove still more water from the web mechanically and to equalize the surface characteristics of the felt and wire sides. The wet web of paper is transferred from the wire to the felt at the couch roll, and is carried through the presses on the felts, the texture and character of which vary according to the grade of paper being made.

The drier section consists of two or more tiers of driers, which are steam-heated cylinders. The web is held firmly against them by means of fabric drier felts. As the web passes from one drier to another, first the felt side and then the wire side are pressed against the heated surface of the drier. The web enters the drier train having a water content of approximately 65%, the bulk of which is evaporated in this section. Moisture removal may be further assisted by hot air blowing onto the sheets and in between the driers to effect removal of water vapor. Within the drier section and at a point at least half way along the drying curve, there is sometimes a breaker stack for use in imparting finish, as well as to facilitate drying. The stack generally consists of a pair of chilled iron and/or rubber-surfaced rolls. There may also be a size press located within the drier section, at a point where the moisture content of the paper has been reduced to approximately 5%.

The calendar section consists of from one to three calender stacks with a reel device for winding the paper onto a reel as it leaves the machine. The calender finishes the paper, i.e., smooths it and imparts the desired finish, thickness, or gloss. Water, starch, wax emulsions, etc., may also be used to obtain additional finishes. The reel winds the finished paper, which may or may not undergo further processing.

The wire, press section, drier section or sections, the calender stacks, and the reel are so driven that proper tension is maintained in the web of paper despite its elongation or shrinkage during passage through the machine. The overall speed of Fourdrinier machines is determined by the grade and weight of the paper being manufactured. (17, 60, 62, 72, 80, 98, 140)

Fourdrinier wire. An endless belt of woven wire used on the wet end of the FOURDRINIER MACHINE, and on which the web of paper is initially formed. The warp wire is generally of phosphor bronze and the shute (weft) wire of brass. In recent years, other metals and nonmetallic materials have been used. The number of warp wires per inch and the number of shute wires determine the mesh of the wire, the warp count varing from 8 to 225, the most common being 55, 60, 70, and 75. (17, 62, 67)

foxing (foxmarks). Stains, specks, spots and blotches in paper. The cause or causes of foxing, which usually occurs in machine-made paper of the late 18th and the 19th centuries, are not completely understood, but in all liklihood, it is fungoid in nature. Fungi, however, are not necessarily visible on foxed areas, nor does prolific growth necessarily imply excessive discoloration, and vice versa. This has been attributed partly to the fact that action may have

been initiated before the examination of the paper, and partly, but less convincingly, to the so-called, action at a distance, which enables an agent to exert its effect at some distance from the object acted upon.

Two significant differences between foxed and clean areas of a paper are the higher proportion of acid and iron in the former, although there does not seem to be any clear and definitive relationship between iron and foxing. Insofar as the acid is involved, it is not clear whether this is produced chemically or as a byproduct of the life function of the organisms present. Iron is attributed to impurities present in the paper, and this conclusion seems to be based largely on the fact that it is seldom found in papers produced before the introduction of papermaking equipment made of iron, e.g., the beater, and improvements in techniques, including bleaching and other forms of chemical treatment. But what role iron has in accelerating foxing, or causing a change from the invisible to visible state, has yet to be demonstrated.

The other factor which controls foxing is relative humidity (R. H.), since these fungi will not develop if the R. H. falls below 75%. The fact that foxing generally starts from the edge of the leaf and spreads inward would seem to indicate that something in the atmosphere is relevant, although air borne organisms may be adequate as an explanation for this effect. In addition, it must still be explained how the center of the leaf is affected most in occasional instances. Perhaps the most logical explanation is that infection by air borne organisms (or by organisms that are natural to the paper) may occur if the conditions, and especially the R. H., are favorable, and that growth, resulting in the generation of fox marks, then occurs. The acid subsequently renders any iron in the paper soluble and therefore visible, with its color being intensified by the presence of organic matter.

The effects of foxing may be reduced to a reasonable extent by use of a reducing agent, such as sodium borohydride ($NaBH_4$) in a 0.5% solution by weight of the paper. This chemical has the advantage of not having to be washed out of the paper (and even depositing a small alkaline reserve—sodium tetraborate ($Na_2B_4O_7$)—in the paper). Foxing may be counteracted to an even greater extent by the use of a 0.1% (by weight of the paper) solu-

tion of an oxidizing agent such as calcium hypochlorite ($Ca(ClO)_2$); however, this chemical is very difficult to wash out after treatment. Unaffected papers may be successfully protected from foxing by maintaining the R. H. of the storage area below 50%. *See also:* DENDRITIC GROWTHS. (43, 102, 143, 218)

frame. 1. Ornamentation of a binding consisting of a simple hollow rectangle placed some distance from the edges of the cover of a book. It is to be distinguished from a BORDER (1). 2. Complete borders which are not, however, compartments, and which comprise enclosures made up of separate cuts or ornaments which show no evidence of having been carved or engraved for use together as a border, and also those made up of separate cast-type ornaments, commonly used in book decoration. (12, 69)

franklin guard. *See:* PHILADELPHIA PATENT-BACK GUARD.

free endpaper. *See:* FLY LEAF. *See also:* ENDPAPERS.

free water-soluble matter (in leather). Soluble matter that can be removed from finely ground leather with very little washing. The free water solubles include gallic acid, quinol, catechol, etc. *See also:* COMBINED TANNIN IN LEATHER; COMBINED WATER-SOLUBLE MATTER (IN LEATHER). (363)

freezing point. The temperature at which the liquid and solid states of a substance are in equilibrium at atmospheric pressure. All adhesives used in archival work are affected by the freezing point, i.e., of water (32° F. or 0° C.). *See also:* GLASS TRANSITION TEMPERATURE.

French cape levant. A type of MOROCCO prepared from the skin of a large Cape (South African) goat. It has a LEVANT grain, which is larger than the small pin-head grain of the usual morocco. (140)

French chalk. Soft, finely powdered magnesium silicate ($Mg_3H_2(SiO_3)_4$), which is dusted between the leaves of a book prior to gilding the edges so as to prevent the leaves from sticking during the gilding process, and also to remove grease stains from paper. (154)

French color. The *third* (or body) color dropped on the marbling size following the dropping of the VEIN COLORS. (217)

French corner. A method of reinforcing the corners of a book cover with leather or cloth, which is subsequently covered on the outside of the board but can just be seen at the corner on the inside of the board. (81)

French curl marble. A marble pattern that has been used for endpapers, particularly in France, since about 1660. The pattern is made on a marbling size of GUM TRAGACANTH, and the colors are dropped on in the same manner as with the NONPAREIL MARBLE. The curls are made with the use of a wooden frame constructed in the form of a small harrow, each parallel bar being set with as many tapering wooden pegs as there are curls required on the sheet to be marbled. The difficulty in executing this pattern is to "catch" the curls before they lose their shape.

Many fine armorial bindings have the large red and blue pattern as linings. Padeloup and Derome both used this pattern for endpapers in books they bound for the French nobility. The French curl pattern remained popular, and continued to be used in Europe and England until about 1870. While it was highly valued for endpapers, it was rarely, if ever, used for cover papers on 17th and 18th century books. (97, 217)

French fillet. A FILLET (1) having three unevenly spaced bands on its circumference.

French finish. Books sewn on raised bands and completely undecorated except for gilt lettering. *See also:* FRENCH KID. (274)

French fold. A sheet of paper printed on one side only and folded over from left and right to form a "section" with uncut bolts. The inside of the fold is blank. (140, 355)

French gold. An alloyed GOLD LEAF, on the light or lemon-colored side. (126)

French guard. A term sometimes applied to the inner margin of an insert, turned over and folded around a section. (25)

French joint. A free-swinging joint produced by setting the board a slight distance (approximately ⅛ to ¼ inch, depending on the size of the book) away from the backing shoulder. This type of joint allows thicker covering material to be used, while still allowing the covers to open easily. The French joint is one of the more notable characteristics of library binding. Also called "open joint." *See also:* CLOSED JOINT (94, 335)

French kid (French finish). A kidskin produced by either tawing or a vegetable tannage. As the name implies, it was produced originally in France and, because of its distinctive finish, the term

was later applied to the same kind of leather produced elsewhere. (325)

French morocco (French levant morocco). A leather similar in appearance to MOROCCO but produced from sheepskin. The term is both inaccurate and misleading. (264)

French paring knife. *See:* PARING KNIFE.

French sewing. A method of sewing a book adapted by French bookbinders in the 16th century, which is essentially the same as the sewing employed in COPTIC BINDINGS. Unlike the traditional Western method of sewing on raised cords (*See:* FLEXIBLE SEWING), each section was sewn through the fold and attached to the next section by a loop similar to a KETTLE STITCH. Cords were not employed. The first and last sections were then laced tightly to the boards. In modern usage, French sewing is the same technique as done by a sewing machine, without the attachment of the boards. Modern French sewing is the principal method employed in edition binding. *See also:* MACHINE SEWING. (69, 89, 154)

French shell marble. A marble pattern developed in the latter part of the 18th century, and particularly identified with France. The pattern is formed by adding oil to the color, which then instead of spreading evenly, forms in drops with an outer circle or "shell" of a lighter shade. Brown and orange as the vein colors and a French (body) color of blue seem to have been the most frequently used colors. Shell papers are commonly found as endpapers of calf- and half-bindings of the early 19th century. Later, when the art

of marbling deteriorated, the shell pattern was executed on very thin paper of poor quality and used for cheap trade bindings. The pattern was also popular for marbling the edges of books. (217, 236)

French standing press. A variation of the regular STANDING PRESS, the major difference being that the platen is lowered by turning a *weighted* wheel, which, when spun, exerts additional pressure by a kind of hammering action against two lugs. Except for the wheel and mechanism, it is made of wood, and, while it does not tighten to the same degree as the iron standing press, it is considerably lighter and does not require the substantial floor required by the heavier iron press. (83, 236)

French varnish. A pale-colored mixture of shellac and oil. *See:* VARNISH.

fret. A continuous border pattern made up of interlaced bands and produced by a fillet. Such patterns can be used for the decoration of either the leaves or covers of a book, or both. (335)

fringed foliage ornament. A bookbinding finishing tool in more-or-less the shape of a lozenge, and cut with a typical foliage design, the principal characteristic of which is a narrow fringe around the edge. (250)

frizzing. 1. The process of removing the fat cell layer prevalent in the corium of sheepskin, subsequent to splitting the skin and fleshing. When sheepskins are to be oil tanned, it is essential that the skins have clean, open surfaces, free from excess fat or grease. This allows the tanning oil to penetrate more freely. 2. Skins limed for a prolonged

FRENCH JOINT

period during which the entire supporting structure of ELASTIN in the grain layer is destroyed. 3. The process in leather manufacture of removing the grain layer of a skin by scraping, either with a knife or by machine. (61, 291, 306)

front. A term applied to horsehides principally to distinguish the forepart of the hide from the butt or hind portion which contains the SHELL from which CORDOVAN LEATHER is produced. A whole "front" represents about two-thirds of the area of the hide. (97)

front cover. *See:* UPPER COVER.

front edge. *See:* FORE EDGE.

frosted. A whitish condition or appearance of lettering or ornamentation in gold which can be caused by the leaf being pressed into the covering material with a tool that is too hot. (335)

frother. *See:* DEVIL.

frothing. The process of foaming glair so as to mix it thoroughly. The glair is not used in a frothed condition, but is allowed to subside, after which the clear glair is poured off.

f. t. p. Abbreviation of *folded, trimmed,* and *packed,* a term applied to books, pamphlets, etc., to indicate that the printed sheets have been folded, trimmed and packed for shipment, usually to a bookbinder. (274)

fugitive colors. Pigments and dyes that fade, especially those that lose color relatively quickly when exposed to natural light. Although still commonly used, the term is misleading because it implies that FADING represents the flight of color, rather than a chemical change. (233, 316)

full. A term sometimes applied to leather made from the unsplit, or full thickness, of a hide or skin, e.g., full calf.

full apron. A leaf the size of the leaves of a book to which a foldout, which must display the entire image beyond the *closed* book, is attached. (339)

full binding. A book which is covered entirely with any one material. In a strict sense, the term is applied only to leather bindings. *Cf:* HALF BINDING; QUARTER BINDING; THREE-QUARTER BINDING (1). (12)

full-bound ends and bands (full-bound ends and hubs). A form of the blank-book, generally full bound in sheepskin and flesher, with overbands. In this style, the leather covering does not extend beyond the head and tail of the boards but is turned in on the fore edges. *See also:* BANDING. (339)

full calf t. e. g. A term sometimes applied to a full calfskin binding with only the TOP EDGE GILT.

full chrome (tanned). Any leather tanned by the CHROME TANNING process. The adjective "full" is added to emphasize the fact that the leather has not been tanned by the semi-chrome or combination chrome process. (306)

full cloth. 1. A book bound in a one-piece cloth cover. The term is not applied to library or edition bindings, i.e., case bindings. 2. A term sometimes applied to a book bound in cloth, as opposed to a binding with a cloth spine and paper sides.

fuller's earth. *See:* ATTAPULGITE CLAY.

full gilt. 1. A book having all three edges gilt, described as a.e.g., for all edges gilt. *See also:* GILT EDGES. 2. A book, usually leather bound, which is heavily tooled in gold on the spine, and with center and corner tools on the covers.

full grain. A leather having the original grain surface exposed by removal of the epidermis, and with none of the grain surface removed by BUFFING (1), SNUFFING, or SPLITTING (1). *See also:* CORRECTED GRAIN. (325)

full law binding (full law sheep). An obsolete style of binding, applied mainly to law books, and distinguished from other types of law binding in that the books were covered entirely in sheepskin, with lace-in boards and raised bands, and the traditional labels on the spine. *See also:* LAW CALF. (274)

full leather. A book covered entirely in leather, whether one piece or several pieces, as with inlays, onlays, etc. *See also:* FULL BINDING; HALF LEATHER; QUARTER LEATHER; THREE-QUARTER LEATHER.

full oil tanning. Any leather tanned by one of the oil processes. The adjective "full" is added to emphasize the fact that the leather has not been tanned by a COMBINATION OIL TANNAGE. (61)

full sheep. A sheepskin of full natural substance. It may be colored, embossed, or left in the natural tanned state, as is the case with BASIL. (274)

full weight (full thickness). A term sometimes applied to an unsplit skin, of natural thickness, but shaved down when necessary on the flesh side to a uniform thickness.

fumigation. The process of exposing archival materials to the vapor of a volatile substance, or with poisonous chemicals, such as thymol, methyl bromide (CH_3Br), chloropicrin (CCl_3NO_2), carbon tetrachloride (CCl_4), ethylene dichloride ($C_2H_4Cl_2$), or hydrogen cyanide (HCN), within a closed (and airtight) container, in order to destroy mold and/or insects. Room temperature is usually sufficient

to vaporize the substances used in fumigation; however, in cases of severe or stubborn molds, heat in the range of 40 to 50° C. will increase the concentration of the vapor and increase its effectiveness. Where no special equipment, e.g., air-tight chambers, is available and the infestation is on a relatively small scale, fumigation may be carried out by means of carbon disulfide (CS_2) in an air-tight box. These methods, while more or less effective, do not confer lasting protection; therefore it may be necessary (assuming it is possible) to fumigate the areas in which the archival materials are stored. *See also:* FUNGI. (143, 198, 233)

fungi. A division or other major group of the lower plants which is often included in Thallophyta coordinate to Algae, that includes a varied assemblage of saprophytic and parasitic plants which lack chlorophyll, and which comprise the classes Phycomycetes, Ascomycetes, Basidiomycetes, and Fungi Imperfecti, and usually, in addition, the Myxomycetes and Schozomycetes.

A large number of the spores of fungi is always present in the atmosphere, and while paper is not a particularly suitable medium to support the growth of molds and fungi, under favorable conditions, such as relatively high temperature and high relative humidity, paper will support the growth of these micro-organisms, some of which have a similar action on paper to that of dry rot fungus on wood. Conditions of storage which permit the prevalence of fungi may require the use of a FUNGICIDE to inhibit and/or destroy them. (198)

fungicide. A substance possessing the power of killing or preventing the growth of FUNGI. No single fungicide possesses all the desired properties of protection, as some of them are mutually exclusive, but it is possible to find one that possesses a range of properties suitable for use in virtually any specific case. Unfortunately, many fungicides are highly chlorinated substances and therefore cannot be washed out if lasting protection is to be conferred. Considerable care must be exercised, therefore, when they are used in or near paper.

While stable enough for most normal uses, the typical fungicide may not be sufficiently stable when it is to remain in paper for decades, even centuries, as paper almost always contains impurities, e.g., iron, which may accelerate the normal slow breakdown of a fungicide. In the usual case, the product of this breakdown is hydrochloric acid (HCl), minute amounts of which are capable of destroying any normal paper; therefore, before using any chlorinated organic fungicide, it must be determined whether or not it is (reasonably) stable in the presence of traces of iron, copper, manganese, etc., and, at the same time sufficiently effective to be of practical value when used in low concentrations, e.g., 0.1% of the weight of the paper. *See also:* COPPER NAPTHENATE; FOXING; MERCAPTO-BENZTHIAZOLE (M. B. T.); MERCURIC CHLORIDE; PENTA-CHLORPHENOL (P. C. P.); SALICYLANILIDE. (198)

funish. The various combinations of materials in the stock suspension used in the manufacture of paper and board. They include the fibrous materials (pulp), i.e., the rag, chemical wood, mechanical wood, esparto, cotton fiber, linen, or other pulps, sizing materials, i.e., rosin, alum-rosin sizes, etc., various additives, e.g., wet strength agents, fillers of various types, e.g., rentention aids, or loading materials, and dyes. (17, 58, 72)

fustic. A natural yellow dye extracted from the yellow Brazil wood (*Morus tinctoria*), and at one time used in the manufacture of yellow marbling color, and also for dyeing leather.

gain. *See:* YIELD.

gallic acid. A white, crystalline acid $(C_7H_6O_5)$, that occurs widely in plants both in the free form, as in GALLS and combined in tannins, from which it may be obtained by the action of molds or an alkali. It is used principally in the manufacture of pyrogallol tannins, dyes, and writing inks. *See also:* VEGETABLE TANNINS. (235)

gallotannin (gallotannic acid). *See:* TANNIC ACID.

galls. The dried excrescences from certain trees and shrubs, especially Oak galls (*Quercus infectoria*), from the Near East and Eastern Europe; Chinese galls (*Rhus semialata*), from the Far East; Tamarisk galls, from several species of *Tamarix,* located from Morocco to India; and Pistacia galls, from several European and Indian species of *Pistacia.* All are relatively rich in tannin (36 to 60%) and are said to contain free gallic acid in addition to tannin, as well as an easily soluble form of ellagic acid. In general, the tannin is not homogeneous and is believed to be built up as a polygallol-ellagic acid.

The galls result from the plants reaction to irritation caused by the larvae of various insects which lay eggs in the cambium area of the plants.

Although galls were used extensively over a period of centuries in the manufacture of certain inks, and in the tanning of leather, they are little used today for tanning outside of the areas where they are collected, largely because of the expense involved in their collection. *See also:* IRON-GALL INK; VEGETABLE TANNINS. (175, 235, 363)

gambier. A tannin obtained from the leaves and stems of *Uncaria gambir,* a shrubby climber found in Indonesia and surrounding areas. It contains catechu-tannic acid (22 to 50%) and catechin (7 to 33%), as well as varying amounts of vegetable acids and their salts, sugar, starch, cellulose, wax, oil, and mineral matter. The catechin is not identical with that of CUTCH. It is one of the condensed tannins and has a relatively high pH value and total salts content. Used alone, gambier produces a rather spongy leather; however, when used in combination with other tannins, such as wattle extract or myrabolans, it is well suited for

both heavy and light leathers. In England, it has been used mainly for the tannage of calf and kip skins. Also known as "catechu," "pale catechu," and "terra japonica." *See also:* VEGETABLE TANNINS. (175)

gamma-cellulose. That portion of a cellulosic material that remains in solution subsequent to neutralization of the alkaline solution obtained in the ALPHA CELLULOSE test. *See also:* BETA CELLULOSE. (17, 72)

gampi. A shrub, *Wikstroemia canescens,* indiginous to the mountain forests of central and southern Japan, the bast fibers of the inner bark of which are used in papermaking. (17)

gang stitching. An automatic or hand fed production line method of fastening leaves together with wire staples. *See also:* SIDE STITCHING.

gape (gaping). A condition in which the covers of a book are not parallel but are further apart at the fore edge than at the spine, i.e., the book does not close properly. Gaping, or yawning, as it is also called, may be caused by improper insertion of folded material without adequate stubbing; by improper covering or casing-in technique, in which the case is in effect too small for the text block or the covering material is drawn on too tightly; or, in the case of vellum books or bindings, by the absorption of moisture, which causes the vellum covers to warp. (99, 236)

gas black. A black pigment used in the manufacture of printing ink, and produced by burning gas with insufficient oxygen for complete combustion to take place. Thick soot is deposited on metal cylinders in much the same manner as LAMPBLACK from oil. Gas black is practically pure carbon. (140)

(Le) Gascon. The name associated with a luxurious style of finishing introduced in France in the early 17th century. The "Le Gascon" style, known as POINTILLÉ, is made up of interlaced bands, enclosing geometrical compartments which are filled with innumerable gold dots, frequently elaborated into lines and curves of remarkable luster and elegance.

Over the years many stories have arisen concerning "Le Gascon." One is that he worked as a bookbinder, or, more likely, as a gilder in the Ève's bindery, from which he took the style later to be called FANFARE STYLE (with its complicated geometrical framework) as the basis of his designs, but worked out all of the scrolls in fine dots instead of solid lines. While finishing tools had begun to become more finely cut with the Èves, they reached the pinnacle of delicacy and perfection with the work of this gilder or group of gilders. It has also been suggested that "Le Gascon" was the pseudonym of a famous binder, and it has been argued that the possibility exists that "Le Gascon" was employed by Gaston, Duke of Orleans.

Despite the speculation, there are no records to indicate just who "the man" may have been. There are documents indicating that someone going by the pseudonym "Le Gascon" was, as early as 1622, producing the most splendid bindings of that time. It is perhaps only natural that attempts should be made to link this name with the finest of the early pointillé bindings, but to date no binding can be said to be the work of anyone by that name. Three very intricate pointillé bindings, signed by FLORIMOND BADIER, do exist, but since Badier did not even begin his apprenticeship until 1630, he cannot have been "Le Gascon." (124, 132, 154, 347, 373)

gatefold. An illustration, map, or other leaf larger in one dimension than the other leaves of the publication and which consequently must be folded, usually at the fore edge or head, to make it the same size as the other leaves. (156, 329)

gathering. 1. The process of collecting, and arranging in proper order for binding, the printed sheets or sections of a publication, which, in the case of sections, takes place after folding. 2. The group of leaves formed by folding and combining the one or more sheets or half sheets which make up a section (signature). The sheet is the printer's unit, while the gathering is the binder's unit. In the case of the octavo, the gathering normally comprises one sheet folded three times; however, in larger or smaller volumes, it may consist of two or more sheets, or sheets and half sheets. 3. *See:* CATCH-UP STITCH. (320, 335)

gathering machine. A machine used mainly in edition binding to collect and arrange in proper order the folded sheets, i.e., sections, of a book, preparatory to binding. The sections are placed in sequence in the pockets or hoppers of the machine and are released individually to a conveying mechanism. Once the machine is in full operation it produces a complete group of sections at every move, i.e., if the book consists of twelve sections, on the twelfth and every move thereafter the machine produces a complete gathering. Every time the conveying mechanism advances, a section is deposited on the conveying mechanism at every feeding station, the complete gathering being assembled at the last station. The total number of stations depends on the number of sections needed for the book being gathered.

All gathering machines designed for uninterrupted operation have continuous feed and remove individual sections from the bottom of the respective piles, thereby making the top of the pile always accessible for the addition of sections.

Three different systems are used in gathering machines: the swinging gathering arm system, the rotary drum system, and the planetary system.

The swinging gathering arm system operates by pulling the section by suction along the fold edge from the pile, gripping it in jaws and dropping it onto the conveyer system. In the rotary drum system, the sections are removed by grippers built into the surface of the rotating drum. In the planetary system, the bottom of the pocket is a drum equipped with rotary vacuum suckers which roll the sections away from the bottom of the pile and transfers them to the grippers on a transfer cylinder, which, in turn deposits them on the conveyer system.

If a section is omitted, or if two sections from the pocket are deposited on one pile, mechanical devices, called calipers, stop the machine and indicate the pocket where the mistake occurred. The calipers are also capable of detecing an incomplete section.

The first gathering machine was introduced by Endicott D. Averell of the United States in 1875. This machine had feed problems which were eventually overcome by a machine developed by F. Wood in 1886. The period of greatest development of gathering machines was 1890 to 1903. (89, 182, 320)

gathering table. 1. A long, narrow table, usually in the shape of a horseshoe, or oval, on which flat sheets or sections are laid in piles in proper order for gathering. 2. A rotating circular table around which gatherers sit and assemble sections as the table rotates, presenting consecutive sections. The variable speed table is rotated by an electric motor operated by a foot pedal. The rotating gathering table is usually used for short runs of edition bindings. (274, 320)

gauffered (gauffred, gaufré, or goffered) edges. The edges of a book, usually gilded, which have been decorated further by means of heated finishing tools or rolls which indent small repeating patterns. Gauffering is most successful on a book printed on hard paper and gilt solid. It may be done directly on the gold, or by laying a different colored gold over the first, and tooling over the top gold, leaving the pattern in the new gold impressed on the original metal. The effect of gauffering is sometimes enhanced by scraping away parts of the gold and then staining the white paper showing through. While this technique was used by a number of European bookbinders, it was especially associated with German bookbinding of the 16th century. The use of color on the edges of books bound in England was less frequent and more restrained. Plain gauffering was done well into the 17th century, usually on embroidered bindings, but appears to have declined sharply after 1650 or so. It was then revived and exploited from the end of the 18th century onwards, and was especially popular in the latter half of the 19th century, when it was found on elaborately bound devotional and other books.

Almost all gauffering was done with pointillé tools, or, as in many examples, the designs were built up with repeated impressions of a large dot. Pointillé tools, as well as those cut in outline, produce delicate effects and are more easily impressed on a hard paper surface than are solid tools. The term comes from the French word for honeycomb, and also applies to the practice of crimping or fluting cloth with heated gauffering irons. *See* PLATE VI. (236, 335, 343)

g clamp. *See:* C CLAMP.

g.e. Abbreviation for GILT EDGES.

gel. 1. A semisolid mass, resembling jelly, capable of deformation by heat or pressure. 2. A system of solid aggregates dispersed through a liquid carrier medium. 3. A non-flowing adhesive mass exhibiting strong cohesive forces having low shear strength. 4. *See:* GELATIN. (198, 306)

gelatin. A complex protein of the scleroprotein class, having a molecular weight varying from about 40,000 to 100,000. It occurs in bones and fibrous tissue in the form of its anhydride, collagen, which is converted into gelatin on boiling with dilute acids. Gelatin swells in cold water, but is insoluble in it. It dissolves in hot water and produces a very viscous solution, e.g., a solution containing 1% or more solidifies to a jelly upon cooling. Gelatin is patricularly rich in glycene and lysine. It is manufactured from hides and bones, principally those of bovine animals, and differs from GLUE in its purity and in the care observed in its manufacture. It is used in the manufacture of glue and photographic film, and in the tub-sizing of paper. (143, 189)

gelation. The partial coagulation of a lyophilic sol which results in the formation of a GEL (1).

gelation time. The interval of time between the introduction of a catalyst into a liquid adhesive and gel formation. The term is used with reference to synthetic thermosetting resins. (233)

gel strength. The strength of a gel or jelly (such as gelatin or glue), often expressed as the weight in grams required to force a plunger into a test sample under specified conditions. The gel-strength test is based on the fact that a solution containing 1% or more of gelatin, when allowed to stand at a temperature of approximately 50° F., will form a firm jelly. If different glue solutions of identical concentration are permitted to chill or set, the quality of the glue will, in general, correspond to the consistency of the jelly formed. (185)

general job binding. A general type of binding in which odd jobs, either for the customer or the trade, are performed. Job binding of this type generally includes some library style binding and small runs of edition binding, i.e., runs under 1,500 copies. (131)

general office stationery binding. A class of binding involving the production of speciality items, including pads, blotters, files, and the like. This type of binding often takes place as a sideline in a binder specializing in STATIONERY BINDING. *See also:* PADDING. (343)

Gentile, Antonio (1519-1609). A Roman goldsmith who produced perhaps the most remarkable silver binding that has come down from the Renaissance. The cover, which protects an equally distinguished Renaissance manuscript, the *Book of Hours,* written by the scribe Francesco Monterchi, and illuminated by Giulio Clovio, for Cardinal Alessandro Farnese, consists of wooden boards covered with parcel gilt silver that is very delicately worked in low relief and openwork. Each cover has a frame of foliage in relief against a pierced ground which is interrupted at intervals by masks, with fleurs-de-lis in the corners. The panel is divided into four sections filled with male and female figures whose bodies terminate in curving foliage. In the center a large oval depicts the annunciate angel on the upper cover and the Virgin Mary on the lower, both in relief. The spine of the binding is covered with a plate of silver decorated with foliate designs in low relief between four double raised bands. The doublures of silver are engraved with Farnese arms and the names of Cardinals Allesandro and Odoardo Farnese. (347)

German paring knife. *See:* PARING KNIFE.

ghatti gum. A gum obtained from the Indian sumac (Country sumac, or "dhawi," as it is called in India), *Anogeissus latifolia,* and used as a substitute for GUM ARABIC. (175)

gift binding. In the usual application, a leather binding produced for presentation, such as a retirement signature book. The term is also applied to that part of an edition run which is bound at the publisher's order for the gift market. (156)

gilder's tip. A camel-hair brush about 3 to 4 inches in width, and used to pick up strips of gold leaf flat on the tips of the hairs. A tip of long hairs is used to pick up whole leaves, while one with short hairs is used for cut pieces of leaf. A tip is not usually needed for metal leaf that is heavier and easier to handle than gold, but one may be necessary for silver leaf, in which case a special tip with double

thickness of hairs is used. (233, 335)

gilder's tub. *See:* RUBBING-OFF CHEST.

gilding. The art or process of adhering thin metal leaf to a surface, e.g., the leather cover or edges of a book, so as to approximate the effect of solid or inlaid metal. Although the term is applied to the decoration of both covers and edges, it is more accurately used with reference to edges, and the term GOLD TOOLING for covers.

Although the term "gilding" ultimately derives from a word for *gold,* it also designates the application of other leaf metal to a surface. Gold, silver, and palladium leaf are the most commonly used metals; however, gold is by far predominant. DUTCH GOLD and ALUMINUM LEAF are imitations of precious metals which give inferior effects and are not sufficiently permanent for archival work. On the other hand, they are superior in both effect and permaence to the so-called gold paint made with bronze power, to the silver paints made of aluminum powder, and to the various imitation gold foils made of various combinations of baser metals. *See also:* GILT EDGES; GILT EXTRA; GILT IN THE ROUND; GILT IN THE SQUARE; GILT MARBLED EDGES; GILT ON LANDSCAPES; ROUGH GILT. (83, 152, 161, 233, 236, 335, 343)

gilding a la antique. *See:* GAUFFERED EDGES.

gilding bench. *See:* FINISHING PRESS.

gilding boards. Finishing boards made of hardwood, and similar to BACKING BOARDS, except that the top edge is flat instead of beveled. They are used to secure the book firmly while the edges are being gilt. (335)

gilding powder. *See:* BLOCKING POWDER.

gilding press (gilder's press). A type of press consisting of two wooden blocks about 6½ inches square and 4 or 5 feet long, fitted with two compression screws operating through brass chucks in each block, and operated by means of a bar inserted in the screw heads. The available DAYLIGHT of the press is generally sufficient to allow the pressing and gilding of the edges of several books at a time. (256, 264)

gilt after rounding. *See:* GILT IN THE ROUND.

gilt all around. A term sometimes applied to a book gilded on all three edges. (335)

gilt edges. The edges of a book which have been trimmed, sized, primed with Armenian bole, covered with gold leaf, and burnished. In this process, the leaves of the book are fanned and dusted with French chalk and the book is then clamped in the gilding press.

The edges are scraped and sanded to give as smooth a surface as possible, and the edges are again primed with bole and polished with a burnishing brush. A dilute solution of albumen or gelatin is applied and the gold leaf is laid on. The edges are then glazed with a burnisher, initially through paper and then directly on the edges. Different qualities of paper require slight variations of treatment. In general, the effect of gilt edges is superior if the gilding is done before the book is sewn. *See:* ROUGH GILT. Following gilding, the edges are sometimes tooled. *See:* GAUFFERED EDGES.

The gilding of the edges of books probably originated in Italy, at about the same time that gold tooling was introduced in that country, or about 1470. The technique appears to have been in use in England by the 1530s.

Aside from appearance, gilding the edges, or at least the head edge, serves the practical function of protecting the book from the incursion of dust. *See also:* EDGE GILDING MACHINE. (140, 236, 335)

gilt extra. A binding which has more gold tooling than is considered normal. *Cf:* OVERCHARGED.

gilt in the round. The fore edge of a book gilded after the book is sewn and rounded, giving the fore edge the appearance of a solid gilt surface. *Cf:* GILT IN THE SQUARE. *See also:* ROUGH GILT. (156)

gilt in the square. The fore edge of a book gilded after sewing but before rounding. This results in a white edge showing at the first and last sections after the book is subsequently rounded and backed. *Cf:* GILT IN THE ROUND. *See also:* ROUGH GILT. (156)

gilt marbled edges. The edges of a book that have been marbled, burnished, sized, gilded, and then burnished again. When it is properly done, the marble can be seen through the gold. In the usual case, however, the marbling is barely perceptible when the book is closed, but appears faintly when the leaves are fanned. This is because the marbling colors penetrate slightly into the paper giving the effect very much like the "hidden" FORE-EDGE PAINTING, although the two techniques are completely different.

Gilt marbled edges is a French invention of the 17th century, and is usually attributed to (LE) GASCON. It is sometimes found on English bindings from about the middle of the 18th

Girdle book. Breviarium, manuscript on paper, written in Southern Germany, probably in the monastery of Kastl, near Nürnberg, in the year 1454. Spencer Collection Ms. 39, New York Public Library.
(10.4 cm. by 7.5 cm.)

century, but it was never used extensively. (236, 241)

gilt on landscapes. A fore-edge decoration consisting of a scene painted on the fore edge, which is then gilded and burnished. Only the gilt edge is seen until the leaves are fanned, whereupon the painting may be seen beneath the gold. The name probably derives from the fact that most of these fore-edge paintings are of landscape scenes. The practice of gilding on landscapes dates from the second half of the 18th century. *See also:* EDWARDS OF HALIFAX; GILT MARBLED EDGES; FORE-EDGE PAINTING. (97, 241, 280)

gilt on red. *See:* RED UNDER GOLD EDGES.

gilt on the rough. *See:* ROUGH GILT.

gilt solid. *See:* GILT IN THE ROUND.

gilt top. *See:* TOP EDGE GILT.

girdle book. A book which has an extra protective covering of soft leather made in such a manner that the book can be hung from the girdle or habit cord of a cleric and swung upward for reading while still attached to the girdle or cord. Doeskin and deerskin were frequently employed for this type of binding, which was used in the middle ages and early Renaissance, especially in Germany. Devotional books or didactic works, or professional reference books, e.g., law books, were most often bound in this manner, and the bindings were almost quite unpretentious. Very elegant bindings, however, were produced in velvet and brocade, to protect illuminated prayer books. Few intact girdle books have survived, as the overlapping leather was usually cut off for reuse when the need for protection had passed. Also called "utilitarian protective bindings." (156, 183, 347)

girdle calendar. A small medieval folding calendar, so made that it could be suspended from the girdle or habit cord of a cleric, or from the belt. Many had covers of stiff vellum sheathed in velvet, sometimes overcast at the edges with silk thread, and ornamented with balls and tassles. Such calendars generally showed the saints' days and other religious observances for each month, as well as various astrological tables. They were generally written on fold-out leaves of vellum. (347)

glacé (glacé (glazed) goat; glacé (glazed) kid). A vegetable or chrome tanned leather having a bright, smooth, glossy or glass-like grain finish obtained, according to the type of leather, by glazing, plating, ironing, or polishing. On the Continent of Europe, glacé is a leather prepared by tawing the skin with a mixture of alum, salt, flour, and egg yolk. Glacé leathers are sometimes used in bookbinding for title labels on a contrasting leather. (306, 363)

glacial acetic acid. A pure form of ACETIC ACID. It is a crystalline, corrosive substance that is miscible with water and alcohol. In solution it is a pungent, hygroscopic liquid and a good solvent.

glair (glaire). The preparation used to secure leaf metal to the covering material or edges of a book. It consists basically of egg white and vinegar, or, for the edges of a book, egg white and water. It may also be purchased in dry form (dry ALBUMEN) and then mixed with vinegar or water. Glair must have the property (and be of the quality) of melting immediately upon the application of heat and then setting quickly upon the removal of heat, so that the impression of the heated letter or finishing tool will melt the glair to permit it to hold the leaf solidly to the surface when the tool is removed.

Two methods of applying glair are generally employed. If the slight gloss produced by the glair is not objectionable, the glair may be sponged over the entire surface to be tooled, and would in any case be applied over the entire edge of the book; however, if the gloss is objectionable, the design and/or lettering are tooled in blind and the glair is then applied to the blind impressions with a GILDER'S TIP. *See also:* BLOCKING POWDER; SHELLAC SIZE. (335, 339)

glair brush. An artists "ground" brush, ¾ inch wide, and with soft bristles set in rubber and used in applying glair to the edges of a book to be gilded. (66)

glairing in. The process of applying GLAIR over the lettering or design that has been blinded in. (115)

glair pencil. A small brush, e.g., camel's hair brush, used to pencil glair directly into the blinded in impressions before laying on the gold leaf.

glass fibers. One of the more unusual man-made fibers being used commercially in the manufacture of special papers, although not at this time being used to make printing papers. Glass fibers are inert, or insensitive, to most external influences, and, in addition, are vermin proof, do not absorb moisture, or burn. Because of the physical nature of these fibers, the properties of glass fiber papers are unique and

different from those of all cellulose papers; however, they do not bond together as do cellulose fibers, and must, therefore, be used in mixtures with cellulose fibers, or bonded with synthetic resins. The two basic types of glass fibers are the drawn glass filaments and the blown glass fibers. (47)

glassine paper. A supercalendered paper manufactured principally from chemical wood pulps which have been beaten to secure a high degree of stock hydration. Glassine paper is grease resistant, has a high resistance to the passage of air, and is almost impervious to the passage of water vapor. It is also smooth and transparent, or semi-transparent. It is made in white and various colors, and may also be made opaque by the addition of fillers. Basis weights range from 12 to 90 pounds (24 × 36 — 500), with the ordinary range being from 15 to 40 pounds. Glassine tape, which is the paper backed, with a water-soluble adhesive, is sometimes used to repair torn book leaves, although it will eventually turn yellow and may damage the paper. It is also used in lieu of cellulose acetate in the SUNDEX PROCESS of lamination. (17, 198, 324)

glass paper. 1. A strong paper faced with powdered glass on one side and used in abrading or smoothing surfaces such as wood or leather, or to remove surface marks from paper. It is sometimes called sandpaper, although sandpaper is actually faced with sand or natural flint and not glass. 2. A paper produced from GLASS FIBERS. (237)

glass transition temperature. That temperature at which an adhesive loses its flexibility and becomes hard, inflexible, and "glasslike." An adhesive which reaches the "glass transition temperature" is subject to failure if flexed. Glass transition temperatures for adhesives vary greatly, from 105° C. (polymethyl methocrylate) to well below 0° C. If flexibility is required of the adhesive, the glass transition temperature can be lowered, either by means of plasticizers, or a polymer with a naturally low glass transition temperature.

glassy layer. The dense fibrous structure found in the butt or SHELL area of horsehide.

glazed. 1. A paper having a high gloss or polish. The gloss is applied to the paper either during manufacture or afterwards, by such means as calendering, friction glazing, plating, etc. Glazed papers are used for book and cover papers, and the like. 2. Any sur-

face finished with a high gloss, such as cloth, leather, or paper. *See also:* GLACÉ; GLAZED BOARD; GLAZING. (17)

glazed board. A MILLBOARD, or other type of board, that has been given a very smooth finish on the calenders. It was used in library binding when standing or hydraulic presses were used for the final pressing of books, its smoothness preventing it from imparting any markings to the covers of the books being pressed. (274)

glazed leather. *See:* GLACÉ.

glazed morocco. A MOROCCO leather which has had its grain flattened by a calendering process, such as GLAZING, as distinguished from CRUSHED MOROCCO.

glazing. The process of producing a bright, glossy, or glasslike finish on leather, paper, board, marbled or decorated papers, etc. Paper glazing may be done by means of calendering, or by applying wax over the surface of the paper and then passing heated iron over it. Leather is glazed, on the grain side, by subjecting it to the action of a non-rotating solid glass (or agate or other suitable material) cylinder drawn across the grain under very high pressure. (17, 335)

gloss (glossiness). The surface characteristic of a material which enables it to reflect light specularly and which causes it to appear shiny or lustrous. Gloss is measured at various angles of illumination, and, although it is subjective in nature, it is clearly associated with the light reflecting properties of a surface. (17)

gloster marble. A marble pattern very similar to the ANTIQUE MARBLE, except that instead of the spot being a flat color, i.e., a color mixed with gall and water alone, it calls for a blue stormont with no white beaten on afterward. (369)

glucose. A crystalline carbohydrate ($C_6H_{12}O_6$), soluble in water, used as a substitute for the more expensive glycerine (glycerol) as a plasticizer for glue, and in making GLUCOSE-GLYCOL PASTE. *See also:* SORBITOL. (339)

glucose-glycol paste. A paste containing glucose, in the form of corn syrup, and diethylene glycol ($C_6H_{14}O_3$), in the proportions of 35% original water, 10% diethylene glycol, 0.1% beta naphthol, 0.3% alum, 20% glucose, 19.6% flour, and 15% water from condensation of steam. The advantages of this paste are stated to be that it is suitable for use on pyroxylin impregnated book cloth and effectively reduces warpage of book covers. (339)

glue. An adhesive consisting of organic colloids of a complex protein structure obtained from animal materials such as bones and hides in meat packing and tanning industries. Glue contains two groups of proteins: chondrin, which accounts for its adhesive strength, and glutin, which contributes jelling strength.

Animal glue is a protein derived from the simple hydrolysis of collagen, which is the principal protein constituent of animal hide, connective tissue and bones. Collagen, animal glue, and gelatin are very closely related as to protein and chemical composition. Gelatin is considered to be hydrolized collagen: $C_{102}H_{149}O_{38}N_{31} + H_2O \leftrightarrows C_{102}H_{151}O_{39}N_{31}$, which gives an approximate chemical composition for glue of 51.29% carbon, 6.39% hydrogen, 24.13% oxygen, and 18.19% nitrogen. There may be minor variations in the composition of collagens from different sources, as well as in the composition of animal glues imparted by variations in processing techniques; however, the composition of glues and gelatins having widely varying case histories are still very similar.

As a protein, animal glue is essentially composed of polyamides of certain alpha-amino acids. It is believed that these acids are not present in glue in the free state, but rather as residues which are joined together by the elimination of water to form long polypeptide chains.

Glue is a polydisperse system containing mixtures of similar molecules of widely differing molecular weights. Because so wide a range of molecular weights is present, the molecular weight of glue is always an average, ranging from 20,000 to 250,000.

Hide and bone glues make up the two major types of animal glue. Hide glue, which is by far the superior of the two, yields a fairly neutral pH in solution, usually in the range of 6.5 to 7.4, although wider variations are possible. Bone glue is generally acidic, having pH values of 5.8 to 6.3. A glue having a high acidity absorbs less water and tends to set more slowly than a glue having low acidity. A glue having a pH greater than 7.0 tends to foam, and has a shorter shelf life than a glue that is slightly acidic.

Animal glues are soluble only in water, and are insoluble in oils, waxes, organic solvents, and absolute alcohol; however, they may be emulsified in water-oil or oil-water systems under proper conditions. One of the more interesting properties of animal glue solutions is their ability to pass from a liquid to a jelled state upon cooling, and then revert to the liquid state upon re-heating.

The important properties of glue include its jelly strength or consistency (gell strength), viscosity, melting point, adhesive strength, tensile strength or elasticity, optical rotation, swelling capacity, rate of setting, foaming characteristics, reactions to grease (whether acid or alkaline), as well as appearance, odor, color and keeping characteristics. Of these, gell strength and viscosity are most often used for determining the grade of a particular glue.

Regardless of the source of the protein, the glue manufacturing process consists essentially of washing the stock, crushing or shredding the bones or hides, soaking in a lime solution to eliminate hair and flesh, boiling to extract the gelatinous material, gelling, and, finally, drying. The resulting hard, brittle sheets of glue are then broken into pieces or flakes, or ground into powder.

Glue as such is much too brittle for use in bookbinding; therefore a plasticizer, such as glycerin, or a less expensive substitute such as SORBITOL, often combined with glycols and tackifiers, are added to improve elasticity and resilience. These so-called flexible glues are usually prepared from high quality grades of hide glue, with the ratio of plasticizer(s) to dry glue controlling the degree of flexibility that is imparted. In addition, glue, being an organic material, is susceptible to mold; consequently preservatives, such as beta naphthol, or the safer phenols, e.g., p-phenyl phenol, are added to prevent mold and bacterial growth. Deodorants, such as terpinol, are also employed in commercial glues.

The wide acceptance of glue as an adhesive stems from its unique ability to deposit a tacky viscous film from a warm water solution, which, upon cooling a few degrees, passes into a firm jelly state producing an immediate, moderately strong initial bond. Subsequent drying provides a permanent, strong, and resilient bond.

The use of glue as an adhesive dates from earliest recorded times. Whoever discovered that a strong adhesive could be produced by cooking pieces of animal hide, or perhaps bone, in water has never been ascertained, but archelogical discoveries indicate that the Egyptians used glue more than 4,000 years ago. The practical manufacture of glue can be traced back directly to 1690 in the Netherlands. Shortly thereafter, or about 1700, the English began making glue and established its manufacture as a permanent industry. Elijah Upjohn is considered by some authorities to have been the first to manufacture glue in the United States, in 1808.

In addition to its use as an adhesive in bookbinding, glue is also used for gumming, for tub-sizing paper, and as a general adhesive in papermaking.

The term "glue" is sometimes used loosely in a general sense as synonymous with "adhesive." (6, 102, 184, 185, 191, 196, 222, 233, 309, 335)

glue brush. A large, circular-shaped brush with long, heavy bristles set in rubber or a composition, and held by a ferrule; it is used for spreading glue over relatively large surfaces. Glue brushes range in diameter from about 1¾ to 2½ inches. (66, 264

glue line. The "line" at which the paper and adhesive meet in an adhesive binding. The fibers of the paper flex at the "glue line," and may work their way loose at this point, regardless of the characteristics of the adhesive that is used. (198)

glue pot. A container, frequently made of copper and usually of a double boiler construction, in which glue is melted and kept at the proper temperature, which is in the range of 120 to 150° F. It is heated by gas, or, more often today, by electricity, either through a water jacket, or directly through insulated walls. It is usually controlled by a thermostat if heated by electricity. Control of temperature is important, as overheating of animal glue results in a loss of gell strength. (183, 335)

glue size. A size made of glue and soap mixed in water, in the proportions of 1 part glue, 1 part soap, and 30 parts water. It is used for resizing papers, and also in sizing endpapers and other sheets following marbling or coloring. (335)

gluing up (glue up; glue off; gluing off). 1. The process of applying glue, or other adhesive, to the spine of a book following sewing. In edition binding, gluing up is a machine operation, but in library and hand binding it is generally done by hand. Usually, one of the polyvinyl adhesives, e.g., polyvinyl acetate, or a hot, flexible animal glue, or even a hot-melt adhesive is used. The major purpose of gluing up is to put the spine of the book in the proper flexible condition for the molding operations of rounding and backing. As these two processes were not introduced into bookbinding until the early part of the 16th century, gluing up was not done before that time.

There are advantages in using a relatively slow drying adhesive in gluing up, as such an adhesive will remain tacky while the spine is shaped and the shoulders are set.

2. The operation of gluing the cloth or paper used for making covers or cases. (102, 236, 256, 335)

glycerol (glycerin). A sweet, colorless, syrupy, hygroscopic trihydroxy alcohol $(C_3H_5(OH)_3)$, that occurs combined as glycerides, and is used as a hygroscopic agent in glue (mainly animal glues) to enable it to remain relatively soft and flexible. Because it is hygroscopic, glycerol can actually absorb so much moisture that mold growths can develop unless an antiseptic is added along with the softening agent. The high cost of glycerol has led to the substitution of other softening agents, such as SORBITOL and diethylene glycol. (339)

goatskin. Leather manufactured from a number of varieties of goats, especially of the genus *Capra*. There is little or no supply of domestic goatskin in either England or the United States; what production there still is, mostly in England, is of skins imported from India, Pakistan, East and West Africa, South Africa, and some from Southern Europe and Central and South America. Supplies are also available from the Far East. The green skins are dry-salted, wet-salted, or simply dried, and then baled for shipment to tanneries. African skins frequently suffer from damage due to disease and improper drying and are usually not suitable for use as bookbinding leather; however, Nigerian goatskins are frequently among the finest available. Some goatskins are tanned, but generally not finished, in the country of origin, principally in India (East India (E.I.) tanned), but also small quantities in Africa. Most goatskin for use in bookbinding is vegetable tanned, but some skins are alum tawed. Some skins are even tanned by a combination vegetable and chrome process.

Goatskin is tougher and more tightly fibered than sheepskin, has a hard-wearing grain, and, when properly tanned, can last for centuries. It colors beautifully and has a distinctive texture identified by ridges and furrows in the grain, and hair pits in groups all over the surface. Straight-grained goatskin is produced by rolling damp skins until all the furrows in the grain run in the same direction, while crushed goatskins have had the ridges flattened by ironing, rolling or plating.

Although MOROCCO, the best known goatskin, was first produced by the Moors, possibly as early as the 11th century or before, the use of goatskin in Europe did not become common until the first half of the 16th century, in Italy, and was not common in France until the second half of the 16th century. It was rarely used in England before 1600. Since its rise to ascendancy, however, it has been the traditional skin used in fine bookbinding. *See also:* LEATHER; LEVANT; NIGER. (83, 102, 164, 207, 236, 291, 335, 363)

goat skiver. The grain split of a goatskin. *See:* SKIVER. *See also:* BUFFING (1); FLESHER.

goat vellum. A "vellum" made from goatskin. Although VELLUM can be, and has been, produced from virtually every type of (relatively small) skin, it is traditionally made from the skin of a calf. (154)

goffered edges. *See:* GAUFFERED EDGES.

go home. A term sometimes applied to the proper and adequate adhesion of the PASTEDOWN in the joint of a cased book. (97)

gold. A very malleable, ductile, yellow trivalent and univalent metal (Au) that occurs chiefly in the free state, is unaffected by most chemicals but is attacked by chlorine and aqua regia, is hardened or changed in color for use in bookbinding and other art work by alloying with copper, silver, or other metals, and which has been used for centuries to illuminate manuscripts, as well as to letter and decorate leather and other bookbindings. *See also:* GILT EDGES; GOLD BLOCKING; GOLD LEAF; GOLD ROLL; GOLD TOOLING. (29, 102, 131, 161)

gold and silver bindings. Bookbindings having boards overlaid with thin panels of gold or silver, often in hammered relief, and sometimes inlaid with ivory, enamel, or jewels. Most of these bindings date from the 6th to the 13th centuries and were frequently executed for wealthy monasteries or churches to enclose their more valuable manuscripts. Very few have survived intact. (347)

gold and silver headband. A double HEADBAND made up of gold- and silver-colored threads. (152)

goldbeater's skin. The prepared outer coat of the caecum of the ox (or other cattle), which is the blind pouch or sac in which the large intestine begins. The gut is soaked in a dilute solution of potassium hydroxide, washed, stretched, beaten flat and thin, and treated chemically to prevent putrefaction. It is then stretched tightly and cemented together, back to back, leaving the clear, smooth, veinless inside of the caecum exposed. The SHODER and MOLD stages of GOLDBEATING are built up with these double skins of the ox. A mold of 1,000 pieces of goldbeater's skin requires the gut of about 400 oxen, and is only 1 inch thick when assembled. The pack is built up by interleaving the skins with leaves of gold. Goldbeater's skin is also used in the repair of holes and tears of vellum. (29)

goldbeater's tissue. An unbleached tissue paper, having a lint-free, hard surface, suitable for use as an interleaving tissue between leaves of the gold book. (17)

goldbeating. The art or process of reducing gold into extremely thin leaves. Goldbeating, which today is done almost entirely by mechanical devices, some of which are designed to duplicate the movement of the human arm, involves melting the gold into a bar, rolling it to a thickness of approximately 1/1,000 inch, and then beating it in three stages: the CUTCH (1), SHODER, and MOLD (2), followed by cutting and booking. When done by mechanical devices, goldbeating is simply a manufacturing process, but when done by hand it is an art.

The origin of gold beating is unknown; however, it is known that the tombs of prominent Egyptians contained artifacts bearing gold leaf, although not of the quality and thinness produced today. *See also:* GOLD LEAF. (29)

gold blocking. The decorative effect produced by blocking the covers of books in gold. The practice began in the early 16th century, probably first with the use of wooden blocks, although metal blocks were also in use during the 16th century. Nearly all gold blocking of that time is very deeply impressed, possibly because of the use of soft pasteboards under the leather, and possibly because the blocking pressure was difficult to estimate accurately because the blocking had to be done in a screw press; if, under these circumstances, the block began to get too cool, very great pressure would have been required. As the impressions made were often very uneven in depth, such refinements as "make-ready" must have been unknown to bookbinders of that time.

Blind lines, forming a cross, were frequently marked on the covers as recently as the early 19th century to assist in positioning the block precisely. The area was coated with glair, the gold leaf was laid on, the heated block was then centered on the intersection of the lines (which can usually be seen extending beyond the gilt impression), and the platen of the press was lowered onto the cover. It is quite likely that the covers were sometimes first blinded in before being blocked in gold. *See also:* BLOCKING PRESS. (236)

gold book. A paper book, usually 3¾ inches square, containing 25 sheets of gold leaf interspersed between leaves of goldbeaters tissues which have been dusted with chalk.

gold cleaner. A pointed instrument of metal or wood used to clean out surplus gold after tooling.

gold cushion. A pad on which a sheet of gold leaf is placed for cutting the pieces required for tooling. It usually consists of a piece of wood padded with blotting paper, cotton wool, or the like, and covered with calfskin, flesh side out, and powdered with brick dust. A stiff piece of paper is sometimes attached to the rear edge, and run around the sides to enclose about one-third of the cushion, as a sort of windshield to protect the fragile leaves from air currents. (233, 335, 343)

gold edges. A term at one time applied to a book when the edges had been gilded. *See:* GILT EDGES. (274)

gold foil. *See:* BLOCKING FOIL.

gold ink. An ink of the color of gold, prepared by mixing gold-colored bronze powder in a size. (261)

gold knife. A flat-bladed knife, the blade of which is about 6 inches long and ¾ inch wide. It has a smooth moderately sharp cutting edge on one or both sides. It is used to manipulate GOLD LEAF and to cut it to the required sizes and shapes. The knife must be sharp enough to cut the leaf with a single back-and-forth stroke but not so sharp as to cut the leather of the GOLD CUSHION. *See also:* GILDER'S TIP. (237)

gold leaf. A sheet of gold 3¼ inches square of an even thickness of 1/200,000 to 1/250,000 inch, and used in lettering and decorating bookbindings, and in other artistic work. The gold leaf used in bookbinding is generally 23 to 23¼ karat, the remaining 1 to ¾ karat being silver and copper. The alloy depends on the finished color desired, ranging from a delicate red through yellow to pale green. Other

types of leaf are also available, including lemon gold (18½ karat) and pale gold (16 karat). Since these are alloyed with the less malleable silver, they are somewhat thicker and consequently easier to handle than the more nearly pure gold. Gold leaf is available in books of 25 leaves, interleaved with sheets of tissue dusted with chalk to prevent them from sticking together. It is also available in ribbon form (*See:* GOLD ROLL). Some gold leaf is made in double thickness, and is believed to be the equivalent of pre-19th century leaf, as old writings and handling instructions indicate a less fragile and more easily manipulated metal than the modern day product. Double thick leaf is especially useful when gilding the edges of books, as it gives a more "solid" effect than is obtainable by using gold leaf of the usual thickness.

Gold leaf is the traditional metal used on books for lettering, edge gilding, and embellishment. In terms of beauty and durability it has never been equalled by any of the less expensive substitutes that have been available for more than a century. *See also:* DUTCH GOLD; GILT EDGES; GOLDBEATING; GOLD BLOCKING; GOLD TOOLING; SHELL GOLD. (29, 140, 236)

gold lifter. A shaped piece of wood, the flat under surface of which is covered with felt. It is used to pick up gold leaf. *See also:* GOLD NET FRAME. (115)

gold marble. A type of cover marble produced by breaking gold leaf into fragments on a piece of cloth, and rubbing the gold through the cloth onto the glaired covers of the book. (152, 241)

goldmark. Gold leaf prepared in a form which permits writing or decorating in gold without the use of heat. Goldmark is laid on leather, plastic, paper, etc., and inscribed with a stylus which produces a gold facsimile. Also called "cold gold." *See also:* BLOCKING FOIL. (234)

gold net frame. A thin piece of cloth, usually nearly transparent, stretched on a frame that can be adjusted for tension on the cloth, and used to pick up gold leaf. *See also:* GOLD LIFTER. (29, 83)

gold powder. Pulverized gold leaf dispersed in an aqueous binder and used in the illumination of manuscripts. Gold powder is both difficult to obtain and more expensive than gold leaf. *See also:* SHELL GOLD. (233)

gold-powdered bindings. Leather bookbindings produced during the period of about 1560 to 1570, and usually tooled with a simple design and then given a "powdered" effect by means of minis-

cule gold dots and (sometimes) gold leaf rubbed into the leather. (347)

gold roll. GOLD LEAF carried on a transparent plastic tape. It is produced by plating the ribbon electrically in a vacuum chamber, and then applying an adhesive to the gold to make it adhere to the surface to which it is applied. Gold in roll form is used extensively in lettering library bindings and in the production of superior edition bindings. (276, 339)

gold rubber. Pure rubber soaked in turpentine, or treated with paraffin to make it absorbent, and used to remove superfluous gold leaf after tooling. Also called "bottle rubber." *See also:* GILDER'S TIP; RUBBING-OFF CHEST. (92, 264, 335)

gold size. *See:* BLOCKING POWDER; GLAIR; SHELLAC SIZE.

gold sprinkle. A 19th century technique of decorating the edges of a book in which pulverized gold leaf is sprinkled on the edges after they have been colored. *See also:* SPRINKLED EDGES. (97, 152, 241)

gold tip. *See:* GILDER'S TIP.

gold tooling. The art or process of lettering and/or decorating the spine and covers of a book with GOLD LEAF (or, at times, other metals, e.g., platinum) impressed into the covering material, usually leather, by means of a heated letter, lettering pallet, or finishing tool.

In the traditional method of gold tooling, the lettering or design is first blinded in, generally first through paper, and then again directly on the leather. The second working of the tool polishes the base of the impression and assists in creating a particular brilliance in the tooling. An adhesive (glair) is applied to the leather (either all over or directly into the blind impressions); strips of gold leaf are laid over the impressions and held in place temporarily with a thin film of vaseline or grease; and the gold is then pressed permanently into place with the heated tool. When done properly, the affinity of the gold for leather is such that it will practically never come off; nor will it tarnish.

Gold tooling must be ranked as one of the most important innovations in the history of bookbinding. Its origins are somewhat obscure, but it was probably introduced into Europe by way of Italy, and spread throughout the rest of Europe and England, eventually arriving in America. There is some evidence that the technique may have been practiced in Morocco in the 13th century, but this is not conclusive. It has also been proposed that gold tooling was introduced into Italy by way of Persia (now Iran), where bookbinding and gilding flourished in the early decades of the 15th century.

Very early gold tooling is difficult to evaluate because it is uncertain whether the gold was actually impressed into the leather with a (hot) tool, or was painted into blind impressions. The evidence offered by some bindings, i.e., the absence of impressions deep enough to indicate tooling, as well as what appear to be brush marks in the gold, would seem to indicate painting. Because of the elapsed time, however, which has led to the inevitable deterioration of the materials, it is difficult to differentiate between the two techniques. In any event, books were actually being tooled in gold in Venice no later than 1470, and possibly several years earlier. Gold-tooled leather bindings were not common in England before about 1530, and not in the United States until about 1669.

The universal adoption of gold tooling was by no means immediate, and, in fact, blind tooling was still the predominant form of decoration until about 1580, or even 1600. *See also:* FINISHING (1). (141, 158, 225, 236, 347)

good seconds. A grade of leather skins which are superior to SECONDS but not as good as FIRSTS (1). "Good seconds" are somewhat less expensive than firsts, the flaws are less numerous than in seconds, and what flaws there are can often be avoided by careful cutting. (335)

Gosden, Thomas (1780–1840). An English bookbinder, book collector, bookseller, and publisher, known as the "sporting binder," because most of his bindings were of books devoted to sports. The pecularity of his style and the reason he is remembered is that he used tools cut in the forms of fish, reels, rods, baskets, and sportsmen. (50, 339)

Gothic tabs. Identifying cloth tabs used with the cut-in or THUMB INDEX. The cloth tabs, each with identifying letter or letters, are glued to the first full leaf of each section devoted to that part of the alphabet. The name derives from the type style used by the firms supplying the tabs. Gothic (cloth) tabs are seldom used today. (264)

gótico-mudéjar style. A variation of the MUDÉJAR STYLE, i.e., mudéjar bindings influenced by Gothic techniques. Such bindings were executed from the 13th to the 15th centuries largely in the northeastern part of Spain. The style has affinities with a class of early Italian bindings in which the plan of decoration is Gothic, but the execution is carried out with small tools similar to those used on mudéjar bindings. The bindings are usually of CORDOVAN LEATHER and most have wooden boards. (330)

gouffered edges. *See:* GAUFFERED EDGES.

gouge. A single-line finishing tool, used either for blind or gold tooling on the covers but not the spine of a book. It has a curved edge which forms a segment of a concentric circle. Gouges are generally made in sets of ten, and, if a series of concentric circles are drawn about 1/10 inch apart, the lines impressed by each succeeding gouge will be longer and flatter. So-called flat curved gouges are those derived from an even larger circle, and are therefore less curved than regular gouges. When tooling, the gouge is always sighted from the concave side. (161, 335)

gouge index. *See:* THUMB INDEX.

governmental style. An obsolete term for full leather bindings in law calf, sheep, or skiver. (256)

grade. Materials listed in an order (or distinguished from other, comparable materials) on the basis of use, appearance, quality, manufacturing, raw materials, performance, or a combination of these factors. Some "grades," such as of cloth, leather, and paper (or board), have been officially identified and described, while others are commonly recognized but are not officially defined. (17)

grain. 1. In machine-made paper and board, the direction in which the majority of the fibers are oriented. *See:* MACHINE DIRECTION. 2. In leather, the term is used primarily to indicate the top or outer, i.e., hair side, layer of a hide or skin that has been split into two or more layers. A "grain layer," is just that portion of a skin that extends from the surface exposed by removal of hair or wool and epidermis, down to about the level of the hair or wool roots. It can also mean the follicle pattern visible on the outer surface of a skin after the hair or wool and epidermis have been removed. *See also:* GRAIN PATTERN. 3. In cloth, the "grain" is the direction of the WARP threads. (143, 234, 291, 320, 363)

grain direction. *See:* MACHINE DIRECTION.

grained jute board. A jute-lined board printed with a grained effect. Rigid and resistant to scuffing, it is used mainly for inexpensive book covers or transfer-file boxes. (17)

grained leather. *See:* BOARDING (1); GRAINED UP.

grained skiver. A SKIVER produced from the flesh split of a sheepskin, dyed and embossed with a grain pattern.

grained up. The process or effect of raising the grain of a leather, usually by wetting and rubbing the grain side with the hand or a piece of cork, causing the grain to rise. Graining up is usually done after the leather has been pared; its purpose is to correct the flattened

GOUGE

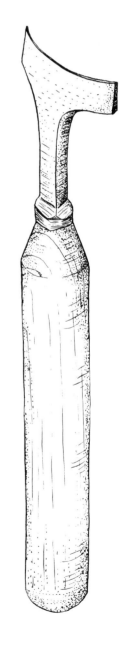

condition of the grain caused by the pressure of paring. "Grained up" usually refers to the process employed by the bookbinder and is not to be confused with BOARDING (1), which is a process employed by the leather manufacturer. (97)

graining. 1. The process of applying an all-over pattern to cloth, either during manufacture or by rolling the cloth between embossing plates. 2. The process or result of printing various designs on paper or board to simulate various wood grains, marble, etc., generally for use as cover papers. 3. *See:* BOARDING (1). 4. *See:* EMBOSSING (1). (94, 164)

graining board. An instrument used for creasing hides and skins, or BOARDING (1), so as to produce certain grain effects in the leather. The implement consists of a curved board faced with a thick sheet of cork, and having a handle on the upper side. Effective use of the graining board calls for considerable pressure, as the greater the pressure exerted, the sharper the creases produced and the closer their spacing, both of which are considered desirable. Graining boards have been largely superseded by the boarding machine. (306)

graining brush. A decorator's brush, about 4 inches in width, used to obtain brush-grained effects on paste-grained endpapers. (335)

graining combs. Combs made of wood, metal, hard rubber, or plastic, or decorator's metal combs, used to produce grained effects on paste-grained endpapers. (231, 335)

graining plates. Plates used to impart a diced pattern to the leather covering of a book. They were invented by John Bohn, a German immigrant in England in about 1796. Early plates were made of brass or wood and were able to impart a deeper impression than that obtained by calendering. Later plates were made of metal. As the lines were placed diagonally in one direction only, two impressions were required to produce the diced effect. They were also superior to calendering in that the dicing could be done following covering. The simple graining plates for dicing soon evolved into more elaborate plates for impressing fish scales, squares, etc. One reason they were popular was their capability for covering blemishes in the leather. (236)

grain layer. That portion of a hide or skin extending from the surface exposed by the removal of the hair or wool and epidermis down to about the level of the hair or wool roots. It is the layer which contains the hair follicles, sudoriferous and sebaceous glands, etc., i.e., the thermostat layer. (363)

grain long. A term sometimes used in paper manufacture to indicate that the grain or MACHINE DIRECTION of the paper is parallel to the larger dimension of the sheet. *Cf:* GRAIN SHORT. (125)

grain pattern. The design on the outer surface of leather produced by the arrangement of the hair follicles and pores, characteristic of the species and age of the animals from which the leather is produced. In general, the younger the animal the finer the grain structure. The skin of the female of the species is usually of a finer grain than the male. The less hair or wool there is on the animal the tougher and stronger the leather, especially the grain surface. Because of their durability, uniformity, beauty, and form, grain patterns represent one of the most appealing and highly prized characteristics of leather, and it is for this reason that imitation grains are often embossed on inferior quality leathers and even printed or embossed on other materials, such as cloth and plastic. (291, 363)

grain short. A term sometimes used in paper manufacture to indicate that the grain or MACHINE DIRECTION of the paper is parallel to the shorter dimension of the sheet. *Cf:* GRAIN LONG. (125)

grain side. The outer, or hair side of a hide or skin. *See:* GRAIN (2); GRAIN PATTERN.

grain split. The outer, or hair layer of a hide or skin that has been split into two or more layers.

grainy. 1. An exaggerated, delicate mosaic pattern of extremely minute depressions in a hide or skin extending inward from the bellies, and consisting actually of the pattern of the blood vessels of the skin projected onto the grain surface. 2. Slight variations in the surface appearance of a paper caused by several factors, including the impressions of wires and felts of the papermaking machine, irregular distribution of color, uneven shrinkage during drying, etc. (17, 363)

grainy edges. A rough surface of a paper which sometimes extends for varying distances in from the edge of a sheet as formed and dried on the papermaking machine. (17)

grangerized. *See:* EXTRA-ILLUSTRATED.

granite board. Any board with an embossed pattern or design resembling granite and used for decorative book covers.

granite marble. A marble pattern produced by sprinkling black (lampblack) coloring in very fine drops over the entire surface of the sheet several times, followed by brown coloring. The paper is then embossed and glaired. The effect is supposed to resemble granite. (152)

grass. *See:* ESPARTO (GRASS).

grass cloth. A lustrous, plain, usually loosely woven fabric manufactured chiefly in the Orient from various grasses and other vegetable fibers, especially RAMIE, and used for lining the spines of books, particularly in the area of manufacture. (142)

gray cloth (gray goods). A fabric which has not been bleached, dyed or otherwise finished. It is the *base fabric* used in the manufacture of BOOK CLOTH.

greaseproof. A descriptive term applied to a book cloth treated in such a manner that it will permit no penetration by oleic acid within a period of 5 minutes, as determined by the RING TEST. (341)

Great Omar. A binding of Vedder's illustrated edition of the *Rubaiyat of Omar Khayyam,* measuring 16 by 13 inches, and decorated according to the designs of the English bookbinder Francis Sangorski. The Great Omar was covered in green levant morocco, and had the same green leather doublures, while brown leather was used for the flyleaves. All were decorated in a most lavish manner, each to a different design, making a total of six designs. In addition to the extremely elaborate gold tooling, there were numerous sunken panels, thousands of colored inlays, as well as some 1,050 jewels, including garnets, olivines, rubies, topazes, and turquoises. The decoration of the lower cover had as its central feature a model of a Persian mandolin made of mahogany, inlaid with silver, satinwood, and ebony.

The magnificent binding, which took nearly 2 years to complete, was probably the most lavishly decorated bookbinding ever produced. The Great Omar was the last of a series of Omars executed by the firm of Sangorski and Sutcliffe, of London. Unfortunately, only reproductions of the binding, also produced by Sangorski and Sutcliffe, now exist, the original having been lost in the sinking of the *Titanic,* and a later copy being destroyed in the Second World War. (236, 319)

Greek style. A 15th and 16th century style of blind tooled binding in which the books had spines rising at head and tail to protect the thick double headbands, which were striped in bright red and blue. The thick wooden boards had grooved edges, and clasp straps of triple braided thongs fastened to pins set in the grooves. Greek texts, or even translations from the Greek, were bound in this manner in France and Italy, probably by Greek craftsmen. (156, 347)

green. 1. An uncured hide or skin, usually one just removed from the animal. 2. An incompletely dried sheet of paper or board.

green agate marble. A cover marble consisting of black sprinkled in large drops; these unite and are followed at regular intervals by green, which is spread on the cover to unite with the black. (97, 152)

green earth. A natural earth similar in composition to the mineral glauconite. It is used mainly as a base for the precipitation of malachite green dye-stuff to form the pigment known as lime green.

green fleshing. A method of applying mechanical action to hides or skins after they have been soaked to a softened condition. It is done by scraping the flesh side with a curved blade on the beam, or, in the usual manner today, in a fleshing machine. In the tanning of heavy leather, FLESHING frequently takes place following liming and unhairing; however, green fleshing, which takes place before liming, has several advantages: 1) it provides a more uniform grain surface for unhairing and helps prevent grain damage during machine unhairing; 2) the physical compression by both the feed rolls and fleshing cylinder materially prevent excessive plumping of the softened hide fibers during subsequent liming; 3) a comparatively thick flesh, particularly one of a fatty nature, reduces soaking, bactericidal, and liming effects; and 4) the formation of calcium soaps during liming and oily matter during tanning is held to a minimum, particularly when poor or insufficient curing has resulted in the presence of free fatty acids in the fatty tissue. Also called "soak fleshing." (306)

green porphyry marble. A cover marble executed by sprinkling green in very fine drops, allowing the color to spread and dry between sprinklings. To form a more elegant vein, the cover is first sprinkled with weak black followed by the green and, when this is dry, by a fine red. (152)

green salted. A hide or skin that has been cured with salt. Many skins are ex-ported from the Indian Subcontinent in the "green salted state." *See also:* BRINING; WET-SALTING. (248)

green salting. *See:* WET-SALTING.

green vitroil. *See:* FERROUS SULFATE.

grid. A decorative ornament often used on heads-in-medallions rolls. It consists essentially of two horizontal lines with a few short vertical bars in between, with foliage on the sides. (250)

Grimaldi, Giovanni Battista. The bibliophile whose collection was long considered to have been brought together by Demetrio Canevari, physician to Pope Urban VIII. The bindings were produced by Venetian bookbinders, probably between 1535 and 1560, and were subsequently inherited by Canevari. The bindings feature fine-figured borders of gold-tooled decoration, with painted oval cameos of Apollo driving his chariot drawn by two horses toward Pegasus. There are two varieties of this elliptical cameo stamp, with the greater diameter of the larger being perpendicular and that of the smaller horizontal. On some of the bindings the title appears on both covers in a cartouche above the stamp. *See also:* CAMEO BINDINGS. (168, 347)

Grolieresque. A term generally applied to the style of binding associated with the name Grolier. *See:* JEAN GROLIER. In many respects it is an ideal style for tooling in gold, depending for its effect on graceful geometrical strapwork. *See also:* MAIOLI STYLE. (156, 286)

Grolier, Jean (1479-1565). The 16th century bibliophile, Jean Grolier de Servin, vicomte d'aquisy. Although Jean Grolier is regarded correctly as a French bibliophile, the bindings executed for him were essentially Italian in their principles of design. Grolier possessed one of the finest private libraries of his time (and possibly any other time), consisting of some 3,000 volumes contained within bindings of superlative richness and beauty.

Grolier lived in Italy, with only a few interruptions, between 1510 and about 1525, and, while there, became the friend of the celebrated printer, Aldus Manutius. It is said that in appreciation of Grolier's friendship and financial assistance, Aldus printed several copies on vellum or large paper for Grolier, several of which were dedicated to him.

Grolier is believed to have patronized several binders over the years he collected, including Claude de Picques, and the so-called fleur-de-lis and cupid's bow binders.

The books which Grolier acquired in his early years (including many of his Aldine volumes) possess the distinguishing characteristics of Italian binding of the time he lived in Italy.

The Grolier bindings, the designs of which have been imitated more than those of any other style, with the possible exception of the *pointillé* bindings, are usually classified into two distinct groups: 1) those executed expressly for him; and 2) those bound before he acquired them either through purchase or gift.

Although the bindings executed for Grolier are distinctly similar in style, they vary considerably in their ornamentation. The designs generally consist of a geometrical pattern, occasionally colored, combined with arabesque work, which is solid, azured, or only outlined. On some of his bindings, however, the geometrical pattern has no arabesques, while in others the arabesque work is found without the geometrical design. Nearly all of the books of the first class, as well as many of those of the second, include the altruistic inscription, *Io. Grolierii et Amicorvm* (of Jean Grolier and his friends), usually at the tail edge of the upper cover, which he apparently borrowed from his contemporary, Mahieu. Both covers of most of Grolier's bindings feature a central compartment, usually containing the title of the book on the upper cover, and the expression *Portia Mea, Domine, Sit in Terra Vivetivm* (Let my portion, O Lord, be in the land of the living), on the lower cover. Other legends also at times appear on his bindings.

Grolier's signature, or his motto, with several slight variations, is frequently found in his own hand inside the books he collected before about 1536. This was usually written at the back.

There are two distinct features to Grolier's bindings which were not consistently practiced by other contemporary collectors: 1) the pastedowns are vellum, followed by two conjugate white paper flyleaves, which are followed by a vellum leaf conjugate with the pastedown, which is followed by a final conjugate pair of paper leaves; and 2) the edges are gilt but not gauffered or otherwise further embellished. *See* PLATE IV. (59, 132, 141, 245, 273, 279, 285, 347)

grooves. 1. The V-shaped or rectangular incisions made on the outside of the boards connecting the holes made for LACING-IN with the edges of the board. The use of grooves in craft bookbinding was not common until the end of the 18th century, which is somewhat surprising because it is an important technique, in that, while the weakening effect on the board is only slight, it permits thick cords to be laced-in without unattractive lumps being seen under the covering leather. In the 19th century, however, the insistence upon neatness and ultra-fine finish led many bookbinders to reduce the thickness of the slips greatly before lacing-in, even though grooves were still cut. Since lacing-in of the cords is one of the major differences between a cased and a bound book, the reduction of cord thickness reduces the strength considerably.

Douglass Cockerell was the first, or one of the first, craftsmen to show that the slight projection of the cords was acceptable not only because it showed that the book was solidly constructed, but because the lumps actually provided a starting point for the decoration of the book.

Grooves in the shape of an inverted V, ending with a hole to take the cord to the inside of the board is the usual method of cutting; however, the tendency today is to cut a groove ending in a rectangular slot at right angles to the groove.

2. The depression along the binding edge of the upper and lower covers of a book. *See:* JOINT (1). 3. The space between the board and spine of a book having an open joint. *See:* FRENCH JOINT. *See also:* CLOSED JOINT. 4 Cuts made in the spine of a text block in the shape of an inverted V, into which cords are recessed when sewing single leaves. *See also:* KERF. (83, 196, 236)

grosgrain. A firm, plain-weave fabric, generally with a silk or rayon warp and a heavy cotton filling that forms pronounced cross ribs. It is sometimes used as a covering material for books. (25)

ground substance. An amorphous background material in which the cells and fibers of collagen are embedded. It is a colloidal substance in the form of a gel, and has the capacity of binding varying amounts of water. The bound water serves as a medium for the diffusion of gases and metabolic substances from the blood vessels to the cells of the tissues, and vice versa, of the living animal. A certain amount of ground substance is removed during the leather manufacturing process. (26, 291)

groundwood free paper. A paper or board that contains no mechanical wood

pulp. "Groundwood free" is actually interpreted to mean that the paper or board contains less than 5% mechanical wood pulp. (17)

groundwood printing papers. Papers of the same general type as BOOK PAPERS. As the name suggests, they contain a proportion of mechanical wood pulp, but it is a pulp carefully prepared, and therefore clean and bright. The use of mechanical pulp for this type of printing paper improves important characteristics of the paper, such as retention of loadings, high bulk, greater opacity for the basis weight, improved softness, and a smoother finish. They are, however, inferior to the chemical wood pulp papers in both permanency and brightness. They are made in a number of furnishes ranging from approximately 75% mechanical pulp to about 20 to 25% mechanical, the balance being chemical pulp. They are sized, finished, colored, loaded, and coated in various ways to make them suitable for virtually any printing process. Their life expectancy, however, even under good storage conditions, is probably under 25 years. (17, 72, 324)

groundwood pulp. *See:* MECHANICAL WOOD PULP.

growing flower. A form of ornamentation of a ROLL (1), consisting of a flattened elliptical base with a stem and leaves ending in two flowers, the tops of which curve outwards. (250)

grubby hides. Hides that have been damaged by grubs of the warble fly. *See also:* PEPPER BOXES; WARBLES.

g.t. (g.t.e.). Abbreviation for gilt top, or gilt top edge. *See:* TOP EDGE GILT.

guard. 1. A strip of cloth or paper pasted around or into a section of a book so as to reinforce the paper and prevent

the sewing thread from tearing through. This type of repair is sometimes required after a book has been pulled for rebinding, either because the folds of the section were torn because the sewing thread pulled through the paper, or the outer fold was damaged during the removal of the old glue on the spine. A guard may also be required for leaves or plates that have become frayed or detached at the inner edge. The material used for the guard must be strong yet thin so as not to cause undue swelling in the spine of the book. When paper is used for the guard, its MACHINE DIRECTION should run from head to tail of the section. 2. A strip of cloth or paper on which an illustration, map, etc., may be attached and sewn through with the section, thus allowing free flexing. Four-page (two folios) plate units are also strengthened in this manner before sewing. A leaf to be positioned at the beginning or end of a section is guarded on the inside, while an interior leaf is guarded on the outside. In both cases the sewing thread passes through the center of the guard. *See also:* COMPENSATION GUARD; CONTINUOUS GUARD; GUARDED IN; PLATE ATTACHMENT; REVERSED V-GUARD; THROW OUT. 3. *See:* STUB (1). (83, 107, 161, 335)

guard book. A book containing compensation guards equal to the anticipated thickness of the additional matter to be added at a later time. The guards are sewn with the book and are intended to prevent gaping of the boards or damage to the spine when the book is filled with photographs, clippings, etc. Also called "stub book." (82, 343)

guarded endpaper. A section which has had a linen GUARD (1) wrapped

GUARD BOOK

around both it and the endpaper so as to effectively make one unit of the two. Its purpose is to provide additional strength at the point where greatest flexing occurs, which is between the endpaper and the first leaf of the section. The guard is usually attached so that not more than 3/16 inch of the linen appears on the exposed leaf of the section, while generally 1¼ inches in on the unexposed side of the endpaper. In a case binding the guard is tipped to both the section and the endpaper, but in a hand-bound book, because both section and endpaper are sewn (through the linen), the guard is tipped only to the section. In case binding the guard also eliminates the necessity of tipping the endpaper to the first leaf of the section and thus eliminates drag on the leaf. In a hand-bound book (where the endpaper is not tipped to the section) one guard strengthens the folds of both the endpaper and section; were two guards to be used instead of the one, the guard would appear on the first printed page of the book.

guarded in. Plates which are inserted into a book without being tipped to one of the leaves of the book. The paper area of the plate is wider than the leaves of the book, the projecting part being wrapped around the fold of the section. A narrow strip of paper appears elsewhere in the book as a consequence.

guarding. The operation of attaching a GUARD (2) for the purpose of providing a hinge for a map, illustration, etc., to strengthen the fold between two conjugate leaves, or to assist in relieving the strain of the endpaper caused by the opening of the book. *See:* GUARDED ENDPAPER; GUARDED IN; GUARDING IN PAIRS; PLATE ATTACHMENT. (335, 343)

guarding in pairs. A method of securing two plates to one GUARD (1). While the positioning of the guard within the section may or may not allow for either or both sides to be located near the accompanying text material, guarding in this manner may help alleviate some of the swelling caused by the thickness of the material used for the guards. (307, 335)

guard sheet. *See:* BARRIER SHEET.

guide boards. A technique employed by some bookbinders when trimming with the plow, in which two binder's boards, each about ½ inch larger than the leaves of the book, are tipped on, one to the front endpaper with its top even

with the trimming line at the head of the text block, and the second tipped to the back endpaper with the edge even with the trimming line at the tail. Guide boards are used to control the squareness of the book in the lying press and to prevent crushing of the shoulders of the text block when the press is closed on it. (196)

guide of fair value. A statement drawn up in 1948 by the Joint Committee of the American Library Association and the Library Binding Institute, establishing "fair" prices for library binding, restoration of valuable books, and the transportation of library materials. The statement is now obsolete. (131)

guide word. *See:* CATCHWORD.

guild of contemporary bookbinders. *See:* DESIGNER BOOKBINDERS.

guilloche. A design used in finishing a book, consisting of two or more bands intertwining and forming a continuous series, leaving circular openings filled with round devices. (94, 261)

guillotine. A machine used for cutting large numbers of sheets of paper and board, and also in library binding for trimming the edges of books. The typical guillotine, which is designed to cut comparatively large edge lengths, is a single-knife cutter, in which a heavy blade descends between vertical runners.

The principal parts of the guillotine are a table on which the material to be cut is piled; a movable back gauge (called the "back fence" in Europe), perpendicular to the table, against which the back edge of the pile rests; a clamp (or press beam) which compresses and secures the front edge of the pile, i.e., the edge to be cut; and a knife (or cutter) fixed in a cutting beam which descends immediately in front of the clamp, cutting through the pile, and stopping at a cutting stick set into the table. Pressure can be applied by hand with a screw spindle, but electric power is usual on both large and small machines.

All guillotines built for the printing and binding trades permit the squaring of a sheet, or section, provided that none of the dimensions exceeds the cutting length of the machine. Generally, on standard models, the size of the material to be placed on the table must not exceed its cutting length in either direction; however, some of the larger cutters are provided with longer back tables as optional equipment. Some cutters allow for trimming the shorter dimensions or splitting sheets. One of the most important features on

some modern cutters is automatic spacing, which causes the back gauge to move a pre-determined distance following each cut.

Modern electronic guillotines have movements which are actuated by a series of relays and contactors brought into operation through the medium of a number of thyratrons, tubes, and photoelectric eye units. All operations are mechanical, and are set into motion by push buttons or by tripping micro switches which control the electronic circuit and, therefore, the cutter.

Modern guillotines also have safety devices which reduce the element of risk, assuming that the proper precautions are taken and the mechanism is not altered. Controls are designed to require that both hands be used to activate the final clamp pressure and cutting operations, and the machines are designed to stop the knife at the top of the stroke without possibility of a repeat cut.

Guillotines came into use in the late 1830s, when, in 1837, Thirault built a model with a fixed blade. In 1844 and 1852 Guillaume Massiquot patented machines similar to those in use today. Since the middle of the 19th century considerable improvements have been made by Fomm and Krause of Germany, Furnival in England, and Oswego and Seybold in the United States. (89, 145, 236, 320)

guinea edge. Ornamentation of the edges of the covers of a book produced by means of a fillet which has an engraved pattern resembling the edge of an old gold guinea. (94)

gum. Any of a number of colloidal polysaccharides of high molecular weight, which can be dispersed in either cold or hot water to produce various mixtures or solutions, and which display good flow and tack characteristics. *See also:* GHATTI GUM; GUM ARABIC; GUM SANDARACH; GUM TRAGACANTH; KARAYA GUM. (175, 309)

gum arabic. A water-soluble gum obtained from several species of the acacia tree, especially *Acacia senegal* and *A. arabica,* and used in the manufacture of adhesives and ink, and as a binding medium for marbling colors. Historically, gum arabic was used to increase the viscosity of ink, or to make it flow well, to prevent it from feathering, and to suspend the coloring matter. It was particularly important in the days of the reed or quill pen. Solutions of gum arabic have long been used as adhesives for paper, but they are little used today.

Gum arabic adhesives produce clear, easy brushing solutions which have no marked initial set but which will pass through a tacky stage on drying. The properties for which they are valued include ready solution in water following drying, readiness for immediate use, cleanliness and ease of application. Gum arabic adhesives, however, are generally too moisture sensitive for use in archival work. Also called "acacia gum." (198)

gum dragon (gum elect). *See:* GUM TRAGA-CANTH.

gum hog (gum hogg). *See:* KARAYA GUM.

gum juniper. *See:* GUM SANDARACH.

gummed cloth tapes. Gummed cloth or transparent adhesive paper used for mending torn book leaves, reinforcing joints, tipping in, guarding, and the like, usually in in-house repair procedures. Such tapes can be difficult to remove and frequently cause extensive damage to the paper when they are removed.

gummed paper (gummed flat paper). A strong, hard-sized, machine-finished, English finish, supercalendered, or coated paper, which is gummed on one side and used for book labels, embossed seals, etc. The paper is made in white, colored, or metallic finishes. Usual basis weight is from 38 to 45 pounds (24 × 36 — 500). Different adhesives are used for gummed paper depending upon the surface to which the paper is to adhere. They should be flat and non-curling. (17, 139)

gum sandarac. A brittle resin obtained from the African sandarac tree, *Tetra-clinis articulata,* in the form of yellowish, faintly aromatic, opaque tears and broken cylindrical pieces. It is soluble in alcohol. It is used in the manufacture of spirit varnishes, and, when dissolved in oil, to make cooked varnishes. It is also used in powdered form to clean vellum and to prepare it for writing purposes. Its most outstanding property is its hardness. Also called "gum juniper." *See also:* POUNCE (1); PUMICE. (233)

gum stripping tapes. *See:* BINDERY TAPES.

gum tragacanth. A gum obtained as a dried exudate from various Asiatic and Eastern European plants of the genus *Astragalus,* especially *A. gummifer.* It consists of bassorin and tragacanthin, and swells in water to form a gel. Gum tragacanth has been used extensively in the preparation of marbling size, and is still used by some marblers. Also called "gum dragon" and "gum elect." (235, 236, 335)

gut. The cured and finished strips of the intestines of sheep, calves, or oxen. The gut of the sheep or calf is used as the core of the HEADBAND, while that of the ox is used in the manufacture of GOLD-BEATER'S SKIN. (335)

gutta-percha binding. *See:* CAOUTCHOUC BINDING.

gutter. The adjoining inner margins of two facing printed pages, i.e., the margin at the sewn fold of a section.

guttering. The ridges that sometimes occur (as a result of use) along the spine of a tight-back binding.

gutter margin. *See:* INNER MARGIN.

gypsum. The naturally occurring hydrous form of calcium sulfate ($Ca_2SO_4 \cdot 2H_2O$), which is used as a filler for printing papers, and serves to fill the spaces between the paper fibers, thereby increasing opacity and smoothness. It is also used in the manufacture of GOLD LEAF. Also called "puritan filler" and "terra alba." *See also:* BRIME. (17, 29, 343)

hair. The coalesced horny cells, which contain the protein keratin along with 0.75 to 2.0% mineral salts. Although hair is an epidermal structure, it is seated deep in the papillary layer of the dermis. It consists of two continuous regions, the root and a long projection, which is the shaft. The lower part of the shaft is enclosed in a follicle which is a sheath of epidermal cells continuous with those in other parts of the epidermis.

Most animal hairs are of two types: primary and secondary. Primary hairs are the more numerous and vary in structure depending on the age and species of the animal. Secondary hairs, which are similar in structure to the primary, are only about one-third their diameter.

The positions which the primary and secondary hairs occupy relative to each other as they enter the surface of the skin, together with their different thicknesses, determine the characteristic grain pattern of the dermal surface after the hair and other epidermis have been removed. Due to the general complexity of the papillary region, including hairs of various diameters at different stages of growth and located at different depths in the papillary layer, their removal by mechanical means is difficult. *See also:* HAIR-ON LEATHER; HAIR SHEEP; SHORT HAIR; UNHAIRING. (248, 291, 363)

hair marble. A marble pattern consisting of but one or two colors, and usually used on the edges of books. The colors are diluted to about one-third of their normal volume with water, and, when two colors are employed, enough gall is added to the first color to make it spread on the size to form a ribbon 5 to 6 inches wide, while the second color is applied evenly in fine drops, followed by a sprinkle of water which forms the hair veins. Carragheen moss is the usual sizing for this marble. Single-color hair marbles include the black, red or blue, while two-color hairs are usually red and black or bluish-brown. (151)

hair-on leather. A leather which has been produced without first removing the hair. SLUNK skins are preferred for this type of leather, although skins of older animals can be used after trimming of

the hair. Hair-on leather has been used occasionally as a covering material for books. (248)

hair sheep. Leather made from the skin of a sheep that grows hair instead of wool. The hair sheep is found in the mountainous regions of India, China, South America, and Africa. The leather produced form these skins has a finer and tougher grain than that made from wool-bearing sheep. *See also:* CABRETTA LEATHER. (61, 164)

hair side. The outer surface of a hide or skin, more commonly referred to in finished leather as the GRAIN SIDE.

hair slips. Hides and skins that have suffered sufficient PUTREFACTIVE DAMAGE so that the hair is loosened.

half bands. Horizontal ridges on the spines of some tight-back bindings. They are generally located at the head and tail of the volume, where they indicate the position of the kettle stitches, and are sometimes also between the raised bands. They are smaller than the raised bands. Half bands are often found on Italian and French bindings of the 16th century. (156)

half binding. A style of binding in which the spine and part of the side of the book, as well as the four corners, are covered with one kind of material, e.g., leather, cloth, etc., and the sides with another material, e.g., cloth or paper. In this style of binding the spine covering usually extends onto the boards about one-fourth of their width, with the corners in harmonious proportion. *See also:* QUARTER BINDING; THREE-QUARTER BINDING. (133, 264)

half cloth. A book bound with a cloth spine, but not cloth corners. The sides are generally paper, which is also used for the spine title label. The style was fairly common on publisher's bindings

from the late 1820s to the early 1840s, for three-volume novels into the early 1850s, and occasionally for general works since about 1890. The style was correctly (though not often) called "quarter cloth" by job binders. Also called at times "half linen." (69, 335)

half extra. 1. In craft bookbinding, "half extra" letterpress binding is defined as any half-leather binding *forwarded in boards,* regardless of any decoration or lack of it. A half extra binding is one usually, but not necessarily, sewn on raised cords. If it is not sewn on raised cords, false bands are usually used. 2. In stationery binding, "half extra" is defined as a blankbook made up of machine-made paper that has been tubsized. Four sections are taped at front and back, and the book is sewn on webbings. It has a SPRING-BACK (1), made endpapers, cloth joints sewn on, leather linings between the webbings, and is covered on the spine and corners with calfskin or roan and on the sides with paper. (152, 236)

half French fold. A modification of the FRENCH FOLD, consisting of a sheet printed on one side only and given two folds, the first of which is half way down the short side of the sheet and the second at right angles to the first across the long side. It is used for brochures, leaflets, etc., but seldom in book work, except for folding maps. (150)

half gilt. An obsolete term used in describing a book sewn on raised cords; the bands appearing on the spine are tooled in gold, usually by means of a broad pallet or roll. The tool was also sometimes worked in the center of each panel between the bands. (97)

half leather. A book having a leather spine, extending over approximately one-fourth the width of the sides, leather corners, and the remainder of the sides covered in cloth or paper.

Half leather bindings covered in calfskin of a tan or other shade of brown, with narrow spines and small corners, marbled paper sides, smooth cut edges which were sometimes stained pale yellow or sprinkled red, and plain endpapers, were common in England in the latter half of the 18th century. The corners of these volumes were occasionally vellum instead of leather.

Stationers also issued cheap half leather bindings, often sheepskin, which were not trimmed and had no headbands, no squares, and were not lettered. Half vellum bindings, which were comparatively rare, were produced throughout the 19th century. *See also:* QUARTER LEATHER; THREE-QUARTER LEATHER. (261)

half linen. *See:* HALF CLOTH.

half-stamp. A finishing tool consisting of a stamp identical with or very similar to a half fleuron, pineapple, etc. It is generally used for tooling compartments at the edges of the frame in lozenge compartment decoration. It is also sometimes used back-to-back to form the lozenges in the center of the cover. The use of the half-stamp was common in Northern Europe and in England during the late 15th and early 16th centuries. (250)

half tanned. *See:* CRUST STOCK.

half vellum binding. A half binding covered on the spine and approximately one-fourth of the sides, as well as the corners, with vellum, with the remaining part of the sides being covered with paper. *See also:* HALF LEATHER.

hammering-down bands. *See:* KNOCKING DOWN.

hand-drawn end- and cover-papers. A term descriptive of custom end- and cover-papers. The design of the papers can be an integral part of the binding in every sense, and can be executed in many kinds of media, including lino- and wood-cut endpapers and covers, which are executed by means of small printing units of repeating designs, or blocks used to print the entire cover or endpaper in one impression. (335)

handle. 1. A somewhat vague term applied to the impression of touch and sound when handling a sheet of paper. It includes such properties as feel, rattle, etc. 2. One or more strips of leather, cloth, or other material, attached loosely across the spine of a book from cover to cover and used to facilitate removal of the book from the shelf. Handles are seldom used today, except for large blankbooks. 3. *See:* FEEL. (17)

hand letters. Individual letters, numerals, etc., cut in brass and attached to wooden or asbestos handles, and used to letter a book by hand. The alternative to hand letters is brass type assembled in a PALLET (2) and used to letter a complete line of type at one time. (161, 236)

handmade paper. A type or class of paper made in hand molds in single sheets, and having a rough or DECKLE EDGE on all four sides. The paper is made by dipping the MOLD (1), of the size required, into the vat containing the stock, and then lifting it out with a particular motion, thus causing the fibers to bond together forming a sheet. Because of the methods employed in lifting and shaking the mold, handmade paper often has very little discernible grain or MACHINE DIRECTION, which means that it has more or less the same strength properties in both (all) directions. It is therefore unlike machine-made paper, which is much stronger in the machine direction than in the cross direction. Handmade paper is also generally superior to machine-made paper in that it is usually sized with gelatin, glue, or similar material, without the use of rosin or alum. It is relatively very expensive because, from the pulp stage, all of the operations are performed by hand and in single sheets; in contrast to the papermaking machine in which paper is felted, couched, pressed, dried, sized, calendered, and reeled in one continuous operation. For general information concerning paper, *see:* PAPER; PAPERMAKING. *See also:* COUCH (1, 2); DECKLE; FELT (1); WATERMARK. (79, 287, 320)

hand mold. *See:* MOLD (1); HANDMADE PAPER.

hand oversewing. *See:* OVERSEWING.

hand sewing. The process of sewing a book by hand. Although it is generally assumed to mean sewing through the folds of the sections, it may also refer to the sewing of sections, or, more often, leaves through the side, i.e., OVERSEWING, SIDE SEWING, the strengthening of the first and last sections or leaves of a sewn book by means of OVERCASTING, or the re-attachment or replacement of endpapers by the same means. *See:* FLEXIBLE SEWING; RECESSED-CORD SEWING; SADDLE SEWING; TAPE SEWING (1).

hand sizing. A method of sizing or resizing paper by dipping the sheets or leaves into a tub of size. Hand sizing was the original method of sizing paper, i.e., handmade paper, and is still used for that class of paper, and also by restorers when resizing documents or the leaves of a book. Old papers, which often contain decomposed size, can be made stronger and safer to handle if resized by hand. (77, 197)

hanging-in. A technique used in edition binding in which the TEXT BLOCK and its endpapers are joined to the case. The text block is positioned in the casing-in machine; the cover drops down over it; and the two are pressed to form the book. (259)

hard bound (hard binding). A book bound in cloth- or paper-covered stiff boards, as opposed to a book or pamphlet in a SELF-COVER, or a LIMP BINDING. The term is not generally applied to hand-bound books covered in leather.

hardener. 1. A substance or mixture of substances added to an adhesive to promote or control the curing reaction by taking part in it. The term is also used to designate a substance used to increase the degree of hardness of the cured adhesive. *See also:* PLASTICIZER (1). 2. A substance added to paints or varnishes to provide a harder finish. (309)

hard glue. A GLUE used in the past in machine case-making where quick setting was the principal requirement of the glue and minimum flexibility was not a serious disadvantage. Such glues are hard in the sense that they contain no plasticizer. They were not used for gluing-up the spine, lining-up, or for flexible cover making, and are now seldom used in book production for any purpose. (256)

hard-grained goat (morocco). A vegetable-tanned goatskin with the characteristic soft and small pinhead grain pattern produced by BOARDING (1) in a wet condition in a minimum of four directions. The grain is much tighter than that of LEVANT and the leather itself is firmer and harder than NIGER. (61)

hard rolled. A term descriptive of the toughness and durability of the board used in bookbinding, e.g., "hard rolled millboard." The term has no meaning other than that the board has been rolled under pressure and is very firm. (365)

hard sized. A paper which has received a maximum of sizing, resulting in a paper having a high degree of water resistance. The term applies only to the sizing characteristics of the paper. *Cf:* SLACK SIZED. (82, 98)

Harleian style. An English style of book decoration which came into vogue in about 1720. The name derives from the books of the Harleian library founded by Robert Harley (1661-1724), and expanded considerably by his son, Edward (1689-1741). Although the name Chapman was once associated with these bindings, along with that of Elliott, it has been established that at least the more important bindings were probably executed by Thomas Elliott. The general characteristics of the bindings are the predominantly bright red color (and inferior quality) of the morocco leather used, and a three-line fillet running around the edges of the covers. Within the fillet is a broad-tooled border made up of two or three sprigs of various patterns, and a large central ornament, usually in the shape of an elongated lozenge, built up from a number of small units. (69, 241, 280)

Harrison method. *See:* REVERSED V-GUARD.

head. 1. The margin at the top of a printed page. 2. The top of a book or leaf. 3. The top of the spine of a book where the HEADBAND is located. 4. The top edge of a bound book. *See also:* TAIL (1). 5. That portion of a hide or skin from the head of the animal.

headband. A functional and/or ornamental band at the head and tail of a book between the sections and the spine covering, which projects slightly beyond the head and tail. Originally, the headband consisted of a thong core, similar to the bands on which the book was sewn, around which the ends of the threads were twisted and then laced into the boards of the book. Today, however, the headband is much simpler and is usually made of colored silk sewn to the book or simply attached after the volume has been forwarded. In edition binding they are almost always manufactured separately and then attached, while in library binding they have been replaced for the most part by a length of cord around which the covering material is rolled at both head and tail.

Headbands at one time were distinguished as the "headband" and "tail-band," but both are now called "headbands" or simply "heads," although the term "endband," to indicate both,

seems to be preferred by some book-binders.

The original headbands were intrinsically a part of the sewing of the book, and were used in lieu of kettle stitches in linking the sections together. They were a part of the construction of the book, which possibly explains why they were (and are) at both the head and tail, rather than just at the head. This type of headband was eventually discarded, however, because it did not permit cutting the edges subsequent to sewing, despite the fact that it had the great advantage of also banding the top and bottom of the sections together tightly.

Techniques of headbanding continued to change, and by the 12th century, or even earlier, it became the common practice to sew the bands independently of the sections. Furthermore, until the end of the 15th century, they were always tied down in the fold of each section, when the increased production of books subsequent to Gutenberg made it necessary to reduce the cost of binding a single book. Thereafter, they were tied down at greater intervals.

Because the boards of early bindings were cut flush, it was the usual practice to cut away the corners of the leaves at head and tail so as to make room for the bands and also to keep them from protruding too far and possibly being damaged.

Headbands of the 12th and early 13th centuries were combined with a leather tab which extended beyond the spine, whereas from the middle of the 13th century to the end of the 15th century, the leather cover at the end of

the spine was frequently cut so that it just covered the headbands. The cover was then sewn through from front to back, or vice versa, underneath and along the length of the hidden headband, resulting in a series of stitches on the spine of the book, as well as a series where normally one expected to see the beading. The binder usually used uncolored thread for both this and the headband, which was usually single and sewn independently of the sewing of the book. The plaited headband, which was made with strips of leather (usually tawed and stained pink), was still another variation. This type was rare in England but often used in Germany in the late 15th and early 16th centuries. This type of headband, which is the strongest ever devised, consisted of two thongs plaited around a core of rolled vellum, which had already been sewn to the book. The thongs also passed through holes made in the leather at the top of the spine where it was cut off instead of being turned in. When using this type of headband, the leather cover was sewn by means of plaited thongs to the primary headband which had already been sewn to the book, thereby making a solid connection at an important point.

The conventional headband, which was sewn with colored silk or other type of thread, and which had the beading showing at the bottom complete with HEADCAP, was introduced very early in the 16th century and quickly became popular. The prevalent colors were blue and white, but pink and blue, pink and brown, as well as other combinations were also used.

Double headbands are not often seen in 16th century English bookbinding, but they were used to some extent on the Continent. They acquired popularity in England in the 17th century, utilizing more interesting colors and superior materials than on the Continent. Until the beginning of the 20th century the double headband usually consisted of two rolls, one smaller than the other, with the smaller placed above the larger; however, early in the 20th century binders began placing the smaller band both in front of and below the larger. It also became the common practice to use a flat strip of material rather than a larger roll.

Only a relatively few bookbinders since the 15th century have taken the trouble to tie down headbands at every section, or even tried to put the needle through the fold of the section where the tie-down was being made; instead

HEADBAND

single headband with core of vellum
or leather

double headband
with core of vellum
or leather

second core of catgut

tie down

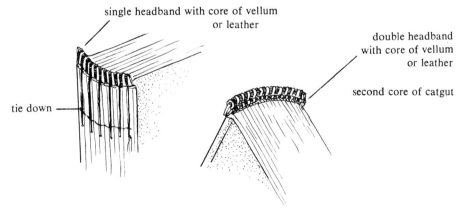

it went between the leaves at intervals of ¼ to ½ inch.

When the headband is an integral part of the book, it serves the practical purpose of taking up much of the strain from the spine covering when the book is pulled from the shelf in the usual manner. The worked headband reinforces that part of the spine covering extending beyond the text block because of the squares. The headband that is only glued on, on the other hand, is merely decorative and often falls short even in that respect, as it usually looks cheap and also as though it were an afterthought. Although it is generally believed that glued-on headbands were unknown before the early 19th century, i.e., the beginning of the rise of edition binding as we know it today, they were being used, at least in Germany, as early as the last decade of the 16th century. They were probably not used in English bookbinding until sometime in the first half of the 17th century. Although it must be assumed that glued on bands were used in that time as an economy measure, they probably required as much time to make as worked headbands. They were made by sewing two threads of the same or different colors in the usual manner with a cross-over beading onto a strip of vellum, which sometimes had its upper edge bent over to provide greater bulk. In many cases about ¾ inch on each side of the core was not sewn but was attached to the boards, usually on the outside. In other cases the bulk of the headband was cut to the thickness of the book and only the part under the sewing extended across the joints or was laced through the joints on some vellum bindings. (141, 172, 236, 241, 335)

headbanding. The process of working or gluing headbands to the text block of a book. *See also:* HEADBAND.

head bolt. The top or "head" folds of a section. *See also:* BOLT.

head box. 1. A large flow box on a Fourdrinier papermaking machine. The furnish of dilute stock is pumped into the head box and from there flows onto the wire where it is formed into the web of paper. The head box is equipped with baffles and other flow-evening devices; it also agitates the stock so as to prevent flocculation of the fibers. The head box is designed to spread the flow of furnish evenly and uniformly the entire width of the wire between the deckles. The box may be open, in which case the height of the stock provides the pressure, or closed, in which case

air pressure is used. 2. A flow-regulating device on a cylinder papermaking machine which controls the volume of stock flowing to the screens and mixing boxes before the vats. (17, 72, 80)

headcap. The leather covering at the head and tail of the spine of a book, formed by turning the leather on the spine over the head and tail and shaping it.

Knocking the dampened leather over the headbands so as to form protective caps was a technique introduced early in the 16th century. Although turning over the leather actually began to be done around 1500, it was not squared and sharply angled, nor was it initially tied around the joints. BACK CORNERING and tying around the joints so as to make indentation at the ends,

HEADCAP

which improved the setting of the headcaps, was introduced during the latter part of the 18th century. The technique of setting the headcaps has been customary in fine binding since its introduction. (161, 236, 237)

headed outline tool. *See:* CUSPED EDGE STAMP.

head trim. The measurement required to determine the position of printed matter before the final trimming of a sewn book. (139)

heat. A somewhat vague term specifically associated with the motion of atoms or molecules, but also applied in a general sense to the condition of excessive warmth or high temperature. Excessive heat results in the lowering of flexibility, strength, and resistance to natural decay through loss of moisture from leather, paper, adhesives, etc., as well as acceleration of decomposition reactions.

heat-set ink. A printing ink manufactured in such a manner as to enable it to dry

quickly, thus allowing for higher speed printing. The materials used in manufacture vary but usually include a concentrated pigment, synthetic resins, and one of the volatile oils. Following printing, the printed web of paper is heated to a temperature of approximately 350° F. (177° C.) which volatilizes the oil, after which the web is rapidly cooled by passing it through chilled rollers which hardens the residue. (140, 276)

heat-set tissue. A lens tissue especially prepared for use in mending tears in paper, strengthening margins, and for laminating weak or badly torn leaves, by means of dry application rather than by the traditional aqueous application. The tissue is made of pure cellulose consisting of more or less 100% rag content, no coating or additives, and a pH of 7.0. The tissue is not structurally uniform in texture, consequently there are small random open spaces and some bunching of fibers. Although its thickness is presumed to be approximately 0.0015 inch, this can vary from one batch to another, although it does not normally exceed 0.002 inch. The tissue is coated on one side with an acrylic resin. It is applied to both sides of tears, but to only one side of a weakened leaf, provided that no adhesive is exposed on the other side. The tissue is tipped on the leaf with a warm iron (approximately 100° F.), and then pressed on firmly through terylene or a textured paper. The iron is not pressed directly on the heat-set tissue because this might result in blocking and may also impart a sheen to the tissue, thus making it more noticeable.

heavy filling. A WEFT yarn that is greater in diameter than those normally used in the fabric. (341)

heavy warp. A WARP yarn that is greater in diameter than those normally used in the fabric. (341)

heel-ball. A shoemaker's composition of wax and lampblack, sometimes used to take rubbings of book spines. (25)

height. The overall dimension of a bound volume from head to tail, including the squares. Library binders frequently base their prices for binding on the height of the volume up to a specified thickness, e.g., 2½ inches. The volumes are priced on the basis of each additional 1 or 2 inches, beginning with a minimum height, usually 8 inches, as for example:

Library Books	Cost
Up to and including 8 inches	Basic price
Over 8 inches and including 9 inches	Higher price
Over 9 inches and including 10 inches	Higher price
Over 10 inches and including 11 inches	Higher price
Over 11 inches	Higher price

Magazines	Cost
Up to and including 10 inches	Basic price
Over 10 inches and including 12 inches	Higher price
Over 12 inches and including 14 inches	Higher price
Over 14 inches and including 16 inches	Higher price
Over 16 inches	Higher price

hemicelluloses. Any of several cell wall polysaccharides present in almost all vegetable fibers. Although impervious to water and almost all natural organic solvents, they may be removed gradually by means of aqueous alkalis. They are hydrolized to simple sugars, uronic acids and acetic acid when heated with dilute acids. Their molecular weights are usually lower than those of various celluloses. The presence of hemicelluloses in paper improves its bonding and folding characteristics. (17, 72, 235)

hemlock (bark). A vegetable tanning material derived from either the Eastern (Canadian) hemlock, *Tsuga canadensis,* or the Western hemlock. *T. heterophylla,* the former being the best known and most used. The bark of the eastern hemlock has an average tannin content of 15 to 16%, while that of the western variety average 10 to 11%. One characteristic of the bark is the lack of any appreciable quantity of sugars, with the result that it does not produce acids by fermentation. Because of this, it is customary to add a small amount of organic acid to hemlock tan liquor. Another characteristic is the reddish color it imparts to the leather, which can be modified considerably by the addition of other tanning materials, such as oak bark or quebracho.

Hemlock bark was for many years the most important tanning material used in the United States and Canada, and was, along with oak bark, the principal material used in tanning leather on a commercial scale. It was responsible for the characteristic "red"

leather produced in America in the 19th century. *See also:* VEGETABLE TANNINS. (175)

hemp. A tall Asiatic herb, *Cannabis sativa,* which yields a tough bast fiber when retted. Hemp fibers are difficult to distinguish from linen by ordinary examination, but their presence may be suspected in a fibrillated paper. Hemp is used mainly for thin, opaque papers of great strength; however, it is almost never used alone. The term "hemp" has also come to be used in a generic sense as fiber and is then preceded by an adjective, e.g., Manila hemp (*See:* ABACA), Seisal hemp (*See:* SISAL), etc. Hemp is also fairly widely employed for the cords used in sewing books. (17, 62, 143, 198)

heraldic cresting. A form of cresting used in decorating bookbindings, the projections of which terminate in heraldic emblems. *See also:* CRESTING ROLL. (250)

herringbone pattern. A pattern on cloth consisting of adjacent rows of parallel lines where any two adjacent rows slope slightly in reverse directions.

Hertzberg stain. A chemical test frequently used to detect the presence of specific fibers in a paper. The Hertzberg stain not only has a greater degree of color selectivity than any other stain, it also brings out the details of the structure very effectively in the case of those fibers which it does not stain with a selective color. It is prepared from: 1) a saturated solution of zinc chloride in distilled water; 2) a solution containing 0.25 gram of iodine and 5.25 grams of potassium iodide dissolved in 12.5 ml. of distilled water; and 3) the entire solution of number 2 added to 25 ml. of number 1. The colors produced are:

Color	indicating the presence of:
Red	Sulfite or sulfate chemical wood pulp, esparto, straw, bamboo, and most other chemically treated fibers.
Yellow-brown	Chemical wood pulp which has been incompletely cooked (so as to preserve strength), with the result that some lignins are still present.
Bright yellow	Materials containing lignin, e.g., groundwood pulp, jute and unbleached manila hemp. (72, 143)

hexane. Any of the five isometric volatile liquid paraffin hydrocarbons, of the formula (C_6H_{14}), the most important

isomer being (CH_3 (CH_2)$_4$ CH_3). Hexane is used as a solvent and thinner for the wax used in some leather dressings, and also a solvent for the adhesive of pressure-sensitive tapes. (130, 173)

hidden painting. *See:* FORE-EDGE PAINTING.

hide. 1. The raw or tanned pelt removed from the adult of one of the larger animals, e.g., cowhide, as distinguished from the skin of one of the smaller animals, e.g., goatskin, or an immature larger animal, e.g., calfskin.

The finest part of a hide is located in the butt area. The shoulder provides good quality although its natural substance is somewhat uneven and falls away toward the cheeks, which are often trimmed. Shoulders also tend to show growth marks which can be conspicuous. The bellies give thinner and sometimes weaker leather.

2. Leather made from hides which have not been split, or from the grain split of a hide. When used in this manner, the name of the animal or the type of leather may be specified, e.g., cowhide. (363)

hide buffing. A very thin film of the grain layer of a cowhide, sometimes used for labels. Also known as "beeswing."

hide glue. GLUE made from the collagen content of hides and skins, particularly of bovine animals, as distinguished from glue made from bones. Hide glue does not include glue made from the skins of fish. (184)

high bulk book paper. A book paper which, in a basis weight of 45 pound, 25 × 38 — 500) bulks 440 to 344 pages to the inch, under 35 pounds pressure. (17)

high finish. A smooth, hard, glossy finish applied to the surface of cloth, paper, etc., during the manufacturing process. (139)

hinge. 1. The strip of fabric (usually linen or cambric), or paper placed between the two parts of a library-style cloth-jointed endpaper, for the purpose of providing additional strength at the point of flexing. 2. Any Japanese copying paper or linen stub that allows for the free flexing of an insert, leaf, etc. 3. An obsolete term for the tongue made by gluing and folding over the waste leaves on which the bands or cords were pasted and then inserted between split boards. (161, 208, 264)

hinged. A map, plate, or other separate sheet which has been folded along the binding edge in order to reduce the possibility of the sheet tearing away from the one to which it is attached, and also to allow it to lie flat and turn easily during use.

hinged and jointed plate. Two contiguous plates each of which has had a strip cut away at the binding edge, and are then joined together by means of a common strip of Japanese copying paper or linen, forming a hinge. *See also:* GUARD (2).

hinged boards. A type of binding having boards attached to a stab-sewn or post binding, by means of a cloth hinge which joins the main board to a narrow board at the spine of the book. The narrow board is secured by the posts or stab sewing. Hinged boards are characteristic of some types of blankbooks. (119, 204)

hinged ledger paper. 1. A LEDGER PAPER that has a flexible (due to the fact that it is thinner) strip running from top to bottom of the sheet about five-eights of an inch in from the edge (binding edge) of the sheet. The strip is a result of the removal of some paper fibers, usually by means of suction, during manufacture. The strip is about 1¼ inch wide. The paper, being thinner at the area of the hinge, is easier to turn and will lie flatter; however, it is also weaker at that point, which may adversely affect writing. 2. A ledger paper having a strip of linen (or cambric) attached to the binding edge of the leaf. Its purpose is to allow the leaf to turn more easily and lie flat. (17)

hinged on a mount. A separate leaf, illustration, etc., attached to a GUARD (2) and bound into the book. (169)

hinge guarding. *See:* REVERSED V-GUARD.

hog's back. 1. An exaggerated curve of the spine of a book, caused by improper rounding, the use of a sewing thread that is too thick, or a combination of the two. 2. An uneven trim of the fore edge of a book that is cut with the plow, caused by the plow knife riding up as it traverses the length of the book. (65, 159)

hogskin. A soft leather produced from the skin of the peccary, genus *Tayassu,* and having a distinctive grain pattern formed by the hair follicles which are arranged in detached groups of three. *Cf:* PIGSKIN.

holdout. The degree to which a material, such as cloth or paper, impedes the penetration of an aqueous or non-aqueous liquid. If the liquid is water, or water vapor, holdout is described as SIZING (1). Non-aqueous liquids include some printing inks, lacquers, etc. (17)

holiday. Any area of an adhesive-covered surface, such as a PASTEDOWN, which

does not adhere properly. *See also:* DRUMMING ON. (140)

holing out (holing). The process of drilling, or more commonly, punching holes in the boards of a book to receive the cords prepared for LACING-IN. (156)

holing-out block. A block of lead or other soft metal on which the board of a book is placed for drilling or punching the holes for the cords or slips in preparation for LACING-IN. *See also:* HOLING OUT. (115)

holland. A cotton or linen fabric, usually in plain weave and heavily sized or glazed, and, when used in bookbinding, gummed. The holland is used in a technique of library rebinding in which a sewing machine automatically feeds two narrow strips of gummed cloth in such a manner that the sewing passes through the holland and the paper. The book to be sewn is prepared as for oversewing, i.e., the leaves are divided into thin "sections," which are run through the sewing machine one at a time, with a strip of gummed holland being sewn simultaneously to each side of the "section." After all of the "sections" have been sewn, the strips of holland are moistened, and the book is jogged and then pressed until the gum has dried. The strips of holland hold the "sections" together along the binding edge. This technique is sometimes employed when the paper of the book

does not adhere properly.

is too embrittled, or otherwise weakened, to allow oversewing; however, it is seldom very successful, as the paper usually fails at the juncture of paper and holland. (339)

Hollis, Thomas (1720-1774). An eccentric English philanthropist and propagandist of the idea of liberty. Hollis distributed books in support of liberty, particularly to libraries abroad, such as those at Berne, Zurich, and Harvard College. The bindings were commissioned from John Matthewman or Richard Montagu, and decorated with emblematic tools designed by G. B. Cipriani, the original drawings for which are now at Harvard. When the first set of tools was destroyed in a fire in Matthewman's shop in 1764 a second set was engraved by Thomas Pingo. These subjects include Britannica, Liberty, the caduceus of Mercury, the wand of Aesculapius, the owl of Minerva, a cock, a liberty cap, and the short Roman sword, or *pugio.* The simpler bindings were by Matthewman, while Montagu executed the more elaborate presentation bindings. (94, 244, 297)

hollow. The lining attached to both the spine of the text block and the inside of the spine of the covering material. It is usually constructed of kraft paper, and consists of a folded sheet, one section of which is glued to the spine of

HOLLOW

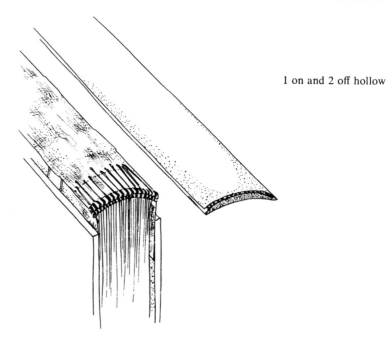

1 on and 2 off hollow

the text block and the other to the covering material. There are many variations of the hollow, however; for example, *see:* ONE ON AND TWO OFF, or TWO ON AND ONE OFF. The purpose of the hollow is to assist in the opening of the book much in the same manner as the SPRING-BACK of a blankbook, though with much less force. The thickness of the paper used for the hollow depends on the size and thickness of the book and the thickness of the paper and sections of the book. (81, 261)

hollow back (hollow back binding). A binding having a space between the spine of the text block and the spine of the cover, resulting from the covering material being attached at the joints (or a one-piece cover in the style of a case binding) and not glued to the spine of the text block. Sometimes a HOLLOW is glued to the text block and covering material; in library binding, however, generally only an INLAY (1) is glued to the covering material, while in edition binding there is usually no support of any kind.

The hollow back binding is believed to have originated in France in about 1770, but it was little used in England before about 1800. It was still comparatively rare in craft binding until about 1820, when the semi-elliptical spine with its pronounced shoulders began to be replaced by the structurally inferior flat spine, which had almost no shoulders and therefore provided little support. The combination of this weaker spine and the use of the hollow back on books which then did not normally need them has resulted in many of the bindings of that time falling apart, while those bound with tight backs years earlier are still in good condition, except for broken joints.

The advantages of the hollow back, which is used almost universally in library and edition binding, are: 1) the tooling or lettering on the spine will not flex and crack; 2) in hand binding, covering is less exacting; 3) in edition and library binding, the cover (case) can be made separately; 4) in hand binding, sewing is faster because it is on tapes rather than cords; and 5) overall, it is a much more economical method than tight-back binding. *See also:* OXFORD HOLLOW. (156, 236, 343)

hollow-punch pliers. Pliers with a tubular sharp-edge cutter, used for punching holes in leather. Such pliers have interchangeable cutters, including eyelet closers. Their principal shortcoming is their limited reach.

hollow tooling. A bookbinding design which is executed in outline, generally in gold. (81)

hooked (hooked on own guard). *See:* GUARDED IN. *See also:* PLATE ATTACHMENT.

horn bindings. Bindings consisting of hard, white, smooth, polished vellum. They were sparsely decorated and had the title written in Chinese ink at the top of the spine.

horn book. A form of child's primer used in England from the 15th century, and in the United States at a later time. The earliest examples were made from "wainscot" (thin panels of oak) and had a label containing the alphabet, simple spelling, numbers, and the Lord's prayer pasted on the wood and covered with a thin, transparent veneer of cattle horn. A wooden handle was attached to the frame. In latter examples the back of the panel was covered with morocco or roan leather blocked with an ornamental device. Other, but rare, examples were made entirely of cowhide with a window cut in the upper portion. *See* PLATE II. (104, 156, 183)

horse. 1. A trestlelike structure of suitable height, traditionally made of wood, but also of a light, non-corrosive, non-staining material such as plastic, on which hides and skins are piled for draining, transportation from one department to another in the tannery, and sometimes for storage purposes. 2. A T-shaped stand, about 3 feet high, on which spoiled sheets from the POST (1) in a handmade paper mill are placed. Being practically of no value as paper, these sheets are subsequently placed at the top and bottom of the salable packs to protect them. (197, 363)

horsing up. The process of piling hides and skins on the HORSE (1) for draining, etc. Because the use of the horse may result in the fibers of the leather setting in a creased configuration, when a flat leather is required hides and skins are placed on a flat surface for draining, transportation, etc. (363)

hot-melt adhesive. A resinous adhesive which achieves a solid state and resultant strength by cooling, as contrasted with other adhesives which achieve the same results through evaporation or removal of the solvents. Before heating, a hot-melt adhesive is a themoplastic, 100% solid material, and is all adhesive. Upon the application of heat, the usual operating temperature being in the range of 175 to 205° C. (350 to 400° F.), the material changes to a

fluid state. Subsequent to the removal of heat, it sets by simple cooling.

When a hot-melt adhesive comes into close contact with the surface to be bonded, a molecular layer of film at the surface of this substrate immediately attains a temperature approaching that of the hot melt. In addition a high degree of wetting, almost coalescence, of the hot melt and the material occurs. Immediately thereafter, the adhesive loses heat to the film over the entire area and temperature equilibrium is attained. Since the adhesive is in contact with a mass much larger than itself, the temperature of the entire system drops to the point at which the hot melt sets to a solid state with sufficient cohesive strength to bond the films together. Thus the uniqueness of hot-melt adhesives stems from the speed with which they produce a bond, which is almost instantaneously.

Although the use of hot-melt adhesives eliminates the cost of solvents required by some other adhesives, the principal cost reduction results from the time saved in their application. In addition, a lesser quantity of the hot melt can usually be utilized to produce an equivalent bond.

Hot-melt adhesives are used extensively in binding books made of loose sheets, especially those that are not rounded and backed, e.g., paperback books, telephone and other directories, etc. For books that are to be rounded and backed, however, the so-called DRYING MEMORY of the hot-melt adhesives causes problems. In addition, hot-melt adhesives alone do not lend themselves well to the binding of heavily loaded or coated paper, from which *all* particulate matter must be removed before application of the adhesive. *See also:* ADHESIVE BINDING; ONE-SHOT METHOD (1); TWO-SHOT METHOD. (81, 89, 179, 219, 309)

hot-melt coating. A method of applying molten plastic materials to a base stock, such as paper or a book cloth without the use of a solvent or other carrier. Rolls, knives, casting, or extrusion techniques are used in this method of coating.

hot-setting adhesive. An adhesive which requires a temperature of 100° C. or greater to cause it to set. *See also:* COLD-SETTING ADHESIVE; ROOM-TEMPERATURE SETTING ADHESIVE. (309)

h pattern. A criss-cross pattern embossed on a book cloth, resulting in small diamond-shaped spaces on the cloth.

hubs. The several thicknesses of board glued together and then to the SPRING-

BACK (1) of a book, usually a large stationery binding. The hubs, which appear as relatively large, raised bands or ridges under the covering material (usually leather) on the spine of the book, strengthen the spine and protect the leather from wear and other damage. The hubs may also serve as an integral part of the decoration of the spine of the book. *Cf:* FALSE BANDS. (264, 339)

hue. That particular attribute of colors which allows them to be classed as bluish, greenish, reddish, yellowish, etc. *See also:* COLOR (1).

humectant. A substance that absorbs and promotes the retention of moisture from the air. The softening (plasticizing) agents in adhesives owe their effectiveness to their capacity to absorb and retain moisture. *Cf:* HYGROSCOPICITY. *See also:* FLEXIBLE GLUE; INTERNALLY PLASTICIZED; GLUE. (184, 198)

humidified. A paper that has been brought to equilibrium with the moisture in the air at a definite relative humidity.

humidity. The actual amount of water vapor present in the air. *See:* ABSOLUTE HUMIDITY. A more relevant term in book work is RELATIVE HUMIDITY.

hung-in. A book that has been glued-in to its cover at the spine only, e.g., a pamphlet glued into its SELF-COVER. (256)

hung on guards. Inserts, such as maps, plates, etc., which have been glued to strips of paper or linen, which are then tipped or stubbed into the book (256)

hyaline layer. A term sometimes used to indicate the smooth surface which is assumed to exist between the epidermis and grain surface of a hide or skin, and which gives the characteristic grain pattern of the leather. *See also:* DERMIS. (363)

hydration. 1. A term applied to the condition of materials containing water of absorption, crystallization, or imbibition. In papermaking, hydration refers to the chemical or mechanical (or both)

treatment of paper fibers, other than cooking or bleaching, which takes place before sheet formation on the papermaking machine. It relates especially to altered sheet characteristics, including density, formation, opacity, and strength. 2. The paper pulp characteristics resulting from the above treatment. (17, 42, 276)

hydraulic press. A STANDING PRESS operated by hydraulic power instead of by hand. Such presses came into use in the first half of the 19th century, and were the principal means of pressing edition and library bindings until the introduction of the casing-in and building-in machines. *See also:* BUILDING-IN MACHINE; CASING-IN MACHINE; REMOVABLE PRESS.

hydrochloric acid. A strong, corrosive, inorganic acid (HCl), manufactured by absorbing hydrogen chloride in water. It is one of the most corrosive of acids, and is particularly destructive to cellulose, breaking the cellulose chain into even smaller units, resulting ultimately in its complete hydrolysis.

The problems with hydrochloric acid began with the use of chlorine in bleaching paper fibers. For many years thereafter, the chlorine substances were insufficiently removed by washing, giving rise to the formation of the acid in paper. Although washing techniques have improved, excess residual hydrochloric acid can exist in paper because of the practice of using chlorine compounds to wash and bleach paper subsequent to its manufacture.

hydrogel. A gel in which the liquid is water.

hydrogen cyanide (hydrocyanic acid; prussic acid). An extremely toxic, colorless liquid (HCN), prepared by reacting methane, air, and ammonia over a platinum catalyst at 1,000° C. It is used to fumigate books.

hydrogen-ion concentration. The concentration of hydrogen ions (more properly hydronium ions—H_3O^+, although

its true structure is probably $(H,4H_2O)$, existing in an aqueous solution. It is a measure of the active acidity or basicity and is expressed metrically as the number of moles or gram-formula weights (1.0078 g.) of hydrogen ions (H^+) per liter of solution. The hydrogen-ion concentration of a solution may also be expressed in terms of its pH, which is defined as the negative logarithm to the base ten of the hydrogen-ion concentration. In aqueous solutions, neutrality is the condition that exists when the concentration of hydrogen ions and hydroxyl ions are equal. At 25° C., neutrality occurs at a pH of 7.0, which is the pH value of pure (distilled) water when condensed hot and shielded from contact with atmospheric carbon dioxide.

Measurement of hydrogen-ion concentration, or pH, may be made colorimetrically, by means of the proper use of suitable neutralization indicators, or, more accurately, by potentiometric methods employing any of various electrodes, which exhibit the proper specificity for hydrogen ions.

Hydrogen-ion concentration is important in archival work because it has been adequately demonstrated that the presence of acid(s) in ink, leather, paper, etc., has or can have, a deleterious effect on such materials, the extent of the effect depending not so much on the *volume* of acid present, as on the *type* of acid and its *concentration*, i.e., a large volume of a relatively weak organic acid, such as formic acid, is less harmful than a smaller amount of a powerful, inorganic acid, such as sulfuric acid. As a decrease of pH means a logarithmic increase in acid concentration, levels of concentration below pH 5.0, or under certain circumstances, even 6.0, become important. Conversely, although not as serious a problem, a high concentration of hydroxyl ions, corresponding to a pH of 10.0 or above, can lead to serious oxydization of cellulosic materials.

The increase in hydrogen-ion concentration as pH declines is given below:

pH	*moles/liter*
7.0	0.0000001
6.0	.000001
5.0	.00001
4.0	.0001
3.0	.001
2.0	.01
1.0	.1
0.0	1.0

See also: ACID; ALKALI. (17, 195, 235)

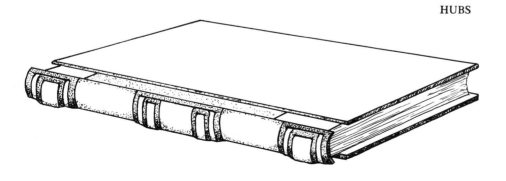

HUBS

PLATES

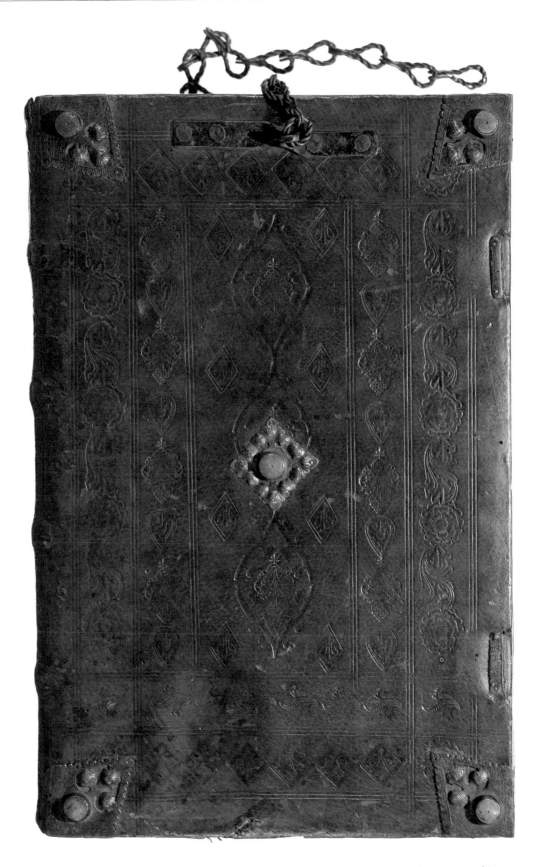

PLATE I.   A contemporary 15th century binding of brown calf over wooden boards, with
two center and four corner bosses. Otto Vollbehr Collection, Library of Congress.
(43 cm. by 29 cm. by 8 cm.)

PLATE II.   An 18th century horn book with a counting device. John Davis Batchelder
Collection, Library of Congress. (28.5 cm. by 18 cm. by 2.7 cm.)

PLATE III.   An embroidered binding in purple satin with seed pearls and bullion on a
copy of *The Whole Book of Psalms,* London, 1641. Lessing J. Rosenwald Collection,
Library of Congress. (8.2 cm. by 5 cm. by 2.5 cm.)

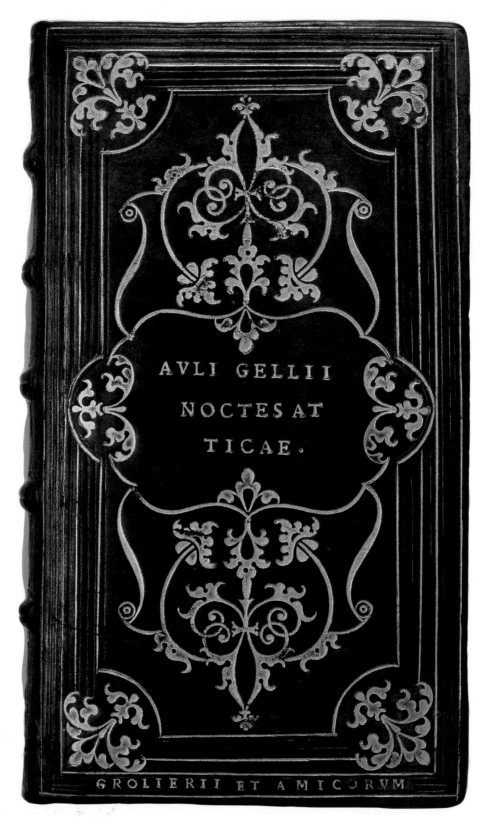

PLATE IV. This Aldine edition of Aulus Gellius's *Noctes Atticae* was executed for Jean Grolier. It is in light brown morocco with tooling on the upper and lower covers. Venice, 1515. Rare Book and Special Collections Division, Library of Congress. (17 cm. by 10 cm. by 5 cm.)

PLATE V.   A tree calf cover from a set of *Systema naturae* by Linnaeus, Leipzig, 1788-1793.
(20.5 cm. by 13 cm. by 4 cm.)

PLATE VI.　　A "fanfare style" binding in the manner of the Ève brothers on a copy of
Horae beatissimae Virginis Mariae. Note the gauffered edge. Printed by Christopher
Plantin, Antwerp, 1570. Lessing J. Rosenwald Collection, Library of Congress.
(21.2 cm. by 13.2 cm. by 4.5 cm.)

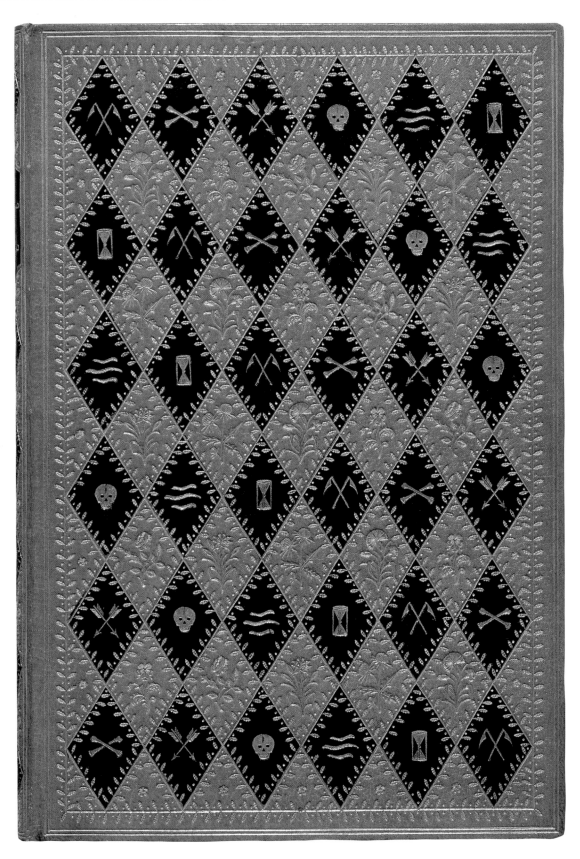

PLATE VII.   A Trautz-Bauzonnet inlaid mosaic binding on a copy of *Les simulachres &*
historiees faces de la Mort, Lyon, 1538. Lessing J. Rosenwald Collection,
Library of Congress. (19 cm. by 13.2 cm. by 1 cm.)

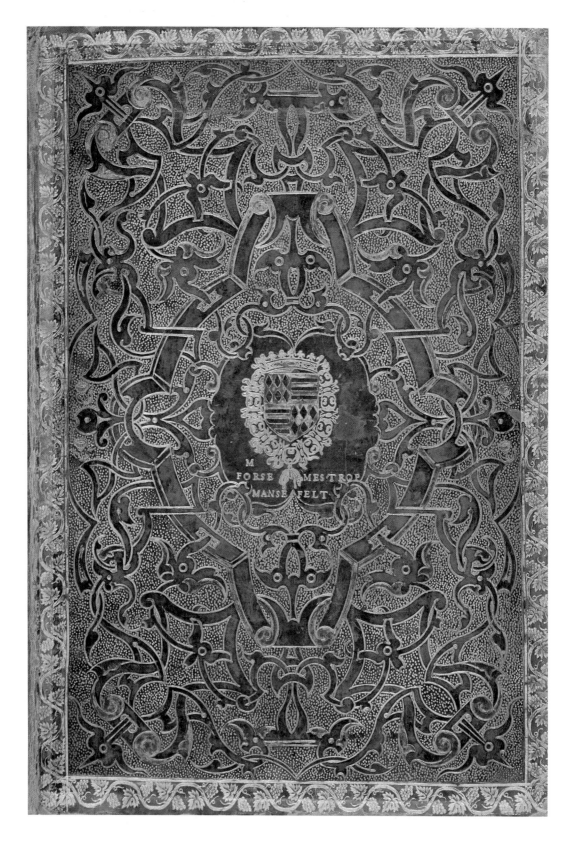

PLATE VIII.   An example of pointillé tooling and strapwork on a 16th century brown calf
binding for *Historiarium adversus paganos libri septem* by Paulus Orosius.
Printed by Pierre Le Rouge for Antoine Vérard, Paris, 1491.
Lessing J. Rosenwald Collection, Library of Congress. (37.5 cm. by 26.5 cm. by 7.4 cm.)

PLATE IX.   A 1950 binding designed by Paul Bonet on a copy of *Le Poète Rustique* by
Francis Jammes. Lessing J. Rosenwald Collection, Library of Congress.
(29 cm. by 24 cm. by 4.3 cm.)

PLATE X.   A Marius Michel doublure on Louis Morin's *Les Dimanches Parisiens,*
Paris, 1898. Lessing J. Rosenwald Collection, Library of Congress.
(26.7 cm. by 19 cm. by 5.2 cm.)

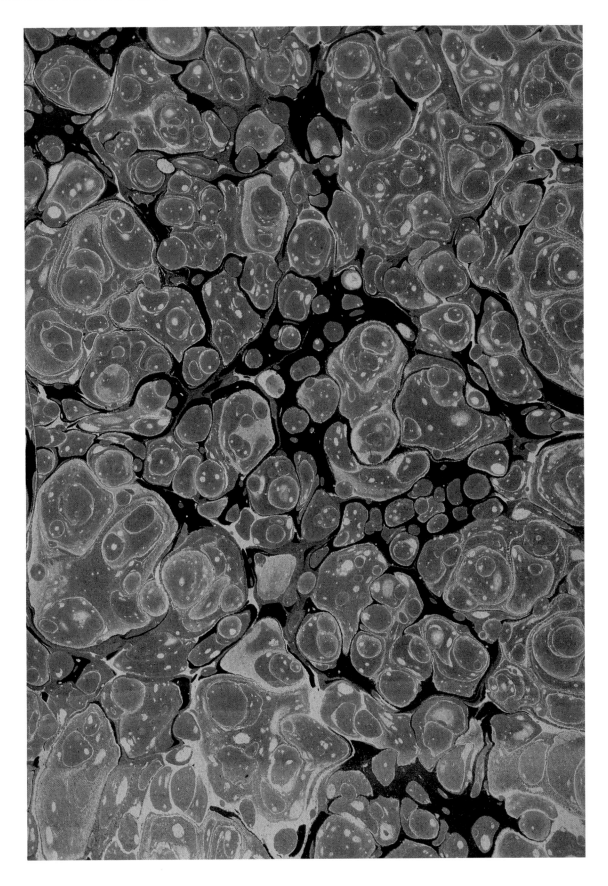

PLATE XI A.   French shell marble pattern.

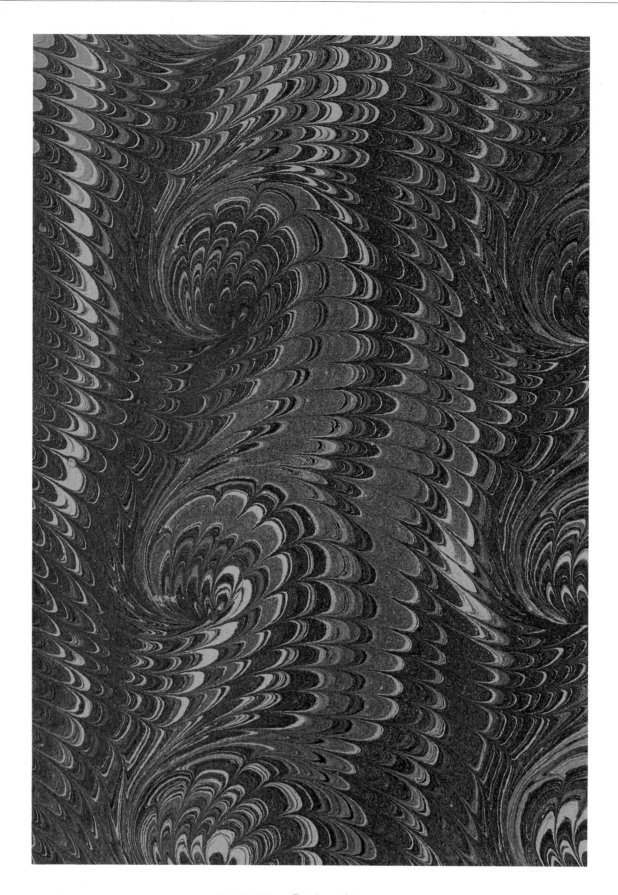

PLATE XI B.   Dutch marble pattern

PLATE XI C.   Bouquet marble pattern

hydrogen peroxide. An oxidizing chemical (H_2O_2), which can be prepared from barium peroxide and dilute sulfuric acid. It is used in bleaching paper pulp, sometimes alone, but more often in combination with other pulp bleaching agents.

hydrolysis. In its broadest sense, hydrolysis indicates a reaction between any substance and water; however, the use of the term is commonly restricted to those reactions due directly to the hydrogen and hydroxyl ions of the water. Due to hydrolysis, for example, nearly every salt yields a slightly acid or alkaline solution. Thus, ethyl acetate in water, for example, forms acetic acid and ethanol: $CH_3CO_2C_2H_5 + H_2O \rightarrow CH_3COOH + C_2H_5OH$.

Hydrolysis is the basis for the manufacture of soap (saponification), whereby fats (glycerol esters of fatty acids) are split with aqueous solutions of sodium hydroxide to form the sodium salt of the fatty acid (soap) and the alcohol (glycerol—more commonly known as glycerine). In reactions involving salts, the neutralization reaction that led to the formation of the salt is partially reversed, forming some free acid and free alkali. If the acid is weak, i.e., poorly ionized, and the alkali is strong, i.e., highly ionized, the aqueous solution of the salt will have an alkaline reaction as a result of the hydrolysis.

In the opposite case, that of a strong acid and weak base, the salt will have an acidic reaction in an aqueous solution. An example of the latter is papermaker's alum (aluminum sulfate), which is hydrolyzed in aqueous solution to form aluminum hydroxide ($Al(OH)_3$), which is insoluble and therefore forms few ions, and sulfuric acid (H_2SO_4), which is almost completely ionized in a dilute water solution. The acid character of alum is well known by its extremely sour, astringent taste, and by its detrimental effect on the permanence of paper.

hydrophilic. A substance that is readily wetted by water. VELLUM is a typical hydrophilic substance.

hydrophobic. A substance that is water repellent, or not easily wetted by water. Nylon is a typical hydrophobic substance.

hygroexpansivity. A change in the dimensions of a material, such as paper, because of a change in the ambient relative humidity of the atmosphere surrounding the material. The phenomenon is usually expressed as a percentage, and is generally several times greater in the cross direction of a paper than in the MACHINE DIRECTION, because paper fibers expand much more in diameter than in length when wetted. Hygroexpansivity is of considerable importance where the dimension of

paper is critical, such as in multi-color offset printing. *See also:* ANISOTROPIC BEHAVIOR; DRIED-IN STRAIN. (17, 72)

hygrometer. An instrument used for measuring the relative humidity, or percentage of moisture saturation of the air, such as the dew-point hygrometer, psychrometer, hair hygrometer, etc.

hygroscopicity. That property of a substance which enables it to absorb water vapor from the surrounding atmosphere. Relative to most materials, vellum and paper, particularly the former, are strongly hygroscopic.

hygroscopic moisture. The amount of moisture retained by a material in the AIR DRY condition.

hymnal style. A style of binding used for church hymnals, or similar publications which utilizes a narrow leather spine, cloth sides, round or square corners, and colored edges. (261)

hysteresis. The differential value of a property, contingent upon approaching a known value of a *related* condition from a higher or lower level. A material such as paper, for example, that is to be conditioned at 50% relative humidity, will contain more moisture when this level is approached from above 50% than when approached from below. Hysteresis has a considerable influence in governing the dimensional stability of paper.

I. The Roman equivalent of 1. *See:* RO-MAN NUMERALS.

ichthyocoll. *See:* ISINGLASS.

illuminated. A manuscript or book embellished with ornamental letters, scrolls, miniature and/or other designs, usually in gold and red, but also in silver and other colors. (169)

illuminated binding. A binding which has extra colors in its scheme of decoration, and especially a binding in which a design was first blocked in blind and afterwards colored. Originally a French innovation, this style was used in England from about 1830 to 1860. Burnt sienna, carmine, gamboge, indigo, sap green and ultramarine were the colors most often used mainly because they were more lightfast. The color was mixed with a suitable gum and applied to the cover; when it was dry, gold leaf was laid on the areas to be gilded, and the entire design was then impressed with the heated block, which fixed both gold and colors, sharpening the edge of the latter. (152, 156, 236, 365)

illumination. The decoration of a manuscript or book with painted pictures, ornamented letters, designs, or a combination thereof, in colors and (usually) burnished gold or silver.

The design was first drawn and then sized with a mixture of clay, gypsum or lime, followed by an adhesive (glair). The gold or silver leaf was laid on and burnished, and the colors were then applied.

Although illumination is considered to be a medieval art, its origins can be traced back to illustrated Egyptian papyrus rolls and especially to Greco-Roman book illustration. Classical artists illustrated the text of codices with continuous chronological sequences of scenes, which often filled the entire page.

The word "miniature," which comes from the Latin *minimum* (red lead, which the Romans used for initial letters), is frequently used with reference to the individual pictures in an illuminated work; however, a "miniature painting" is not synonymous with "illustration," because illuminations are usually executed in gold or silver while miniatures generally are not. (140, 156, 365)

illustration board. A board used primarily

for the application of ink and water color. It is made by pasting drawing paper to one or both sides of a board, one that is usually filled, pulp-lined, or pasted. The usual properties of the drawing paper, such as finish and sizing, are essential, but hard sizing and good erasing quality are of greatest importance. The finished board should be as free as possible from warping. The basis weight is 150 pounds ($17 \times 22 - 500$), and the thickness is 0.0325 inch. (17)

imbrication. A form of embellishment of a book featuring a pattern consisting of overlapping leaves or scales. The term is also applied to any decorative pattern composed of overlapping elements. (156, 233)

imitation art paper. A printing paper containing a high percentage of china clay, kaolin, etc., in the paper furnish. It has a very high water finish, which provides the required surface opacity, and absorbency suitable for the printing of some halftones. Imitation art paper differs from ART PAPER (1) in that the clay is mixed with the fibers, and is thus an entirely on-machine operation. Coated art paper, which is the superior product, may be determined by the black mark which results from rubbing it with a silver coin. Imitation art paper is not usually suitable for halftone printing where the screen is finer than 133 lines. (17, 58)

imitation cloth. A material other than a woven fabric, e.g., paper or plastic, which has been embossed to give it the surface appearance of a fabric. (102)

imitation gold. A metallic composition used as a substitute for gold leaf or foil in the lettering and decorating of books, particularly in edition binding. It is usually made of powdered bronze.

It lacks the richness and depth of genuine gold and eventually tarnishes due to oxidation. Also called "artificial gold." (147, 164)

imitation leather. A coated fabric, rubber or plastic composition, or absorbent paper, manufactured so as to resemble genuine leather. Of the many efforts to find a satisfactory substitute for leather, both proposed and actually manufactured, only a few have any extensive use in bookbinding today, and, as they usually contain cellulose nitrate or polychlorides, their permanence is suspect. Also called "artificial leather." (198, 264)

imitation parchment. A type of relatively strong paper first produced by W. E. Gaine in 1857. It is made entirely of chemical wood pulp and is called imitation parchment in order to distinguish it from parchment paper made in imitation of true (animal) parchment. Imitation parchment now bears little resemblance to that paper, nor does it possess any of its qualities. The paper may be rendered partially transparent, greaseproof, and somewhat waterproof by prolonged beating (hydration) of the pulp or by treating the paper with sulfuric acid. The usual basis weight is 30 pounds ($24 \times 35 - 500$). (17, 156)

imitation Russia. A vegetable-tanned split cowhide finished with oil of birch to impart the odor characteristic of true RUSSIA LEATHER.

imitation vellum. A paper made so as to simulate true VELLUM, and produced in much the same manner as IMITATION PARCHMENT, except that it is thicker.

imperfect. 1. A book having leaves or sections omitted, duplicated, misplaced or bound in upside down, damaged, etc. 2. An obsolete term for reams of paper that have not been made up of the full number of a printer's ream. (83, 156)

imperfection note. The bookbinder's list of shortages encountered as he proceeds through to the end of an edition run. Certain sections or plates may be missing because of spoilage or short printing, and it is customary to print the requisite extra copies of these when, and if, the book is reprinted. (307)

imperfections. 1. Printed sheets rejected by the binder because of some kind of imperfection, and which must be replaced before the work can be completed. 2. Additional sections, i.e., those printed and folded in excess of the number required to complete the run. (339)

imperial morocco cloth. A linen cloth finished with a grain pattern resembling leather, usually a straight-grained morocco.

imposition. The plan of arrangement of the pages of type in a chase so that they will read consecutively when the printed sheet is folded. It is a term which means literally "in position," and originated in letterpress printing.

There are four standard methods of imposition: 1) sheetwise; 2) work-and-turn; 3) work-and-tumble; and 4) work-and-twist. The purpose of having different schemes is to obtain maximum economy in printing.

Sheetwise imposition, also known as "work-and-back," "front-and-back," or "print-and-back," requires two image carriers per color, one each for the front and back of the sheet. This method is used for printing jobs where the number of pages to be printed on each side of the sheet is large enough to utilize the full capacity of the press.

Work-and-turn imposition, also known as "print-and-turn," is used where it is practical to print both sides of the sheet from a single image carrier per color. It is frequently used, and requires relatively large presses because the sheet will carry two complete units, each occupying one-half of the sheet. The sheet is either slit during backup or is cut apart after printing. Work-and-turn imposition cuts the number of sheets to be printed by 50%, but it generally requires larger and more expensive presses than sheetwise imposition.

Work-and-tumble imposition, also known as "print-and-tumble," "work-and-roll," or "work-and-flop," is used less frequently than either of the two previous methods. It is selected when a work-and-turn form cannot be used, or when two sheetwise forms would have to be run on a sheet of difficult dimensions. This method needs only one image carrier for printing both sides of the sheet, and in this respect it is similar to work-and-turn.

Work-and-twist imposition, also known as "work-and-twirl," differs fundamentally from all three previous schemes. While the first three are methods designed to produce sheets printed on both sides, work-and-twist imposition solves problems pertaining to one-side printing, e.g., printing blank rule and tabular forms, with cross rules in one section and vertical rules in the other. In this method, two separate sections, or divisions, of an individual form are imposed and locked up together in such a manner that they may be printed side by side on a double-sized sheet in one impression. After completion of the run, the already printed paper is repositioned face up for the second printing from the same image carrier. Work-and-twist imposition is actually rarely used, as it requires nearly perfectly square stock for execution. (234, 287, 289, 316, 320, 339)

impregnated fabrics. Fabrics in which the interstices between the yarns are completely filled with the impregnating compound throughout the thickness of the material, as distinguished from sized or coated fabrics, where the interstices are not completely filled. Sometimes the reverse side of impregnated fabrics are sized to insure the adhesive sticking to the cloth. When a grain or pattern is applied to impregnated fabrics, it is worked directly into the cloth, rather than on a surface coating as is the case of coated fabrics. *See also:* BOOK CLOTH. (208, 260, 341)

impregnated paper. A paper in which a material such as latex or plastic is made to permeate the paper rather than merely coat it, thus adding to the wet strength, tearing resistance, and oil or grease resistance of the paper. The untreated paper used in its manufacture is known as saturating paper. (102, 139)

impressed watermark. *See:* WATERMARK.

impression. 1. The pressure required to transfer ink from one surface to another, as, for example, plate to paper, or plate to blanket, etc. It is usually expressed in terms of thousandths of an inch beyond that needed to produce first contact between two printing cylinders. 2. A printed copy or the result of impressing ink upon a receiving surface. 3. The indentations remaining in paper as a result of the pressure used in letterpress printing plus the dampness of the paper. These impressions were often quite pronounced in early letterpress printing. *See also:* CONVEX COVERS. 4. The effect produced by stamping, blocking, printing, or tooling a design or lettering on the covers of a book. 5. All copies of a work printed at one time from one setting of type. There may be several impressions (presumably unaltered) of one edition, each new printing from standing type

or original plates constituting a new "impression" of the work. If, however, the pages are reimposed to produce a different format, the resultant impression is a different edition. 6. A single copy of a print or map. 7. A print taken by means of a special engraving press, from an enlarged plate. (12, 17, 83)

in boards (in-board binding; in-board forwarding). 1. A book which has had its edges cut *after* the boards have been laced-in. In-board forwarding, although infrequently used today, was the principal method of craft bookbinding for centuries and in many respects is still the finest technique of forwarding, as it treats bookbinding purely as a craft. It also enables the bookbinder to achieve more accurate SQUARES. It is an abbreviation of "cut in boards." *Cf:* OUT OF BOARDS. 2. A term occasionally applied to an economical style of binding common in 18th and early 19th centuries, consisting of pasteboards covered with paper, usually blue sides and a white spine. (343)

in-boards extra. An in-board binding with solid gilt edges.

incised leather. *See:* CUIR-BOUILLI; CUIR CISELÉ.

incunabula (sing. **incunabulum;** anglicized: **incunable**). Books and all printing from movable metal type which can be dated before the year 1501. The date limitation probably derives from the earliest known catalog of incunabula, an appendix to Johann Saubert's *Historia bibliothecae Noribergensis . . . catalogus librorum proximis ab inventione annis usque ad a. Ch. 1500 editorum,* 1643. "Incunabula" derives its name from the Latin "cunae" (cradle) and refers to books produced in the infancy of printing. The term may also be used to designate works created during the earliest stages in the development of an art form or technique or at the beginning of any new period of artistic productivity.

In a general sense, the term "incunabula" can be used to refer to printed works of a time so early in the history of printing in a given locality that such printing may be said to be in its infancy; thus it is possible to speak of American incunabula, Arizona incunabula, etc. With regard specifically to printing, however, and unless stated otherwise, the term is used to refer to the products of the European press of the 15th century.

Incunabula were usually simply bound in leather-covered boards with decoration in blind. However, their collectors later often had them rebound in more sumptuous covers; consequently original bindings are now relatively rare. (69, 140, 255)

independents. Books or pamphlets published separately and later bound together into one physical volume.

index. In bookbinding, the words, letters, numbers, etc., printed, stamped or pasted in alphabethical, numerical, or other order: 1) in spaces cut or gouged in the fore edge of the book; 2) tabs attached to the leaves at the fore edge; or 3) printed on the leaves of the book, or on separate sheets to be inserted in their proper position in the book. The purpose of the index is to facilitate quick reference to the contents. *See also:* CUT THROUGH INDEX; ONE-LETTER INDEX; TAB INDEX; THUMB INDEX; TWO-LETTER INDEX.

index board. A type of single- or twin-wire pulp board, in white and colors, used for index cards and other record keeping. The board has a good, even, well finished surface suitable for writing, and is smooth, hard-sized, and of an even LOOK-THROUGH. The usual basis weights are 180, 220, 280, 340, and and 440 pounds (25.5 × 30.5 − 1000). (17)

indexing. The process of attaching index tabs to the leaves of a book, or the cutting, stamping, gouging or printing of indices in the fore edges of books. When tabs are used for the index, the top one is cut larger than the others when the steps are small, because, being at the top of the leaf, a small step may break away during use unless it is large enough to be secured firmly to the leaf. In blankbook tab indexing, under average conditions, certain letters of the alphabet will have more accounts listed under them than will other letters. Analysis of this had led to the development of tables that give the proper number of pages to meet the requirements of each letter. Thus, more pages are required for the initial letter S, followed by B (or vice versa in some cases), then H, and so on down to X, which requires the fewest.

Indicies for reference books are usually of the thumb type, while blankbooks generally have cut through or tab indicies.

In indexing format, a ONE-LETTER INDEX usually consists of 24 letters or divisions, while a TWO-LETTER INDEX has 13 divisions. Some indices have supplementary indices for the five vowels cut into the leaves of each letter of the main index.

Although these terms are used, an index may be made with any number of divisions and leaves to each division, or may be cut through the entire book. (264, 343)

index rolls. Alphabetical brass rolls used for lettering indices. (264)

index shears. A curved or ordinary pair of shears with an adjustable gauge, used for cutting step indices. (264)

index tab. A small piece of leather, paper, card, or fabric attached to, and projecting from the fore edge of a book and bearing in progressive order, usually from head to tail, letters, words, symbols, or other indexing information. *See also:* THUMB INDEX. (274)

India Bible paper. *See:* BIBLE PAPER.

India ink. *See:* CHINESE INK.

Indian tragacanth. *See:* KARAYA GUM.

Indian yellow. A yellow coloring matter prepared from the evaporated urine of cows that have been fed on mango leaves. It is less fugitive than most other yellow lakes. In 1938, however, its production was prohibited on humane grounds, as mango leaves are harmful to the cattle. The term is also applied to a brilliant yellow pigment made from naphthol yellow and used in coating paper. (233)

India Oxford paper. *See:* BIBLE PAPER.

India paper. From about 1768 to 1875, a soft absorbent paper imported from China for use in making proofs of engravings. Since 1875 it has been made from chemically processed hemp and rags. Today it is generally a thin, opaque sheet made in a basis weight of 20 pounds, bulking approximately 1,000 pages to the inch. (82, 182)

India proof paper. *See:* CHINA PAPER. (1)

India red (Indian red). *See:* VENETIAN RED.

India rubber. A substance obtained from the latex of many tropical plants, especially of the genera *Hevae* and *Ficus,* and characterized by its elasticity, although this property varies widely depending upon its source and preparation. It was at one time used in the production of adhesive bindings. *See also:* CAOUTCHOUC BINDING. (25)

India tint. A term commonly applied to printing papers to indicate a light buff color.

indicator. A ribbon, usually of steel, on a GUILLOTINE cutter, ruled to sixteenths of an inch. It is used to read the distance from the front face of the back gauge to the cutting edge of the knife. (145)

indigo. A blue vat dyestuff, with the formula $(C_{16}H_{10}N_2O_2)$, formerly derived by fermentation of the leaves of the herbaceous shrubs *Isatis tinctoria, Polygonum tinctoria,* etc., but now

manufactured from anthranilic acid $(C_7H_7NO_2)$, and used, along with wood ashes, mainly in northern Nigeria, in the removal of hair from goatskin. In the 19th century the natural product was used, in conjunction with sulfuric acid, to make a blue coloring matter for use in the production of leather cover marbles. (130)

industrial binding. A term sometimes applied to early machine produced (edition) bindings of the 19th century.

infusorial earth. *See:* DIATOMACEOUS SILICA.

ingrain. A descriptive term applied to a mottled, rough, or granite appearance in a type of paper used for pamphlet covers.

inhibitor. 1. A substance used to reduce the rate of a chemical reaction. Inhibitors are sometimes used in certain types of adhesives to prolong storage- or working-life. 2. Substances that retard or prevent the accumulation of acid in paper or leather, or the growth of mold or fungi on leathers, paper, cloth, adhesives, etc. (198, 309)

in hubs. A term applied to a blankbook when the HUBS have been glued to the SPRING-BACK (1), the book then being ready for covering. (264)

ink. A general descriptive term for a fluid or viscous material of various colors, but most often black or blue-black, that is composed essentially of a pigment or dye in a suitable vehicle and used for printing or writing.

The earliest inks were essentially suspensions of soot (carbon) in a gum. They were very suitable for use with papyrus, which was porous enough to absorb the vehicle and entrap the pigment between the fibers. Under these conditions the writing would be permanent, indelible, and harmless to the papyrus. This type of ink was in common use until the 11th century when IRON-GALL INK began to come into prominence.

The introduction of PARCHMENT as a writing material was probably the reason why an ink other than a carbon-gum solution became necessary. Carbon ink would not adhere to the greasy surface of a material such as parchment, and, in any case, it was too easily removed by sponging. *See:* PALIMPSEST. Examination of parchment manuscripts from the 9th to 15th centuries indicate that all were written with iron-gall inks in which no trace of carbon could be found. Carbon inks, however, continued to be used for documents, probably until the advent of the "blue-black" ink period. From these somewhat indefinite beginnings, simple iron-gall inks were the predominant inks until about 1860, when the introduction of aniline dyes brought about radical changes in ink manufacture, stemming largely from the fact that in the case of an ANILINE INK, the need for partial oxidation of the ink no longer existed. Since then the manufacture of ink has become extremely complicated.

Most modern inks are manufactured to overcome one or more of the disadvantages inherent in blue-black inks, including their acidity, muddiness, and less than adequate permanence. When considering permanence it is important to distinguish between printing inks and writing inks, because, as prepared today, the former are more permanent than the latter. Writing inks, having a high degree of permanence, can be made to meet special requirements, but such inks are harmful to the fountain pens. In general, the introduction of writing inks colored with an aniline dye has made the typical modern writing ink less permanent than its predecessor of a century earlier. The stability of good quality printing ink, on the other hand, is such that it usually outlasts the paper, and this is as permanent as it need be. *See also:* CARBONACEOUS INKS; CARBON INK; CHINESE INK; COLORED INKS; PRINTING INKS; SEPIA INKS. (20, 21, 143, 198)

ink absorption. A measure of the extent to which an ink will penetrate into a sheet of paper before it dries.

ink and fold papers. Decorative end- and cover papers produced by laying a sheet of plain rice paper on a lined glass surface to aid in the placement of the design. The glass can be wetted before the paper is laid on, or the paper itself can be thoroughly wetted. The design is laid on with colored inks and a brush, and the paper is then folded twice along its long dimension and then over, forming a square. The square is squeezed tightly to make the color blend, and the paper is then unfolded and allowed to dry. Dots with circles and stripes are commonly used designs for this paper. (183)

ink blocking. The process of blocking titles, or other information, on book covers in black or colored inks. An unheated press and quick-drying printer's ink are used. Drying can be a problem in climates experiencing high relative humidity. (140)

ink holdout. *See:* HOLDOUT; INK RECEPTIVITY.

ink receptivity. That property of a paper, cloth, etc., that allows it to accept ink in printing and blocking. The capability of the ink to wet the printing surface is essential and in many cases the ability of the paper to absorb the ink vehicle is also important. *See also:* ABSORBENCY; PRINTABILITY; RECEPTIVITY. (17, 98)

inlaid. A leaf or plate that has been placed within a larger and usually thicker leaf, for the purpose of enlarging its margins and thus its overall size. This is sometimes done to make it as large as the other leaves in a composite volume, in which case it is usually described as "inlaid to size." The term is also applied to the laying down, or re-margining of all four edges, of a damaged leaf. The overlapping edges are sometimes shaved thin to prevent bulkiness at the laps. (69)

inlaid binding. *See:* INLAY. (4)

inlaid ornaments. *See:* INLAY. (2)

inlay. 1. A strip of kraft or other relatively stiff paper, used to stiffen the spine area of the case of a library binding. The paper used should be between 0.012 and 0.025 inch in thickness, depending on the size of the book. Edition bindings generally do not have inlays. *See also:* HOLLOW. 2. An illustration, photograph, picture, or other decoration inlaid in the cover of a book. 3. A manuscript, letter, leaf, etc., mounted in a cut-out frame to protect it and/or permit both sides to be viewed. The edges of the plate, etc., are beveled and pasted to the beveled edges of the sheet cut out to its size. 4. A piece of leather, of the same thickness as the leather covering of a book, but usually of a contrasting color, grain, or both, cut to a desired shape for placing into the leather covering, from which a piece of the exact same size and shape has been removed. If the scheme of decoration calls for tooling over the area of the inlay, the leather for the inlay is cut on a bevel so that the grain surface is slightly larger than the flesh side, while the leather covering is cut in the opposite manner. If, however, the area of the inlay is not to be tooled, the inlay and leather covering are cut vertically. Inlaid bindings were produced in great numbers in the 17th and 18th centuries, especially in France. Onlaid bindings are often mistakenly described as inlaid. *Cf:* ONLAY. 5. The setting of a leaf or plate into a larger leaf by cutting out a portion of the latter, beveling, and pasting the leaf or plate over the gap. (161, 183, 335, 343)

inline binding machine. A term borrowed from the packaging field where it is used to indicate a continuous manufacturing process combining many different operations. An example of inline machine work in bookbinding would be in the backer, triple liner and headbanding machine, casing-in machine, book forming and pressing machine, and jacketing machine, all aligned as to speed, controls, etc., and connected to each other by a specially constructed linking conveyor. An "inline" binding machine, therefore is a single completely integrated machine used for the mass production of books. It operates intermittently, the conveying mechanism moving a uniform and predetermined distance, then stopping for a short interval during which the books are subjected to the action of all processing stations at the same time. As each book moves on, it passes through the production steps selected for a specific job. (302)

inner lining. 1. *See:* SPINE LINING (1). 2. *See:* INLAY (1).

inner margin. That margin of a page adjacent to the binding edge of a book. It is the left hand margin of the recto and the right hand margin of the verso of a book that reads from left to right. *See also:* GUTTER. (131)

inorganic aids. Acids, such as hydrochloric, sulfuric, nitric, etc., that are usually very corrosive and are often relatively nonvolatile. Also known as "mineral acids." *Cf:* ORGANIC ACIDS.

in quires. *See:* IN SHEETS.

insect wax. A WAX such as that obtained from China, where insects such as *Coccus ceriferus* deposit the wax on trees. The wax is scraped off and washed on the surface of hot water before being cast into molds and set in blocks. It has a softening range of 80 to 84° C., and is very firm, like beeswax, and consequently is useful in providing body for leather dressings to be used in very hot climates. (291)

insert. 1. A piece of blank paper or card laid between the leaves of a book and not secured. Inserting is sometimes required to compensate for the swelling of the spine caused by the added bulk of the sewing thread. 2. An additional printed leaf or leaves, circular, etc., placed between the leaves of a book, pamphlet, newspaper, etc. 3. *See:* INSET (1). (82, 164, 316)

inserted. A term describing folded sections on which pasting or inserting has been accomplished, the sections then being ready for gathering.

inserted after binding. Bulky maps, plans, etc., which require many folds and which are to be tipped into the book subsequent to binding, as they might otherwise interfere with trimming. In order to compensate for the bulk of this material, and thus prevent gaping of the covers of the finished book, a COMPENSATION GUARD is usually included in the binding of the book. *See also:* LIPPED; THROW OUT.

inset. 1. A section placed within another section so that the subsequent sewing passes through the folds of both. The inset may be four pages only or multiples of four pages and may be placed in the center of the outer section, or on the outside, where is is wrapped around the main section. In rare cases it is sometimes located in some intermediate position. Insetting is of considerable importance as a method of incorporating plates into a section without resorting to tipping-in. Where the plates are on the outside of the section they are sometimes referred to as "outserts" or "wrap arounds." If the section to be insetted is required to complete the succession of pages, it is called an "offcut." 2. A small map, illustration, etc., set within the border of a larger one. (58, 82, 287)

in sheets. Unbound printed sheets, especially when unfolded. The term is also used loosely to indicate sheets that have been processed up to the point of folding and gathering. "In sheets" is gradually superseding "in quires," with which it is synonymous. *See also:* QUIRE (2); SHEET STOCK.

inside borders (inside margin). *See:* TURN-INS (1).

inside dentelle. *See:* DENTELLE.

inside rolling block. A block of wood the thickness of a book so that its opened cover will lie perfectly flat on its top. It has a concave edge into which the rounded spine of the book fits, thus providing support for the entire cover up to the joint. It is used when finishing the inside of the cover, and tooling the turn-ins. Several sizes of block are required for books of different thicknesses. (115)

inside tins. *See:* PRESSING TINS (2).

in signatures. The gathered but unsewn sections of a book. *See also:* QUIRE (2).

in straps. The condition of a blankbook when the leather or cloth, usually the former, has been glued underneath the SPRING-BACK (1) between the tapes or webbings. *See also:* CLOTHINGS. (264)

intaglio. 1. The impression formed by a ROLL (1) cut in relief in which the sunken part of the leather forms the design. 2. A type of watermarking with a DANDY ROLL. Also called "shadow watermark." *See:* WATERMARK.

integral cover. *See:* SELF-COVER.

integrated bookbinding. A craft bookbinding which displays surface imagery that is intended to interpret and project the essence of the communication of the author of the book. This imagery is also inseparable from the style of any illustrative matter contained in the text, and sympathetic to the typographical format. The design elements work consistently throughout the book and its binding. Integrated bookbinding excludes unrelated surface decoration. (311)

interleaved (interleaved plate; interleaving). 1. An extra leaf, usually blank, inserted between the printed leaves of a book, generally for the writing of notes, or, if thin tissues, to prevent text and illustration from rubbing together, in which case it is more appropriately called a BARRIER SHEET. 2. A plate which has a thin leaf bearing a descriptive caption pasted to the inner margin. A leaf of cellophane is a modern version of this. (82, 234)

interleaving blotting paper. A thin blotting paper used between freshly printed sheets to prevent ink from being OFFSET (2) to other sheets, or to absorb (dry) fresh writing in ink. It is produced in a basis weight of 20 pounds (19 $\times$ 24 — 500). (17)

interleaving paper (interleaving tissue). *See:* BARRIER SHEET.

interlocking clamp and back gauge. Recesses in the clamp and back gauge of a GUILLOTINE cutter which permit the back gauge to push the pile to be cut

further forward than would be possible if both clamp and back gauge were solid. Its purpose is to allow for cutting narrow strips. In normal cutting, a flat solid plate fits over the clamp to prevent it from indenting the stock. (145)

intermediate colors. The six colors located between the primary and, secondary colors of the spectrum, and which are green-blue, blue-violet, red-violet, red-orange, orange-yellow, and yellow-green. (233)

internal bond strength. The strength of the adhesion between body stock and coating of a paper. Low internal bond strength will sometimes result in picking of the clay coating from paper when it is printed with a tacky ink.

internally plasticized. An adhesive which has had the plasticizing agent introduced as part of the adhesive molecule during the manufacturing process, as contrasted with an adhesive to which the plasticizer is added by the user. The adhesive is copolymerized with the plasticizer to form the internally plasticized adhesive.

internal stress. Stress created within an adhesive film because of different rates of movement of the joint, or by the contraction or expansion of the adhesive itself.

international paper sizes. Standard sizes of paper that are recognized internationally. The international "A" series of paper sizes, which are now widely recognized throughout the world are:

Designation	Trimmed Size	
	Millimeters	Inches
4A	1,682 by 2,378	66.22 by 93.62
2A	1,189 by 1,682	46.81 by 66.22
A0	841 by 1,189	33.11 by 46.81
A1	594 by 841	23.39 by 33.11
A2	420 by 594	16.54 by 23.39
A3	297 by 420	11.69 by 16.54
A4	210 by 297	8.27 by 11.69
A5	148 by 210	5.83 by 8.27
A6	105 by 148	4.13 by 5.83
A7	74 by 105	2.91 by 4.13
A8	52 by 74	2.05 by 2.91
A9	37 by 52	1.46 by 2.05
A10	26 by 37	1.05 by 1.46

(156)

in the crust. Hides or skins that have been preserved (cured) in the dry, salted state. *See:* DRY-SALTING.

in the pickle. Hides or skins that have been preserved (cured) thoroughly soaked in a brine solution. *See:* BRINING.

in the round. *See:* GILT IN THE ROUND; SEWING IN THE ROUND; TRIMMED IN THE ROUND.

in the square. *See:* GILT IN THE SQUARE; TRIMMED IN THE SQUARE.

invading the print. *See:* CROPPED (1).

inverted pages. The arrangement of a book or periodical issue containing two separate works issued together, and bound or imposed in such a manner that one is inverted with respect to the other, each beginning at one end of the volume or issue and concluding in the interior. Each may have its own title page and perhaps blank leaves between the two works. *See also:* DOS À DOS BINDING.

invisible joint. The joint of an endpaper consisting of a reinforcing fabric, usually linen or cambric, so constructed that it cannot be seen in the finished book. Sometimes called a "concealed joint." (102)

invoice. An itemized statement, in greater or lesser detail, furnished by the binder to the library, specifying the work done, the prices for the work, and (sometimes) the terms of payment.

Irish moss. The dried and bleached plants of two red algae, *Chrondrus crispus* and *Gigartina mamillosa,* used to some extent in the production of MARBLING SIZE. *See also:* CARRAGHEEN MOSS. (217)

iron. 1. A heavy, malleable, ductile metal (Fe), of which some papermaking beaters are constructed. Minute specks of iron, which is chemically active, sometimes break off, enter the papermaking slurry, and become part of the paper. Iron may act as a catalyst in the conversion of sulfur dioxide into sulfuric acid, which is highly destructive to paper. 2. An old measure of the thickness of a leather, one iron being equal to $\frac{1}{48}$ inch. *See also:* LEATHER SUBSTANCE TABLE.

iron acetates. Ferric acetate $(Fe(CH_3 CO_2)_3$, and ferrous acetate $FE(CH_3 CO_2)_2$, deep red and pale green respectively and used, largely in the 19th century, to treat leather bindings for "sprinkled" and "tree" effects. *See also:* TREE CALF.

iron bindings. Bookbindings, usually of German origin, which have covers of iron, cast in the form of grillwork composed of bars and scrolls and riveted onto the boards. The style was also employed in England in the 19th century. (152)

iron-gall ink. An INK produced by the reaction of tannic acid with an iron salt, such as ferrous sulfate $(FeSO_4)$. The reaction produces no immediate change in the color of the solution, but, when the ink is applied to paper and is thus exposed to air, it darkens by oxidation, forming ferric tannate. The difficulty of writing with a colorless fluid was partially overcome by the addition of gum arabic to the solution, as well as some pre-exposure to air, so as to form of the ferric tannate before use. The gum arabic served to prevent the ferric tannate from settling out of solution. There were disadvantages to this procedure, such as the tendency of the ferric tannate to settle out despite the gum arabic, and the tendency of the ink to remain on the surface of the writing material instead of impregnating the fibers. This was due to the fact that the ink had formed before meeting the paper, and the result was that it could be removed rather easily by washing once the water had loosened the gum. In an effort to overcome these problems, various coloring matters were added to the original solution, including extracts of logwood, and, at a later date, indigo. Other than being colored at the outset, iron-gall inks treated in this manner had several advantages: the oxidation and consequent deposition of solid matter was restrained and the ink therefore penetrated the fibers more readily; the penetration was assisted by the absence of gum arabic because the ink could then flow more freely; oxidation occurred only on the paper, and the ink then changed from blue to black; and the addition of the indigo also increased the resistance of the ink to fading and bleaching.

Iron-gall ink does have one serious disadvantage. Free acid is often present, which not only corrodes steel pens badly, but, far worse, attacks the paper, as well as certain of the dyes used to color them.

There is also the so-called Japan ink, which consists of almost completely oxidized iron tannate with large proportions of gum, which gives a black glossy effect immediately; and an ink made from logwood and iron, without the addition of tannic acid, which has a greenish shade which eventually changes to black.

Iron-gall inks came into use in the 9th century and by the 11th century had largely replaced carbon inks as a writing medium. (143)

ironing. The process of smoothing the grain surface of finished leather. Ironing customarily follows BOARDING (1), and, although the grain is again made smooth by the ironing, the pattern produced by the boarding remains. The ironing makes the boarded leather softer and more flexible. It may be done by hand (much in the same manner as clothes are ironed), or, more commonly today, in rotary ironing machines, in which the leather is passed over a polished, heated steel cylinder, which is thermostatically controlled at a pre-set temperature. The fine effect of ironing seemingly cannot be obtained by other processes, such as smooth-plating. (363)

isinglass (ichthyocoll). A semi-transparent whitish substance consisting of a very pure form of gelatin, produced from the sounds (swimming bladders) of the sturgeon (*Acipenser huso,* and other species of *Acipenser*), found in the Caspian and Black Seas. After removal, the bladders are cut open, soaked in water, spread out and the outer silvery membrane removed by rubbing. The isinglass contains about 80% collagen. It is used as a clarifying agent, in the manufacture of fish glue, and as a size for handmade paper. Its use in recent years has greatly diminished, due to the rise in use of synthetic materials and gelatin. (102, 195, 335)

isometric colors. Colors that appear to be identical but actually have different chemical and/or physical properties. Burnt umber and a mixture of burnt sienna, black, and a small part of green, for example, create an exact imitation of the mass tone of burnt umber. (233)

Italian style. *See:* ALDINE (ITALIAN) STYLE.

ivory. The hard, creamy-white, opaque, fine-grained, elastic, modified dentine, that makes up the tusks of elephants and other (large) land and marine animals. Ivory has been used as a writing and decorating medium because of the fineness of its grain, its warm tone, the ease with which it can be given a high polish, its adaptability for writing and carving, and, when properly cared for, its remarkable durability.

Ivory was used for the covers of books in the Middle Ages, but not by English bookbinders until the mania for novelty and commercial advantage led to its use in about 1860. It has also been used in the manufacture of superior diptychs, as clasps for books, and for the folders used in bookbinding. (102, 236, 280)

ivory black. A fine, velvety, carbonaceous, black pigment, prepared by calcining ivory scraps; at one time, used in the production of black marbling color, and, until recently, in the production of an ink used in copperplate printing. (152)

ivory bristol. A bristol board used for a variety of purposes, including light-weight binders' board. It is an uncoated board with a high finish and a clear formation, and is somewhat translucent. The board is produced from cotton fibers and chemical wood pulps in basis weights of 70 to 90 pounds (22½ × 28½ — 500). (17, 82)

jacket. 1. *See:* BOOK JACKET. 2. A detachable outer cover for a bound book, designed to protect the binding from wear and soiling. It is frequently made of a clear plastic and is more or less easy to remove. 3. *See:* JOB TICKET. (256, 329)

jaconet (jaconette). A lightweight cotton cloth with a semi-glaze finish which enables it to resist briefly the penetration of adhesives. It is often used as a reinforcing material in bookbinding because it provides strength without excessive bulk. (237)

Jaffé, Mair (fl 1468-1480). An itinerant Jewish bookbinder of Ülm who worked at Nürnberg and was a master of the art of CUIR-CISELÉ, as applied to the embellishment of books. Jaffé bound a Hebrew Pentatuch manuscript which was decorated with beautifully designed animal figures, and he also bound books for wealthy Nürnberg patricians. It is notable that none of Jaffé's bindings include any Christian symbols, but instead were decorated with heraldic and ornamental designs composed of unicorns, flowers, hounds, and motifs of a similar nature. (141)

Jansen, Cornelius. *See:* JANSENIST STYLE.

Jansenist style. Originally, a French style of book decoration of the late 17th and early 18th centuries, named after the followers of Cornelius Jansen (1585-1638), the Bishop of Ypres, who advocated personal holiness and austerity. The books were embellished only by a centerpiece (often armorial) and corner fleurons, or by elaborate doublures tooled with dentelle borders but with no decoration at all on the spine and covers. (69, 172)

Japanese copying paper. A very thin, strong paper made in Japan from long-fibered stock, such as mitsumata and the paper mulberry. It is a very versatile paper, and depending on the thickness, may be used for mending torn book leaves, for the overall lining of paper as reinforcement, for reinforcing the folds of sections, or for mending hinges. Japanese copying paper is for the most part handmade, the fibers being pulped by hand and the sheets made on molds of bamboo or hair. The length of the fibers gives the paper exceptional strength and wearing characteristics, and when it is torn, the

fibers pull apart rather than tear. Also called "long-fibered Japanese tissue." (17, 237)

Japanese sewing. A method of sewing leaves or sections which, despite the name, was actually developed in China. The method involves gathering and jogging the leaves, and then drilling a hole through the entire thickness of the pile in the center anywhere from ¼ to ¾ inch from the edge of the spine, or more depending on the size of the book, the nature of the paper, and the extent of the binding margin. Additional holes are then drilled on either side of the center hole at uniform distances, the total number, including the one in the center, being an odd number. The sewing proceeds from the center hole to the head of the book, over the head and then down over the spine past the center hole to the tail and then back to the center. When the sewing is completed, the ends arc tied in a flat knot on the out-

side. An alternative method is to begin at either end, in which case the number of holes may be even or odd. Thread, cord, string, yarn, tape, or rope fibers can be used. Japanese sewing may be considered as a form of SIDE SEWING (or stabbing) and, although it does not allow much flexibility, especially with small books, it is an extremely strong method of sewing, possibly one of the strongest ever devised. (183)

Japanese silk. A type of SILK that is more closely woven and of finer threads than the usual silk. It is also a double warp fabric, i.e., the warp and filling threads are of the same thickness. Japanese silk is less likely to fray along cut edges than ordinary silk, which makes it useful for SILK FLYLEAVES. (236)

Japanese vellum. A thick paper produced in Japan from native fibers that are of relatively great length. The paper has a very cloudy formation and is tough and durable. The color is usually cream or natural, and the paper is finished with a smooth surface. Japanese vellum is suitable for engravings, etc., or where a very durable paper is required. An imitation, made by treating ordinary paper with sulfuric acid, is sometimes called "Japon." (156)

Japan ink. *See:* IRON-GALL INK.

Japan marble. A cover marble of a shaded red, produced by coating the leather with potash water (potash alum), brazilin and glair, followed by copperas water (ferrous sulfate) and

JAPANESE SEWING

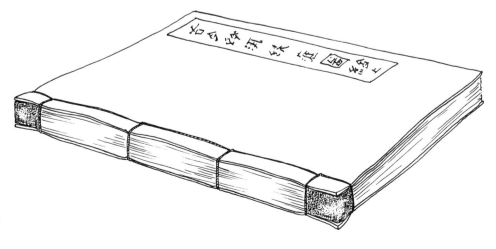

the red coloring in large drops, which were made to run down the covers. After the colors had dried, the covers were then washed several times with more of the brazilin, which added gloss. (95)

Japanned ox hide. Virtually the same leather as ENAMELED HIDE but finished with a plain, flat surface.

Japan wax. A soft, yellowish WAX having adhesive properties. It is obtained from the berries of the Japanese sumac (*Rhus verniciflua* and other species of *Rhus*), and used in some leather dressings. It is not a true wax but a glyceride, and contains palmitin with free palmitic acid. It has a softening range of 50° to 56° C., but upon being solidified, is likely to have an erratically lower softening point for some time thereafter. (173, 291)

japon. An imitation JAPANESE VELLUM.

javelle water. A dilute bleaching solution prepared either from sodium hypochlorite (NaOCl) or potassium hypochlorite (KOCl), the former being the stronger of the two. It was at one time widely used for bleaching purposes, but its use in the bleaching of archival papers has been superseded by the use of milder agents, such as calcium hypochlorite (CaOCl). (197)

jeweled bindings. Bookbindings having gilt metal plates covered with enamel work and plaques in metal or ivory, and embellished with jewels. Jeweled bindings were produced in many areas of the Continent of Europe, notably in France and Germany, from about the 6th to the 14th centuries, and in England during the Middle Ages. Very few, however, have survived intact. These jeweled covers actually represented the work of the jeweler, goldsmith, and silversmith, more than the bookbinder. Jewels were also at times used on leather bindings in the 19th century, but it was not until shortly after the turn of the century that the jeweled binding became an established style, culminating in Sangorski's GREAT OMAR. (236)

jiggering. 1. The procedure employed in BLIND TOOLING, in which, after an initial quick application of the heated finishing tool to "set" the leather in the impression, the tool is impressed a second time and rocked slightly, imparting a polished and darkened surface to the base of the impression. 2. The process employed in imparting dark lines on the spine of a book, usually on either side of the raised bands, by means of a string or strings drawn back and forth rapidly across

the leather. The device used in this procedure is known as the "jigger bands," and usually consists of one or two lengths of cord stretched between two wooden handles. (97, 335)

job backer. An iron screw press with opposing steel jaws and a screw that operates horizontally. It is used in backing books by hand, usually those too large to fit into the ROUNDING AND BACKING MACHINES. (164)

job binding. A general term applied to small binding jobs of a miscellaneous nature. Job binding does not utilize fully automatic equipment, as is found in large edition binderies, but relies instead on handwork, either alone or in conjunction with some machine operations. The job binder produces smaller lots of edition bindings and also binding that cannot be accommodated by automatic equipment, such as Bibles and prayer books bound YAPP STYLE. By accepted definition, job binding does not include LIBRARY BINDING, although the two are similar in many respects. (320, 339)

job ticket. A printed form, often in the form of an envelope, on which instructions pertaining to a printing or binding job are recorded. Also called "jacket." *See also:* BINING SLIP. (139)

jog (jogging). The operation of producing a smooth-sided pile of sheets or sections by knocking or vibrating the material against a smooth, flat surface, either by hand or by means of a mechanical device known as a JOGGER. *See also:* KNOCKING UP. (190)

jogger. A vibrating device used to produce a smooth-sided pile of paper stock before trimming, folding, binding, etc., or to align and position any material for any purpose during a production run. The jogger may be a unit or a part of a printing press delivery system. Joggers are employed at the press or cutter in small printing shops and binderies, in label factories, and in the gathering machines of newspaper printing plants. (320)

joint. 1. The exterior juncture of the spine and covers of a (usually) case-bound book. Although the term "joint" is often used to indicate the internal juncture of the board paper and fly leaf of a book, the more appropriate term here is HINGE (1). *See also:* CLOSED JOINT; FRENCH JOINT; LACING-IN; SUPPORTED FRENCH JOINT. 2. The sections at the front and back of a blankbook, consisting of one plain and one waste sheet, connected by a strip of linen, buckram, or other relatively heavy material, and lined with a plain or

marbled paper. The plain sheet is glued to the first (and last) leaf of the book and the waste leaves to the boards. 3. Any location at which two adherends are joined by a layer of adhesive. (83, 209, 335)

joint rod. A strip of wood or plastic, flat on one side and curved on the other, and placed between the board and SPRING-BACK (1) of a blankbook to form a groove when the book is pressed. To prevent the rod or board from pressing on the spring-back, the board is set a distance from the edge of the rod, usually ⅛ inch. (264, 339)

jordan. A type of REFINER consisting of a conical plug which fits into a matching conical shell. The outside of the plug and the inner surface of the shell are fitted with knives or bars. The plug is pushed into the shell to the point where the knives or bars of each are almost touching. When fibrous stock in solution enters the shell, usually at its smaller end, the knives or bars of the rotating plug and stationary shell mascerate the fibrous material and help reduce it further. (17)

journeyman bookbinder. A bookbinder who has learned the aspects of the trade of bookbinding. The term "journeyman" refers to the previous practice of workmen journeying from place to place to work in different shops in order to acquire a thorough and comprehensive knowledge of the craft. The term no longer has much significance in the United States, although it is used in some trades in describing a person who has completed a training program.

j pattern. A pebbled pattern in a book cloth similar in appearance to a morocco grain in goatskin. (256)

jump (jump out). 1. A term applied to the problem of books slipping from under the guillotine clamp during trimming. 2. A section or sections of a book which slip out of position during the backing operation. *See also:* START. (256)

jute. An Indian bast fiber obtained from white jute, *Corchorus capsularis*, the Tossa jute, *C. olitorius*, and other species of *Corchorus*. It is used in making burlap, gunny sacking, etc., which in turn have been used to provide fibers used in papermaking. Jute fibers are weaker and less durable than flax or hemp, and relatively easily rotted by water. An average clean sample of jute contains approximately 69.35% cellulose and 18.82% lingnin. (17, 72, 143)

jute board. A board used occasionally as a binder's board, produced from jute stock, along with chemical wood pulp. The board is said to be strong and lightweight.

juvenile picture-book binding. A style of binding in which the illustration of the BOOK JACKET is usually incorporated in the case and the book itself is given a sturdy binding suitable for use by children. *See also:* SCENIC BINDING.

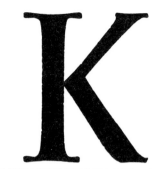

Kairouan bindings. *See:* COPTIC BINDINGS.

kangaroo skin. The skin of the herbivorous marsupials (family *Macropodidae*) of Australia, New Guinea, etc., which when properly tanned, makes a supple and durable bookbinding leather. Today, it is generally chrome tanned with a glazed finish, thus making it unsuitable for use as a bookbinding leather. It is said to be stronger, weight for weight, than any other leather. (325)

kaolin. A fine clay mass, usually white in color, and made up principally of clay mineral kaolinite. The kaolin clays have the approximate formula $(Al_2O_3 \cdot 2SiO_2 \cdot 2H_2O)$; however, they also contain small amounts of other minerals, as well as impurities. Kaolin is used extensively as a coating and filling clay in the manufacture of paper. *See also:* PAPER CLAY. (17, 60)

karaya gum. A gum derived from the dried exudation of the Indian tree *Sterculia urens*. In the deacetylated form, it is used as a fiber deflocculating agent for the long-fibered paper pulps. Karaya gum is also used as an economical substitute for GUM TRAGACANTH, as the size for marbling water. It is also known as "Indian tragacanth," and colloquially as "gum hog." (17, 233, 339)

keratin. The fibrous protein material of the hair and epidermis of a hide or skin, which represents approximately 2.0% of the protein composition of the skin. (305)

keratose. The degradation product of KERATIN. During the action of the lime liquors on the epithelial cells of the epidermis and sebaceous glands, degradation products are formed which remain in the hides and skins after unhairing, scudding, and washing. They are present, in the form of viscous solutions or jellies adhering to the structures of the thermostat layer, in the region just under the grain surface. They are not readily visible under the microscope, but are precipitated as flocculent masses upon contact with acid solutions. They are removed by the action of enzymes during BATING, and, if not properly removed, will result in a grainy surface that is thick, spongy, and irregular, suggesting the presence of keratose precipitated in the grain layer. (306, 363)

kerf. A shallow cut, approximately $\frac{1}{32}$ inch deep, made between $\frac{1}{4}$ and $\frac{1}{2}$ inch from the head and tail on the backs of the gathered sections of a text block. The loops of the kettle stitches fit into the kerfs and consequently do not show as lumps under the leather of a TIGHT BACK binding. The term is also applied, although somewhat inaccurately, to the saw cuts made for the cords used in RECESSED-CORD SEWING. (335)

kettle stitch. The stitch made near the head and tail of a book sewn on tapes or cords, and which holds the sections (other than the first and last) together. The term may be a corruption of "catch-up stitch," or "Kettel stitch" (the stitch that forms a little chain). Sometimes called "ketch stitch." (106, 156, 236)

key. A bookbinder's tool, consisting of a device that somewhat resembles the prongs of a blunt fork with a circular hole at the top. It is used to secure the sewing cords to the base of the sewing frame. (335)

KETTLE STITCH

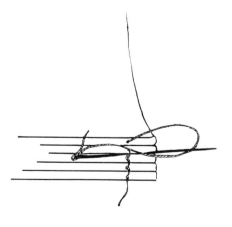

khaki. A strong, durable light olive-brown to light yellowish-brown cloth, usually made from cotton and similar in texture to canvas. It makes a reasonably satisfactory covering material for books subject to hard usage, such as blankbooks; however, it is not as durable as canvas or impregnated buckram. (196)

khari. A salt which occurs as an efflorescence on the ground in certain areas of India. It contains approximately 60% sodium sulfate, 20% magnesium sulfate, and 5% sodium chloride. It is used in DRY-SALTING hides and skins largely in the area where it is found.

kid seal. A SEALSKIN, dressed with alum and salt and oiled. It makes a soft, tough, hard-wearing leather.

kidskin. The skin of a young goat. It has a fine grain pattern, and makes a strong and flexible leather.

kieselghur. *See:* DIATOMACEOUS SILICA.

kinky filling. A place in a fabric where a short length of WEFT has spontaneously doubled back on itself.

kip (kip calf; kipskin). 1. A small cattle hide, i.e., the hides of fully mature cattle, other than the buffalo, native to the Indian Subcontinent and some parts of Africa, which are smaller than those of Europe and America. 2. The skins obtained from immature European and American bovine animals that have been grass fed and which are larger than calves but smaller than fully grown cattle. Among cattle hides, a kip is one weighing between 15 and 25 pounds in the green salted state. Generally, a kip is considered to be intermediate between a hide and a skin. Leather made from kips generally has a fine, tight fiber. 3. As an abbreviation of the full term "East India tanned kip," or "E. I. kip crust," a vegetable tanned leather made from cowhide originating in the Indian Subcontinent and tanned in India, mainly in the south, and especially around Madras. (61, 248, 264, 363)

kissing the bookbinder's daughter. A trick played on a young bookbinder just finishing his apprenticeship, in which, as part of the ceremony, he must kiss the daughter of the owner of the bookbinding establishment. The prettiest girl in the shop is actually chosen for the part, and as the new journeyman steps forward to perform his part of the ceremony, which he is required to do with his eyes closed, a well-filled paste brush is substituted for the girl and the young binder gets a mouthful of paste. *See also:* RINGING OUT.

kiss marks. Light or white patches on vegetable tanned leathers, caused by hides and skins touching each other in the tanning pits, thus preventing the tan from penetrating the areas of contact. Kiss marks are prevented by rocking the frames which hold the skins while in the pits. (306)

knife folding machine. *See:* FOLDING MACHINES.

knockers. A name given bindery workers around the turn of the century who jogged (knocked) and stacked sections as they came from the folding machines. Knocking up sections, in which some 15,000 workers were employed in the United States at the turn of the century, was one of the last hand operations in the large edition bindery. (89)

knocking down (knock down). The process of flattening any lumps or other high places on the covers of a book caused by the cords laced into the boards. (256, 335)

knocking-down iron. A heavy, T-shaped piece of iron, which, when clamped in a press, forms a solid base for hammering down the cords used to lace the boards to the book, or for a similar type of binding operation. (237)

knocking out the groove. The process employed when rebinding a book that was backed in the original binding, in which the bend in each section caused by the backing is removed. In library binding this is frequently accomplished by nipping the book before the sections are separated. In hand binding, one method is to hammer (three) sections together on the knocking-down iron, but a more gentle (and safer) method is to bend each section individually over the edge of a board thus reversing the backing fold. In the latter method there is no danger of disturbing the conformation of the paper fibers, as can happen when the section is hammered. (161, 355)

knocking out the swell. The process of reducing the "swell" in the spine of a book sewn through the folds by hand or on a sewing machine. The swell may be caused by the addition of thread in the folds of the sections, and also, at times, by the thickness of the paper used to guard damaged sections. Reducing the swell is a somewhat delicate operation, as it is necessary to have additional thickness in the spine in order to be able to round and back the book properly; too much swell, however, produces undesirable results, including a wedge shape, a greater tendency for the spine of the book to fall in, and a book that is lacking in firmness and solidity. Excessive swell may be reduced by clamping the text block in a lying press, placing the knocking-down iron against it, and tapping the side at the spine with a backing hammer, or, as in the case of library and edition binding, by smashing or nipping. (339)

knocking up. The process of evening up one or two edges of a pile of sheets so that they can be cut squarely, or for some other purpose requiring squared-up sheets. *See also:* JOG. (140)

Koberger, Anton (1440-1513). A Nürnberg printer and publisher and one of the most productive of all Nürnberg craftsmen of his time. Koberger's books are often in fine bindings, characterized by a floral diaper in the center panel of the upper cover, flanked by stems of ornamental foliage wound around a ragged staff. On the lower cover, there is usually no diaper; instead there are lozenge compartments formed by diagonal fillets often enclosing a characteristic tool—a griffin with scaly extended wings. Koberger's books frequently have the title lettered in large Gothic letters in gilt on the upper cover. The panels on the spine often contain large rosettes scattered in an irregular manner. While it has been suggested that the books published by the Koberger firm were bound there, the correspondence of the firm from 1493 to 1525 mentions neither bookbinding nor anything relating to the binding process. (141, 347)

kozo. *See:* PAPER MULBERRY.

kraft paper. A paper produced by a modified sulfate process, and employing only wood pulp. It is a relatively coarse paper and is known especially for its strength. Kraft paper is usually manufactured on a Fourdrinier machine and is generally given a regular machine-finished or machine-glazed surface. It can be watermarked, striped, or calendered, and has an acceptable surface for printing. Its natural unbleached color is brown, but it can be produced in lighter shades of brown, cream tints, and white, by the use of semi-bleached or fully bleached sulfate pulps. Kraft paper is generally made in basis weights from 25 to 60 pounds (24 × 36 − 500) but it is also made in weights ranging from 18 to 200 pounds. (17, 81, 323)

kraft process. *See:* SULFATE PROCESS.

Krause, Jacob (1526/7-1585). A German bookbinder who learned the craft in the workshop of the famous Augsburg merchant bankers. Krause was summoned to Dresden in 1566 and appointed "Binder to the Elector of Saxony." In the electoral decree appointing him to this position it is specifically stated that he should bind books in the "German, French, and Italian fashion." Among his numerous bindings there are a great number of blind-stamped pigskin bindings decorated with panels and rolls, as well as a group of richly gold tooled morocco and calfskin bindings which he bound for the Elector. Krause's bindings are noted for the technical excellence of their gold tooling, no gilder outside of France producing "à petits fers" gilding of such accuracy and perfection. In artistic merit, however, while a few of his bindings are considered to be excellent, most are thought to be very much overloaded with gold tooling and are too rich and "restless" to be considered completely successful. Krause's work, as well as that of his pupil and successor, Caspar Meuser, is also remarkable for the elaborately tooled and printed edges, on which there is often the arms of Saxony and his signature—I. K. F.—in small letters. (104, 141)

krieg block. A composite wooden block, about 30 inches square, composed of small uniform pieces of clear white pine, cut approximately 2 inches square and 3 inches long, all set on end, glued together and enclosed by a band of metal. Such a block is used by some bookbinders for cutting leather. (256)

L. 1. The Roman equivalent of 50. *See:* ROMAN NUMERALS. 2. A lower case letter l is the abbreviation for LEAF. (1)

label. A square or rectangular piece of leather, cloth, or paper, usually of a different color from that used for covering, and attached to the spine, or (occasionally) the upper cover of a book. Labels display, usually in gilt tooling or blocking, the title of the book, the volume number (if any), the author's name (sporadically before the late 18th century, but regularly since), and, since about 1800, the date of publication.

Labels came into use in England in about 1680 and by 1700 had generally replaced direct lettering on the spine of books. Two labels, one for the title and the second for the volume number came into use in England (probably from France) in about 1730. The title label was usually red and the volume label blue, and later green. Red and black labels have also been used. The so-called open-sided label, i.e., one without vertical side fillets was uncommon before 1795 and was probably introduced by ROGER PAYNE.

Originally, labels were almost always of leather, generally a thinly pared skin, and later SKIVER. Paper labels, printed from type, or occasionally engraved, began to be used in the second half of the 18th century on the paper spines of boarded books (the earliest known examples dating from 1765). They continued to be the usual method of titling boarded books even after this style of binding was for the most part superseded by publishers' cloth, i.e., the first quarter of the 19th century. They were also used on early cloth bindings, with decreasing frequency after 1832, when the technique of applying gold directly onto the cloth became feasible. *See also:* FLYSWING. (69, 156, 205, 236, 320)

label paper. A machine finish or English finish paper used for a variety of types of labels. Some such papers are supercalendered while others are coated on one side. They are specially sized for gumming and printing. (17)

lac. A resinous substance of insect origin, collected from twigs of several trees of the *Acacia* family. The substance is secreted as a form of protective scale

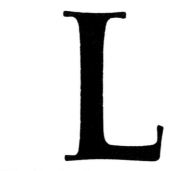

on the bodies of the insects *Coccus lacca,* which attach themselves to the twigs. The crude resin (stick lac) consists of twigs encrusted with the excretion of the insects' remains, and is processed in several steps to produce SHELLAC.

The blood-red dye obtained from lac was at one time the most valuable product of the refining process. It has been used a a dyestuff since very early times and was the dye used in Indian lake pigment.

The word "lac" and the term LAKE are derived from the Sanskrit *laksa,* meaning "a hundred thousand." One of the host trees referred to in Sanskrit writings is "Lakshatarn," the tree which nourishes a hundred thousand insects. (195, 233)

lace binding. A style of embellishment of leather bindings introduced in France in the 18th century. The border in use in the 17th century was enlarged until it became the predominant element of the design, so much so that often only space for an armorial shield was left. Edges, which formerly had been straight, were now tooled in a wavy pattern, thus giving a "lacy" effect at times described as "à la dentelle," but actually looking more like the wrought ironwork of fancy balconies and gates. The style was very popular and was used by many bookbinders and gilders, including the Derome family and Pierre-Paul Dubisson, who used metal plates instead of tools, so as to be able to block the design and thus increase production. (158)

laced on. *See:* LACING-IN.

laces. The single-twist knitting cotton about 1/16 inch in diameter, or double-twist cotton about 3/32 inch in diameter, with or without tags; it is used for

loose-leaf bindings and also for attaching leaves loosely in temporary covers. The tags, if used, may be straight or crossed.

lacework. A border decoration on a book cover, executed by tooling in gilt in resemblance of lace. *See:* LACE BINDING. *See also:* DENTELLE.

lacing. A form of book decoration usually used on blankbooks, and consisting of narrow strips of vellum laced to the outside of the covers. The vellum laces pass through the boards and are hammered flat inside so as not to appear as lumps under the board papers. *See also:* BANDS (2). (343)

lacing-in. The process in craft bookbinding of attaching the boards to the text block by passing the bands or cords on which the book is sewn through holes punched or cut into the boards. The bands are first frayed out and moistened with paste and then passed through the holes or slots.

For more than a thousand years lacing-in has been the customary method of attaching the boards in craft bookbinding. The Stonyhurst Gospel, a Coptic style binding of the 7th or 8th century, has the sewing thread laced through its boards, while in bindings of the 11th century or earlier, which were sewn on raised thongs, the thongs run along tunnels and through holes, and are held in place by pegs. By the 13th century, or even earlier, thongs were run over the upper sides of the boards, sometimes in grooves cut to receive them. This technique persisted up to the 15th century.

Wooden boards usually had two or three holes in a straight line out from the location of the thong on the spine; later on, however, the holes were cut straight, sometimes at a diagonal, or at right angles to the thong. Diagonal holing and lacing-in became the favored technique, and was the superior method because it strengthened the binding, particularly since boards made of paper had largely replaced wooden boards. The right angle method has the disadvantage of weakening the board.

Although the cords in fine binding were frayed out so they would not be noticeable under the leather, fraying out was not done in other styles of binding, and the technique of cutting grooves to receive the cords was not introduced until the end of the 18th century. Grooving is a superior technique because it does not weaken the board to any extent and yet allows thicker cords to be used in sewing.

The practice of lacing-in began to decline in the 19th century in favor of split boards and the French joint. *See also:* HOLING OUT. (236)

lacquer. A surface coating of an organic material that dries solely by the evaporation of the solvent and without any chemical change taking place in the film. The most important lacquers are based on cellulose derivatives, e.g., a cellulose ester, such as cellulose acetate or cellulose nitrate, or a cellulose

ether, such as methyl or benzyl cellulose, etc., together with modifying agents, such as plasticizers, resins, waxes, and pigments. Lacquers are used in coating cloth, leather, and paper to decrease water vapor transmission rates and provide heat-sealing properties, water and grease resistance, and gloss, as well as decorative effects. Their use in archival work is questionable, however, as the solvents used in them emit toxic fumes, and the films themselves begin to deteriorate after a relatively short time, particularly if exposed to ultraviolet light.

lacquered bindings. A method of decorating bookbindings by means of scenes painted and then covered with

lacquer. The technique was probably a Persian (Near Eastern) invention of the second quarter of the 16th century, and while they are still being produced today, the technique reached its pinnacle in the 16th century. Lacquered bindings are actually more the work of the miniature painter than the bookbinder. The designs were painted in watercolors on leather, and later pasteboard, that had been dusted with chalk and given a thin coat of clear lacquer. After painting had been completed several more coatings of lacquer were applied. (347)

lactic acid. A hygroscopic, usually syrupy, alpha-hydroxy acid ($C_3H_6O_3$), usually manufactured by the bacterial fermentation of milk, cane or grape sugars, corn, starch, etc., by means of *Lactic bacilli*, and used in leather manufacture to control pH, in mordanting dyes, and in the potassium salt POTASSIUM LACTATE.

lacuna (pl. **lacunae;** anglicized: **lacunas**). An area of a manuscript, painting, or other material, that is completely missing as a result of any type of damage. The word derives from the Latin expression for "gap."

laid lines. The closely spaced watermark lines in LAID PAPER, produced by the laid wires of the MOLD (1) in handmade paper, or by the DANDY ROLL of the papermaking machine. Laid lines usually run parallel to the long side of a sheet of handmade paper and across the grain of machine-made paper; however, SPIRAL LAID paper has lines parallel with the grain. Also called "wire lines" or "wire marks," as opposed to CHAIN LINES (1). (52, 225)

laid mold. A MOLD (1) having the sieve made up of wires laid parallel to each other, as compared with a woven mold formed of wire cloth. It is used in making handmade LAID PAPER.

laid paper. A paper which shows thick and thin lines at right angles to each other, and produced by the weave of the DANDY ROLL in machine-made paper, or, in the manufacture of handmade paper, by the MOLD (1) having thin wires placed very close together and fastened to thicker wires running at right angles at intervals of about 1 inch. The thin wires are the LAID LINES, or "wire lines," "wire marks," while the thicker wires are the CHAIN LINES, or "chain marks," "wide lines." Laid paper, whether hand- or machine-made, has no advantage over WOVE PAPER except perhaps appearance. (58, 156, 182)

lake. A term used with reference to any

LACING-IN

slots are parallel to square grooves

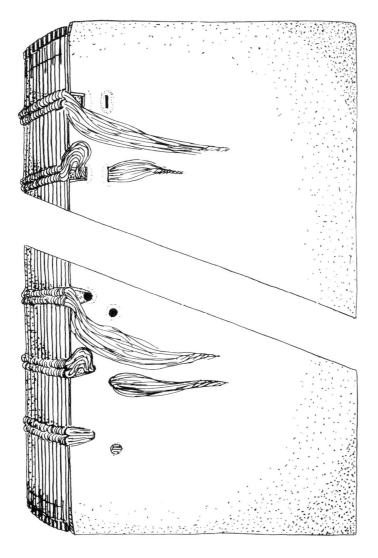

holes are diagonally placed

of a large group of organic pigments that are generally bright in color and are more or less translucent when in the form of an oil paint. Lakes are obtained by precipitating dyestuffs and other coloring matters, e.g., cochineal, madder, logwood extract, etc., onto a substrate in the presence of tannic acid, casein, sodium phosphate, etc., or with a metallic hydroxide. Aluminum hydroxide, for example, reacts with many soluble organic coloring matters, precipitating them as so-called lakes in cloth printing and dyeing, with the hydroxide acting as the mordant; the same dye, however, can produce different colored lakes depending on the mordant employed. Because many salts of calcium, chromium, magnesium, tin, zinc, etc., are used in producing lakes, a great number of pigments can be obtained. Substrates used include alumina, which gives a pigment that is rich and transparent in color, such as those used in printing inks; china clay, where a light, soft material with bulk and good suspension properties is required; barytes, which are used in the manufacture of paint; blanc fixe, which is usually a more finely divided baryte than the natural crystalline ones; and green earth and precipitated hydroxide of iron, which are used according to color requirements.

Many excellent pigments having good light fastness are now made from artificial dyestuffs; therefore, because they are expensive and/or insufficiently light fast, many lakes formerly produced from natural dyestuffs are no longer in demand.

The term "lake" may derive from the Italian "lacca," used by medieval Italian craftsmen to indicate the scum they removed from their dye vats and sold to painters. The Italian word, in turn, is related to "lac," which derives from the Sanskrit. *See:* LAC. (17, 195)

lambskin. The tanned skin of a young sheep. Vegetable tanned lambskin was highly prized in the latter part of the 19th century as a bookbinding leather because of its delicate colors, and also for limp bindings because of its softness and freedom from scratches and other blemishes. Lambskin is similar in appearance to calfskin but is less durable. *See also:* SHEEPSKIN. (261)

laminate. 1. To unite (superimpose layers of material) by the use of an adhesive, or by other means, such as heat, pressure, or both. 2. A product made by bonding together two or more layers of material or materials. (309)

laminated board. A binder's, or other

type of board built up in layers by pasting or gluing two or more plies of board together either with the grain (machine) direction of the boards running in the same direction (parallel laminated) or at right angles to each other (cross laminated), or by applying paper, plastic film, or other sheet material, to one or both sides of a board. Laminated boards are often used in the binding and rebinding of large books, such as art folios, large periodicals, and the like.

laminating film. The film used to encapsulate a leaf, map, etc., undergoing LAMINATION. The "ideal" laminating film should: 1) be flexible, i.e., capable of withstanding all the flexing and folding that is required of the paper being protected throughout the useful life of the document; 2) be (considerably) stronger than the paper it protects. (Since the majority of papers found in archival collections exhibit an elongation of about 2% upon rupture, the film should offer satisfactory strength at an elongation of less than 2% to protect the document, and should also have sufficient strength to make reinforcement with tissue unnecessary); 3) have considerable elongation beyond the yield point of a stress-strain curve. (Because high edge tearing resistance is usually associated with high elongation, a narrow margin of film around the edges of a document would protect it in case of strain at the edges); 4) have properties enabling it to resist degradation; 5) be capable of being joined to the document with minimum effort, preferably without application of heat and pressure; 6) permit separation of the film from the paper with minimum effort and without damage to the document; 7) be resistant to abrasion; 8) be transparent to light, at least throughout the visible spectrum; and 9) contain no elements or other substances which might in any way damage the document it protects. (303, 364)

lamination. A method of protecting and preserving embrittled or otherwise weak papers, maps, etc., by placing them between sheets of thin, transparent thermoplastic material, which, when subjected to heat and pressure, with or without an adhesive, seals the paper in and protects it by making it more or less impervious to atmospheric conditions. It also increases its effective strength.

The paper is first deacidfied and dried. It is then placed between two layers of cellulose acetate film ap-

proximately 0.001 inch thick. Layers of Japanese tissue or lens tissue are then placed over the film. The "sandwich" is then fed through heated rollers under pressure, emerging as a sheet slightly thicker and heavier than the original document and considerably stiffer and stronger.

Lamination is an excellent method of improving the mechanical strength of documents which are to receive considerable handling, but it also has both real and potential disadvantages. Unless the document is properly and adequately deacidified before it is laminated, it will continue to deteriorate despite the illusion of protection afforded by the laminating film. In addition, there is the slight but definite loss of clarity and sharpness of the printed matter, especially in the case of colored illustrations. It is also difficult to remove the document from the laminates. *See:* DELAMINATION (2). Finally, there is potential damage from the cellulose acetate itself, which may be more vulnerable to the action of the atmospheric gases such as sulfur dioxide, particularly if the acetate contains metallic impurities. *See also:* BARROW, WILLIAM J.; LAMINATING FILM; SUNDEX PROCESS. (33, 35, 72, 173, 198, 218, 303, 364)

lampblack. A finely divided, bulky, black soot, at one time the most important black pigment used in the manufacture of printing inks. It is produced by the imperfect combustion of pitch resin or tung oil, or fatty substances, such as naphthalene, in a vessel within a tent made of paper or sheepskin. The smoke is deposited on the inside of the tent which is then beaten to cause the soot to fall off. The soot is then heated several times to a very high temperature in a metal container having a small opening in the top, through which the impurities escape. *See also:* CARBONACEOUS INKS; CHINESE INK. (156, 235)

landscape. *See:* OBLONG.

landscape binding. A style of decoration featuring landscape scenes, executed either by freehand drawing with Chinese ink or acid, printing, or by some form of painting. The earliest recorded is 1777, while others are mentioned in the 1820s. (156, 236)

landscape gilding. *See:* GILT ON LANDSCAPES.

lanolin. A widely occurring crude preparation of cholesterol and its esters. Some lanolins are derived by solvent extraction from the sebaceous glands of wooled sheepskins. The molten wax is washed with alkaline (carbonate) solutions followed by water alone. When pure, lanolin is white and odorless, has excellent emulsifying properties and does not readily turn rancid. It has a softening range of 58 to 62° C. Lanolin is employed as one of the constituents of leather dressings, and is valuable because of its powers of penetration, its favorable softening range, and its ability to supply body to the dressing. Also called "wool wax." (218, 235)

lapis-lazuli. 1. A deep blue, semi-precious stone, which, when ground into a powder, was used as ultramarine, a pigment now produced synthetically. It is a metamorphic rock, and its color stems from the blue feldspathoid lazurite, which is normally (NaAlSiO₄ · Na₂S); however, the properties may vary significantly in both the natural and synthetic products. It is used from time to time in the ornamentation of bookbindings and the coloring of paper. 2. A clear blue marble veined with gold. The blue is in the form of large irregular spots, of a cloudlike appearance, becoming an increasingly darker shades of blue as the color is applied several times. The gold veins are produced by gilding. (152, 235)

large paper copy (large paper edition). A copy of a book printed on larger and (frequently) a better quality paper than that used for the usual trade edition, thus giving it more extensive margins. Large paper copies are printed from the same type as the rest of the edition, but often margins have been reset to provide a wider margin at the gutter as well as the other edges. Large paper copies are recorded in England dating from the 1590s, becoming increasingly popular until well into the 19th century. *See also:* FINE PAPER COPY; LIMITED EDITION; SMALL PAPER COPY. (12, 156)

last fold. A term sometimes applied to the final or back fold which completes the section, bringing it to the proper page sequence for gathering. (256)

lateral porosity. The POROSITY of paper in a direction parallel to the plane of the sheet. It is usually very much less than the porosity through the plane of the paper. Sometimes called "transverse porosity."

latex. A colloidal water dispersion of high polymers derived from sources related to natural rubber or of synthetic high polymers resembling natural rubber. Although originally applied to the milky sap found in the cells of certain plants, of which *Hevea brasilienes*

(from which natural rubber is obtained) is the most important, the term is now applied to many synthetic rubbers, paints, coatings, etc. Latex is used in paper manufacture as an adhesive and barrier coating, and also for impregnating book cloth. (17)

lattice stamp. A finishing tool, the distinguishing feature of which is a central diamond formed of lattice and crisscross work. It is generally found on blind stamped bindings of the late 15th and early 16th centuries. (250)

law binding. 1. A term applied from the 1830s until recently to a full leather binding (usually a vegetable tanned, lightweight, cream-colored sheepskin), having laced-in boards and two or more gold-blocked title labels on the spine (usually red above black); or a binding with creased bands on the spine and blind lines around the edges of the boards. 2. A modern version of the above, i.e., a case binding consisting of a light tan buckram made to resemble sheepskin, with red and black paper labels blocked in gold. *See also:* LAW BUCKRAM. (12)

law buckram. An obsolete term for a calf- or fawn-colored buckram made to resemble sheepskin, but without any graining. (256)

law calf. 1. A general term applied to an uncolored calfskin. 2. A cream-colored vegetable-tanned calfskin with a smooth grain surface, at one time used in covering the better grades of law books, but now largely superseded by buckram. Also called "fair calf," and, incorrectly, "law sheep." *See also:* LAW BINDING (1); LAW BUCKRAM. (154, 156, 264)

law sheep. A natural-colored, vegetable-tanned sheepskin, at one time used for covering law books, but now largely superseded by buckram. *See also:* LAW BINDING (1); LAW BUCKRAM; LAW CALF (2). (12)

law skiver. A very thin SKIVER, tanned and finished to a russet or natural color, and at one time used for title labels of law and medical books, but now largely superseded by paper labels. (274)

law super. A SPINE LINING FABRIC reinforced at intervals with heavier threads running across the width of the cloth, and consequently across the spine of the book. It was used in the past for lining the spines of large, heavy books. (339)

lay bands. 1. *See:* LAY CORDS. 2. *See:* CORDS; FLEXIBLE SEWING.

lay cords. The loops on the top bar of the SEWING FRAME to which the sew-

ing bands or cords are attached. *See also:* KEY. (304, 335)

lay down. An obsolete term applied to the process of embroidering a binding.

laying-away. The process of tanning hides and skins in layer vats over a long period of time in order to assure a full tannage. The hides or skins are dusted with finely ground raw vegetable tanning materials to provide additional tanning material. Laying-away, which was practiced in situations where only weak tan liquors were available, has been little used since the introduction of concentrated tan liquors. (363)

laying-bye. The process of covering a hide pack with salt during the curing process, and then allowing the hides to stand in order to permit the strong brine to thus penetrate the entire pack. (363)

laying-on. The operation of placing gold leaf on a surface prior to the application of a heated tool. The gold leaf is transferred from the GOLD CUSHION by means of a wad of cotton-wool, or a piece of felt. When the gold is in roll form, it is transferred directly from the roll to the surface to be gilded. In edge gilding, the leaf is transferred from the cushion by means of a GILDER'S TIP. (140, 256)

lay on (laying-on boards). An obsolete term for the process of cutting and fitting the boards to the text block in preparation for LACING-IN. (256)

layout. 1. The process of arranging piles of sections in proper sequence in an "aisle" or "alley" for gathering by hand. 2. The plan of an entire book. 3. A plan, prepared by or for a printer, giving the arrangement of the matter, type faces, size of type, position of illustration and captions, etc. for a job of printing. (12, 156)

leaching. In leather manufacture, the process of extracting the tannin from finely ground raw, vegetable-tanning materials by means of steam and/or water.

leaf. 1. One of the units resulting from folding a sheet of paper, vellum, etc., into a section (signature). A leaf consists of two pages, one on each side, either or both of which may be blank, or may bear printing, writing, or illustrative matter. Blank leaves generally are not numbered. 2. A newly formed sheet of handmade paper before it is dried and finished. It is more appropriately called a WATERLEAF (3). 3. *See:* ALUMINUM LEAF; DUTCH GOLD; GOLD LEAF; PALLADIUM LEAF; PLATINUM LEAF; SILVER LEAF. (156, 234)

leafcasting. A system by which archival papers can be repaired by mechanical means rather than manually. The principal of the method is similar to that of papermaking itself: paper pulp in a water suspension is pulled through areas of loss in a document so as to fill the lacunae with freshly cast paper. Varying combinations of fibers are mixed in amounts proportionate to the missing areas in the leaf to be repaired, and gravity or vacuum pressure pulls the paper slurry through the leaf to be repaired as it lies on a mesh support in the leafcaster. The new fibers settle only in the areas of loss.

For certain kinds of materials, particularly those of large format, e.g., newspapers and maps, leafcasting is a much more efficient and economical method of repair than the traditional manual methods. Its use can also strengthen the entire leaf, as leafcasting not only fills in the holes but also fills cracks, joins fragments, repairs

margins and may also be used to provide linings. In contrast to hand repairs, these procedures have the additional advantage of requiring little or no use of adhesives.

leaflet. In a restricted sense, a publication consisting of two to four pages printed on a small sheet folded once, but not stitched or bound. In a broader sense, a small thin pamphlet. (156, 256)

leather. The outer covering from an animal (usually a mammal) tanned, or otherwise dressed and prepared in such a manner as to render it usable and resistant to putrefaction, even when wet. Leather is a unique and flexible sheet material that is somewhat analogous to textiles, and may in fact be considered to be the first and only *natural* fabric.

The unique characteristics of leather are due largely to its structure, which is an interwoven, three-dimensional network of fibers inherent in the nat-

ural raw materials—hides and skins. This raw material is principally a fibrous protein called collagen and is composed of one continuous network of fibers.

In the raw skin, at least four distinct structures can be distinguished: 1) the thin outermost layer termed the EPIDERMIS; 2) the grain layer or dermal surface; 3) the juncture between the grain layer and the dermis or corium; and 4) the major portion of the skin (the DERMIS or corium), which is the part converted into leather. In addition, there is the flesh layer, or hypodermis, which is the structure adjacent to the body tissues.

Before tannage, the *approximate* composition of a freshly flayed hide is:

Water	64 %
Protein	33 %
Fats	2 %
Mineral salts	0.5%
Other substances (pigments, etc.)	0.5%

The 33% which is protein consists of:

1) Structural proteins, or		
Elastin (yellow fiber woven in the collagen fiber)		0.3%
Collagen (which tans to give leather)	29	%
Keratin (protein of the hair and epidermis)	2	%
2) Non-structural proteins, or		
Albumens or globulins (soluble, non-fibrous proteins)	1	%
Mucins or mucoids (mucous materials associated with fibers)		.7%

While *all* mammalian skin is made up of these constituents, the figure for keratin will vary widely, depending on the amount of hair present; the figure for fat will also vary. The division between albumen and mucins is debatable.

Beginning with the outer surface of a skin, there are: 1) the hairs, embedded in the skin, each in a sheath of epidermis known as the hair follicle and each with a hair root at its end, fed by a tiny blood vessel. Chemically the hairs consist of the protein keratin, and penetrate deeply into the papillary layer of the dermis. *See:* HAIR. Most animals have hair of two types, primary and secondary. The positions which these hairs occupy relative to each other as they enter the surface of the skin, together with their different thicknesses, determine the characteristic marking or *grain* of the

LEATHER

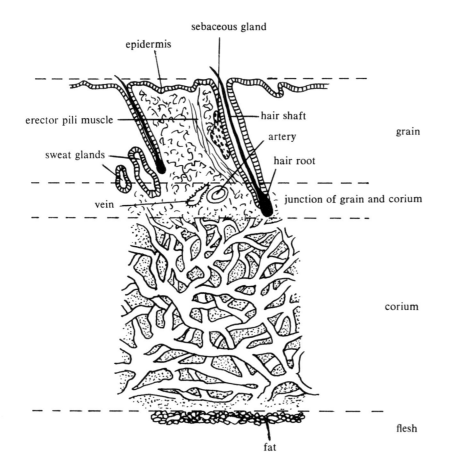

dermal surface, i.e., the grain pattern of the leather, which is exposed upon removal of the hair and other epidermal structures; 2) the epidermis, which is a protective, hard-wearing layer of keratinous cells. Those on the outside are dead and, upon drying and shrinking, fall off the skin. On the underside, adjacent to the skin proper, they consist of soft, jellylike living cells, which have little resistance and are readily attacked and degraded by bacterial action or enzymes, as occurs with stale skins or in enzyme unhairing. They are usually disintegrated by alkalis, especially sodium sulfide or hydrosulfide. *See:* LIMING; UNHAIRING; 3) the sudoriferous (sweat) glands, which are also lined with epidermal tissue and discharge sweat from the skin through the pores in the grain surface, and the sebaceous glands, which are located at the side of the hair follicles and discharge into them an oily, waxy substance, which protects the hair. (The gland is operated by a muscle, called the erector pili, which also causes the hair to stand upright); 4) the skin proper or dermis (corium), consisting of a network of collagen fibers, very intimately woven and joined together. In the grain layer these fibers become thin and tightly woven and are so interlaced that there are no loose ends on the surface beneath the epidermis. Thus, when the epidermis is removed, a smooth layer is revealed (sometimes known as the HYALINE LAYER), which gives the characteristic grain surface of the leather. Toward the center of the dermis the fibers are coarser and stronger, and the predominant angle at which they are woven indicates the properties of the resultant leather. If the fibers are more upright and tightly woven, the leather will be firm and hard, with little stretch, while if they are more horizontal and loosely woven, the leather will be softer and stretchier. The dermis is also the strongest part of the skin; and 5) the flesh of the dermis, i.e., that layer next to the body wall of the animal, where the fibers have a more horizontal angle of weave, and fatty (adipose) tissue may also be present.

In the living skin, the collagen fibers and cells are embedded in a watery jelly of proteinlike substance, called the GROUND SUBSTANCE. The living collagen fibers are formed from this substance, which ranges in constitution from the blood sugars to substances which are almost collagen. The

latter fibers have been called "inter-fibrillary" proteins, also known as non-structural proteins, or pro-collagens. These are essential for the growth of the skin and also render the fiber structure nonporous. When the skin is dried (as in some forms of curing), they dry to a hard, gluelike substance, which cements all of the corium fibers together and makes the skin hard and horny. In producing a leather which is to be soft or supple, it is essential that these inter-fibrillary proteins be removed.

The corium fibers are composed of ropelike bundles of smaller fibrils, which in turn consist of bundles of sub-microscopic micelles. These in turn are made up of very long, thread-like molecules of collagen twisted together. All together, this gives a very tough, strong, flexible, three-dimensional structure, forming a network on which many of the qualities of leather depend. It is this structure which makes leather unique for, as of today, it has not been possible to produce it artificially. It is also unquestionably the basis for the remarkably high tensile strength of leather.

The skin also contains small arteries and veins which convey blood to the living tissues, as well as the nerve structures necessary for the sense of touch.

While all mammalian skins are structured along this basic pattern, they vary tremendously in size, e.g., from the hide of an elephant or ox to the skin of a rabbit or mouse, and they also vary considerably in shape and thickness. In addition, some animals have but little hair or wool and a thick epidermal layer—e.g., the pig—while others, such as the sheep, have a heavy fleece with curly wool and curly hair follicles but a relatively thin epidermis. The state of development of the animal is also important. A calf, for example, has finer structured hair than a full grown cow, consequently, leather made from the skin of a calf is relatively smooth and very fine-grained, while that of a cow is rougher and has a very pronounced grain pattern.

The skins of certain animals (at certain times of their lives) also contain considerable quantities of fat in globular cells, which lie approximately in the center of the dermis. Notable examples are the pig and sheep. Sheepskin may actually contain fat of this type, that is, in the interior of the skin and not merely on the flesh layer,

amounting to 25% of the weight of the skin. Such excessive growth of fat cells disrupts and weakens the dermal fiber structure to such an extent that some sheepskins can be split into two layers along the line where the fat is located.

In general, the younger the animal at time of slaughter the thinner and smaller the skin, the smoother and finer the grain structure, and the less liklihood of damage due to disease, scratches, insects, etc. *See:* LEATHER DEFECTS. The more natural the animal's feeding and living conditions, the better the quality of the resultant leather; overfeeding, for example, produces greasier, weaker skins, while starvation results in thin, weak, mis-shapen skins showing skeleton markings. The skin of the female is usually finer grained than that of the male, and has a looser fiber structure, especially in the flanks, giving a somewhat softer, stretchier leather. The less hair or wool there is on the animal the tougher and stronger the resultant leather, especially in the grain layer. Heavily wooled Merino sheep, for example, are inferior in this respect to goats and pigs.

Leather occupies a unique position among the covering materials used by bookbinders. Its structure gives it a very desirable softness and strength, while its chemical nature gives it the property of adhering well to paper, board, linen, etc. Its outstanding characteristics include its durability (when properly prepared and cared for), suppleness, porosity, beauty, temper and feel, in addition to its strength and softness. In terms of permanence, when properly tanned, stored, and maintained (*See:* LEATHER DRESSINGS), it is probably the most permanent covering material known at this time.

The manufacture of leather predates recorded history. There is evidence that some leather samples found in Northern Germany may have been produced perhaps 12,000 years ago. Leather artifacts believed to date from the Neolithic and European Bronze Ages have been discovered, and it is an established fact that the Egyptians knew the art of vegetable tanning, as well as alum tawing, as long ago as 2000 B.C., and that tanning practices there were well established by 1600 B.C.

Leather has been used for covering books since at least as early as the 3rd century A.D. (*See:* COPTIC BINDINGS), and its use in craft bookbinding continues to this day. Although virtually every conceivable type of skin has been used, calf, deer, goat, pig, and sheepskin, as well as horsehide (RUSSIA LEATHER) have been used most often, at least in Europe and the United States. Pigskin, as well as goatskin and deerskin, were often alumtawed; however, vegetable tannage was and is the predominant method of preparation. Goatskin has been used to cover books in Europe for more than a thousand years and has been used extensively in Europe since the 16th century. *See:* VEGETABLE TANNING; VEGETABLE TANNINS. *See also:* ALLIGATOR LEATHER; AMERICAN RUSSIA; BABY CALF; BUCKSKIN; BUFFALO; CABRETTA LEATHER; CALFSKIN; CHAMOIS; CHEVRETTE; CHEVROTAIN; CORDOBAN LEATHER; CORDOVAN LEATHER; COWHIDE; DEERSKIN; DOE SKIN; GOATSKIN; HAIR SHEEP; HOGSKIN; KANGAROO SKIN; LAMBSKIN; MOROCCO; PARCHMENT; PIGSKIN; SEALSKIN; SHEEPSKIN; VELLUM; WALRUS HIDE. (26, 83, 207, 236, 248, 282, 291, 292, 306, 343, 351, 352, 353, 362, 363)

leatherboard. An imitation leather typically produced by pulping and compressing scrap leather and wood pulp. (310)

leather bound. A general term applied to a book bound in full or part leather.

leather cloth. A polyvinyl chloride- or cellulose nitrate-surfaced fabric, usually made of cotton, or a plastic material with a similar surface. It is used principally in covering blankbooks. (81, 353)

leather defects. Imperfections in the grain surface or structure of a hide or skin resulting in unsightly appearance and/ or weakness of the resultant leather. Such defects may have arisen during the life of the animal, or may have developed in the flaying and/or preparation of the stock.

Damages caused during life include: 1) scars, resulting from scratches or cuts. (When the cut is healing, the fibers grow densely packed together, and the healed skin is often hard, raised, and lacking hair follicles. Scar damage is also caused by branding the animal for ownership purposes, usually in the butt area, which is the best part of the hide); 2) infestations, such as ticks, warble flies, and mange. (Ticks pierce the skin to suck blood, leaving holes that look either like pin pricks or minor scars in the grain of the leather. This defect occurs mainly in the belly areas of the skin. Sarcoptic mange mites enter the epidermis and tunnel around, causing the cells to multiply

and the hair to fall out. The grain surface becomes roughened, and the animal generally compounds the damage by rubbing to relieve the itching. In demodectic, or follicular, mange, the mites penetrate into the dermis itself, where a wall of fibers is formed to surround and "encyst" them. The cysts generally are seen on the grain of unhaired skins as small swollen nodules. Tanning and drying processes shrink the contents of the cysts, causing the grain surface to sink over the cavity so that the defects are seen as shallow depressions, though the grain surface itself is not generally damaged. *See also:* WARBLES); 3) infections. (If ringworm, which is a fungus, heals it leaves no scars, but if the animal is slaughtered while still infected, the grain appears coarse at the site of the infection); and 4) cockle, which occurs in wooled sheep immediately before shearing. (This defect appears as boil-like hard spots, of varying size, which occur in rows at right angles to the spine from the shoulder to the butt, and, while the defect disappears rapidly after shearing, it cannot be eliminated during manufacture of the leather.)

Damages caused after death include: 1) flaycuts and gouges, which cut into the fibers of the dermis. (In thin leathers they show through and thereby spoil the grain. Some flaycuts go completely through the hide or skin, ruining it completely. These kinds of cuts are usually the result of careless or improper flaying); 2) putrefaction, which is the result of bacterial growth which starts almost immediately once the animal is dead, unless the skin is properly cured, especially on the exposed flesh side. *See:* PUTREFACTIVE DAMAGE; 3) veininess, in which branching lines of blood vessels can be seen on the flesh side. (If, because of poor curing or old age, for example, the structure around them becomes loose, the skin is said to be veiny, and the branching pattern of the veins usually shows through on the grain side. Veininess can actually at times be attractive in some skins, such as VELLUM, for example); and 4) damage from heat, which may occur on hides and skins in tropical areas. (It is a common fault with ground-dried skins.) *See:* SUN DAMAGE. *See also:* BLEEDING (5); BLOOM (1); CRUSTY BREAK; DRAWN FLANKS; KISS MARKS; PIPEY LEATHER; PIPING (1); SLACK TANNED; SPEW. (248, 291, 306, 363)

leather dressings. Substances, or mixtures of substances, applied to leather book-

bindings to prevent or retard deterioration, preserve, and, to limited extent, restore flexibility to leather. Over the past one hundred years or so a great number of different leather dressings of varying degrees of effectiveness have been used to impart new life to deteriorating leather. These treatments have ranged from simple paste-washing and/or coating with varnish to more-or-less carefully formulated and tested preparations. Most of the latter contain an oil which may be of animal, vegetable, or mineral origin, in order of probable decreasing relative value as preservatives. While such dressings may preserve, and to some extent restore, the flexibility of the leather, they cannot prevent *chemical decay,* nor can they restore leather that has become decayed because of chemical influences.

The majority of leather dressings contain lanolin as their principal fatty component. Lanolin has sufficient capability to exchange water with the surrounding atmosphere and to maintain relatively long-term flexibility and softness of HANDLE in the leather. Most dressings also contain one or more of the following substances: beeswax (or some other harder or softer wax, such as candellila, spermaceti, carnauba, etc.), cedarwood oil, n-hexane (or benzene), potassium carbonate, potash alum, isopropanol (or ethanol), thymol (or p-nitrophenol or o-phenylphenol), and neat's-foot oil. Beeswax is said to give body to the surface of the leather which can then be polished to impart a glossy finish. (See further comments below concerning the use of wax.) Cedarwood oil provides protection against mold growth and insect attack. The n-hexane or benzene acts as a solvent to get the lanolin into the leather, but according to some authorities, usually evaporates so rapidly that it actually is of little benefit. Furthermore, such hydrocarbons are flammable as well as toxic, and benzene is extremely toxic. The alcohols, isopropanol and ethanol, are sometimes added to a dressing to promote the penetration of the lanolin, and also to permit the use of a wider range of organic substances—e.g., fungicides, such as thymol—to be included. The metallic salts, such as potassium carbonate or potash alum, are said to help in binding the fats to the leather fibers. Neats'-foot oil is another fat used to lubricate the fibers of the leather.

The use of hard waxes in leather dressings is very controversial. Some argue that their use reduces the danger of penetration of harmful atmospheric gases into the leather, e.g., sulfur dioxide, which can be converted into destructive sulfuric acid. Others, however, contend that wax decreases the capability of the lanolin to exchange water with the surrounding atmosphere and that the lanolin itself will reduce the ingress of harmful gases. It is also argued that the wax causes treated volumes to stick together on the bookshelf, and even worse, that repeated applications may result in building up a heavy wax surface which eventually cracks and flakes, taking pieces of leather with it.

A simple, economical, and certainly widely used, dressing consists of a mixture of 60% neat's-foot oil (20°C, cold test) and 40% anhydrous lanolin, or 60% lanolin and 40% neat's-foot oil, depending upon the temperature and relative humidity in the area of use. This dressing offers some important advantages over many other preparations. It is (relatively) less expensive, easy to prepare and apply, non-toxic, non-flammable, and contains nothing, insofar as is known at this time, that could possibly damage the leather. *See also:* P. I. R. A. TESTED; POTASSIUM LACTATE. (148, 265, 291)

leatherette. A covering fabric produced from a strong, machine-glazed base paper, which is coated and embossed, or printed and embossed, in imitation of grained leather. (139)

leather fillers. Substances, such as starch paste, isinglass, etc., used to fill the pores of leather before gilding, so as to cause the gold leaf to adhere better. The filler helps keep the glair on the surface of the leather. (194)

leather flyleaf. A free flyleaf made of leather, generally of the same type of skin as used in covering, although thinner and possibly of a different color. The leather flyleaf is generally used in conjunction with the leather DOUBLURE (1). (343)

leather gauge. An instrument used to measure the thickness of leather, either in ounces or millimeters. *See also:* IRON (2); LEATHER SUBSTANCE TABLE; OUNCE.

leather glove. A heavy leather "glove" which fits over the thumb only, and is used to steady the finisher's hand in starting the heated lettering or finishing tool. (130)

leather hinges (leather joints). Endpaper hinges made of leather and designed to add strength at the point where the endpaper flexes. They are used with simple folded endpapers in either of two ways—by sewing them in with the endpapers while the book is being sewn, or by pasting them down on top of the endpapers after covering. Leather hinges (or joints) have been used since the 17th century in Europe, and between 1750 and 1800 they were a fairly common feature of the best English morocco and Russia bindings. They were usually heavily embellished with fillets, rolls, and small tools. (83, 236, 335)

leather marble. A method of coloring leather so as to obtain something of a marbled effect. The skins are dampened and rolled into a ball, each skin being carefully arranged so that no large area of any one is hidden in the folds. The ball of skins is then immersed in the dye, which colors the skins at the edges only, resulting in a kind of marbling effect. (164)

leatheroid. An obsolete name for an IMITATION LEATHER consisting of chemically treated paper combined with rubber and sandarac. *See also:* LEATHERETTE. (256)

leather substance table. The measurement of the thickness of a finished leather, in millimeters (1 mm. = 0.03937 inch), irons (1 iron = 1/48 inch), or ounces (1 ounce = 1/64 inch):

Inch	Ounces	Irons	Millimeters
1/64	1	.75	0.4
1/32	2	1.5	.8
3/64	3	2.25	1.2
1/16	4	3.0	1.6
5/64	5	3.75	2.0
3/32	6	4.5	2.4
7/64	7	5.25	2.8
1/8	8	6.0	3.2
9/64	9	6.75	3.6
5/32	10	7.5	4.0
11/64	11	8.25	4.4
3/16	12	9.0	4.8
13/64	13	9.75	5.2
7/32	14	10.5	5.6
15/64	15	11.25	6.0
1/4	16	12.0	6.4
17/64	17	12.75	6.8
9/32	18	13.5	7.2

(306)

leaves. 1. Finishing tools cut in the shape of leaves that are symmetrical in shape and generally curving in different directions. 2. *See:* LEAF. (161)

lecithin. A lipoid, or fatty acid, substance found in all animal and vegetable cells. Commercial lecithin is a mixture of phosphatides and glycerides obtained in the manufacture of soybean oil. It is soluble in mineral oils and fatty acids and is dispersible in animal and vegetable oils. It is one of the most effective materials used to assist in the formation and stabilization of emulsions.

lederschnitt bindings. *See:* CUIR-CISELÉ.

ledger binding. *See:* BLANKBOOK BINDING; STATIONERY BINDING.

ledger paper. Originally, a writing paper used for pen and ink records, as in ledger or blankbooks, but now also used for printing purposes. Ledger papers are generally made from cotton fiber, bleached chemical wood pulps, or mixtures thereof. High quality ledger papers are animal sized, and the usual ledger paper is made in basis weights ranging from 24 to 36 pounds (17 × 22 − 500). As it is subjected to considerable usage, it requires a high degree of durability and permanence. Significant properties include strength, especially tearing resistance, erasibility, water and ink resistance, uniformity of surface and color, smoothness, and a good surface for ruling. (17, 58, 339)

legal buckram. *See:* ENGLISH LINEN.

Legrain, Pierre (1889–1929). An outstanding French bookbinding designer of the 20th century. Legrain's early career was that of illustrator and theater painter, and it was not until 1917 that he became associated with the bibliophile Jacques Doucet and became interested in bookbinding. Under Doucet's encouragement Legrain literally established the profession of artist-designer of bookbindings in France. Although he never himself bound a book he abandoned the restrictions of tradition in book decoration, and established, by means of his adaption of artistic traits of contemporary art, the course of creative bookbinding in France for decades to come. Letter forms (titles, etc.) were an important part of his designs, and in his most mature style, he used color and texture of leather, as well as conventional tools and onlays of traditional binding, in new and imaginative designs related to abstract art. (89, 347)

Leighton, Archibald (1784–1841). An English bookbinder who is generally credited with the introduction of the first practical cloth for covering books. Although William Pickering may have introduced cloth earlier, and though woven flax canvas had been used for covering school books in England as early as 1770, it was not until about 1823 that a cloth more-or-less impervious to glue was used as a covering material. Leighton's first cloth was a dyed and glazed calico, with a starch filler. He dyed, stiffened, and patterned small rolls of calico in his own shop, and, by 1832, was embossing cloth with die-stamped patterns, and even blocking cloth with gold leaf. (89, 236, 286)

lemon. 18½ karat gold leaf. Because of the alloys used to reduce the gold from 24 to 18½ karat, it is lighter in color and somewhat thicker than the 23 or 23½ karat leaf more commonly used in book decoration, although not so much as PALE leaf. See also: GOLD LEAF. (130)

lemon oil. A fragrant yellow essential oil obtained from the skins of lemons. It is one of the several oils used to secure gold leaf temporarily to the covering material of a book before blocking or tooling. (264)

length of the book. A term used by some bookbinders to indicate the distance between the "X" points of the gathered sections marked up for sewing by hand. The "X" points indicate where the head and tail are to be trimmed, i.e., the "length of the book" being the distance between the "X" points. It is actually the height of the text block but not that of the finished book, unless it is a cut flush binding. (335)

lengthwise lettering. Lettering which runs vertically rather than horizontally on the spine of a bound book. The lettering generally runs from head to tail so that it may be read if the book is shelved horizontally with the upper cover uppermost. Lengthwise lettering is used for books meant to be shelved flat, e.g., newspapers, and also on books which are too thin for across the spine lettering without undue hyphenation or abbreviation. In the latter case it is common for library binders to make an additional charge for the lettering.

lens tissue. A thin paper made from long-fibered stock which contains no unbleached or mechanical wood pulps. The paper is usually soft and is free from abrasiveness, lint, or dusting. It is not calendered and is generally made in basis weights of 5½, 8½, and 16 pounds (24 × 36 — 500). Some lens tissues contain silicone, while others receive some form of wet strength treatment. The tissue is used in lamination and paper repair. (17)

Lesné, François A. D. A 19th-century French bookbinder who referred to himself as the "Poet-binder" because of his poems eulogizing bookbinding. Lesné is better known, however, for his development of a temporary soft-cover binding of plain calfskin which was said (by Lesné) to be an improvement over the BRADEL BINDING, developed earlier in the 19th century. Lesné's bind-

ing consisted of calf-covered boards sewn to a strip of linen; the sections themselves, however, were not sewn. It is not clear how the sections or leaves were secured to the linen, unless, as in a later American binding which infringed on Lesné's method, the boards were sewn to the linen at both spine and fore edge, thus creating a form of wrapper binding. In order not to deceive the buyer, Lesné stated that books so "bound" would bear the blind stamped inscription "Exposition de 1834. Cartonnages conservateurs de Lesné." (It was at this exposition that he received a bronze medal for his invention.) (89)

less-used materials specifications. See: LUMSPECS.

lettering. The process of marking a binding with author, title, or other distinguishing bibliographical information, and, in a loose sense, with accompanying ornamentation, e.g., lines, library imprints, etc. The lettering of hand-bound books is usually done either with individual letters (as in the best work), or with type set in a pallet. It is also done at times with straight lines or gouges. See: BUILT-UP LETTERING. Edition and library bindings are usually blocked (stamped), either in an automatic or hand-blocking machine.

Type sizes for lettering books generally range from 6 point (very small) to 36 point (relatively large), depending on several factors, including the size of the book and the relative degree of legibility desired. Design of the type face and proper arrangement of the lettering, however, are as important for legibility as is the size of the type. As a general rule, the factors governing lettering are: 1) only one type face should be used on an individual book or set of books; (2) spacing between lines should be logical and pleasing to the eye; 3) spacing between letters should be the same on all lines; and 4) the type size should be appropriate for the size of the volume. (83, 161, 259, 307, 343)

lettering pallet. A hand type-holder used to letter books by hand. The pallet has two viselike jaws which screw in from each end of the pallet and clamp the type securely in place. 2. An engraved device used to inscribe the same lettering, e.g., a library imprint, on the spines of books. (74, 130)

lettering size. A preparation used for sizing coated or impregnated book fabrics before blocking with gold leaf. It consists of equal parts of orange shellac and alcohol, one-fourth part ordinary

ammonia and one-fourth part ethyl acetate. Cloths that are to be blocked with gold or pigment foils do not have to be sized in this manner, as the foil contains its own size. (259)

letter piece (lettering piece). See: FLYSWING; LABEL; SKIVER.

letterpress. 1. See: LETTERPRESS BINDING. 2. The text of a book as distinguished from its illustrations. 3. Matter printed directly from a raised surface. See: LETTERPRESS PRINTING.

letterpress binding. One of the two major composite styles of bookbinding, the other being STATIONERY BINDING. Letterpress binding refers to the binding of books intended to be read, as distinct from books used for written records, i.e., books meant to be written in. The name derives from the time when all printing was done by letterpress. The major forms of letterpress binding include: EDITION BINDING, LIBRARY BINDING, and PAMPHLET BINDING, as well as the binding of books by hand. See also: BOOKBINDING. (343)

letterpress printing. Any printing produced from a raised, or relief, surface, as distinct from planographic or intaglio printing. It employs type or plates, or any letter or image cast or engraved in relief on a suitable surface. The ink is applied to the printing surface which is above all nonprinting areas or spaces (the exact opposite of gravure or intaglio printing). Impressions are then made by pressing the paper against a flat area of type or plate, e.g., on a platen press, by the pressure of a cylinder rolling across a flat area of type, as on a flat-bed cylinder press, or by having the flat printing area stereotyped (molded into a curved form with cast metal) against which another (impression) cylinder revolves carrying the paper web, as in newspaper (rotary web) printing. Flat sheets may also be printed by the rotary method by having the printed areas electro-typed, i.e., duplicated in a copper or other metal plate, and then curving the plate to fit a cylinder.

Letterpress printing includes both hand-set and machine composition. Foundry type, cast in individual pieces, is used in hand composition, whereas in machine composition the type may be cast in slugs of equal length or measures by linecasting machines, such as the linotype or intertype, or cast in a single piece of type, as in the monotype machine. The advantages of single-type composition are quick correction of individual letters, flexibility in spacing between letters, and the relative ease by which any portion of a line may be increased or decreased to obtain a justified right-hand margin.

Letterpress printing is the oldest, and still the more commonly used, method of printing; it is employed for practically all newspaper printing, as well as the printing of many periodicals and books. It is capable of producing both very fine and very cheap results, in either very short (e.g., 750-copy) or very long (e.g., 250,000-or-so-copy) runs. It is considered the standard with which other printing methods are compared. (17, 316)

levant. In general, a descriptive term applied to a leather having a characteristic drawn-grain pattern, originally produced by an astringent tannage, but now produced by hand or machine BOARDING (1) of vegetable or semi-chrome tanned goatskins and sheep-skins, or vegetable tanned sealskin. The traditional "levant" used in bookbinding is a vegetable tanned goatskin. When the pattern is produced by embossing, as it frequently is, it is called "levant grain." The original levant, which during the past one hundred years or so was considered to be the finest of the morocco family, was always goatskin obtained from the Near East. In recent years, however, the best levant has been tanned in the northern and northwestern areas of Africa and usually finished in France. Today the great bulk of genuine "levant" goatskin comes from South Africa and is called "cape levant." *See also:* GOATSKIN; MOROCCO. (61, 69)

levant marble. A type of cover marble produced by applying brown coloring in broad streaks, followed by washing with aqua regia. (152)

levers. Strips of millboard or pasteboard, each about $\frac{1}{16}$ inch thick, 2 inches wide, and slightly longer from head to tail than the end webbings, and used in conjunction with SPRING-BACK (1) to give added resistance to the opening of a blankbook and thus cause the spine of the book to spring up and lie flat, thus facilitating writing in the book.

In attaching the levers, the outside of the leaf adjacent to the board papers is glued out and the levers are placed approximately $\frac{1}{8}$ inch from the spine of the book. The webbings are then glued to the levers and the endpapers are folded over and glued down on themselves, the levers, and the web-bings. The clothings are then glued across the spine and onto the folded endpapers. The entire assemblies are then slit at the points of the kettle stitches, the end sections being glued to the insides of the boards and the middle sections between the split boards. The spring-back clamps over the edges of both levers near the spine, and, when the boards of the book are opened, the pull of the levers causes the spring-back to throw the spine of the book up so that the conjugate leaves present a flat surface for writing. To impart added stiffness to the levers,

LETTERING PALLET

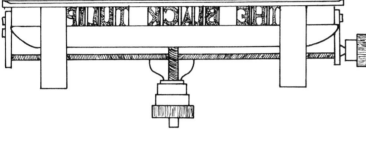

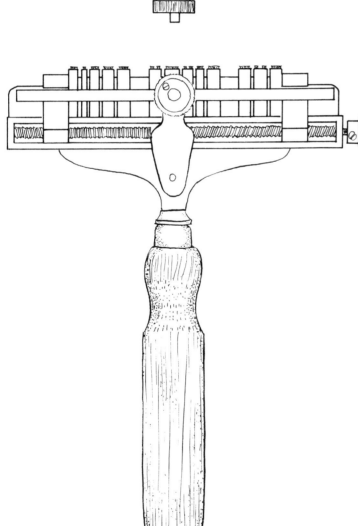

they are cut so that the grain (machine direction) of the board runs at right angles to the spine, which is one of the very few instances in bookbinding where it is desirable to have the grain in this direction. Also called "stiffeners."

library binding. The business of providing specialized binding services to public, private, institutional, and other libraries. Library binding, like job binding, relies heavily on handwork, supplemented by the use of specialized equipment, such as sewing machines, rounding and backing machines, board cutters, blocking presses, smashing and nipping machines, etc. The services offered by library binders include prebinding, rebinding, serial (periodical or magazine) binding, pamphlet and adhesive binding, box and portfolio construction, general repair work, and, in some binderies, rebinding and/or restorating rare or valuable books, Bibles, etc.

Library binding must provide a book which will open fairly easily and retain its shape after repeated openings. It must also possess sufficient durability to last as long as the paper on which the book is printed, and be priced in accordance with the quality of the work. *See also:* BOOKBINDING; LIBRARY SEWING; OVERSEWING. (58, 81, 121, 209, 293)

Library Binding Institute. A trade association of commercial library bookbinders of the United States and Canada, suppliers to the bookbinding industry and institutional bookbinders. One of the Institute's principal objectives is to inspect and certify library binderies as to the quality of materials and level of workmanship in the books they bind. No library bindery whose binding fails to meet the Institute's standards promulgated on January 1, 1958, can warrant its binding to be Library Binding and, therefore, to be in compliance with all the requirements of the Library Binding Institute standard for library binding. (208)

library buckram. 1. A heavy weight cotton fabric possessing the qualities called for in the minimum specifications for Class "A" library binding. *See also:* BOOK CLOTH; BUCKRAM. 2. A trade name sometimes incorrectly applied to all book cloths of a similar nature, e.g., all coated cloths, all impregnated cloths, etc.

library corners. A book corner in which the covering material, instead of being cut and abutted, has the excess taken up in two diagonal folds, one under each turn-in. The library corner is the standard corner used by library binders in the United States. Also called "Dutch corner." *Cf:* SQUARE CORNER. *See also:* CORNER MITERING; ROUND CORNER. (68, 150, 156)

library edition. 1. A more or less obsolete term for an edition, series or set of books, produced in a uniform format to differentiate it from another edition. 2. A book supposedly or actually printed on a better quality of paper, bound in a stronger manner than the customary edition binding, and intended for use in a library. *See also:* PRE-LIBRARY BOUND. (156)

library sewing. A method of sewing the sections of a book on tapes that stemmed originally from the relaxation of the (high) standards set for craft bookbinding, in which a book was always sewn on raised bands (*See:* FLEXIBLE SEWING), and had a TIGHT BACK. The need for both economy and the HOLLOW BACK, which caused the open book to lie flatter, led to the introduction of sewing on (four) tapes, which was the basic sewing for library books for many years. Today, however, and especially in the United States, OVERSEWING is more nearly synonymous with library sewing. *See also:* TAPE SEWING. (12, 343)

library stamp. A rubber stamp cut with the name of the library in relief, and used to indicate ownership on the title page or other pages of a book. In some cases it is used to identify the publication upon receipt by the library, i.e., before the book is processed, and is sometimes used in lieu of a BOOKPLATE.

library style book. A book that is sewn through the folds, usually on (four) tapes but sometimes on the same number of cords, and has split boards, a leather spine with vellum tips, cloth or paper sides, and French joints. The term is now obsolete. (204, 276)

library style endpaper. An endpaper with a visible cloth joint, consisting of two folded white sheets attached by the cloth strip, and with decorative marbled or colored sheets glued to the opposing white sheets. The waste sheet is not cut completely away, a stub or tongue being left for insertion between split boards. This style of endpaper is associated with library binding of the 19th century. (335)

lift. 1. A quantity of sheets of paper or board which can readily be lifted from one operation to another. 2. The maximum number of sheets of paper placed at one time under the knife of a cutting machine. 3. The thickness of a "section" sewn in an oversewing machine. (139, 316)

lifting. *See:* PICKING.

light fast. *See:* FAST COLORS.

LIBRARY CORNER

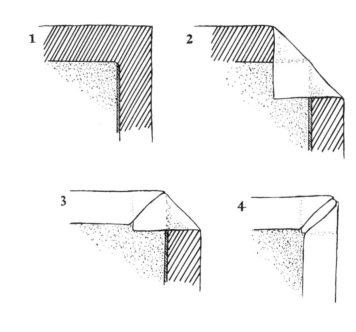

light Italian marble. A marble pattern characterized by a network of fine veins or lines. The usual marble of this pattern consists of four colors, each successive color requiring more gall and water than the preceding, so that each will spread into large spots in such a manner as to drive the other colors into veins. When the different colors and gall water have been properly adjusted to each other and dropped on the surface of the size, clear gall water, of an even stronger concentration than any contained in the colors, is sprinkled evenly over the entire surface; this drives the colors into the fine hair veins for which this marble is noted. Light Italian is closely identified with the country from which it derives its name, being found often as endpapers in Italian books of the late 18th and 19th centuries, and occasionally as cover papers. The size for this marble is usually a mixture of gun tragacanth and flea seed. (217)

lignin. A highly polymetric material occurring with cellulose in plant material, and which is considered to be largely responsible for the strength of the wood. Lignin is usually determined as the residue left on hydrolysis of the plant material with strong acids after resins, waxes, tannins, and other extractives have been removed. Softwoods give from 26 to 34% lignin with a methoxyl content of about 15%, while hardwoods give 16 to 24% lignin with a methoxyl content of about 21%.

The nature of lignin is not fully understood, but it is considered to be a complex cross-linked, highly aromatic structure of high molecular weight, i.e., about 10,000. It cannot be hydrolyzed by acids, but is readily oxidizable. It is soluble in hot alkali and bisulfate, and condenses readily with phenol and thio compounds. Lignin is not a compound but a *system,* and its composition varies both with the method of isolation used and with the species, age, growing conditions, etc., of the tree or lignified material. It is more or less completely removed during chemical pulping operations in paper manufacture but none is removed by mechanical pulping. It is further removed or modified by bleaching sequences to give pulps of greater brightness.

So-called sulfite cellulose (which is more appropriately called "sulfite lignin extract"), when adjusted to a pH of between 3.0 and 5.0, has a tanning action resembling that of the vegetable tannins. When used alone, however, it produces a brown leather that tends to

be thin and hard, with low tan fixation. It is used chiefly at the end of some vegetable tannages to improve the fullness and firmness of the leather, especially in those cases where the leather is to be sold by weight. (17, 72, 198, 268, 306)

lime blast. A defect in leather, characterized by a rough grain surface and/or hard or dark colored patches, or patchy dyeing. It is caused by excessive exposure to air of a limed skin, resulting in some of the lime being converted by atmospheric carbon dioxide into insoluble calcium carbonate. Prolonged exposure may also cause some drying of the skin, resulting in hard, brownish, translucent patches in the finished leather. (306)

limed rawhide. A translucent or opaque material produced from cattle hide after the limed hide has been dried, subsequent to unhairing and fleshing. No tanning process is employed. (61)

lime fleshing. The process of FLESHING hides and skins subsequent to the liming operation. *See also:* GREEN FLESHING.

lime liquor. A saturated limewater containing slaked lime (calcium hydroxide) greatly in excess of saturation and used, usually along with sodium sulfide, for loosening and degrading the hair and other epidermal structures of hides and skins. *See also:* LIMING. (363)

lime slaking. The process of treating caustic lime or calcium hydroxide with water to produce slaked lime for use in LIMING. *See also:* LIME LIQUOR. (363)

liming. One of the beamhouse operations employed in leather manufacture. Its purpose is to degrade, and thereby loosen, the epidermal structure of hide or skin, including the hair, epidermis, sweat glands, etc., so that they may be removed. Methods of liming vary both in the chemicals used and in procedures. Unhairing and liming can be carried out simultaneously by immersing the skins in the lime and water mixture, often with the addition of other chemicals known as sharpeners, e.g., sodium sulfide.

Lime, which is calcium oxide (CaO), reacts violently with water to form hydrated lime (calcium hydroxide ($Ca(OH)_2$)), which can be used with safety in liming and unhairing because it will not damage the collagen fibers of the skin, assuming it is properly used. This is because calcium hydroxide is not very soluble in water, and, in fact, a *saturated* lime solution contains only approximately ⅛ part lime

per 100 parts water. Even this limited solubility, however, is sufficient to produce a solution with a pH in the range of 12.4 or 12.5, and, under such very alkaline conditions, some of the young keratin protein decomposes to produce sulfur compounds in the lime liquor. These compounds, in conjunction with the lime, accentuate the further breakdown of keratin. The lime therefore promotes unhairing, and the more keratin breakdown impurities it contains, the more rapidly it unhairs. Liming, however, must be carried out with extreme care, as the alkali also modifies and will eventually degradate the collagen fibers of the skin. Skins limed for an overly prolonged time produce thin, loose, and weak leather.

Liming also causes the hide or skin to swell. In order to promote gradual and uniform swelling, so as to avoid distortion or buckling of the stock, the skins are left in the lime solution for 1 to 2 days, following which a sharpener is usually added to promote the process. The addition of sodium hydrosulfide (NaSH), sodium cyanide (NaCN), sodium hydroxide (NaOH), sodium carbonate ($Na_2(CO)_3$), dimethylamines, etc., quickens the process in two ways: 1) by attacking the keratin, resulting in faster loosening of the hair; and 2) by increasing the alkalinity, and, therefore, the rate of swelling. If too much sharpener is added too quickly, however, rapid unhairing results, accompanied by excessive swelling of the *surfaces* of the skin, while the interior remains unswollen. This results in buckling, which makes subsequent unhairing, fleshing (if not done before liming), or splitting difficult. It may also result in permanent distortion and weakness of the grain, and, in addition, any naturally occurring wrinkles or "growth marks" may become accentuated. After liming, the skins are then ready for UNHAIRING. (248, 298, 363)

limited edition. An edition of a book that is frequently printed on superior paper and bound more luxuriously than other editions. It is, by definition, printed in relatively limited numbers (seldom more than 1,500, usually about 150 to 500, and at times as few as 10) and sold at a premium price. The copies often contain a printed notice, which usually faces the title page, indicating the number of copies issued and a space in which to write the copy number of an individual copy. The copies may be signed by the author. A copy of a limited edition may or may not be more valuable than a copy of another edition. (12, 69)

limp binding (limp cloth; limp covers; limp leather; limp vellum). A book which does not have stiff boards but instead has flexible cloth, leather, vellum, or paper sides, which may or may not be lined. The term, however, is seldom applied to paper sides. (*See:* SELF COVER.) Limp vellum bindings for blankbooks were being produced at least as early as the 14th century and probably earlier. This type of binding was not a craft binding, however; it was more convenient to bind the thin blankbooks of that time in limp covers. Other limp vellum bindings were produced in relatively great numbers in the 16th and 17th centuries, but the limp vellum binding declined thereafter until revived by the private presses near the end of the 19th century. In the last quarter of the 18th century and the first quarter of the 19th, limp leather was commonly used for books to be carried in the pocket, but for the past century or so limp bindings have been largely restricted to devotional books, diaries, and sentimental verse, sometimes in the YAPP STYLE. (69, 236, 264)

limp suede (limp ooze). An obsolete term applied to an OOZE LEATHER finished in gray, and sometimes used as a book covering material. (274)

limp vellum. *See:* LIMP BINDING.

linen. A cloth (and sewing thread) made from straw of the flax plant, genus *Linum*, and especially *L. usitatissimum*. The stems are steeped in water to remove resinous matter and allow fermentation to take place. After fermentation is completed, the fibrous material is separated from the woody matter and spun into thread. The cellulose content of linen fibers ranges between 70 and 80%. The fibers, which appear flat like those of cotton, are thicker than cotton fibers, have knots and joints, as well as transverse markings and creasings, and are very tough, can be bleached white, and take dyes more readily than cotton. The chlorine test stains linen fibers a claret red. (93, 143)

linen buckram. A BUCKRAM made with a base of linen rather than cotton.

linen paper. A paper made from LINEN rags with or without the addition of other pulps.

liner. 1. A sheet of paper of an appropriate thickness attached to the inner surface of the board of a book, usually one that is to be fully covered in leather. The liner causes the board to

curve convexly to the text block. This curvature will be straightened by the shrinkage of the leather which covers the outside of the board. In order to prevent warping of the cover at a later time, the grain direction of the lining paper should be parallel to the spine of the book. 2. The outer layers of any kind of paperboard which varies in color or quality from the middle or other parts of the board. (139, 335)

liner and headbanding machine. An edition binding machine which lines the spines of books with cloth or paper and attaches the headbands. It has a capacity of 4 to 11½ inches, head to tail, 2½ to 8½ inches in width, and ¼ to 2 inches in thickness. *See also:* TRIPLE LINER AND HEADBANDING MACHINE. (343)

line tool. *See:* FILLET (1); GOUGE; PALLET (1).

lining. *See:* SPINE LINING.

lining paper. *See:* PASTEDOWN.

lining skiver. A leather split somewhat thinner than the usual SKIVER and used for lining the inside of the limp leather covers of Bibles and other limp bindings.

link sewing. *See:* CATCH STITCH.

linotype. A typesetting machine that casts an entire line of type in one slug. The machine holds a number of single matrices in a magazine, which are released as the keyboard is operated, and are assembled in proper sequence with appropriate spaces separating the words. The spaces justify the completed line as it is brought to the orifice of a mold, where it is cast as a single type-high slug. Linotype is one of the typecasting machines used by library binders. The linotype machine was invented by Ottmar Mergenthaler and has been in use since 1890. *See also:* MONOTYPE. (156, 316)

linseed oil. A pale yellow drying oil extracted from ground flax seed genus *Linum*, and especially *L. usitatissimum*, and used occasionally in the 19th century as a marbling size. It was never used as extensively as GUM TRAGACANTH or FLEA SEED. Linseed oil is also used in the manufacture of some printing inks and in some finishing processes in leather manufacture.

linson. The trade name of a particularly strong type of paper used in the manufacture of edition bindings. It is sometimes embossed in imitation of linen cloth, and is manufactured in many colors and finishes. It is used as a substitute for woven cloths. (161, 258)

linters. *See:* COTTON LINTERS.

lipped: A method of accommodating a

THROW OUT that is longer than the trimmed height of the book. A portion of a leaf to be folded adjacent to the gutter margin is cut away, i.e., lipped, so that the remaining portion may be folded without buckling and creasing the binding margin.

list of signatures. *See:* REGISTER (2).

lithograph paper. A paper made for use in lithography. It is produced from bleached chemical wood pulps, or a combination of chemical and mechanical pulps. In England it is produced mainly from ESPARTO (GRASS). The principal characteristics required of this paper relate to the printing process to be used, and include, water resistance, pick strength, curl resistance, and the like. Both coated and uncoated lithograph paper are produced, in basis weights of 45 to 70 pounds (uncoated) and 50 to 100 pounds (coated) ($25 \times 38 - 500$). Because any stretch of the sheet to be printed must be along the narrow dimension, lithograph papers are usually positioned the narrow way across the printing press. (17, 58)

lithophone. A white pigment consisting of a mixture of zinc sulfide (ZnS), barium sulfate ($BaSO_4$) and some zinc oxide (ZnO), and prepared by the cross precipitation of zinc sulfate ($ZnSO_4$) and barium sulfide (BaS), plus the addition of heat. It is used in the manufacture of ink, paint, etc., and as a pigment filler in paper. *See also:* ZINC SULFIDE.

Little Gidding bindings. Early 17th century bookbindings produced by the members of the Anglican community founded by NICHOLAS FERRAR and his nieces, in Huntingdonshire, England, in 1625. The bindings they produced included albums (concordances) of Biblical texts taken from printed texts, to which the Ferrars added illustrations. The bindings themselves were of gold tooled velvet, vellum or morocco. Ferrar died in 1636, but the community continued on for another 20 years.

Little Gidding was an abused term among dealers and historians of bookbinding, just as with Mearne and Ève, and at one time virtually *any* English embroidered binding of the early 17th century was called Little Gidding. (132, 165)

lizarding. A technique employed in embroidering bindings which involves the cutting of strips of flat metal into shapes which are held in place by small stitches at regular intervals. (111)

lizard skin. A leather made from the skins of various lizards, usually those found in India and Indonesia. The skins are tanned by various processes, including vegetable (sumac), alum and salt (tawing), and chrome tannages. The resultant leather has a pleasant color and a grain pattern produced by tiny scales. While usually fawn or gray, they are sometimes dyed. Lizard skin has been used from time to time in decorating book covers. (351)

load. 1. The total physical force applied to a specimen of a material when measuring a certain property, such as the compression resistance of paper, the tensile strength of leather, etc. 2. A maximum handling unit, e.g., a full platform of sheets, sections of books, etc. (17, 256)

loading. 1. The operation of incorporating finely divided, relatively insoluble, white powders into a papermaking stock, either directly or by chemical processes, so as to improve the printing surface and ink absorption, to give a higher finish and greater opacity, to improve formation and flatness, and to improve dimensional stability. Loading is usually done prior to sheet formation. Loading was first used in the 19th century, apparently surreptitiously, to save pulp and reduce the cost to the papermaker; however, it was then discovered that restricted quantities of loading improved the paper. 2. Mineral matter, such as clay, barium sulfate, calcium carbonate, china clay, calcium sulfite, magnesium silicate, titanium oxide, etc., used as filler materials in paper. (17, 58, 143, 365)

localized watermark. A WATERMARK so arranged that it is impressed at definite intervals on a sheet of paper. *See also:* CUT TO REGISTER.

locks. Locking devices placed on books whose contents are considered to be confidential or private, such as personal accounts, confidential credit ratings, diaries, etc. Book locks are made in several sizes and are adjustable over the distances between sizes. They are riveted to the covers after binding. (339)

lock stitch. 1. Any method of sewing with thread whereby the stitching at each operation is "locked" and cannot unravel if cut on either side of the completed stitch. 2. *See:* KETTLE STITCH. (164)

Lofton-Merritt stain. A test used to determine the presence of unbleached sulfate or sulfite fiber in paper. The stain consists of two grams of malachite green in 100 ml. of water, plus one gram of basic fuchsin in 100 ml. of water, 50 ml. of the former being mixed with 100 ml. of the latter. The

specimen is treated with a drop of the mixture and then with a 0.1% solution of hydrochloric acid, followed by the application of distilled water. A blue or blue-green stain indicates the presence of unbleached sulfate fiber, while purple or lavender indicates unbleached sulfite. (143)

logwood. An aqueous extract obtained from the heartwood of the logwood tree, *Haematoxylon campechisnum,* of Central America and the West Indies. Logwood contains approximately 50% haematoxylin ($C_{16}H_{14}O_6 \cdot 3H_2O$), a colorless crystalline material when pure, but which turns blood red when exposed to air. It is only slightly soluble in water, but dissolves in aqueous solution of alkalis to give a range of colors from violet to black. It was taken to Europe soon after the discovery of America, and was one of the most important of the natural coloring matters until the 19th century, when it was superseded by synthetic dyestuffs of greater brilliance. Logwood dye was used in producing black ink, marbling colors, including purple and violet, and is still used in dyeing leather and textiles black. (233)

Longepierre, Hilaire Bernard de Requeleyne, Baron de (1679–1721). A book collector who had his books elaborately bound and embellished with the Golden Fleece, in commemoration, it is said, of the success of one of his dramas. This device, which formed the sole decoration of his bindings, was usually located in the center and at the corner of the covers, as well as in the panels on the spine. The books were bound in morocco, the edges were marbled under gilt, and some of the volumes had finely tooled doublures decorated with the same motif as the covers. The superior craftsmanship of these bindings has prompted some authorities to conjecture that they were bound by Luc Antoinne Boyet. (94, 347)

long-fibered Japanese tissue. *See:* JAPANESE COPYING PAPER.

long fold. A sheet of paper, which, if folded lengthwise, will be folded with the machine (grain) direction of the paper. *See also:* BROAD (1).

long way. *See:* PORTRAIT.

look-through. A term describing what a paper looks like when viewed by means of transmitted light. This type of examination gives an indication of the formation and texture of the paper, its watermark, whether paper is laid or wove, and whether it is marred by impurities, shives, and the like. (17)

looping maching. A machine used to at-

tach looped cord to hangers, calendars, etc. The machine punches the hole, inserts the cord, draws it to the desired length, ties the loop, cuts it off, and delivers the finished product—all in one continuous operation. Looping machines are used by the job binder. (247)

loose back. *See:* HOLLOW BACK.

loose-leaf binding. The business of binding individual sheets of paper in an exchangeable form, for leaves to be added, removed, or relocated in the book. Loose-leaf bindings are used wherever records of repeatedly changing information must be kept. Instruction manuals, catalogs, and accounting forms are often loose-leaf bound. Loose-leaf binding includes the construction of the covers (although not the manufacture of the binding mechanism, which is, in general, purchased from companies specializing in its manufacture), the punching or drilling of the paper, as well as the assembly of the various parts. Loose-leaf binding, which is classed as miscellaneous binding, is a part of STATIONERY BINDING. (320, 343)

loose section. One or more sections of a book which have become loosened in the binding, usually because of breakage of the sewing thread. *See also:* START.

lop-sided. Any section or part of a book that is folded or backed with one side out of true with the other. (256)

lower cover (lower board). The back or under cover of a book, or the cover nearest to the last leaf of the book. Also called "back cover," "reverse cover," or "end board."

lower edge. The TAIL of a book. Also called "bottom edge" or "tail edge."

lozenge. A diamond-shaped stamp, or a square stamp turned 45° on its axis, and used in decorating bookbindings. (156)

l pattern. A LEVANT pattern embossed on a book cloth.

Ludlow. A machine designed by the Ludlow Typograph Co., and used for casting entire lines of type in a range of sizes from 4 to 90 point, and, for special purposes, even up to 240 point. Ludlow composition is actually hand composition, except that the compositor sets matrices (molds) instead of actual type and casts the line from these matrices. Ludlow machines are used in library binderies for casting the type used for lettering books. (156, 234)

lump. 1. A defect in a paper caused by an

agglomeration of fiber or other materials. 2. A small, hard, pill-like substance in paste or glue, caused by imperfect mixing, lack of proper dissolution, or screening. (256)

Lumspecs (Lesser Used Materials SPECS). Specifications for the binding of library materials that are expected to receive little use and need not, therefore, be bound according to Class "A" specifications, but which are expected to be used to the extent that they require greater protection than that afforded by a pamphlet box. Essentially, Lumspec binding differs from Class "A" in three respects: 1) the Lumspec book is side sewn instead of oversewn or sewn through the folds; 2) only the spine and a small part of the sides are covered in buckram, with the remainder of the boards not being covered at all; and 3) the volumes are not lettered. The bindings so produced are called Lumbindings. Lumspecs were devised in 1957 by a subcommittee of the American Library Association's bookbinding commitee and were approved that same year by the Library Binding Institute. (11, 211)

lw pattern. The code name for a "linen weave" applied to a book cloth embossed to give the coarse appearance of linen cloth.

lying flat. That characteristic of a binding that enables the leaves of the book to lie more or less perfectly flat when the book is opened in its center. It is a particularly necessary characteristic for music scores, books which are to be photocopied, and books which are to be written in. *See:* SPRING-BACK (1). Lying flat is generally associated with the HOLLOW BACK, which permits a greater degree of throw-up in the spine.

lying press. A small, portable press, usually made of wood, with two steel or wooden screws operating through bronze chucks, in which books to be backed by hand, trimmed with the plow, lettered or decorated, etc., are clamped. The lower face of the block on the bookbinder's left has a groove in which the plow runs. It is not known when the lying press was introduced into bookbinding, but since it was unusual for the edges of books to be cut and spines backed before the last part of the 15th century, it was probably invented sometime after 1500. (161, 236)

Lyonnaise (Lyonese) style. A 16th century style of book decoration featuring broad interlaced geometrical strapwork, usually gold tooled and then painted, lacquered, or enamelled in different colors. Lyonnaise was also a style in which the binding was decorated by blocking the cover with large corner ornaments and a predominant center design, roughly lozenge shaped, the all-over background being filled in with dots. The name is misleading, as neither style had any connection with Lyons. (69, 156, 347)

M. 1. A thousand sheets of paper or board. 2. The Roman equivalent of 1,000. *See:* ROMAN NUMERALS.

machine binding. A term sometimes applied to the type of bookbinding in which equipment is employed extensively, as contrasted with the type in which relatively little machinery is employed. Machine binding would include mainly edition and pamphlet bindings, and possibly library bindings. (339)

machine direction. The direction in which the greater number of the fibers of a sheet of paper tend to be oriented as a result of the forward motion of the wire of the papermaking machine. The paper so produced is stronger in the machine direction, and also experiences less dimensional variation in the machine direction due to changes in humidity. The direction at right angles to the machine direction is known as the CROSS DIRECTION. Also called "grain" or "grain direction." (82)

machine ruling. The process of applying faint blue, red, or blue and red lines to paper that is to be used for blankbooks, note books, check books, etc., by means of RULING MACHINES, as distinguished from that produced by printing (58, 343)

machine sewing. The operation of sewing a book by mechanical means rather than by hand. Although in its broadest sense machine sewing includes OVERSEWING and SINGER SEWING, as well as some forms of SIDE SEWING, it is commonly accepted that the term refers specifically to the various methods of sewing through the folds of the sections by means of sewing machines. Machine sewing is a product of edition binding, and reaches its greatest efficiency (economy) in the sewing of relatively long runs of books of identical size.

The basic principal of machine sewing is that one needle does not go "all along" the length of the section, taking its thread with it, as in hand sewing; instead, a series of needles operate, each with its own kettle stitches.

In the usual type of sewing machine, one section after another is placed on a feeding arm which brings each to the part of the book already sewn. Fully automatic machines feed sections by means of vacuum suckers and/or

mechanical grippers which are electronically programmed to reject imperfect sections. The feeding arm forms a saddle with a pronounced ridge over which the half-open section is so placed that the fold is immediately above the edge of the saddle. The saddle has a row of holes through which punches rise and puncture the section. Immediately thereafter, threaded needles descend from above and pass through the holes created by the punches. The thread is then gripped by the side needles of the feeding beam and drawn double for a set space along the back fold to the hook-needles descending from above. The hook-needle grips the loop of thread, and also draws it up through the paper and also through the corresponding loop of the preceeding section. The feeding arm then swings out to pick up the next section, repeating this process until the sewing is completed.

Sewing with thread alone is sometimes referred to as "ordinary French sewing." Most machine sewing can be done on spine lining material or tapes fed from reels across the spine of the book. The sewing is accomplished in the same manner, but the thread passes through the lining material or tapes. Some machines are so designed that the thread passes around the tape. In addition, some machines work with an off-and-on stitch, which is suitable for books made up of thin paper and/or sections, and corresponds to the two-on method used in sewing by hand. While ordinary sewing is done with two needles for each stitch, the off-and-on method requires three needles working in combination, the thread being drawn alternately to one or the other of the outer needles. In the "staggered stitch"

method the needle changes its position for each section, so that the thread forms a zig-zag pattern across the tapes which are thus more solidly secured to the sections.

In ordinary French sewing, the books are sewn to each other until the machine is filled, whereupon the books forming a span are taken out and separated by cutting, a process carried out automatically on some models and by a second operator on others. In sewing on linings or tapes, the width of the cloth for each book must be greater than the thickness of the book. This is accomplished by inserting a split after each book, i.e., a wooden strip of a suitable width, usually with a metal gutter to facilitate cutting. In order to allow the sewn book to move forward with the necessary thread corresponding to the width of the split, a free stroke is made after each book, or the spare tape or lining is dropped in a fold between the books. *See also:* DAVID MCCONNELL SMYTH. (89, 203, 259, 315, 320)

machine stitching. A variation of SIDE SEWING, in which holes are drilled or punched through the gathered leaves and the book is then sewn twice, up and down through the thickness of the book. *See also:* JAPANESE SEWING. (259)

madder lake (turkey red). Any of several herbs of the genus *Rubia,* and especially an Eurasian herb, *R. tinctorium.* It contains the glycoside ruberythric acid, which gives xylose, glucose, and the dye alizarin upon hydrolysis. Madder lake is used for dyeing and in the manufacture of marbling colors.

made boards. Book boards consisting of two boards of unequal thickness pasted together, the thinner board being on the inside next to the book. Made boards are useful when binding a large book, one requiring boards that are thicker than normal. The advantages of using two boards rather than one very thick board are that the thinner board will tend to cause the boards to curve towards the text block rather than away from it, and the use of two boards provides greater stability for them. (172, 335)

made endpaper. A type of endpaper consisting of two decorative leaves, e.g., marbled, colored, etc., and two or three plain leaves. The decorative end is pasted to one of the plain leaves, and, on larger books, a linen guard, through which the sewing passes, is wrapped around both. One decorative leaf becomes the board paper, the other, as well as the plain leaves, being the free flyleaves. If a waste sheet is desired, another plain folded sheet is tipped to the innermost plain leaf and one leaf is swung around on top of the board paper. This method also gives an additional free flyleaf. (81, 335, 343)

made flyleaves. Flyleaves made from colored, marbled, or otherwise decorated paper, lined with uncolored paper that is sometimes similar to that of the text. (237)

made-up copy. A book having IMPERFECTIONS (1) which have been replaced by parts from other copies of the same edition. (69, 156)

magazine binder (magazine case). A form of case, generally having a transparent plastic upper cover, and used as a temporary binding of pamphlets or current magazines. It can be removed for use with the succeeding numbers. (156)

magazine paper. A paper suitable for printing of periodicals. It is manufactured in a wide range of grades and finishes, two or more of which are frequently used in a single issue. Both coated and uncoated grades are used, depending mainly on the requirements for illustrations and halftones. (17)

magnesium bicarbonate. A bicarbonate $(Mg(HCO_3)_2)$ used in deacidifying papers. The bicarbonate is produced by passing carbon dioxide through a solution of magnesium carbonate. The document to be deacidified is immersed in a bath or sprayed with a solution of about 10 grams of magnesium carbonate per liter of water that has been treated with CO_2. The advantage of this method is that it is simple and effective.

magnesium carbonate. A carbonate $(MgCO_3)$ produced in paper by the action of atmospheric carbon dioxide on magnesium hydroxide. See: NON-AQUEOUS DEACIDIFICATION.

magnesium hydroxide. A white precipitate $(Mg(OH)_2)$ produced in paper by the action of moisture in the paper on magnesium methoxide. See: NON-AQEUOUS DEACIDIFICATION.

magnesium methoxide. An organic salt $(Mg(OCH_3)_2)$, insoluble in water, and produced by dissolving magnesium in dry methanol. When dissolved in alcohol and freon, it can be used in the NON-AQUEOUS DEACIDIFICATION of pa-

per. The magnesium methoxide reacts with moisture in the paper to form magnesium hydroxide, which slowly carbonates to form magnesium carbonate. A common method of application is by aerosol spraying.

magnesium silicate. An insoluble white powder $(Mg_3H_2 (SiO_3)_4)$, used in gilding. See: FRENCH CHALK.

magnesium sulfate. A colorless, crystalline salt $(MgSO_4)$, soluble in water, which occurs naturally as white, granular, fibrous, or earthy masses, and is readily obtained in solution. It is used in leather manufacture to improve the color and feel of leather. See: SOUR DIP.

Mahieu, Thomas (active 1549-65). The 16th century bibliophile, who, along with Grolier, was the most celebrated collector of his day. Mahieu's collection, which belongs to the period 1550 to 1565, included bindings, some of which were done by Claude de Picques, with punched and gilded backgrounds for designs, or curved strapwork and arabesques, with ornaments in outline or azured. Some bindings are lavishly ornamented with colored onlays on a gilt background. Many are inscribed "Tho. Maioli et Amicorvm," (the Latinized form of his name being Maiolus). About 90 bindings survive, ranging in quality from adequate to very superior.

Mahieu, who may have been a native of Italy, was secretary to Catherine de Medicis from 1549 to 1560 and later a treasurer of France, as was Grolier, whom Mahieu probably knew. (168, 347, 373)

mahogany marble. A "tree marble" produced by sprinkling black and brown coloring, mainly the former, on the covers of a book, and when dry, coating the entire cover several times with red coloring. See also: TREE CALF. (97, 152)

Maioli, Thomas. See: MAHIEU, THOMAS.

make up. 1. The sections and other gatherings needed to make up one complete book. 2. A list of the contents of a book supplied by a publisher to the printer and bookbinder to serve as instructions as to the positioning of plates, plans, map endpapers, etc. See also: DUMMY (1). 3. A general term applied to the process of taking type from galleys, arranging it into page form, inserting illustrative cuts, dividing the matter into page lengths, adding running heads, titles of subdivisions, footnotes, etc., and securing with cord. The pages of type are then ready to be locked in the chase. (264, 365)

maleic anhydride. A colorless crystalline

substance $(C_4H_3O_2)$, soluble in acetone and chloroform. It is manufactured by the oxidation of benzene by air at 400 to 450° C. over a vanadium catalyst. Maleic anhydride is used in the manufacture of paper. See: FORTIFIED SIZE.

malleable. A term applied to a metal capable of being beaten or rolled in all directions without breaking or cracking. Since the molecules of the metal must remain locked to each other during the beating or rolling, a malleable metal must exhibit a high degree of structural plasticity. The most malleable of all metals is gold, which can be beaten into a sheet (leaf) only 1/300,000 inch thick. Other malleable metals used in bookbinding include silver, aluminum, platinum, and palladium. (233)

malpighian layer. The layer of epithelial cells in the epidermis of a hide or skin next to the grain surface of the derma, whose protoplasm has not yet changed into horny material.

mangrove (bark). Trees of the family *Rhizophoraceae*, especially those of the genera *Rhizophora, Bruguiera, Avicennia* and *Ceriops*, the barks of which are rich in tannin. The tannin content of mangrove barks varies widely, however, from less than 10% to more than 40%, depending upon a number of factors, including the species, as well as the age, exposure to sun and air, location on the tree where the bark is removed, etc.

As a tanning material mangrove bark has both advantages and disadvantages. Its principal disadvantage is the reddish color it imparts to leather (*See also:* HEMLOCK), although this can readily be overcome by mixing mangrove with other tanning materials which modify or reduce the intensity of the color. The leather produced by the use of mangrove alone also tends to be harsh and thick-grained. When used with other tannins, however, as it usually is, mangrove provides a very satisfactory tannage. The rate of penetration of the tannin is slower than with such tannins as wattle or quebracho, but can be increased by sulfiting.

Mangrove is considered to be the most economical and abundant vegetable tannin available today. It is one of the condensed class of tannins, has a fairly high pH and a relatively low acids content. It is very soluble and develops a minimum of insoluble matter. It also produces very little sludge in the tanning liquor.

Mangrove is inaccurately (but persistently) referred to as "cutch" or "kutch." *See also:* VEGETABLE TANNINS. (175, 306, 363)

manifold binding. The business of binding multiple business forms, such as sales records, billheads, purchase orders, etc. It may also include the punching of custom-made forms that are used in one of many proprietary loose-leaf, record keeping systems. Manifold bindings are usually padded or wire stitched, and are seldom sewn. They are also frequently of a temporary nature, e.g., a common style consists of marbled boards with a paper spine (although it may be cloth). Since this style of binding frequently includes sheets of carbon copy, perforation is usually necessary. Other manifold bindings sometimes require page numbering. Manifold binding usually employs power-driven, hand-operated equipment. (320, 343)

manifold paper. A thin, translucent paper used for typewriter carbon copies, or as tissue overlay for correction or protection of other work. It is produced from chemical and/or rag pulp, the rag pulp content generally ranging from 25 to 100%. The finish may be dull or glazed, and basis weights are 7 to 9 and sometimes 10 pounds (17 × 22 − 500). Manifold paper is also used for map overlays and, in a slightly waxed form, for interleaving tissue. (17, 58)

manila. A color and finish of a paper resembling that at one time obtained in paper manufacture from manila fibers, but which contains no manila, i.e., hemp stock. Manila paper is sometimes used for the covers of brochures and like publications, and for lining the boards of leather bookbindings. (17, 339)

manila board. A thin, strong board, generally made from chemical wood pulp ranging in thickness from 0.016 to 0.035 inch. It is used for cover stiffeners, fences for blankbooks, and covers for notebooks. (17)

manila hemp. *See:* ABACA.

Mansfield, Edgar (1907-　). An English bookbinder and sculptor, who was born in London, settled in Hastings (1911) and Napier (1965), New Zealand, and is presently living in that country. He studied binding under William Matthews and design under Elsa Taterka and taught art and crafts at the Feilding High School from 1929 to 1933, proceeding to London for further study in 1934. There he taught design and color at the London College of Printing from 1948 to 1964. Mansfield was the first foreign member to be elected

to the German Guild (M. D. E.— 1949) and the first president of the British Guild, 1955-1968. He was also the first president of DESIGNER BOOK-BINDERS. His bindings are to be found in numerous libraries, including the British Museum Library, Victoria & Albert Museum, Klingspor Museum, Royal Library of Stockholm, New York Public Library Spencer Collection, and the Victoria State Library, as well as many public and private collections.

Mansfield's designs, while difficult to evaluate, are enormously pleasing to view. His bindings are subtle but forceful, and convey almost a feeling of tranquility that brings about a common understanding between artist and viewer. Considering the trends of today, he has done with relatively sober means, that which many have failed to convey with the most elaborate of devices.

Mansfield is also the author of several articles dealing with teaching of bookbinding design, contemporary approach to bookbinding design, as well as new directions in bookbinding design. (50)

manuscript binding. A method used occasionally when a manuscript (or type-script) made up of single leaves is to be bound in sections. The leaves are pasted in pairs in such a manner that if there are 16 leaves, for example, the binding edge of leaf 1 (recto side down) would be pasted to the binding edge of leaf 16 (recto side up), leaf 2 to 15, and so on, the 8 double leaves then being folded to make a section. At best it is an awkward method and is probably not as effective as a GUARD (2). (355)

manuscript cover paper. A lightweight cover paper used on legal documents, and similar publications. It is produced from chemical wood pulps, which sometimes contain cotton fiber, in basis weight of 40 pounds (18 × 31 − 500). (17)

Manutius, Aldus (c 1450-1515). The leading publisher and printer of the Venetian High Renaissance, Aldus set up a definite scheme of book design, produced the first italic type, introduced small and handy pocket editions of the classics and applied several innovations in binding technique and design for use on a broad scheme. He established his press in about 1490, and his printer's device of anchor and dolphin has been copied by numerous printers since. Between 1515 and 1533 the press was managed by his father-in-law, Andrea Asolano, until Aldus' son,

Paulus (born 1511) came of age. Aldus' grandson, Aldus the Younger, took over the press upon the death of Paulus (1574) and subsequently closed it in 1590 when he was appointed director of the Vatican Press. *See also:* ALDINE (ITALIAN) STYLE. (104, 154, 252, 313, 334)

map endpapers. Endpapers on which maps are printed. While frequently adding to the attractiveness of a book, it is somewhat difficult for the reader to refer to such maps, a throw-out map being much superior for practical use. In addition, map endpapers make rebinding of the book more expensive, as the old endpapers must be saved, though generally not again for use as endpapers. The term is also generally applied to endpapers printed with charts, graphs, etc.

map paper. A paper used for the production of maps of all types, including atlases. It is a superior grade of paper produced from linen, cotton fiber, chemical wood pulps, or combinations thereof, in basis weights ranging from 16 to 28 pounds (17 × 22 −500). Required characteristics include finish, printability, dimensional stability to assure good register, good folding properties, and, in some cases, e.g., road maps, high opacity. Map papers are also sometimes produced in a manner that affords high wet strength, water repellency, mildew resistance, luminescence, abrasion resistance, and other properties pertinent to a particular use. (17, 324)

marble. To impart a veined or mottled appearance to the edges of a book or the surface of a paper, cloth, leather, in order to simulate an appearance of marble.

marble board. A pasteboard stained on one side with veined or mottled colors in imitation of marble, and used in bookbinding for checkbooks and marbleboard bindings. (339)

marbled. The edges of a book or the surface of paper, cloth, etc., which have been given a veined or mottled appearance in imitation of marble.

marble calf. A calfskin leather treated with acid so as to produce an effect of marble. *Cf:* MOTTLED CALF. *See also:* TREE CALF. (264)

marbled cloth. A book cloth patterned with variegated colors in imitation of marble. The cloth is colored by throwing on the colors in a manner similar to the "marbling" of leather, or by laying the cloth on the surface of the marbling size as in the marbling of paper. Marbled cloth was first introduced in about

1851 but went out of fashion before the turn of the century. (236, 369)

marbled edges. Veined or mottled coloring on the edges of a book in imitation of marble, and produced by touching the edge of the book under compression on the surface of a size on which marbling colors have been floated and patterned, or by transferring the pattern to the edge.

Marbling of book edges was introduced near the end of the 17th century, mainly on trade books bound in calfskin and sheepskin. Fine bindings were not so marbled until the closing years of the 18th century. These latter bindings were usually half or full bindings of Russia leather, usually of quarto or folio size. All classes of books bound in morocco continued to be gilded until well into the 19th century, i.e., the 1830s, when cheaper morocco bindings began being marbled. Marbled edges were common until the First World War, when the practice began to decline, except for stationery bindings. *See also:* MARBLE ROLLERS; MARBLE TRANSFER; MARBLING. (236, 241, 327)

marbled grain. A mosaic pattern, corresponding to the pattern of the network of tiny underlying blood vessels, which sometimes occurs on the grain surface of a leather. It has a rough, wild, or grainy appearance. (363)

marbled leather. The leather covers of a book which have been decorated with veined or mottled colors in an effort to imitate marble. Unlike the technique used in edge and paper marbling, leather marbles are produced by sprinkling or throwing the marbling water and colors directly onto the paste-washed and glaired leather. *See the following examples:* COMMON MARBLE; GREEN AGATE MARBLE; GREEN PORPHYRY MARBLE; LEVANT MARBLE; PORPHYRY VEIN MARBLE; PURPLE MARBLE; RED MARBLE; RED PORPHYRY MARBLE; ROCK MARBLE; STONE MARBLE. *See also:* TREE CALF.

marbled top. A book which has had only the head (top) edge marbled.

marble rollers. A mechanical device consisting of two layers of rollers, one above the other. The top roller or rollers hold the colors, distributing them to the lower roller or rollers which, in turn, apply the colors to the edges of the book. (264)

marble transfer. A marble pattern that has been transferred from ordinary marbled paper, or a marbled paper made expressly for transfer purposes, usually to the edges of a book. The transfer of ordinary marbled paper involves coating the edge of the book with an egg size somewhat thicker than the size used for gilding, placing the surface of the marbled paper against the edge, and then applying dilute hydrochloric acid to the back of the paper. When the design appears clearly through the paper, the marble is transferred by rubbing or beating the paper. Marbled paper made especially for transfer is treated with rectified ethyl alcohol (spirit of wine), pressed on the edge and daubed with hot water. Transfer marbling is still done to some extent on blankbooks, dictionaries, etc. (236)

marbling. The art or process of producing certain patterns of a veined or mottled appearance in imitation of marble by means of colors so prepared as to float on a mucilaginous liquid which possesses antagonistic properties to the colors prepared for the purpose. The colors are floated and formed into patterns and are taken off by laying a sheet of paper (or touching the edge of the book) on the surface of the size. The size is usually prepared from carragheen moss or gum tragacanth, boiled in water, but it may also be made from flea seed, linseed, etc., although flea seed and linseed are not as effective as the two gums and cannot be used in the production of certain marbles, e.g., the combed marbles.

Water colors are generally used in marbling, although oil colors can also be used; however, they do not permit as fine control or produce the clean, sharp lines of water colors. Mineral colors are seldom used because of their tendency to sink to the bottom of the trough due to their weight.

Little is known of the origin of marbling, but there seems to be little doubt that it was introduced into Western Europe from the East. Examples of Japanese marbling produced as early as 800 A.D. exist under the name of *Sumingagashi*. The Persians are considered to have been the first to use marbled papers in books, and examples of their work are found on the borders of some of their 16th century manuscripts. Marbled paper was in use in Holland by 1598, but its earliest use in England dates from about 1655; in America it was in use by 1679. By the 1670s it was in common use in England, although not in trade bindings. The most commonly used pattern was what we call OLD DUTCH MARBLE, most of it actually coming from Holland.

Beginning in about the last quarter of the 18th century the Old Dutch pattern was gradually superseded by the French Shell, Stormont, Antique, Spot, and others, all of which were uncombed. These then declined in popularity by about 1840, and were replaced by the Nonpareil and Spanish patterns. Both of these were revivals of the 17th century patterns which did not have the "set" look and high glazing of their 19th century counterparts. The Spanish marble is believed to have been used in England towards the end of the 18th century. Both revivals were used extensively throughout the 19th century, and then, later, mainly for the endpapers and sides of inexpensive half-calfskin bindings, and for the sides of cheaper stationery bindings. Other patterns, used mainly during the second half of the 19th century and generally for cheap or medium cost bindings, included the Gloster, Italian, Spot, Antique, West End, and Gold, the last being introduced in about 1880. During this same period, German marbles, which tended to be drab and heavily spotted with black on a colored background, were also used extensively, but seldom for the superior grades of work. The most frequently used pattern was a modern variation of the Dutch pattern. See the following marble patterns: AMERICAN; ANTIQUE; BLUE STORMONT; BOUQUET; BRITISH; CURL; DRAWN; DUTCH; FANCY; FANCY DUTCH; FRENCH CURL; FRENCH SHELL; GLOSTER; HAIR; LAPIS-LAZULI (2); LIGHT ITALIAN; NONPAREIL; OLD DUTCH; PEACOCK; REVERSED NONPAREIL; SNAIL; SPANISH; SPOT; STORMONT; TURKEY; WAVE; WEST END; and ZEBRA. *See also:* MARBLED CLOTH; MARBLED EDGES; MARBLING BRUSHES; MARBLING COMBS; MARBLING MACHINE; MARBLING SIZE; MARBLING TROUGH. *See* PLATE XI. (151, 152, 161, 217, 236, 327, 333, 369)

marbling base. *See:* MARBLING SIZE.

marbling brushes. Fine bristle brushes, set in hard rubber and secured in metal ferrules. They are generally from ⅜ to ½ inch in diameter. The larger brushes are used for the ground color in drawn marbles, while the smaller ones are used for the subsequent colors. The bristles of marbling brushes should be formed into a curved shape so as to give a freer motion when dropping the colors.

marbling combs. Instruments, generally with wire teeth, used for combing marbling colors while on the surface of the size. They are usually of two basic types: those with relatively short teeth, used for combing on the surface of the size (and sometimes called "top combs" because the teeth are allowed to touch the floating colors); and those with relatively long teeth, which touch the bottom of the trough while the comb is being drawn (and sometimes called "bottom combs"). In the production of comb patterns, four combs with variously spaced teeth are used; the most common are: four teeth to the inch, two to the inch, and double combs, in which the spacing of the teeth is alternately wide and narrow. (335, 369)

marbling gum. *See:* MARBLING SIZE.

marbling machine. A machine used to drop marbling colors on size. It consists of a four-compartment reservoir and a system of tubes connected to it, which serve as outlets and distribute drops of color at regular intervals. Three and five outlets, respectively, are provided for the two main colors, and two outlets each for the secondary colors. (264, 317)

marbling rods. A pair of rods sloping toward the marbler, and used when marbling the covers of a book. The book is placed on the rods so that the extended boards rest on them, with the leaves hanging between. The tail of the book is lower than the head so that the colors will flow from head to tail. (97)

marbling size. The gelatinous liquid upon which the marbling colors are dropped and formed into patterns. GUM TRAGACANTH over the years has been the most frequently and successfully used marbling size gum, but other gums and substances have also been used with varying degrees of success, including CARRAGHEEN MOSS, IRISH MOSS, FLEA SEED, and even LINSEED OIL. The last, however, was very seldom used because, although it is easier and more economical to prepare, it deteriorates quickly. Flea seed is stronger and lasts longer but it is of little use in the nonpareil and other combed patterns because the colors are dragged off by the comb. Carragheen moss, which was first used sometime after the middle of the 19th century, is still popular; however, it quickly decomposes unless a preservative such as sodium sulfate, glycerin and water, or formalin is added. (217, 264)

marbling trough. A metal or wooden trough about 3 inches deep and about 1 inch larger all around than the largest sheet to be marbled, and designed to contain the MARBLING SIZE and colors. It is usually rectangular in shape, and has an additional compartment about 4 inches wide partitioned off at one end

which acts as a spillway to receive the coloring matter left after the sheet or book edge has been marbled. (335)

marbling under gilt. *See:* GILT MARBLED EDGES.

marbling water: *See:* MARBLING SIZE.

margin. 1. The area of a page between the printed, written, or illustrative matter and the edges of the leaf. The four margins are usually called the "head" (or top); "fore edge" (or outer, outside, side); "tail" (or bottom, foot); and "inner" (or back, inside, gutter, binding). The proportional width of the margins is an important element in a properly balanced book page. A good (and standard) ratio is: head 2 units, fore edge 3 units, tail 4 units, and inner 1½ units (the opposing inner margins making a total of 3 units). In order for these ratios to exist following trimming, the head, fore edge, and tail margins must be greater by the extent of the trimming, which is usually ⅛ inch for each. 2. The area of a map, drawing, or print, between the line enclosing the information and the edge of the paper. (156, 234)

maril. An acronym for *ma*rbled *i*nlaid *l*eather. It is a method of utilizing waste leather consolidated in stages by mixing scraps of different colored leathers with an appropriate adhesive, e.g., polyvinyl acetate, pressing, and then veneering. Maril is a collage method devised by the English bookbinder PHILIP SMITH, and is used in expressive bookbinding imagery. (311)

marking. 1. The process of stamping or writing identification marks, binding instructions, or other information, on the side of the board paper which is eventually glued to the inside of the board. Marking is done to avoid errors in binding, or to identify the particular library owning the book. 2. The individual marks or a colored thread used by hand- or machine-sewers, collators, or inspectors, to establish their responsibility for the work done. (256)

marking up (marking out). 1. The process of marking the position of cords or tapes on the spine of the gathered sections before sewing. 2. The preliminary marking before the binding in of the design to be followed in decorating or lettering a bookbinding. (156, 256, 335)

mastic. An aromatic, resinous exudation obtained usually in the form of yellowish to greenish lustrous, transparent, brittle tears from incisions in the bark of the mastic tree, *Pistacie lentiscus*, and used, along with sandarach and rectified ethyl alcohol (spirit of wine),

to make a varnish used to impart a high gloss to leather bookbindings. (97)

matching sets. A term indicating that each succeeding year of a periodical is bound as nearly as possible like the preceeding years, with regard to trimmed height (called trimming to recorded size), binding title, lettering format, color and type of covering material, etc. *See also:* RUB (1).

mature. Paper or board which has been seasoned for a period of time before being used. Maturing is important in preventing excessive warping of such materials as binder's board, as well as to have the moisture content of paper and board attain equilibrium with the surrounding atmosphere. *See also:* SEASONING.

mbt. *See:* MERCAPTO-BENZTHIAZOLE.

m.e. Abbreviation for MARBLED EDGES.

mean tensile strength. The average value of the results obtained by testing the tensile strength of a material. Where the material has a warp or machine direction, the testing is conducted in both the machine, or warp, direction and the cross, or weft, direction. (197)

Mearne, Samuel (1624-1683). An English publisher, bookseller, and bookbinder, about whom little definitive knowledge exists. While Mearne's name is associated with the splendid COTTAGE STYLE, some authorities have expressed doubts that he actually bound any books himself, but rather that the famous Mearne bindings were executed by the Dutch bookbinder Suckerman, and that Mearne was a publisher, not a bookbinder. It has been established, however, that Mearne's second apprenticeship was with Jeremy Arnold, a bookbinder, and it is therefore argued that he must have learned the craft, the question being how many books he actually bound. It is probably unlikely that he would have taken the time to bind books following the Restoration, because he quickly became an important figure in the book trade. Mearne acquired the posts of Stationer and Bookseller to the King, and thereafter became Master of the Stationers' Company. It is probably reasonable to assume, however, that, considering his knowledge of bookbinding, he would have continued to take an interest in the work of his bindery.

Regardless of its origin, the cottage style came to be regarded as distinctively English, and attained a popularity which endured with minor variations until the first quarter of the 19th century, thus lasting for a longer period than any other style of book decoration.

Mearne's second son, Charles, was his partner from 1678, and when Charles Mearne died in 1686 the shop seems to have gone to Robert Steele, one of Samuel Mearne's apprentices, who is last recorded in 1710. Steele's daughter, Jane, then took over the business, and was in turn followed (in about 1718) by THOMAS ELLIOTT. The same set of tools can be traced from Samuel Mearne to Elliott, by way of Charles Mearne, Robert Steele, and Jane Steele.

At one time the most elaborate of the Restoration bindings were attributed to Samuel Mearne. *See also:* RECTANGULAR STYLE. (109, 253, 347)

mechanical adhesion. The adhesion that exists between surfaces in which the adhesive secures the adherends by means of interlocking forces. *See also:* SPECIFIC ADHESION. (309)

mechanical binding. The business of binding single leaves in a non-exchangeable form. In such a binding, leaves cannot be added, removed, or relocated in the book, as is possible in the case of LOOSE-LEAF BINDING. Mechanical binding may be done on many levels of technology, and is usually part of the services of the job bindery. The forms which mechanical binding can take include spiral, coil, ring, cercla (a binding consisting of connected plastic rings), and comb. Mechanical bindings have several advantages, including: 1) the leaves open flat; 2) pages may be arranged in any order, and may be of varying weights and sizes; 3) there is no need to impose and print in even forms, as 8, 16, 32, etc., pages; and 4) the bindings are simpler and less expensive than sewn and/or adhesive bindings. They also have disadvantages, however, some of which are: 1) they are more expensive than simple wire stitched bindings; 2) when the book is open, the left hand page is usually (higher) or lower than the right, by half the distance between the holes; 3) they do not provide the support and protection often desired in permanent bindings; and 4) pages are more easily lost, torn out, or stolen. Mechanical bindings are frequently used for calendars, diaries, price books, notebooks, catalogs, instruction books, etc. (320)

mechanical deckle-edge paper. An imitation DECKLE EDGE produced in a paper by applying mechanical abrasion, or other treatment, to the edges of the sheet. (17)

mechanical fasteners. A general term applied to books with paper covers held together (either permanently or temporarily) with metal or plastic fasteners, such as staples, nails, coils, posts, and plastic or metal strips. (259)

mechanical marblers. *See:* MARBLE ROLLERS.

mechanical wood pulp. A papermaking pulp produced by mechanical means only. The resultant fibers, which are produced by abrading the de-barked logs against a grinding wheel, are short, the average length being about 3 to 4 mm, with an average diameter of about 0.03 mm. Paper made from 100% mechanical wood pulp has relatively low strength, discolors fairly rapidly upon exposure to air and light (possibly because no lignin is removed from the fibers), and has very little permanence. It does, however, possess good bulk, opacity, and compressibility, which are desirable characteristics in some boards, book papers, and printing or writing papers. The wood used is almost always one of the softwoods, although in certain instances hardwoods are also used. The most important physical properties of mechanical wood pulp are freeness, relative length of fiber, uniformity of fiber length, strength, color, and cleanliness.

This type of pulp is generally used with a proportion of chemical wood pulp, the percentage ranging from about 15 to 50. Chemical tests for determining the presence of mechanical wood pulp include the iodine-zinc chloride test, which gives a yellow result, as does aniline sulfate, and phloroglucinol, which gives a bright red. (17, 143)

meeting guard. *See:* REVERSED V-GUARD.

mellowing. A term sometimes applied to the process of allowing the leather used for covering a book to absorb the first application of paste so as to saturate the pores of the leather before the second application of paste immediately before covering. (115)

mending. A somewhat contradictory term which, in its most elementary sense, refers to the minor restoration of a book with no replacement of any material or the separation of the text block from its case or covers. In this sense mending is not so complete a rehabilitation as RESTORATION. In a more complex sense, however, "mending" can be a long, involved process. The mending of torn leaves, for example, in which the tears occur in the folds, involves a process which necessarily includes taking the book

completely apart. (173, 335)

mercapto-benzthiazole (m. b. t.). A crystalline heterocyclic compound (C_7H_4NS (SH)), which is prepared by the treatment of thiocarbanilide with sulfur, or by heating aniline, carbon disulfide, and nitrobenzene. M. B. T. is useful under certain conditions as a paper fungicide, generally in a concentration of 0.1% by weight of the paper. It contains no chlorine and can be applied either as an aqueous or non-aqueous solution. (198)

mercuric chloride. A colorless, odorless, and non-volatile compound ($HgCl_2$), which is the oldest and perhaps best known of the paper fungicides. It can be applied in an aqueous or non-aqueous solution and is usually used in concentrations as low as 0.1% by weight of the paper. It is liable to liberate hydrochloric acid under certain conditions; however, since it contains only a small percentage of chlorine, and is usually effective in very low concentrations, it is not very likely to be dangerous in this respect. Its major disadvantage is its violently toxic nature, which has led to its use being legally restricted in the United States. (198, 235)

merrythought. A finishing tool in the form of a wishbone, or "merrythought," usually embellished with cusps or foliage. It was used on late 15th century and 16th century blind stamped bindings. (250)

metal back binders. Binders of the expanding-post type, generally with a steel or aluminum spine. Each side post has four alternately solid and tubular telescopic posts attached. The posts alternate so that a thin solid post is adjacent to a thick hollow post, which prevents looseness in any part of the binder. A key at one end of the spine plate operates a transmission rod to widen the distance between the clamping bars, thus allowing leaves to be inserted or removed. Because of the telescopic posts, this type of binder has a fixed minimum capacity, while the maximum is always twice the minimum. *See also:* LOOSE-LEAF BINDING; MECHANICAL BINDING. (276)

metallic inks. Printing inks used to produce colored effects, such as gold, silver, copper, or bronze. Unless used on coated paper, and initial printing of a sizing material is done, the results will be unsatisfactory. (140)

metallic thread. *See:* WIRE THREAD. *See also:* PURL.

metalwork. A decorative ornament found

on numerous rolls; it consists of fancy work in imitation of wrought and curved ironwork filling a small panel. (250)

methylated spirit. Ethyl alcohol (ethanol, or grain alcohol) denatured with methonol, or other denaturant, e.g., benzene, and used to dilute spirit stains.

methyl bromide. A colorless volatile liquid (CH_3Br), prepared by the action of bromine in methyl alcohol in the presence of phosphorus, followed by distillation. It is used as a fumigant for books and other materials.

methyl cellulose. Cellulose methyl ether, produced by treating cellulose from wood or cotton with an alkali, such as sodium hydroxide, followed by methyl chloride. The resulting product is a white granular solid, soluble in cold water but insoluble in hot water. It is used as a thickening agent for aqueous preparations and as a substitute for natural gums, and particularly as a stabilizer in emulsions. It has also been used to greaseproof paper and as an additive in adhesives to increase film strength, flexibility and adhesion. (198)

methyl magnesium carbonate. An organic compound, ($CH_3OMgOCO_2CH_3 \cdot xCO_2$), with x being variable depending on the solvent used. It is prepared by treating a solution of magnesium methoxide with carbon dioxide until saturation is attained. The resulting solution is clear, colorless, and has a pH of approximately 7.0. It has been recommended as a non-aqueous deacidifying agent for paper, preferably in low concentrations, e.g., 0.7 to 1.0%. Its advantages are said to be: 1) a mild pH, due to the neutral character of the solution and direct conversion to magnesium carbonate upon hydrolysis; and 2) convenience of use due to the decreased sensitivity of the solution to water, which assists in preventing premature precipitation.

mica paste. An adhesive produced from ISINGLASS dissolved in a suitable solvent. It is used in guarding.

Michel, Marius. The name employed by Jean Michel (1821-1890) and his son, Henri François (1846-1925), who were distinquished Parisian bookbinders. The work of the elder Michel, while technically excellent, was largely traditional. Henri François, on the other hand, was more enterprising, and used curved stamps instead of small dies and fillets to work exotic flower and leaf forms, and also attempted to relate the decoration of the book cover to its contents. He was the first bookbinder to suggest that the mood of the

book should be continued in the design and color of the binding. He may, in fact, be called the founder of the 20th century French school of binding. The designs of the two binders were often based on natural forms and the ornament is often expressed in color, outlined in blind, and very often without the use of gold. *See* PLATE X. (140, 347)

microcrystalline wax. A WAX obtained from the heavy lubricating oil fraction derived from crude oil, subsequent to the removal of PARAFFIN (WAX). Its characteristics resemble those of the natural waxes closely, including its high melting point, high viscosity, flexibility at low temperatures, and high cohesion and adhesion. It is used as a substitute for other waxes in laminating paper and foils, as well as for polishes, etc.

microencapsulated adhesive. An adhesive employing microencapsulation (a procedure for containing liquids, e.g., the dye in carbonless copy paper, in microscopic pods which are crushed to release their contents) so as to cause it to act instantly, i.e., the adhesive sets the instant the capsules are crushed. The "adhesive," for example, could be applied to the boards or board papers of a book at any time during binding. Pressing the book would crush the capsules creating the adhesive. The process would have particular use in edition binding, as it would solve the problem of timing inherent in most modern machines, where the glue (at the correct temperature and viscosity) must reach its application area (in correct film thickness) an instant after the work is properly positioned but before machine pressure is applied, which is a set of circumstances very difficult to keep in proper adjustment. The use of microencapsulated adhesives would also be of considerable benefit to library binders. As of this time, such adhesives are only in the experimental stage. (89)

microfilm. Generally, a 35 mm film bearing a photographic record in reduced form of print or other graphic material, such as books, newspapers, documents, etc. Although originally intended to save both space and the handling of the originals, microfilm is currently being used extensively as a method of "preserving" the literary content of deteriorating materials.

micrometer. An instrument used for measuring thickness of materials such as paper, cloth, leather, and board.

microscopy. The use of, or investigation

by means of, a microscope. A microscope consists of an optical device containing one or more lenses and is used to view minute objects, generally those larger than .005 mm. A one-lens instrument is known as a simple microscope, while one with two or more lenses is called a compound microscope. Instruments which interpose oil of the same refractive index as glass between the object and the objective are used for high power work. The limit of resolving power is equal approximately to the wavelength of the light source used, i.e., points separated by 4×10^{-5} cm. Objects smaller than this can be detected as bright points in the ultramicroscope, while their actual shape and dimensions can be examined in the electron microscope, in which a beam of electrons is used in lieu of light and is focused by electrostatic or magnetic fields. Resolution down to 5×10^{-8} cm is theoretically possible with such an instrument, which is, however, difficult to use because of the necessity of mounting the specimen in a vacuum. The microscope is a valuable instrument for the study of paper and leather fibers, etc. (195)

Middleton, Bernard C. (1924-). One of the outstanding modern day bookbinders and conservationists, Middleton won a Trade Scholarship to the Central School of Arts and Crafts, Southhampton Row in 1938, and was apprenticed to the British Museum Bindery in 1940. He was a City and Guilds Silver Medalist in 1943. Middleton was later bookbinder at the Royal College of Art and, for a short time, managed the Zaehnsdorf bindery. He started his own business as a book restorer in 1953.

Middleton's forwarding is considered to be superlative, while his designs and tooling, though restrained, are always in good taste and are superbly executed. He is also considered to be one of the most skillful book restorers at work today.

Aside from being a gifted bookbinder, Middleton is recognized as an outstanding scholar in the field of bookbinding history, and is the author of a comprehensive work entitled *A History of English Craft Bookbinding Technique,* as well as *The Restoration of Leather Bindings.* He is unique among historians of bookbindings because he writes with such a vast knowledge of technique, largely overlooked by others.

migration. A condition or process of extraction, in which an aqueous or organic solvent selectively dissolves part of an adhesive film, and carries it to a different location as the solvent evaporates. The term also refers to the penetration of an adhesive plasticizer into the adherends due to the attraction of the adherend for the plasticizer. *See also:* ACID MIGRATION.

mil. A unit of linear measurement, equivalent to 0.001 inch.

mildew. A growth caused by micro-organisms, whose spores, in a moist, warm environment, become molds. They derive their food from the substance on which they form, e.g., the materials of a book. During their growth they produce citric, gluconic, oxalic, or other organic acids, that can damage paper, leather, cloth, etc. They also at times produce color bodies, leading to staining which is difficult to remove.

In counteracting mildew, every part of the affected book must be treated with the inhibitor most suited for it. The best preventatives, however, are thorough cleanliness, sunlight, dry circulating air, and relatively low temperature. *See also:* FUNGI; MOLD (4). (144, 363)

millboard. A high grade of hard, tough binder's board, dark brown to black in color. It has a smooth finish produced by rolling or milling under high pressure. Originally, millboard was produced from old tarred rope, sacking, and similar materials and was called "black board" or "rope board"; however, genuine rope millboard is now virtually impossible to obtain, except from covers discarded from old bindings. It is now made from waste paper, various wood pulps, screenings, with the better grades containing some hemp and flax fibers. The sheet is produced on a wet machine and is calendered by passing it through a board calender several times. The final thickness of the board generally ranges from 0.036 to 0.144 inch.

Old millboard contains sufficient iron impurities to promote the formation of sulfuric acid due to the presence of sulfur dioxide in the atmosphere, much in the same manner as in paper, although at a much slower rate. Millboard, furthermore, often suffers from an additional defect from the point of view of the bookbinder, namely, excessive lamination stemming from the pressure used in calendering. This excessive lamination can cause the corners of the boards to be subject to splitting and mashing.

Rope fiber millboards were first produced in the late 17th century, but they were not in general use until per-haps the first and possibly the second decade of the 18th century, and even then only in the superior grades of binding. The cheaper machine-made boards were in use as early as the 19th century. Millboard was used continuously until the Second World War in the better grades of binding. (82, 161, 198, 236, 335)

millboard machine. *See:* ROTARY BOARD CUTTER.

mimeograph paper. A type of paper used for producing copies on a mimeograph machine. The paper is produced from numerous furnishes, including those containing cotton fibers and bleached chemical wood pulps, mechanical wood pulp, and combinations thereof. Absorbency, absence of fuzz, finish, and opacity are desired characteristics. The usual basis weight is 20 pounds (17 × 22 − 500) but basis weight may range from 16 to 24 pounds. (17)

mimosa. *See:* WATTLE (BARK).

mineral acids. *See:* INORGANIC ACIDS.

mineral tanning. A method of converting hides and skins into leather by the use of metals, e.g., chromium, aluminum and potassium (alum), iron, and zirconium. The first mineral tannage, called "tawing," involved the use of alum and salt. *See:* TAWING. *See also:* CHROME TANNING; ZIRCONIUM TANNING.

miniature book. A small to very small book, generally up to 3, or perhaps even 4 inches in height, in which the principal, if not only, interest lies in its small size. It is designed on a small scale (although some consider books reduced in size by photographic means to qualify as miniatures), printed with small type, bound and decorated on a small scale, and, if illustrated, provided with reproductions appropriate to the size of the book.

The idea of a miniature is artificial, although they are very popular. Many Bibles, devotional works, almanacs, classics, etc., have been issued in miniature form from an early date. (69, 156)

minium. A red lead (ground cinnabar) of Iberian origin, mixed with water and egg white, and used in the rubrication of Egyptian papyri and in the production of miniatures. (140)

mint. A book which is in the same new and unblemished condition as when it was first published. A "mint" condition of a book usually implies that it still has its book jacket, if provided originally, which is also new and unblemished. (69)

mirror binding. A style of decoration featuring a dark marbled central panel (the mirror), surrounded by a gold tooled frame and, outside of that, a lighter area that is also surrounded, but by a blind rather than a gold tooled line. The spine is usually heavily gilt. So-called mirror bindings were popular in Denmark in the 18th century. (104)

misbound. One or more leaves or sections of a book which have been incorrectly folded, bound in the wrong place, or bound in upside down. Text blocks bound in upside down are a common occurrence in edition binding.

miscellaneous binding. 1 Primarily a British term applied to a style of hand binding that is not of as high a quality as extra binding, but considerably superior to edition binding. Under this category may be included work done for a book collector who desires something better than the regular publisher's (edition) binding. 2. *See:* JOB BINDING. (343)

missing leaves. Any leaves not included in, or removed from, a section, gathering, or bound book.

missing picks. The contiguous pick (filling) threads missing from a portion of the width of a fabric.

mistletoe tool. A finishing tool which, despite its name, impresses a design more like a feather than a mistletoe leaf. Apparently it was first used on Irish bindings about 1766, and was afterwards used on the spine panels of Irish bindings of about 1780. (96, 156)

mitered. 1. A binding ornamentation on the spine or covers of a book, either in gold or blind, consisting of straight lines that meet but do not pass beyond the vertical panel or "run-up" lines on either side. A fillet or pallet may be used to make the lines; however, the fillet is not generally used on the spine of a book except when executing the RUN-UP GILT BACK. 2. The juncture at the corners of the turn-ins edged to an angle of 45°. *See:* CORNER MITERING; NICKED CORNER. 3. The connection at the angles of an outer frame to an inner frame or panel by the diagonal use of a fillet or roll. (161, 183, 236, 335)

mitsumata. A shrub, *Edgeworthia papyrifera*, found in temperate Asia and cultivated in Japan for its bark, the fibers of which are used in papermaking.

m. m. system. A method of computing the basis weights of all grades of paper on a sheet size of 25 by 40 inches (1,000 square inches) and a 1,000-sheet count, i.e., the 1,000, 1,000 or m. m. system. The traditional writing paper basis weight of 20 pounds (17 × 22 − 500) becomes 107 pounds on an m. m. basis (25 × 40 — 1000), while regular 60-pound book paper (25 × 38 — 500) becomes 126 pounds, and so on. The m. m. system, which originated in the 1920s, is not in general use but printers, paper buyers, as well as others, often find it advantageous to use. In applying the m. m. system, a conversion chart is used which lists various grades with their traditional basis weights and corresponding m. m. factors. (17, 320, 329)

mocha (mocha suede). A leather produced from the Arabian blackhaired sheep (commonly called blackhair mochas). It is a chrome-tanned leather, with the grain removed by mechanical abrading rather than by hand frizing. It is suede-finished on the flesh side. This leather retains most of the fibers of the skin, and its particular fineness is due to the closeness of the fibers of the skin. (351)

mock flexible. A more or less obsolete term which has been interpreted to mean either a binding with a tight back and false bands, being "mock" because it is flexible but has false bands, or a binding with a hollow back and false bands, being "mock" for both reasons (371)

modeled-leather covers. A method of decorating a book in which the leather cover is molded, cut, or hammered to raise a design in relief, or in which the leather is laid over a decorative foundation attached to the boards. The style is found on the Stonyhurst Gospel (7th or 8th century) and on some Coptic bindings of 100 or 200 years later, but is not seen again, at least in British craft bookbinding, until the end of the 19th century. (236)

modern monastic. A style of bookbinding which characteristically employed very thick boards, red, brown, or gilt edges, and unusually high raised bands. The usual leather used was divinity calf, as well as brown or red morocco. The design was blocked in blind, or tooled in blind with rolls, fillets and stamps. It consisted of a center pattern featuring heavy lines and solid figures within a rectangle, which, in turn, was within an elaborately embossed rectangle surrounded by a mitered border. Modern monastic was very popular in the middle of the 19th century. (241)

modified starches. Starches that have undergone certain biological, chemical, or physical treatment which changes their viscosity and/or chemical characteristics and which are used in the manufacture of paper. (17)

modifier. Any chemically inert ingredient which when added to an adhesive changes its properties. *See also:* EX-TENDER (1); FILLER (5); PLASTICIZER (1).

modulus of elasticity. The ratio of stress to strain within the elastic range of a material. In an adhesve, it is an empirical measurement of the elastic deformation of which an adhesive film is capable. (222)

Mohs' scale. A scale used to determine the hardness of solids, especially minerals. It is named after the German mineralogist Friedrich Mohs. The scale reads as given below:

Hardness	Material
1	Talc—easily scratched by the fingernail
2	Gypsum—just scratched by the fingernail
3	Calcite—scratches and is scratched by a copper coin
4	Fluorite—not scratched by a copper coin and does not scratch glass
5	Apatite—just scratches glass and is easily scratched by a knife
6	Orthoclase — easily scratches glass and is just scratched by a file
7	Quartz—not scratched by a file
8	Topaz
9	Corundum
10	Diamond

The scale has been extended as follows:

Hardness	Material
1	Liquid
2–6	As indicated above on the chart
7	Vitreous pure silica
8	Quartz
9	Topaz
10	Garnet
11	Fuzed zirconia
12	Fuzed alumina
13	Silicon carbide
14	Boron carbide
15	Diamond

(195)

moiré book cloth. A book cloth having an irregular, wavy finish produced by embossing in such a manner as to resemble watered silk. Prayer books and Bibles sometimes have endpapers consisting of a folded sheet of black moiré cloth mounted on a paper flyleaf. Moiré book cloth was at one time used fairly frequently for doublures. It was also one of the earliest decorative effects applied to the calico used for publishers' bindings. (339)

moiré effect. The optical illusion observed when curved parallel lines are superimposed, forming an illusionary pattern. WATERED SILK is an example of the moiré effect. (233)

moisture content. The amount of actual moisture in a material. The moisture content varies according to prevailing natural or controlled atmospheric conditions. *See also:* HUMIDITY; RELATIVE HUMIDITY.

moisture proofness. The ability of a material to resist the passage of water, either in the liquid or vapor form. In book materials, generally, it indicates a material with unusually low WATER-VAPOR PERMEABILITY. *See also:* WATERPROOF; WATER RESISTANCE.

moisture vapor transmission. A measure of the ability of an adhesive or plastic film or coating to resist the penetration of moisture through the film or coating into the substrata. It is usually measured in grams per square meter over a period of 24 hours. Abbreviated M. V. T. (233)

mold. 1. The rectangular wooden frame over which the brass wires or a wire cloth is stretched and through which water drains away from the pulp fibers in the formation of a sheet of handmade paper. *See also:* DECKLE (2). 2. A packet of leaves of gold interleaved into 1,000 goldbeater's skins, each 5 inches square. The mold stage of goldbeating is the final and most exacting of the three stages of beating. *See:* GOLD LEAF. 3. In printing, a device in two parts used for casting movable type. 4. A multi-cellular, microscopic vegetable plant which forms cobweblike masses of branching threads from the surface of which tiny fertile threads project into the air bearing the part of the plant from which spores develop. Mold may be of brilliant colors or black and white, depending on the type. Molds can develop on leather, cloth, paper, etc., especially in the presence of relatively high heat and relative humidity. *See also:* FUNGI; MILDEW. (29, 198)

molding iron. *See:* BACK-MOLDING IRON.

mold-made paper. A deckle-edged paper resembling handmade paper but actually produced on a cylinder machine or a cylindrical mold revolving in a vat of paper pulp. The sizes of the sheets are determined by dividing the surface of the cylinder with rubber bands which also create the deckle edges. The deckle edge may also be simulated by cutting the web with a jet of water. Mold-made paper is used in limited editions where a handmade or simulated handmade paper is desired. (58, 307)

mold resistant paper (and board). A paper or board which has been rendered mold resistant by treatment with mold-inhibiting chemicals, such as the chlorophenates. (17)

moleskin. A heavy, durable cotton book cloth made in satin weave, usually with a smooth twilled surface on one side, and a short, thick, velvety nap on the other. At one time it was used for covering blankbooks. (264, 276)

monastic bindings. *See:* ECCLESIASTICAL BINDINGS.

Le Monnier family. A group of some twenty French bookbinders, of whom Louis François and his son, Jean, were the best known. The family was involved in bookbinding from the first half of the 17th century to about the middle of the 18th century. They used floral decorations and designs suggestive of Chinese lace, and their bindings were beautifully tooled, often with fantastic designs, but not always in the best taste. They also made extensive use of mosaics. *See:* MOSAIC BINDING. (342)

monotype. A machine used for casting individual pieces of type. It was invented by Tolbert Lanston (1844-1913) in about 1889 and was put into commercial operation in about 1897. The monotype is a distinct improvement over the LINOTYPE in that the individual types produced facilitate replacement in case of error. The monotype composing machine is the most successful thus far developed, its product being almost equal to that of hand composition. (313).

Montagu style. A style of book decoration deriving its name from Montagu of the firm Montagu and Johnson, London bookbinders, who flourished in the later half of the 18th century. The principal features of the style are corners and centers filled with stops, etc., similar to illustrations. The tools used are mainly of an open leafy description, flowing from a stem of scroll or curl. (241)

mordant. A compound, such as a salt or hydroxide of chromium, iron, aluminum, or tin, used to fix a dye in or on a substance, such as a fabric, leather, or paper, by combining with the dye to form an insoluble compound. *See also:* LAKE. (130, 195)

mordant dyes. Dyes of varied constitution, all of which possess an acid character. Because of the presence of hydroxyl or carboxyl groups in their molecules they are capable of forming lakes with metallic mordants. The methods by which the mordant colors can be attached to a fiber depend on the nature of both the dyestuff and the fiber. (235)

morocco. A vegetable tanned leather having a characteristic pinhead grain pattern developed either naturally or by means of graining or boarding, but *never* by embossing. The most common and characteristic grain pattern is known as "hard grain."

By long usage, the term "morocco" is taken to denote a goatskin, tanned by *any* vegetable tannage, and boarded in the wet condition; in a more strict interpretation, however, morocco is defined as a goatskin tanned exclusively with SUMAC, and boarded in the wet condition. Leather made from vegetable tanned goatskin having a grain pattern resembling that of genuine morocco, but produced other than by hand boarding, is more properly termed "morocco grained goat" or "assisted morocco."

When properly produced, morocco goatskins are very durable, flexible, beautifully grained, and relatively strong, making them eminently suitable for use as a bookbinding leather. The skins are (or, at least, have been) obtained from several areas, including: wild goats, principally from Africa, which generally produce heavy skins with a very bold grain, e.g., LEVANT; domestic goats, which produce a leather with the more familiar hard grain or PINHEAD MOROCCO; and true PERSIAN MOROCCO, which is produced from Indian or East Indian goatskins. The term, however, is also applied (incorrectly) to East Indian sheepskin tanned with condensed tannins and dressed in imitation of goatskin; so-called Cape morocco (produced from goatskins from the Cape of Good Hope), which, when obtainable, were of high quality and had the most pronounced grain pattern and the richest finish; and NIGER goatskins, which are soft and can be obtained in a wide range of colors.

Alum-tawed "morocco" stained pink, was first produced by the Moors, possibly before the 11th century. Vegetable-tanned morocco was in use in some part of Europe in the 16th century, particularly in Italy where the goat was more common than in the north of Europe, where calfskin was more abundant. Morocco leather was rarely used in England before 1600.

Straight-grained morocco was popular in the late 18th and early 19th centuries. Bright red and green were the most popular colors, with dark blue, black, citron, and even purple skins also being used.

Throughout the 19th century, morocco, in its various grain patterns, was used in the finest bookbinding, and it is still used for much of the better binding, although it is very expensive and is also becoming more and more difficult to obtain.

Today, to refer to a leather as "morocco" gives no indication as to the subspecies "Levant," "Niger," etc., since most of the morocco now used in bookbinding comes from other parts of the world. The only common denominator among the numerous varieties of leather which now go under the name morocco is that they are all goatskins. (236, 291, 343, 351)

morocco cloth. *See:* IMPERIAL MOROCCO CLOTH.

morpholine. A colorless organic liquid ($Na \cdot (CH_2)_2 \cdot O \cdot (CH_2)_2$), which boils at 128° C., and has a characteristic ammonialike and slightly fishy odor. It has been proposed as a vapor-phase deacidifying agent, mainly because it is inexpensive, easily used, and deacidifies rapidly in suitable chambers. Its main disadvantage, other than its highly disagreeable odor, is the tendency of the treated paper to revert to an acid condition in the presence of high relative humidity.

Morris, William (1834-1896). An English poet, painter, architect and printer, who led the movement in search of higher standards of workmanship among craft bookbinders in the latter years of the 19th century. It was Morris' wife who recommended that Cobden-Sanderson take up bookbinding. Later Cobden-Sanderson founded the Doves Bindery to bind books produced by the Kelmscott Press. Morris and his group also sought to improve the quality of the materials used in bookbinding, and, under his influence, great emphasis was placed on both utility and beauty. While Morris' name is best remembered for his revival of fine printing, some outstanding bindings were executed on editions of beautifully printed books produced at his Kelmscott Press, which he founded in 1891. These vellum bindings were not ornamented except for the title in gold on the spine, and had projecting covers which were bent over the fore edge. Ribbon ties held the covers closed. They had flat spines, and were sewn on tapes, which were extended to the fore edge to form the ties. (339, 347)

mosaic bindings. Bookbindings decorated by inlaying or onlaying small pieces of leather of various colors to form patterns. The technique is particularly associated with the work of the 19th century French bookbinders, Antoine Michel Padeloup, Louis François, and Jean Le Monier. This form of decoration has been used for a considerable length of time; examples of mosaics of inlaid leather, while extremely rare, date back to the 16th century. Painted mosaics consist of geometrical interlacings filled with a colored and varnished incrustation, with borders of gold lines. Very brilliant when first executed, the composition in time cracks and peels off, thus damaging the line work of gold encircling it. *See* PLATE VII. (90, 150, 329, 334)

mossing. The process of finishing the flesh side of leather with a mixture of (Irish) carragheen moss and French chalk, which leaves the surface smooth and white. (338)

mottled. A variegated effect produced on the surface of a material, such as paper; by the addition of heavily dyed fibers, called mottling fibers, to the papermaking stock. Mottled papers are used for endpapers, pattern papers, cover papers, and other kinds of decorative papers. (17)

mottled calf. A calfskin binding which has been decorated with an irregular pattern produced by staining the covers of the book with dabs or flecks of ferrous sulfate. *See also:* TREE CALF. (69, 264)

mottled edges. A form of edge decoration produced by daubing color lightly over the edges of a book, generally by means of a sponge which leaves its natural markings on the edges. The edges may be colored over first, or the mottling may be applied directly to the white edges. Red and black are frequently used combinations. Mottled edges are found mainly on large blankbooks but seldom on letterpress bindings. (256)

mottled sheep. A sheepskin treated with colors in an irregular pattern.

mottling. 1. The process of decorating the covers of a book by applying color or acid to the leather. *See, for example,* MOTTLED CALF. *See also:* TREE CALF. 2. In printing, a defect appearing: 1) on a solid print as a variation in color intensity across the sheet or as a variation in gloss; or 2) as a blotchiness due to frothmarking. Mottling may be caused by localized variations in either ink receptivity or penetration; in the former it may be predominantly a difference in hue, while in the latter it will generally be a result of a difference in gloss. 3. The uneven dyeing of paper pulp fibers resulting from the coloring of a small number of fibers before complete dispersion of the dye. This is due to the manner of addition of a hot concentrated solution of dyestuff to the beater, or of dyeing a combination furnish containing fibers which take up the dye more readily than others. 4. An uneven dyeing of a paper due to the application of drops of dye on the web while it is on the Fourdrinier wire or on the finished sheet after it has left the papermaking machine. (17, 93, 159, 172)

mounted and tipped. A plate that is smaller than the leaf to which it is to be attached, and which is positioned above the caption and secured by tipping along the top or side edge, or at the corners. The entire plate is not usually pasted down because of the greater danger of cockling, particularly if the grain directions of the two papers are in opposition. (276)

mounted on guards. *See:* GUARDS (2).

mounts. *See:* BOSSES.

mucilage. An aqueous adhesive consisting of GUM ARABIC or fish glue, plasticized with glycerin, glycol, or sorbitol, with a small amount of a preservative and odorant added. In a more general sense, mucilage is a liquid adhesive having a low order of bonding strength. The terms mucilage and mucilaginous are also commonly used as generic terms describing gummy or gluey watermiscible substances. (235, 309)

mucilaginous liquid. *See:* GUM; MARBLING; MUCILAGE.

mudéjar style. A style of Spanish bookbinding of the 13th and early 14th centuries. In the most typical of such bindings the main decorative feature consists of a blind geometrical pattern with double outline interlacings (strapwork), with either all or part of the background being filled in with dots, small tools, and the like. Various types of small oblong or square stamps were also used, not all mudéjar in character. In typical Muslim tradition, however, tools representing living creatures were avoided. Although the characteristic mudéjar binding was decorated in blind, later bindings were decorated in both blind and gold. Most of the mudéjar bindings have wooden boards (and the remainder pasteboards) and the majority are covered in CORDOVAN LEATHER. The name derives from the Mudéjares, or Moors, who remained in Spain during and after the Christian reconquest of that country. *See also:* GÓTICO-MUDÉJAR STYLE. (245, 330)

mull. An English term for the coarse, loosely woven cotton fabric used principally to line the spines of edition bindings. Also called CRASH or "super." *See also:* SPINE LINING FABRIC.

mullen. A term used with reference to the bursting strength of paper. It is so called from the the name of the instrument used in conducting the test, invented by John W. Mullen, in 1887.

multiple spindle drill. A paper drill which can be fitted with a number of adjustable heads. It is used for drilling several holes in a lift of paper or along the binding edge of a pile of sheets to be side sewn.

murex. A purple dye obtained from marine gastropods (Family *Muricidae*), and used in the Middle Ages for embellishing manuscripts.

muriatic acid. The old name for HYDROCHLORIC ACID.

music manuscript (music paper). A paper printed with staff lines and used for the writing of musical scores. It is produced from rag and/or bleached chemical wood pulps. It is stiff enough to stand in a music rack and has a surface that will take pencil or pen and ink. Basis weights generally from 60 to 80 pounds ($25 \times 38 - 500$) or 24 to 30 pounds ($17 \times 22 - 500$). Erasability is an important characteristic. Music printings are used for reproducing music, and are produced mainly from bleached chemical wood pulp. The paper is well formed and is sized and processed to insure good pick strength and minimum curl. The basis weights range from 60 to 90 pounds ($25 \times 38 - 500$). (17)

muslin. A plain woven cotton fabric, made in various qualities ranging from coarse to sheer. For use in bookbinding, it is usually sized, starched, or blued to reduce stretching or shrinking. (237)

mustard plasters. *See:* YELLOWBACK.

mutton thumper. An old term for an incompetent bookbinder.

mutton thumping. An old term applied in England to the binding of school books in sheepskin.

mutual solvent. A volatile solvent so called because it is miscible with more than one class of liquids. Acetone, for example, is miscible with water, alcohol, and ether, as well as with oil, alcohol, or ethereal fluids. Such a material is also known as a coupling agent because it can cause two ordinarily immiscible liquids to combine with each other, forming a clear solution. (233)

M. V. T. *See:* MOISTURE VAPOR TRANSMISSION.

myrabolans (myrobalans). A vegetable tanning material obtained from the dried astringent fruits of certain species of *Terminalia,* and used extensively in the tanning of leather. The dried fruit is rich in tannin, averaging 30 to 32%, but the percentage varies greatly with different grades and sources.

One of the principal advantages of myrabolan extract, which has to a large extent replaced sumac and plant galls in European tanneries, is its acid-forming properties. It contains 3 to 5% sugars, which is much more than most other tannins contain; consequently fermentation takes place readily in the tan liquor and satisfactory plumping of the hides and skins is obtained in the early stages of tanning. Myrabolan tannin also contains a large proportion of ellagitannic acid, and thus readily deposits bloom. The disadvantages of the tannin are its slow penetration, and its tendency to produce a spongy leather of poor wearing quality. Because of these characteristics, myrabolans is usually blended with other more astringent tannins, e.g., wattle, quebracho, or mangrove, which penetrate faster.

Myrabolans is a pyrogallol class of tannin, with low viscosity, a medium pH (3.2) and salts content, and very high acids content. The tannin also contains chebulinic acid and a fairly high proportion of ellagitannin.

In addition to its used in the tanning industry, myrabolan tannin is also used as a black dye and in the manufacture of some inks. *See also:* VEGETABLE TANNINS. (175, 298, 306)

nailing. A method of securing the leaves or sections of a book (usually a newspaper or a book in sheets that has an ample binding margin) in which ordinary flat-heated nails, or specially designed nails or staples, are driven through the paper near the binding edge from both sides. The nails are slightly shorter than the thickness of the pile of leaves, so that they do not emerge from the paper on the reverse side of the pile. This style of binding is cut flush and is not rounded and backed. Unless the book is very large, and is made up of suitable paper, a nailed binding usually has poor to very poor OPENABILITY. (146, 259)

naphthylene. A crystalline aromatic hydrocarbon ($C_{10}H_8$), obtained from coal tar, that is sometimes used to destroy or inhibit the spread of bookworms, and is also spread among dried goatskins to lessen the danger of attacks by insects during shipment and storage. (83, 363)

nappa leather. A soft, full grain leather made from an unsplit sheepskin, lambskin, or kidskin, usually tanned with alum and chromium salts and dyed throughout.

nap side. The soft, fibrous surface of a leather or cloth, as opposed to the smoother reverse side, i.e., the grain side of a leather. The term is usually applied to velvet cloth and ooze or suede leathers to indicate the face of the material. Normally, the side opposite the grain side of a leather is termed the "flesh side." (102, 256)

natural dyestuffs. A class of dyes extracted and processed from plant or animal sources, as distinguished from dyestuffs manufactured from derivatives of coal-tar. The use of natural dyes predates recorded history. Other dyestuffs were later developed in ancient Greece, Rome, and the Orient, while still others were used in medieval and Renaissance times. Although still used to a limited extent for specialized work or for reasons of economy, their use in archival work is now virtually obsolete.

Few, if any, of the natural dyestuffs are resistant to external influences, such as light; they do, however, fade at different rates. Upon fading, they

either darken or undergo a change in hue.

Some of the natural dyestuffs are: blues—indigo, woad, chemic, and Prussian blue; reds—madder, cochineal, brazilwood, alkanet, annatto, and safflower; yellows—fustic, quercitron, dock, goldenrod, sassafras, and tumeric; browns—butternut, catechu, alder, and hemlock; purples—orchil and cudbear; blacks—logwood; and neutral colors—barks of various trees, including birches and oaks, galls and sumac. (4)

neat's-foot oil. A pale yellow, fatty oil produced by boiling the feet and shin bones of cattle, horses, sheep, and pigs, and skimming the oil from the surface of the water. Like all natural fats, neat's-foot oil is a mixture of substances, many of which deposit on cooling. "Cold-tested" neat's-foot oil is a material that has been held at the freezing point for a period of time and then filtered. Neat's-foot oil is used in the preparaton of some leather dressings, and in the fatliquoring of leather. (143)

necking. The process of shaving the flesh side of a finished leather to equalize the thickness of the different parts of the skin, and to remove loose adhering flesh. (298)

needle point lace stitch. See: BUTTONHOLE STITCH.

needles. 1. The long, slender, round steel instruments pointed at one end and with an eyelet at the other and through which the thread passes. They are used to carry the thread through paper or cloth in sewing a book through the folds. The eyelet should be designed so as not to cut the thread and yet allow it to pass freely through the holes made in paper or cloth. 2. The special

straight, curved, spiral and/or hollow needles used in machines which sew through the folds of sections, through the side of a pile of leaves, or in lacing sheets together. Most of these needles have the eyelet at the pointed end or carry the thread through the hollow. (183, 256)

needlework binding. See: EMBROIDERED BINDINGS.

network. A term sometimes applied to a finishing design consisting of intersecting lines forming squares. (94, 156)

neutral color. A color that is not dominated by blue or red and which, therefore, is neither warm nor cold. Medium grays and browns are usually classed as neutral colors. (233)

neutral size. See: ROSIN SIZE.

neutral sulfite process. A paper pulping process that dates back to at least 1880, when a method was developed for using an alkaline solution of sulfite in iron digesters. The process employs sodium sulfite with sufficient alkali added, to neutralize the acids developed during the cooking process. The alkali may be caustic soda, soda ash, or sodium bicarbonate. (17, 324)

neutral syntans. SYNTANS which have been adjusted to a pH of 6.0 by the addition of an alkali. They are often miscalled synthetic mordants, whereas they should be referred to as "synthetic leveling agents." (306)

neutral tint. A color which approximates gray. Specifically, it is a nearly neutral, slightly purplish black that is slightly bluer and lighter than slate or sooty black. (233)

newsprint. A generic term applied to the type of paper generally used in printing newspapers. The paper is machine finished and slack sized and has little or no mineral loading. It is made in basis weights of 30 to 35 pounds (24 × 36 — 500). Thirty-two-pound basis weight, which has proven to be the most satisfactory in that it represents a practical compromise between cost and printability, is the most commonly produced weight.

Newsprint is produced at very high machine speeds, which causes the fibers of the sheet to be very directional; however, the fact that the majority of the fibers are oriented in one direction is actually an advantage from the point of view of printing, because it helps the paper take the strain of the high-speed press run, and, from the point of view of production, "runability" is the most important characteristic in newsprint. Other important characteristics include: smoothness, which is the controlling factor for halftone fineness in all direct-printing methods; softness, which is especially important in newsprint because the image carrier forces the ink into the pores of the paper during impression; opacity, which is important in all lightweight paper and particularly so in newspaper relief printing where the ink does not remain on the surface but is forced deep into the paper; and brightness, or whiteness, which is important because it contributes to good contrast between ink and paper in black-and-white printing and is of great importance in full-color printing.

The usual furnish for newsprint is 75 to 85% mechanical pulp, and 15 to 25% unbleached or semibleached chemical pulp. The mechanical pulp adds the desired properties of high opacity, smooth surface, and high oil (ink) absorption, while the chemical pulp adds the necessary strength required to run the paper through fast rotary presses without breaking.

The high percentage of mechanical pulp in newsprint, which makes it very satisfactory for newspaper printing, makes it unsatisfactory from the point of view of permanence. (17, 72, 287, 320)

nibbed. *See:* LIPPED.

nicked corner. The corner of the cover of a book which has the turn-in on the fore edge overlapping the turn-in at head and tail. This type of corner is made by cutting the covering material at a 45° angle at a distance of about three times the thickness of the board from the corner. The head and tail are turned over first, followed by the fore edge. A small tuck forms a smooth edge at the corner. (150)

Niger. A soft vegetable tanned goatskin that has a natural grain pattern resulting from the nature of the skin, the tanning processes employed, and, especially, boarding in the wet condition. Niger, which is now difficult to obtain, is tanned and finished from native skins in Nigeria and surrounding districts by primitive methods, usually employing babul bark as the principal tanning material. The most common colors, which are seldom uniform, include crimson, orange to brick-red, green, as well as the natural buff. The

slight variations in grain surface and color which give Niger its characteristic appearance, are seldom successfully imitated in other skins, such as that of the sheep, which is being increasingly offered as genuine Niger. *See also:* GOATSKIN; MOROCCO. (61, 69)

nip. The point of contact between two rolls, as in a folding machine, rolling press, calender stack, etc.

nipped-in. A term sometimes applied to hand sewing that has been drawn too tightly, resulting in the sections being unduly compressed at the points of the kettle stitches. When the book is subsequently rounded and backed, the hammering may cause the kettle stitches to break. (335)

nipper (nipping machine). 1. A machine used in edition binding to compress the spine of a newly sewn book and in library binding to remove the original backing shoulders of a book that is to be rebound (and usually when it is to be resewn through the folds). The nipping machine in a library bindery is usually a hand-operated, power-driven device, while in the edition bindery it is usually a continuously running, power-operated machine. In its typical design and operation, the book is secured by a spring-operated clamp to prevent the sections from slipping. The front jaw of the nipper is split lengthwise, the top half being held open by heavy springs. It projects beyond the lower half and can be slipped back flush with it. When the book is inserted and the jaws are closed, the upper half catches it and secures it while the lower half applies pressure to the sewing swell or shoulders at the spine.

The first nipper, a hand-operated and power machine, was introduced in 1882.

2. The flanges of a BUILDING-IN MACHINE which form the joints of the book.

3. *See:* BAND NIPPERS. (320, 339)

nipping. 1. The process of reducing the swell caused by the sewing of a book, or the removal of the backing shoulders of a book to be rebound, by applying pressure to the book at the spine *only*, usually between the jaws of a NIPPER (1). *See also:* KNOCKING OUT THE GROOVE; KNOCKING OUT THE SWELL. 2. The process of applying heavy pressure of short duration to a case-bound book for the purpose of setting the joints before the adhesive used in casing-in sets. *See also:* BUILDING-IN MACHINE. (179, 339)

nipping press. A small press consisting essentially of a fixed, horizontal iron base plate, and an upper, movable platen that is raised and lowered by means of a relatively long, vertical screw. The nipping press is used to apply quick and uniform pressure in a variety of bookbinding operations. While the nipping press does not have the available DAYLIGHT or the pressing power of the STANDING PRESS, it is relatively easy to open and close which makes it very useful for a quick pressing operations. The true nipping press does not release its pressure until released by the turning of the screw; however, substitute "nipping presses," which are really "letter-presses" or "copying presses," once used in business offices for "copying" letters, are limited in their ability to apply pressure because they have a tendency to ease the pressure when the handle is released. (203, 335)

nipping up. A covering technique which involves pressing the leather around the raised bands after it has been drawn over the spine of the book. BAND NIPPERS or a BANDSTICK (1) are usually used for this operation.

nitric acid. A corrosive, non-volatile, inorganic acid (HNO_3). It is a strong acid, with most of its important reactions being due to its oxidizing action. Nitric acid reacts violently with cellulosic materials, and can be formed in them by the conversion of nitric oxide (an air pollutant) into nitrogen dioxide, and then into nitric acid: $2NO + O_2 \rightarrow 2NO_2$; $3NO_2 + H_2O \rightarrow 2HNO_3 + NO$. As the amount of nitric oxide in the atmosphere is very small, relative to sulfur dioxide, the formation of nitric acid in archival materials is relatively slow; however, it also functions as a catalyst in the conversion of sulfur dioxide into sulfuric acid.

nitrocellulose. *See:* CELLULOSE NITRATE.

non-aqueous deacidification. A method of deacidifying paper which utilizes alcohol, or some other non-aqueous solvent, for the deacidifying chemical. Aqueous methods cannot be used to treat archival materials in cases in which the ink is susceptible to the action of water; therefore, in such cases a non-aqueous method is essential. One such method involves treating the document with a solution prepared by dissolving 19 gm of crystalline barium hydroxide octahydrate ($Ba(OH)_2 \cdot 8 H_2O$) in one liter of methyl alcohol (which corresponds to a 1% solution of barium hydroxide as a free base). The normal procedure is to immerse the document in the solution, but it may be brushed or sprayed on if the document is too fragile for immersion. While drying, any excess barium hydroxide is converted into barium carbonate ($BaCO_3$) by the action of atmospheric carbon dioxide, giving a final pH of approximately 8.0. Another method is to treat the document with a 1.0 to 1.5% solution of magnesium methoxide in methyl alcohol. In this process the magnesium methoxide is converted by the moisture in the paper into magnesium hydroxide ($Mg(OH_2)$), which is the effective deacidifying agent. Excess magnesium hydroxide is converted into magnesium carbonate ($MgCO_3$) by the action of carbon dioxide in the atmosphere. The final pH is approximately 8.5 to 9.0. *See also*: ALKALINE RESERVE; DEACIDIFICATION; DOUBLE DECOMPOSITION; VAPOR-PHASE DEACIDIFICATION. (198, 366)

non-commingled. A term used with reference to the transportation of unbound or bound books by a library or binder on an unmixed, or separate basis. Binderies which do not operate their own trucks, but rely instead on a common carrier, may be instructed by the library to ship the library's books on a separate basis, that is, not together with other materials not destined for or owned by the library.

non-curling gum. An adhesive used for PADDING work, consisting of gum arabic dissolved in water and mixed with small quantities of glycerin and honey.

nonpareil marble. A marble pattern consisting or red, black, yellow, blue, and buff, executed on a size of gum tragacanth. The red is dropped first so as to cover the entire surface of the size, followed by the black, yellow, blue, and buff. A peg rake the length of the trough is drawn across the surface, followed by a fine comb drawn from left to right across the width of the trough. The paper is then laid on. The reversed nonpareil is executed in the same manner except that the comb is drawn from left to right and then back again.

The nonpareil marble represents a revival of the early comb pattern. It came into use in about 1838 and was used throughout the middle of the 19th century for endpapers and later for cover papers on all classes of stationery bindings. It was also used for edge marbling from about 1840 to the 1920s when edge marbling virtually went out of existence. Nonpareil marbles were less artistic than the earlier combs, and, although executed by hand, suf-

fered from a sort of mechanical appearance. (217, 236, 369)

non-sewn binding. *See:* ADHESIVE BINDING.

non-tannin. That portion of the water-soluble matter in a vegetable tanning material, other than the tannin, that is non-volatile. Non-tannins, or non-tans, as they are usually called, may include hydrolysis products of the tannins, starches, gums, hemicelluloses, polysaccharides, hexoses, pentoses, uronic acids, organic acids, including lactic and acetic, together with their salts, inorganic salts, proteins and zymoproteins (enzymes), if the temperature is not too high, as well as coloring matters such as brasilin, fisetin, and quercetin. (248, 291, 306, 363)

non-woody fibrous material. Vegetable and synthetic materials used in the manufacture of paper and board. Of the many such materials, both organic and inorganic, the most important today are cotton, esparto, linen and straw. For a number of reasons the types of fiber which have proved commercially worthwhile are somewhat limited, and have become even more so as the size and productive capacity of papermaking mills have increased. Among the qualifications which satisfactory materials must possess are: 1) sufficient fiber length to provide the desired strength in the paper; 2) ready reducibility to the fiber form, and separation from accompanying impurities and ingredients which might be harmful to the paper; 3) availability in very large quantities and within a reasonable distance from the mill; 4) not too great bulk per unit of fiber produced; and 5) low cost per ton of fiber produced. (324)

non-woven covering materials. 1. *See:* LEATHER. 2. Natural and synthetic materials used in the manufacture of covering materials for books. They include granulated leathers and paper fibers bonded with latex, impregnated paper fibers, matted polyethylene fibers, and the like. 3. A clothlike material composed of paper fibers longer than those normally used in papermaking, but which are not woven but matted by felting on a fine mesh screen from a suspension of water or air, and with or without binders. (17, 220)

normal moisture. *See:* AIR DRY.

nose. A term sometimes applied to the point at either side of the top of a text block caused by the head being knocked up out of square. (97)

novel paper. A class of paper once used extensively in the production of so-called pulp magazines, and now popu-

lar in the manufacture of paperbacks and children's coloring books. It is produced from 75 to 85% mechanical wood pulp plus 15 to 25% chemical wood pulp, and in such a manner to provide a rough surface and maximum bulk. The usual basis weight is 32 pounds ($24 \times 36 - 500$). Thickness ranges from a minimum of 0.004 inch to as high as 0.0055 inch. (17)

n pattern. The code designation of a book cloth finished so as to resemble the grain pattern of sealskin leather.

numbering. The process of printing or stamping figures in consecutive or other order, on sheets, leaves of a book, or the spines of bound volumes. Numbering in this context is one of the processes of stationery binding, principally that of blankbooks and manifold books, including check books. Blankbooks are usually numbered subsequent to sewing and trimming. Where every page contains a separate record, the pages are numbered consecutively throughout the book and the book is said to be "paged." Where facing pages are used for the record, the two pages are numbered as one and the book is said to be "folioed."

Numbering bound books is more difficult than numbering sheets, and may be done by machine only where the figures are to be located at the top corner of the leaves. If the numbers must be located elsewhere, the book is numbered before binding. Numbering before binding may be done either as a separate operation in the bindery after the sheets have been ruled or printed, or on the printing press by means of a numbering machine in the form, a process called "numbering at press."

Sheets on which the same number appears two, three, or more times are described as double-numbered, triple-numbered, etc., while sheets on which the same number repeats on more than one sheet are described as being numbered in duplicate, triplicate, etc.

Numbering machines may be designed to impress the same number over and over, consecutive numbers, or, in the case of the skip-wheel numbering machine, may omit numbers as desired. (264, 320)

nylon. Synthetic materials developed by E. I. du Pont de Nemours & Company in 1938, consisting of polyamides prepared from a dicarboxylic acid and a diamine, or from omega-amino acid or its lactone, that can be formed from a melt or solution in fibers, fabrics, filaments, or sheets.

Soluble nylon is a chemically modified form of nylon produced by treating nylon with formaldehyde. It is soluble in alcohol, or alcohol and water, and is particularly useful when flexibility and penetration are required, as in an adhesive. Soluble nylon film is used in archival restoration as an adhesive backing for fragile documents, in which case it is applied by heat. It is also used in resizing paper. *See also:* NYLON SIZE; SEWING THREAD. (198, 235)

nylon size. A size for paper prepared from soluble nylon dissolved in an industrial methylated spirit. A 2% solution is used for sizing very weak paper, and as a fixative for water colors and manuscript inks when paper is being bleached or subjected to other aqueous treatment. *See also:* SIZING; RESIZING. (237)

nylon thread. *See:* SEWING THREAD.

oak (oak bark: oak wood). The bark and wood, principally the former, of several species of *Quercus,* including the pedunculate oak *(Q. robur)* and sessile oak *(Q. petraea)* in England and Europe; the evergreen oak *(Q. cerris),* wooly oak *(Q. pubescens)* and kermes oak *(Q. coccifera)* in Europe; and the white oak *(Q. alba),* chestnut oak *(Q. prinus),* tanbark oak *(Q. densiflora),* and black oak *(Q. kelloggi)* in the United States. As the bark has a much higher tannin content than the wood, generally only it is used for tannin extraction, but at times both the heartwood and bark are utilized.

Oak bark is not as high in tannin content as many other materials, and its use, which has extended over many centuries, has been due more to its ready availability than to any other factor. A high quality oak bark will contain 12 to 14% tannin, while old oak heartwood will contain 6 to 9%.

Despite its relatively low tannin content, oak bark was at one time used extensively in the manufacture of some very fine leathers, especially in England. In fact, the English leathers of the past, which were known throughout the world for their high quality, were produced largely by means of high quality stock and a long, slow, oak tannage. Slowness of penetration, however, along with declining availability, are important reasons why its use is not nearly so extensive as in the past.

Oak tannin is a combination of the pyrogallol and condensed tannins, in the ratio of one to two, but the real nature of the tannin is still somewhat obscure. The tanning has a medium pH and moderate salts and acid content. *See also:* VEGETABLE TANNINS. (175, 306)

oak-bark tanned. A lightweight, unbleached, bark-tanned leather, which is defined as having been pit-tanned, without hot-pitting, for not less than 5 to 6 months. The process involves layering the skins for not less than 6 months, with OAK bark being used as the basis for tannage. (61)

oakum board. A loosely twisted fiber, usually of hemp or jute, impregnated with tar and used up until about the Second World War to produce a better

quality binder's board. *See also:* MILLBOARD (1); TAR BOARD. (65)

oasis (oasis goat). A trade name for a second quality NIGER goatskin tanned and processed in England. It has a smoother surface than the usual goatskin.

oblique corners. A half-leather binding with corners at an angle other than 45°. Oblique corners are usually associated with oblong books. (86, 234)

oblong. A book of a width greater than its height. This can result from folding a sheet of paper across the long way, i.e., halving the short side, or by putting together a THIRTY-SIXMO gathering. Also called "cabinet size" or "landscape." (12)

octavo. The book size resulting from folding a sheet of paper with three right angle folds, thus producing a leaf one-eighth the size of the sheet and forming a 16-page section. To define fully, the paper size must also be stated. The typical book paper, for example, which is 25 by 38 inches, will give an untrimmed book size of 12½ by 9½ inches. Also called 8vo or 8°.

octodecimo. *See:* EIGHTEEN-MO.

offal. The leather trade term for the shoulders, bellies, cheeks, face, or tail rounded from the choicer parts of a cowhide.

off and on. *See:* TWO ON.

offset. 1. A printing process which involves the transferral of the image from a litho stone or a plate to a rubber-covered cylinder, which is then offset by pressure onto the paper. The image area of the plate is receptive to ink, whereas the balance of the plate is water receptive. 2. The inadvertent transfer of (printing) ink from one printed sheet or illustration to another sheet. Offsetting of this nature may

occur during printing, in the printing warehouse storage area, during folding of the sheets, or during binding (pressing) before the ink is completely dry. Offsetting from illustrative matter onto text matter is probably more common than that from text sheet to text sheet. Also frequently called "rub off" or "set off." *See also:* BARRIER SHEET. 3. The result of undried ink or excess ink accumulating on some part of the printing press after the paper leaves the impression cylinder. This ink is transferred to the paper at the second impression and, if the registration is not absolutely accurate, the offset will give a shaded edge effect to the print. *See also:* DOUBLING. (17, 69, 316)

offset ink. An ink used for offset lithography. Such an ink is very finely ground, free from water soluble particles, and contains only lithographic varnish or certain lacquers as the binding medium. It is necessary that the ink be insensitive to sulfur, since this is one of the ingredients of the rubber printing rollers. (140)

offset paper. A printing paper designed for use in offset lithography. The offset printing process is based on the antipathy of grease (ink) for water, consequently offset paper must be free from excess water soluble chemicals and particularly surface active agents. The paper, which may be coated or uncoated, is produced in basis weights of 50 to 150 pounds (25 × 38 − 500). Uncoated offset paper may be used for periodicals, brochures, etc., and for single or multi-color work. (52, 58, 182)

oiling off. The process of coating the grain surface of a wet leather with oil before drying.

oil of egg. A leather dressing obtained by extracting egg yolks with ether or chloroform. When oil of egg is used, it is usually followed by a dressing of beeswax to impart a polished surface. Oil of egg is seldom used today as the sole ingredient of a leather dressing, although LEATHER DRESSINGS making use of it are still used to a limited extent. (218)

oil of neroli. A fragrant, pale yellow essential oil obtained by steam distillation from fresh blossoms of *Citrus* *aurantium,* and at one time used to perfume books. (152)

oil tanning. A "tannage" which involves the incorporation of fish or marine mammal oils into inner splits or frizzed-grain skins, usually wooled sheepskins. The tanning agent is generally raw cod liver oil, which, subsequent to being incorporated into the skin, is induced to undergo oxidation and other chemical changes while in contact with the fibers, leading to a chemical combination of oil derivatives with the fibers. The liberation of heat accompanies and speeds up these chemical reactions; however, there is the danger of the oiled skins being heated to the point where they may smoulder or even burn. Cod liver oil is not readily taken up by the skins; therefore, for the success of this process, it is essential to bring the oil into the closest possible contact with the fibers; this is accomplished by vigorous mechanical action. Oil tanning is used principally in the manufacture of chamois leather. At one time it was referred to as "chamoising." (248, 291, 306, 363)

old Dutch marble. A comb marble pattern executed by placing the colors on the size in a particular sequence and manner. The four colors, red, yellow, green, and blue, are placed in a series of small pots which are set in a frame so that they stand in a row about 3 inches apart from center to center. The total number of pots of color is determined by the length of the rake, which must be as long as the trough is wide. Two rakes are used in the execution of this marble; the first takes up the colors so they may be dropped on the size with precision, while the second is used to put the Chinese white on the size. The red is dropped first, and the second rake is then dipped in the Chinese white and lowered onto the surface of the size, each peg of the rake dropping a spot of the white onto the red, which has already spread out. The points of the first rake are then dipped into the pots of color and then placed on the surface of the size so that a single drop of color is placed as near the center of the white spots as possible. A stylus is then drawn through the center of the colors from front to back of the trough, followed by a fine or coarse comb which is drawn through the colors from left to right, causing the pattern to form with well distributed colors in even scales of red, white, yellow, green, and blue. Although probably a more mechanical

pattern than virtually any other marble, the Old Dutch has been used since about the middle of the 17th century. The marble is executed on a size of GUM TRAGACANTH. *See also:* DUTCH MARBLE. (217, 269)

oleic acid. A colorless liquid ($C_{18}H_{34}O_2$), soluble in alcohol and ether, but insoluble in water. It occurs naturally in greater quantities than any other fatty acid, being present as glycerides in most fats and oils. It is used in determining the oil penetrability resistance of book cloths, especially buckram. (209)

one-letter index. An INDEX consisting of 24, 26, or (rarely) 27 divisions for the letters of the alphabet. The 24-division index generally omits the letter X and either omits I or combines it with J; the 26-division index includes all the letters, or adds Mac and omits X; while the 27-division index includes X along with Mac. *See also:* TWO-LETTER INDEX. (264)

one on. *See:* ALL ALONG.

one on and one off. One of the simplest forms of the HOLLOW, consisting of a strip of paper, linen, jaconet, etc., twice the width of the spine of the book, one half of which is glued to the spine, the other half being folded over the first and glued to it only along the edge. The one on and one off method does not give fully adequate support to the spine in most cases, but it is useful when fastening a book back into a tight cloth case. Additional strength may be gained by folding the paper across the grain. *See also:* ONE ON AND TWO OFF; TWO ON AND ONE OFF. (339)

one on and two off. A method of constructing a tube for a HOLLOW, in which a strip of paper, linen, cambric, etc., three times the width of the spine of the book is cut, the middle width of which is glued to the spine, the two end widths being folded over the middle and glued to each other. This method is generally superior to ONE ON AND ONE OFF, and, although it does not offer adequate support to the spine of a large book, it is adequate for some light, thin volumes, depending upon the weight of the paper. *See also:* TWO ON AND ONE OFF. (236, 335)

one piece cover. A term used in edition binding to indicate a book completely covered in one type and color fabric only. (329)

one sheet on. *See:* ALL ALONG.

one-shot method. 1. The trade name for a method of applying adhesive in high-speed paperback binding, in which *one*

application of a hot-melt adhesive is applied to the spine of each book, in distinction to the application of both hot and cold adhesives. The one-shot method is extremely rapid, as the adhesive begins to set almost as soon as it is removed from the source of heat and has practically fully set within a matter of seconds, depending on the type of adhesive used. This allows the book to be handled and trimmed straight from the adhesive binding machine. Problems develop, however, when the one-shot method is used in binding heavily coated or loaded papers, because if *all* of the coating or loading dust is not removed from the paper, the adhesive may not adhere well to the leaves. 2. A colloquial term for the process of deacidifying paper through the use of one alkaline solution, as opposed to methods requiring the use of double treatments. *See also:* ADHESIVE BINDING; DEACIDIFICATION; DOUBLE DECOMPOSITION; HOT-MELT ADHESIVE; TWO-SHOT METHOD. (294)

onion skin. A durable lightweight paper that is thin and usually nearly transparent—so called because of its resemblance to the dry outer skin of an onion. It is used for making duplicate copies of typewritten material, permanent records where low bulk is important, and for airmail correspondence. It is produced entirely from cotton fibers, bleached chemical wood pulps, or combinations of these. The fibers of the paper are long and the paper is sized with rosin, starch or glue; it is usually supercalendered or plated to a high finish, or is given a cockle finish. Basis weights range from 7 to 10 pounds ($17 \times 22 - 500$). *See also:* MANIFOLD PAPER. (17, 316)

onlay. A method of decorating a leather binding by means of thin, variously colored pieces of leather, usually of a different color than the covering leather, which are attached by means of paste or P.V.A. to the surface of the covering leather, thus giving it a kind of mosaic effect. The pieces of leather are usually, but not necessarily, of the same type of leather as that covering the book. The onlay was certainly in use in England by the 17th century and was also a technique occasionally adapted to publisher's cloth bindings between 1840 and 1860, with onlays sometimes made of paper. *Cf:* INLAY (4), for which the onlay is often mistaken. (69, 236, 335)

ooze. An obsolete term for the vegetable tanning liquor used in converting hides and skins into leather. Also called WOOZE. (*See also:* VEGETABLE TANNING.)

ooze leather (ooze calf). Originally, a leather produced from calfskin by forcing OOZE through the skin by mechanical means, producing a soft, finely grained finish like velvet or suede on the flesh side. The term is also used incorrectly with reference to sheepskin. Today, ooze leather is a vegetable- or chrome-tanned skin of bovine origin, generally calfskin, with a very soft, glovelike feel and a natural grain, which is sometimes accentuated by BOARDING (1). (61, 363)

opacimeter. An instrument used to measure opacity. It is, in effect, a reflectometer designed especially to measure the opacity of paper. The reflectance of the sheet is first measured using a black background and then with a standard white background behind it. The instrument can be designed to give the ratio of the two measurements directly. (93)

opacity. That property of a material which restricts the passage of light and thus prevents one from seeing through it or seeing objects on or in contact with the reverse side. Opacity is of considerable importance in paper that is to be used for printing. In printing papers opacity is measured in percentages, e.g., a lightweight bond paper may have an opacity as low as 79%, i.e., 21% of the light that strikes it passes through, while a 24-pound bond paper of high opacity may rate a percentage of 93, meaning that only 7% of the light penetrates it. Different opacities may be obtained by: 1) varying the paper pulp; 2) varying the degree of hydration; or 3) using loading materials and special opacifying agents. (17, 350)

opaque. The property of being impervious to light, i.e., non-transparent. *See:* OPACITY.

openability. That characteristic of a bound book which allows the leaves to lie relatively flat when the book is open, with no weight or pressure applied (especially along the binding edge). Openability depends to a certain degree on the size of the book, and to a considerable degree on the weight and thickness of the paper, its grain direction in the book (which should be parallel to the spine), the method of sewing, and the overall quality and structure of the binding. *Cf:* LYING FLAT.

open assembly time. The time interval between the spreading of an adhesive on the adherend and the completion of the assembly of the parts for bonding. In general, the use of paste and glue allows a greater assembly time than does the use of the polyvinyl adhesives. *See also:* ASSEMBLY TIME; CLOSED ASSEMBLY TIME. (309)

opened. A book which has not had the bolts cut during the binding process but which has had the leaves separated with a paper knife, or other instrument. *Cf:* UNOPENED.

opening boards. The operation in hand binding of opening the boards of a book when the leather covering is well set but not completely dry. As each board is opened it is pressed toward the joint, both being pressed at the same time so that the boards will open just at the top of the shoulders.

opening up. The process of "opening" a newly bound book (other than an edition binding), in order to improve its flexibility. The usual method is to hold the book fore edge up, then by regular, uniform motions, a few leaves at a time, pressing the leaves down, first at the front, then at back, and then repeating, until the center of the book has been reached. "Opening up" helps avert strain on the binding and also permits freer opening of the book. *See also:* BREAK (1). (127)

open joint. *See:* FRENCH JOINT.

open warbles. *See:* WARBLES.

opisthograph. An ancient manuscript inscribed or written on both sides of the leaves. The term was also applied to early printed books bearing letterpress on both sides of the leaves. (156, 192)

optical spacing. 1. The spacing of the raised bands on the spine of a book in such a manner that the bottom panel is slightly larger (the amount depending on the size of the book) than the other panels, so as to give the spine a balanced appearance. If the bands were so spaced that all of the panels were in fact the same size, the lowest (bottom) panel would appear to be much smaller. The bottom panel usually has the date, or extra (and different) tooling of some nature, at the very tail of the spine, and the size of the panel above this tooling is the same as the panels above it. 2. The spacing of the lettering on the spine of a book in such a manner as to make all of the letters of a word appear as though they are the same distance apart. In the combinations OO, OL and NN, for example, the OO combination would be spaced closer together than the OL, which in turn would be closer

together than the NN, in the relative distance of 1 to 1½ to 2 spaces.

optimum binding method. An expression sometimes applied to the method used to secure the leaves or sections of a book, e.g., fold sewing, oversewing, adhesive binding, side sewing, etc., which will offer the best (optimum) binding for a given book in terms of usability, including openability and durability (strength and longevity). It is conceded that there is no one method which can satisfy all requirements for all books.

orderbook style. A style of blankbook binding in which the book has a leather spine and rounded corners, canvas sides, ink blocking on the sides, and gold blocking on the spine. (256)

ordinary book-volume. A book defined by the Library Binding Institute to be an ordinary-sized graphic work consisting of an appreciable number of leaves or sections produced originally as a unit and submitted for binding, rebinding, or prebinding as such a unit and not requiring special handling. An ordinary book-volume ranges in height from approximately 6 to 12 inches, a proportional width and a thickness not exceeding 2 inches. (209)

ordinary periodical-volume. A (periodical) volume defined by the Library Binding Institute to be a series of multi-leaved, like-constituted, serially numbered graphic units submitted for binding or rebinding into a scheduled multi-unit volume and not requiring special handling. An ordinary periodical volume ranges in height from about 8 to 16 inches, a proportional width and a thickness not exceeding 2½ inches. (209)

organic acids. The class of acids, such as acetic, formic, lactic, oxalic, tannic, etc., which are usually found in living organisms or which can be made from them. These acids are characterized by being relatively volatile and weak, consequently they are considered to be less harmful to archival materials, especially paper and leather, than the more powerful inorganic acids; however, they can be very destructive if allowed to remain in contact with leather or paper, especially the latter, for long periods of time.

organic pigments. Originally, pigments obtained from vegetable or animal materials, as distinguished from the inorganic pigments obtained from minerals. More recently, however, pigments have been classed as organic if they contain the element carbon in their composition. Most modern organic pigments are prepared synthetically from coal-tar derivatives, such as phthalocyanine blue, alizarin crimson, and the lakes produced from synthetic dyes. (233)

oriental leaf. A type of imitation GOLD LEAF composed of brass and bronze. *See also:* DUTCH GOLD. (169)

original binding (original boards). The binding of a book which has been bound only once, or, in edition binding, the earliest of several bindings used for a particular edition of a book.

orihon. 1. A strip of paper, papyrus or vellum accordian folded so that writing or printing, which appears on only one side, is formed into pages or columns. The resulting "book" is then secured by cord passed through holes punched along the length of the binding edge. Covers were also at times laced on. Single sheets, folded but also uncut, were also at times treated in this manner. 2. A "stabbed" binding of Oriental origin. *See:* JAPANESE SEWING. (156, 370)

ornamental inside lining. *See:* DOUBLURE.

ounce. A measurement of the thickness of leather, one ounce being equal to 1/64 inch. Originally, it meant the thickness of 1 square foot of finished leather that weighed 1 ounce avoirdupois. *See also:* LEATHER SUBSTANCE TABLE. (325, 363)

outer joint. The grooves in the covering material at which the boards open. Also called (outer) hinge. The term "joint" is sometimes used to indicate the ridge or abutment formed by the backing operation to accommodate the boards; however, this ridge is more appropriately referred to as the SHOULDER(S) (1) of the book. *See also:* FRENCH JOINT. (237)

out of boards. A book that is cut (trimmed) before the boards are secured to the text block. It is an abbreviation of "cut out of boards." *Cf:* IN BOARDS. (335)

out of register. An imperfect REGISTER (3), meaning that the two sides of a printed sheet do not back each other perfectly, or the impression is not in correct position in relation to the other matter already ruled or printed on the sheet. *See also:* FOLD TO PRINT. (365)

outsert. An additional folio placed around the outside of a section.

outside margin. *See:* FORE-EDGE MARGIN.

ovals, in. An oval arabesque centerpiece decoration blocked or tooled on both covers of a book. This was a popular method of decoration of the late 16th and early 17th centuries, and was executed in both gilt and blind. (156)

overbands. *See:* BANDS (2).

overcast cloth joint. A reinforcement used to strengthen the attachment of the cover to a text block. One side of a strip of cloth is sewn to the shoulder of the text block and the other side is pasted to the inside of the board. (237)

overcasting. A method of hand sewing in which groups of single sheets are sewn together using a single length of thread which passes through the paper and over the back edges of the leaves. Overcasting is sometimes used when sewing a book made up of single sheets, the "sections" created being sewn flexibly. It is also a method used by library binders when attaching new endpapers to a book being recased, or to reinforce the first and last sections of a book being rebound without resewing.

Overcasting is a strong form of sewing, but it results in considerable strain on the leaves and frequently cuts the paper, partly because of the diagonal at which the thread passes through the paper. In addition, when groups of leaves are overcast and then sewn on cords or tapes, unsightly gaps are seen between the "sections." (84)

overcharged. A leather or other binding having too much ornamentation, usually gilt, giving the entire decoration a crowded and overburdened appearance. (203)

overdried. Paper which has been dried to the point of brittleness and loss of strength. It is usually assumed that the term applies to paper which is dried excessively during manufacture, but it may also be applied to paper, i.e., books, documents, etc., stored in an excessively dry (and usually very hot) environment. The expression "brittleness" is appropriate here even though in a strict sense brittleness refers to a breakdown of the cellulose linkages in a paper, generally as a result of chemical degradation. (72)

oversewing. A method of sewing the leaves of a book by hand or machine, almost always the latter in library binding. The sewing thread passes through the edges of each "section," in consecutive order, using pre-punched holes through which the sewing needles pass.

The oversewing process generally entails the removal of the original spine lining cloth, glue, original sewing, and the folds of the sections, which is usually accomplished by planing, grinding, sawing, or cutting the spine of the book, thus removing an eighth of an inch or more of the binding margin. Sometimes the spine is first nipped to remove the original backing shoulders before the folds are removed. The book, having been reduced to individual leaves, is then jogged, and a very light coat of glue is applied along the binding edge to hold the leaves together temporarily. A number of leaves, or a "section," between 0.055 and 0.065 inch in thickness (depending upon the thick-

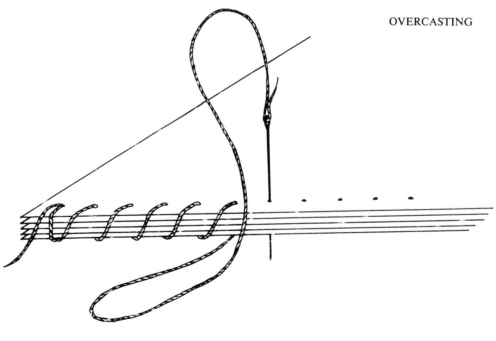

OVERCASTING

ness of the paper) is then sewn, either by hand, or, more commonly, in an oversewing machine. The thread passes through the section perpendicular to the plane of the paper (Holloway method) or obliquely. This later, diagonal method, is known as the CHIVERS method, which is employed in oversewing machines. Altogether, about ⁵⁄₁₆ or ⁶⁄₁₆ inch of the binding margin is consumed by the process.

Hand oversewing was in common use by the end of the 18th century and the beginning of the 19th, particularly for large books and those with loose plates. The oversewing machine, which was invented and perfected in the first quarter of the 20th century, is the principal sewing machine employed by library binders in the United States. (22, 236, 255)

oversize. 1. A book which is too large to be shelved in normal sequence in the bookstack. In the United States, books over 30 cm. (11.81 inches) are generally included in this category. 2. Paper made to allow for trimming to the size offered.

overstitching. *See:* OVERCASTING.

over-tanned. A condition in which the grain and flesh sides of a hide or skin have received an excess of tannin in relation to the interior, or corium, of the skin. It results from the grain and flesh sides being exposed to a strong tannin liquor and becoming over-tanned while the corium has had insufficient exposure. The problem can be avoided by using weaker liquors initially, and building to stronger solutions as tanning progresses. Over tanning produces a hard, thin leather, often with

a cracky, distorted (drawn) grain. *See also:* CASE-HARDENING. (306)

overweight kip. A cattle hide weighing from 25 to 30 pounds in the green, salted state.

ownership mark. A bookplate, rubber stamp, label, perforation, or other means of marking the ownership of a book. (156)

oxalic acid. A dibasic, highly toxic acid ($H_2C_2O_4$), soluble in water and alcohol, and slightly soluble in ether. It occurs as the free acid in beet leaves, and as potassium hydrogen oxalate in wood sorrel and rhubarb. Commercially, oxalic acid is prepared from sodium formate (HCO_2Na). It can also be obtained as a byproduct in the manufacture of citric acid and by the oxidation of carbohydrates with nitric acid (HNO_3) in the presence of vanadium pentoxide (V_2O_5). It is used by some bookbinders to clear the leather before applying paste for tooling. It must be applied in very dilute solution, otherwise it will bleach the leather. It is also used in the manufacture of dyestuffs for cloth, in bleaching cotton linters, and in the manufacture of ink. Potassium hydrogen oxalate is sometimes used to remove ink stains from paper. (152, 195)

Oxford corners. Border lines that cross and project beyond each other, as on title pages and (sometimes) book covers. (81, 156)

Oxford hollow. A particular form of the HOLLOW consisting of a simple flat paper tube which is glued to the spine of the text block on one side, and to the inside of the spine of the covers, leaving a hollow opening between. The term presumably derives from the fact

that Oxford binders were the first to use it, namely for leather-bound Bibles. It is actually a ONE ON AND ONE OFF hollow. (140)

Oxford style. *See:* DIVINITY CALF (1).

ox-gall. The bile obtained from the gall bladder of a bovine animal, usually a domesticated cow. It consists of a ropy, mucous, semi-transparent liquid, and contains sodium salts of taurocholic and glycocholic acids, cholesterol, lecithin, etc. Ox-gall is used as the expanding and binding medium for the colors used in MARBLING. It is necessary in all marbling, and it is important that it be pure and free from water. When in its original state it is yellowish or greenish brown, but becomes clear and dark brown when allowed to settle. The liquid is then drawn off and mixed with alcohol. Its effect on the colors is to make them spread out in large flat rings when they are dropped on the size. Ox-gall is also used in engraving and lithography. (217, 264, 369)

ox hide. Leather made from the hides of domestic cattle. *See:* COWHIDE.

oxidization. The chemical reaction in which a material combines with oxygen to form an oxide, i.e., the positive valence of the material increases. Oxidization results in the deterioration of an adhesive due to atmospheric exposure, to the breakdown of a hot-melt adhesive because of prolonged heating, and to the deterioration of paper due to an excessive amount of alkali which results in an excessively high pH. *See also:* HYDROGEN-ION CONCENTRATION.

oxycelluloses. A degraded form of cellulose produced by oxidation. Oxycelluloses vary in chemical nature according to the oxidation agent used. (17, 72)

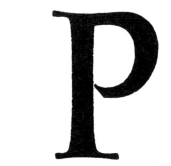

Pablos, Juan. An Italian printer (Giovanni Paoli), appointed by Juan Comberger, the leading printer of Seville, to serve as compositor and manager of a printing establishment in Mexico. Pablos thus became the first known printer in the Western Hemisphere. The first book issued by the press, of which there is any definite record, was dated 1539, the same year the press was established. Records do not indicate that any bookbinder was associated with the press; therefore it is possible that Pablos himself did the binding.

Some authorities contend that printing in the Western Hemisphere began even before 1539. Early Mexican records mention a printer by the name of Estaban Martin, but there is no record of anything he may have printed. An early letter from the Archbishop to the King of Spain, however, would seem to indicate that attempts were made to establish a press before Pablos arrived in Mexico. (235)

packing. *See* STUFFING (1).

packthread. A strong thread or small twine over which the PURL was sewn on embroidered bindings.

pad. A number of sheets of paper (printed, ruled, or blank), generally backed with thin board, secured at one edge (frequently the top) with a padding compound, and sometimes reinforced with a cloth or other type of lining. *See also:* PADDING (2). (264)

pad counter. 1. A simple type of gauge used to divide the leaves of a book into "sections" of the appropriate thickness for oversewing. Two gauges are generally used, one to divide the leaves into sections 0.055 inch in thickness, the other to divide bulkier paper into sections 0.065 inch thick. 2. A device consisting of two flat blades, one of which is adjustable to any distance from the other, and used to determine the number of sheets in a pad. The number of sheets wanted in each pad of a production run is counted out (five extra sheets being added to allow for a snug fit when setting the gauge). The counted pile is placed between the two blades and the movable blade is tightened, following which the five extra sheets are removed. If the fixed blade is placed directly on top of the pile of stock and firm pressure is applied as

the adjustable blade is slid into the pile, the counter will pick up approximately the number of sheets desired. *See also:* CHECK PILE. (74, 164)

padded boards (padded leather; padded sides.) A book which has boards padded with cotton batting, blotting paper, or other compressible material, so that they are thicker than normal boards, especially toward the center, and are soft to the touch. Such boards are generally covered with genuine or imitation leather, and are used for diaries, presentation books, and the like. (264)

padding. 1. The blank leaves added at the end of a thin publication so as to form a volume with sufficient thickness to be rounded and backed and/or to be lettered on the spine. Unfortunately, the paper used for this purpose is usually of an inferior quality, and becomes embrittled and transfers its acidity to the leaves of the publication. Also called "filler," or "filling." 2. A method of securing ruled, printed or blank leaves by the application of a padding compound, and sometimes a cloth or other reinforcing liner, to one edge (frequently the top) of the sheets which have been jogged even on the binding edge and placed under pressure. Special padding troughs, clamps and presses are used to facilitate padding large quantities at one time. *See also:* PAD COUNTER (2); PADDING COMPOUND. 3. A method of applying dyestuff to the grain surface of a leather or tawed skin, particularly the latter, in cases where it is not feasible to immerse the skins in the dyestuff liquor because of the increased fullness and decreased stretch which will result from such immersion. (179, 196, 234, 291)

padding clamp. A compression table clamp designed to secure pads on two

edges, leaving either of two edges, one long and one short, available for PADDING (2).

padding compound. A liquid adhesive, usually consisting of gum arabic plasticized with glycerin, glycol, or sorbitol, and used in PADDING (2) work. (142, 269)

paddle dyeing. A method employed in dyeing the more fragile leathers, including bookbinding leathers, skivers, etc., that might otherwise be damaged by the vigorous mechanical action involved in drum dyeing. Paddle dyeing requires considerably higher ratios of dye solution to weight of leather than are used in drum dyeing, and utilizes the dyes less effectively; however, it does have the advantage that the leather is visible during dyeing and adjustments to shade and strength can be made continuously. (248)

Padeloup, Antoine Michel (1685-1758). A French bookbinder who was probably the outstanding craftsman of a distinguished family that was associated with the craft for more than 150 years. Padeloup was apprenticed to his father, Michel (c 1654-1725), and probably became a master bookbinder in about 1712. More commonly known as Padeloupe "le jeune," he was appointed royal binder to Louis XV in 1733, succeeding Luc Antoine Boyet. Padeloup was esteemed both for the solidity of his forwarding and the embellishment of his bindings. He had an eclectic taste and most of his bindings displayed several diverse styles of ornamentation mingled together. Padeloup often decorated his books with DENTELLE (lace-work) borders, and has even been credited by some with the introduction of this border, although there is no real proof of this. He also executed, but with less success, several bindings with onlaid work in different colored leathers. Although these mosaics were well executed, the tilelike design of many of them is considered by some authorities to be too feeble. He is also credited with the introduction of the "repetition" design. Some of Padeloup's bindings are in imitation of the work of FLORIMOND BADIER, sometimes repeating the silver-threaded headbands of that period. Padeloup was also one of the first binders to

An 18th century binding with dentelle borders by Antoine Michel Padeloup.
Dentelle borders are sometimes called Derome style after the work of Nicolas
Derome. This binding is on *Les Amours Pastorales de Daphnis et Chloé,* by
Longus, printed by Quillau, Paris, 1718. (17.2 cm. by 11.5 cm. by 2.3 cm.)

"sign" his bindings, by means of a ticket bearing his name and address. (109, 342, 347)

page. One side of a leaf, whether blank or containing letterpress or writing, and regardless of sequential arrangement.

page flex test. A binding endurance test designed to determine the number of times a leaf of a bound book can be flexed under light tension before it becomes detached from the book. The book is placed open on a flat plate, with both covers flat on the surface. A single leaf is selected and held in a vertical position, while the remaining leaves on either side are clamped down. The vertical leaf is passed between two bars approximately 3/16 inch in diameter, ¼ inch apart, and longer than the leaf, and positioned at a fixed distance of 2 inches above the gutter of the book. A clamp is attached to the leaf to hold it in a vertical position, as well as to exert an upward force of 3 to 5 pounds. The bars on either side of the leaf are moved back and forth a distance of 3½ inches, causing the leaf to flex at an angle of 45° to either side of the vertical, or a total of 90°. The flexing is at the rate of 88 per minute, and the test continues until failure of the leaf, or a maximum of 1,000 flexes. To accelerate the test, the upward force exerted on the leaf can be increased.

page pull test. A binding endurance test designed to determine the force required to pull a leaf from a bound book; its purpose is to determine the strength of the method used to secure the leaves or sections of the book. The leaf is pulled with uniform force along its entire length, usually by means of an Instron tester. The book is clamped into position by the bottom jaw of the testing device with a single leaf held in a vertical position by the top jaw. The jaws are separated and the force required to tear the leaf or pull it from the adhesive or adhesive-thread layer is measured. The total force in pounds is divided by the length of the leaf in inches to give the page-pull unit of measurement as pounds per linear inch. The page-pull test does not measure individually the binding strength of a book, e.g., an adhesive binding, having a stiff, high-bulking paper, may display a satisfactory page-pull test of 5 to 7 pounds, yet if the volume is subjected first to the SUBWAY TEST, and then the page-pull test, it may show a much lower value, even as low as 1 to 2 pounds.

pagination. A system of numerals or other characters, or a combination thereof, assigned to the pages of a book or manuscript to indicate their order. Numbering of the leaves of both manuscripts and printed books began in about 1470, and by 1480 the practice had become general. Page numbering, however, was comparatively rare until 1500, and did not become general until 1590. *See also:* FOLIATION (3).

"painted" bindings ("painted" leather). 1. A late 17th and early 18th century method of ornamenting the covers of books, consisting of landscapes "painted" with a chemical (possibly an iron salt, e.g., ferrous sulfate) on the cover or covers. The paintings were usually executed on fawn-colored leathers that had been paste-washed. *See also:* EDWARDS OF HALIFAX. 2. Leather and vellum bindings of the mid and late 16th century, which were tooled and painted in various colors, including gold, silver, green, purple, red, etc. (124, 236, 347)

painted edges. *See:* FORE-EDGE PAINTING.

painted papers. Decorative cover papers or endpapers produced by painting designs directly onto the paper, either freestyle or in a controlled and organized plan. Paint alone, or paint mixed with black or colored inks, is generally used in the execution of these papers.

pale. Sixteen karat gold leaf. Because of the alloys used to reduce the gold from 24 to 16 karat, "pale" leaf is much lighter in color and somewhat thicker than the customary 23 to 23½ karat gold leaf. *See also:* LEMON.

palette knife. A blunt-tipped knife with a very flexible steel blade having no cutting edge, and used for mixing the colors, paste, etc., for marbling, decorative endpapers, etc. (261)

palimpsest. A manuscript consisting of a later writing superimposed upon the original writing, which was first removed to the extent possible. A double palimpsest is one that has two subsequent writings, and therefore two removals. The extent to which the earlier writing could be removed depended to a great degree on the ink used. Early carbon inks, which merely lay on the surface of the parchment, could be removed more or less completely simply by sponging, but the later iron gall inks were much more difficult to remove because of the interaction with the fibers of the tannin present in the ink. They had to be scraped and then treated with a weak acid, such as the citric acid of an orange. Even then traces of the original writing remained. Wetting

the parchment in this manner softened it to such an extent that it was necessary to treat the skin with dry lime to make it dry and white once again. The word "palimpsest" derives from the Greek roots meaning "rub away again." Also called "rescript." (143)

palladium leaf. A silver-white, moderately ductile, malleable metal (Pd) of the platinum group. It can be beaten into leaf form, although not as thin as gold leaf, for use in lettering and decorating books. It is suitable for use alone or in combinations with gold leaf. Although it is somewhat duller than silver and has a slightly leaden quality, unlike silver, it does not tarnish under normal circumstances. (130, 233)

pallet. 1. A finishing tool having a long narrow face bearing a line or design, and used for decorating books, usually those bound in leather. Straight-line pallets are available in various lengths, and a complete set, used for building designs, ranges from 1/16 inch to a maximum of 2, 3, 4, or more inches, increasing (in *very* complete sets) by as little as 1/16 inch at a time. Pallets are generally used to impress lines on the spines of books, although they are also used on the covers, especially to finish off lines impressed with fillets, or other tools. Very short pallets are usually referred to as "short-line pallets" or, occasionally, as "short-line tools." The edge of the pallet is made very slightly convex in order to avoid cutting the leather in the process of tooling. A decorative pallet is called a "band pallet," while one with more than one line on its face is called a "two-, "three-," etc., "line pallet." 2. A tool used for holding and heating type for lettering a book. *See:* LETTERING PALLET (1). (161, 236, 335)

palleted. A term sometimes applied to a binding which is "signed," usually in gilt, at the tail of the inside of the upper cover, generally by means of a stamp or pallet. The term does not include paper tickets, which are often used in lieu of a pallet. *See also:* LETTERING PALLET (2); SIGNED BINDINGS.

palm leaf book. A manuscript book, produced in India, Burma, and contiguous areas, consisting of strips cut from the leaves of the palmyra, or talipot palm *(Corypha umbraculifera)*. Each strip is about 16 to 36 inches in length, and about 1½ to 3 inches in width. The leaves were first inscribed with a stylus, the incisions then being filled with an ink prepared from charcoal and oil. The strips were then gathered, pierced through the middle, secured with cord or twine, and attached to a board. (156, 225)

palm oil. A semisolid or solid, red or yellowish-brown oil obtained from the flesh or fruit of the oil palm, especially the African palm, *Elaeis guineensis,* and used to dress Niger goatskin before drying. (130, 280)

pamphlet. In a limited sense, an independent publication consisting of a few leaves of printed matter stitched together but not bound, and with or without self-, or other paper, covers. While independent in the sense that

PALLET

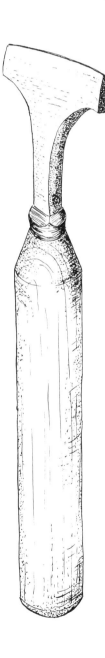

each is complete in itself, it is not uncommon to issue pamphlets in a series, usually numbered consecutively. In a bibliographical sense, a pamphlet has been variously defined as a publication of not more than 8 pages, one not exceeding 5 sheets, one not more than 100 pages, one less than 80 pages, one not less than 5 nor more than 48 pages, and as a publication consisting of one folded section (signature), regardless of the number of pages (but generally never more than 128). In early 18th century England, a pamphlet was described as work consisting of 20 leaves in folio, 12 in quarto and 6 in octavo. A periodical issue is not generally regarded as a pamphlet. *See also:* PAMPHLET BINDING (1). (12, 139, 142, 234)

pamphlet binder. A cover of pasteboard, with a gummed and stitched binding strip, used to hold one or more pamphlets. The quality of the board generally used for this type of binder, which is used in many libraries as a permanent binding, is such that it sooner or later (and usually sooner) becomes highly acidified, transferring its acidity to the first and last leaves of the publication, thus acidifying them, also.

pamphlet binding. 1. The business of binding sheets as they come from the press. The folded sheet (or sheets) is wire-stitched, or the leaves are secured by an adhesive, usually a hot-melt. The binding may include a cover of a stock heavier than that of the publication itself. Pamphlet binding includes the binding of pamphlets, periodical issues, and other publications, and represents, in total volume, the largest branch of "bookbinding." The term, however, which stems from the days when the writing of political pamphlets was popular, is unfortunate, in that the binding of telephone books, directories, and similar publications, is classed as pamphlet binding. 2. The style in which such publications are bound when they are issued by the publisher, i.e., saddle stitched, side sewn, or side stitched. (320, 339)

pamphlet box. An open or closed box designed to hold a number of pamphlets, sheets, and the like. *See also:* PRINCETON FILE.

pamphlet-cover paper. A type of cover paper for small publications produced from mixes of cotton fiber and chemical wood pulps in a wide range of thicknesses, colors, designs, and finishes.

pamphlet-style library binding. A style of bookbinding used for PAMPHLET pub-

lications or a group of such publications, which are expected to be little used. The typical publication is side stitched, covered with plain boards, heavy paper, paper-covered boards, or limp cloth, usually with no lettering. (12, 102)

panel (paneled, paneling). 1. A form of decoration consisting of single, double, or triple lines, rectangular in shape, formed by a fillet or pallet, in gilt or blind, either on the sides or between the bands on the spine of a book. *Cf:* BORDER (1); FRAME (1). 2. *See:* CAMBRIDGE STYLE. (99, 105)

panel stamp. A relatively large block of metal or wood, usually the former, engraved intaglio, and used to impress a design on the cover of a book. Although little used today, the panel stamp dates back perhaps 700 years or more, to the 13th century where it was used in Antwerp. The panel stamp was in use throughout the 14th century in the Netherlands, in Cologne before 1400, and in Paris before 1500. The first use of such stamps in England was the period 1480 to 1490. Except in Germany and the Netherlands, they were used very little, if at all, after 1550 until revived in the 1820s for use in embossing bindings. The designs created by the use of panel stamps were almost invariably in blind. (156, 236, 347)

panel stamp bindings. A method of decorating leather bindings by means of panel stamps. Throughout the middle ages the normal method of decorating a book was by means of repeated impressions of variously arranged small stamps. The great increase in book production near the end of the 15th and beginning of the 16th centuries, however, led to various methods of reducing the labor involved in bookbinding, of which the panel stamp was one. The large stamp required the use of a press because the pressure required was considerable, particularly for the octavo and folio size stamps. The earliest stamps were employed in the Netherlands, and Flemish binders continued to use finely designed and engraved stamps well into the 16th century. The French began using the technique near the end of the 15th century, when, in Paris and Normandy, they began producing bindings of great beauty, often pictorial in design. Panel stamped bindings were not produced in England to any great extent until near the end of the 15th century.

Virtually all panel stamp bindings produced in England were calfskin, which, of all leathers, best produces the details of the engraving, mainly because of its fine, smooth-grained surface. The panel stamp binding declined in popularity in England after 1550 until revived in the 1820s when stamps were used to emboss bindings. These were usually small books, covered in roan or morocco of a dark color, blocked in blind, and usually with gilt edges. The lettering on the spine was in gilt. The covers were often embossed in huge fly-embossing presses before covering. The impressions made by the blocks on the dark leather were striking in their effect, particularly so because they were in blind. This type of binding appears to have been popular for about 20 years, although blind blocking continued into the 1850s. (141, 236, 347)

pane sides. *See:* CAMBRIDGE STYLE.

paper. In general, all types and categories of matted or felted sheets or webs of fiber formed on a fine screen from a water suspension. The word "paper" is derived from PAPYRUS (although papyrus is by no means paper), and is one of the two broad sub-divisions of paper as a general term, the other being BOARD. The distinction between paper and board, however, is not sharp, but, in the usual case, paper is lighter in BASIS WEIGHT, thinner, and more flexible than board. Usually, all sheets 12 points (0.012 inch) or more in thickness are classed as boards, while those less than 12 points are classed as paper. The exceptions to this include blotting paper, which is greater than 12 points in thickness, and chipboard, which is less than 12.

Paper may be produced from animal fibers, e.g., wool, fur, hair, silk; mineral fibers, e.g., asbestos; synthetic fibers, e.g., rayon or nylon; and even ceramics, metals, glass, and other materials. Most paper, however, is produced from cellulosic plant fibers, principally those obtained from wood pulp (trees), cotton and linen (rags), ESPARTO (GRASS), and cereal (straw). Other materials used at times and in specialized places include: Abaca, Addar grass, Arundo donax (Spanish grass), bagasse, bamboo, baobab, carob, cotton linters, hemp, henequen, Johnson grass, jute, manila hemp, sisal, and sunflower stalks.

The earliest known paper was made in China, by Ts'ai Lun, although whether he actually invented the process or simply recorded its importance is debatable, and, while its origin has been tentatively established to be 104

to 105 A.D., there is evidence that it may have been known a hundred or more years earlier. Nearly a thousand years later the invention spread from China, moving eastward to Japan, south to India, and west to the Near East. From there is spread to Egypt, Morocco, and Spain (Toledo) in the 12th century. At about the same time the Italians learned the process in Palestine and returned with it to Italy. From Spain it spread to France, Holland, Germany, and the rest of Europe. In 1490, papermaking was begun in England by John Tate at Stevenage in Hertfordshire. William Rittenhouse established the first paper mill in the United States (Philadelphia) in 1690, some 100 years after paper was first made in Mexico.

The quality of early European paper (all of which was made from linen or cotton rags, or a mixture of the two) was very superior. Most of it seems to be of a relatively heavy substance with considerable character in the texture of the surface. It was also well sized. Subsequent to the invention of the stamping mill, in Valencia, Spain, in the 12th century, which shortened and facilitated the maceration of the pulp, the fibers of paper became shorter and the character of paper gradually changed, becoming smoother and thinner.

Very early in the 19th century, the manufacture of paper became mechanized, an event which was to have a profound effect on the craft of bookbinding. Whereas in paper made by hand the stretch caused by pasting or other moistening is virtually the same in all directions, the stretch in paper made on a machine is far greater in the cross direction than in the MACHINE DIRECTION. This affects the bookbinder in many important ways; e.g., if the machine direction of the paper making up the leaves of a book runs the wrong way—at right angles to the spine—the leaves will probably not lie flat under their own weight, unless the paper is very thin or the surface area of the leaves is very great.

When the shortage of rags became chronic late in the 18th century, papermakers were forced to turn to other potential sources of vegetable fiber. Experimental papers were produced, but nothing new was adopted on a large scale until early in the 19th century when straw was first used. ESPARTO (GRASS), the first really successful substitute for linen and cotton fibers, was put into commercial production early

in the 1860s, and about 20 years later chemical and mechanical wood pulp papers were being produced in great quantities for use as book papers.

Early in the 19th century papermakers discovered that it was more economical to add rosin to the pulp while it was being beaten instead of dipping the sheet of waterleaf into a solution of gelatin in the manner practiced since the 12th century. Rosin reduced the absorbency of the paper, but, unlike gelatin, did not increase its strength. A great deal of the machine-made paper of this period is of low quality, having little tensile strength. It is also subject at times to severe FOXING. The weakness, however, is probably due more to the ALUM used to precipitate the rosin than the rosin itself.

Paper coated with one of the clays, e.g., china clay, came into common use at the end of the 19th century. This type of paper is ideal for printing fine halftones, but it lacks strength, is easily damaged by moisture, and unless synthetic resins instead of starch are used as binders, the surface strips off easily. *See:* HANDMADE PAPER; PAPERMAKING. *See also:* ABSORBENT PAPERS; ACCELERATED AGING TESTS; ACID-FREE PAPER; AIR PERMEABILITY; BASIC SIZE; BASIS WEIGHT; BREAKING LENGTH; BRIGHTNESS; BRIGHTNESS REVERSION; BRITTLENESS; BULK (2, 3, 4); BULK EQUIVALENTS; BURST FACTOR; BURSTING STRENGTH; COMPRESSIBILITY; CONDITIONING; COTTON FIBER CONTENT PAPER; DECKLE EDGE; DUPLEX (1); FOLDING ENDURANCE; FORMATION; FOURDRINIER MACHINE; FOURDRINIER WIRE; GROUNDWOOD FREE PAPER; M. M. SYSTEM; MOLD-MADE PAPER; SIZES OF PAPER; WATERLEAF; WATERMARK. (17, 58, 77, 79, 80, 143, 144, 176, 268, 323)

paperback. A book generally defined as a flat back book with a paper cover that is usually, but not always, of a heavier stock than that used for the leaves of the publication itself. Paperback books are often made up of single leaves secured by a hot-melt adhesive. They usually have relatively narrow binding margins, are often printed on paper of poor to very poor quality (frequently with a high proportion of mechanical wood pulp), and are generally cut flush. (123)

paper board. *See:* BINDER'S BOARD; BOARD.

paper boards cut flush. An old style of bookbinding in which the spine of the book was slightly rounded and covered with skiver. Pulp boards were pasted on and covered with manila paper. The book was then cut flush. (256)

paper clay. A white to light-colored clay having a very low free silica content. Most paper clays are processed to obtain properties required for their use as fillers or coatings for paper. (17, 58)

paper cloth. 1. A cloth faced with paper. 2. A fabric made by the Polynesians from the inner bark of the PAPER MULBERRY and other trees. 3. Twisted paper woven or knitted in a fabric. 4. Any of several types of paper specially processed for use in bookbinding.

paper converting. 1. An edition binding term used with reference to the binding and finishing of publisher's books. 2. The processing of raw paper, as produced on the papermaking machine, to obtain an improved grade or a finished product, such as a coated or laminated paper.

paper covered and overlapped. A binding consisting of a paper cover glued to the spine of the text block and endpapers, both of which extend beyond the edges of the leaves. *See also:* YAPP STYLE.

paper covers. An economical style of binding used for reprints, or, especially in Europe, a temporary binding of original works, in which the cover consists of stiff paper attached at the spine. The cover may overlap the edges, or it may be trimmed and turned so that in effect it is flush with the edges of the book. *See also:* BRADEL BINDING; LESNÉ, FRANÇOIS A. D.; STIFFENED PAPER COVERS. (140, 169)

paper cutter. Any machine or device used to divide a sheet, or sheets of paper, or board into smaller sizes, for squaring paper or board, or for trimming the edges of books. *See, for example:* GUILLOTINE; PLOW; ROTARY BOARD CUTTER; THREE-KNIFE TRIMMER.

papermaking. The craft or process of producing a sheet or web from the matted and felted fibers of vegetable and/or other materials. Although paper is still produced in small quantities by hand (*see:* HANDMADE PAPER), the great bulk of paper is now made by machine.

After the paper stock (consisting of the fibrous material, and, usually, sizing materials, loadings and coloring matter) is compounded, it is collected in the machine (or mixing) chest where it is further diluted from about 3 to 6% down to about 2 to 3%. The stock is then pumped into a regulating box which controls the flow of the stock to the papermaking machine.

Subsequent to further dilution of the stock with white water (which is water containing fibers and other materials retrieved from the papermaking machine), the stock is screened through sand traps or other purifying devices to remove lumps or clumps of fibers, impurities, etc. The screened stock then enters the flow (head) box of the papermaking machine, where it is agitated and spread onto the wire, which, by means of forward movement and lateral agitation, forms the fibers into a matted web of paper. The wire, which is endless, is supported by the breast roll, followed by a series of foils or table rolls. It also moves over several suction boxes which remove water from the suspension, and then under the DANDY ROLL, before returning over a suction couch roll. The breast roll and the suction couch roll represent the two extremes of the wire. On its return to the breast roll the tautness of the wire is controlled by a number of stretch rolls. The water draining through the wire, i.e., the white water, is collected and returned to the head box. The fibrous slurry is prevented from running off the edges of the wire in various manners, e.g., by means of a DECKLE on either side of the wire. When the paper web passes under the dandy roll it is still sufficiently wet to receive an impression. It is at this point that the web is given a WATERMARK, or, if desired, a laid or wove finish. The former is produced by covering the roll with evenly spaced parallel wires, while the wove finish requires that the roll be covered with woven wire. The paper web proceeds from the wire to a series of wet presses. When the web reaches the couch roll it still contains approximately 80 to 85% water and therefore cannot support itself. The required support is provided by woolen felts which carry the web through the presses, each press being supplied with its own felt. Suction boxes are also usually provided to remove water from the felt. The wet presses reduce the water content of the web to about 70%, and at this point the web is self supporting. The web than passes from the "wet end" of the papermaking machine to the "dry end." This section consists of a series of cast iron driers arranged in two or more rows. The web is held tightly against the drying cylinders by means of felts. By the time the web emerges from the last drying press, its water has been reduced to less than 10%. Depending on the finish desired, the paper may pass from the drying section to the

calender stack or it may be reeled initially without calendering. Thus, modern papermaking involves essentially seven basic operations: 1) fiber pretreatment; 2) fiber blending; 3) furnish cleaning and screening; 4) slurry distribution and metering; 5) web formation and water removal by mechanical means; 6) web compaction and water removal by means of heat; and 7) sheet finishing, by means of calendering, sizing, coating, or glazing.

The method used today to prepare cellulosic material for papermaking is almost entirely mechanized. Wood chips are treated with chemicals, under heat and pressure (*see:* SULFATE PROCESS; SULFITE PROCESS), various impurities (notably LIGNIN) being removed in the process. The chips are partially processed into pulp and are then bleached to the desired brightness and washed. Following washing, the partially processed pulp is ready to be processed into paper pulp. The pulp, at this stage called "half stuff," is ground in a beater, by means of refiners (*see:* JORDAN; REFINER), and, in the usual process, loading agents, sizing and coloring materials are also added.

The properties of the finished paper depend largely on the loading agents, as well as the fibrous materials used and the degree of their treatment. These agents consist of mineral substances, principally one of the clays (*see:* KAOLIN), which affect the opacity of the paper, its suitability for printing, etc. SIZING (2) materials are usually added to the pulp to impart water (ink) resistance. *See also:* ADDITIVES (2); AIRDRIED; ALKALINE FILLER; ALKALINE PROCESS; ALKALINE RESERVE; ANIMAL SIZED; ASH; ATTAPULGITE CLAY; BEATER SIZED; CALENDER; CELLULOSE; CELLULOSE CHAIN; CELLULOSE FIBERS; CHAIN LINES; CHEMICAL WOOD PULP; CLAY; COATED; COATING; COATING CLAY; COUCH (3, 4); COUCH ROLL; DIGESTER; FILLER CLAY; HARD SIZED; MACHINE DIRECTION; MECHANICAL WOOD PULP; NEUTRAL SULFITE PROCESS; PULP; ROSIN SIZE; SEMICHEMICAL PULP; SIZING; SLACK SIZED; SUPERCALENDER; SURFACE SIZED; TUB SIZED; UNBLEACHED SULFATE PULP; UNBLEACHED SULFITE PULP; WELL-CLOSED FORMATION. (58, 140, 144, 162, 176, 177, 230, 324, 340)

paper mulberry. An Asiatic tree, *Broussonetia papyrifera*, the bast fiber from the inner bark of which is used in the manufacture of paper, especially handmade paper. Also called "kozo."

paper sizes. *See:* SIZE (3); SIZES OF PAPER.

paper-stiffened cover. A binding consisting

of a paper cover attached to the spine of the text block and stiffened on the sides by means of heavy paper or card inserted between the cover and the board paper. *See also:* CLOTH-STIFFENED COVER.

paper substance. The weight of paper per unit area, as contrasted with density, which is the weight per unit volume. *See also:* BASIS WEIGHT. (93)

paper tree. Various trees from which paper is made in the Far East (and other areas), including *Broussonetia papyrifera* (*see:* PAPER MULBERRY); *Daphne cannabina, Edgeworthia cardneri,* and *Trophis aspers,* the last three found in the East Indies. There is also the paperbark tree, *Melaleuca leucadendron,* as well as species of *Callistemon,* which are Australian trees from which the bark peels off in layers. (197)

paper wrappered and overlapped. A binding consisting of a paper wrapper secured to the spine of the text block only, the covers of which extend beyond the edges of the leaves. (343)

paper wrappered, turned over. A binding consisting of a paper wrapper secured to the spine of the text block only, and folded over onto itself or the endpaper so as to be flush with the edges of the leaves. (343)

papeterie. A class of papers normally cut to size, boxed, and used for writing. Papeteries are produced from cotton fiber or chemical wood pulps, or mixtures thereof, and are given many special treatments, such as embossing, mottling, watermarking, aniline printing, and the like, to obtain desired colors and appearance. The majority of them have low strength, high bulk, and good folding qualities. They normally carry a considerable percentage of filler, in order to give them the required finish and opacity, and are sized to give satisfactory pen-and-ink writing qualities. Basis weights normally range from 16 to 32 pounds (17 × 22 − 500). (17)

papyrus. A giant sedge, *Cyperus papyrus,* native to the region of the Nile, the pith of which was used to make a writing material by the ancient Egyptians, Greeks, and Romans. Papyrus was the forerunner of paper and the origin of the word, although it is not paper because it is not a matted or felted sheet made from a fibrous material. After the pith was sliced, the strips were laid out in a row with the edges slightly overlapping. Another row was laid crosswise on top of the first, and the two layers were moistened with water and pounded into a sheet of

writing material. Presumably, the sheets were then sized, dried, and otherwise finished. When of a high quality, papyrus was very supple and flexible. The individual sheets were generally glued together side by side to form long sections which were usually rolled up.

Papyrus was sold in large quantities in the form of bales or rolls from which sheets could be cut off as required. The size of the sheets ranged from 6 or 7 inches up to about 18 to 20 inches. The better grades were more brownish in color.

One common characteristic of papyrus, regardless of quality, is the difference between the two sides of the sheet, which stems from the strips being at right angles to each other. The recto side, on which the strips run horizontally, was the side generally preferred for writing, while the verso, which had vertical strips, was less frequently used. A material as pliable as papyrus was well suited to be rolled, and when this was done the recto became the inner side and the verso, with no writing, the outer side.

The greatest use of papyrus as a writing material was between the 4th century B.C. and the 4th century A.D. (192, 218, 236)

paraffin (wax). A waxy crystalline substance that in the pure form is white, odorless and translucent and has the approximate chemical formula of $C_{20}H_{42}$ (and above). It is obtained from petroleum by distillation and is then purified by sweating or solvent refining. Paraffin, which is not a true wax, consists mainly of a mixture of saturated straight-chain solid hydrocarbons. Its melting points range from 50 to 57° C. It is used in the manufacture of certain types of paper, in leather dressings, in marbling, in producing paraffin prints, etc. (17, 183, 335)

paraffin prints. Decorative cover paper and endpaper prints produced by etching a paraffin (or other waxy material) surface with a stylus, inking, and pressing on paper or cloth. Only an oil-base printer's ink will work on the wax surface. (183)

parallel fold. A method of folding in which each fold is parallel to the preceding. Parallel folding is generally used for narrow book formats, for books printed two-up, and for maps. Printing should be done so that the folds can be made along the machine direction of the paper. *Cf:* RIGHT ANGLE FOLD. *See also:* FOLDING; FOLDING MACHINES. (320)

parallel laminated. A board or other laminate having both or all layers oriented, with the grain direction of each running in the same direction. *See also:* CROSS LAMINATED. (17, 309)

parallel transmittance. The degree to which light beams reflected from an object pass through a material, such as paper, within a predetermined small range of angles. It is measured by means of a standardized instrument designed specifically for the purpose. Parallel transmittance is important in determining the transparency of transparent papers, i.e., the more parallel the light beams, approaching 0° angle, the more transparent the paper. (17)

parchment. A translucent or opaque material made from the wet, limed, and unhaired skins of sheep, goats, or similar smaller animals, by drying at room temperature *under tension,* generally on a wooden frame known as a stretching frame. Wood is used because a frame of iron, for example, is likely to cause blue iron stains which are difficult to remove. Good parchment must be fine—that is, thin, strong, yet flexible—and must have a smooth surface if it is to be used for writing.

In the manufacture of parchment, the skin is first limed and unhaired (or dewooled), a process generally accomplished by scraping the skin with a blunt knife. Following unhairing, the skin is dried under tension. While this is taking place, more lime is applied to remove moisture and grease, particularly the latter in the case of sheepskins. Finally, the parchment is finished while still in a taut condition; the surface is smoothed by shaving it with, a semi-circular (often semi-lunar) knife, and rubbing it with pumice. Despite this treatment, the flesh side can usually be distinguished from the grain side of an unsplit skin by its rougher texture and often darker color. In books, the pages are usually arranged grain- to grain-side and flesh-to flesh-side in order to provide a more uniform appearance.

Parchment manufacture, which subjects the fiber network of the skin to the simultaneous action of stretching and drying, causes changes in the skin very different from those which take place in the manufacture of leather. The dermal fiber network is reorganized by the stretching, and the network is then permanently set in this new and highly taut form by drying the fluids— i.e., ground substance of the skin—to a hard gluelike consistency. The fibers of the skin are thus fixed in a stretched condition and, as long as the skin remains more or less dry, they will not revert to their original three-dimensional network. This gives a taut, highly stressed sheet that is relatively inelastic and has a stiff handle. In addition, the alignment of the fibers into layers parallel to the grain and flesh surfaces of the skin (resulting in very low or virtually zero angle of weave) involves a certain extent of breakage of fibers in the dermal network. It is this variation in mechanical processing that results in the fundamental difference between parchment and leather. The extent of the alteration of fiber orientation depends on several factors, including the species of the animal; the age, sex, diet, etc., of the skin being processed; the intensity of the liming it has received; and the tension and rate at which the wet, stretched skin is dried. The fiber orientation of parchment is such that it tends to tear fairly easily into a number of thinner sheets, whereas leather cannot be torn in this manner because it retains its original three-dimensional network.

Originally, parchment was made from the full thickness of a skin, and was made thinner in the Middle Ages by shaving. The modern practice, however, is to use only the flesh layer of a split skin, which means that neither side of the finished parchment has any grain pattern. The remaining grain split is generally used to make a thin leather, usually a skiver.

As in leather manufacture, it is usually the skins of animals slaughtered for their meat that are used in making parchment. As the blood drains from the animal, the minute network of dermal blood vessels becomes colorless and is usually undetected in the flayed skin. Proper drainage of the blood vessels is essential, otherwise the iron compounds of the blood will react with the lime liquors to form dark colored pigments which are extremely difficult, if not impossible, to remove. If, however, some blood does remain in the vascular system during the processing of a skin into parchment, so that a colored pattern of blood vessels is left on the finished material, the parchment is said to be "veined." Assuming the veining pattern is of an attractive character, it may actually enhance the aesthetic appeal of the parchment for use in bookbinding. The colors and depths of shading of finished parchment vary with the animal skin, ranging from the greenish markings of goatskin, through the light brown patterns of calfskins,

to the brown-black shades of sheepskins.

Contrary to the process in leather manufacture, the lime used for unhairing skins in parchment is not subsequently removed. The presence of so much alkaline substance may explain why parchment is not affected as much as leather is by the action of acids resulting from atmospheric pollution, mainly from the presence of sulfur dioxide (SO_2). Parchment, however, is readily affected adversely by water, and water can very easily permit the multiplication of bacteria, which can rapidly degrade and even destroy parchment. In addition, if parchment is permitted to absorb large quantities of water, the setting and fixing action of its dried ground substance will eventually break down allowing the fiber network to relax since it is no longer fixed in a taut condition. When the parchment is subsequently dried in this relaxed condition, the very properties that made it parchment initially are lost, and a hard, horny sheet, not unlike rawhide, is all that remains. It follows then, that parchment should not be washed, at least in the manner that leather may be washed, or allowed to remain in an environment saturated with water vapor.

Medieval scribes usually pounced their parchment a second time (also with pumice) before writing. It was also given a coat of glue sizing before it was illuminated. In the 18th century, however, a new method of sizing parchment was developed in which the size was actually formed in the surface of the sheet by dissolving it with hot water. As a result of this new technique, pouncing is no longer usually required.

In the modern method of parchment manufacture, the shaving knife is still used, but the skins are rapidly unhaired by the use of sodium sulfide, split by machine, and dried in an oven under tension. If a transparent skin is required, the tension is relaxed somewhat. Transparent parchment was at one time used in decorative schemes displaying paintings underneath the covering material of books. A patent for making transparent parchment (vellum) was issued to James Edwards in 1785. *See:* EDWARDS OF HALIFAX.

Ideal storage conditions for parchment are temperatures between 0° and 20° C. (32° and 68° F.), with a relative humidity of 50 to 65%. Although, under no circumstances should parchment be allowed to become saturated

with water, neither should it be allowed to dry out.

The manufacture of parchment dates back to at least the Middle Kingdom of Egypt, or approximately 2000 B.C. Its manufacture arrived in Northwestern Europe along with Christianity, where it became the most important writing material of the Middle Ages. From the 12th century onwards, however, its use slowly declined in favor of paper. Its use today is limited, being restricted largely to state and legal documents, certificates, and the like; in the construction of musical instruments; and in certain aspects of archival conservation.

Some authorities use the terms parchment and VELLUM interchangeably, contending that vellum is simply a superior form of parchment—one made from the unsplit skin of a calf. Others, however, maintain that, whatever the historical derivations may be, parchment is a material made from the flesh split of a sheepskin, while vellum is made specifically from an unsplit calfskin. In either case, both materials are produced by the same process. *See also:* GOLDBEATER'S SKIN; IMITATION PARCHMENT. (198, 236, 263, 291)

parchment bond. A class of writing paper used in lieu of genuine or vegetable parchment for bonds, legal documents, etc. It is a superior grade of paper made from cotton and bleached chemical wood pulps which are usually well beaten to produce adequate hydration of the fibers. The paper is tub-sized, and loft, air, or machine dried. The basis weights range from 24 to 40 pounds (17 × 22 — 500). Durability, toughness, and good surface for writing are significant properties. (17)

parchment size. A resizing material made from scraps of parchment. It is prepared by boiling 21 grams of parchment scraps soaked in 2½ liters of water for 45 minutes, or longer if a stronger size is required. It is used at a temperature of 35 to 45° C. for resizing archival papers that have been washed. An alkaline buffering agent is sometimes added to the size to provide an alkaline reserve in the paper.

parchment writing paper. A VEGETABLE PARCHMENT PAPER used for various handwritten documents. It is produced from cotton fiber or cotton plus chemical wood pulps, in basis weights of 28 to 32 pounds (17 × 20 — 500). Permanence, strength and durability are required characteristics. (17)

paring. The process of thinning leather

by cutting away the flesh side, or shaving the edges, i.e., beveling the edges that are to be turned in. A PARING MACHINE is generally used for the thinning process (or a SPOKESHAVE if no paring machine is available), while a PARING KNIFE is used for shaving or beveling.

Very little if anything is known of the method or methods used by binders to reduce thickness in the early days of covering books with leather, but it is entirely possible that from about the latter part of the 16th century they purchased leather from the manufacturer in the required thickness and then simply pared the edges.

During the 19th century there were no paring machines in use in binderies, nor were there any spokeshaves. There is no evidence of any paring of leather other than edges during the first half of the 19th century; consequently it must be assumed that the leather was purchased already pared, or was purchased and then sent out to be pared as required. (161, 236, 335)

paring knife. A knife used for paring the edges of leather to be turned over the edges of the boards. The knife has its cutting edge at the end, and is ground flat on the underside and beveled on the upper. There are several varieties of this type of knife: the English paring knife has a flat cutting edge; the French knife is rounded; the German knife, while rounded like the French version, is also ground at an angle. Except for paring the edges of leather, the paring knife has been largely superseded by the SPOKESHAVE. (154, 204, 236, 335)

paring machine. A hand-operated, power-driven machine used for paring leather to the required thickness. Any required width within the scope of the foot above the feed roll may be pared. The feed roll is always close to the inside edge of the circular knife (which is constantly sharpened by a grinding stone beneath it), but not touching. When the foot pedal is depressed, a feed roller propels the leather against the knife. The depth of cut is controlled by stops, which limit the distances between roller and knife edge. The leather pared falls away in thin scraps. In the use of the paring machine the condition of the skin is important; it must be flexible and pliable enough to bed down flat on the feed rollers, but if it is too soft or loose the fibers tear and drag rather than cut cleanly. (154, 264)

paring stone. Usually a lithographic stone on which the binder cuts and pares

leather, or performs any other operation requiring a smooth, hard surface. (237, 335)

Parks, William (d 1750). A printer and bookbinder, who, between 1726 and 1737, was printer to the Lord Proprietor of the Province of Maryland. Parks, an Englishman by birth, was one of the most influential figures in the history of printing in Colonial American times, and had an important role in American literary history as well. He did bookbinding as well as printing in his establment, advertising that "Book-Binding is done reasonably, in the best manner." In 1730 Parks established a branch business in the Province of Virginia at Williamsburg, and operated both businesses until disagreement with the Assembly at Annapolis in 1737 caused him to move his entire operation to Williamsburg. He was the first successful printer in Virginia, and *The Complete Mariner,* a manuscript volume of

PARING KNIFE

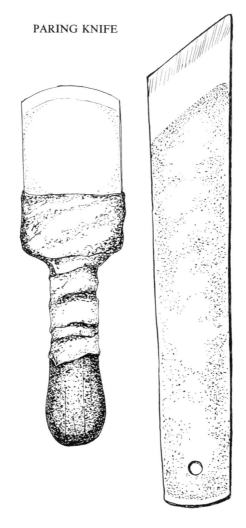

French   English

navigational exercises with a title page printed in Williamsburg in 1731, was one of the first products of his press. The binding of this work is skillfully decorated in blind with a roll and two other ornaments that were also used on books issued by his Annapolis shop and later on bindings executed in Williamsburg. (200, 301, 347)

part binding (parti binding). An obsolete style of library binding consisting of a cloth spine, paper sides with no corners, or, at times, a paper spine, with sides of a different type of paper, but again no corners.

parts of a book. The different segments of a book, gathered in the following order: half title page, frontispiece, title page, printer's imprint and copyright notice, dedication, preface, acknowledgments, table of contents, list of illustrations, introduction, errata, text, appendices, author's notes, glossary, bibliography, index, and colophon. Publishers sometimes vary the order of inclusion, and not all works contain all segments indicated. (140)

passing. A metallic thread worked through the material of an embroidered binding or sewn to it with silk thread of the same color. *See also:* TAMBOUR (2). (280)

paste. A soft, plastic, adhesive composition, having a high order of yield value, and generally prepared by heating a mixture of starch and water and subsequently cooling the hydrolized product.

Paste has been used for centuries to join porous, non-greasy materials. At one time it was made from flour (frequently wheat flour) mixed with water, but other materials now are frequently added to achieve particular results. The present-day tendency is to use ready-made paste in which the proportions of the ingredients are scientifically blended.

Paste has many uses in bookbinding, although its use is declining in favor of the increased use of cold resinous adhesives, such as polyvinyl acetate. It is still used, however, in covering, for pasting down endpapers, and in casing-in, etc. It is also used for decorative work (*see:* PASTE PAPERS), in repairing torn leaves, and the like. In paper conservation, rice starch and wheat starch pastes are used for hinging, lining, and in long-fiber repairs. (183, 186, 218, 309, 339)

pasteboard. 1. A class of board produced by laminating (pasting) sheets of (brown) paper and used for the boards of books, or, if lined, for printing. Originally pasteboards were generally of three types: 1) those made by pasting together sheets of plain paper, leaves of books, or printing spoilage; 2) a better grade produced by matting together sheets of newly made hand-made paper; and 3) an inferior grade produced from shavings and even floor sweepings. The last named was not actually "pasteboard," by definition, as it was not built up of laminated layers.

Pasteboard was not in general use in Europe before about the first quarter of the 16th century, although in the East its use for book boards originated centuries before. By the second quarter of the 16th century, however, the use of pasteboard for books exceeded that of wood. Pasteboard continued to be used in economy trade binding until late in the 18th century, even though it had begun to be replaced by rope-fiber millboards in the latter part of the 17th century. Genuine pasteboards are seldom used in bookbinding today. (*See also:* BINDER'S BOARD.)

2. A general term applied to those paperboards and cardboards formed by pasting a liner on stock of a different grade. The term also denotes any stiff board or cardboard of medium thickness. (58, 198, 236, 339)

pastebox. A wooden box lined on the inside with zinc or galvanized iron, and fitted with a rod across one end to enable the bookbinder to work surplus paste from his brush into the box (264)

pastedown. The plain, colored, fancy, or marbled paper attached to the inside of the board of a book after it has been covered, or when it is cased-in. The pastedown serves several purposes: 1) it hides the raw edges of the covering material where it is turned over the edges of the board; 2) it forms the hinge between the text block and the board or case; and 3) in edition and library binding, particularly the former, the pastedown and hinge are frequently the only means by which the text block is secured to its case. If the pastedown is laid down indepedently of, and is separate from, the flyleaf, it is called a DOUBLURE (1), in which case it is joined to the flyleaf by means of joint, usually of leather. The pastedown is frequently referred to as the "board paper." It is also sometimes called the "endpaper" (singular), "end lining," "end sheet" (singular), or "lining paper." *See also:* PASTING-DOWN OPEN; PASTING-DOWN SHUT. (83, 237)

paste drying. A method of curing freshly flayed hides or skins by means of a watery paste of *natural* salty earth (*see:* KHARI) rubbed into the skin on the

flesh side. This treatment rapidly draws water from the skin, resulting in a quick cure. The salts also have a bacteriostatic effect so that drying need not be as thorough as in the case of air drying. Paste-dried stock is also easier to rehydrate than that which is air dried. Paste drying as a method of curing has been used for centuries and is still employed in India, Pakistan, Iran, and Turkey. (291)

paste-grained roan. A tanned grain split of a sheepskin, split while in the limed state. When in the finishing stage, a flour paste is applied to the flesh side, which causes the skin to plump, enabling it to take a bright cross or straight grain. The flesh split is either tanned or converted into parchment. Paste-grained roan is sometimes referred to as "French morocco." (335)

paste papers (starch papers). Decorative endpapers and cover papers produced by pressing or sliding objects into a wet paste or starch mixture that has been spread on the paper. When dry the paper is then glazed. The paste is usually colored with poster paints, dyes, colored inks, or the like, worked into the thinned paste. Paste papers, which were one of the earliest forms of decorative papers, were used for both cover papers and endpapers from the 16th through the 18th centuries, and are still used to some extent today. (133, 217)

paster. 1. A machine used for pasting sheets together, either in a continuous roll or as separate sheets. 2. A device for applying a fine line of paste or other adhesive on one or both sides of a web of paper, the web then being cut, printed, and folded to produce booklets in which paste is used in lieu of sewing or stitching. The adhesive can be applied only in the direction the web travels. (17, 339)

paste tins (paste boards). Zinc-covered boards used mainly in trade binding for pasting guards and cloth joints. The zinc is pasted and the guards and/or cloth joints are laid down, a sheet of waste paper is laid on top and rubbed down, resulting in the laid down material picking up the adhesive. (256)

paste-washing. 1. The process of applying a coating of thinned paste to the flesh side of leather, so as to cause the leather to shrink slightly and also to help it maintain its shape when covering. 2. The process of applying thinned paste to the grain surface of calfskin and sheepskin bindings before tooling so as to clean the leather and fill in the pores to prevent absorption of the glair. 3. *See:* CLEANING OFF. (236, 335)

paste water. Paste that has been thinned down to the consistency of milk. *See:* PASTE-WASHING.

pasting. 1. A general term applied to the process of joining two or more sheets of paper or board, cloth and board, leather and board, cloth and paper, etc., by means of an adhesive. 2. The application of paste to a surface, either by hand with a brush, or by machine. Pasting machines are used to a considerable extent, either as independent units or built into other machines, e.g., casing-in machines. The pasting machine usually consists of a rotating cylinder to which the adhesive is carried from a container or through transfer cylinders, and against which the paper is fed. (140, 234)

pasting down. In hand binding, the process of pasting the board papers to the insides of the boards of a book. In library and edition binding, the proper term is CASING-IN. Also called "pasting off," or "pasting up." *See also:* PASTE-DOWN; PASTING-DOWN OPEN; PASTING-DOWN SHUT. (335, 355)

pasting-down open. The traditional method of pasting the board papers to the boards in hand binding (and almost always when it is a leather binding), while the boards are open and resting on the block. (161, 335)

pasting-down shut. A method of pasting the board papers to the boards in hand binding. The board papers are spread with adhesive and the boards are closed onto them and pressed. In hand and edition binding, this technique is used for cloth or case bindings, respectively. (310, 335)

pasting off (pasting up). *See:* PASTING DOWN.

patent leather. A cattle or horse hide, which is coated, usually on the flesh side, with a flexible, waterproof film having a lustrous and highly glazed surface produced by successive coatings of daubs, varnishes, and lacquers, some of which may be pigmented. These were formerly based on boiled linseed oil ("Japanning") but some or all may now consist partly or entirely of plasticized cellulose nitrate and/or plastic resins. (351, 363)

pattern. 1. *See:* RUB. 2. In edition binding, the base used as a pattern for the entire edition. 3. Metal plates, the exact size of the covers of a book, and used as guides in cutting leather covers or spines. (256, 261)

pattern board. A board on which the bookbinder mounts a specimen of the covering material to show the titling layout, color, size, etc., to ensure uniformity in the binding of a series of books. *See also:* RUB (1). (156)

patterned papers. Papers printed or patterned in relief with a design and used for book jackets or covers. One of the more common patterns has been a simulation of leather. Patterned papers are produced by passing the web of paper through rollers engraved with the pattern on the papermaking machine. For linen or crash patterns the rollers may be wrapped with the material itself. (182)

paumelle. A wooden toothed instrument sometimes used to impart a straight or cross grain pattern to MOROCCO leather. (172)

pawl press. A very powerful type of STANDING PRESS, equipped with a pawl (a device which permits motion in one direction only until released) to enable the press to maintain constant pressure. It was used in the past by printers and bookbinders. (274)

Payne, Roger (1738-1797). The most accomplished and influential of the 18th century English bookbinders. Payne was born in Windsor, England, and was probably apprenticed to an Eton bookseller named Pote. Later he was employed by the Holborn bookseller, Thomas Osborne. In about 1770 Payne was set up in business by Thomas Payne (no relation), the principal bookseller of London.

Roger Payne was an outstanding craftsman. His books were very well forwarded and his style of finishing displayed not only a high level of skill but also very good taste. He usually sewed his books with silk thread and lined the spines with leather. He frequently used elaborately designed doublures, made his endpapers with leather joints, and covered the books with russia leather or morocco. Since Payne was usually short of cash, he cut his own (iron) finishing tools, building up beautiful designs with a relatively meager assortment of small ornaments.

Payne developed a style of splendid simplicity, perhaps made necessary by having to cut his own tools, which gave his design a simplicity and individuality which they otherwise might have lacked. His style consisted essentially of the repetition of small floral forms in borders of radiating corners, the background being formed with dots and circles.

Payne described his bindings as "bound in the very best manner," or "finished in the most magnificent manner," not because of mere vanity on his part, but simply as the only true de-

scription of his work. Oftentimes he presented his customers with highly detailed invoices describing the work he had done. He made his ornamentation appropriate to the subject matter of the book and while the spines were often richly embellished, the covers were generally quite simple.

The leathers he used were generally olive, red or blue morocco, or brown Russia. Payne's endpapers were nearly always solid in color. He preferred purple (sometimes pink) and generally used endpapers which clashed with the covers. His headbands were flat (upright) and sewn with green silk which sometimes had a gold thread in it. The edges of his bindings were rough gilt or plain. (112, 347)

p. c. p. Abbreviation for PENTA-CHLORO-PHENOL.

peacock marble. A drawn marble pattern that is essentially a variation of the NONPARIEL MARBLE, the difference being that after the colors (black, blue, yellow, and red; or black, brown, yellow, and white) have been drawn by the stylus into wavy lines, they are then drawn with a comb, which is extendible in such a manner that it is made wider and narrower at intervals of ½ inch. This widening and narrowing is continued until the entire surface is crossed by this opening and closing comb, resulting in a pattern resembling the tail of a peacock. (264)

peacock roll. A ROLL (1) cut in the shape of the raised and spread tail of a peacock as part of the design. This type of design is characteristic of some English Restoration bindings, as well as some 18th century Irish bindings. (96, 156)

pearl ash. A crude form of potassium carbonate (K_2CO_3) leached from wood ashes, purified by partial crystallization and then dried by evaporation. It is dissolved in water and used to wash the covers of leather bindings before marbling. (97, 159)

pearl edge. A 19th century method of edge decoration executed by gilding the edge of the book, tooling a pattern on the gilt and then removing the gold where the tools have not impressed a pattern. At one time pearl edge bindings were considered to be ideal wedding gifts.

pearl filler. CALCIUM SULFATE.

pearl-sewn bindings. EMBROIDERED BINDINGS incorporating seed pearls.

pebbled-grain. *See:* BOARDING (1).

pebbling. A rough finish on a coated paper, produced by passing the paper between roughened rollers under high

pressure. Because it is more difficult to print on roughened paper than on paper which is smooth, paper is usually pebbled subsequent to printing. A fine-screen halftone cannot be printed on eggshell or antique paper by letterpress processes, but it can be printed on smooth paper that is later pebbled to an antique finish.

Pebbling is often employed to improve the appearance, bulk, or pliability of paper so that a cheaper paper may be substituted for more expensive stock. It may be used to finish small quantities of paper which otherwise could not be purchased with a pebbled finish except in large quantities. (234, 278)

peccary. Leather made from the skin of the wild boar, genus *Tayassu*, of Central and South America, i.e., South American PIGSKIN. (363)

peel. A wooden implement in the shape of a "T" square, used mainly by printers, but also by bookbinders for carrying washed sheets and book leaves to the drying lines. (83, 94)

peeling. 1. A form of leather decay characterized by peeling off of the grain surface. Peeling seems to be particularly associated with those leathers tanned with the condensed class of vegetable tannins, although at this time the cause or causes of the defect are unknown. 2. A defect in paper in which the surface scales or peels off.

peg rake. An implement consisting of a series of round wooden pegs set in a frame. The pegs are smooth and taper slightly at the points and are set about 1¼ inch apart. The device is used to "rake" marbling colors on the size. The pegs should be of sufficient length to touch the bottom of the trough. (159, 217)

pelt. A contradictory term defined both as the skin of an animal with the hair, wool or fur still on, and specifically in the leather trade, as a hide or skin prepared for tanning by the removal of the hair or wool, epidermis, and flesh. (61, 261)

pencil case (pencil box). A colloquial expression for a fold of unadhered paper in the hinge of a book caused by the endpaper not adhering properly, by too loose a turn-in, or by a spine inlay that is too large, etc. (97, 133)

pencil in. The process of applying glair directly into the blind impressions of a decoration before laying on the gold leaf. (130)

penetration. 1. The entering of an adhesive into an adherend. This property is measured by the depth to which the adhesive penetrates the adherend. *See also:* ABSORBENCY; PERMEABILITY; STRIKE IN. 2. A general term for the infusion of a tanning material into the thickness of a hide or skin. 3. The entering of an ink vehicle into the surface of a paper or cloth. (17, 143, 309)

penning. The process of blackening the blind impressions of a decoration with carbon or Chinese ink, in order to accentuate the blind lines. (130)

pen ruling machine. *See:* RULING MACHINES.

penta-chlorophenol (p. c. p.). A crystalline compound (C_6Cl_5OH), produced by the reaction of hexachlorobenzene with sodium hydroxide, or of chlorine with phenol, and used, in concentrations of 0.1% by weight of the paper, as a fungicide. It is applicable either as an aqueous or non-aqueous solution. Being a highly chlorinated substance, it must be used in the presence of sufficient alkali to compensate for the probable liberation of hydrochloric acid, or in such small quantities, i.e., less than 0.1%, so as not to endanger the paper severely even if it does decompose slightly. To avoid the danger of acidity, p. c. p. is sometimes used as the sodium salt, sodium pentachlorophenate, which is less likely to produce difficulty because of acidity. P. c. p. is colorless and is not likely to produce an appreciable odor. (198)

pepper boxes. The pattern appearing on the grain surface of a leather produced from grubby hides. The pattern actually consists of grub holes, and often resembles (in miniature) the holes produced by shotgun pellets. *See also:* WARBLES. (363)

per cent points. A method of expressing a strength factor in paper. It is calculated to a basis weight of 100 points by dividing the actual test results by the actual basis weight and multiplying by 100. (17)

percent wet tensile strength. The tensile strength of a paper when it is completely saturated with water. It is expressed as a percentage of the dry tensile strength of the same paper. *See also:* WET STRENGTH PAPER. (17)

perching. The process in the manufacture of some leathers wherein the skin is clamped in a wooden frame (the "perch") and flexed by a scraping action on the flesh side with a moon knife (or arm perch). Perching is done on very soft, delicate skins, as well as on some furred or wooled skins. Essentially, it is a variation of STAKING. (306)

perfect binding. *See:* ADHESIVE BINDING.

perfected. An edition binding term indicating that both sides of the sheet (i.e., the outer and inner forms) have been printed. The sheet is then ready to be folded and gathered with other perfected and folded sheets to form a book ready to be bound.

perforating. 1. The process of punching round or slotted holes in paper, either during printing or as a separate operation, so that one portion of the sheet may be detached from another, e.g., checks from a checkbook. 2. The process of punching holes, generally arranged in the form of a letter or letters, symbol, etc., in one or more leaves of a publication, for the purpose of identifying the ownership of the material. *See also:* EMBOSSING (3). (189, 264, 339)

perforating at press. PERFORATING (1) done on a printing press by means of a special perforating rule in the printing form. Perforating at press generally does not produce as satisfactory results as perforating as a separate operation, but it is more economical. (274)

perforating machine. A machine used for perforating paper. Two types of perforating machines are in general use: 1) the vertical, or flat-bed perforator, in which the punches and dies are set in a straight line, with the punches set in a moving bar and the dies in the surface of the table. Several sheets may be fed at one time between the punches and dies against adjustable guides. When the machine is activated, the bar descends and punches a series of holes in the paper. The punches are adjustable so that some may be removed when the holes are to be punched only part way across the sheet; and 2) rotary perforators, which are capable of punching round holes, slots, or slits. The punches and dies are mounted on discs that revolve against each other, the paper being fed between them, with one edge against a guide. This type may be set to perforate struck lines as well. Some types of perforators raise the punches for struck lines, while others drop the dies; however, in either case, the punches do not enter the dies, so the sheets are left unperforated. This movement of dies or punches is synchronized with the opening of a paper gate so that the perforating will start at the desired point. The same result may be obtained on other machines by removing some of the punches. Rotary perforators can accomodate several perforating heads which are adjustable

laterally on the spindles to change the spacing between the lines of perforations. The minimum spacing varies with different makes of machines.

The angle perforator can punch in both directions at one feeding. This machine is actually a combination of two rotary perforators at right angles to each other, with feed rollers to carry the sheets of paper from one set of perforating heads to the other.

By means of special attachments, most rotary perforators can also perform other operations, such as scoring, crimping, and slitting. (320, 339)

perforator. A punch or stamp which perforates a mark of ownership in the leaf of a book. They may be hand- or power-operated, the latter usually by means of compressed air.

performance standards. Standards that measure the performance of a product as a unit, e.g., a binding, but which do not specify materials and methods of manufacture. Performance standards, at least as related to edition and library binding, are largely meaningless, because by implication, if not fact, they measure the durability of the binding in the short run only, while the need for the book, and therefore its binding, may extend well into the long run.

period binding. *See:* CONTEMPORARY BINDING (2).

permanent-durable paper. *See:* DURABILITY (OF PAPER); PERMANENT PAPER.

permanent materials. Those (book) materials, as defined by the Library Binding Institute, which a library considers basic to its collection. Literary or monetary value, replaceability, age, accuracy of information, etc., may be pertinent criteria, but the essential criterion is the importance of a specific volume to a particular library's collection. (208)

permanent paper. A paper manufactured in such a manner as to resist chemical action which may result from impurities in the paper itself, as a result of materials or methods used in manufacture, or agents from the surrounding atmosphere while in storage. A "permanent" paper, therefore, is one which resists the effects of aging to a greater degree than is usual in ordinary paper.

Several levels of permanence have been arbitrarily established. In descending order, they are:

1. The greatest degree of permanence obtainable, within the limits of present-day technology. These papers would be used for state or other archives, treaties, political records, etc. This quality of paper would be manufac-

tured from 100% rag (new linen), flax, cotton, or hemp, undyed and unbleached, and produced by hand or machine. It would contain no loading or color additives, and beating and drying would be controlled so as to obtain maximum folding and tearing strengths. The physical and chemical criteria of permanence would be:

pH value—minimum of 7.0, maximum 9.5

acidity—maximum of 0.04%

folding strength decrease after 72 hours at 100° C.—maximum of 25%

alpha-cellulose content—minimum of 95%—decrease after 72 hours at 100° C.—maximum of 1.5

copper number—maximum of 1.2; maximum after 72 hours at 100° C.—.5

rosin content—maximum of 1.2%

iron content—maximum of 0.005%

chlorine content—maximum of 0.05%

2. Intermediate level, providing a high degree of permanence, yet considerably lower than that of the highest level. This type of paper would be used for important documents, including letters of government officials, and special editions of books intended for permanent retention (and which are to be retained under the best of environmental conditions while still being made available to readers). This class of paper would consist of 100% rag (clean, undyed rags of linen, cotton, or hemp), with any materials used for coloring to be as lightfast as possible and free from acid. The maximum decrease in folding endurance after 72 hours at 100° C. should not exceed 30%, and the alpha cellulose minimum should be 92%.

3. The lowest level, used principally for printing first editions, issues of important books, periodical publications, important reference books, and the like, all of which will be stored under relatively good storage conditions. This paper would consist of 30% rag, mixed with 70% carefully bleached sulfite wood pulp, or 35% wood pulp and 35% other fiber, e.g., esparto, straw, etc.; maximum ash content to be 10%, except for coated and other special papers required for color printing, etc. The coloring material would not be poorer in light fastness than ultramarine, or poorer than Prussian blue in its resistance to acidity. Alpha cellulose minimum would be 87% and the maximum decrease in folding endurance after 72 hours at 100° C. would be 40%. Other specifications would be the same as the intermediate type.

These specifications do not of course have any bearing on the permanence (or lack of it) of papers already in existence. The prevailing opinion today seems to be that *any* paper can be made more or less "permanent" by the addition of a suitable alkaline reserve. Modern papers containing, for example, at least 3% (by weight of the paper) of calcium of magnesium carbonate are sometimes classed as archival, since they are expected to last in the range of 300 to 500 years. The addition of an alkaline reserve into any given paper, however, will not restore strength to the paper if it has already been weakened by deleterious influences, either during manufacture, or thereafter. Furthermore, the length of time an alkaline reserve will retain its effectiveness depends, at least to a certain extent, on the level of pollution in the atmosphere, and the quantity of harmful chemicals added to the paper during manufacture. Finally, while an alkaline reserve may retard or prevent chemical deterioration, it has no influence on the fundamental durability of the paper, i.e., its inherent strength, which is enhanced, for example, by the use of long-fibered stock, and decreased by the use of excessive loadings, filler clays, etc. (17, 143, 198)

permanganate bath. A solution of one of the permanganate salts, such as salts of permanganic acid, potassium permanganate, sodium permanganate, etc., used to remove stains from paper. Thirty grams of the permanganate in one liter of slightly warm water is the usual concentration. The sheets, subsequent to treatment, are washed under running water until as much of the purple stain of the permanganate as possible is removed. Not all of the salt can be removed by washing; therefore, the sheets are generally placed in a bath of 1 ounce of sulfurous acid to ½ liter of water until the original color is restored. The sheets are then washed again in running water and resized. (198, 364)

permeability. The rate at which a fluid (in either gaseous or liquid form) penetrates into a material. The rate may be a result of pressure differentials and/or capillary forces. Permeability is of considerable importance in both papermaking and printing. (17, 58)

Persian. A vegetable-tanned leather produced from sheepskins originating in the Indian Subcontinent, and tanned in India, mainly in the south, and especially around Madras. *See also:* E. I. (61)

Persian calf. A vegetable-tanned leather closely resembling calfskin, at one time produced in Persia (Iran) from the skins of mountain sheep. (291, 306)

Persian morocco. Reputedly, a vegetable-tanned leather produced originally from goat skin and subsequently from the skins of various hair sheep. It is said to be tough and strong but lacking in permanence, supposedly because it is tanned from the condensed class of tannins. The leather is finished with a smooth grain surface in imitation of calfskin, which makes the expression "morocco" misleading. (264)

Persian skiver. A thin grain-layer split of leather taken from a PERSIAN sheepskin. (61)

petits fers. "Small irons." Small hand finishing tools.

pH. *See:* HYDROGEN-ION CONCENTRATION.

phenol (carbolic acid). A soluble, crystalline compound (C_6H_6O), that is acidic, forms metallic salts, and is readily halogenated, sulfonated, and nitrated. It is used in the manufacture of phenolic and epoxy resins, various dyes, and the like. Phenol, even in its purest form (ice crystals), has a tendency to turn a pinkish color. It is also used at times as a preservative in paste. In concentrated forms it must be carefully handled, as it can cause severe burns. (198)

Philadelphia patent-back guard. A heavy cloth guard to which a folio of a large blankbook is sewn before being sewn to webbings. It is used mainly where the sewing must have greater flexibility than that afforded by sewing on webbings alone. It also contributes considerably to the strength of the sewing.

phloroglucinol (phloroglucin stain). A sweet, crystalline phenol ($C_6H_3(OH)_3$), used in conjunction with hydrochloric acid and alcohol as a test solution to detect the presence of mechanical wood pulp in paper, which it turns red. It has no advantage over the HERTZBERG

STAIN other than that it can be applied directly to the paper. (143)

photocopying paper. A base paper of superior quality that is coated with a fast light-sensitive emulsion for use in photocopying machines, and also for designs and layouts. The paper is produced from pulps ranging from 100% cotton fiber to 100% chemical wood pulps, the latter being generally of papermaking alpha grade. The pulp must be highly purified as all metallic residues must be removed. The paper is also given wet strength treatment to enable it to withstand the acids and alkalis and other photographic solutions used in photographic processes. Inertness to photographic sensitizing solutions is important, as are uniformity of color and surface. The base paper is finished with gelatin sizing so as to prevent the photographic emulsion coating from penetrating too deeply into the sheets. (17)

photographic paper. Paper used as the base for various photosensitive systems which use silver halide crystals as the light sensitive receptors. It is a carefully made paper produced either from cotton fibers or highly purified chemical wood pulp. The paper must be free of all substances, especially chemicals, which might adversely affect later processing and it must also possess high wet strength so as to permit processing in both acid and alkaline solutions. Photographic paper ranges in thickness from 0.0025 to 0.015 inch. (17)

pick. 1. Paper pulp or fibers which adhere to the wet or dry sections of the papermaking machine. *See also:* PICKING. 2. A particle of hardened ink, dirt, or paper, or a piece of composition roller, embedded in the hollow of printing type, filling up its face and causing a dark spot to appear on the printed sheet. 3. A small particle of metal on an electrotype or stereotype plate, caused by a slight defect in the mold, and resulting in a spot or blot on the printed sheet. 4. A white spot on the printed surface of a sheet, and caused by ink adhering to the form and pulling a particle from the surface of the paper. 5. The condition in an adhesive which causes it to transfer unevenly from an adhesive applicator due to high surface tack.

picking. A lifting of the coating of a paper, or even the paper fibers themselves, from the surface of a sheet. It generally occurs during printing and is caused when the lifting stress resulting from tackiness of the ink exceeds the strength of the paper or its coat-

ing. The defect itself does not register from sheet to sheet, but its effect may be seen on succeeding sheets. Picking can usually be overcome by reducing the viscosity of the ink and/or running the press at a lower speed. (17, 323)

pickling. The process in leather manufacture of bringing hides and skins into a condition of equilibrium in preparation for tannage. Pickling, which is a process developed specifically for use in modern chrome tannages, takes place following LIMING, UNHAIRING, and DELIMING (and BATING), and is used particularly in the case of sheepskins. The skins are de-wooled (the wool being more valuable than the skins) and are then pickled, drained and packed, ready for transportation to the tannery. Pickling takes place in a solution of 12% salt and 1.2% sulfuric acid (previously diluted with water). The salt solution should remain above 10% and the acid above 0.8%. Furthermore, if the proportion of salt to acid is incorrect the skins may be damaged; consequently, both must be carefully controlled. Pickled skins also must not be allowed to become dry, as drying may cause the acid to weaken the skin structure, and the crystallization of salt on, or in, the grain may lead to SALT SPROUT.

The salt serves to preserve the skin, just as in the case of salting for the purpose of curing, while the acidity, if below a pH of 2.0, inhibits nearly all known putrefying bacteria. The treated skins, therefore, may be stored for several months, provided they are kept cool; however, at temperatures above 32° C., the acidity may cause damage to the skins. Pickling, while stopping bacterial damage, does not stop the formation of molds, which favor pH values of less than 5.0, and which can cause green, black, or white discolorations, as well as a loss of gloss or face on the finished leather. This is due to their attack on the grain structure, and often manifests itself in uneven dyeing. Mold growth can be prevented by the use of fungicides added to the pickle liquor in a concentration of about 0.001% of the weight of the liquor. A typical pickle fungicide is paranitrophenol. (248, 306, 363)

pick strength. *See:* BONDING STRENGTH.

pictorial bindings. Wrapped bindings with pictorial decorations, generally executed in one color, and usually on a black or colored background. Gilt pictorial decoration on the spines of publishers' cloth bindings was common

in the late 1830s and the 1840s. A similar technique was used on cloth, and although glazed pictorial cloth bindings were never as common as those boarded or wrappered, they were used occasionally until the end of the 19th century. (69)

pictorial calf bindings. Bookbindings produced in the early 19th century, executed by painting the leather a brown or black color, generally by means of acid, or by transferring a decoration to the leather from copperplate prints. *See also:* "PAINTED" BINDINGS.

pieced. 1. Any space on the cover of a book which has a piece of another material attached to it. The term is most often applied to leather used for labels and titles. Also called "titled." 2. A book cover made up of several different parts or pieces of different materials. 3. The process in fine binding of joining two smaller pieces of the same leather to make a full cover by using pieces which individually are not large enough to cover the book. (12, 25, 94)

pigment. A natural or synthetic, organic or inorganic substance that imparts color, as well as black and white, and is used in the manufacture of paint, printing inks, etc. A pigment is insoluble in its liquid medium, and imparts its coloring effect simply by spreading over the surface to which it is applied. A pigment produced by precipitating a dye on a colorless, or inert, base, thus rendering the dye insoluble, is called a LAKE, while a synthetic organic compound that is insoluble and can be used directly as a pigment is called a "toner."

Pigments are generally classified according to their origin. Those produced by processing colored earths are referred to as EARTH COLORS, while those produced by chemical processes from inorganic raw materials that are not in themselves coloring matter are called artificial inorganic pigments. The finest grades of earth colors occur in specific areas, e.g., French yellow ochre, Italian raw and burnt sienna, etc. Early pigments included the native earths, e.g., red iron oxides and yellow ochre, as well as manufactured pigments, such as crimson lake, lampblack, and white lead.

Pigments should be chemically inert, so as not to react in an undesirable manner with other pigments or liquids with which they may be mixed, and they should also be lightfast and not fade or darken when exposed to typical indoor lighting, such as indirect sunlight, artificial light of normal intensity, and controlled temperature and humidity variations. All pigments of very high quality will endure indefinitely under proper conditions, although some may undergo loss of color if exposed to direct sunlight. *Cf:* DYE. (17, 195, 233)

pigment leather. A leather finished with materials containing opaque pigments which obscure the grain pattern, including any defects it may have. When a leather is buffed very deeply in order to remove grain defects, it is often necessary to apply large amounts of pigment in the finish to obtain a uniform appearance. An increase in the amount of pigment used requires an increase in the amount of binding material used, so as to prevent the pigment from chalking and flaking off. *See also:* ANILINE LEATHER. (363)

pigment properties. The characteristics or attributes of a pigment in addition to its color properties, and used in evaluating or describing it. (233)

pigskin. A leather produced from the skin of the domestic pig (*Sus scrofa*). For use in bookbinding, it is vegetable tanned (or alum tawed). Pigskin has the characteristic grain pattern produced by the hair follicles, which are arranged in (roughly) triangular groups of three. The nature of pigskin is such that the holes remaining following removal of the bristles can be seen on the flesh side as well as the grain side. Pigskin is a tough and durable leather (and is even more durable perhaps when alum tawed) but is somewhat stiff and intractable. In addition, it does not tool readily, except in blind, although very fine bindings tooled in both blind and gold have been produced. It is a rugged leather best used on large books which can more readily emphasize its rugged characteristics. Pigskin was used extensively as a bookbinding leather in Germany from about 1550 to 1640, usually on books having wooden boards.

The term "pigskin" does not apply to leather produced from the FLESH SPLIT (1) of a pigskin. (69, 236, 351, 363)

pile-up. The volume of leather per unit weight, i.e., the number of square feet of leather ⅛ inch (8 iron, or approximately 10.67 ounces) thick per 100 pounds of leather of 12% moisture, or 115.5 divided by the apparent specific gravity of the leather of 12% moisture. (363)

piling. *See:* CESSING.

pineapple. A decorative ornament cut to look something like a pineapple, and used in the same position as a FLEURON. *See also:* TWISTED PINEAPPLE. (250)

pin grain. A small pebbled grain pattern in a leather, characteristic of such leather as MOROCCO.

pinhead morocco. A MOROCCO of the hard-grained type, but with a grain pattern smaller and less distinct than that of the morocco commonly referred to as hard-grained. As genuine morocco leather always has this "hard-grained" surface, the so-called pinhead morocco is a misnomer. (154)

pinhead style. A style of decoration executed by means of a stamp cut with fine dotted lines on its face. The fine curved or spiral lines are broken into a series of small dots and are arranged to form a web or network over the entire cover or around a central panel surrounding a coat of arms. This style came into existence in France in the later years of the reign of Louis XIII. In this type of ornamentation there were faint traces of baroque ornaments. The dotted stamps were also used on the spines of books and inside the covers when doublures were used. *See also:* POINTILLÉ (1). (104)

pinholes. 1. Defects in paper appearing as small punctures which are caused by fine particles of alum, clay, sand, etc., being crushed and falling out when the paper is calendered. Very hard grit may also be imbedded in the steel rolls of the calender itself and produce pinholes at each revolution. 2. Large pores in a thin paper where fine fibrous material or fillers fail to fill the voids between larger fibers. 3. Minute, almost imperceptible pits in the surface of a coated paper. 4. Very small transparent dots which appear in a lithographic paper after development and which, unless covered by an opaque medium, may affect printing. 5. Very small holes in a fabric. 6. Small punctures found in the untrimmed margins of printed books and caused by the pins attached to the tympan used in obtaining perfect registration of inner and outer forms. They are usually not seen in folios because they are in the fold, unless, as in some very early books, there are two pairs of pins, in which case they will be seen in the center of the top and bottom margins of each leaf. In quartos they will be in or very near the crease of the head BOLT, and evidence of them can often be found even if the bolt has been opened. In octavos they appear in the lower fore edge margins of the first four or last four leaves of

each GATHERING (2) and are also discernible even if the bolt has been opened. *See also:* POINT (5, 6). (17, 341)

pin seal. 1. A leather produced from the skin of a baby or very young seal. It has a much finer grain and a more lustrous finish than the usual sealskin. 2. A very small, fine-grained leather effect resembling the natural grain of a young seal. (156, 256)

pipey leather. A leather having a grain surface that forms coarse, sharp, and loose wrinkles when it is bent grain surface inward. It is a defect caused by the action of bacteria on the grain surface of the hide or skin. *See also:* PIPING (1). (363)

piping. 1. A defect in leather appearing as a double-skin effect when the leather is bent or flexed, and resulting from the grain layer of the leather separating from the corium. It is caused by excessive staking during manufacture, or by too great pressure during burnishing. Sheepskin, because of the excessive fatty tissue in the interior of the skin (especially in older animals), is particularly affected. 2. A type of crease or ribbing in paper caused by irregular tension in reeling, by moisture, or because the paper was wound too tightly after sizing. (60, 291, 363)

P. I. R. A. tested. An accelerated deterioration (decay) test designed for vegetable-tanned bookbinding leathers, and developed by the Printing Industries Research Association of Great Britain. Essentially, the test involves treating a specimen of leather with sulfuric acid and hydrogen peroxide. The P. I. R. A. test is actually an ACCELERATED AGING TEST and it is said that it will reveal (in the course of seven days) whether the leather is likely to undergo greater deterioration in a polluted atmosphere than in one that is not polluted.

A sample of leather 2½ inches square and weighing from 2 to 6 grams is placed on a glass plate, flesh side up, and evenly dampened with a 5% solution of sulfuric acid in the proportion of 1 ml of acid solution per gram of air dry leather. After remaining at room temperature overnight, hydrogen peroxide (10 vol. strength) is applied uniformly to the specimen, in the proportion of 0.6 ml per gram of leather. The specimen is then given additional treatments with hydrogen peroxide every 24 hours. This procedure is said to cause unsatisfactory leather (leather lacking in permanence) to become blackened and gelatinized whereas satisfactory (permanent) leather will be unaffected, except for possible discoloration of the edges. Changes in the color of dyestuffs are said to be immaterial. (237, 351)

plain binding. A style of binding executed in Colonial America and characterized by the use of sheepskin and calfskin decorated sparsely in blind. This austere and rugged "style" of binding certainly accounted for the largest number of books bound in Colonial America. A limited number of plain vellum and half sheep bindings with leather corners and marbled paper sides were also produced. (115, 200)

plain edges. *See:* WHITE EDGES.

plain-finished fabric. A finished fabric which has been given no surface design, such as embossing, graining, etc. (341)

plain finishing. A book decorated entirely with a single or double fillet border in gilt on the covers, and only the author and title lettered on the spine. (256)

plain gilt. The edges of a book that are gilded with no color, marbling, or pictorial images under the gold, and no tooling or gauffering following gilding. (154, 371)

plaited headband. A HEADBAND consisting of strips of skin, usually alum-tawed and stained pink. The plaited headband, while rare in English fine bindings, is common in German examples of the late 15th and early 16th centuries. It represents the strongest type of headband ever constructed. Two thongs were plaited around a former of rolled vellum which was already sewn to the text block. In addition, the thongs were threaded through holes made in the leather at the head of the spine where it was cut off instead of being turned in. The closely formed and set appearance of these headbands indicate that the thongs were worked while wet. (236)

plant wax. A WAX obtained from various plants, including *Rhus verniciflua,* as well as species of *Euphorbiacea,* which is frequently included in leather dressings. Plant waxes are cheaper and generally more easily available than many of the organic waxes, and are said to be useful in providing body to the dressing at a slightly higher softening temperature. In addition, unlike the animal waxes, they are more resistant to rancidity, and they also emulsify well with water. *See also:* CANDELILIA WAX; CARNAUBA WAX; JAPAN WAX. (291)

plaquette. A small tablet of metal having a design in relief and cast from a wax mold. The principle was adopted in France during the 15th and 16th centuries as a center decoration for book covers. Hand-painted specimens are to be found on books bound for Jean Grolier, the plaquette being impressed in gesso, painted, and then fitted into the upper board. *See also:* CAMEO BINDINGS. (347)

plasticity. That property of a material, such as an adhesive, which permits continuous and permanent deformation without failure upon the application of a force which exceeds the yield value of the material. (309)

plasticized cover material. A transparent film laminated to a decorative cover paper. A heavy cartridge paper is generally used as the base paper to avoid the possibility of the paper splitting after the book has been in use for some time. Some library binders laminate the jacket of a book and incorporate it in the cover of the case. (139)

plasticizer. 1. A material, such as glycerin (glycerol), sorbitol, triethylene glycol, etc., incorporated into an adhesive during manufacture to increase its flexibility, workability, or distensibility. The addition of the plasticizer may cause a reduction in melt viscosity, lower the temperature of the second-order transition, or lower the elastic modulus of the solidified adhesive. 2. A material added to the stock in the manufacture of a paper such as glassine, or used in the papermaking mixtures, to impart softness and flexibility. Usual papermaking plasticizers include glycerol, sorbitol, invert sugar, phthalic acid esters, various minerals oils, organic esters of phosphoric acid, and the like. (17, 235, 309)

plastic jacket. A removable plastic cover or sleeve designed to protect books expected to receive hard use. It is often used on school books.

plastic welding. The process of sealing two or more layers of material by means of the introduction of a high frequency voltage field between two electrodes. The electrodes conduct the high frequency current through the material and also bring the surfaces in close contact, thus ensuring an efficient weld. When power is applied, the agitation of the molecules within the plastic causes a rapid rise in temperature until the softening point is reached, whereupon the plastic sheets fuse along the seam of the electrodes. Because the line of fusing must be outside the area of the document being sealed, it is necessary to cut the plastic sheets somewhat larger than the document. (276)

plate. 1. An illustration printed separately from the text of the book, often on a different type of paper. Plates may be

PLAITED HEADBAND

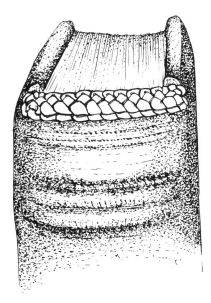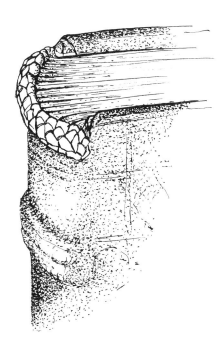

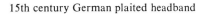

15th century German plaited headband

bound into a book, tipped onto a blank leaf (or a leaf bearing a printed caption), loose in a pocket or portfolio, or bound in a separate volume. Plates are not generally included in the pagination of the book. *See also:* PLATE ATTACHMENT. 2. A flat block of wood or metal, usually of copper, nickel or zinc, on the surface of which is a design or reproduction of a type form, and which is used for printing, engraving, embossing, etc. The method of printing may be relief, intaglio, or planographic. 3. To make an electrotype or stereotype. (156, 234)

plate attachment. The method used to attach a plate to a leaf or section of a book. The various methods include: 1) an illustration printed on a separate sheet and pasted to a narrow guard of paper or linen which is then folded around the section and sewn with it (plate guarded and hooked); 2) a plate secured by folding the margin of the edge of the leaf on which it is printed around the section and sewing it with the section (plate hooked on own guard); 3) plates printed to form a section of two or more leaves and inserted into or folded around a section and sewn with it (plates folded in or around sections); and 4) two plates joined together by means of a strip of paper or linen, thus forming a section which is inserted into or folded around a section and sewn with it (plates guarded and joined). (82, 343)

plate folding. An alternative name for buckle folding. *See:* FOLDING; PLATE ATTACHMENT.

plate mark (plate line). An impressed line denoting the boundary of a plate used in making an engraving. It is caused by the pressure applied to make the impression on the sheet. The part of the paper on which pressure was applied is depressed and smoother than the surrounding area. Occasionally faint traces of ink can be seen along the plate line if the plate was not properly cleaned before printing. (156)

platen. The flat part of a printing press which presses the sheet against the form; also the movable plate of a standing or nipping press which descends and presses books or other materials against the bed of the press.

plate folded in or around sections (plates guarded and joined). *See:* PLATE ATTACHMENT.

plate stamp. *See:* PANEL STAMP.

plates volume. The volume or volumes of a set containing the illustrations pertaining to the text. The plates volume usually has no printed matter other than that which identifies it and/or which relates specifically to the illustrations. (156)

platina. *See:* PLATINUM LEAF.

plating. 1. The process of imparting a smooth, glossy surface to a leather by pressing it against a highly polished, heated metal plate under very great pressure. The process is analogous to embossing except that in the latter process the plate is engraved with a "grain." The term also refers to the process of imparting a smooth and polished surface to the leather covers of a book. *See also:* POLISHING PLATES. 2. The process of imparting a special finish to a paper by subjecting it to heavy pressure (and sometimes slight friction) between plating rollers while it is interleaved between metal plates that are polished or covered with a material different from the paper itself, e.g., linen, thus producing on the paper an impression characteristic of the material used. (17, 306)

platinum leaf. A very heavy metallic element (Pt), that is typically grayish white, non-corroding, ductile and malleable, and which can be beaten into leaves, although not as thin as gold leaf. It is used with, or in lieu of, gold leaf in decorating bookbindings. It is suitable for the best work and, being thicker than gold leaf, is easier to handle.

pleat (pleating). Any series of folds, parallel but in alternating directions, such as the fold frequently used for large inserts. *See also:* CONCERTINA FOLD.

pleated corner. The folds in the cloth or leather made when the covers have rounded corners. *See:* ROUND CORNER.

plow (plough). A device used for trimming the leaves of a book, usually one bound by hand. It consists of two parallel blocks of wood about 4 inches wide and 8 inches long connected by two guide rods and one threaded rod, with a cutting blade attached to the lower edge of one of the blocks. The

PLOW

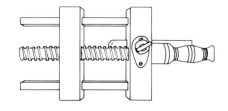

left hand part of the plow fits into a runner on the left cheek of the LYING PRESS, while the other block is fitted with the adjustable knife. The knife is generally moved inward by the turn of a screw, cutting into the leaves as the plow is moved back and forth.

When, where, or by whom the plow was invented is unknown, but in all likelihood it was not used to any great extent before the early part of the 16th century. Its use thereafter, however, was widespread in all classes of binding until sometime around 1840, when the GUILLOTINE cutter was introduced. The plow is now used very little except in the best of fine leather binding. (236, 237, 339)

ply. 1. One of the separate layers of paper or board comprising the sheet formed on a multi-cylinder papermaking machine. Each cylinder adds one layer (web), which is then pressed to another, both or all of which adhere firmly upon drying. The thickness of the resultant board is generally expressed in the number of layers of which it is composed. The equivalent ply ratings in thousandths of an inch are given below:

Ply	Inches
2	0.012
3	0.015
4	0.018
5	0.021
6	0.024
8	0.030
10	0.036
12	0.042
14	0.048
16	0.056

2. One of the sheets laminated to build up a pasted board of given thickness. (17, 278)

pneumatic press. A type of press in which pressure is applied by means of compressed air. Such presses are used in mechanized binderies for a variety of purposes, and, although they cannot supply the extreme pressures available with the HYDRAULIC PRESS, they do offer the advantages of speed of operation and cleanliness. (140)

pocket. *See:* BOOK POCKET.

poetical binding. A bookbinding decorated with looped banderoles impressed with poetical inscriptions in gothic type. It was a style of decoration believed to have been executed in Austria in the latter half of the 15th century. (347)

point. 1. One thousandth of an inch. The point is used in expressing the thickness of paper or board, as well as other materials, but not leather. *See:* LEATHER SUBSTANCE TABLE. 2. The expression of certain values of the properties of paper, e.g., points per pound, or pounds per point. 3. The unit of measure for printer's type. A point is approximately $\frac{1}{72}$ inch, 12-point type, for example, being 12/72 or $\frac{1}{6}$ inch in body. One inch equals 72.25433 points, while 72 points equal 0.9962 inch. The width of a line of type (or "measure") is determined in pica (12-point) ems. The depth of a page of type is similarly measured in picas or ems. 4. A book collector's term for a particular characteristic of text, type, form, etc., that distinguishes states, issues, and editions from one another. 5. A thin piece of metal with a point projecting from one end, and secured at its other end to the tympans of some printing presses; it is used to insure accurate register in feeding. 6. A mark or hole made on or in sheets in printing to serve as a guide in folding. (17, 42, 156)

pointillé. 1. A luxurious style of finishing consisting of dotted lines and curves impressed on the covers of a book. In the first half of the 17th century, pointillé was used by numerous French bookbinders and/or gilders, including Florimond Badier and Macé Ruette, although in terms of sheer magnificence of execution, it reached its pinnacle earlier in the bindings associated with the name (LE) GASCON. 2. A generic term indicating a form of dotted book decorations. 3. A small dotted finishing tool. *See also:* FANFARE STYLE; PINHEAD STYLE. *See* PLATE VIII. (94, 140, 280)

points per pound. A ratio derived by dividing the basis weight of a sheet of paper in pounds by its thickness in mils. It is used to describe the density of paper or board. *See also:* APPARENT DENSITY. (17, 60)

poker-work. A form of decoration involving the burning of designs into the leather with hot pokers or electrically heated tools. (261)

polaire. The leather case or satchel in which monks in earlier times placed their books. Polaires were usually lacking any decoration, unless made for wealthy persons, in which case they were usually decorated with a design stamped in relief. (94, 280)

pole mark. *See:* BACK MARK.

polished calf. A calfskin bookbinding that has been polished to a high gloss.

polisher (polishing iron). A hand tool used to crush down or polish the leather covers of a book. Polishers are generally made of brass, and are either round on in the shape of a wedge, the former being used on the covers, the latter on the spine. *See also:* BURNISHER(S) (2); POLISHING. (130, 152)

polishing. The process of smoothing and adding gloss to the covers of a book by mechanical means. The process involves working the leather at first with a slightly warm tool, followed by repeated workings with polishers heated to higher temperatures. Small circular motions are used to prevent wide areas of darkened streaks from showing. The technique of polishing leather covers dates back at least to the second half of the 14th century. (161, 236, 335)

polishing iron. *See:* POLISHER.

polishing plates. Large smooth plates, usually of metal, used in the final pressing of a book to impart smoothness to the leather. The use of polishing plates was probably infrequent before the 19th century. Early plates were made of tin or horn, while later materials included japanned tin, iron, nickelled steel, and German silver. In more recent times, stainless steel and polished aluminum have been used. Also called "crushing plates." (236)

polychrome decoration. A style of decoration characterized by the use of gold and various colors painted over the design. (347)

polychrome plaque-embossed bindings. A 15th century (Persian) style of decoration characterized by covers embossed with panel stamps or plaques, and then painted. The coloring gives the effect of cutwork tracery to the raised design. (347)

polycondensation. *See:* CONDENSATION (1).

polyester fibers. Synthetic paper fibers prepared and spun by procedures similar to those used in producing nylon. The long polymer chains in the filaments are arranged randomly and have very little orientation in line with the longitudinal axis of the filament; consequently the filaments have relatively little strength. Strength is added by drawing or stretching the filaments approximately two to five times their original length. The polymer chains become oriented in this stretching, with an accompanying decrease in filament diameter along the major axis of the filament. In addition, it is possible to develop a relatively high degree of lateral order (crystallinity) of the polymer chains by means of heat or solvent treatment. The filaments assume the cross-sectional configuration of the spinneret hole, which is usually

POLISHER

circular, although non-circular cross sections are also used. The drawing process leaves the circular cross-sectional configuration unchanged; however, it does reduce the sharpness of the non-round cross section. (42)

polyesters. Resins, plastics, and synthetic fibers based on resins produced by condensation of polyhydric alcohols with polybasic acids. Linear polyesters, e.g., polyethylene terephthalate, are saturated thermoplastic materials that are widely applied in the form of drawn melt-spun fibers and orientated cast film. Unsaturated polyester resins, such as the polycondensate from phthalic anhydride, propylene glycol, and maleic anhydride, will copolymerize with minor proportions of styrene and methyl methacrylate under the influence of an organic peroxide catalyst, to produce thermoset materials.

polyethylene (polythene). A waxy, translucent, somewhat flexible thermoplastic, prepared by polymerizing ethylene at high pressure (1,000 to 4,000 atm) and high temperature (180 to 190°C.) in the presence of a trace of oxygen. It is one of the lightest of the plastics, having a specific gravity of 0.92 to 0.93. Below 60° C., polyethylene is insoluble in all solvents and is resistant to the action of most reagents, other than strong oxidizing acids. Above 115° C., the polymer changes from a clear solid to a relatively low-viscosity melt. At this temperature and above, exposure to air causes relatively extensive oxidative degradation, unless antioxidants are included with the polymer.

Polyethylene is widely used as a film by itself or as a hot extrusion onto paper to provide additional strength and moisture-resistant characteristics. It is also applied to printing papers to provide finish and strength. The material is also made in sheets for use as a facing to prevent materials from sticking to a surface in operations requiring the application of pressure. The film which does not adhere permanently to waxes and many plastics in the unhardened state, is easily peeled off when the operation is completed. In sheet form, it is used in conservation work, in lieu of cellulose acetate lamination, to protect brittle paper, in which case the paper is placed between two sheets of the film, which is then sealed with double-sided adhesive tape around the edges. It may also be sealed by means of plastic welding. (81, 233)

polymer. A synthetic or natural substance having a structural basis of a number of identical molecules linked together. The polymer form of a particular type of molecule has both a higher molecular weight and a different set of physical properties than a monomer, which is composed of single molecules. An example of a polymer is POLYVINYL ACETATE, while another polymer, LINSEED OIL, contains triglycerides, i.e., molecules of glycerides of linolenic acid ($C_{18}H_{32}O_2$) linked together in threes. Virtually every film-forming material is a polymer.

polymerization. A chemical reaction involving the linkage of the molecules of a monomer to form large(r) molecules with a molecular weight greater than that of the original monomer. When two or more monomers so react, the process is termed copolymerization or heteropolymerization. *See also:* CONDENSATION (1).

polyvinyl acetate. A vinyl resin, one of the clear, water-white, thermoplastic synthetic resins produced from its monomer by emulsion polymerization. Polyvinyl acetate, abbreviated PVA, has the advantage over the other resinous adhesives in that it is available in the form of an emulsion that is readily diluted with water, is easily applied, and is safe to use because it contains no flammable solvents. In addition, there is no need to use preservatives or fungicides because it does not deteriorate quickly and is unaffected by mold or fungi. The emulsion does slowly hydrolyze, however, and should not be stored for more than one or two years before use. Freezing also destroys the emulsion; therefore, precautions must be taken to avoid exposing it to temperatures near or below the freezing point. (37, 198, 235)

polyvinyl alcohol. A polymer obtained by alcoholysis with methanol of POLYVINYL ACETATE. The polymer is compounded with glycol plasticizers to give thermoplastic compositions that are available in the form of clear films, sheeting, and other sections, as well as monofilaments. These materials are all distinguished by their elastomeric properties, complete resistance to hydrocarbon solvents, and ready solubility in hot water (unless specially insolubilized). Polyvinyl alcohol solutions are used as sizes, in water-based adhesives, and as aqueous suspending agents. (235)

polyvinyl chloride. An ethenoid polymer produced as a fine white powder by both emulsion polymerization and suspension polymerization of the gas, vinyl chloride, when liquified under nitrogen pressure. The terms "PVC" and "vinyl" are commonly used with reference not only to the polymer, but to all materials of which polyvinyl chloride is a constituent. PVC compositions are prepared by hot mixing the polymer with plasticizers and small proportions of stabilizers, stearate lubricants, and coloring materials to give materials of a wide range of hardness, from rigid (with little or no plasticizer) to very soft (equal proportions of plasticizers and polymer), and in a wide range of colors, as well as crystal clear. Unplasticized flexible PVC foils are normally produced from vinyl chloride-acetate copolymers by calendering and stretching. The product is usually flexible, relatively nonflammable, hard wearing, and resistant to water and corrosion.

PVC film can be heat sealed, either by high frequency vibration (*see:* PLASTIC WELDING), or by means of a press equipped with a special barrier to prevent the film from adhering to the heated jaws. Another method of sealing is to sew the sheets together, which is possible because of the remarkably high tear strength of the material when properly plasticized.

PVC film has an attractive matte surface; however, in the more hardwearing grades it is slightly opaque. The grades used for the protection of archival materials are readily available in a wide range of thicknesses and widths.

As with other highly chlorinated materials, the use of PVC should be very carefully considered in view of the possibility of the formation of hydrochloric acid. (81, 198, 235)

porosity. That property a material has of containing interstices. It is defined as the ratio of the volume of the interstices to the volume of the mass of the material, and depends upon the number, shape and distribution of the voids, as well as their shape and orientation. The term is sometimes used incorrectly to indicate permeability. (17, 139)

porphyry vein marble. A cover marble consisting of black in large drops, a brown sprinkle, followed by a scarlet sprinkle, followed by large spots of yellow and weak blue. The colors are followed by applications of aqua regia, all of which is made to flow down the covers of the book to form a distinct vein. (97, 152)

portfolio. 1. A case used to protect loose drawings, plates, papers, and the like. It usually consists of two sheets of board covered with paper or cloth, with a wide cloth or paper joint forming the "spine." It generally has flaps of cloth or cloth lined with paper, attached to the three edges of the lower board which turn in to contain the material enclosed. Tapes are attached at the head, tail, and fore edge, or at the fore edge alone, to secure the contents. Abbreviated pf. 2. A size of board 27 by 34 inches. (102, 156, 183)

portrait (portrait way). A leaf that is taller than it is wide, i.e., the ordinary upright or folio leaf. Also called "long way." (276)

post. 1. A pile of WATERLEAF (2) sheets, fresh from the mold. The post is built up of recently formed sheets couched with alternate felts, which are then pressed. The "post" is actually the quantity, which varies with the area of the sheets, that can be conveniently pressed, and usually ranges from 130 to 144 sheets. A "white post" is a pile of several posts of pressed paper after the removal of the felts. 2. The solid or sectional device, usually threaded, used in a POST BINDER. (140, 256)

post binder. A form of loose-leaf (mechanical) binder. The screw posts for the binders may be either solid or sectional, the former being used for storage binders, the latter for books being actively used. As the volume of the book increases, half-inch or inch-long sections are added to the posts.

The typical binder has two posts, which may either be self-locking or locked by caps or knurled thumb screws. In the so-called flexible chain post binder, the book is compressed by a link mechanism operated by a key or crank. It is also possible to construct post binders that cannot be tampered with. A lock in the back of the binder which must be opened with its own key is provided for this purpose.

Post binders use punched or slotted leaves, the latter allowing exchange of sheets without the binding having to be removed. A superior type of post binder has the top and bottom strips of metal, with the posts fastened to the bottom plate, the top plate sliding on them. The top plate has a lock which grips both posts, which can be released by turning a key or sliding a latch. Also called "transfer binder." (320, 339)

post-mortem changes. Chemical and structural changes that occur naturally in a hide or skin between the time the animal is slaughtered and the curing

or other preservative operation. *See also:* PUTREFACTIVE DAMAGE. (363)

potassium carbonate. A white deliquescent salt (K_2CO_3), which dissolves readily in water to give a strong alkaline solution. It was used in the execution of BEDFORD STYLE bindings, TREE CALF bindings, etc. Also known as "pearl ash," and "salts of tartar."

potassium ferrocyanide. A yellow, crystalline salt ($K_4Fe(CN)_6$), prepared by the reaction of potassium cyanide with ferrous salts, and used in combination with other substances as a paper fungicide. Although only slightly toxic under normal circumstances, it can form extremely toxic gases if heated strongly or mixed with hot, concentrated acids. Also called "yellow prussiate of potash." (198)

potassium lactate. A potassium salt of lactic acid ($KC_3H_5O_3 \cdot H_2O$), used to treat leather in order to counteract acid present in the leather due to manufacturing processes or because of air pollution (sulfur dioxide), or as a safeguard against the future incursion of acid or acid-forming materials. It is used in an aqueous solution of 7% potassium lactate, 0.25% paranitrophenol (to inhibit mold growth), and distilled water. The potassium lactate is said to act as a buffering agent, e.g., $2KC_3H_5O_3 + H_2SO_4 \rightarrow K_2SO_4$ (potassium sulfate) $+ 2C_3H_6O_3$ (lactic acid).

There is some controversy over the use of this salt as a leather/acid buffer. The major arguments against it seem to be that it may cause a whitish discoloration to appear on the surface of the leather (potassium sulfate discoloration) and, unless applied to *both* the flesh and grain sides of the leather, it is ineffectual. If the latter argument is correct, it would mean that leathers used for bookbinding could be treated only one time.

Potassium lactate should not be applied to powdery (red rot) leathers, nor to suede leathers, as it will result

in the blackening of both. (173, 265, 366)

potassium metabisulfite. A white, crystalline salt ($K_2S_2O_5$), used (infrequently) in bleaching paper, and also in conjunction with sodium hypochlorite to neutralize any residual chlorine in paper.

pot life. *See:* WORKING LIFE.

pouch binding. *See:* GIRDLE BOOK.

pounce. 1. A finely ground powder, generally prepared from GUM SANDARAC mixed with pumice or cuttlefish bone. Originally, it was used to prevent ink from spreading on unsized paper or over an erasure, as well as to prepare vellum to take writing ink. *See:* POUNCING. It is now sometimes used as an adhesive in gold tooling and in the coloring of the edges of books. 2. *See:* REPOUSÉ.

pouncing. The process of roughening the surface of vellum or parchment with POUNCE (1) or pumice to counteract the natural greasiness of the material and enable it to take ink readily. Pouncing, which has a tendency to spoil the grain surface of vellum, has been made less necessary by the use of special sizes. (140)

powdered. A background decoration consisting of minute dots in gold. *See also:* GOLD-POWDERED BINDINGS; SEMÉ.

powdering. A printing defect caused by the vehicle and pigment separating during or following printing. The vehicle penetrates the paper but the pigment is left lying loosely on the surface. The defect is caused either by an ink that is too mobile, or by a paper that is too absorbent. (140)

Powell, Roger (1896-   ). An English bookbinder and restorer, born in London and educated at Bedales. Powell did not become seriously interested in bookbinding until 1930, when he studied for a year at the Central School of Arts and Crafts under Douglas Cockerell and others. In 1931 he established his own bindery in Welwyn Gar-

POST BINDER

den City and maintained it for 4 years, before joining the firm of Douglas Cockerell & Son in 1935. The following year he became a partner, continuing on with the firm until 1947. He succeeded Douglas Cockerell as tutor in charge of bookbinding at the Royal College of Art, remaining there until 1956, when he left formal teaching to devote himself full time to his bookbinding and restoration business.

Powell has maintained a long standing interest in the field of restoration and repair, together with an abiding interest in problems relating to the durability and permanence of materials, sewing methods, and forwarding in general. Because of this, as well as his outstanding craftsmanship, he has been commissioned to restore many priceless (and irreplaceable) volumes, including *The Book of Kells,* for the Trinity College Library in Dublin (1953), *The Book of Durrow* (1954), *The Book of Armagh,* and *The Book of Dimma* (1956-1957), as well as numerous comparatively early books in the Aberdeen University Library. In recognition of his outstanding service, he was awarded the degree of Master of Arts, *honoris causa* (1961), from Trinity College, Dublin, and the O. B. E. (Officer of the Order of the British Empire) in 1976.

Roger Powell places soundness of construction, in both materials and method, ahead of decorative design. He believes that the actual design of a binding must be an integral part of the binding itself, because a book is a tangible object meant to be used. His desire to make bookbinding a work of artistic merit, and his ability to carry out this desire have made him one of England's outstanding bookbinders. (50, 205)

practice block. A device on which to practice lettering and decoration of the spine of a book. It consists of a block of wood, the edge of which is rounded to simulate the curved spine of a book. This edge is covered with leather that has been pasted over a strip of board the width of the spine. The board gives a resiliency and response to the pressure of the finishing tool similar to that of the spine of a book. (130)

pre-bound (pre-binding). *See:* PRE-LIBRARY BOUND.

pre-forwarding. The processes in bookbinding preliminary to the gluing-up of the spine, including folding, gathering, insertion of illustrations, collating, and sewing. Sewing is often considered to be a forwarding operation, rather than a pre-forwarding one. (157)

pre-library bound. A new book either in soft or hard covers, which has been bound by a library binder prior to, or at the time of, the original sale, but in either case before being placed in use. Abbreviated "pre-bound." (12, 129, 156)

preliminary leaf. Any leaf preceding the text of the book, whether numbered (often with Roman numerals) or not. Many times a preliminary leaf will be blank, although it is a part of the first gathering of the book as issued.

presentation copy. A copy of a book having an inscription of presentation, usually by the author. The term is also applied to a copy of a book presented by the publisher.

preservatives. Chemical additives that prevent or inhibit the development of spoilage organisms in paper, glue, leather, cloth, etc., or prevent or retard the deterioration of leather or paper.

press. 1. A relatively simple piece of machinery used to apply pressure evenly over the surface of a material, e.g., one of the various screw presses used to keep a book or books in position under pressure to effect adhesion of pasted or glued adherends, or for some other purpose. *See:* ARMING PRESS; BACKING PRESS; BUNDLING PRESS; FINISHING PRESS; HYDRAULIC PRESS; LYING PRESS; NIPPING PRESS; PNEUMATIC PRESS; REMOVABLE PRESS; STANDING PRESS. 2. The machine, or apparatus, used to press paper onto the type, plate, engraving, or block. 3. In a papermaking machine, a pair of rolls between which the web of paper is passed in order to: remove water in the wet press, smooth and level the sheet in the smoothing press, or apply surface treatments to the sheet in the size press. (17, 156, 261)

pressboard. A tough, dense, highly glazed rag or chemical wood pulp board used where strength and stiffness are required of a relatively thin sheet. It is produced in several colors, including brown, black, red, and gray, with a mottled surface that is smooth and highly polished. It is almost as hard as a sheet of fiber board and is used for the covers of notebooks and tablets. (339)

pressing. 1. The process in leather manufacture of removing the bulk of water from wet leather by means of a hydraulic press. 2. A paper, usually machine glazed, used for the covers of pamphlets, notebooks, etc.

pressing blocks. Blocks of wood used to fill up the space in a standing press, for the purpose of reducing the effective DAYLIGHT of the press and thereby the distance the platen must be lowered. (261)

pressing boards. Flat boards of solid or laminated wood, or fiberboard, used to insure even pressure when books are pressed. Since they are placed between covered books, they must be smooth and lined with clean waste. *See also:* CASING-IN BOARDS.

pressing tins. 1. Sheets of tin or zinc used to separate gatherings that are to be compressed before sewing. 2. The thin sheets of metal used between the free endpapers and the board paper during final pressing to insure even pressure of the entire surface of the text block, to prevent any dampness from the adhesive used in pasting down the board papers from reaching the flyleaves, and to prevent indentation of the turn-ins into the text block. (237, 335)

press mark. 1. A design impressed into a wet web of paper, usually at the second or third roll of the papermaking machine, by means of a rubber collar which carries the design. *See also:* WATERMARK. 2. The symbol given to a book to indicate its location in British (rarely American) usage. In the late medieval period manuscripts were often kept in large chests (presses), and when books later came to be shelved in book cases, the term press continued to be used. The press mark is still used in some older libraries to indicate the "press," and often the shelf and the numerical position of the volume on the shelf. As a location system it indicates the precise position of the volume (and it can also be used to maximize the number of volumes that can be shelved in a given area), but it lacks flexibility and is completely useless as a browsing system. The simplest form is a letter followed by two numbers, indicating the section, the shelf, and the volume on the shelf, as A.2.13, or section A, second shelf, thirteenth volume. Other, more complex, systems are also used, sometimes to indicate subjects, sizes, etc. Press marks are found on the spine of the volume, on a label attached to the spine, on the flyleaf or the pastedown, on the title page or its verso, or on the fore edge of books that were at one time shelved fore edge outward (usually because they were chained). Press marks can often be a valuable indication of provenance. (17)

press pin. An iron bar used to tighten a

large standing or lying press. Such pins come in two sizes—a short pin used by one man, and a long pin operated by two or more persons. The long pin permits the application of very great pressure. (97, 335)

pressure bulker. An instrument used to determine the bulk, or the ratio of weight to thickness, of paper, or to determine the number of leaves of a stipulated stock that will be required to make a book bulk to a specified thickness, under application of a specified pressure. (274)

pressure-sensitive adhesive. An adhesive that will adhere to a surface at room temperature by means of briefly applied pressure only. (309)

pressure-sensitive tape. Strips of paper, plastic, etc., opaque or transparent, coated or impregnated on one or both sides (usually the former except for use in encapsulation) with a pressure-sensitive adhesive. In the form of cellophane tape, which is a clear plastic that is glossy on one side and coated with adhesive on the other, it is sometimes used in the repair of torn leaves, documents, etc., and for encapsulating archival papers. In the usual case it darkens with age, is difficult to remove, removes the print when it is detached, and stains the paper to which it adheres. The acetate tape, or transparent mending tape, which has a matte surface and appears colorless when in the roll, has a much higher degree of permanence and does not change color; however, it, too can be damaging to archival materials.

Masking tape is strong brown paper tape of crinkly texture, made in rolls of various widths. Its pressure-sensitive adhesive secures the tape firmly to any hard, dry, non-fibrous surface, and it is easily peeled away. It is used to mask areas that are not to be treated. Masking tape generally becomes difficult to remove if left in place for more than a few days or if exposed to high temperature.

Benzene or ether, both of which are toxic (especially the former), flammable, and therefore dangerous to use, are solvents capable of removing pressure-sensitive tapes. (233, 309)

primary binding. The earliest of any different publisher's binding styles found on copies of the same edition. The term is applied only to edition bindings, and, as a matter of practice, is seldom used with reference to anything other than publisher's cloth, although it could perhaps be applied to a "boards-and-label" copy of a book published between 1820 and 1830, assuming copies issued later were bound in gilt-lettered cloths, i.e., after 1832. (69)

primary colors. The three chromatic colors—red, yellow, and blue—from which all other hues, tones, and shades may theoretically be obtained by mixing, sometimes with the addtion of black and white. To obtain another color, however, it is necessary to use secondary and intermediate colors, e.g., green and violet, as well as red, yellow, and blue pigments of various shades to obtain many hues because pigment is not pure color. *See also:* COLOR (1). (233, 316)

Princeton file. A free-standing, boxlike container open at the top and back, as well as the lower half of the front. It is used to hold pamphlets, single sheets, etc., usually for storage on the book shelves. *See also:* CUT CORNER PAMPHLET FILE. (156)

print. 1. A copy (reproduction) of a drawing, photograph, etc., done by any printing process. The term is generally applied to etchings, engravings, mezzotints, etc. 2. To apply ink and then paper to blocks, plates, or type to make an "impression" or a "print" of an image. 3. *See:* NEWSPRINT. (12, 17, 156)

printability. That characteristic of a material, such as paper, which permits high quality printing, and which, though not capable of precise definition, is generally judged visually in terms of uniformity of color of the printed areas, uniformity of ink transfer, quality of "black on white," and rate of ink setting and drying. In paper, hardness, smoothness, opacity, color, and pick resistance are some characteristics which lend themselves to good printability. (17, 139)

printed edges. The edges of a book that have been printed by means of rubber type. This is done at times on the fore edge as a means of indexing, and is frequently done on one or more edges of directories, and the like, for purposes of advertising. (140)

printed papers. Decorative end- and cover papers printed or stencilled with designs, figures, borders, etc. Many of these original papers, printed in the 18th century by the dominotiers (from the Italian *domino,* little cloak or hood, part of the costume of the men who did marbling) of France, had their origin in early wall papers, except that most had smaller designs than those used for wall decorations. They were printed on small sheets of paper in a wide variety of designs, ranging from simple, almost crude woodcuts in one color only to patterns printed in two or more colors. There were papers in a multitude of stripes, including wide bands of color with a floral stripe between, horizontal lines broken up with sprays of flowers tied in knots of ribbon, designs of small flowers on cream backgrounds, bold patterns with conventional carnations, grapes, roses, intricate strapwork in three colors, etc. (183, 217)

printed paper warehouse. The area in which printed sheets are stored while awaiting instructions for binding. In book printing, it is not unusual for a number of printed sheets to be left unbound, so as to avoid the additional expense of binding (and costs of inventorying) if the full quantity of books should not be required. Printed sheets were stored from an early date by their printers, and later by booksellers. There were professional warehousemen who were employed sometimes by several booksellers to store their sheets. Usually they were stored unfolded, but there are many indications that they were sometimes stored folded and gathered. (58)

print finishing processes. A generic term for the wide range of pre-printing and post-printing operations involved in converting paper into the printed book, or other salable item. These include: 1) actual print finishing processes, such as the storage and preparation of unprinted paper, the cutting to correct size of unprinted and printed sheets, the production of booklets and periodicals (pamphlet binding, stationery and file material, stationery, miscellaneous binding, etc.), the production of labels, posters, calendars, etc., assembly work (boxing, set-making, etc.), as well as gumming, varnishing, laminating, packing, and shipping; 2) BOOKBINDING; and 3) box and carton manufacture. (229)

printing inks. Inks used in printing, consisting of a coloring agent, which may be a plant dye, mineral, or an earth, in a medium (or vehicle) of oil, water, or varnish.

Printing inks are categorized according to the process for which they are intended, and, within each category, they may be further divided according to color and categories of quality. Letterpress inks, for example, include colored inks and black inks (halftone ink, jobbing ink, ornamental printing ink, rotary printing ink and special ink). There are also newspaper inks, lithographic printing inks (collotype ink, litho ink and offset ink), photogravure inks (either actual photogravure ink or copperplate ink) and die stamping ink, aniline printing ink, and special inks of various kinds, e.g., carbonizing ink.

Printing inks are also categorized according to the manner in which they dry, because rate of drying is considered to be one of the most important properties of an ink. Lithographic and ordinary letterpress inks dry by oxidization, and partly by penetration and evaporation; newspaper ink dries by absorption; and aniline and photogravure inks dry by evaporation.

Modern inks which dry on contact with the paper have been perfected, and are used principally on high-speed rotary presses. A recent development in inks is the monomeric ink which dries instantaneously when exposed to certain radiations, such as ultraviolet light or gamma radiations. This type of ink is designed to be used on ultra-high-speed presses. There are also heat-set inks which dry when the paper is passed through a heating chamber at a temperature of about 300° C. (infrared radiation is also used for heating). Cold-set inks, which are solid at room temperature, and which must be heated for printing, dry when the paper is conveyed, following printing, over a cooling cylinder. Steam-set inks, which consist of artificial resins dissolved in a hygroscopic solvent, such as ethylene glycol, dry when the paper web is passed through a steam chamber, where a small quantity of water is absorbed by the layer of ink causing the artificial resin to be deposited in solid form. Another type of quick drying ink is one which is combined with a vehicle which ordinarily solidifies at room temperature but is prevented from doing so by an admixture of substances. In printing, the admixtures are absorbed by the paper and the impression then dries quickly.

Consistency of a printing ink is also of considerable importance. Ink is said to be thin when it is easily set in motion, and stiff when it offers comparatively strong resistance to changes in form. A so-called long ink is viscous and can be drawn out into threads, while the opposite is a "short ink." In printing varnishes, a distinction is made between weak, medium, and strong (rigid) varnish. Oils are also used as vehicles, and at one time linseed oil was used most often because of its good drying properties, although tung oil was also used extensively. Tung oil dries very rapidly but loses its gloss in the process. Both have been largely replaced by tar and mineral oils. Inks for newspaper printing are compounded in mineral oils, and are very thin. *See also:* ANILINE INK; CARBONACEOUS INK; CARBON INK; CHINESE INK; DOUBLE-TONE INK; HEAT-SET INK; IRON-GALL INK; METALLIC INKS; OFFSET INK; SEPIA INK. (21, 140, 143, 195)

printing processes. The various processes by which printing jobs are done. There are, in general, four fundamental printing processes: letterpress (relief printing); intaglio (gravure printing); planography (flat-surface printing); and silk screen. Letterpress includes printing from raised type, halftone, or woodcuts on a platen, cylinder, or rotary press printing. Intaglio includes printing from engraved plates, etching, photogravure, or rotogravure. Planographic printing includes lithography, offset, aquatone, collotype, etc., printing. Silk-screen printing utilizes a stencil (silk or other material) through which ink or paint, e.g., is forced. (17)

printing sticks. Small pieces of wood, usually about three inches in length and of various cross sections, made of close-grained wood in order to impress an even print, and used in the execution of decorative end- and cover papers. (86)

processing. A term sometimes applied to the finishing operations performed on printed literature, such as trimming, folding, punching, die-cutting, perforating, and laminating. (139)

prong binder. *See:* RING BINDER.

proof. 1. A leaf or leaves of a book purposely left untrimmed by the binder as evidence that the book has not been unduly trimmed. Proof assumes that at least one of the sections of the book is shorter than the others. The practice, which is now virtually obsolete, stems from the time when binders, and even very fine binders, had the reputation of cutting down the leaves of a book as much as possible. 2. An impression made from type before the printing run is begun. The first proof is corrected by the printer's reader or corrector and returned to the compositor. After the printer is satisfied with the type as set, a proof is sent to the author for correction. This proof is usually on a long sheet of normal width, called a galley proof. After the author has made his corrections the type is made up into pages, page numbers and running heads are added, and a final page proof is sent to the author. In modern practice the author often sees only the galleys. 3. A preliminary impression taken from an engraved plate or block, or a lithographic stone. Usually called a "trial proof." 4. An impression taken from a finished plate or block before the regular impression is published and usually before the title or other inscription is added. Also called "proof print" or "proof impression." (12, 156, 241)

protected leather. A leather which has had chemical incorporated into it in an effort to render it more resistant to deterioration. *See:* P. I. R. A. TESTED; POTASSIUM LACTATE. (261)

protection tissue. *See:* BARRIER SHEET.

protective containers. A BOX (1), PORTFOLIO (1), PULL-OFF BOX, SLIPCASE, SOLANDER BOX, or other container, designed to contain and protect a book, pamphlet, manuscript, map, or other archival material. (173)

protective sheet. A sheet of paper temporarily attached to the endpapers of a book during forwarding processes to protect them. If it is part of the endpapers it is known as a WASTE SHEET (1).

proteinaceous. A substance having a protein base, such as animal glue, casein, leather, etc., all of which are proteinaceous materials.

provenance. A record of previous ownership (of a book or manuscript). A bookplate, inscription, signature, motto on the title page or elsewhere, PRESSMARK (2), price notation, manuscript date, coat of arms on the covers, and sometimes even a style of binding may indicate previous ownership of a book.

provinical made endpaper. A modification of the conventional MADE ENDPAPER, designed to overcome the tendency of that endpaper to drag at the first and last sections of the book. *See also:* ZIG-ZAG ENDPAPER. (81)

Prussian blue. A blue pigment used in dyeing and the manufacture of ink and paint. It is produced from potassium ferrocyanide and ferric salts. Also called "ferric ferrocyanide," "bronze blue," and "Chinese blue."

prussic acid. *See:* HYDROGEN CYANIDE.

psychrometer. A hygrometer used for determining relative humidity. It utilizes wet and dry bulb temperature readings which are compared with a chart which shows the measure of dryness of the surrounding air. (269)

publisher's binding. *See:* EDITION BINDING.

publisher's cloth. The cloth used as the covering material for edition bindings. The use of cloth has been widespread in edition binding since about 1850. Originally introduced as a novel alternative to paper-covered boards and, like them, looked upon as only a temporary covering (the purchaser having the book bound in leather according to his own needs), its possibilities as a "permanent" covering material became apparent by the early 1830s. Although many collectors continued to have their books bound in leather, this practice has steadily diminished over the years. (69, 299)

publisher's decorated wrappers. Cover wrappers, generally decorated with a woodcut, and usually produced on the same paper as the text. These covers appear to have been issued by the publisher as a means of making unbound books more attractive to the customer, and were intended simply to advertise the book, not to serve as a permanent or usable binding. As such, they seem to have been an experiment by several competitive Augsburg printers, the earliest examples being issued by Schonsperger in 1482. (347)

publisher's dummy. *See:* DUMMY (1, 2).

publisher's endpapers. Ordinary edition ENDPAPERS on which the publisher printed advertisements, and especially the titles of other books he published. Publisher's endpapers were a fashion of the middle 19th century, and were used on almanacs, inexpensive editions of the classics, popular novels, publishers' series, and the like. In a strict sense they are not really endpapers at all. (217)

publisher's reinforced binding. A now more-or-less obsolete term, used at one time in the publishing trade to identify bindings purported to be strengthened for use in (circulating) libraries. Misuse of the term, in that it was used by some publishers for bindings that were actually no stronger than regular bindings of other publishers, has made it virtually meaningless. (16)

publisher's trade edition binding. *See:* EDITION BINDING.

pucker. 1. The tendency of the inner leaves of a section to become wrinkled at the corner folds when thick paper is folded at right angles. 2. A cocklelike condition in the surface of a paper that has contracted unevenly while drying.

puckered leather. Leather which, while still tractable, during the covering of a book is pushed into wrinkles or folds, induced at times by thinning leather on the flesh side in areas where folds are required. Sometimes higher folds are so located as to take the wear and abrasion such bindings are likely to suffer, thus protecting the remaining surface areas of the covers. The leather is first impregnated with paste which, when dry, imparts a high degree of rididity

and solidity to the fold areas. (311)

puering. A process now included with BATING. Formerly, it consisted of the treatment of unhaired skins with solutions of fermented dog dung in a heated infusion, the purpose being to effect the removal of certain undesirable constituents and to further prepare the skins for tanning. Puering was a faster and more powerful method than bating because of the greater strength of the puering liquor, but for this very reason it was also potentially more dangerous. (363)

pull. 1. A tie secured to the inside of a slipcase in such a manner that the enclosed material may be removed from the case by pulling the tie. 2. A trial print produced before the printing of an edition. 3. *See:* DRAW (1, 2). (156, 256)

pulled. A book which has been taken apart for rebinding. A book has been "pulled" when the case or covers have been removed, the spine lining and/or old glue has been cleared off, the sewing threads have been cut, and all the sections have been separated from each other.

pulled paste papers. Decorative end- and cover papers produced by applying colored paste to the surface of two sheets of paper, pressing the pasted surfaces together, and slowly pulling them apart. The result is a veined or feathery design on both paste-covered surfaces, and, if more than one color of paste is used, the various colors blend in a free design. Blue, red, and yellow

PULL-OFF BOX

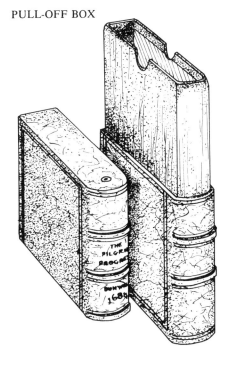

pastes were freqeuntly used in the execution of these papers.

Pulled paste papers were used as cover papers on German and Italian pamphlets and as endpapers for the heavily blocked or plain leather bindings of the 18th century. A variation of the technique consisted of laying a soft string or thin strips of felt between the two sheets. When these were rubbed down, the material which had been laid over left white areas on the paper in whatever pattern it had been arranged. These papers seem to have been produced most often in a single color, usually dull blue or terra-cotta; however, there are also examples, often found in German and Italian books of the 18th century, in red, yellow, and violet, in which circles of felt were used to produce an effect of small round doughnutlike patterns. (217)

pulling. The process of reducing a bound book to individual sections (or, in the case of a book in sheets, to loose leaves). 2. The condition arising from DRAW (2) during trimming or cutting.

pull-off box. A simple or elaborate book-shaped box designed primarily to hold a book, but also used to contain pamphlets, manuscripts, etc. Occasionally it opens at the side or front, but it more often consists of two separate parts, one telescoping over the other, hence its name. In its most elaborate form, it often has a rounded back (spine) with raised bands, projecting squares, a leather covering, and possibly one or more spring catches. When properly constructed, it provides nearly air-tight protection. The book is generally provided with a separate wrapper. Also called "pull-off case" or "pull-off cover," and frequently, though incorrectly, a SOLANDER BOX.

pulls. Metal handles, or pieces of tape or ribbon, attached to the tail of a book or the base of a shelf, case, or file box for convenient removal. Pulls were used frequently on large blankbooks in which case they were usually riveted or laced to the center band.

pulp. The mechanically and/or chemically prepared mixtures obtained from vegetable fibers and used in the manufacture of paper and board. The general classes of paper pulp are listed below. Any of the various pulps listed may be further classified as unbleached, semi-bleached, or bleached.

    I. Wood pulp
        A. Mechanical
            1. Groundwood
            2. Defibrated
            3. Exploded

B. Chemical
  1. Sulfite
  2. Neutral sulfite
  3. Sulfate
  4. Chemical cellulose (sulfate and sulfite)
    a. Papermaking alpha pulps
    b. Chemical conversion pulps
  5. Soda
  6. Semi-chemical
  7. Chemigroundwood
  8. Screenings
  9. Miscellaneous

II. Cotton fiber or rag pulps

III. Reclaimed papers
  A. Paper stock
  B. De-inked paper stock
  C. Paper shavings and cuttings

IV. Other fibrous pulps
  A. Manila hemp
  B. Jute
  C. Esparto
  D. Cereal straw
  E. Seed flax straw
  F. Bagasse
  G. Bamboo
  H. Reeds
  I. Leaf fibers
  J. Kenaf
  K. Miscellaneous fibers (17, 72, 143)

Conifers (softwoods)		
Black spruce	*Picea mariana*	North America (N. A.)
Douglas fir	*Pseudotsuga taxifolia*	N. A.
Jack pine	*Pinus banksiana*	N. A.
Norway spruce	*Picea abies*	Europe (E.)
Radiata pine	*Pinus radiata*	New Zealand
Red spruce	*Picea rubens*	N. A.
Scots pine	*Pinus sylvestris*	E.
Silver fir	*Abies alba*	E.
Sitka spruce	*Picea sitchensis*	N. A.
Slash pine	*Pinus caribaea*	N. A.
White fir	*Abies concolor*	N. A.
White spruce	*Picea glauca*	N. A.
Broadleaf trees (hardwoods)		
Aspen, poplar	*Populus tremula* and	E.
	P. tremuloides	N. A.
European birch	*Betula verrucosa*	E.
European oak	*Quercus robur*	E.
Paper birch	*Betula papyrifera*	N. A.
Red maple	*Acer rubrum*	N. A.
Red oak	*Quercus rubra*	N. A.
Saligna gum	*Eucalyptus saligna*	South Africa
Sycamore	*Acer pseudoplatanus*	E.
Tasmanian oak	*Eucalyptus regnans* and *E. obliqua*	Australia

(60, 72)

pulpboard. A type of BINDER'S BOARD produced either in a single web, a one-ply board, or from two webs on the same machine, that is, a twin-wire board. Pulpboard quality depends on the furnish used, which may be mechanical or chemical wood pulp, or a combination thereof. It differs from PASTEBOARD in that the pulpboard is made directly from the pulp, whereas pasteboard is built up from thinner sheets of paper or board laminated together. Pulpboard is the principal board used in library and edition binding. (17, 58, 156, 264)

pulping. The process of reducing cellulosic raw materials, e.g., pulpwood, rags, straw, esparto, reclaimed papers, etc., to a condition suitable for further processing into paper materials, or for chemical conversion into some other cellulosic product. Pulping may vary from a simple mechanical action to complex digesting sequences and may be done in batches or by means of continuously operating equipment. (17, 72, 320)

pulpwood. Those woods suitable for the manufacture of chemical and mechanical wood pulp. The principal trees from which wood pulp is obtained include:

pumice. A cellular or highly porous volcanic glass used in "stone" form to smooth vellum and parchment for writing or when preparing them for re-use, and also to smooth the gold cushion. It is also used in very finely powdered form in the manufacture of vellum and parchment. It is composed largely of aluminum silicate. *See also:* PALIMPSEST; POUNCE (1). (130, 198)

punch and tie. *See:* JAPANESE SEWING.

punching gauge (punching guide). A template, consisting of a strip of card, wood or metal, punched with holes in the required positions and used for punching sheets in exactly the same positions, as in loose-leaf work.

punching machine. A machine used to produce holes in paper. It consists of a flat plate on which the pile to be punched is placed, an arm which carries the hollow punches, and lay guides to which the sheets are fed, so that the holes are punched in the same positions throughout. The punches, which are generally positioned about ⅛ to ¼ inch from the back edge of the sheets, descend and punch the holes. The discs of waste paper produced are left in the hollow center of the punches and eventually clear through their open tops. The punching machine has been largely superseded by the paper drilling machine. (179, 189)

puppy. An alternative name for the GOLD RUBBER.

pure dressed. A leather which, subse-quent to tannage, has been dressed solely by the introduction of grease, which is usually DUBBIN applied by hand. (61)

puritan filler. *See:* GYPSUM.

purl (purfling). The spiral wires cut into lengths, threaded on silk, and sewn down (generally on packthread), in the raised areas of the designs of an embroidered binding. Purl was sometimes manufactured with a colored silk twisted around the metal but which did not conceal it. The small corkscrew-like rings made by this coiled process sparkled with reflected light. (111, 280)

purple marble. A type of leather cover marble consisting of solid purple, which is glaired and then followed by a sprinkle of sulfuric acid, which produces red veins in the purple. (97, 152)

pustaka. A type of book consisting of long strips of thin bark, or an imitation paper produced from the bark of trees. The Sanskrit word "pustaka" is used for this kind of book in North Sumatra, Java, and other areas, while the word "pustaha" is used in South Sumatra. Pustakas were written in brilliant ink on long strips, which were folded concertina-wise and tied together with string woven from rushes. (164)

put out. The removal of tanned skins from the drying drum or paddle and their placement on a low, slanting bench to have the wrinkles pressed out.

putrefactive damage (putrefaction). A general source of hide and skin damage caused by bacterial action on the stock following flaying and before curing, or, at times, following soaking, but before tanning. A wet, unsalted skin at any point before tannage is in a very perishable state and is very susceptible to the invasion of putrefactive bacteria, especially on the flesh side of the skin. This is particularly the case under the climatic conditions generally prevailing in areas where skins are dried, rather than being cured by one of the salting processes. Often the bacteria will develop along the vascular system and leather produced from such stock is said to be VEINY LEATHER.

Putrefactive damage is often obvious before a skin is dried (but not necessarily during or subsequent to wet-salting, brining, etc.); however, subsequent to drying the damage is not readily perceptible and therefore may not be suspected. Once the affected skins reach the tannery, however, the damage is usually detected before they reach the limed condition. Once they are in soak they display a pitted condition, often honeycombed with small holes that may penetrate through the entire thickness of the skin. They may also be pitted and corroded, mainly on the flesh side.

This type of damage is not intensified by liming, but it is not unusual for both putrefactive and SUN DAMAGE to be present in the same skin, in which case even greater damage will be apparent after liming than before. Moreover, the presence of fatty tissue left after flaying may encourage putrefactive as well as sun damage.

The first indication of putrefaction (aside from odor) is hair slip, usually accompanied by a sensitive condition of the grain surface, so that the grain layer tends to rub away during normal processing of the stock. Slight rubbing gives a "dull grain," generally accompanied by blotchy finishing. Putrefaction also causes the general structure of the skin to become loose and flabby. (248, 363)

putting out. *See:* SETTING OUT.

PVA. *See:* POLYVINYL ACETATE.

PVC. *See:* POLYVINYL CHLORIDE.

pyrethrum. An insecticide derived from the chrysanthemum (*Chrysanthemum coccineum* or *C. cinerariae*), at one time used to inhibit bookworms.

pyrocatechin; pyrocatechol. *See:* CATECHOL.

pyrogallol. A crystalline, toxic phenol ($C_6H_6O_3$), having weak acidic properties, prepared by heating gallic acid with water. It is readily soluble in water, alcohol, and ether. Alkaline solutions rapidly absorb oxygen from the atmosphere, becoming dark brown in color. Pyrogallol is used in photography, as well as in the manufacture of dyes and in dyeing processes. (175, 195)

pyrogallol tannins (pyrogallols). *See:* VEGETABLE TANNINS.

pyroligneous acid. A crude brown liquor obtained by the distillation of wood. Its acidic properties are due chiefly to its acetic acid content. It is used as a substitute for sulfuric acid in some PICKLING processes.

pyroxylin. 1. A substance consisting of lower-nitrated cellulose nitrate, usually containing less than 12.5% nitrogen. It is used in the manufacture of pyroxylin coated and impregnated book cloths. 2. The cellulose plastics and solutions, such as lacquers prepared from cellulose acetate. (164, 235)

pyroxylin-coated paper. A paper coated with pyroxylin lacquer, i.e., cellulose mono- or di-nitrate in a suitable solvent, and used for book covers, labels, imitation leather, etc. The lacquer may be clear or colored. (17, 316)

pyroxylin-treated fabrics. A cotton fabric completely and (usually) heavily coated with the cellulose nitrate compound, pyroxylin; or, a fabric completely filled with the same compound. The former is usually called a "pyroxylin-coated fabric," and the latter a "pyroxylin-impregnated fabric." *See also:* BOOK CLOTH. (102, 208, 366)

quad mark. *See:* BLACK STEP.

quadrigesimo-octavo. *See:* FORTY-EIGHT-MO.

quadrille. Paper ruled in such a manner as to form a large number of small squares, e.g., graph paper. While this type of paper was formerly produced by ruling, today it is largely produced by offset printing. (156)

quadruple folder. A folding machine designed principally for book production, which produces either four 16-page or two 32-page sections. It has three folding levels and six sets of folding rollers. The sheet is folded on its longest dimension in the first section, and is folded in a parallel fold in the second, while at the same time being slit into four units, each of which is folded at right angles in the third section. When insetted sections are required, the two center sections are conveyed to positions under the right and left outside sections by means of hickey rolls before the final fold is made. Here the two sections are folded together with one operation of the right- and left-hand folding knives, and are then delivered to the receiving hopper as two 32-page sections. *See:* FOLDING MACHINES. (320)

quagga. A wild ass, *Equus quagga,* found in the southern part of Africa, the skin of which was once used in the manufacture of an imitation sealskin leather. (261)

quaker colored. Drab or gray colors, or the dulling effects produced by modifying brighter shades, sometimes by the addition of black pigment. The term refers to shades of book cloth sometimes used on devotional books, and is presumably derived from the predilection of members of the Society of Friends for muted colors. (197)

quarter binding (quarter-bound). A binding having the spine and a small part of the sides (about one-eighth the width of the boards) covered with one material, with the rest of the boards covered with another. A quarter binding may consist of leather and paper, leather and cloth, cloth and paper, vellum and paper (with or without vellum tips at the corners), etc. In fine bindings, leather and paper, as well as vellum and paper, are the most common quarter bindings. *See also:* HALF BINDING; THREE-QUARTER BINDING. (161, 264)

quarter-bound cut flush. A type of stationery binding that is wire stabbed and has cloth-jointed endpapers. The boards, which are placed approximately one-quarter inch from the wire stabbing are glued to the endpapers before trimming. The cloth covering is then attached to the spine overlapping the paper-lined boards. The book and its covers are then trimmed flush. This style of binding, which is now virtually obsolete, was used mainly for order books. (58)

quarter cloth. A binding having a cloth spine and paper sides, with the cloth extending from one-eighth to one-third across the width of the boards. (204)

quarter flush, edges turned in. A style of stationery binding similar to QUARTER-BOUND CUT FLUSH, but with the boards lined and turned in all around.

quarterfoil. A finishing tool consisting of a conventionalized representation of a flower with four petals or a leaf with four leaflets, or an ornamental design having four lobes or foils.

quarter leather. A binding having the spine and a small part of the sides (about one-eighth the width of the boards) covered with leather, and the remainder of the boards covered with a different material, usually paper but sometimes cloth. *See also:* HALF LEATHER; THREE-QUARTER LEATHER.

quarternion. A gathering consisting of four sheets folded once, and insetted. This was the form in which some manuscripts and early printed books, especially those of vellum, were assembled, with the first and eighth, second and seventh, etc., leaves being conjugate. *See also:* QUINTERNION; SEXTERNION; TERNION. (225, 278)

quarto. A book in which the sheets have been folded twice, the second fold at right angles to the first. The result is often squarer than the upright rectangular characteristic of the FOLIO, OCTAVO, and DUODECIMO. In books with laid paper the chain lines are horizontal. In England the quarto became an elegant format for published works in the first half of the 18th century.

In the 19th century, when the rapid mechanization of the printing industry took place, librarians began to apply the term format according to size rather than the way a book was put together. This has contributed considerably to the general confusion concerning format.

quarto leaf. One-fourth of a sheet of paper of any size.

quebracho. A South American tree, genus *Schinopsis,* the wood of which is relatively rich in tannin. The name "quebracho" (pronounced "kay-brat-sho") derives from a contraction of the colloquial Spanish or Portuguese term "quiebra-hacha" (ax breaker), and refers to the extreme hardness of the wood (specific gravity 1.12 to 1.39). The trees exploited for tannin include *Schinopsis balansae* (quebracho colorado chaquerno) and *S. lorentzii* (quebracho colorado santiagueno).

The heartwood of *S. balansae* averages 20 to 25% tannin, while that of *S. lorentzii* averages 16 to 17%. Untreated quebracho tannin is relatively insoluble in cold water and is usually sulfited to overcome this disadvantage. The untreated tannin also has a high pH value and low salts and acids content, while the sulfited product is the same except that the salts content is high. Quebracho belongs to the condensed class of tannins.

Quebracho tans very rapidly, converting hide substance into leather in about one-third the time required by a tannin such as oak bark. Used alone, however, it produces a leather that is light, lacking in firmness, and with poor resistance to wear; therefore, it is commonly mixed with other tannins, such as hemlock, mangrove, oak bark, myrabolans, and sumac.

Quebracho has been used extensively in the tanning of leather since it was first introduced over one hundred years ago. It has been used so extensively, in fact, that its use has declined sharply in recent years largely because of over-exploitation. (175, 306, 363)

quercitron. A tannin, and yellow coloring material, obtained from the bark of the black oak, *Quercus velutina,* and used to a very limited extent in tanning and dyeing leather. The bark contains about 6 to 12% tannin. *See also:* OAK. (197)

quick-drying inks. PRINTING INKS which have had driers added for the rapid conversion of the ink vehicle (varnish) to a solid film. (140)

quick-set inks. PRINTING INKS containing thin mineral oil and varnish. The thin oil is quickly absorbed into the paper during printing, while the pigment and varnish remain on the surface of the paper, thus allowing the sheets to be handled sooner than if regular linseed oil-based inks were used. Since the final setting time of the varnish is in-creased, the surface of the sheets re-main more receptive to subsequent printings, as in multi-color printing. (140)

quinternion. A gathering consisting of five sheets folded once, and insetted. This was the form in which some manuscripts and early printed books, especially those of vellum, were as-sembled. The first and tenth, second and ninth, etc., leaves were conjugate. *See also:* QUARTERNION; SEXTERNION; TERNION. (258, 278)

quire. 1. One-twentieth of a ream of paper, or 25 sheets (sometimes 24 sheets plus an outside sheet) in the case of a 500-sheet ream, or 24 sheets in the case of a 480-sheet ream. 2. A gathering (section), particularly when unfolded (i.e., printed but unfolded). A quire was originally a gathering of 4 sheets, forming 8 leaves or 16 pages after one folding. It is thus synony-mous with QUATERNION. The low-Latin word quarternum was shortened to "quair" or "guaer." When parchment was the prevalent book material, quires of 4 sheets made convenient gather-ings for sewing; however, when the use of paper spread it was possible to use from 5 to 7 sheets without forming too thick a gathering for sewing, and the original association of "quaire" with "four" eventually became ob-scured. *See also:* IN SHEETS. 3. To lay together two or more folded sheets, one within the other. *See:* QUIREWISE. 4. In blankbook binding, a term indi-cating 80 pages. 5. A small book or pamphlet consisting of, or as if con-sisting of, a quire of paper. (94, 234, 316)

quirewise. A method of imposing a book or pamphlet, in which the folded sheets fit one within another, and are saddle sewn or stitched, instead of be-ing gathered side by side and side-stitched or sewn through the folds. (142, 179)

rabbit back. A text block that has been rounded and backed in such a manner that, instead of forming the arc of approximately one-third of a circle, the spine is peaked in the center and slopes steeply to the shoulders. The "rabbit back" is generally a result of improper rounding and backing procedures, too much swell in the spine because of added bulk of the sewing thread, or loose sewing. *See also:* HOG'S BACK (1). (97)

rabbit skin glue. A high quality animal GLUE produced from the unhaired skins of rabbits.

raddle. *See:* RED OCHER.

rag board. Originally, a hard-calendered paper board used as a support for the leather covering of carriages, and produced from rags and waste paper in thicknesses of approximately 0.125 inch. Today the term refers to a general type of binder's board used for mounting prints, art works, matting, etc., or as the boards for fine bindings. Its outstanding characteristic is its high dimensional stability and permanence. (17)

rag book paper. A wide range of book papers having a cotton fiber content of 25, 50, 75, or 100%, the one with 100% being known as "Extra No. 1." A "rag content" paper is one that contains a minimum of 25% rag or cotton fiber. Such paper is used for currency, ledger, manifold and onionskin, blueprint and other reproduction papers, maps and charts, etc. *See also:* BIBLE PAPER; COTTON FIBER CONTENT PAPER. (17, 350)

raised bands. The cords or thongs on which the sections of a book are sewn. The cords, of which there are traditionally five (but which historically have varied from two to as many as fourteen) are seen as ridges across the spine of the covered book. Raised bands have long been associated with the best of fine hand binding and the TIGHT BACK. False raised bands, which are generally glued to the hollow of the spine, are sometimes used to give the impression of FLEXIBLE SEWING. Such books are generally sewn on sawn-in cords. (236)

raising. *See:* DRENCHING; SWELLING.

ramie. A tall herb of the nettle family, native to tropical Asia and cultivated in

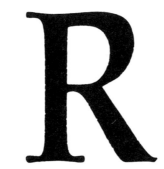

other suitable areas. The fibers are obtained by decorticating and degumming *Boehmeria nivea* (white leaves) and *B. tenacissima* (green leaves), the latter being the more important of the two. The degummed material is practically pure cellulose and is identical in composition with bleached cotton and linen. Ramie fibers are among the strongest vegetable fibers known, and are durable and not as much affected by moisture as are many other fibers. It is used in the East as a textile fiber and in Europe for banknote paper. It is a potential source of papermaking fibers. Also called "rhea." (17, 77, 143)

range. A strip of leather cut from a hide. A "butt" range is a strip of convenient width cut from the fore end of a range usually after, but sometimes before, the hide is tanned. (61)

Ranger, Edmund (d 1705). A bookbinder of Colonial New England, and a contemporary of JOHN RATCLIFF. Ranger was admitted as a freeman of Boston and established his business in 1671 as a publisher, bookbinder, and bookseller. The earliest known gold-tooled bindings of his date from 1682. Ranger was one of the first American bookbinders to use silk headbands in lieu of linen threads and, like Ratcliff, he sewed his books on both raised and sunken cords (thongs). Ranger covered his books in leather and employed marbled endpapers, gilt edges, and gold tooling, all in addition to his work in so-called PLAIN BINDING. (171, 200, 301)

raspail test. A method of determining the presence of rosin size in paper. One drop of a strong solution of ordinary sugar is applied to the sheet, the excess being blotted after one minute. A drop of concentrated sulfuric acid is then applied, which turns the area treated a bright red color if rosin is present in the paper. (143)

rasped. 1. A book that has had the sharp edges of its boards rounded but not beveled. 2. The roughened edges of sheets that are to be adhesive bound instead of sewn.

Ratcliff, John. A bookbinder of Colonial America who came to this country from England between 1661 and 1663 to bind copies of the Indian Bible of John Eliot. A number of other books exist that documentary evidence indicates were bound by Ratcliff, including a blind-tooled binding executed in 1677, as well as a binding produced two years later, which was tooled in gold wtih the same tools. Ratcliff sewed his books on both raised and sawn-in cords (thongs), gilded the edges of some of his bindings, used marble endpapers, and covered the books in leather. Nothing is known of John Ratcliff after 1632, and it is surmised that he returned to England in that year. (171, 200, 301)

rattle. That property of a sheet of paper which produces noise when the sheet is shaken. While rattle is generally considered to be dependent on such characteristics as density and stiffness of the sheet, recent investigations indicate that the property is primarily associated with the presence of numerous extremely short fibers among the normal (longer) fibers of the paper, as well as a high proportion of hemicelluloses binding them together. (17, 139)

rawhide. A (cattle) hide rendered resistant to putrefaction by unhairing, liming, stuffing with oils and greases, and sometimes by other preparatory processes. As the name implies, it is not tanned. It is sometimes used for lacings or trimmings, of books, but it is far too stiff and intractabe to use as a covering material. (291, 325, 363)

rayon. A fine, smooth, hygroscopic textile fiber made from various solutions of modified cellulose, such as wood pulp or cotton linters. The rayons were among the first, if not the first, of all the man-made fibers considered for use in papermaking from which simulated paper structures were produced on conventional papermaking equipment. Rayon fibers are among the better synthetic papermaking fibers because: 1) they are far less expensive than most of the organic or inorganic synthetic fibers; 2) being cellulosic, and, therefore, compatible with water slurries of other cellulosic fibers, they can be handled by conventional papermaking equipment and techniques; and 3) they have most of the inherent advantages of synthetic fibers, such as control of denier, length, strength, elongation, cleanliness, and optical uniformity.

The compatibility of rayon fibers with less expensive pulp furnishes, as well as the ease with which their diameters can be controlled, make them useful for adding bulk to paper when an improvement of porosity is required. In addition, their cleanliness, strength, and bulking properties also make them valuable components in saturating papers. (42, 143)

r. e. Abbreviation for RED EDGES. *See also:* RED UNDER GOLD EDGES.

reactive dyes. Dyes which are bonded to fibers by irreversible, covalent bonds, rather than by the usual hydrogen bonding, electrovalent bonding, or solvation effects, all of which are reversible. Most reactive dyes may be used to color fibers other than cellulose, the only criterion being the presence in the substrate of a reactive hydrogen atom, which is present in wool, nylon, and cellulose acetate. (195)

ream. 480 or 500 sheets of paper, according to grade. Handmade and drawing papers may "ream" at 472, 480, or 500 sheets. Originally, a ream was 526 sheets, while today a "short" ream consists of 480 sheets, and a "long" ream 500 or 516 sheets. (17, 316)

rebacked (rebacking). The renewal or replacement of the material covering the spine of a book. The term is used primarily with reference to books covered in leather, as this type of repair is seldom feasible in the case of paper-covered books, or a publisher's cloth (edition) binding, unless the book is rare or has a binding of unusual attractiveness, e.g., a Victorian illustrated cover. Used in a strict sense, however, it refers to the renewal of the original spine covering. The term may also be applied to the reattachment of the original spine material, usually after repair or restoration. Unless a substantial portion of the original spine can be restored and reattached, it is usually replaced in its entirety. In either case, it is customary to lay a new strip of leather over the spine of

the text block, over which the original spine is glued. The leather beneath is extended under the leather on the sides, thus effectively creating new joints. (69, 237)

rebind. As a noun, a volume that has been rebound; as a verb, to subject a book to REBINDING.

rebinding. The more-or-less complete rehabilitation of a worn and/or damaged book, the minimum amount of work involving resewing and the attachment of new covers. For the general steps in rebinding a book, *see:* BOOKBINDING.

rebound. A book that has had its (original) binding removed and replaced with another, usually after resewing.

rebuilding corners. The repair and reconstruction of the corner or corners of the covers of a book that have become worn, soft, bent, mashed, or broken. Corner rebuilding generally involves the application of paste or other adhesive between the plies of the board. The adhesive is sometimes injected between the plies by means of a hypodermic syringe. If a part of the corner is missing, or so badly damaged that it cannot be rebuilt as described above, the covering material and board paper are lifted, permalife paper cut to proper size is glued to both sides of the board, and the corner is then rebuilt by packing the space between the permalife paper with shredded blotting paper mixed with an adhesive, plastic wood, etc. (173, 236)

rebuilding old covers. *See:* COVERS BOUND IN (1).

recased. In a strict sense, a text block that is separated from its case, and, following repair to text block and case, is then placed back into the *same* case, perhaps with new endpapers, or possibly simply with new hinges. In a more general sense, a book is recased when the text block is removed from its original case (usually a publisher's binding) and placed in a new case made specifically for it. The first method might be said to be the work of the hand binder, and the second the work of the library binder. (69, 94)

receptivity. The acceptance of a substance, such as oil, water, or other liquid, by the surface of a material, e.g., paper or cloth. Receptivity depends upon the ability of the liquid to wet the surface, as well as upon the initial rate of penetration of the liquid into the surface of the material. In the usual interpretation, receptivity connotes penetration occurring under the action of capillary forces only; however, in some printing processes, pene-

tration is abetted by the pressure of a nip. *See also:* ABSORBENCY; HOLDOUT. (17)

recessed-cord sewing. A method of sewing a book by hand which involves cutting grooves into the spine of the gathered sections and recessing the cords into those grooves. A single length of thread is carried from kettle stitch to kettle stitch, as in FLEXIBLE SEWING, but passes across the cords instead of encircling them. The sewing may be done ALL ALONG, TWO ON, etc., as in flexible sewing.

Sewing on recessed, or sawn-in, cords is relatively old, having been used in France as long ago as 1580. It continued in use in France until about 1650, and in England, particularly for thin books bound in sheepskin, until about 1770. The technique seems to have died out after that time until revived, some fifty years later, by Nicolas Denis Derome. *See:* DEROME STYLE.

Recessed-cord sewing has been used extensively in craft bookbinding since the latter part of the 18th century. Although inferior to flexible sewing in soundness of technique, it has several advantages over that method in that: 1) the sewing proceeds faster, thus effecting savings in time; 2) it reduces the cost of subsequent forwarding operations in that there is no need to fill in between bands, the bands do not have to be straightened, and there is no necessity of molding the covering leather about the bands; and 3) in combination with the HOLLOW BACK, it usually allows more THROW-UP in the spine, thus facilitating opening of the book. *See also:* FLEXIBLE NOT TO SHOW; TAPE SEWING (1). (236, 355)

reclaimed papers. A paper and/or board made from paper stock, reclaimed "waste" (so-called recycled papers), de-inked paper stock, and paper shavings or cuttings. Somewhat over 20% of the total fibrous raw material employed in the manufacture of all grades of paper and board is secondary fiber obtained from reclaimed paper and board.

The reclaimed papers are mechanically disintegrated in water to produce a pulp suspension, after which foreign materials are removed. This type of pulp is characterized by low color, as well as low strength, unless produced from carefully selected long-fibered stock.

De-inked paper stock is used in the manufacture of several grades of paper, including book papers, groundwood specialty papers, newsprint, etc. It may be used either alone or combination with virgin fiber. It is produced from printed and/or unprinted reclaimed papers by means of mechanical disintegration, and treated with chemicals and dispersing agents which make possible the removal of most of the ink, filler, and other undesirable materials during subsequent washing. The cooking and washing operations are usually followed by bleaching. In general, the secondary pulp is of shorter fiber length and is somewhat lower in strength than the original pulp; therefore, it is given a minimum of beating and refining. Use of de-inked paper stock results in paper which possesses good formation, opacity, bulk, dimensional stability, and printability.

Paper shavings and cuttings—e.g., from binderies—are used to produce another grade of reclaimed paper stock, which is used extensively in the manufacture of writing and printing papers, as well as board and board linings. These are converted into pulp by mechanical disintegration in water. Their qualities depend upon the grade of paper from which they are made. In general, their physical strengths are lower and the formation superior to those of the original stock.

reconstructed binding. A now virtually obsolete form of library binding applied to a pre-library bound book, in which the volume is removed from its case, resewn, and then placed back into the original case. In general, a reconstructed binding may be either a rebinding or a first binding, depending on whether the book is received in a hard cover, or in a self-cover or gathering. The purpose of this type of binding supposedly was to provide the book with a form of sewing (oversewing) that was stronger than the original, thus enabling the book to withstand more circulations. (102, 164)

rectangular style. A style of binding decoration executed in the bindery of SAMUEL MEARNE for Charles II of England, while Mearne was the Royal bookbinder. It consists of a simple three-line gilt rectangular panel with a crown or similar emblem at each corner, often with a roll on the inside of the rectangle in blind. Although the usual leather used was crimson morocco, many such bindings were in calfskin or sheepskin. (156)

recto. 1. The right-hand page of an open book or manuscript, usually bearing an odd page number. 2. The first side of a printed or ruled sheet as distinct from the VERSO (2). 3. A term sometimes

applied to the outside of the upper cover of a book. (12, 208)

red decay. A type of deterioration of leather (bookbindings), which generally takes two forms: 1) a hardening and embrittling of the leather, which occurs most often in leathers up to about 1830, i.e., books published (or at least bound) up to that date, and which is especially noticeable in calfskin bindings; and 2) a powdering of the leather, which can be so severe as to destroy it completely. This latter deterioration appears to affect virtually all leathers, and is apparently influenced by several factors, including (possibly) the tanning agent or agents used, light (ultraviolet radiation), atmospheric conditions (air pollution—sulfur dioxide), and, finally, how frequently (or, more accurately, how infrequently) the book is handled. *See also:* POTASSIUM LACTATE; REDS; VEGETABLE TANNINS. (237, 298)

red earth. A hard, deep red clay found in tropical areas. It is usually leached and low in combined silica and is used, in powdered form, to chalk goldbeater's tissue when assembling the gold book, and also on the gold cushion—in both cases to prevent the leaf from sticking. (130)

red edges. The edges of a book that have been trimmed smooth, colored red, and burnished. "Red edge" would be a more appropriate term, as the treatment is largely restricted to the head edge. (156)

red heat. A defect in hides and skins, appearing as red or colored patches on the flesh side of the skin, and caused by the action of halophilic bacteria, which are bacteria acclimated to living in salt solutions. The presence of "red heat" suggests putrefaction and consequent damage to the skin. The presence of halophilic bacteria in the cured skin may result from the use of marine salt, or the reuse of salt previously used in wet salting. (306)

red marble. A cover marble executed by coating the leather before covering with a heated mixture of Brazil dust (brazilin, i.e., Brazil wood), alum and vinegar, and, after covering, a coating of glair followed by potash water and vinegar black. Aqua regia added to the basic Brazil dust solution supposedly produced a brighter and more "permanent" red. *See also:* ROCK MARBLE. (95)

red ocher. A red, hematite, used either in paste or solution form for sprinkling the edges of books, and in powdered form by type casters to coat the inner surfaces of their molds to make the

metal flow more freely when casting very small sorts. Also called "raddle." (156, 310)

red porphyry marble. A cover marble excuted by sprinkling black color over the covers in small spots, glairing when dry, and then sprinkling with red and scarlet. When dry, scarlet was again sprinkled on in small spots. (152)

reds. A thick, reddish sludge deposited by certain vegetable tannins when diluted and allowed to stand. The sludge stems from part of the phlobaphenes found in plant materials which yield the condensed tannins. *Cf:* BLOOM. *See also:* RED DECAY. (298)

reducing the grain. *See:* IRONING; PLATING (1); ROLLING.

red under gold edges. The edges of a book that have been trimmed, colored red, and then gilded. "Red under gold edge" would be a more appropriate term, as the treatment is largely restricted to the head edge. (156)

red wallet. A relatively thin, flexible board, used for file folders, expanding envelopes, and in some libraries as a temporary cover for periodical issues. It is produced from rope, jute, chemical wood pulps, and in some cases, with the addition of mechanical pulp. Thicknesses vary from 7 to 20 points. (17)

reed. A tall grass, a species of which, *Phragmites communtis*, covers vast areas of some river deltas in Europe, Asia, and the Middle East, and which is used in the manufacture of paper. Reed produces a pulp of medium fiber length, that is soft and bulky, and which is particularly useful in making printing and writing papers, as well as unbleached papers and board. Reed pulp is almost always blended with stronger, longer-fibered wood pulps. (144)

refiner. A unit in which cellulosic raw material in a water suspension is macerated, rubbed, cut, etc., in order to reduce it to a fibrous state as part of the process of converting wood into paper. *See also:* DISC REFINER; JORDAN. (17)

refining. The operations involved in the mechanical treatment of cellulosic material in a water suspension designed to develop the papermaking properties of HYDRATION (1) and FIBRILLATION and to cut the fibers to the desired length. *See also:* REFINER. (17, 42)

reflectance. The ratio of the fraction of light reflected by a specimen to the fraction similarly reflected by a standard reflector, under specified conditions. The spectral reflectance curve gives the reflectance of a specimen as it varies with wavelength throughout the entire visible spectrum. Reflectance is important in the physical measurement of color brightness and opacity. (17)

refraction (refractive index). A term indicative of the bending or deflection of a ray of light from a straight course as it passes obliquely from one medium to another, e.g., form air to water, with the extent of deflection being related to the speed of light in the two mediums. The refractive index (RI), or index of refraction, of any substance is the ratio between the speed of light in air and its speed in the substance. The greater the difference between the refractive index of a substance and its surrounding medium, the more light will be reflected and the less absorbed, while the smaller the difference, the less light will be reflected and the more absorbed. (233)

register. 1. The ribbon or cord marker attached to a book to serve as a bookmark. It is usually run under the headband (if any) and glued to the spine. Generally, the register is about 1 inch longer than the distance from the head of the book at the spine, taken diagonally to the outer corner of the tail. Registers are not used as often as in the past, possibly because of the rising cost of edition binding. They are still found fairly frequently in devotional books, especially Bibles, and cookbooks. When two registers are used, as with some cookbooks and other publications, they are called "double registers." Also called "bookmark." 2. A list of the quires or sections of a book, often printed at the end of early printed books, particularly those printed in Italy, to assist the binder in assembling and collating a complete copy in the correct order. The list may contain catchwords, signature marks, or a combination thereof. 3. In printing, a term used to indicate that the type area of the recto of the sheet coincides exactly with that of the verso; also the adjustment of color blocks so that colors are superimposed with exact accuracy. Register is of considerable importance in multi-colored printing. 4. In folding, the exact alignment of images so that the print of one leaf is exactly over that of the preceding and following leaves. 5. A book in which binding and other records are kept. 6. In paper ruling, a sheet is said to be in register when ruled on both sides the lines coincide exactly. (17, 83, 107, 156, 241)

registered cutting machine. A type of cutting machine which operates on the same principle as that of the lying press and plow, except that it has a table on which the work is placed and a gauge at the back for the accurate positioning of the pile to be cut. When in the correct position, the top beam is screwed down and the paper is plowed. The registered cutting machine is seldom if ever used today.

rehinged. A book that has had a strip of linen attached across the hinge from the flyleaf onto the board paper, so as to reinforce a torn or broken hinge. If the board paper has been lifted from the board for some other operation, e.g., the insertion of an overcast cloth joint, the new hinge can be secured to the board. In cases where the book is also to be strengthened across the joint with a new strip of leather, it is preferable to replace the hinge first, otherwise the additional thickness of the linen inside may exert pressure on the outer joint when the book is closed and create severe strain across the joint. *See also:* REJOINTED.

reinforced. Any section, endpaper, hinge, joint, or cover that has been strengthened by means of stitching, pasting, mounting, guarding, etc.

reinforced binding. A term sometimes used for "pre-library binding." *See:* PRE-LIBRARY BOUND. *See also:* PUBLISHER'S REINFORCED BINDING.

reinforced library binding. A type of replacement (secondary) binding in a "pre-library bound" style. The term, which is now virtually obsolete, is properly used only with reference to so-called Class "A" pre-library binding; however, it is sometimes also used with reference to a pre-bound book which retains the publisher's original case. (12)

reinforcing fabric. A fabric, such as cambric or linen, used for strengthening endpapers at the hinges. The Library Binding Institute standards call for a fabric that is the standard 80 by 80 thread count, print cloth construction, prorated to 39 inches, 4.0 yards to the pound. (209)

rejointed. A leather binding that has had one or both joints repaired or replaced. Replacement joints are the length of the book and about ¾ inch wide, the exact width being determined by the size of the book and the distance the strips are to extend underneath the spine and sides. The strips, which are pared moderately thin, have a long feathered bevel on all sides. While paring does weaken the leather, if it is too thick along the line of the joint, it will tend to lever itself off the spine

each time the cover is opened. (69, 236)

relative humidity. The ratio of the amount of water vapor in the air to the amount which would be present at the same temperature were the atmosphere to be fully saturated. Relative humidity is expressed as a percentage. Saturated water vapor pressure for various temperatures is given below:

Temperature in ° C.	Saturated Vapor Pressure (mm. of mercury)
0	4.58
5	6.54
10	9.20
15	12.78
20	17.51
25	23.69
30	31.71
35	42.02
40	55.13

Thus, at 25° C., for example, if the pressure of water vapor actually present in the atmosphere is 13.77 mm of mercury, the R. H. is:

$$\text{R. H.} = \frac{\text{actual vapor pressure}}{\text{saturated vapor pressure}} \times 100,$$

or $\dfrac{13.77}{23.69} \times 100$, or 58%

All organic fibers, including paper and leather, are hygroscopic and absorb or emit water vapor so as to adjust their moisture content to that of the air in which they are stored. Although the R. H. factor varies with different kinds of organic fiber, it remains constant for the same kind of fiber. Since the moisture content of paper affects its weight and printing properties, its R. H. must be known. It may be measured by a sword hygrometer inserted in a pile of paper.

R. H. of the Air	Corresponding Water Content of equal Weights of a Cellulose Fiber
30%	5%
40%	6%
50%	7%
60%	8.5%
70%	10%
80%	13%

The change in rate of increase, e.g., between 50 and 60%, stems from the fact that the curve is not flat but "S" shaped; and, also, because of hysteresis, equilibrium water content is higher when approached from the wet side than from the dry side.

Any changes in water content of a fiber immediately manifests itself as changes in its dimensions, especially in the cross direction of the paper. The fiber diameter swells considerably at increased moisture content resulting in stretching of the paper. Other properties of the paper are also affected, but the most significant change affecting printing is the change in dimension. The absorption and emission of moisture require time, absorption generally requiring less than emission. The edges of paper in storage come into contact with the atmosphere to a greater extent than other areas, and are therefore exposed initially to changes in R. H. A rise in R. H. will cause the edges of the paper to buckle, while a decrease may cause undulations in the middle of the pile. In order to avoid dimensional changes in paper it is not unusual to hang it before printing. In offset printing, where attention must be given to the moisture transferred to the paper directly from the dampened plates (by way of the rubber cloth), a relative humidity of approximately 60% has been found to be suitable for purposes of register, while in other printing methods and paper handling firms, a lower moisture content may be more suitable.

remainder binding. The business of binding unsold copies of a book that are in sheets or gatherings. These are sold to a jobber, bound in a different format from the original binding, and offered for sale, sometimes with a different title. Such bindings are usually very economically priced. For 19th and 20th century books, the term "remainder binding" is used correctly only with reference to a book bound for the wholesale book trade by someone other than the original publisher of the book. A later (and sometimes less expensive) publisher's binding was a SECONDARY BINDING. (69, 70, 261)

remargined. The replacement or restoration of part of one or more of the outer margins of a leaf, either by means of paper cut to size and pasted to the leaf or by LEAFCASTING. If all four margins are replaced, the leaf is said to have been INLAID. (69)

remboîtage. A French term applied to the process of transferring a book, i.e., text block and endpapers, from its original binding to another. The new binding may be more luxurious, more nearly contemporary, or simply more appropriate, than the original. The term also refers to the process of transferring a superior text of a work into a better

binding than the one originally made for it. There is not a comparable English word for this expression, re-casing being the closest; however, in craft bookbinding, "recasing" connotes a book that has been removed from its covers, repaired and/or re-sewn, and then returned to the original covers, while in library binding, it indicates a new, but usually just ordinary, case. (69)

removable press. A type of press that is not designed to exert pressure but simply to hold pressure that is applied. In the days when standing presses were used in edition and library binding, many presses were required because books were generally kept under pressure for 24 hours. Use of the removable press reduced the number of (hydraulic) standing presses required because it divided the *application* and *maintenance* of pressure between two implements. The books were loaded on a separate base supported on casters instead of the base of the press. When the press was filled, a special board was placed on top of the last pressing board, and, after the pressure was applied, threaded steel rods connected the top board and the caster-mounted base. The pressure of the hydraulic press was then released and the entire load of books rolled out of the press. With this equipment it was necessary to have only one press for each casing-in machine; however, sufficient special bases, top boards and pressing boards for the day's work were required. *See also:* BUILDING-IN MACHINE. (339)

Renaissance ornament. A conventional finishing tool cut in the shape of columns, urns, vases, beasts, birds, garlands, or foliage found in Renaissance architecture. (250)

repoussé. A book cover of metal, usually silver, produced by hammering or shaping the metal into a design from the reverse side, generally into a mold of wood, or other solid material, that has been carved intaglio. The metal is then attached to the book board, which is usually made of wood. Repoussé work is often refined by chasing. (233)

reproduction paper. A base paper used in numerous reproduction processes or systems. It may be sensitized, as in the case of negatives, blueprints, photographic paper, etc., or plain, as that used for electrostatic reproduction paper. It is usually produced from high grade bleached chemical wood pulps and/or cotton fiber pulps in basis weights ranging from 11 to 32 pounds (17 × 22 — 500). It is generally well

sized and its more important properties include chemical purity, good wet and dry strengths, and a relatively high degree of permanence. (17)

reptile calf. An imitation lizard skin produced from calfskin, the grain pattern being created by embossing. (278)

rescript. *See:* PALIMPSEST.

reset. A leaf, leaves, or an entire section of a book which has become detached and has been glued back into place. Although the technique is used by some bookbinders, it is a poor and usually ineffective method of repair. The term is also used (improperly) to describe an entire text block that has become loosened in its case and has been reset. (69)

resewing. The process of removing a text block from its case or covers, removing the spine lining (if any), old adhesive, as well as the original sewing thread, and then resewing the sections. In conservation bookbinding, "resewing" usually implies the same method of sewing as the original; in library binding, however, the term generally implies the substitution of OVERSEWING for edition sewing. (130)

resilience of leather. The degree of percentage rebound of a standard plunger dropped onto the surface of a leather under specified conditions. Resilience of leather is a property closely associated with TEMPER. (363)

resin. Any of various hard, brittle, solid, or semi-solid amorphous, organic, fusible substances that are insoluble in water but soluble in organic solvents, and which are classified as natural or synthetic. Resins contain a high proportion of carbon but little oxygen, and have an indefinite and often high molecular weight. The natural resins are excretion or exudation products principally of plant origin (a notable exception being shellac), fusible, usually yellowish to dark brown in color, and transparent to translucent. "Recent resins" are those obtained from living plants, while those dug from the earth where they were deposited, are known as "fossil resins."

Chemically, resins consist of complex mixtures of organic (resin) acids and alcohols, which are generally aromatic in nature, and inert substances (known as resenes), together with extraneous fatty, mineral, or other materials. Gum resins contain carbohydrate gums, while oleoresins are mixtures of resins and volatile oils. The non-volatile residue of conifer resins is called ROSIN, which is the most important resin used in the manufacture of paper. Other more-or-less familiar resins include copal and dammar, which are natural resins used in the manufacture of varnish, accroides, amber, elemi, ester gum, manila copal, mastic, sandarac, and shellac. *See also:* SYNTHETIC RESINS. (17, 233, 235, 309)

resin milk. A RESIN that has been finely divided in the form of an emulsion before being used as a sizing material. (197)

resinoids. A class of thermosetting resins, either in their initial temporary fusible state or in their final (infusible) state. (309)

resinous adhesives. A group of adhesives containing as their principal constituent a water emulsion of POLYVINYL ACETATE (PVA) resin. There are several formulas for PVA resinous adhesives, some of the principal ones used in conservation work being listed below:

1. PVA   95%
   Plasticizer   5%
   Water (sufficient to thin as
      required for best working
      consistency)

This composition is used both in hand binding operations and in gluing machines, and is particularly suitable in those operations involving the use of pyroxylin coated or impregnated fabrics, e.g., buckram, which are difficult to attach by means of ordinary glues.

2. PVA   78.0%
   Dibutyl phthalate   6.3%
   Gamma valerolactone   7.8%
   Water   7.9%

This formula produces an adhesive which will adhere paper, leather, plain cloths, or pyroxylin coated or impregnated, starch filled, or rubberized cloths to cellulose acetate surfaces.

3. PVA   90%
   Gamma valerolactone   10%
   Water (sufficient to thin as
      required for best working
      consistency)

This is a quick drying adhesive.

4. PVA   32%
   Isopropyl alcohol   39%
   Plasticizer   4%
   Water   25%

This adhesive provides excellent penetration.

5. PVA   89%
   Hexylene glycol   7%
   Isopropyl alcohol   2%
   Water   2%

This is an adhesive that is quick drying and has excellent penetration. (37, 309)

resistance of leather to acid. The maximum percentage of acid that a leather is capable of absorbing without deteriorating with time. Experiments involving both chrome- and vegetable-tanned calfskins indicate that rapid destruction of the chrome-tanned leather may be expected if the percentage (by weight of leather) of (sulfuric) acid exceeds 10%, while a percentage greater than 4% of the same acid will cause rapid deterioration of the vegetable-tanned skin. Most of the acid found in the chrome-tanned skin is probably in chemical combination with the chromium, whereas in the vegetable-tanned skin it exists as free acid. (363)

resistance to grain cracking. The extent to which leather may be stretched or flexed without causing the grain surface to crack. (363)

resistance to wear. That property of a material that enables it to withstand abrasion or other forms of wear, or, in a more general sense, degradation during use. *See also:* ABRASION RESISTANCE. (17)

resite. *See:* C-STAGE.

resitol. *See:* B-STAGE.

resizing. The process of applying sizing material to paper that has had part of its original sizing removed, either accidently—e.g., by wetting—or deliberately during washing to remove stains, deacidification, etc. Regardless of the original size, the material used for resizing is generally some form of gelatin or glue, or, more frequently today, carboxy methyl cellulose. Vellum or parchment size is used occasionally, as is nylon, when the paper is very weak and cannot be immersed in water. (237)

resol. *See:* A-STAGE.

restoration. The process of returning a book, document, or other archival material as nearly as possible to its original condition. The entire scope of "restoration" ranges from the repair of a torn leaf, or removal of a simple stain, to the complete rehabilitation of the material, including, at times, deacidification, alkaline buffering, resizing, filling in missing parts, resewing, replacement of endpapers and/or boards, recovering or restoration of the original covering material, and refinishing in a manner sympathetic to the time of the original binding of the publication. Restoration, therefore, encompases virtually the entire range of book work—mending, repairing, rebinding, and reconstruction. *Cf:* CONSERVATION. (102, 233, 237)

restored. A book that has been repaired or rebound in such a manner as to retain all, or at least as much as possible, of the original covering material, and (frequently) the original boards and endpapers. It is generally accepted that everything possible should be done to retain as much as possible, and that added materials should be functional, chemically safe, strong, durable, and unobtrusive (although with no attempt at deception).

restrike. A second or subsequent impression of a lettering or finishing tool, or a second impression in a blocking press. (310)

retanning. The process of subjecting a hide or skin, which has been more-or-less completely tanned by one process (or one kind or blend of tanning agents), to a second tanning process, involving similar, or, more usually, different tanning agents. A typical retanning process is CHROME RETAN. (61)

retention. The quantity of filler or other material remaining in a finished paper. It is expressed as a percentage of the quantity of those materials added to the paper stock prior to sheet formation. (17)

reticular layer. The fibrous part of a hide or skin located between the grain layer and the flesh.

reticulin. Fibers in a hide or skin that are believed to compose a network which surrounds the collagen fiber bundles and assists in holding them together. Reticular fibers are found in most connective tissue (skin) as a network of fine fibrils which, in sharp distinction to collagen fibers, exhibit marked branching anastomosis. (26, 248)

retrogradation. A reversal to a simpler form, such as a physical reaction involving vegetable adhesives, characterized by a reversion to a simpler molecular structure. An example of retrogradation would be a change in starch pastes from low to high consistency upon aging, and, in extreme cases, a separation of more-or-less solid gel from the aqueous solution. (309)

retrospective binders. Bookbinders who imitate earlier styles of binding. In the 18th and 19th centuries, many celebrated and not so celebrated bookbinders imitated earlier styles, including Padeloup and Thouvenin, who were perhaps the most famous, as well as Cape, Trautz-Bauzonnet, Lortic, Chambolle-Duru, Taffin-Lefort and Gruel among the French, and Rivière,

Zaehnsdorf, Lewis, and Clark among the English.

In the 19th century, the demand of antiquarian book collectors for retrospective bindings was so great that there was a concerted effort on the part of bookbinders to copy earlier styles. Many of these binders produced outstanding designs of earlier years, offtimes surpassing their models in the precision and brilliance of their tooling. The vogue for such lavish bindings continued well into the 20th century. (363)

retting. 1. The process of soaking or exposing a substance, such as flax or hemp, so as to promote the loosening of the fiber from the woody tissue by bacterial action. The term also refers to chemical treatment to loosen fiber from the woody tissue. 2. The rotting or damage to a material caused by exposure to moisture.

reverse calf. A calfskin finished on the flesh side by light buffering. The skin is used flesh side out. Reverse calf was sometimes used in place of suede leather as a covering material for ledgers and blankbooks during the latter 18th and early 19th centuries. Also called "rough calf." (173, 325)

reverse cover. *See:* LOWER COVER.

reversed cloth. A book cloth used with the reverse (unfinished) side out. The practice of covering books in this manner began in the late 1880s and was important at the time because, while washable cloths were not common, the reverse side of the fabrics then in use were not affected by water. (236)

reversed fold book. A method of binding single sheets without sewing, the leaves instead being glued to a continuous stub folded concertina-wise. *See also:* CONTINUOUS GUARD. (58, 183)

reversed nonpareil marble. A NONPAREIL MARBLE executed by drawing the comb through the colors on the size from right to left instead of left to right, as in the nonpareil. (159)

reversed v-guard. A folded GUARD (1) to

REVERSED V-GUARD

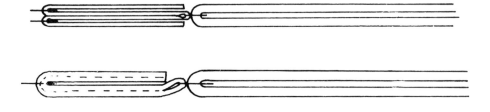

which a section is sewn, the folds of the guard meeting in reverse. The guard consists of several strips of paper folded with the two open ends being folded back on the guard, either together or in opposite directions; the guard may be folded over in one direction on itself and the section sewn at either end, or it may be folded over in opposite directions on itself and one or two sections sewn to it, depending on the thickness of the sections and amount of sewing swell required. Generally, the paper used for the guard (before folding) should be one-fourth the thickness of the section, so that when it has been folded it will be of equal thickness. The reversed V technique is used if the paper of the book is too thick to be sewn in the usual manner, and if it is not possible or desirable to hinge the leaves on linen guards, such as in an album. In addition, such a guard may be required because there is writing in the folds of the sections which would be made inaccesible by the usual manner of sewing and binding. The reversed v-guard technique places considerable strain on the sewing thread and folds of the section, particularly if the guards throw out far from the spine. Also called "meeting guard." (236)

reversible cloth. A book cloth that is finished on both sides, so that either side may be used as the "outside" of a book cover or case. (261)

reversion. The condition of shrinkage and the exuding of clear water from a paste following gelling. *See also:* RETROGRADATION. (198)

rexine. A strong, coated cloth, usually in the form of an imitation leather, and used as a covering material for books. The weave and composition of the base (gray) cloth depend on the grade of cloth being manufactured at the time, and may be cotton or a cotton and rayon mixture. The cellulose nitrate coating is colored by mixing powdered pigments with synthetic oils and is applied in several layers, each being dried before the next application. Polyvinyl chloride may also be used for the coating. Embossing is done with engraved steel rollers, usually to imitate the grain pattern of a leather, but sometimes with modern geometric designs. This type of cloth has been in use since the first decades of the 20th century. (25)

Reynes, John (d 1544). A native of Holland who by 1510 had established himself as a bookseller in London. Reynes was active as a publisher and bookseller, and the bindery under his direction was the most prolific of his time. His bindings usually bear his device, initials, or, in many cases, both. Besides using panels depicting emblems of the Passion, etc., Reynes also employed a fine roll cut with his trademark—a hound, a falcon, and a bee, amid sprays of foliage and flowers. His name is also associated with the early use of gold tooling in England. (132, 347)

R. H. *See:* RELATIVE HUMIDITY.

rhea. *See:* RAMIE.

rheology. A term pertaining to viscosity behavior, e.g., the viscosity of an adhesive under conditions of shear, or the plastic flow properties of an adhesive. Rheological behavior may be thixotropic, where viscosity decreases greatly with shear; dilatant, where viscosity increases greatly with shear; or Newtonian, where viscosity is directly proportional to shear. (221)

rice glue. A type of glue (actually a paste) prepared by boiling ground rice in soft water. The resulting adhesive is white in color and dries to a film that is almost transparent. (371)

rice marble. A "marble" executed by scattering particles, such as rice, bread crumbs, etc., in a random manner on the edges of a book, or, more commonly, on the covers of calfskin bindings, and then sprinkling the edges or covers with color. This decoration was popular on calf bindings of the first half of the 19th century. When used on the edges of books, the edge was sometimes first colored, the particles were scattered over, and a lighter color was then sprinkled over the first. (152, 236, 241)

rice paper. A non-fibrous, delicate, paper-like material made from the pith of the rice paper tree, a small Asiatic tree or shrub, *Tetrapanax papyriferum*, that is widely cultivated in China and Japan. The pith is cut into a thin layer of ivorylike texture by means of a sharp knife. (17, 156)

Richenback, Johann (fl 1467-1485). A

German bookbinder and chaplain of the church at Geislingen (Wurtemberg). Richenback generally included his name and address on his bindings, as well as the name of the person for whom the book was bound. Some 40 or more of his bindings have been authenticated, most of which are covered in white pigskin, a favorite leather of the early German binders. The use of coloring on many of his bindings gives them a bright appearance, making them stand out from the blind-tooled calf and pigskin bindings of his time. He was using rolls, as well as stamps, as early as the 1460s, and had a font of 7 of the former and some 49 of the latter. (94, 339, 347)

ricing. A mottled or grainy LOOK-THROUGH of a paper, especially one produced largely from esparto, caused by the crowding or crushing of the fibers. The term is generally used when the paper displays characteristic small knots caused by over cooking and/or by the wet beating of the pulp. (197)

right angle fold. One of the principal methods of folding, in which at least one fold is at right angles to the others. Right angle folding is the most commonly used fold in book work. *Cf:* PARALLEL FOLD. *See also:* FOLDING; FOLDING MACHINES. (320)

right reading. 1. An image that appears in the normal reading position and not laterally reversed. 2. The arrangement of the papers that are to be printed on one side of a sheet so that, when cut and folded, they will be "right reading," i.e., in correct numerical sequence. (156, 316)

right side. The so-called correct side of a sheet of paper. It is the wire (mold) side in a handmade paper, and the upper (felt) side of a machine-made paper. In both, it is the side from which the WATERMARK is read correctly. Printers often have to know which side of the paper is the "right side" because of differences in surface, as well as the undesirable effect of using sheets laid one way with those laid another way in the same publication. Flat papers are usually packed with the right side uppermost, while, if folded, the right side is outermost. In blue and azure papers, the right side is usually darker in color than the reverse side.

ring binder. One of the earliest forms of LOOSE-LEAF BINDING. The ring binder is a form of mechanical binding similar to the ring notebook paper binder, only much larger. This type of binder has declined in popularity in recent times because it is prone to accidental opening, and, in addition, the bulk of the spine is large in proportion to the quantity of paper it can hold. The binder is usually constructed with two or three rings mounted on a metal backpiece. A mechanism inside the metal back links the rings together so that they all open and close simultaneously, being held closed by spring tension. Some binders open when a small latch at the end of the backpiece is pressed, and close when the latch at the other end is depressed, while others have fiber strips designed to slip over the rings. When these strips are pulled in opposite directions the rings snap open. In the usual case, the bindery produces the binding, but purchases the assembled mechanism. (276, 339)

ring color test. A test designed to determine the presence of different tanning agents used in the manufacture of leather. Concentrated sulfuric acid is added to a small quantity of the test solution of ground leather fibers mixed with water. A dark red ring will form at the juncture of the two liquids in the case of a condensed tannin, while a pyrogallol tannin gives a yellow or brown ring. (291)

ringing out. A ceremony observing the apprentice's last day as an apprentice. On noon of that last day, the next senior apprentice begins the ringing by banging his press pin on the platen of a press, or some other metal object. Following the ringing, the new journeyman puts on his jacket and walks into the office of the owner of the establishment to ask for a job. *See also:* KISSING THE BOOKBINDER'S DAUGHTER.

ring test. A test designed to determine the water resistance of a (book) cloth. The Library Binding Institute standards call for a book cloth that will permit no penetration of water within a period of 10 minutes, or oleic acid (grease) within 5 minutes. (341)

Rivière, Robert (1808-1882). An English bookbinder of French descent. Rivière was an accomplished craftsman and excelled in imitating the best historical styles with a fidelity and technique that have not often been surpassed. His craftsmanship is evidence by the fact that he restored and rebound the Domesday Book.

Rivière established himself at Bath in 1829, relocated in London in 1840, and died in 1882. His grandson, Percival Calkin, became a partner in 1881, and thereafter the firm was known as Rivière and Son, until it closed in 1939. (94, 140)

roan. A variety, or varieties, of leather produced from a superior grade of unsplit sheepskin. Roan is softer than BASIL, and is colored and finished in imitation of MOROCCO. The typical roan has a close, tough, long, boarded grain, a compact structure, and is usually dyed a red color. Originally, roans were leathers tanned exclusively with sumac (as were the moroccos); however, in later years they were often tanned with other vegetable tannins. They were used extensively for covering books from about 1790 until well into the 19th century, but have been seldom used since that time. (69, 264, 343, 351)

rock marble. A cover marble executed by throwing large drops of black color on the leather, which, when partially dry, was followed by diluted potash water. When this was dry, scarlet was sprinkled on in small drops, followed by aqua regia, which was supposed to brighten the scarlet. *See also:* RED MARBLE. (152)

roll. 1. A finishing tool consisting of a brass wheel, the circumference of which is engraved so as to impress a continuous repeating pattern as it revolves under (considerable) pressure. The decorative roll was used in Germany at least as early as the 1460s, and was in common use by the second decade of the 16th century. Most of these early rolls were cut intaglio, so that the design on the leather was raised, but many were also cut in relief. The average length of the pattern impressed by early rolls was approximately 5 to 6 inches, which would give a wheel diameter of approximately 1.6 to 1.9 inches. The common diameter of rolls used today is about 3.5 inches, which is capable of producing an impression of about 11 inches in length. The smaller size, however, is still in use. Rolls have been produced in an enormous variety of designs, including simple lines, simple and intricate patterns, as well as edge and title rolls. 2. The design impressed by a roll. *See:* SCROLL (2). (69, 83, 94, 301)

rolled-back. A type of SPRING-BACK consisting of a thin strip of millboard that is wetted and glued to a strip of paper that is wrapped around it. Both are then rolled to the shape of the spine of the text block. If the book is unusually thick, two boards are used, the outer one being cut slightly wider than the inner so as to compensate for the larger arc it must transverse. The "shoulders" of the rolled-back are formed before the glue hardens. (99)

rolled edges. 1. The edges of the covers

of a book which have been decorated with the roll, usually in gilt. 2. Paper which curls on the edges. (17, 156)

rolled pattern. A blind or gilt decoration produced with a ROLL (1).

roller backer. A bookbinding machine, invented by the American, Charles Starr and exhibited by him in 1851 at the London exposition. It is used to create the backing shoulders of a text block which has previously been rounded, usually by hand. It consists of a heavy roller pivoted above a pair of jaws. The book is clamped with that part of the text block equal to the extent of the backing shoulders projecting above the jaws. The roller is adjusted so that it swings back and forth across the jaws in an arc that corresponds to the round of the spine. The roller is then lowered so that it presses on the spine and is rocked back and forth to shape the spine into the proper shape, bending the sections over the jaws and thus creating the shoulders. If too great a pressure is applied directly to the spine, the sections may be buckled and creased on the binding edge; in addition, the endpapers and several leaves of the first and last sections may be cut by the edges of the jaws. *See also:* BACKING; ROUNDING AND BACKING MACHINE. (164, 339)

roller basil. A leather with a smooth finish, a very fine grain pattern, and a compact, firm structure. While of a natural color, it is sometimes dyed red. Roller basil is produced from vegetable tanned sheepskin, and is used to some extent in the binding of blankbooks. (61)

roller shoes. The SHOES for large and/or heavy books which have been fitted with tiny rollers, enabling the book to roll off the shelf instead of sliding. Roller shoes have been in use since about 1857. (339)

rolling (rolling machine). The process of smoothing and compressing the grain surface of leather by subjecting it to the action of a metal roller under pressure. Unlike GLAZING, rolling involves the use of a revolving steel roll and is usually done in a rolling machine, or rolling jack, which is very much like the glazing machine, except that the latter has a stationary roll made of solid glass in place of the revolving steel roll. While the steel roll strikes the leather with considerable pressure, there is no great friction, as in glazing, and no measurable heat is generated. While being rolled, the leather is usually rotated so that the entire area is rolled twice, a process referred to as "rolling twice around." (363)

rolling machine. A bookbinding machine at one time used to flatten and consolidate the sections of a book before sewing. It consists essentially of two iron cylinders, each of which is about a foot in diameter. The distance between the rolls can be adjusted by means of a screw. The sections are gathered into packets of anywhere from two to four and placed between tin plates. The number to be rolled at a time depends on the thickness of the sections. The "book" of sections is then passed between the rollers and removed by the workman turning the crank. Before the invention of the rolling machine (in 1827), which was the first machine to be used in the craft of bookbinding, sections were compressed by pounding them with heavy beating hammers. Not all books were suitable for rolling, e.g., old books with a heavy type impression and deep corrugations across the type area; therefore the hammer continued to be used during the remainder of the 19th century, although its use diminished steadily. The modern counterpart of the rolling machine is the BUNDLING PRESS. (83, 203, 236)

Romanesque bindings. A group of bookbindings dating from the 12th and early 13th centuries. These bindings, of which more than a hundred examples are recorded, are always in leather, usually of a dark brown color. Their decorative patterns were not incised with a knife or graver, as was common in that time, but were produced by means of repeated impressions made with engraved metal stamps. The finest examples are of French or English origin, but the style was also prevalent in Germany, although not in Italy or Spain. Romanesque bindings are the earliest of the blocked bindings and represent a fully developed art of book decoration by means of deeply engraved metal dies, which left excellent impressions in relief in the leather. These 12th century stamps are well engraved, and seem to have no known antecedents. There is evidence indicating that they were produced by the members of a small group of monasteries, and within a relatively short period of time. Most of the extant examples are bindings of individual books of the Bible, each usually having a different design on the upper cover. (69, 167)

Roman numerals. The capital letters used as numbers in books, for chapter headings and the designation of part numbers, appendices, on title pages for

ROLL

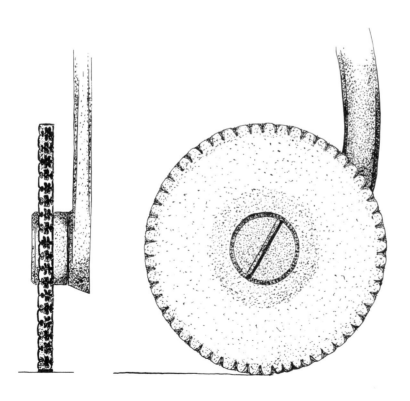

dates of publication, etc. They are also used in lower case for the pagination of preliminary pages. The Roman capitals most commonly used as numerals are:

I—1	C—100
V—5	D—500
X—10	M—1,000
L—50	

Combinations of numbers are made by the addition and substraction, e.g., XX = 20, XIX = 19, XXI = 21, MCMLXXVI = 1976, etc. 1,000 was at first represented by the Greek letter *phi* ϕ, which in lettering and architectural inscriptions became CI, which then became M. 500 was half a *phi*, or IƆ, which later became D. 100 was represented by the symbol for *theta* θ, which later became T, then C, while 50 was represented by the Chaleidian form of the letter *chi* Ѱ, which became ⊥ and later L. Below are listed most of the known numerals:

B	300	IƆƆ	5,000
C	100	L	50
CIƆ	1,000	M	1,000
CIƆCIƆ	2,000	N	900
D	500	Q	500
E	250	R	80
F	40	T	160
G	400	V	5
H	200	X	10
I	1	χ	1,000
IƆ	500	∞	1,000

A bar or dash placed over a letter increased its value a thousand times.

Roman numerals were used by early printers because they had no Arabic numerals; their use today, however, especially for dates of publication, is largely an affectation. (156)

room-temperature setting adhesive. An adhesive which sets in the temperature range of 68 to 86° F. Such adhesives encompass the majority of those used in bookbinding. (309)

rope pattern. A form of decoration introduced into Italy from the Near East in the 15th century. It consisted of an interlaced, or reticulated, design, usually of a very intricate nature, formed by a narrow fillet, and decorated with a series of oblique lines, in imitation of the twist of a rope. The rope pattern continued to be used frequently in the gauffering of book edges during the first 30 years of the 16th century, and was used from time to time into the 19th century. The technique was probably an Oriental innovation. Also called "cable pattern." (172, 347)

rosin. A residue derived from the distillation and subsequent removal of volatile materials (notably turpentine) of the gum of the southern pines, *Pinus palustris* and *P. elliottii.* Gum rosin exudes from the living tree, while wood rosin is obtained from the wood by steam and solvent processes. Rosin is essentially an organic acid, the main constituent being abietic acid ($C_{20}H_{30}O_2$). *See also:* ROSIN SIZE. (17, 143, 235, 309)

rosin size. A solution or dispersion obtained by treating ROSIN with a suitable alkali. The resulting size may be fully saponified or it may contain free rosin acids. When properly converted in the papermaking process, usually by the addition of ALUM, the size precipitates and imparts water (ink) resistance to paper. Since in its natural state rosin is insoluble in water; it must be altered chemically before it can be used as a sizing material. Although several methods of treatment exist, the one in general use today is basically the same as that used in the manufacture of soap, i.e., saponification of a portion or all of the rosin with caustic soda or soda ash to form a soluble rosin soap. Unreacted rosin, which is held as an emulsion, is known as free rosin. The percentage of free rosin has been found to affect the sizing efficiency of a material to a certain degree, the extent depending on variations in conditions in local paper mills. (17, 98, 143)

rotary board cutter. A machine used extensively in library binderies, and to some extent in edition binderies, for cutting boards to trimmed size. The circular blades of the cutter are fixed on an axle, and the board passes beneath them on a flat bed. One pass cuts the boards to the set length, and, after adjustment of the setting, a second pass cuts them to the required width. (81, 203)

rotary gatherer. *See* GATHERING TABLE (2).

rough calf. *See:* REVERSE CALF.

rough cut (rough edges). The edges of a book that are left rough intentionally in cutting, i.e., the opposite of CUT SOLID (1). During a part of the 19th century rough cutting was the fashion, but more as a matter of affectation than to indicate PROOF (1). The edges of books are cut solid to facilitate turning of the leaves, for aesthetics, and to reduce the incursion of dust. Also called "rough trimmed." *See also:* DECKLE EDGE. (256, 433)

rough gilt. The edges of a book that have been cut solid and gilded *before* sewing, so that when the book is later sewn the edges are slightly uneven (rough), although usually to an almost imperceptible extent. This technique has been widely used in England and America, especially by those bookbinders who do not care for the solid "block of metal" appearance of edges gilt subsequent to sewing. *See also:* GILT IN THE ROUND; TRIMMED BEFORE SEWING. (156, 236)

rough tanned. Usually, a vegetable-tanned leather which has received no further processing following tannage, other than drying. The term is used mainly with reference to hide leathers. (61)

rough trimmed. *See:* ROUGH CUT.

roulette. An alternative term used in the United States to indicate a FILLET (1).

round back. 1. The natural configuration of a thin booklet, the individual folios of which have been inserted inside each other and saddle stitched, sewn, or corded to the cover through the center fold. 2. A book which has been shaped during the binding process to give it the familiar convex spine. The opposite of "flat back." *See:* ROUNDING. (156, 256)

round corner. A book cover which has had the corners at the fore edge and head and tail cut off before covering. The round corner is used extensively in the binding of Bibles, passports, diaries, as well as some ledgers, blankbooks, and the like. (139, 339)

round cornering. The process of trimming the corners of a lift of paper to a rounded shape to prevent the edges from becoming frayed or dog-eared.

round cornering machine. A hand- or power-operated machine used for cutting round corners on lifts of paper. Power-operated cornering machines can make two round corners simultaneously on lifts of paper up to 6 inches in height. (256, 278)

round corner lapper. A device shaped something like a bent trindle, with two tines, and used in shaping leather over a ROUND CORNER. (264)

rounded and backed. A rounded text block that has had its spine further shaped with a shoulder at front and back to receive the boards. (256)

roundel. A finishing tool consisting of a double ring, usually surrounding a dot in the center. (156, 172)

rounding. The process of molding the spine of a text block into an arc of approximately one-third of a circle, which in the process produces the characteristic concave fore edge of the book. Rounding takes place after the spine has been given a light coat of adhesive, and is accomplished by means of light hammering along the spine with a round-headed hammer. It may also be done by pushing in on the fore edge while holding the sides of the text block firmly, or, in the case of library or edition binding, by means of a rounding—or more commonly, a rounding and backing machine. Edition bindings are generaly rounded after the spine lining has been applied.

A book is rounded to help prevent the spine from falling in, i.e., assuming a concave shape (and a convex fore edge), which would result in severe strain on the hinges of the book. It also facilitates the outer sections being knocked over to form the backing shoulders, and, in conjunction with this backing process, helps accommodate the swell in the spine resulting from the bulk added by the sewing threads.

The practice of rounding the spines of books dates back to at least the middle of the 15th century, and, during the course of years, the "proper" shape of the round has ranged from a nearly flat spine to a highly exaggerated arc. *See also:* BACKING; ROUND BACK. (161, 196, 236, 335)

rounding and backing machine. A book-binding machine which performs the two operations of rounding the spine of a text block and forming the shoulders for the boards. The book is placed in the machine fore edge down, and is drawn along until it arrives over a forming bar, where it is gripped between facing rollers revolving in opposite directions while the bar is pushed up against the fore edge. The two sides of the text block are dragged downwards while the middle is being pushed up, forming an arc of approximately one-third of a circle. The text block is gripped between jaws that serve the same function as the backing boards in hand backing, and a rocker above swings in an arc against the spine,

ROUNDING

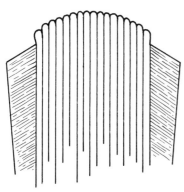

finishing off the rounding and forming the shoulders. The rocker is a heavy piece of metal with a concave edge, and is brought down until the concave is in contact with the spine. In library binding, the rounding and backing machine operates in a similar manner, except that each book is inserted by hand, fore edge up, and the mechanism must be adjusted to the thickness of each book. The text block is both rounded and backed by the action of the concave rocker arm. (203, 320, 339)

roundlet. A finishing tool cut in the shape of a small circle.

round plow. A hand-operated, hand-powered cutting machine with a circular cutting blade. It was usually employed when a number of books were cut together. *See also:* PLOW. (371)

Roxburghe style. A particular style of quarter binding characterized by plain flat spines covered with brown and green calfskin, no raised bands, and dark red cloth or paper sides. The lettering, which is in gilt, is near the head within a border. Only the head edge was gilt and the other edges were rough cut. The style was originally designed for the publications of the Roxburghe Club, founded in England in 1812 by a group of wealthy bibliophiles, and named in honor of John Kerr, Duke of Roxburghe. (69, 94)

royal bindings. A general term applied to bindings which have a sovereign's arms in the upper or upper and lower covers. Despite the presence of a sovereign's arms, so-called royal bindings did not necessarily have any royal provenance, as such bindings were produced rather frequently, especially in the 16th and 17th centuries. English bookbinders used royal arms indiscriminately as a means of decorating their books well into the 19th century. The blind-stamped bindings produced in the reign of Henry VIII, for example, which are embellished panels of the royal arms, are all trade bindings, as are almost all of the plain calfskin bindings bearing the arms of Queen Elizabeth, or her crowned falcon badge. Large prayer books or Bibles with royal arms may have come from one of the Royal Chapels, or they may have been bound for any (loyal) local parish. (69)

Roycroft. An old term applied to full leather or paper-bound books bound by the Roycroft Bindery, in East Aurora, New York, and founded by Elbert Hubbard in 1896. The books were not backed and had the covers glued to the lined spine. The covers

were flexible and were not turned in but overlapped the head, tail, and fore edge. Sometimes the covers were not attached to the text block by any other means other than cords laced through holes drilled from front to back of the entire text block at the binding edge. This style was popular for suede leather bindings. (256)

rub. 1. A representation of the spine or sides of a book, showing the lettering bands, lines, decoration, etc. The rub is made by placing a piece of paper, tracing tissue, or linen against the part of the binding on which the impression is to be made, and rubbing it with a cobbler's heel ball, lead pencil, or soft crayon until a recognizable copy of all details is obtained. The rub is used principally in library binding to enable the binder to match sets when binding a serial publication, or when rebinding one volume of a set. Also called "pattern," or "rub-off." 2. To take an impression by rubbing a sheet of paper placed on an ink block or inked type form. (12, 156)

rubber adhesives. Adhesives consisting of solutions of rubber and naphtha or carbon tetrachloride. They are used as temporary adhesives for paper or thin board. Upon drying, the film of rubber which remains has but little holding power, but is often sufficient for certain purposes. Their principal advantage is that the rubber film can readily be peeled off when it has served its purpose without damage to the surface of the adherend. (198)

rubber-back binding. *See:* ADHESIVE BINDING; CAOUTCHOUC BINDING.

rubbing-off chest. A large chest of wood that was part of the equipment of every gold blocking firm of the latter decades of the 19th century. It was topped with a grill upon which surplus gold was cleaned off blocked cases. Once or twice a year the contents of the chest were sent to the refiner for reclamation. In the great days of gold blocking, the saving was considerable, for the sides as well as the spines of books were often covered almost entirely with gold. (106)

rubbing-up stick. *See:* BANDSTICK (2).

rub-off. 1. The wearing away by abrasion of the cloth covering of a book. The Library Binding Institute standards call for a cloth that will resist rub-off to the degree that the loss by abrasion will not exceed 8% of the weight of the fabric, when subjected to abrasion for 2 minutes by fine flint paper (2/0), on a disc 2 inches in diameter turning at 1,250 r.p.m. under 3 pounds pressure.

2. Printing ink which has rubbed onto the fingers from a printed sheet which has not dried sufficiently. *See also:* OFFSET (2). *See:* RUB (1). (34)

rubric. The heading of a chapter or section of a manuscript or printed book written or printed in red. The term is also used at times with reference to borders, underlined words on title pages, etc., of books of the 16th and 17th centuries, although this usage would better be called *ruled in red*. A book having rubrics is said to be "rubricated" and the rubrication is done by a "rubricator" or "rubrisher." (69, 165)

rubricated; rubrication; rubricator; rubrisher. *See:* RUBRIC.

Ruette, Macé (fl 1598-1644). A Parisian bookbinder and bookseller who succeded Clovis Eve as royal binder to Louis XIII in the early part of the 17th century. Ruette was at one time given credit for the invention of MARBLING, but as that art is known to have come to Europe by way of the Near East, his part may have been to introduce it into Parisian bookbinding. He and his son, Antoine, who was royal binder to Louis XIV, produced many bindings tooled in the "au pointillé," i.e., the POINTILLÉ style. (94, 100, 140)

ruling. 1. The process of marking or ruling lines on paper, usually by means of one of the types of RULING MACHINES. Ruled paper is used for county, court and other record books, forms, notebooks, checkbooks, loose-leaf books, etc.

It is also possible to print patterns of lines similar to those produced by ruling. Ruling, however, has several distinct advantages over printing, including: 1) the absence of glare. (Glare in this context refers to the effect produced when more light is reflected from the printed lines than the paper itself, and results in strain on the eye of the user. Ruled lines do not produce glare because the ruling inks are aqueous liquids, and their color, therefore, does not stem from insoluble pigments, but from dyes which are absorbed into the surface of the paper. Modern offset lithography appears capable of producing less glare than other printing methods, and today, certain kinds of ruled lines are now often produced by web offset printing. Loose-leaf books, checkbooks, and other mass produced items are today always printed); 2) the simplicity of multi-color work. (The ease with which various colors can be ruled side by side in one operation is also closely related to the nature of

ruling inks. Essentially, ruling uses the same technique commonly known as SPLIT FOUNTAIN printing, in which the reservoir is compartmented, each section containing ink of a different color. Printing ink, on the other hand, is a highly viscous material that must pass through a series of rollers before it can be applied to the image carrier. Ruling ink is of low viscosity and can be fed to the ruling pens or discs by capilliary action; therefore many different colors can be ruled extremely close to each other); and 3) writing done in ink will not skip as it may if the ruled lines are printed.

2. The ruling on the printed pages of letterpress books for the purpose of setting off the text from headlines, pagination, notes in the margins, etc. This type of ruling was prevalent from about the mid-16th century on the continent to the end of the 18th century in England. The color of the ruling is almost always red, now often faded to brown, particularly in the earlier continental books. The practice was usually reserved for large paper copies or special copies. Professional rulers were available for this work. (256, 320)

ruling inks. The special aqueous, low viscosity, rosin and dye fluids used in ruling machines. *See also:* RULING.

ruling machines. The machines used to rule lines on paper according to a predetermined scheme. There are two basic types of ruling machines in use today: the pen ruling machine and the disc ruling machine. The pen ruler applies ink in lines by means of multiple pens. It is the most common type of ruling machine in general use, and is also the one usually regarded as producing the best results. It is used for short-run general ruling and is capable of producing lines in the most intricate patterns. Its operation is relatively simple. The paper is fed from the feed board onto an endless moving blanket, each sheet being kept in position on the blanket by means of thin cords stretched around a series of plain and grooved rollers. The pens are held in a slide fitted on the carriage and positioned according to the pattern to be ruled. The pens rest lightly on the paper and rule the lines as the sheet passes beneath. After passing under the pens, the sheet is carried on cords underneath the machine and onto another blanket to permit the ink to dry before delivery to the pile at the end of the machine. The pens on the carriage are arranged to rule along the length of the

sheet for RUN THROUGH ruling. For "struck work" the carriage may be lowered or raised at any required position on the sheet. It is automatically operated by a system of cam wheels at the side of the machine that are synchronized with a gate in front of the feed board which retains and releases each sheet in such a manner that it passes under the pens at the proper time. The pens may be set in a slide in a straight line so that they drop and lift in a straight line, or they may be staggered so that they drop and lift in different alignments, e.g., for box headings. Different colors of ink may be ruled at the same time from the same set of pens on the same carriage provided they are not too close together. Pen rulers are designed with one or more carriages, which permits additional sets of pens to be used on the same sheet if required by the pattern, or separate carriages may be used for different colors of ink.

The disc ruler transfers the ink to the sheet by means of thin revolving discs instead of pens. Its principal advantage over the pen ruler is that, on two-sided machines, *both sides* of the sheet can be ruled in one operation; in addition, some disc machines will rule, count, perforate, slit, and jog the sheets, all in one operation. Despite these advantages, however, they are still considered to be less versatile than pen rulers in the combinations of intricate patterns they can rule. In addition, disc rulers have a tendency to produce broken lines. On one-sided disc rulers, the discs are arranged on spindles according to the pattern of ruling required. The spindles are set around a cylinder over which the paper is conveyed by means of thin cords. On "striker" machines the spindles are arranged so that they can drop and lift the discs as required by the ruling pattern; however, since each row of discs is set on one spindle, and therefore in one line, a separate spindle has to be used for each "step" (and also for each color on most machines), whether or not the lines run off one end of the sheet. Two-sided (perfecting) machines have an additional cylinder and after the sheet has been ruled on one side it is carried by the cords to the second cylinder to be ruled on the reverse side before being conveyed to the delivery pile. (190, 320)

run in. The tendency of the sections of a book, particularly the sections at or near the center of a large book having considerable sewing swell, to collapse inward, causing the book to lose its shape, and (generally) to become loose in its case. Run in is usually caused by excessive swell in the spine, or by sewing that is too loose.

running out. *See:* FANNING OUT.

run out. 1. The fading or "running out" of the pattern lines in paste-graining. It is caused by the use of paste that is too thin. 2. *See:* FANNING OUT.

run pelts. Sheepskins with grain surfaces pitted or otherwise damaged in de-wooling by SWEATING.

run-through ruling. Down line ruling in which the lines run the full length of the sheet without a break. (256)

run-up gilt back. The double gold lines produced by a two-line fillet which runs along sides of the spine of a book, and which are intersected at intervals by double gold lines on either side of each raised band. The horizontal lines are not mitered, and they cross the vertical lines, extending to the edges of the spine. The run-up gilt back represents one of the few cases where the fillet is used on the spine of a book. (339)

russet (russet leather). The condition of a vegetable-tanned hide leather that has been dressed and is ready for staining or finishing by other processes. Such leather is also frequently referred to as "skirt" or "skirt leather." (61, 325)

Russia bands. *See:* BANDS (2).

Russia calf. Originally, a leather produced in Russia from calfskin, vegetable-tanned with tannin obtained from the bark of willow, poplar, or larch trees, curried from the flesh side with a mixture containing birch-bark extracts—which gives it the characteristic odor for which it was famous—and dyed red or reddish brown. It was often given a grain pattern of latticed lines. Genuine Russia calf was at one time highly valued as a bookbinding leather, particularly between 1780 and 1830, partly because its pleasing odor was supposed to repel insects. It was first introduced into Europe before 1700.

Russia cowhide. *See:* AMERICAN RUSSIA.

Russia leather. A more-or-less obsolete trade name originally applied to a shaved cowhide, and later calfskin, horse hide, goat skin, or sheepskin, vegetable-tanned with tannins obtained from willow and other barks, curried on the flesh side with a mixture containing birch-bark extract to give it its characteristic odor, and dyed black and in colors other than the original red or reddish brown. Russia leather (or imitation Russia calf) was produced as early as the 17th century. Its use as a bookbinding leather in the 20th century has been mainly for BANDING blankbooks. (94, 172, 264)

sabai grass. A fiber grass, *Ischaemum augustifolium,* indigenous to India, and used in the manufacture of paper similar in characteristics to that produced from BAMBOO. Also called "bhabar." (143)

saddle. The part of a sewing or stabbing machine on which sections are placed to be brought up under the sewing needles and loopers, or the stitcher head. (139)

saddle sewing. The process of sewing a section, e.g., a periodical issue or pamphlet, through the center fold by means of thread. The term "saddle" derives from the SADDLE of the machine. Saddle sewing affords full openability of the section, i.e., to the gutter of the binding margin. Saddle sewing may also be done by hand, usually employing a figure-eight stitch, but it is more often done by machine, usually one which has the capability of varying the length of the stitch. *Cf:* SADDLE STITCHING.

saddle soap. A mild soap made with some additional unsaponified oil and used in removing dirt from vellum bindings and in cleaning and conditioning leather bindings. (173)

saddle stitching. The process of securing the leaves of a section, e.g., a periodical issue or pamphlet, through the center fold by means of wire staples. The term "saddle" derives from the SADDLE of the machine. The machine cuts the wire, forms the staple, drives it through the paper and clinches it from the other side. The section is stitched in two or more places depending on the height of the publication. The number of leaves that can be satisfactorily stitched in this manner depends to a great degree on the thickness of the paper. Saddle stitching, which is fast and, therefore, more economical than SADDLE SEWING, enjoys the same advantage of that method, namely, full openability to the gutter of the binding margin. The staples used in saddle stitching are usually formed from round wire and are generally made of copper, galvanized iron, or aluminized iron. Also called "wire stabbing." *See also:* SIDE STITCHING. (179, 234)

sailcloth. A strong, heavy CANVAS sometimes used for covering very large blankbooks. (183)

salicylanilide. A crystalline compound ($HOC_6H_4CONHC_6H_5$), used as a fungicide. It is applied either as an aqueous (weak alkaline) solution, or as a non-aqueous solution, in a concentration of 0.1% by weight of the fabric or paper. Since it does not have a great affinity for cellulose fibers, it can be washed out fairly easily if necessary, and, being both colorless and odorless, it is not likely to alter the appearance of the material treated. As it is relatively non-volatile, it should make the material treated immune to attack for long periods of time at normal atmospheric temperatures. It does not contain chlorine. (198)

salicylic acid. A crystalline phenolic acid ($C_7H_6O_3$), soluble in alcohol, ether and hot water, but less soluble in cold water. At 200° C. it decomposes into phenol and carbon dioxide. It is used in the manufacture of dyes, and as a preservative for paste. (142, 371)

salimeter (salometer). A hydrometer especially graduated to indicate the percentage of salt (sodium chloride), in a pickling or brine solution. It is used in developing pickling solutions and in measuring the salt concentration of brining solutions used in curing hides and skins. (363)

salt. *See:* SODIUM CHLORIDE.

salts of tartar. *See:* POTASSIUM CARBONATE.

salt sprout. The crystallization of salt on, or in, the grain of a hide or skin, which may cause damage to the grain surface. It is caused by allowing a pickled skin to dry out. *See also:* PICKLING. (305)

salt stains. Discolorations which appear on the grain surface of hides and skins that have been cured by wet salting. The stains, which are usually greenish-blue or rusty-brown in color, may develop in the corium of the skin, in which case they are usually flat, oriented parallel to the skin surface, and surrounded on all sides by normal hide fibers. They may also develop on the flesh side, or on the grain surface of the skin. All three types are characterized by a hardening of the fibers caused by a grainy deposit which can be removed by treatment with strong acid solutions. As bacteria are found only in the stains which form on the flesh or grain surfaces and not in the corium, it is not believed that they are caused by these organisms, but by deposits formed from alkaline earth salts present in the salt and autolytic decomposition products of blood and non-collagenous hide proteins. Their presence reduces the value of the finished leather significantly; however, the addition of 3% soda ash and 1% naphthalene by weight of the salt virtually eliminates the problem. (248, 363)

sammying (sam; sammie; sammy). A method of conditioning newly tanned hides or skins with water to bring about a uniform distribution of moisture of approximately 30 to 40%. A leather is sammed to condition it for STAKING. (306, 363)

sample back. A strip of material such as leather, cloth, etc., intended to represent the spine of a book and used as a sample for matching colors, material, lettering, etc. *See also:* RUB (1). (12, 156)

sandarac gum. *See:* GUM SANDARAC.

sanding. 1. The process of rubbing down the edges of a book with fine sandpaper, or a sanding machine, so as to remove as small an amount of margin as possible. 2. The process of sanding down the paper or leather spine lining of a book to make it smooth, chiefly so that no undulations or lumps will be seen under the leather covering. 3. The process of sanding the edges of book boards to impart smoothness.

Sangorski, Francis (1875-1912). An English bookbinder apprenticed to Charles Ferris and employed in the workshop of Douglas Cockerell in 1899. In 1901 Sangorski and the English bookbinder GEORGE SUTCLIFFE opened their own bindery, which is still in operation, and commenced producing the fine jeweled bookbindings on which, over the course of years, their great reputation was largely built. Of the hundreds of such volumes they executed, the most outstanding, and their crowning achievement, was a binding known as the GREAT OMAR. (94, 236, 347)

saponification. The hydrolysis of esters by alkalis, and especially the hydrolytic action by which fats and oils containing glycerides are converted into soap and an alcohol, which, in the case of glycerides, is glycerin. *See also:* FAT-LIQUORING; ROSIN SIZE. (195, 233)

satin. A smooth fabric woven in satin weave, and having a very lustrous face and dull back. Satin is woven of silk and other fibers and at one time was used extensively in the production of EMBROIDERED BINDINGS. The fabric lacks the durability of velvet or canvas, which were the other principal cloths used for such bindings. (111, 280)

satin stitch. A padded or unpadded embroidery stitch that is nearly alike on both sides and is worked in various lengths and parallel lines. It is closely woven and evenly made so as to resemble satin. (111)

satin white. A paper filler prepared from aluminum sulfate ($Al_2SO_4)_3$) and calcium hydroxide (slaked lime) ($CaOH)_2$). It is used as a coating pigment in coating mixtures, particularly in coated paper of high white color requiring an enamel finish. Satin white is difficult to handle, and does not keep well; therefore it is usually prepared immediately before use. Very close control of its preparation is necessary to obtain fully satisfactory results. (17)

sawing in. The process of sawing grooves across the spine of the gathered sections of a book for reception of the cords used in sewing a book on recessed (sawn-in) cords. "Sawing-in" was introduced as part of the search for economical binding processes which began as early as the 16th century. Centuries later, in combination with the HOLLOW BACK, it was to have a significant effect on the future of craft binding. *See also:* RECESSED-CORD SEWING.

saw kerf binding. A method of binding single sheets by means of both thread and adhesive. Kerfs (dove-tailed grooves) are cut across the spine at an angle and are filled with adhesive. Sewing thread is then woven around the kerfs to supplement the adhesive, following which the kerfs are again filled with adhesive. This technique

was the forerunner of SMYTH-CLEAT SEWING. (183)

sawn-in cord sewing. *See:* RECESSED-CORD SEWING.

scaleboard (scabbard). The thin wooden boards, which are only slightly thicker than modern pasteboard, made of oak, maple, or birch wood, and used by bookbinders in Colonial America in lieu of paper boards, principally because of their availability and ease of use. It was used, even after paper became generally available, for the cheaper sort of work well into the 19th century. Scaleboard is not to be compared with the pasteboard of earlier times, which was sometimes very thick. (115, 200)

scales binder. An anonymous London binder active from before 1460 to about 1491, so called because one of the stamps he used most frequently represents a pair of scales. The scales binder used decorative stamps on his bindings and is believed to be the only English bookbinder to have used both the stamped- and cut-leather methods of decoration. (167, 236)

scenic binding. A style of library binding which utilizes the book jacket or cover illustration as part of the case. *See also:* JUVENILE PICTURE-BOOK BINDING. (123)

scent of Russia. The particular spicy scent characteristic of genuine RUSSIA LEATHER, and imparted by the application of an oil obtained from the bark of birch trees. (152)

school prize binding. A style of fine binding employed in northern France and the Netherlands as early as the 17th century, in Ireland (Trinity College, Dublin) from the 18th century, and in England from the last quarter of the 19th century until the First World War. In England, the bindings were produced in a common pattern consisting of a full calfskin cover (usually of a dark color), worked headbands, run up gilt backs and colored title labels, two-line fillets on the covers ending with a rosette, and with the arms of the particular school blocked on the upper cover. The endpapers and edges were marbled, often matching in both color and pattern, while the turn-ins and edges of the boards were decorated with a roll in blind. The books often included, inserted before the title page, a printed or manuscript form giving the subject in which the prize was awarded, the name of the recipient, the date, etc. (236)

score (scored; scoring). To impart a linear indentation or crease in a sheet of heavyweight paper or lightweight board

by pressing it between two metal surfaces, one of which has a recessed groove and the other a tongue. The scoring may also be done with a dull blade. The score is made along the line at which the sheet is to be folded or turned. It alters the sheet structure by compressing the fibers in such a manner as to provide a hinge and increases the number of times the sheet can be flexed before failure. Scoring may be done on the printing press, folding machine, or in the bindery. In bookbinding, and especially library binding (when a book is to be oversewn), scoring is frequently necessary because of the weight of the paper (particularly cover papers), incorrect machine direction of the paper, i.e., vertical to the binding edge, or both. (17, 58)

scored calf. A calfskin subjected to an embossing process (subsequent to the covering of the book) so as to produce on the grain surface an indented effect that was supposed to simulate straight-grained morocco. This type of embossing was popular in England from about 1800 to 1830. (69)

scored hides. Hides damaged during flaying by cuts that do not completely penetrate the hide. (363)

scoring. *See:* SCORE.

scoring machine. A machine used to score heavy paper or lightweight board. There are two basic types in use: the rotary scorer and the bender scorer. Each produces a blind impression in the sheet compressing and stretching the fibers. The machine may be a separate unit, or part of the printing press or folding machine. (58)

Scotch grain. A pebbled grain pattern in leather produced by embossing. It is usually applied to cow hide or calfskin and is intended to resemble the heavy coarse-grained leather originally produced in Scotland. (325)

Scotch knife. *See:* SLIDING KNIFE.

Scottish style. A style of decoration developed by Scottish bookbinders of the 18th century. The designs, which are referred to as "wheel" and "herringbone," were well established by 1725 and continued in use until about 1775. The central design on the upper cover consisted of either a large wheel-shaped device with radiating spokes, surrounded by numerous sprays of foliage, the idea for which derived from the fan bindings of the previous century, or a vertical pattern, often enclosed, with branching ornaments radiating outward, i.e., a herringbone pattern. The bindings often had DUTCH GILT

PAPERS with embossed floral ornaments. (1, 312)

scouring. 1. The process of removing the sediment of tannin particles which become fixed in the grain of the skin following a prolonged tannage. The machine used in scouring is similar to the regular unhairing or fleshing machine, except that the cylinder has carborundum cemented in place in lieu of blades. The speed of the machine is also much slower. *See also:* SCUDDING. 2. The removal of surplus oil from an oil-tanned leather, e.g., CHAMOIS (2), by washing in water and a 2 to 4% solution (by weight of the skins) of soda ash. (306)

scraper. A steel implement with slightly rounded ends, used to scrape the edges of books before gilding. (154, 161)

scratted paper. An imitation marbled paper, produced by "spiriting" or spotting various colors on paper by means of a brush. Scratted papers date back to at least the 17th century. (17)

screw binder. *See:* POST BINDER.

scrinium. A receptacle in the shape of a cylinder with a removable lid, and used in ancient Rome as a container for scrolls. (156)

scroll. 1. A roll of material, e.g., parchment, usually bearing writing and rolled onto rods, which were usually fitted with handles. The scroll, and early forms of manuscript, was called *volumen* (roll) by the Romans, and is the word from which *volume* is derived. The scroll (or roll) consisted of a number of sheets of papyrus, parchment, etc., glued together to form a long strip and wound on a rod. The scroll was generally fitted with a parchment cover, fastened with laces, and finished with a "sittybus", or title label. Sometimes the scroll or scrolls were kept in a SCRINIUM. The text was written in relatively narrow columns on the recto side of the material, which in the case of papyrus was the side having the horizontal strips. 2. A decorative motif consisting of any of several spiral or convoluted forms, resembling the cross section of a loosely rolled strip of paper and generally used between flowers on a ROLL (1). (12, 183, 250)

scrow. Strips, clippings, or other waste parts of hide or skin used in the manufacture of glue, and at one time used by papermakers as a source of animal gelatin for sizing paper. (197)

scud. The remnants of epithelial tissues, hair pigments, glands, lime soaps, etc., left in the grain layer of a skin following unhairing. *See also:* BATING; SCUDDING.

scudding. A process used to remove remnants of hair and hair sheaths, hair pigments, fat, and undesirable protein constituents, lime soaps, etc., from a skin when a very clean grain for both smoothness and level dyeing properties is required. A skin is usually scudded following unhairing, and, while it may be done following bating, it is always done before tanning. The process is carried out over the beam with a curved, blunt-edged knife, or, more often today, in a machine which squeezes and pushes the unwanted material (scud) out of the skin. (291, 363)

scuffing. The lifting of the fibers on the surface of a material when one piece of the material is rubbed against another or comes into contact with a rough surface. (17)

scuff resistance. The resistance a material offers to scuffing, usually measured in terms of the number of cycles required to produce a specified degree of abrasion when abraded by an object of designated size and weight (or pressure applied) rotating or reciprocating at a designated speed. (17)

sealskin. A light, tough leather of very fine quality and distinctive appearance, with excellent wearing qualities, produced from the skins of various species of seals. It may be finished with its own delicate grain pattern and lustrous surface, or with a bold grain produced by a combination of embossing and boarding. While customarily black it is also produced in colors. Although its use as a covering material for books goes back hundreds of years, it is little used today because of the declining number of seals, and the excessive oiliness of the skin. *See also:* FLESHER; PIN SEAL (1). (83, 295)

seasoned splits. Split sheepskins, of a natural or dyed color, that have been treated with milk and white of egg, which impart a soft, semi-bright finish without the hardness produced on the brighter, machine-glazed skins.

seasoning. The process of exposing paper or board to relatively uniform atmospheric conditions so that its moisture content will attain to equilibrium and become evenly distributed throughout the sheet. *See also:* CONDITIONING; MATURE. (17, 287)

sebaceous gland. An oil producing gland of the skin located in the grain layer. The glands are effectively removed from the skin by liming, scudding, and bating. (363)

secondary bevel. An extra narrow bevel, honed on the cutting edge of a paring knife.

secondary binding. A second or subsequent binding of a publication. Although the term may also be applied to hand or library bindings, it is used principally with reference to different times of edition binding. When a publisher does not know how many copies of an edition will be sold, and does not want to assume the cost of binding and inventorying copies which may not sell, he may have copies bound in segments, and, as this may spread the binding of the full edition over a period of time, the different bindings may vary because of changes in cloth color, spine lettering, etc. The practice of deferred binding was more prevalent, and the periods of time much longer, in the 19th century than today, as edition binding is now very highly mechanized and standardized. A REMAINDER BINDING is not a secondary binding. (69, 140)

secondary colors. The colors which result when the three primary colors are mixed. The secondary colors are green (blue and yellow), orange (red and yellow), and violet (red and blue).

second impression. The second working of the finishing tool following blinding-in through the paper on which the design is drawn, immediately before tooling in gold. *See also:* BLIND TOOLING; RESTRIKE. (130)

second lining. A strip of paper, usually kraft, the full width of the spine and about 1/8 inch less than the length at both head and tail. It is glued over the first (cloth) lining. The second lining is applied to large and/or thick books to provide additional support to the spine. (156, 343)

seconds. Materials such as cloth, leather, or paper, that are below the established standard of quality, and which are sorted out and sold at a lower price. *See also:* GOOD SECONDS. (17, 82)

section. 1. The unit of paper that is printed and folded, and which, together with other like units, makes up a complete book. A section is usually folded from 1 sheet of paper, but it may consist of 1½ or 2 sheets, or even one sheet and an additional leaf or leaves. Each section of a book bears a different SIGNATURE (1) identification. *See also:* FOLDINGS. 2. In library binding, a group of leaves of a book, suitable for oversewing, not exceeding 0.055 inch in thickness, except those of flexible, pulpy paper which may be

0.065 inch in thickness. (173, 208, 264)

sectional post binder. *See:* POST BINDER.

section B. The first section or gathering of a book following the preliminary matter, usually beginning with the first page of the text proper. (97)

sectioning machine. *See:* PAD COUNTER (2).

selection factors. The condition of hides or skins as to soundness, good cure, pattern, and freedom from defects, etc., as related to stock bought or sold on futures contracts. (363)

self-cover. A cover printed on the same stock and in the same format as the text, with the cover pages being so imposed that when the sheet is folded they will appear as the upper and lower covers of the book, which is usually a single-section pamphlet. Also called "integral cover." (339)

self-endpapers. Endpapers which are also leaves forming part of the first and last sections of the book. (156, 365)

self heating. A condition wherein skins burn or smolder during tannage. It applies especially to the oil tannage of sheepskins and is caused by the oxidization of the cod liver oil used in the tannage with the accompanying liberation of heat. (306)

self-vulcanizing. An adhesive that achieves vulcanization without application of heat. (309)

se-lin labeling system. A method of preparing labels for books developed at Battelle Memorial Institute under the sponsorship of the Library Technology Program of the American Library Association. The system utilizes a regular typewriter (but with a special platen and usually with larger than normal type), special plastic strips, and a transparent laminating material.

The base tape is fed into the typewriter from a reel, the appropriate information is typed on the tape and the clear (laminating) strip is applied over the tape by means of a pressure laminating roll assembly. After the strip of combined base and clear tapes is cut into label size, the backing release paper is removed, the label is placed in the proper position on the book, a shield is held over the label, and heat is applied by means of a hot iron or plate. Although the labels can subsequently be removed by the application of heat, which softens the adhesive, in practice this is difficult to do without damaging the fabric covering of the book.

selvage (selvedge). 1. The border of a roll or section of book cloth to which the filler has not been applied and which is meant to be cut off and discarded. 2. The edges or an edge of a fabric so woven as to prevent raveling.

semé (semeé; semis). An heraldic term indicating a form of decoration consisting of a scattered (sown) pattern of diminutive figures—flowers, leaves, sprays, etc., often repeated at regular intervals by means of one, two, or three small tools, resulting in a sort of powdered effect. Sometimes a coat of arms, or other vignette, is added in the center of the cover, or at the corners. There may also be a tooled fillet around the edges of the cover. Early examples of this style date from 1560 on books bound for Charles IX of France. (81, 156)

semi-chemical pulp. A paper pulp produced by mild chemical treatment of the raw materials followed by a mechanical fiberization operation. Delignification is only partially accomplished; consequently the individual cellulose fibers are not completely separated. The stock coming from the digester is made up of either softened chips or a mixture of free fibers and softened chip centers; therefore, it must be mechanically fiberized in attrition mills to produce a pulp that can be readily felted. (17, 320)

semi-chrome box calf. A black calfskin leather having a grain pattern of fine box-shaped creases produced by boarding the skins in two directions—head to butt and belly to belly. (61)

semi-chrome tannage. A complete vegetable tannage followed by retannage by the chrome method. In this particular tannage, most of the available space between the protein chains of the skin will be occupied by the large vegetable tannin molecules, consequently, unless the vegetable tannage is heavily stripped out, the principal effect is likely to be the coordination of chromium with the vegetable tannins, so that the characteristics of the leather will tend to approximate those of a vegetable tanned leather. *Cf:* CHROME RETAN. (248, 306)

semi-elliptical spine. A book rounded in the form of an ellipse and having pronounced shoulders. This type of spine shaping began in fine binding in the last quarter of the 18th century. The technique gives the spine additional support because the sections are knocked well over on either side. (236)

semis. *See:* SEMÉ.

separate cover. A pamphlet cover printed separately from the text and usually on a different paper stock. Separate-

cover pamphlets, of which the usual periodical issue is a typical example, may be saddle stitched, side stitched, of (rarely) saddle sewn. The covers are usually of a heavy stock stitched to the publication; however, at times the pamphlet is sewn or stitched and the cover is then glued on. (339)

sepia inks. Inks that are compounded from the dark pigment discharged by the common cuttle-fish and other cephalopods, family *Sepiidae,* in order to mask retreat. The effect of this fluid is somewhat remarkable, in that 1 part ink in 1,000 parts of water is sufficient to make the latter opaque. It was used as an ink in ancient Rome, but is little used today except as an artist's coloring. The dried ink is pulverized and boiled with alkali, which is subsequently neutralized with acid so as to precipitate the pigment. The pigment is then washed, dried, and incorporated with oil. The main feature of this process, with regard to permanency, is the amount of acid used to precipitate the pigment, because acid in ink is as detrimental to paper, as is acid in the paper itself. Although sepia inks are reasonably permanent in dull light, they tend to fade rapidly when exposed to bright natural light. (20, 143)

set. 1. A term used with reference to the transformation of an adhesive into a solid (hardened) condition by means of chemical or physical processes, such as condensation, polymerization, oxidation, vulcanization, gelation, hydration, or evaporation of the volatile constituents. Adhesives vary greatly in their "sets," both in time and conditions under which they take place. Glue sets by cooling, paste by evaporation of the volatile constituents, e.g., water, etc. The final set of most adhesives used in archival work usually takes place by evaporation. This type of setting almost always results in shrinkage which, if severe, may cause the adhesive to withdraw from the surface of the joint, leaving it weakened or defective. 2. The distance between the left- and right-hand sides of a piece of movable type. Type is said to have a wide or narrow "set" according to the width of the body. 3. The peculiarities of a sheet of paper, as manifest during folding. 4. The permanence or "set" of the fibers in a sheet of paper produced by heavy calendering. (16, 154, 156, 309)

set-off. *See:* BARRIER SHEET; OFFSET (2).

set-off boards. Boards with a greater than normal space between the shoulder and the inner edge. They are used on side-stitched text books so as to allow for easier opening of the covers. (256)

set out. To attach an insert to a guard so that it stands out from the binding edge. (102)

set square. A modified try square having an adjustable head. It is used by some bookbinders in taking precise measurements, including marking off the head of the text block for trimming with the plow or guillotine, board cutting, cutting of mats, etc. The critical part of this implement is the sliding arm (or head), which must move freely but not wobble.

setting meters. *See:* MITERED (1).

setting out. The process of smoothing, stretching and removing excess water from newly tanned skins. Setting out is similar to SLICKING (1), except that the skin is placed flesh side down and a much blunter blade is worked over the grain side. Setting out may also be done in a machine similar to a fleshing or unhairing machine; the skin is fed against a rotating, blunt, helically bladed cylinder while being supported on a soft rubber roller. Another type of setting-out machine clamps the skin over a half cylinder covered with rubber, and rotates it forward and backward against a bladed cylinder. While setting out removes some water, its distinctive purpose is to "set" the grain, i.e., flatten and smooth the grain surface to remove any irregularities, and also stretch the skin to its maximum area. Also called "putting out." (306)

setting temperature. The temperature to which an adhesive, or adhesive assembly, is subjected to set the adhesive. The temperature of the adhesive in the process of setting (adhesive setting temperature) may differ from the temperature of the surrounding atmosphere (assembly setting temperature). *See also:* CURING TEMPERATURE; DRYING TEMPERATURE. (309)

setting the caps. The process of adjusting the leather at the head and tail of the spine of a book so as to form a protective cap over the headbands. The caps may also be set at an angle, usually 45°, when there are no headbands. In blankbook binding, as well as quarterbound bindings with French joints, the cap is usually molded over a length of cord the width of the spine. *See also:* HEADCAP. (274)

setting the joint. 1. In hand binding, the process of positioning the boards against the shoulders of the text block at such a distance and in such a manner that the boards open easily with no strain on the joints when the leather has dried. Setting the joint is done following covering but before setting the headcaps so as not to damage the headcaps by the opening of the boards. 2. In library and edition binding, the process of creating the joints of the book by pressing it between layers of boards ridged with bands of metal, or by applying pressure in a casing-in machine, or heat and pressure in a building-in machine. (276)

setting the squares. A fine binding process of placing the boards in such a manner that the SQUARES are equal in extent at head, tail, and fore edge. (335)

setting time. The time interval during which an adhesive is subjected to heat and/or pressure to set it. *See also:* CURING TIME; DRYING TIME. (309)

Settle, Elkanah (1648–1724). An English playwright and hack versifier, who composed topical poems which he bound himself, or, more likely, had bound, as there is no direct evidence that he was a bookbinder. Settle's bindings were in leather and were decorated with a rectangular frame within which he had the binder set the arms of a likely patron. If the book did not sell, he had the original coat of arms covered with leather and tooled with a different arms for another prospective purchaser. (158)

du Seuil, Augustin (1673–1746). A celebrated Parisian bookbinder who held the position of royal binder to Louis XV of France. Du Seuil employed lavish doublures and rectangular panels with an armorial panel in the center. He was one of the first bookbinders to execute MOSAIC BINDINGS, although PADELOUP is generally credited with their introduction. He is the only French binder written of in English literature, being mentioned in Pope's fourth moral essay:

His study! With what authors is it stored?
In books, not authors, curious is my Lord;
To all their dated backs he turns you round;
These Aldus printed, those du Seuil bound.

Du Seuil married into the Padeloup family and worked with Antoine Michel Padeloup at the beginning of Padeloup's career. (94, 732)

sewing. The process of securing the sections or leaves of a publication by means of thread in such a manner as to insure a consecutive and permanent unit. There are two basic approaches to sewing a book: 1) through the center folds of the sections, e.g., FLEXIBLE SEWING; and 2) through the sides of the leaves, e.g., OVERSEWING. There is also a subdivision of the latter, one which involves penetration of the sewing thread through the entire thickness of the text block, e.g., SIDE SEWING.

For many years sewing was distinguished from stitching, in that sewing involved joining groups of leaves or sections to each other, gradually building up a complete text block; whereas stitching involved uniting the entire group of leaves or sections from front to back through the entire thickness of the text block, as in JAPANESE SEWING or side sewing. Both types, however, involved the use of thread. Today, on the other hand, sewing is considered to be construction of a text block by means of thread, while stitching is done by means of wire staples. *See also:* OVERCASTING; RECESSED-CORD SEWING; REVERSED V-GUARD; SINGER SEWING; SMYTH-CLEAT SEWING; TAPE SEWING (1). (22, 161, 179, 335)

sewing bench. *See:* SEWING FRAME.

sewing clamp. 1. *See:* SEWING FRAME. 2. A device consisting of two narrow metal plates with small holes about one inch apart, clamped together at one end and secured to the bench. By means of the clamp, books, pamphlets, or sheets to be stabbed through the side are held securely while the sewing holes are drilled through the holes in the plates. (183)

sewing frame. A frame or press on which books are sewn by hand. It consists of a flat baseboard, two uprights threaded on both ends, a crossbar and two supporting wooden nuts. Tapes, cords, or bands are stretched from the slotted baseboard, where they are secured by keys, to the crossbar, where they are attached to loops (laycords), or, in German models, to hooks.

The sewing frame was certainly in use in Northern Europe by the 12th century, and probably as early as the

SEWING FRAME

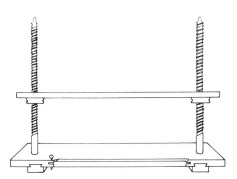

SEWING

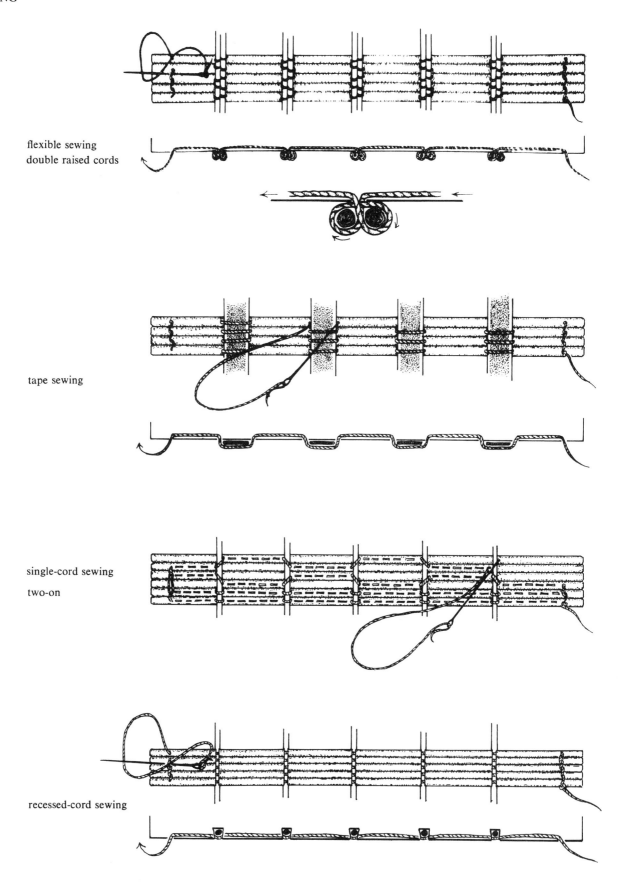

flexible sewing
double raised cords

tape sewing

single-cord sewing
two-on

recessed-cord sewing

11th, because in all likelihood the need for some type of frame became apparent as soon as flexible sewing was introduced. Also called "sewing bench," "sewing press," and "sewing rack." (161, 236)

sewing heart. A piece of card, roughly the shape of a heart, cut with a flap, and used to facilitate locating the center fold of a section when sewing a book TWO ON.

sewing in the round. A method of sewing the sections of a book on cords or tapes which utilizes a special sewing frame having a base which curves at the back, thus allowing the sections to form into a round as they are sewn to each other. Some frames of this type have a sliding block with a convex edge, against which the fore edges of the sections are placed, thus assisting in forming the round as the book is being sewn. Sewing in the round helps the sewn book to maintain its proper shape better than rounding after sewing because: 1) it does not have to be *put* into a rounded configuration after sewing, as it originated in the round; and 2) a book sewn with the correct amount of thread tension, and in the ordinary manner, will tend to have a concave shape to the spine when it comes off the sewing frame, which makes rounding even more difficult. In addition, a book rounded after sewing stands a greater chance of losing its round. The disadvantages of sewing in the round are: 1) the sewing takes longer (and is therefore more expensive); 2) a special or (adapted) sewing frame is required; and 3) several special convex blocks are needed to accommodate different thicknesses of books.

sewing key. *See:* KEY.

sewing machine. *See:* MACHINE SEWING.

sewing not to show. A method of sewing a book consisting of one section, which is sewn through the fold without the cover, the cover then being attached, thereby covering the sewing. *See also:* SEWING TO SHOW.

sewing on cords. *See:* FLEXIBLE SEWING; RECESSED-CORD SEWING.

sewing on tapes. *See:* TAPE SEWING (1).

sewing press (sewing rack). *See:* SEWING FRAME.

sewing stick. A length of wood, weighted at one end, and used to knock the sections of a book down as they are being sewn. *Cf:* BUNDLING (1). (65)

sewing thread. The filament or group of filaments used for securing the leaves or sections of a book. Book sewing threads include linen (with a glazed finish), cotton, nylon, terylene, and a combination of cotton and terylene. Sewing thread is available in a range of thicknesses, which are designated by number, e.g., 1 pound of flax spun to a length of 300 yards is Number 1; if spun to 600 yards, Number 2; 900 yards, Number 3; and so on. Number 16 is 4,800 yards. For example, 16–4, is made from four cords of Number 16. Number 50 is a strand of 15,000 yards, which, if doubled, becomes Number 50–2 thread.

Whether the thread is of one (knotted) continuous length, as in hand sewing through the folds, or consists of a number of individual threads, as in the usual machine sewing, it is a fundamental part of the make-up of a book. When consideration is given to the strain imposed on the sewing in the course of the normal handling of a book, especially a large volume, it is obvious that the thread used in sewing a book must be both strong and durable.

Sewing thread, whether for a publisher's binding or a book sewn by hand, is selected with regard to the thickness (and softness) of the paper, as well as the number of sections to be sewn. A thread that is too thin will not give sufficient swelling in the spine to enable the book to be properly rounded and backed, while thread that is too thick will produce a book that has too much swell, and that leads to difficulties in nipping and rounding and backing, as well as a tendency to produce creases in the inner margin.

Cotton thread is a fine continuous strand produced by plying two or more lengths of cotton strands with a tight twist and smooth finish. It is also made in varying thicknesses for various types of sewing. Although it is usually bleached, and bleaching is detrimental to the durability of thread, it is, and has been for more than 100 years, the most widely used thread for book sewing, especially in edition and library binding. The breaking strength of cotton thread commonly used in bookbinding is as follows:

Thread Size Number	Breaking Strength (in pounds)
50—4	2.5
36—4	3.4
24—4	4.4
12—4	8.5
10—4	11.0
10—5	14.0

One of the disadvantages of silk and terylene thread is their tendency to unravel and "catch-up" during sewing.

This can be overcome by soaking the thread in polyvinyl acetate, diluted to about three times its original volume with water, followed by drying of the thread in air under normal conditions. This cements the individual filaments together slightly, and also insures that the tension is shared equally among all of the filaments and not thrown onto only one, as might otherwise occur if one filament in a loose bundle is slightly shorter than the others. The use of PVA does not appear to have any adverse effect when the accelerated aging test is applied to the thread, although it naturally reduces the softness and flexibility of the thread to some degree. For the most part, these threads are used only in machine sewing.

Linen thread is produced from straw of the flax plant. *See:* LINEN. It is usually unbleached and is superior to cotton thread in both strength and durability. Thicknesses of threads used vary from Number 12, which is relatively thick, to Number 30, which is very fine and suitable for most books. At one time linen thread was used extensively in library binding, but it has largely been replaced by cotton, synthetics (principally nylon), and combinations of cotton and synthetic sewing threads.

Nylon thread maintains a smooth, knot-free surface and is stronger than thread made from either cotton or linen. It has the advantage of being relatively inexpensive and can be manufactured in finer grades so that books sewn with it can be more easily nipped, rounded, and backed, as the swell caused by the sewing is not excessive. Its principal disadvantages seem to be that it may cut the paper if the diameter of the thread is very small, and it has a tendency to contract upon release of tension, so that when a group of sewn books is cut apart the nylon thread tends to contract and loosen the end sections. (81, 92, 198, 259, 335, 339)

sewing to show. A method of sewing a book that consists of one section in which the cover is first placed over the section and is sewn with it, thus being visible on the outside. The three- or five-stitch method, using fancy thread or cord, is frequently used for this type of sewing. *Cf:* SEWING NOT TO SHOW. (335)

sewn regular. An obsolete library binding expression applied to the sewing of books through the folds, generally on tapes, as distinguished from oversewing. (129)

sexternion. A GATHERING (2) composed of six sheets, each folded once and insetted. This was the form in which some bound manuscripts and early printed books, especially those of vellum, were assembled. The first and twelfth, second and eleventh, etc., leaves being conjugate. *See also:* QUARTERNION; QUINTERNION; TERNION. (140)

shade. A term used in describing or comparing colors to indicate a full or definite degree of difference between two colors. A particular red, for example, may be a shade darker, lighter, deeper, more bluish, yellowish, etc., than another red. The term applies also to a chromatic color darkened by the addition of black. (233)

shade-craft watermark. A WATERMARK produced by means of a design on the dandy roll of the papermaking machine that is intaglio instead of in relief, thus thickening the sheet at the point of contact. It causes the watermark to appear darker than the rest of the sheet, rather than lighter, as is the case with the true watermark. The earliest shade-craft watermark (known as a "light-and-shade" watermark) was produced by the Frenchman Jannot in about 1812. His, of course, was not produced by a dandy roll. (17)

shaded tool. A finishing tool cut partly in outline and partly solid. (156)

shadow watermark. *See:* INTAGLIO (2).

shagreen. A somewhat obscure and ambiguous term which seems to have been used, at different times, for very different materials. The word, along with its French and German equivalents, *chagrin,* is said to have been derived from the Persian expression *sāgharī,* which applies to a leather produced from an ass, and which had an indented grain surface caused by spreading seeds of *Chenopodium* (goose foot) over the surface of the moist skin, covering the skin with a cloth, and trampling them into the skin. When the skin was dry the seeds were shaken off, leaving the surface of the leather covered with small indentations.

In the 17th and early 18th centuries, however, the term "shagreen" (or "chagrin") began to be applied to a leather made from sharkskin having a curious grain surface of lonzenge-shaped, raised and spiny scales of minute size, the character of which is difficult to perceive without optical assistance. The term was also applied to the skin of a rayfish (probably *Hypolophus sephen*), which is covered with round, closely set, calcified papillae resembling small pearls. In its natural form it has been used for many years in both the East and the West for a variety of purposes, including bookbinding; however, in the early years of the 18th century it became the practice to grind the surface flat and smooth, leaving only the pattern of small contiguous circles. The leather was dyed from the flesh side so that the dye did not reach the small circles of calcified substance but only colored the epidermis where it could be seen between the circles. This is the leather which for a century has been called "shagreen"; how confusion arose with sharkskin, which is completely different both in character and in appearance, is not clear. (97, 261, 351)

shake. A device on the wire of the Fourdrinier papermaking machine which causes the wire to oscillate in a plane at right angles to the forward movement of the wire. Its purpose is largely like that of the vatman's shake of the mold in hand papermaking, which assists in securing the desired intermingling of fibers of the sheet. The oscillations may be varied in frequency and length of stroke to obtain the required results. (17, 60)

shaken back. The loosening or breaking of the sewing of a book, particularly in edition binding, resulting in gaps appearing between the sections. Brittleness of the glue on the spine, inadequate spine lining, loose sewing, and careless use can, individually or collectively, lead to this condition. *See also:* START. (64)

shammy. *See:* CHAMOIS (2).

sharkskin. A leather covered with minute scales bearing short spines. It has been used frequently as an abrasive material and was popular during the 18th century for covering boxes of various types. For this latter purpose it was usually vegetable tanned, with the spiny scales being ground down leaving a slightly roughened surface which, under magnification, could be seen to be composed of tiny, detached, lozenge-shaped scales which sparkled. Sharkskin was usually stained black. *See also:* SHAGREEN. (291, 351, 363)

sharpening agent. A material added to the lime liquor to accelerate the loosening of the hair of hides and skins during LIMING. Sharpeners are usually one or more of the alkali sulfides, of which sodium sulfide is frequently used. (248, 306)

shave. 1. To take a very slight trim from the edges of a book. *See also:* SANDING (1); TRIMMING (1). 2. To pare or skive leather. The term is also applied to the areas of the leather covering of a book that have been pared or skived, usually the turn-ins and the area covering the spine. *See also:* PARING. (256)

shaved weight. The weight of a pack of leather taken after shaving or when its water content is approximately 50%. (363)

shaving. 1. *See:* PLOW. 2. The process of reducing the overall natural substance of a tanned hide by removing small pieces with a currier's knife (the sharp edge of which is at right angles to the blade), the blade being held at right angles to the flesh surface of the leather. The operation is performed over a special beam, one having a flatter surface than that of the beam used for other leather-making processes. The pieces shaved off are useless as leather and were sometimes boiled in water to make glue or gelatin sizing for paper. The purpose of shaving is to make the skins even in thickness, as well as to smooth and clean them. Virtually no hides and very few skins are shaved today, the process having been replaced by splitting. Any shaving that is still done is usually of light skins and is done by machine. (363)

shaving machine. A machine used to shave part or all of the flesh side of a tanned skin. The shaving cylinder consists of spiral blades set in a revolving cylinder. The portion of the skin to be shaved is fed between a bolstered backing roll and the shaving cylinder, with the flesh side facing the cylinder. The skin is forced against the revolving knife blades and moves forward until stopped by the operator. The same area can be fed into the machine repeatedly so as to reduce its thickness gradually. (363)

shaving tub. A receptacle used in hand binderies, located beneath the lying press and plow, into which the shavings fall from edges being trimmed. (152)

shea butter. The solid, grayish, yellowish or whitish fat obtained from the seeds of the shea tree, *Butyrospermum parkii,* and used for oiling leather during the process of tanning.

shearing strength. 1. The shear force required to produce failure in a paper or board. The shear force is the internal force causing two contiguous parts of a body to slide relative to each other in a direction parallel to their plane of contact. 2. The relative resistance of an adhesive film to a stress in such a manner that the adherend surfaces slide in a plane parallel to their plane of contact. (17, 222)

shears. 1. A hand-operated, single, curved cutting device for cutting single sheets of paper or light board. 2. A large pair of scissors used for cutting leather and cloth for covers. (183)

sheepskin. A soft, porous leather produced from the skins of wooled or hair sheep. It is usually vegetable-tanned and grained in imitation of other (more expensive) skins, e.g., morocco, a process to which it lends itself very well. The term "sheepskin" always indicates an unsplit skin, and is not applied to split sheepskin or SKIVER. Split sheepskin is the traditional material used in producing PARCHMENT.

Sheepskin is somewhat difficult to describe because the individual skins differ so greatly in size, fat content, and general quality of the dermal network. From the standpoint of leather, the closer a sheepskin approaches the hair sheep, the tighter and firmer the fiber network, and, therefore, the better the skin for producing leather. This is the case because the numerous fine wool fibers, as opposed to the lesser number of coarse fibers of the hair sheep, cause the skin to be more open and loose in texture. In addition, the wool follicles are associated with extensive glandular structures, consisting of sebaceous and sudoriferous glands, which also interrupt the dense packing of the connective-tissue fiber network in the papillary layers, as well as the dermis itself.

The grain layer of sheepskin occupies more than a half of the total thickness of the skin; furthermore, in the reticular layer, the collagen fibers are not as compact and run in more closely horizontal directions.

The proportion of adipose tissue to collagen fibers in sheepskin varies widely according to the feeding of the animal. There is frequently an almost continuous layer of fat cells separating the grain layer and the reticular layer. Because much of the fatty tissues is destroyed or removed in the liming, bating, and scudding operations, it is not unusual to find the grain layer and reticular layer of sheepskin leathers separated, sometimes over wide areas. The tanner at times separates these two layers by splitting after liming, and then tans the grain layer for bookbinding purposes, etc., and the reticular layer for chamois.

During the beamhouse operations, the glands in the grain layer are destroyed, leaving the grain layer rather spongy in structure. This, together with the relatively loose and empty structure of the reticular layer, places sheepskin leather in a class by itself.

Sheepskin is a reasonably durable leather if properly prepared and cared for. It has been used as a covering material for books for more than 500 years. *See also:* LAW SHEEP; ROAN; SKIVER; SMYRNA MOROCCO. (161, 207, 291, 306, 363)

sheepskin split. A sheepskin that has been split after liming but before tanning and finishing. *See also:* SKIVER.

sheep vellum. A term sometimes applied to VELLUM produced from the split skin of a sheep rather than the skin of a calf. (154)

sheet. 1. A single piece of paper, board, paper pulp, cellulose acetate film, etc. 2. The continuous web of paper as it is being manufactured by machine, or the single unit as it is being made by hand. 3. A general term applied to paper and/or board in any form and in any quantity which, when used with appropriate modifiers, indicates general or specific attributes of that sheet, including quality, class, use, grade, or physical properties, such as an opaque sheet, etc. 4. To cut paper or board into sheets of desired size from a roll or web. 5. A piece of paper printed in such a manner that it may be folded to form consecutive pages for publication of the required size. *See:* IMPOSITION. 6. To place freshly printed sheets between unprinted sheets for drying and to prevent OFFSET (2), i.e., to slipsheet. 7. As used in collation, a separate sheet of any size printed to be read unfolded, i.e., with the text or illustration imposed on a single page on one side or on each side of the paper. 8. A sheet of any material, such as a leaf of gold, silver, etc. 9. Another term for the surface or cover of the mold or dandy roll, but sometimes restricted to this before it is placed in position. (17, 264, 343)

sheeting. 1. The operation of cutting sheets from a web or roll of paper. A rotary cutter, which is somewhat similar to a web-fed cylinder press, with a steel cutting edge, is attached along the length of a cylinder, to which the web of paper is fed. At every revolution of the cylinder, the cutting edge cuts a sheet of paper off the roll. Several rolls may be fed to the cutter simultaneously, thus cutting multiple sheets.

Rotary cut paper is usually referred to as "machine trimmed" paper and the cut is sufficient for the requirements of most booklets, pamphlets, etc., that are to be printed "work and turn" and folded as a full sheet. *See:* IMPOSITION.

For printing that is done on a full sheet and then slit, however, "machine trimmed" paper will not always suffice. Broadsides, folders, labels and similar forms of printing that must be accurately trimmed require guillotine trimmed paper. Uncoated paper intended for such printing is usually ordered guillotine trimmed on at least two edges. Coated papers are guillotine trimmed as a regular practice. 2. The formation of a sheet on the papermaking machine. (17, 198, 350)

sheet stock. Unbound printed sheets of a publication which are inventoried by the printer until receipt of a binding order from the publisher. *See also:* SECONDARY BINDING. (156)

sheetwork. A term used in edition binding for the binding operations of folding, tipping, gathering, endsheeting, sewing, and smashing. *Cf:* FORWARDING. (101, 287)

shelfback. That part of a bound book seen when the book is on the shelf, i.e., the spine.

shelf life. *See:* STORAGE LIFE.

shell. A kidney-shaped section occurring in the butt area of an equine animal hide which contains the dense mass of fibers known as the glassy layer. The collagen fibers of this area are so dense (perhaps the most dense of any leather) that the leather made from it is nearly air-tight and weatherproof. It is isolated by removing the skin layer above and below it. The remaining part, the shell, is frequently split, both splits being finished on the cut surfaces. Although the butt area of the hide is extreme in its tightness and solidity of structure for a large hide, the remainder of the hide is extremely loose. The shell is used in producing CORDOVAN LEATHER. (363)

shellac. A resinous secretion of the insect, *Tachardia lacca,* which breeds on the twigs of certain Indian trees. It was originally used as a source of dyestuff, but is now used almost entirely for its content of resinous matter. Shellac has a softening temperature of 60 to 75° C., but decomposes if heated much above 100° C. It is soluble in alcohol, except for about 4% wax, which is insoluble in cold alcohol. It represents the most highly refined form of LAC and is prepared in the form of thin orange or yellow flakes. The term is also used with reference to the varnish prepared by dissolving shellac in alcohol. Shellac is used in the manufacture of leather, in lithography, in the preparation of finishing sizes, etc. *See also:* SHELLAC SIZE. (233, 235)

shellac size. A size prepared by dissolving shellac flakes in alcohol. It is used as an adhesive in gold tooling and blocking. After being painted into the blinded-in impressions on the leather, the alcohol evaporates, leaving a thin layer of shellac which serves the same purpose as GLAIR. (102)

shell gold. Gold leaf that has been reduced to powder form by grinding it with honey, which is then washed away. It is used to produce powdered effects on leather bindings, to repair or restore gold tooling, and for gilding manuscripts. Very early gold "tooling" of the Near East may have been shell gold, or something like it, painted on the leather. The name derives from the mussel shells it was once stored in. Today it is available in tablet form. *See also:* GOLD-POWDERED BINDINGS. (152, 236)

shingling. A technique used to prevent creep or push-out in a sewn or stitched pamphlet made up of a great number of folios of thick paper. The page sizes are selected with the idea of allowing sufficient material for variation in binding margins and outside margins whereby creep is counteracted. This means that the page (leaf) size diminishes from the outside folio moving inward. In some cases an adjustment is necessary in order to properly align page numbers for folding and trimming. (320)

shive. 1. A group of incompletely separated fibers. A shive is seen in the finished sheet as small dark specks or splinters. These are particularly prevalent in groundwood papers. In the case of esparto and straw pulp papers they often appear as transparent spots. 2. The non-bast fiber portion of the flax plant. (17)

shoder. The packet of 1,160 gold sheets interleaved between sheets of goldbeater's skin 4½ inches square. The "shoder" is the second beating stage in the the manufacture of GOLD LEAF, and is a more delicate stage than the CUTCH (1) but less so than the MOLD (2). *See also:* GOLD BEATING. (29)

shoes. Metal attachments fixed on the tail edges at the corners of the covers of large books, e.g., ledger books, to prevent abrasion of the leather, which may otherwise occur when the book is slid off the shelf. *See also:* BOSSES; ROLLER SHOES. (339)

short hair. A defect in leather stemming from a very fine, deeply embedded young (newly formed) hairs in a hide or skin, which are not removed by unhairing and scudding, and which are

carried throughout the leather manufacturing processes, appearing on the finished leather. Short hairs can actually enhance the appearance of a skin such as vellum. (291)

shortness. Said of an adhesive that does not string, cotton, or in other manner form filaments or threads when applied to an adherend. (309)

shorts (short copy; short set). 1. The copies of different printed sheets required to complete an imperfect or incomplete edition. *See also:* CANCEL (1). 2. A copy of a book having margin greatly trimmed by the binder. *See also:* CROPPED (1, 2). 3. A multivolume work that lacks one or more volumes. (69, 156)

shoulder(s). 1. That part of the spine of a text block at the outer extremities which is bent over in the backing process to form the projection at right angles to the text block to accommodate the board. 2. The portion of a cowhide covering the shoulders and neck of the animal together with the two cheeks, and the leather produced therefrom. A squared shoulder is obtained by cutting off the cheeks. Shoulders usually provide good, firm leather; however, that part of the hide is prone to growth marks and creases which cannot be entirely eliminated during manufacture. 3. The top of the shank of a piece of movable type. Its parts include the bevel, beard, line, and side bearing. 4. A term sometimes applied to the upper, outer corners of a leaf of a book. (151, 161, 313)

show side. The side of a paper, cloth, etc., which will be seen, i.e., will show, when the binding or other operation is completed. The term is used especially with reference to book cloths, which are generally finished only on the one side. (140)

show through. Printed matter which can be seen from the other side of a leaf when viewed by reflected light. It is caused by excessive ink penetration, insufficient opacity of the paper, or excessive pressure during printing. Show through may be particularly noticeable if the printer has failed to achieve proper REGISTER (3). *See also:* STRIKE IN; STRIKE THROUGH. (17, 316)

shrinkage. 1. The decrease in the width of a paper web as it travels through the papermaking machine. The degree of shrinkage varies, depending upon the weight of the paper, and the degree to which the pulp is refined, the nature of the fibrous material used, and the tension in the wet driers. 2. Any de-

crease in the dimensions of paper, leather, etc. *See also:* YIELD. (17)

shrink temperature. The water temperature at which a specimen of leather begins to shrink. Shrink temperature will differ for each kind and degree of tannage, although, in general, tannage usually increases the resistance of a leather to heat in the wet condition. Most chrome-tanned leathers are resistant to the action of boiling water, while vegetable-tanned leathers are not. If leather that cannot withstand the boiling test is placed in cold water and the temperature of the water is gradually increased one degree at a time, a point will be reached where the leather suddenly begins to shrink, which is the "shrink temperature." Shrink temperature is generally taken as a measure of the degree of tannage of a leather. (291, 363)

shut. 1. An expression used by the vatman when the liquid pulp in the mold is formed into a uniform sheet of handmade paper. "Shut" also takes place on the papermaking machine, assisted by the action of the suction boxes and dandy roll. It is the point at which fiber movement within the web ceases. (197, 335)

shuttle mark. A fine line parallel to the filling in a cloth, caused by damage in the shuttle to a group of filling yarns.

shuttle threads. The threads in the OVERSEWING method which pass through each loop created by the needles of the machine. Punches descend from above, penetrate the paper, and then withdraw. The needles then enter from below and, when they reach the top of the pile of leaves making up the "section," they drop slightly leaving a series of loops of thread through which the shuttle needles carry their thread from left and right, meeting in the center. As they reach the center, two catch teeth emerge and snag the threads, holding them until the shuttles retract. The cycle is then completed and the head of the machine drops, tightening the loops around the shuttle threads. It is, therefore, the shuttle threads which secure the individual oversewing stitches in the "section."

side. 1. The outside surface of the upper or lower cover of a bound book. 2. The paper, cloth, or other material used on the sides of a book. 3. The half of a cowhide, either in full weight or as a split. Cowhides are frequently cut in half down the backbone for ease of handling, so that they may be hung in the tanning pits without being folded, etc. 4. The left- or right-hand of a piece of movable type when the printing surface is uppermost and facing the viewer. The front is the belly and rear the back. (102, 156, 363)

side cut. An obsolete term applied to the cutting or trimming of the fore edge (only) of a book. (256)

side papers. The paper sides of a quarter, half, or three-quarter binding. (302)

side sewing. A method of securing the leaves of sections of a book with thread near the binding edge, from front to back through the entire thickness of the text block. When a book is said to be side sewn, it is implied that the text block does not consist of individual sections which are first fastened by themselves and then to each other, but that all of the leaves are sewn through at one time. Side sewing is an extremely strong form of sewing; however, it affords very little openability, unless the inner margin is very extensive, the paper is very flexible, e.g., JAPANESE SEWING, or the book is very large, e.g., an unabridged dictionary. Also called "stab sewing." Cf: SIDE STITCH-ING. (92, 183, 320, 339)

side stitching. A method of securing the leaves or sections of a book with wire staples or sections of a book with wire the thickness of the text block. Side stitching is one of the strongest forms of construction and is frequently used in binding textbooks; it is also a common method of binding periodical issues made up of leaves or more than one section, and which, therefore, cannot be saddle stitched. The stitching is done by means of a machine that cuts the wire, forms it into a staple, drives it through the paper, and clinches it from the other side. Flat-wire staples of galvanized iron or aluminized iron are usually employed. Flat staples are used to provide flatter surface on the side of the publication than could be obtained with round staples.

The disadvantage of side stitching is that it affords almost no openability in the book; consequently the publication must be designed with wider margins and more flexible paper in order to compensate for the lack of flexibility. Also called "stab stitching." Cf: SIDE SEWING. (179, 316, 339)

side title. A title lettered or blocked on the side, i.e., the upper cover of a book. (156)

siding. 1. See: SIDE (2). 2. The process of siding-up, or attaching, the paper sides to quarter, half, or three-quarter bindings. See also: FILLING IN (1). (92, 236)

sifted chalk. A finely powdered chalk

used in removing excess grease from skins in process of being converted into PARCHMENT. (130)

sighting. The procedure of observing where the finishing tool is to be impressed or "struck." Sighting is usually done over the top of the shank of the tool. It is not an uncommon practice to file a notch in the top edge of the shank to give a better view of the letter or ornament.

signature. 1. A section or GATHERING (2) of a book, either in the flat or folded state, to which a SIGNATURE MARK has been assigned. Technically, the sets of 4, 8, 16, 32, 64, or 128 printed pages, when folded, constitute a "section," while a "signature" is only the sequential mark of identification printed on the initial page of the section; today, however, little if any distinction is made between the two expressions. The term is not altogether synonymous with SHEET (5), because a sheet as printed may contain more than one section (see: FOLDING), and, in the case of a half sheet, may constitute a section of fewer pages than others in the same publication. Thus books consist of many sections but those sections may not consist of the same number of leaves. 2. The name or initials, written in a person's own hand, for the purpose of authenticating a document. (69, 140, 189, 287)

signature and catchword line. The line of type in an old book which bears both the signature and the CATCHWORD. It is usually located below the lowest line of the text. If the signature and catchword are on separate lines, the lower is called the DIRECTION LINE. (156)

signature mark. The letter or number, or the combination of letters and numbers, printed at the foot of the first page (and sometimes on subsequent leaves of a section) as a guide to the bookbinder in the process of gathering. Signature marks were written or stamped in until 1472, when Johann Koeloff of Cologne printed a signature as the last line of a text page. The binders of manuscripts usually cut off the signature letters.

Each section has a different signature, and when letters are used for identification, as is the usual practice, they progress in alphabetical order, with J, V, and W usually omitted to avoid confusion, although their exclusion does have an historical basis, in that manuscripts and early printed books were usually in Latin, in which I stands for both I and J, V for both U and V, and there is no W.

When all designated letters of the

alphabet have been used, a lower case sequence or a new sequence of double letters followed by triple letters, or sequences combining capital and lower case letters are used, e.g., AA, BB, Aa, Bb, 2A, 2B, etc. If the same sequence is used again, it is known as duplicated or triplicated signatures.

The preliminary leaves are sometimes not signed, in which case the text may begin with section B; however, the preliminaries are sometimes assigned a lower case letter or letters and are occasionally signed with an asterisk (*) or similar symbol. The title leaf is almost never signed (especially in 16th and 17th century English publications). In the United States, when they are used at all, which today is very infrequently, printers have tended to use all the letters of the alphabet.

When the quire includes additional sheets or a portion of a sheet (inset), these are also signed to indicate how they are to be folded and inserted. Also called "signature" (1). See also: COL-LATION (1); DESIGNATION MARK; VOL-UME SIGNATURE. (140, 278)

signed bindings. Bookbindings signed by the binder. Several forms of "signatures" have been used over the years, including: 1) the initials, cypher, or name of the binder tooled in blind on the outer surface of one of the covers, either by means of a tool or with a roll; 2) BINDER'S TICKET; 3) a stamped name, mainly on the inside edge of the lower cover, but also at the tail of the spine, inside the upper cover, on the inside of the front hinge, and, in modern times, in ink at the edge of one of the flyleaves; 4) a note inserted in the book by the owner; and 5) sometimes external evidence, such as a description of the work done, as with Roger Payne, or correspondence; or a famous style—Edgar Mansfield, Paul Bonet, etc. (69)

signet. A type of REGISTER (1), consisting of a silk ribbon, often lavishly ornamented with precious stones, and used frequently by French bookbinders of the 16th century. (140)

sig water. An alkaline solution of soda ash, borax or ammonia, used to wash the grain surface of leather preparatory to the application of dye solutions. Formerly, sig water was a solution of stale urine. (363)

silica. A powdered quartz prepared in several degrees of fineness. It is inert, has a sharp grain, and is used to impart tooth to coating materials. (233)

silica gel. A colloidal form of silica, available in the form of pale amber colored, highly absorbent granules, and used as a dehumidifier. It is generally kept in small cloth bags near objects on display or in storage that are prone to cockling or other damage. By absorbing moisture from the atmosphere, silica gel helps prevent formation of mold, softening of water-soluble coatings, cockling, warping, etc. When saturated, it can be dried by heating. Sometimes color-coded particles are added which change color when the gel has become saturated. It is also available in an air-floated, extremely fine powder form that is useful for adding slip resistance to coating, and dulling effects to varnish and similar finishes.

silk. The elastic, hygroscopic protein fiber produced by the larvae of many species of moth of the natural order *Lepidoptera,* the most important of these being the *Bombyx* moths, and especially *Bombyx mori* (the silkworm or mulberry worm). Raw silk threads consist principally of sericin and fibroin, which are proteins containing carbon, nitrogen, hydrogen, and oxygen but not sulfur. Silk is widely used in spinning thread and weaving fabrics, and is used in bookbinding for sewing, for doublures, for covering books (generally embroidered bindings), and in the repair of torn leaves, etc. Silk as a covering material is somewhat extravagant, particularly since books covered with it usually must have boxes to protect them, as it does not wear well and is particularly susceptible to deterioration in natural light. Silk used for doublures, however, is protected from the deteriorative effects of light and air and often out-lasts the covers. *See also:* JAPANESE SILK; MOIRÉ BOOK CLOTH; SEWING THREAD; SILK GAUZE; SILKING; SILK-SCREEN PRINTING; SILK-SCREEN PRINTS; WATERED SILK. (81, 143, 280, 335)

silk cord (silk floss). Braided and twisted strands of silk used for tying or sewing booklets, brochures, pamphlets, etc. (256)

silk flyleaves. The free flyleaves and board paper of an endpaper assembly made of silk. While very attractive, the use of silk for flyleaves causes problems because it tends to fray at the edges and must, therefore, be turned in. Since this can only be done after the book is trimmed, they must be attached as one of the last operations. This problem can largely be overcome, however, by the use of JAPANESE SILK, which has less tendency than ordinary silk to fray. Silk flyleaves are fre-

quently used in conjunction with leather joints. *See also:* DOUBLURE (1); DRUMMING ON. (343)

silk gauze. A very thin, transparent, strong, finely meshed silk cloth, which is used in archival work for reinforcing paper and other materials. Pure silk is one of the strongest materials available for reinforcing paper, and is almost invisible when properly applied. It is stronger than either Japanese copying paper or lens tissue, but its permanence is much less than that of a high quality paper because it tends to deteriorate relatively quickly, especially if exposed to natural light. Deterioration proceeds even more quickly if the adhesive used to attach the silk contains alum as a preservative. The use of silk gauze in archival work has declined over the years in favor of various cellulose products, e.g., CELLULOSE ACETATE. (237)

silking. The process of applying a thin, transparent, finely meshed silk cloth to one or both sides of a leaf as a means of repairing or preserving it. A leaf so treated is said to have been "silked." In general, the process may be said to be reversible. *See also:* SILK.

silk pattern. A book cloth embossed with small diagonal lines, imparting an appearance of silk. (264)

silk-screen printing. Essentially a stencil process used to duplicate original designs, largely in situations where the run is too short to justify the expense of lithography. A fine mesh material, such as phosphor bronze, steel gauze, bolting silk, etc., is used in the process. The design is cut in a stencil (or the areas not be reproduced are painted out on the screen itself) which is secured to the underside of the screen. Ink, paint, or another material is then forced through the screen onto paper, glass, or another material. (17, 146)

silk-screen prints. Decorative end- and cover papers produced by the same principle as the stencil print, except that the paint is forced through a cloth, producing a printing quality. Paint used for these papers can be made from a mixture of frothed wallpaper or wheat paste and water, to which poster or powder paint has been added. It should be the consistency of whipped cream, but thin enough to flow freely and not clog the screen. Silk-screen paint may also be used. The less pigment used the more transparent the color will be. (183)

silk sewn. An expression sometimes applied to books sewn with silk thread. At one time it was common to indi-

cate Bibles and prayer books sewn with silk by means of a tiny gold stamp "silk sewn" on the inside of the upper cover. (256)

silk stitch. A style of sewing at one time used extensively for sewing booklets of a superior quality in lieu of wire stitching. (256)

silk thread. *See:* SEWING THREAD.

silvered. A term used to describe a book whose edge or edges have been covered with silver leaf instead of gold. (156)

silverfish. A small wingless, silvery insect, of the order *Thysanura,* and especially *Lepisma saccharina,* which flourishes in a damp environment, feeding on the glazed surfaces of photographs, and the starchy content of paper, board, and paste. It has done extensive damage to book collections in the past. It can be controlled by the use of proper fumigants, such as ethylene oxide, methyl bromide, hydrogen cyanide, etc.; however, as the use of these chemicals can be dangerous, a better procedure is to create a cool, dry environment which the insects cannot tolerate. *See also:* BOOKWORMS.

silver leaf. A thin sheet of silver (Ag) metal used in lieu of gold leaf for tooling books. Because silver is somewhat less malleable than gold, silver leaf is usually about three times as thick as gold leaf and is, therefore, easier to handle. Unlike gold, however, it requires lacquering or varnishing to prevent tarnishing. Because of this, palladium or platinum leaf is often used instead of silver when a silvery effect is desired.

Silver was used in the very early days of tooling with metal, and its use in England has been recorded as early as 1550. Silver paint was used occasionally in the 17th century, although the silver was not painted into blind impressions to simulate tooling, but was used to supplement the tooled areas so as to provide a more solid effect of the tooling. (83, 236)

Singer sewing. A method of side- or fold sewing pamphlets, periodicals issues, textbooks, etc., with thread. Despite the fact that the term implies the use of a particular machine, it has come to be more-or-less a generic term for sewing of publications which ordinarily would be stitched. Pamphlets are generally Singer sewn through the fold, while multi-section journals and books, especially textbooks, are sewn through the side. The machine used for this sewing utilizes a single needle and can side sew books up to 1½ inches in thickness with stitches up to one inch in length. A high-speed drill is located in front of the needle and they are raised and lowered simultaneously. The drill produces a hole in the sheets and is then withdrawn. The book is then moved forward for the length of the stitch desired and the threaded needle enters the hole while the next hole is being drilled for the succeeding stitch. *See also:* SIDE STITCHING. (179, 234)

single coated paper. A paper which has received but one application of coating, either on one or both sides. The term does not indicate a paper coated only on one side, which is a paper properly termed "coated one side." (17)

single-section book. A book, pamphlet, etc., consisting of one folded section. Most periodical issues are single-section publications. (335)

single-shear stroke. A paper cutting machine which utilizes a knife that moves with a sidewise motion at the same time that it descends. Because its edge is always parallel to the top of the table, the single-shear knife cuts the entire width of each sheet at the same time all the way down through the pile. *Cf:* DOUBLE-SHEAR STROKE. (145)

single spread. The process of applying an adhesive to only one adherend of an assembly. *See also:* DOUBLE SPREAD (2). (309)

singleton. A vague expression used with reference to a single leaf, especially where a conjugate pair is normal in a gathering. This single leaf will be the leaf remaining after the other has been removed, the removed leaf itself in a new location, or an additional leaf printed for insertion. (69)

sisal (sisal hemp). A West Indian plant, *Agave sisalana,* or *A. rigida,* whose leaves yield a fiber used in making hard fiber cordage. Some of it is used in rope papers obtained from cordage waste. Also called "sisal hemp." (17)

six on. A rarely used technique of sewing a book on raised cords, the number of cords being the same in number as the sections to be sewn with a single length of thread. Because each of the sections is sewn to only one of the six cords does not mean that the method is unduly weak, because when all six sections are sewn they are pierced and fastened together at head and tail. (236)

sixteenmo. A book size produced by folding a sheet with four right angle folds, giving a leaf size 1/16 the size of the sheet and forming a section of 32

pages. For a full definition, the size of the sheet must also be given. A sheet 25 by 38 inches produces a book size (untrimmed) of 6½ by 9½ inches. Written as 16mo or 16°. Also called "sextodecimo."

sixty-fourmo. A book size produced by folding a sheet with six right angle folds, giving a leaf size 1/64 the size of the sheet and forming a section of 128 pages. As it is both difficult and impractical to fold a sheet with six right angle folds, the 64mo is generally composed of a sheet folded with both parallel and right angle folds, or by using more than one sheet of paper and insetting. Written as 64mo or 64°.

size. 1. The dimensions of a book as measured by its height. Size is usually given in centimeters (or inches), or, in the case of miniatures and fine bindings, in millimeters. The fold symbol, e.g., f°, 4°, 8°, etc., is used as an indication of approximate size. A book is said to be "narrow" if its width is less than three-fifths of its height, "square" if more than three-fourths, and "oblong" or "landscape" if the width of the cover is greater than the height. The width of a book is generally given only when unusual, or for old books, fine bindings, and in restoration work. When both are given, height is given first. In describing fine bindings it is not unusual for the thickness to be given also. *See also:* BOOK SIZES; FOLDINGS; SIZES OF PAPER. 2. A glutinous substance prepared by boiling the hides and bones of animals. It is sometimes used for sizing paper. *See:* GELATIN; GLUE. 3. Any material used in the internal sizing or surface sizing of paper or board. Typical sizing agents include rosin, gelatin, glue, starch, modified celluloses, synthetic resins, latices, soluble nylon, waxes, etc. 4. A material, such as GUM TRAGACANTH, boiled in water and used as a base (size) to support marbling colors. *See also:* ALBUMEN; EGG ALBUMEN; GLAIR; LETTERING SIZE; SIZING. (82, 139, 259)

sizes of paper. The common or standard sheet sizes of paper. They are:

in the United States (in inches)
Bible: 25 x 38, 28 x 42, 28 x 44, 32 x 44, 35 x 45 and 38 x 50;
Blotting: 19 x 24 and 24 x 38;
Bond (wood pulp and cotton content): 8½ x 11, 8½ x 13, 8½ x 14, 10 x 14, 11 x 17, 17 x 22, 17 x 28, 17½ x 22½, 19 x 24. 20 x 28, 22 x 25½, 22 x 34, 22½ x 35, 23 x 29, 24 x 38, 28 x 34, 34 x 44, and 35 x 45;

Book (uncoated): 17½ x 22½, 19 x 25, 22½ x 35, 23 x 29, 23 x 35, 25 x 38, 28 x 42, 28 x 44, 32 x 44, 35 x 45 and 38 x 50;
Book (coated two sides): 22½ x 35, 24 x 36, 25 x 38, 26 x 40, 28 x 42, 28 x 44, 32 x 44, 35 x 45, 36 x 48 and 38 x 50;
Cover (wood pulp and cotton content): 20 x 26, 23 x 29, 23 x 35, 26 x 40 and 35 x 46;
Document manila: 22½ x 28½ and 24 x 36;
Glassine: 24 x 36, 25 x 40 and 30 x 40;
Index bristol (woodpulp and cotton content): 20½ x 24¾, 22½ x 28½, 22½ x 35, 25½ x 30½ and 35 x 45;
Label (coated one-side book): 20 x 26, 25 x 38, 26 x 40, 28 x 42, 28 x 44, 32 x 44, 35 x 45, 36 x 48, 38 x 50 and 41 x 54;
Ledger (wood pulp and cotton content): 17 x 22, 17 x 28, 19 x 24, 22 x 34, 22½ x 22½, 22½ x 34½, 24 x 38, 24½ x 24½ and 28 x 34;
Litho label (coated one side): 25 x 38, 28 x 42, 28 x 44, 32 x 44, 35 x 45, 36 x 48, 38 x 50 and 41 x 54;
Manifold: 17 x 22, 17 x 26, 17 x 28, 19 x 24, 21 x 32, 22 x 34, 24 x 38, 26 x 34 and 28 x 34;
Manuscript cover: 18 x 31;
Newsprint: 21 x 32, 22 x 24, 24 x 36, 25 x 38, 28 x 34, 28 x 42, 34 x 44, 36 x 48 and 38 x 50;
Offset book (uncoated): 17½ x 22½, 22½ x 35, 25 x 38, 28 x 42, 32 x 44, 35 x 45, 36 x 48, 38 x 50, 38 x 52 and 41 x 54;
Offset book (coated): 22 x 29, 22½ x 35, 25 x 38, 28 x 42, 28 x 44, 32 x 44, 35 x 45 and 38 x 50;
Photomount board: 23 x 29
Rotogravure: 25 x 38, 28 x 42, 28 x 44, 32 x 44, 35 x 45 and 38 x 40;
Text: 23 x 29, 23 x 35, 25 x 38, 26 x 40, 35 x 45, and 38 x 50;
Writing: 17 x 22, 17 x 28, 19 x 24, 22 x 34, 24 x 38 and 28 x 34.

in Great Britain (in inches)

Foolscap	13½ x 17
Foolscap, oblong double	13½ x 34
Pinched post	14½ x 18½
Crown	15 x 20
Post	15¼ x 19
Large post	16½ x 21
Foolscap, double	17 x 27
Demy	17½ x 22½

Medium	18 x 23
Post, double	19 x 30½
Royal	20 x 25
Crown, double	20 x 30
Large post, double	21 x 33
Imperial	22 x 30
Demy, double	22½ x 35
Medium, double	23 x 36
Royal, double	25 x 40
Foolscap, quad	27 x 34
Crown, quad	30 x 40
Imperial, double	30 x 44
Demy, quad	35 x 45
Medium, quad	36 x 46
Crown, double quad	40 x 60

(17, 52, 140, 316)

sizing. 1. A property of a material stemming from an alteration of its surface characteristics, which, in the case of paper, pertains to fiber characteristics. In so far as internal sizing of paper is concerned, it is a measure of the resistance of the paper to the penetration of water and/or various liquids, e.g., ink; while in terms of surface sizing, it refers to the increase of properties such as water and abrasion resistance, abrasiveness, creasibility, finish, printability, smoothness, and surface bonding strength, as well as a decrease of porosity and surface fuzz. 2. The process of adding materials to a papermaking furnish or the application of materials to the surface of a paper or board to provide resistance to the penetration of liquids and, in the case of surface sizing, to affect one or more of the properties listed under 1. Traditionally, papers are BEATER SIZED, SURFACE SIZED and TUB SIZED.

Papers are generally classified into three groups according to sizing; unsized, weak-sized, and strong-sized. Unsized papers are WATERLEAF (1); weak-sized papers are SLACK SIZED; and strong-sized papers are HARD SIZED. Blotting paper is an example of waterleaf, while sized newsprint is slack sized, and bond paper is hard sized.

Rosin sizing is the principal size used for machine-made papers, while gelatin is often used for handmade papers. 3. The application of a sizing material, e.g., albumen, to the edges of a book before laying on the gold leaf. 4. The process of applying size (glair) to the covers of a book or directly into the blind impressions before tooling in gold. 5. The process of sorting books similar in size into batches for treatment. (17, 52, 62, 67, 161, 309, 320, 350)

skeleton guard book. A type of guard book consisting entirely of guards, and meant to contain photographs, clippings, etc. (274)

skeleton marked. An unevenness in leather produced from an underfed animal, especially in those areas of the skin that covered bony structures, such as the ribs. (363)

skewings. Waste gold leaf generated in the process of blocking and sent to the refinery for recovery. *See also:* GOLD RUBBER; RUBBING-OFF CHEST. (140)

skimming. The process of removing film from the surface of marbling size. The film results from evaporation and must be removed before the colors are placed on the size, otherwise they will not expand properly. It must be done quickly and the colors dropped on immediately so as to prevent another film from forming. Skimming may be done with a skimmer, a device attached to the marbling trough, and which is raised and lowered on both ends, according to the quantity of size in the trough. The rubber blade which skins the size allows for a clean skim, and, being supported on the rim of the trough, assures an even and quick pull which does not disturb the size. (264)

skin. 1. The raw integument of a mature, fully grown animal of the smaller type, e.g., goatskin, sheepskin, pigskin, etc.; or the covering of an immature animal of the larger type, e.g., calfskin. The term also applies to a small hide; among cattle hides, for example, it would include one weighing less than 15 pounds in the green salted state. For a description of the physiology of the integument, *see:* LEATHER. 2. The leather produced from such a material which has not been split. *See also:* BASIL; ROAN. 3. The covering of a fur-bearing animal, dressed and finished with the fur on, i.e., a PELT. 4. A high, hard finish on paper or board. 5. An expression sometimes used to indicate the tearing of paper, with reference to the fact that when paper is torn the fibers are not broken but pulled apart, i.e., the paper "skins" better when torn along the length of the MACHINE DIRECTION rather than across it. (17, 26, 363)

skin dresser. An obsolete term for the workman who shaved or pared leather. (241)

skinned. 1. A pasted or glued surface on which the adhesive has been equalized by being rubbed over through another sheet of paper. 2. An adhesive which has been allowed to stand too long allowing the surface to partially dry and form a non-tacky "skin." (309)

skipped coating. A defect in a coated paper caused by failure of the coating machine and seen as areas on the web or sheet that are not coated. (17)

skirt (skirt leather). *See:* RUSSET.

skive (skiving). The process of cutting leather more-or-less horizontally for the purpose of thinning it for a particular end use. When performed by hand it is done with a PARING KNIFE or SPOKESHAVE. *See also:* SHAVING (2); SKIVER.

skiver (skiver label). The outer grain split of a sheep-, lamb-, or (occasionally) goatskin, vegetable-tanned, and usually from 0.25 to 1.0 mm thick. Skivers are finished in a wide variety of colors and embossed grains, as well as with a plain, smooth surface. At one time skiver was used very extensively for labels of many kinds of bindings, e.g., the red and black labels of law books. *See also:* FLESHER. (164, 343, 363)

slack sized. A lightly sized, somewhat absorbent sheet of paper. Slack sized also refers to below standard degree of water resistance. Newsprint is an example of a slack-sized paper. *See also:* HARD SIZED; SIZING; WATERLEAF. (17)

slack tanned. A hide or skin which has undergone an insufficient degree of tannage—i.e., less than that necessary to produce the desired characteristics in the leather. (363)

slicker. A blunt blade of brass, steel, glass, or plastic, used for the more delicate procedure in SETTING OUT, i.e., SLICKING. The slicker is also used to work DUBBIN into a skin. (306)

slicking (slicked). The process of SETTING OUT very thin, delicate leathers and/or those with very high requirements of smoothness of grain surface. The operation is done by means of a SLICKER and its primary purpose is to remove water and stretch the leather, thus making it perfectly flat and smooth. The slicker is applied with considerable pressure to the flesh side of the skin (called "setting on the flesh") and then lightly on the grain side (called "setting on the grain") to remove any final slight irregularities. 2. The process of smoothing and removing residual hair from a skin that is being stretched and dried in the process of making PARCHMENT or vellum. (306, 363)

sliding knife. A PLOW knife that slides along in a dovetail groove. Any length of the sliding knife may be exposed for cutting, unlike the BOLT KNIFE, which, being attached to the shoe of the plow is unavoidably a fixture and must be worn down by cutting before it will trim accurately. The sliding knife was invented toward the end of the 19th century and rapidly superseded the bolt knife. Also called "Scotch knife." (236, 371)

slip. 1. A fluid or semi-solid mixture of a pigment, such as clay and water. 2. Any printed leaf considerably smaller than the leaf of the book to which it is attached or inserted into, including errata sheets, a CANCEL (1) notice, and the like. Also called "slip cancel." 3. The ease with which papers or boards slide over one another. Too much "slip" is undesirable in paper because it then becomes more difficult to stack, whereas too little is also undesirable because it makes the material too difficult to sort and handle. (69, 222)

slipcase. A more-or-less elaborate box made to order for a specific book, or other archival material, and used for protection. The simplest form of the slipcase is a cloth- or paper-covered box with one open edge into which the book is slipped with its spine exposed. The addition of a cloth dust wrapper or chemise affords additional protection; however, since the spine is then covered, the title must either be blocked directly on the closed edge of the box or a label must be attached to the chemise. The substitution of an inner box for the chemise is a further elaboration. The inner box is usually made of chipboard covered with cloth, and frequently it is lined with felt or a felt substitute to protect the contents against friction within the inner box. A cloth tab may be attached as a means of pulling the inner box from the case, or the sides of the case may be thumb-notched to permit grasping of the inner box. Simple slipcases, which have no inner box or chemise, should not be notched as this places considerable strain on the joints of the book when it is removed and also causes soiling of the covering material.

The outer case may be improved in appearance by rounding the closed edge to give the appearance of the spine of a book, but this is seldom done, except for very valuable books. The booklike appearance may be further enhanced by attaching false bands to the closed edge to give the effect of sewing on raised bands, and by covering the case with a leather spine and cloth sides.

A slipcase should fit the book it protects. The inner box, if any, other-wise the case itself, should hold the book snugly so that it cannot move and rub against the board, which in turn should provide a sliding fit in the case. But the case (or box) should not be so tight that the book must be pulled from it, nor so loose that the book will fall out. *See also:* PULL-OFF BOX. (81, 173, 339)

slippage. A physical property of an adhesive manifest in the ability to move or reposition the adherends, such as the movement of the leather when covering a book.

slips. 1. The free end of the cords, thongs, or tapes on which a book has been sewn, that are used to attach the boards (or case) to the next block. Tapes may be glued to the inside surface of the boards, or they may be glued into boards that have been split horizontally (or between two boards glued together); this is "split-board binding," that was at one time the traditional method for library binding. In library binding today, when tapes are used, the slips are glued to the overhanging spine lining cloth and both are then glued to the insides of the boards of the case. *See also:* SPLIT BOARDS. When cords or thongs are used, as in craft binding, they are strung through holes punched in the boards, in which case they are said to be "laced-in." *See also:* HOLING OUT; LACING-IN. 2. A term sometimes applied to the paper forms used in writing instructions to the binder. 3. Matter not set up into pages, but pulled as proofs, on long slips of paper called galley proofs. *See also:* PROOF (2). (156, 236, 335)

slipsheet (interleaf). The paper or other material inserted between printed sheets in order to avoid offsetting an image on one sheet onto the back of the next sheet. In terms of the preparation of copy, "slipsheet" means to insert pages into proper sequence to indicate the placement of illustrations that have not yet been prepared. Each page, or slipsheet, identifies its particular illustration, along with information as to whether the illustration is line or halftone, foldout or horizontal, as well as the size, the negative or art file number, the figure number and titles, and any other information that might serve to key illustration to its proper page for printing or collating. *See also:* BARRIER SHEET. (17, 156)

slitting. The operation of cutting a fold or BOLT by hand for the purpose of inserting a map, plate, etc., within the section at a place other than the center. *See also:* BONE CUTTING. (339)

slunk. The skin of an unborn or prematurely born animal. The term is applied particularly to calves, from which the very finest grade of PARCHMENT is produced. Slunks are also used in making SUEDE LEATHER, and the smaller the fibers, the finer the nap that can be produced. The skins of unborn or prematurely born animals have skins with very fine fibers and a much less highly developed vascular network. (363)

small paper copy (small paper edition). A copy, or edition of a book printed on paper of a smaller size than that of a LARGE PAPER COPY. The paper, however, is usually the *normal* size for the edition and therefore perhaps should be called "plain paper copy," or not be given a designation at all.

smalt. A potassium cobalt silicate glass of a deep blue color. It is pulverized under water for use as a coloring material in papermaking. It consists of 50 to 70% silica, 12 to 22% potassium oxide, and 6 to 16% cobalt oxide, and is prepared by fuzing crude cobalt oxide (called "zaffre") with silica and potassium carbonate. It must be pure; otherwise its color is adversely affected. It is usually used as a loading agent, and because of its resistance to acids, alkalis, heat, and moisture, its fastness is excellent; however, because of its relatively low coloring power it is expensive to use, and is, therefore, used mainly for the more costly hand-made and better machine-made azures used for writing papers. Its high specific gravity usually causes it to sink through the pulp and color one side (the wire side) more than the other. At one time the term "smalt" was used to describe the vitrified pigment used for painting on glass and was not necessarily limited to blue. (156, 197)

smash. A relatively large hole in a fabric characterized by many broken warp ends and floating picks. (341)

smashing. The operation of reducing the bulk of the entire text block, as opposed to NIPPING (1). Smashing compacts and consolidates the text block, driving the air from between the leaves. Smashing is particularly important in edition binding because it is essential that the books be of uniform thickness so that the machines, e.g., rounding and backing, casing-in, etc., can be set up just once for the entire run of the edition. (182, 320)

smashing machine. A vertical press that is used to apply enormous pressure to material. Smashers are often provided with automatic conveyer belts, the books being piled at one end of the press on the belt in equal numbers in several piles and automatically conveyed under the smasher head. There the books are smashed either once or twice, as required, and then moved out of the press by the same conveyer, from which they are removed manually. The smasher remains for a pre-set time in its compressed position (DWELL TIME). It has no clamp to prevent the slippage of sections and can therefore be used to smash only those books that have so little swell in the spine that they will not RUN IN, otherwise they must first be nipped. *See:* NIPPING PRESS. At times it is possible to smash books with considerable swell by feeding them in pairs of two with the spines alternating and the fore edges projecting beyond the spines. *See also:* BUNDLING PRESS. (320, 339)

Smith, (Charles) Philip (1928-). An English bookbinder and painter who received his education at Ackworth School and his art training at the Southport College of Art. He also studied under Roger Powell at the Royal College of Art, and was awarded a 1st Class diploma in 1954. Smith worked with Sydney Morris Cockerell from 1957 to 1960, and since then has worked as a free-lance creative bookbinder and painter. His bookbindings have been exhibited widely both in Great Britain and abroad, and are to be found in the collections of the British Museum, the Victoria & Albert Museum, the New York Public Library Spencer Collection, and other libraries and museums, as well as numerous private collections.

Smith has been responsible for many innovations in construction and covering technique, design, and the use of materials. He created the BOOK WALL, as well as several new techniques in cover treatment, including the feathered ONLAY, and re-constituted and sectioned onlays, which allow a greater variety, subtlety, and fluidity of color and surface, all essential to his particular mode of expression.

Smith is a member of the Crafts Centre of Great Britain (1956), the Guild of Contemporary Bookbinders (1959), and the Society of Artists and Designers (1967). He is also the author of *The Lord of the rings and other bookbindings* (1970), and *New directions in bookbinding* (1974).

smoked tool. A finishing tool, the face of which is covered with carbon black, which is deposited on the leather to darken the impression in blind tooling a book. Originally, the carbon was deposited by holding the tool over a smoking flame; today, however, carbon paper is usually used to blacken the tool. (83, 152)

smoke tanning. A method of tannage used in combination with an oil tannage, whereby the fat-saturated skins are subjected to the smoke of wood fires. The smoke from the charring wood contains aldehydes, acetaldehyde, and formaldehyde, which have tanning properties. The heat also assists in the oxidation of the oil, promoting further aldehyde and polymer production. Some volatile tarry substances also often become included in the skin. Smoke tanning, simply because it involves aldehyde formation from the partial oxidation of woody materials, can be used to tan hides and skins without the need to use fats. Although a minor tannage method, it is still being used in North and South America, as well as in China. (291)

smooth calf. A smooth, uncolored calfskin, used rather extensively in the latter years of the 19th and early part of the 20th centuries for covering books when the binding was to be marbled, or sprinkled, or just left plain. *See also:* SMOOTH CALF BINDING; TREE CALF. (264)

smooth calf binding. A full calfskin binding lacking any tooling or other decoration, except for the title in gilt on the spine. This type of binding was popular in the latter 19th and early 20th centuries. *See also:* PLAIN BINDING.

smoothness. That property of a surface, e.g., cloth, board, paper, or other material, as determined by the degree to which it is free of irregularities, depressions, etc.

smut tape. A tape used to prevent the offset of ink when pages are being numbered in a numbering machine. When numbers are printed on both sides of the sheets, the second number will cause the first to offset on the table, so that when the next sheet is laid in place it will be smeared. Smut tape prevents this by taking up the ink as it offsets and then moving before the next impression is made, so that a clean surface is brought into position for every sheet. (339)

smyrna morocco. A sheepskin, split and embossed with an imitation MOROCCO grain pattern. (156)

Smyth-Cleat sewing. A method of machine sewing or lacing adapted from an earlier European method by the Smyth Manufacturing Co. in the late 1960s and early 1970s. It combines thread and adhesive to secure the leaves of a book. In a separate machine, the back of the sections are planed off leaving the spine as smooth as possible. This is a very critical part of the operation, because if the cut spine is not smooth and even, subsequent operations are affected detrimentally. The block of leaves is then placed spine down in the Smyth-Cleat machine and is moved into position where a circular saw cuts a number of cleats completely across the back from head to tail (the number depending on the long dimension of the book). The sawn leaves then move into the sewing position where a single hollow needle laces thread around the cleats in the manner of a fiddle or figure-eight stitch. The sewn text block is then ready for the application of adhesive to the spine. The adhesive used may be one of the hot-melts or cold polyvinyl adhesives. For books that are not to be rounded and backed, the hot-melt may be preferable because of its extremely rapid

SMYTH-CLEAT SEWING

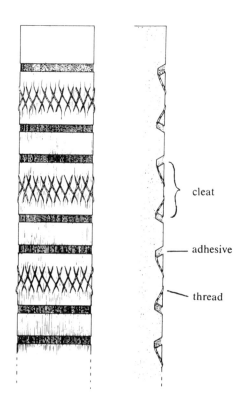

cleat

adhesive

thread

rate of setting; however, if the book is to be rounded and backed, an adhesive other than a hot-melt is required, because of the DRYING MEMORY of hot-melt adhesives.

Smyth, David McConnell (1833-1907). An Irish-American, who was for the most part self taught, and who become a prolific inventor and one of the foremost pioneers in the design of bookbinding equipment. One of his first machines was an "all along" sewing machine which he patented in 1868. This machine used straight needles, the number depending on the long dimension of the book (but always one more than the number of tapes used). The notched (sawn) sections, open and flat, were fed by hand above the needles and positioned so that the needles protruded through the saw cuts. A spring-loaded, hand-operated rod passed thread to the hooked needles and retracted. The operator had to refold the section, closing it over the stitch before feeding another.

Smyth also patented a multiple-stitch, off-and-on book sewing machine in 1879, the same year the Smyth Manufacturing Company was organized. Since that time, the Smyth Company has developed more than fifteen versions of the Smyth sewing machine, including a machine that will simultaneously sew "two-up," i.e., two separate, but not yet cut apart, books (imposed for printing "two-up.") This model can take sections from 3 to 10½ inches in width, up to 7½ to 19 inches in height at a speed up to 85 sections a minute. The company has also designed and produced a number of other bookbinding machines, including case-making, gluing and pasting, book trimming, casing-in machines, etc.

David Smyth's contribution to book sewing was such that his name is virtually synonymous in the United States with machine book sewing. *See also:* MACHINE SEWING. (89)

snail marble. A drawn marble pattern executed by dropping the colors on the size as for the NONPAREIL MARBLE and then drawing them into wavy lines, one by one with the aid of a stylus, thus producing snail-like forms. Variations of this pattern, which is usually used on the edges of books, include: 1) the gray snail, with green added to the gray until the desired tone is obtained; 2) the common green-gray snail, with black, light blue, yellow, pink, light red, gall water, and finally, the body color, which consists

of one part black and two or three parts sprinkling water, all dropped on in the order given and drawn into snails; 3) the dark blue snail (a brilliant marble designed for light-colored bindings), which consists of black, light brown, light blue, lemon yellow, gall water and the body color, which consists of one part black and two parts indigo blue, sprinkling water plus a solution of shellac and ammonia; 4) the dark red snail (which was frequently used with half bindings having light colored spines and endpapers of the same pattern), consisting of black, light red, pink, light gray, gall water and the body color, which consists of two parts carmine lake, one part black and two parts sprinkling water plus the shellac-ammonia solution; and 5) the gray-green snail, consisting of black, claret red (two parts carmine lake and one part black), pink, gall water (which forms the required white veins) and the body color, which consists of one part black, three parts sprinkling water, as well as green. (151)

snakeskin. Leather produced from the skins of the larger snakes, and tanned by processes that include sumac, alum, and salt (tawing), and chromium salts. The skin of the python has a striking pattern of black and white; however, its scales are rather large. A more delicately patterned skin is that of the watersnake. Snakeskin has been used for covering books upon occasion and also for decorative bands on leather-covered books. (261, 351)

snuffing. The process of lightly BUFFING (2) the grain surface of a leather, usually by means of carborundum paper wrapped around a revolving cylinder. Snuffing is a degree of sandpapering between buffering and CORRECTED GRAIN, and the leather treated is said to be "snuffed." (363)

soak-fleshing. *See:* GREEN FLESHING.

soaking. 1. The process of treating raw hides and skins with water. The restoration of moisture lost during curing and storage, as well as the removal of extraneous matter are of prime importance in converting raw stock into leather. The restoration of moisture is essential because: 1) the stock may otherwise be physically damaged by the action of washing under agitation, and flexing during green or lime fleshing; 2) sufficient moisture within the stock is necessary for solution and elimination of salts and globular proteins contained within the fibrous hide structure; and 3) the replenished water

serves as a diluent as well as a vehicle for penetration into the fibrous structure of the astringent chemicals employed to effect hair loosening, plumping, and required alkaline action. Removal of extraneous organic and inorganic matter, except epidermis and flesh, by soak-washing is essential because: 1) solid matter in excessive amounts can result in both stock and machine damage during fleshing and unhairing; 2) manure and urine are ideal foods for bacterial growth during soaking. (Such matter, along with certain salts in the soaks, can result in discoloration and stains on the stock that cannot subsequently be removed); 3) the cementing effect of globular proteins upon dried tanned fibers reduces fiber mobility necessary for softness and good handle in the final leather; 4) curing salts transferred to the lime liquors affect the alkaline plumping action, reduce the rate of unhairing, and cause a contraction of the grain surface of the stock; and 5) the presence of extraneous matter presents a false and variable hide substance weight in determining the amounts of materials required for liming.

Because of many variable conditions, the time and temperature of soaking varies considerably according to the kind of stock being treated. Generally, few soaking aids are used in soaking cured and brined stock unless a considerable number of a given lot have been stored under exceptionally dry and warm conditions. In such cases, either sodium sulfide (63%) or sodium hydroxide may be used to the extent of 1.0 to 0.5 pound respectively per 100 gallons of water. These chemicals are frequently employed in the soaking of dry stock. Excessive amounts will cause a high grain in the leather.

2. The process of wetting the grain side of a leather with water and the flesh side with paste to improve the pliability of the leather preparatory to covering. (161, 248, 291, 298, 306, 363)

soda. 1. SODIUM CARBONATE. 2. *See:* SODA PULP.

soda ash. A commercial anhydrous SODIUM CARBONATE. It is used in the manufacture of leather to neutralize acids and to clean and prepare vegetable-tanned leather for acid bleaching. (306)

soda pulp. A chemical wood pulp produced by high temperature digestion of papermaking material with sodium hydroxide. The soda pulp method is used in making paper from poplars, birches, oaks, and other deciduous trees. Papers containing a high proportion of soda pulp are very white and soft, and possess high bulk and opacity but low strength. Soda pulp is frequently used to give a soft finish to a sulfite-pulp base paper. (17, 143, 198, 320)

sodium bifloride (sodium hydrogen floride). A white salt ($NaHF_2$), prepared by dissolving sodium floride in aqueous or anhydrous hydrofluoric acid. It is used to disinfect restricted-import hides and skins. (363)

sodium bisulfite. An acid salt ($NaHSO_3$), usually prepared by passing sulfur dioxide through a solution of sodium carbonate. It is unstable and is generally known only in solution. It is used to sulfite oils employed in fatliquoring leather, and, because of its capability of liberating sulfur dioxide, in bleaching leather. (306, 363)

sodium borohydride. A white solid ($NaBH_4$), prepared by reacting sodium hydride or sodium methoxide with diborane. It is soluble in water, and is stable under alkaline conditions. It is used to reduce the effects of FOXING.

sodium carbonate. A mild alkaline (Na_2CO_3), also known as "soda" or "soda ash." It is prepared by dissolving ammonia in purified brine, the resulting solution being treated with carbon dioxide. It is used in leather manufacture, particularly in chrome tannages, to control pH, and, in the manufacture of paper, in the preparation of chemical pulps. (144, 306)

sodium chlorate. A white, crystalline salt ($NaClO_3$), formed either by the action of chlorine on hot aqueous caustic soda, or by the electrolysis of sodium chloride in solution. It is used in bleaching paper pulps and also to remove stains from archival papers. Its chlorine content, which is extremely difficult to remove, makes it detrimental to the permanence of paper. Its bleaching action stems from its strong oxidizing potential. It also supports combustion.

sodium chloride. Common salt ($NaCl$), which occurs naturally as rock salt, and is distributed over the land surfaces of the earth, as well as in sea water. It is used in very large quantities in brining, wet-salting, and dry-salting (curing) hides and skins for transporation and/ or storage. It is also used to pickle sheepskins, and in deliming, bating, and other leather manufacturing processes. (363)

sodium chlorite. The sodium salt of chlorous acid ($HClO_2$). Sodium chlorite ($NaClO_2$), an oxidizing agent, is used for bleaching and the delignification of wood pulp, dyeing, and other purposes. When an acid is added to an aqueous solution of sodium chlorite, it liberates chlorine dioxide.

sodium cyanide. A salt ($NaCN$), usually prepared by reacting methane with hydrogen cyanide, followed by neutralization with sodium hydroxide, or by passing carbon monoxide and ammonia over finely divided sodium carbonate at 600 to 650° C. It has been used to some extent as a (powerful) sharpening agent in lime liquors; however, its extremely toxic nature makes it dangerous to use. (363)

sodium formate. A white, crystalline salt (HCO_2Na), prepared by passing carbon monoxide through heated sodium hydroxide. It is soluble in water and forms complex compounds with chromic salts. It is used in chrome tannages to bring about greater tan fixation. (363)

sodium hydrosulfide. A salt ($NaSH$), the anhydrous form of which is generally prepared by saturing a solution of sodium in alcohol with dry hydrogen sulfide. It is used as a sharpening agent in lime liquors and is equally as effective as, but less caustic in its action than, SODIUM SULFIDE. (363)

sodium hydrosulfite. A crystalline salt ($Na_2S_2O_4$), prepared by the reaction of sodium bisulfite with zinc, or by the action of sulfur dioxide on sodium amalgam. It is used in bleaching paper pulps, especially mechanical pulps, and in leather manufacture as a reducing agent in dyeing. (17, 306)

sodium hydroxide. A white, translucent, highly deliquescent, extremely caustic alkali ($NaOH$), prepared mainly by the electrolysis of sodium chloride. It is used in the manufacture of paper pulps, and can also be used for the rapid degradation of hair and other epidermal structures of hides and skins; it is seldom if ever used for this purpose in practical tannages, however, as it dissolves the hair (which is commercially valuable) and can severely damage the collagen of a skin unless very carefully controlled. Also called "caustic soda." (144, 306)

sodium hypochlorite. A salt ($NaOCl$), formed, together with the chloride, by the reaction between chlorine and cold dilute sodium hydroxide. It is used as an oxidizing agent in bleaching archival materials. Its chlorine content, however, which is extremely difficult to remove from the paper, makes it detrimental to paper permanence.

sodium nitrite. A colorless to nearly yellow salt ($NaNO_2$), usually formed by the absorption of nitrogen oxide in a solution of sodium carbonate, and used in the application of developed dyes. (363)

sodium peroxide. A nearly white compound (Na_2O_2), having vigorous oxidizing properties, and used in bleaching mechanical paper pulps and as a final stage in the bleaching of chemical paper pulps in some multi-stage bleaching sequences. It is dangerous to use because, when in contact with organic matter, it reacts so vigorously with atmospheric moisture that sufficient heat can be generate to cause organic matter to burn or even explode.

sodium p-toluenesulphon-chloroamide. *See:* CHLORAMINE T.

sodium silicate. An alkaline salt, prepared by calcining diatomaceous earth, quartz, or sand with sodium hydroxide or sodium carbonate. The salt consists of varying proportions of sodium oxide and silica, such as Na_2SiO_3. It is used in the manufacture of paper for improving physical tests, increasing the retention of fine particles, and pH control. In this final use, it provides another means of increasing alumina in the stock preparation system, one that is accomplished by raising the pH value of the stock, thereby forcing the use of additional alum to lower the pH. Also called "water glass." (98, 235)

sodium sulfide. A reddish-yellow compound (NaS), generally prepared by the reduction of sodium sulfate with carbon monoxide or hydrogen. It is soluble in water and is used as a sharpening agent in lime liquors. It forms both sodium hydrosulfide and sodium hydroxide when dissolved in water. Its action is much more caustic than that of SODIUM HYDROSULFIDE. (291, 363)

sodium thiosulfate. A salt ($Na_2S_2O_3$), prepared by treating a solution containing sodium carbonate and sodium sulfide with sulfur dioxide, or by boiling sodium sulfite with sulfur. It is used extensively in photography because of the ability of its solutions to dissolve silver halides, and as an anti-chlor when sodium hypochlorite is used in bleaching archival papers. It is also used extensively in the chrome tannage of leather. (144, 306)

soft. Said of a paper of a soft nature and surface, which has little or no sizing. Such a paper requires but little pressure during printing. (17)

soft cover. Sometimes said of a book cover other than one that is hard or a SELF COVER. It is produced from any type of paper other than that on which the text is printed. A soft cover is not the same as a LIMP BINDING. *See also:* PAPERBACK. (316)

softener. *See:* PLASTICIZER.

softening the back (spine). The process of applying water or paste to the spine of a book in order to soften the glue preparatory to rounding and backing, or to remove the old glue when pulling a book for rebinding. (196)

soft sized. *See:* SLACK SIZED.

Solander box (Solander book-box portfolio). A more or less elaborate book or document box invented by Dr. Daniel Charles Solander, a botanist, during his tenure at the British Museum (1773–1782). The Solander box, which is generally of a drop-back construction, is made of wood, has dovetailed joints and a back shaped from a single piece of wood. The top and bottom are held in place by screws and glue. The box is secured by two spring catches fixed in the "fore edge" frames near the head and tail. When properly constructed the Solander box is very nearly dustproof and almost waterproof. The box, which can be made as elaborate as the maker desires, is generally covered in cloth, or, in more elaborate instances, full morocco. It may even have raised bands on the back (corresponding to the spine of a book) and may be tooled.

The drop-back Solander is intended to house a book. For document storage, specifically to facilitate removal from the box, a drop-front box may actually be preferable, although in a strict sense it may be argued that such an arrangement is not really a Solander box. Aside from this, however, the drop-back box has a distinct advantage over the drop-front type in that the former imposes virtually no strain on the hinge of the box because it is in a right-angle position when closed and assumes a straight line position when opened. The drop-front box, on the other hand, with its fixed back, strains the hinge at the back because of the approximate 60° angle at the top when the box is open. If the top is accidently struck when the box is open the top may break off. (155)

solid. 1. *See:* BUNDLING (1); NIPPING (1); SMASHING. 2. *See:* CUT SOLID; GILT IN THE ROUND. 3. *See:* SOLID TOOL. 4. GOLD TOOLING which has no breaks, cracks, or other imperfections. 5. That part of a printing surface printed in full color as distinguished from parts that are grained, stippled, or otherwise made to print in gray or a light color. (12, 83, 335).

solid board. A board made of the same stock throughout, as distinct from a combination board where two or more stocks are used. A PASTEBOARD (1) is not considered to be a solid board even though the same stock may be used throughout. (17)

solid fraction. That part of a paper which consists of the fibrous material, as well as sizing, loading, pigments, etc. It is the ratio of solids to total volume. *See also:* VOID FRACTION. (17, 72)

solid gilt. *See:* GILT IN THE ROUND.

solids content. The percentage by weight of the non-volatile matter in an adhesive. (309)

solid tool. A finishing tool cut so that it produces a solid or completely filled-in impression, as contrasted with an outline tool, which impresses an open figure, or an AZURED TOOL. (94, 335)

solid tooling. The solid ornamentation of a book with metal, usually gold, but sometimes aluminum, paladium, platinum, or silver.

soluble nylon. A N-methoxymethyl nylon prepared by treating nylon 66 with

SOLANDER BOX

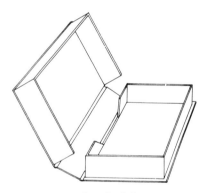

drop back box

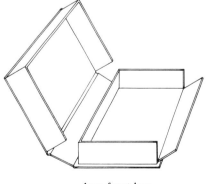

drop front box

formaldehyde, and used in non-aqueous resizing of paper. Its major importance is that it can be used in a 2% solution in methyl or ethyl alcohol and sprayed or brushed on the document (depending on the fragility of the paper) in cases where the paper is too weak to handle easily when wet or where it is suspected or known that the ink may be sensitive to water. It also imparts strength to weak papers. (265)

solvents. Liquid substances which, to a greater or lesser degree, are capable of dissolving or dispersing other substances. In addition to water (the so-called universal solvent), acetone, ethyl alcohol, normal and isopropyl alcohols, ethylene glycol, naphtha, carbon tetrachloride, carbon disulfide, many esters, etc., are used as solvents. The fact that water is neither flammable nor toxic makes it a very valuable solvent; unfortunately, its adverse effect on some inks, colors, etc., makes the use of other solvents necessary at times.

solvent sizing. A method of sizing paper in which the size (rosin) is dissolved in a suitable solvent, and applied to the paper; the solvent is then recovered for reuse. (17)

solvent tannage. A non-aqueous tannage system which utilizes organic solvents, e.g., acetone, in lieu of water as the vehicle for the tanning agents. (325)

sorbitol. A hexahydric alcohol ($C_6H_{14}O_6$), corresponding to glucose. It occurs naturally, and is also produced by the reduction of glucose in an aqueous solution. It is used in lieu of GLYCEROL as a plasticizer in certain adhesives, notably animal glues, and as a softening agent for textiles, paper, and leather. Sorbitol is cheaper than glycerin and its plasticizing effect is said to last longer because it is less volatile. *See also:* INTERNALLY PLASTICIZED. (198, 235)

sorghum guineense dye. A reddish-purple dye obtained from the leaf sheaths and stems of plants of the genus *Sorghum,* and used in dyeing Niger goatskins. (130)

sour dip. An acid solution containing magnesium sulfate and fermenting corn sugar, into which some leathers are dipped before drying to improve their color and enhance their feel. (363)

spangles. Small discs and geometrical shapes of shining metal used for the further ornamentation of embroidered bindings. Spangles were never used to any great extent on velvet, but found their greatest use on satin embroidered books. They were usually held in position either by a small section of PURL, or by a seed pearl, in both cases very effectively, so that the use of gimp or pearl was not only ornamental but served the same protective purposes as bosses. (111)

Spanish. The name by which the best grade of ESPARTO (GRASS) is known. *Cf:* TRIPOLI. (156)

Spanish grain. A grain pattern on leather produced by embossing the skin with a modified natural grain surface. This type of grain was formerly produced by drawing a hide or skin in a strong tan infusion so as to shrink the grain, resulting in a particular grain pattern due to the unequal shrinkage of the different parts of the skin. (325)

Spanish leather. *See:* CORDOBAN LEATHER; CORDOVAN LEATHER.

Spanish marble. A marble pattern of soft colors, including pale green, old rose and brown (or fawn), with a MOIRÉ EFFECT. It was used in Spain from the early 17th century and is found on the more familiar later Spanish marble papers that have been used in both England and the United States since the end of the 18th century.

The best size for executing the Spanish pattern is said to consist of a combination of gum tragacanth and flea seed. In mixing the colors for this pattern, each successive color requires more ox gall than the preceding one. The main, or body, color must also be thicker and mixed with more gall than any of the other colors.

The wavy effect of the early Spanish marbles was not nearly as even as in the later examples, and was almost invariably executed on a relatively heavy laid paper. The distinguishing moiré or watered effect, which sets the Spanish marble apart from all other types, is produced by a series of lines, shading from dark to light, crossing the entire sheet in a diagonal direction, and is the result of the method by which the paper is laid on the size after the colors have been dropped on. The sheet is held at two diagonally opposite corners and is kept in as upright a position as possible. With the sheet inclined toward the left, the corner held by the right hand is lowered until it barely touches the floating color. As soon as the paper starts to fall on the surface, it is slightly agitated with a regular motion, while at the same time being gradually lowered with the left hand until the entire sheet is on the size. If properly done, shaded stripes will appear on the paper when it is removed from the size. These strips vary in width, depending on how much the paper was agitated while it was being lowered. (152, 217, 241, 369)

s pattern. The code name for a fine-grained, silklike pattern embossed on a book cloth. (256)

spatter papers. Another form of PASTE PAPERS. A very thin mixture of colored paste is applied to the paper by rubbing a stiff paste-charged brush across a hair sieve, which is held well above the paper and moved across the surface of the sheet as the fine specks of color are sprayed through it. Three or four colors are generally used in making these papers, which are often executed on a colored paper background.

This simple form of decoration was used for the sides of half bindings in calfskin and sheepskin in the early 19th century. They were produced all over Europe until about 1850, and were used as endpapers in books with marbled-paper covers but seldom for bindings in full leather.

A variation of this paper, used in France, England and the United States in the latter part of the 19th century, consisted of dull gray-blue or lavender-purple paper spattered with coarse black spots. This was done by striking a brush filled with color on a bar and distributing the color as it fell over the surface of the paper. These papers were used as covers for inexpensive books but seldom for endpapers. The earlier examples had a dull finish, but others, used mainly for music scores, had a glossy surface. This type of spatter paper was sometimes hung up before it was dry, the surplus color running down across the paper in uneven streaks. This dribbled pattern is almost always found in tones of brown or orange and black, and is considered by many to be less appealing than the simpler spatter papers. (217)

special edition. To the bookbinder, an edition of a work that differs from a regular edition because of some distinctive feature, such as superior paper and binding, more extensive margins, illustrations not to be found in another edition, etc. (143, 156)

special volume. A book defined by the Library Binding Institute as one that is undersized, oversized or odd-sized, or any volume that requires special handling. (208)

specific adhesion. The adhesion which exists between surfaces which are held together by VAN DER WAALS forces of the same type as those which give rise to cohesion. *See also:* MECHANICAL ADHESION. (309)

specification slip. *See:* BINDING SLIP.

specific gravity. The ratio of the weight of an object to the weight of an equal volume of pure water at its maximum density, which is at 4° C. Because paper, leather, cloth, etc., do not lend themselves well to measurement of specific gravity, density is used more often as the reference in describing these materials.

specific heat. The number of calories of heat required to raise the temperature of one gram of a material by one degree centigrade.

speckled calf. *See:* SPRINKLED CALF.

speckled sand edge. A book with edges that have been abraded with fine sandpaper and then colored by sprinkling or spraying. *See also:* SPRINKLED EDGES.

spent tannin. A vegetable-tanning material or solution from which all, or practically all, tannin has been removed.

spermaceti wax. A pearly white, fatty substance obtained from the cavities of the head of the cachalot (sperm) whale, *Physeter macrocephalus,* by hot water treatment. Upon cooling, the wax separates out and is pressed to remove some of the (sperm) oil. The wax is then remelted and washed with a weak carbonate solution before being cast into molds for setting into blocks. It has a softening range of 40 to 44° C. and is easily emulsified with water. It is sometimes used as a lubricant for leather bindings, usually in combination with other materials in LEATHER DRESSINGS. (195, 291)

sperm oil. A pale yellow oil found with spermaceti in the cachalot (sperm) whale, *Physeter macrocephalus.* When spermaceti wax is obtained by treatment with hot water, the sperm oil is pressed out. It is classed chemically as a liquid wax and is sometimes used as a lubricant for leather bindings, generally with other materials in LEATHER DRESSINGS. (173, 291)

spew. Material that exudes or is exuded. In the manufacture of leather, it is seen as a portion of the oily constituents of a leather that appears on the grain surface in the form of white crystalline fatty acids, or as a gummy deposit in the form of dark oxidized fatty acids. (325)

spine. 1. The collective fold-areas sections of a gathered book after sewing. Sometimes called "back." 2. That part of the covering material of a book which covers the folds of the sections of a book and which is the part usually visible as it stands on the shelf. It generally bears the title, author, name of the publisher (when an edition binding), and (in a library) frequently a location (classification) number, or a symbol of some kind. Also called "back," "backbone," or "shelfback." (69, 173)

spine fold. *See:* BOLT.

spine lining. 1. The process of reinforcing the spine of a sewn book, after gluing-up, rounding and backing, and before covering or casing-in. The spine lining material (which is usually a fabric) does not generally extend closer than within ⅛ inch of the head and tail of the text block. In edition and library binding, the lining material, or initial liner, if there is more than one, extends beyond the edges of the spine, and is attached to the boards of the case; any subsequent lining, however, stops at the shoulders of the spine.

The purpose of lining the spine is to support it and to impart a certain degree of rigidity, while still maintaining the necessary flexibility for proper opening; consequently the weight and stiffness of the spine lining material is of considerable importance. *See also:* SPINE LINING FABRIC; SPINE LINING PAPER.

2. A term used incorrectly with reference to the strengthening or stiffening of the area between the boards of the covering material of case bindings. This lining is more appropriately called the INLAY (1). (236, 339)

spine lining fabric. The fabric used to line the spine of a book. It is generally made of cotton, napped on the side which goes against the spine, and of a weight that will help support the spine while not decreasing its flexibility.

The Library Binding Institute's Specifications for Libary Binding call for cloth of a weight not less than 4.0 ounces per yard, a thread count of not less than 45 in the warp and 38 in the filling, and a breaking strength (by the strip method) of not less than 42 pounds per inch for the warp and 53½ pounds for the filling. For books less than ½ inch in thickness, these specifications may be reduced to a cloth with a weight of 2½ ounces per square yard, plain weave, single ply yarn, a thread count of not less than 33 in the warp and 25 in the filling, and a breaking strength (by the grab method) of not less than 44 pounds per inch for the warp and 40 pounds per inch for the filling. *See also:* SPINE LINING; SPINE LINING PAPER. (208)

spine lining paper. A relatively heavy paper, usually kraft, sometimes coated, and with either a creped or flat finish. The paper, which is applied with the machine direction running from head to tail of the text block, should be of a thickness appropriate to the size and weight of the book. It is generally applied over the initial cloth lining of large and/or heavy hand- and library-bound books. Spine lining paper is seldom used in edition binding.

spine marking. The spine area of a tanned skin, which is sometimes of a darker shade than the remainder of the skin.

spinner. A marbling comb having a handle attached in such a manner as to allow the comb to be twirled in the marbling size in order to form particular patterns. (335)

spiral binding. A form of MECHANICAL BINDING used for art reproductions, commercial catalogs, instruction books, books in single sheets, etc. The leaves are drilled or punched near the binding edge to take a spiral-twisted wire or plastic coil which is drawn through the holes. A tendency for the coil to be torn through the holes makes this type of mechanical binding unsuitable for publications likely to be subject to much use or careless handling. The binding margins of such publications are frequently less than ½ inch, and part of that is taken by the holes, which makes rebinding difficult if the publication must be sewn, as the holes can cause breakage of the needles and punches of an oversewing machine. Furthermore, in many cases, the type of paper used for these publications does not lend itself well to adhesive binding. Also called "coil binding," or "spirex binding." (139, 234, 338)

spiral laid. A special type of DANDY ROLL, having the laid wires running around the circumference of the roll, producing lines parallel to the machine direction of the paper. This laid mark is characterized by the absence of chain lines. (17)

spirex binding. *See:* SPIRAL BINDING.

spirit of salts. An old name for HYDROCHLORIC ACID.

splash papers. Decorative end- and cover papers produced by sprinkling the paper with alum water, followed, after pressing for several hours, with colors, e.g., yellow, dark red, bright red, green, purple, and brown. Generally the lighter shades are splashed on first. Usually one or two colors, sometimes in combination with black ink, are used for these papers, which are burnished after being colored. (95)

splice. 1. A join made by bringing together two pieces of film or paper, by means of an adhesive or heat, so that they function as one piece when run through a camera, processing machine, or other apparatus. Lap splices are those in which the two pieces overlap and are joined, while butt splices are those where the two pieces are abutted and welded with no overlap. 2. The joining of the ends of two or more webs of paper to make a continuous roll. Materials used for this include adhesives, gummed tapes, or splicing tissue. (17, 156)

split. Any one of the several layers of a hide or skin produced by the mechanical operation of SPLITTING (1), e.g., grain split, middle split, or flesh split. In ordinary usage, however, the term usually indicates an under layer of a hide or skin, i.e., a layer other than the grain layer, or the leather made therefrom. A grain layer split is generally referred to as a SKIVER. If the name of the animal from which the split originates, or the word "hide" or "skin," or the part of the animal from which it is taken, is included in the description, then the word "split" must be used as a noun, e.g., pig split, hide split, butt split, and not as an adjective, e.g., split pigskin. *Cf:* SPLIT HIDE. (61)

split back-gauge. A type of movable BACK GAUGE of a paper cutting machine made up of two or more sections. Split back-gauge machines are designed especially for trimming books and pamphlets (in edition and pamphlet binding), and are unlike machines designed for cutting piles of paper, which have solid back gauges. Each of the sections of the split gauge may be set at a different distance from the knife, so that the trimming gauge for two or three different margins of a book may be set simultaneously. This permits trimming a book or a pile of books or pamphlets without changing gauges or waiting for entire lots to go through the trimming of one edge. If the split gauge is in three sections, the middle section is generally set for trimming the fore edge, and the left and right hand sections for trimming the tail and head edges, respectively.

The split gauge trimmer was used extensively in edition binding until largely superseded by the THREE-KNIFE TRIMMER. When both types are used in one bindery, the three-knife machine is generally used for pamphlets (periodical issues) and the split gauge machine for books. (142)

split boards. The boards of a book that are made up of two or more plies of board glued together, except for a distance at the inner edge into which the slips or tapes are glued when the boards are being attached. Generally, if two boards are used they are of different thicknesses, with the thinner of the two adjacent to the text block. If three boards are used, the thinnest is placed in the center and does not extend all the way to the inner edge, thus providing the space for the tapes or slips. In the past some "split boards" were made by splitting a single ply board, either by hand or by machine, thus eliminating the cost of laminating.

SPLIT BOARDS

The split stopped an inch or so short of the head and tail of the board (in case binding), which made it possible to make the case separately and then attach it to the text block by gluing the tapes into the splits of each board.

Split boards are used today almost exclusively in hand binding and then only for books sewn on tapes, although the technique has also been used occasionally for books sewn on recessed cords. (161, 236, 335)

split cover. A two-piece pamphlet cover consisting of separate sheets for upper and lower covers side stitched to the pamphlet. A strip of cloth is glued to the spine and onto the sides, thus covering the stitching. (142)

split fountain. A type of ink fountain by means of which two or more inks of different colors may be run simultaneously on the same printing press or ruling machine. The trough of ink that feeds the press or ruling machine is the "ink fountain," which may be split into two or more compartments by means of dividers. (320)

split hide. The outer or grain layer of a hide from which the under or flesh side has been removed to produce a reasonably uniform thickness of less substance than the entire hide. The resultant leather is generally slightly thicker than 1.5 mm. (351)

split stitch. A fine chain stitch used on embroidered bindings, and executed by beginning each successive stitch slightly within the one immediately preceding. (111)

splitting. 1. The process of dividing a hide or skin horizontally into two or more layers. Before the introduction of splitting machines, a hide was reduced

in thickness by SHAVING (2) after tanning. The modern splitting machine has a flexible knife in the form of an endless band moving at high speed over a pair of large pulleys. When the leather to be split is placed on the bed of the machine and pushed forward, it is gripped by pairs of rollers and propelled forward in such a manner that the band knife cuts it into two layers. The propelling rollers are made up of a large number of small ring rolls with rubber centers which allow for initial variations in the thickness of the hide. The knife can be adjusted to slice through the thickness of the hide at any desired depth below the grain surface by adjusting the level of the rollers. While the machine is in operation, the band knife is automatically sharpened by grinders on its underside.

Splitting may be done while the hide is in the limed or partially limed condition, or following tannage. Hides are sometimes split in the limed condition so that a grain layer of desired thickness may be taken off and tanned separately from the splits. A gain in yield of the resultant grain leathers may be expected as a result of the slight "letting-out" of the fiber structure consequent to splitting before tannage. In certain tannages, such as vegetable tannage of leather for purposes not requiring the full thickness of the hide, savings in materials and shortening of processing time may also be effected.

When the hides are to be split in the unhaired or limed condition, the stock is plumped to a condition of sufficient firmness or solidity so as to be fed through the splitting machine smoothly in order to split off the grain layer of desired thickness uniformly across the full width and length of the hide. The fibers have a more vertical position when the hide has been plumped and will stand up against the beveled cutting edge of the band knife with less tendency to leave gouges or uneven ridges and valleys.

Although it may be highly desirable (or necessary) to reduce the substance

of a hide or skin by splitting, the operation may also have undesirable effects. The strength of leather is not uniform throughout its thickness, and the grain layer, which contains the thermostat mechanism of the living skin, is relatively weak. As nearly all of the strength of leather lies in the corium, the strength of a grain split will depend upon the thickness of the corium layer which it contains. Splitting always causes a loss of strength per unit width and the sum of the strengths of the splits is *always* less than the strength of the unsplit leather. In fact, the breaking strength of the grain split of a vegetable-tanned calfskin, for example, will be between 3.5 and 12% of the unsplit skin, while the breaking strength of the flesh split will be between 54 and 70% of the unsplit skin; thus the leather loses between 18 and 42.5% of its strength because of splitting.

2. Separating the plies of a paper or board. (291, 306, 363)

spokeshave. A wheelwright's drawing knife used for shaping and finishing spokes, and used by bookbinders for paring leather and beveling boards. It has an adjustable blade which may be flat or curved. The tool is modified for paring by widening the gap between the blade and the guard to prevent

SPOKESHAVE

clogging. In addition to this, the bottom of the blade is generally ground at a shallower angle, because a steep angle would result in too much of a scraping action. Because it is safer (in that there is little or no possibility of cutting completely through the leather), as well as faster, the spokeshave has largely replaced the paring knife. (92, 154, 236)

spot binding. An economical form of SPIRAL BINDING, consisting of a short spiral at the head and tail of the book or, sometimes, a short spiral at the head and tail and in the center. (54)

spot marble. A general type of marble consisting of a base or "ground" color, usually of a dark shade, followed by colors of lighter shade. The color containing the greatest amount of gall is dropped on the size last so that it will spread out and crowd the other colors together. (371)

spotting. 1. *See:* FOXING. 2. A form of geometrical powdered decoration on a leather binding, with the background occupying a larger area than the ornament. *See also:* GOLD-POWDERED BINDINGS; SEMÉ. (94, 261)

sprays. A cluster or mass of leaves, branches, etc., tooled in blind or gold on the covers of a book. They are generally built up with a combination of tools and gouges. (83)

spread. 1. Two facing pages. *See also:* CENTER SPREAD. 2. The quantity of adhesive used in the joint area of an adherend. *See also:* DOUBLE SPREAD (2); SINGLE SPREAD. 3. The entire inside section, when unfolded, of a folder or broadside. (309, 365)

spreading. The tendency of an oil to creep over the entire surface of water on the fibers of a hide or skin. This behavior is of importance in the process of fatliquoring and stuffing leather. (363)

spready hide. A hide or skin with a poor or ill-defined shape, or a hide with a large area in relation to its weight. (363)

spring-back. 1. A device or technique invented by the Englishmen John and Joseph Williams, in about 1799 and used ever since in the binding of large blankbooks. The spring-back consists of a strip of millboard, or other hard binder's board, the length of the boards of the book and of a width that, when curved, will fit around the spine and onto the sides of the text block at least one fourth of an inch on both sides. The board is first soaked in water and a strip of kraft paper four times its width is then glued around it. The purpose of the paper is to stiffen the board further so that it will maintain its form after it is curved to the proper shape. The assembly is curved around a core (the thickness of the book), or by means of a BACK-MOLDING IRON. A cloth liner is then glued to the interior of the curve, overlapping the edges by 2 inches on either side. These overlaps are glued to the LEVERS. After the spring-back is attached, both ends are softened, paste is applied, and the ends of the spring-back are bent over to form the headcaps.

The purpose of the spring-back is to cause the book to lie flat so as to facilitate its being written in. It acts as a spring, and its pressure on the sides of the book near the spine causes the book to snap open and shut. The levers assist in this snapping effect, which is enhanced by the fact that the machine direction of the lever boards is at right angles to the length of the spine.

2. The degree to which a sheet of paper will assume its original flat condition after being folded and then released. (241, 264, 339, 343)

spring channel binder. A mechanical binding used to hold less than ½ inch thickness of paper. The back of this type of binder has a spring steel channel, the leaves being held between the sides of the channel by spring pressure. The boards are hinged to the edge of the channel, and, when both are thrown back and pressed together, the channel is forced open for removal or insertion of sheets. It is not necessary to punch or drill the paper for this type of binder. (339)

sprinkled calf. A calfskin that has been given a speckled appearance by a sprinkling of coloring matter, or, more often, ferrous sulfate. It has been used in England since the 17th century, if not earlier. *See also:* MOTTLED CALF; TREE CALF. (83, 264)

sprinkled edges. The head, or all three edges, of a book which have been cut solid and sprinkled, usually with an earth pigment, such as bole, dissolved in a non-spirit solvent. Sprinkled edges are intended to be decorative and to prevent the edges from appearing to be soiled. The technique has been used since the 16th century, generally on trade and edition bindings, ordinary library bindings, and also on dictionaries and similar publications. Venetian red has always been the color most often used, possibly because it does not clash with other colors, such as endpapers or the leather covering. A good deal of the early sprinkling is very fine and even, so much so that at first glance it appears to be a solid color. (343)

sprinkling. The process of sprinkling or spattering irregularly shaped spots or splotches of coloring matter on the leather covers of a book, usually calfskin or sheepskin, or on the edges, to achieve a decorative effect. Traditionally, sprinkling was done by means of a large brush knocked against an iron bar, but it is now usually done with a brush and sieve, or by means of a mechanical device. *See:* MOTTLED CALF; SPRINKLED CALF; SPRINKLED EDGES. (236, 264)

sprinkling water. A mixture of soap dissolved in alcohol, boiled, and mixed with water for use as a size in the execution of certain marble patterns. Hair vein and Turkish marbles require a stronger expanding medium than ox-

SPRING-BACK

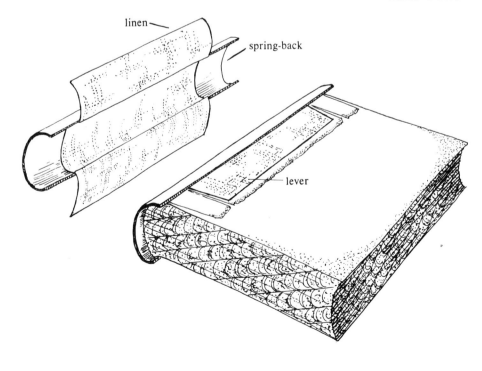

linen
spring-back
lever

gall for the first color, and sprinkling water forces the color and gall into veins. In addition, sprinkling water produces oval spots which enhance the attractiveness of the vein. *See also:* VEINING LIQUID. (264)

square. 1. The name applied to a book when the width of the cover is more than three-fourths of its height. 2. An L-shaped measuring device, made of steel, and used both for measuring and for obtaining square or right angle corners. 3. A book which has had its boards (covers) cut at perfect right angles. (183, 335)

square back. *See:* FLAT BACK BINDING (1).

square blanks. The length of brass on the face of which the bookbinder or tool cutter cuts the design of a finishing tool. (335)

square corner. A book corner in which a piece of the covering material is cut at the corner so that one turn-in overlaps the other considerably without the need of additional folding. *See also:* CORNER MITERING; LIBRARY CORNER. (156, 256)

squared. 1. Paper or board that is trimmed on at least two sides to ensure exactness of angle. For all high quality printing and folding jobs, and particularly in a work-and-tumble imposition, the paper must be squared before printing. In other impositions it is only necessary that the side guide edge and the gripper edge are at a right angle. 2. Another term for sectional and/or scale paper.

square form. A cattle hide with a minimum amount of tissue in the neck, leg and belly areas. The "square form" has resulted from programs of breeding cattle to produce a body conformation which will yield the greatest amount of lean beef per unit weight of animal. Dairy breeds, on the other hand, have an overall distribution that is much less than "square." (363)

squares. The marginal difference between the edges of the text block and the edges of the case or boards of the book. Normally, squares vary both in proportion to the size of the book and according to taste. They are described relatively from the least extensive, or *pinhead,* to the most extensive, *bold,* with *neat, ordinary,* and *full* being intermediate sizes. Books with projecting index tabs will have very extensive squares on the fore edge. *Cf:* CUT FLUSH; YAPP STYLE. *See also:* STILTED. (97, 173, 306)

square sheet. A paper or board which has equal tensile strength and tearing resistance in both machine and cross directions. Although not so stated, the impli-

cation of "square sheet" is that the paper is handmade. (17)

stabbing (stabbed; stab holes). 1. *See:* JAPANESE SEWING; SIDE SEWING; SIDE STITCHING. 2. *See:* HOLING OUT. 3. The process of punching or drilling holes for the sewing needles, as in oversewing, overcasting, etc. (58)

stabbing machine. A hand- or power-operated device for the simultaneous punching of holes through the sides of a pile of leaves preparatory to SIDE SEWING or SIDE STITCHING. *See also:* JAPANESE SEWING. (259)

stability. The permanence of a paper or board as reflected in its ability to resist

changes in any of its characteristics upon exposure to various conditions during use or storage. *See:* BRIGHTNESS REVERSION; BRITTLENESS; COLOR FASTNESS; DIMENSIONAL STABILITY; DURABILITY (OF PAPER); PERMANENT PAPER; YELLOWING.

stabilized. A material, such as leather or paper, whose moisture content is in equilibrium with that of the surrounding atmosphere. *See also:* CONDITIONING.

stab sewing. *See:* SIDE SEWING.

stab-sewn endpaper. A type of endpaper consisting of a single leaf and a folio attached to a strip of linen. The end-

STAB-SEWN ENDPAPER

A = height of backing shoulder plus 1/16 inch   B = height of backing shoulder

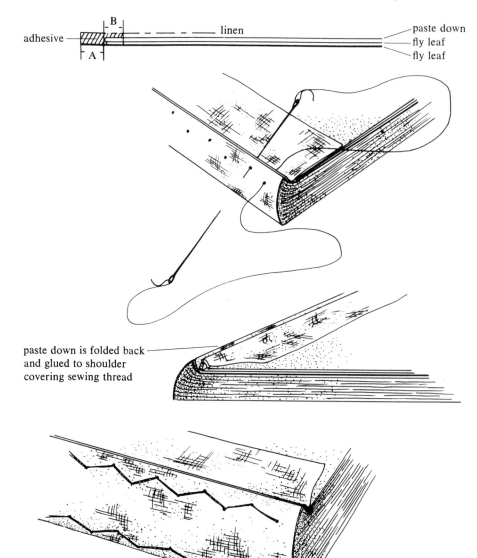

paper is attached to the text block by sewing through holes drilled through the leaves of the book in a staggered pattern. The thread is passed back and forth through the holes in a crisscross pattern using two needles. This type of endpaper is said to be useful when a book is to be re-covered (recased) but not resewn. It provides a strong endpaper attachment and reinforces the first and last few sections or leaves of the book.

stab stitching. *See:* SIDE STITCHING.

stag hide. The hide of an ox that is castrated later in life than a steer, often when a year old. The longer castration is delayed, the more the hide will resemble that a bull. It has no recognized designation on the hide market, but is classed as steer or bull depending on which it more nearly resembles. (363)

stain. A suspension or solution of a dye or other coloring matter in a suitable vehicle. The principal difference between a stain and other coloring agents is that the former has little or no power to opacify; consequently, when applied to leather, for example, a stain imparts color while still allowing the grain pattern of the leather to remain clearly visible. The two types of stains most often used in coloring leather in restoration work are *spirit stains,* which are dyes dissolved in methylated spirit, and *water-soluble* stains, which are dyes dissolved in water. Those most often used today for this purpose are the synthetic dyes, such as those prepared from aniline tars. Spirit stains tend to give greater penetrating power and are faster drying than water-soluble stains. Both types are available in powder form, or as prepared solutions. (64, 236)

stained edges. The edges of a book that have ben stained a uniform color, as distinguished from SPRINKLED EDGES, marbled edges, etc. If only the head edge is so treated, it is termed "stained top." (156)

stained label. A colored (usually rectangular) panel printed or painted directly on the spine covering of a book as a background for the lettering. It is intended that it have the appearance of leather. (156)

stained top. *See:* STAINED EDGES.

staking. The process whereby the fibers of a leather are separated to a degree, thus softening the leather and improving its feel and handle. The process involves flexing the skin, either by hand or machine. Staking by hand is done by pulling the skin in all directions across a blunt blade fixed in a stake.

The staking machine consists of a table that is divided into two parts with an opening of about 10 inches between them. The machine is equipped with two jaws, one above and one below the table. The upper jaw has a rubber roll at its end, while the lower jaw has a bladed opening into which the roll of the upper jaw may sink. The operator slides a portion of the skin between the jaws, which then come together and pull back. As they do so, they force the leather to flex sharply over the blades of the lower jaw and around the roll of the upper jaw. The operator holds the skin in place against the backward movement of the jaws and shifts the position of the skin after each motion of the jaws. There are also machines with automatic clamps that hold the skin when the jaws are staking it. Instead of a roll in the upper jaw, some machines have a smooth blade which forces the skin into a slot; both blade and slot pull backward with the skin betwen them, flexing it sharply along their path. (306, 363)

staling. Another term for putrefaction. *See:* PUTREFACTIVE DAMAGE.

stamp. 1. A finishing tool, cut in brass, bearing figures or patterns in relief. Stamps range in design from a simple dot to the most intricate lacework design, and can be used by hand or in a blocking machine. In a more restricted sense, however, the simpler tools, or those meant to be used by hand; they are probably more correctly referred to as hand tools, fancy hand tools, or UNIT TOOLS. 2. An engraved design on a block, or the impression of a block or stamp on the covers of a book, as distinct from a decoration executed by a roll, or one cut into the leather. *See:* ARMORIAL BINDINGS; BLOCKING (1); BLOCKING FOIL; BLOCKING PRESS; PANEL; STAMP. (25, 137)

stanchgrain. A hard, firm sheet of very white PARCHMENT, produced by means of special finishing compositions. Stanchgrain was an English technique of modifying parchment to produce a firm, smooth, grease-free writing surface of uniform whiteness. The composition used for this consisted essentially of lime and flour; or lime, quicklime and flour, eggwhite and milk, all mixed together and spread on the skin, which was then dried slowly outdoors in the sun. (291)

standardized lettering. A simplified method of lettering the spines of library-bound serial publications, in which all unnecessary words, abbreviations, and decorative stamping are omitted. Years

and months are placed in alignment on volumes of all sizes and titles are placed in alignment within each group size. (131)

standing instructions. The overall instructions pertaining to the binding of a library's books, given to the binder in lieu of preparing a binding slip for each volume. It is in effect a "blanket order" to the binder. (326)

standing press. A large floor press, at one time used extensively in virtually all binderies for operations requiring the application of great pressure; it is used today almost exclusively in hand binding. Pressure is applied by means of a platen which usually is powered by turning a screw, first by hand, then with a short bar, and finally, in operations requiring very great pressure, by means of a long pin. The size and weight of this type of press permit exertion of very great pressure.

The standing press is used not only for the final pressing of a book, but also during the operation of cleaning off the spine and to press the backing shoulders out of the sections of a book pulled for rebinding.

It is not known for certain if standing presses existed in binderies before the end of the 15th century; however, as the use of paper in bookmaking had become more widespread by this time, resulting in increased production of books, the importance of a large press capable of simultaneously pressing a number of books may have become apparent. In addition, a heavy press was needed because the paper of that time was bulky and spongy as compared with parchment.

The form of the early standing press, with its single screw and descending platen, changed very little until the introduction of the hydraulic press. *See also:* BOOMER PRESS; BUILDING-IN MACHINE; FRENCH STANDING PRESS; REMOVABLE PRESS. (161, 236, 320)

staple. One of the several wire fasteners used in SADDLE STITCHING and SIDE STITCHING pamphlets, periodical issues, and the like. Staples for this type of work are of two general types: those already formed and fed automatically, and a continuous roll of wire that is snipped off, formed into a staple, and clinched. Round wire staples are used for saddle stitching, and flat wire staples for side stitching. (234)

staple binder. A hand-, treadle-, or power-operated machine for saddle stitching pamphlets and periodical issues with wire staples. (199)

stapled. Describes a thin book, pamphlet,

periodical issue, or similar thin publication, secured with wire staples. Wire stitching (stapling) in lieu of thread sewing was introduced by publishers in about 1880. Unless bronzed, or otherwise treated, the staples tend to rust. While inadequate for securing the leaves or sections of larger books and/or books of quality, they are probably adequate for many pamphlets (if rust resistant), and are in fact used extensively for securing the leaves of many periodical issues. (69)

starch. The carbohydrate $(C_6H_{10}O_5)_x$, which is being continuously formed and broken down in the living cell and which also serves as a reserve material. Like CELLULOSE, it is made up of a long chain of glucopyranose units joined together through oxygen by x-glucosidic bonds. Chemically, starch is a polymer of glucose, and yields glucose alone on complete hydrolysis, maltose when broken down by enzymes, and dextrine under other conditions. The starches commonly used in papermaking are obtained from corn, potatoes, tapioca and wheat, the last named being the principal source of starch for paste used in bookbinding. Starch was the original material for sizing paper and may have been the first adhesive. *See also:* PASTE. (143)

starched edges. Decorative book edges produced by the use of colored starch (paste), which is sprinkled on the edges in very fine drops. When the starch is dry a darker color is sprinkled on, and, when that is dry, the starch paste is brushed off. Blue-gray (mixed with the paste) and dark brown were the colors commonly used for this decoration. Unsized book paper was best for this technique because it permitted absorption of the paste and color. When sized papers were used, the colors did not adhere well and often ran together unless the edge was first treated with gall water. (151)

starched-filled fabric. A BOOK CLOTH having the interstices of the cloth filled with starch. *Cf:* IMPREGNATED FABRICS.

starch place (starch lume). A section in a book cloth where the WARP contains an excessive quantity of sizing.

start. A section of a book that projects beyond the other sections at the fore edge. A start is generally caused by: 1) the sections being too thick; 2) a large number of sections; or 3) the sewing thread being too loose. (140, 256)

starting charge. A term sometimes used by edition binders to indicate the amount included in their bid or price to cover the costs incidental to beginning the binding of an edition, especially those costs relating to setting up the machines for the run. (140)

starved joint. A joint having too little adhesive to permit a satisfactory bond.

A starved joint may be a result of the adhesive being spread too thin to allow complete filling of the gap betwen adherends, by excessive penetration of the adhesive into the adherends, by inadequate assembly time, or by too great pressure. (309)

static electricity. A condition of electrical charge associated with friction, which is a phenomenon occurring in paper and other non-conductors. In the paper mill it may be due to circumstances involving its manufacture, such as evaporation, friction against the cylinders and felts during shrinkage which takes place during drying, or when it is being glazed, calendered, etc. It also occurs when the paper is on the printing press, folding machine, or other converting equipment. The electricity causes the sheets of paper to adhere to each other or to machine parts, and may cause operating slowdowns. The drier the paper the more easily it retains static electricity, so that increasing the amount of water vapor in the air and storing the paper under carefully controlled conditions in an atmosphere of 65 to 70% relative humidity may reduce the problem.

Static electricity in the papermaking or processing machine may be reduced by passing the paper through electrical fields or by having grounded netting or trailing wires by the paper web.

stationery binding. One of the two broad subdivisions of bookbinding, the other being LETTERPRESS BINDING. By definition, stationery binding is that branch of bookbinding which deals with books meant to be written in, such as ledger, record, and account books, and the like; however, it also encompasses the binding of manifold and duplicate books, receipt books, check books, passports, bankbooks, loose-leaf volumes, and other forms of mechanical binding, as well as punching, perforating, padding, ruling, and other miscellaneous binding operations.

The style of binding applied to books used for written records, e.g., blankbooks, is by necessity much different from that for books meant to be read. Their shape, size, and durability depend on the purpose for which they are intended; consequently, stationery bindings vary greatly in style, complexity, and quantity. Blankbooks, including court record books, which are generally required for permanent records, are bound in a different style from letterpress work because not only must the binding withstand heavy use, it must also open very flat for writing purposes. *See:* SPRING BACK. To a large extent, loose-leaf books are replacing sewn blankbooks, but this branch of stationery binding is rather specialized and is not often undertaken by printing establishments. Manifold and other books designed for use with carbon paper, of which there is a tremendous variety, are generally of a less permanent nature and in most cases are bound in various styles of CUT FLUSH bindings appropriate to the intended use. Stationery binding is sometimes referred to as "vellum binding" because at one time the books were generally covered in vellum. *See also:* BLANKBOOK BINDING; MECHANICAL BINDING; RULING. (58, 95, 276, 339, 343)

stationery endpapers. Endpapers that are tipped on to, rather than being sewn to, the text block. (335)

stave. A folded sheet of a blankbook. (99)

steamboat boards. Any boards used for cutting books OUT OF BOARDS. (241)

steamboating. The process of cutting or shearing a pile of books OUT OF BOARDS. (241)

steamset. A trade name for an English process of edition binding, in which the spine of the book is lined with an expandable cloth before rounding and backing. The lining and the adhesive on the spine are softened by the application of steam, and the book is rounded and backed while the adhesive is in the softened state. Full rounding with good formation of the shoulders, together with durability and good openability, are said to be merits of the process. (89, 140)

steenbok. A small antelope of the genus *Rhaphicerus,* especially *R. campestris,* which lives on the plains of Eastern and Southern Africa, and is used in producing a fine, soft leather. (261)

steer hide. The hide of the male bovine animal that was castrated when only several months old. The hide of such an animal is finer, tighter in structure, and more uniform in thickness than the hide of a bull. (363)

stencil. 1. A method of printing which utilizes wax, silk, or other material. The ink, paint, etc., is applied to the back of the stencil, and covers the paper, cloth, etc., only where the stencil is open. *See also:* SILK-SCREEN PRINTING. 2. A thin cut metal plate which allows the transfer of a design, letter, etc., to a surface when an inked brayer or brush is passed over its surface. (156)

stencil prints. Decorative end- and cover papers produced by the application of paint to paper through a stencil. Prepared transparent wax stencil paper can be used for the stencils. The paint is applied very sparingly with a stiff-bristled brush by starting at the edge of the cut-out at the top of the stencil and then into the open area. This prevents the paint from seeping under the cut edge and leaves a sharper outline. The paint can also be applied with a spray gun, or by rolling an inked BRAYER over the stencil. Either watercolors or dyes may be used for these prints. (86, 183)

steps. Irregularities in the fore edge of a book usually resulting from the sections of the book being too thick, or because of starts in the sections. *See also:* START. (154)

stiasny test. A chemical test designed to determine the type of vegetable tanning agent used in tanning a leather. It consists of boiling the specimen in a solution of formaldehyde and hydrochloric acid, which causes any condensed tannins present to be completely precipitated, while any pyrogallol tans remain in solution. The test solution is obtained by extracting a fragment of the sample (a piece 4 by 4 mm) by refluxing, for 4 hours, first in a 50% aqueous solution and then equal volumes of 6N hydrochloric acid, acetone and water.

Even under the best of conditions this test is difficult to use. Since most vegetable tannins contain both pyrogallol and condensed tannins, it is frequently impossible to judge the colors and precipitates with any degree of certainty. Usually more information of a qualitative nature can be obtained by paper chromatographic separation of the tannin constituents. (291)

stick. 1. A device used to hold the leaves of a current issue, or several current issues, of a newspaper. It is, in effect, a split stick which grips the newspaper at the fold both inside and outside, and is held at the end by a thong or ring, or other type of fastener. 2. The metal holder in which type is set for stamping titles in a blocking press. 3. The implement used in setting printing type by hand, and called a composing stick. (12, 259)

stick mark. *See:* BACK MARK (1).

stick prints. Decorative end- and cover papers produced by the application of wooden doweling, spools, bamboo, and wood scraps of various kinds that have been dipped in color to the paper. Poster paint mixed with paste, glue, or rubber cement is used for printing. The results are improved if the color is used sparingly and the stick is rocked slightly to form a good impression. (86, 133, 183)

stiffen. 1. The process of making a glue or paste more dense, or stiff, by increasing the ratio of solids to solvent. 2. To increase the rigidity of a board by gluing paper or another board to it.

stiffened paper covers. A temporary form of binding consisting of paper covers glued to thin boards, cut flush at head and tail, with the fore-edge flaps turned over.

stiffener. A thin millboard used for stiffening another board or other material. The term is also applied to an INLAY (1). *See also:* LEVERS. (133, 371)

stiff leaf. 1. The blank leaf of an endpaper pasted directly to the first leaf of a book. The first folio number is then on a left-hand page. It is a technique used in blankbook binding. 2. Two ruled leaves pasted together at any place where the ruling changes, so as to have uniform ruling at any SPREAD (1) to which the book is opened. Leaves are also glued between the front fly leaf and the first page of the index, as well as between the index and the main part of the book. (276)

stiffness. A term relating to the ability of a material such as paper or board to resist bending while under stress. Resistance to the bending is called flexural stiffness, and may be defined as the product of the modulus of elasticity and the moment of inertia of the section. Other factors being equal, stiffness of paper and board varies as the cube of its thickness and directly with the modulus of elasticity. Stiffness is improved by increasing the degree of hydration of the pulp used in making the sheet, because a high degree of hydration makes paper dense and hard, and provides cohesive strength. The property is obtained more readily with some pulps than with others. Soda pulp, for example, does not produce particularly stiff paper because the relatively long beating period required to develop the degree of hydration required virtually pulverizes the short soda pulp fibers. Sulfite pulp, on the other hand, can be hydrated to the point of hardness before the fibers are entirely broken down; consequently, long-fibered sulfite pulp is more often used in the production of stiff, hard papers. (17, 98, 350)

stilted. The SQUARES of a book that are unusually extensive. A book is stilted so as to make it of the same height as other books on the same shelf. Stilting may be required when one volume of a set is rebound (and trimmed), in order to make it range with other volumes of the set. In addition, books issued in parts were sometimes stilted by a binder who trimmed excessively. (66, 69)

stippled edges. The edges of a book which have been spotted irregularly with color mainly to keep them from appearing to be soiled. *See also:* SPRINKLED EDGES; STAINED EDGES. (91, 156)

stitcher-trimmer machine. A hand-fed machine that collates, stitches, and trims up to 7,000 units per hour. It can be made to accommodate up to eight hand feeding stations. Two or four wire-stitching heads for stitching through the folds are available and are laterally adjustable. The machine can handle a maximum size of 17½ by 11½ inches and a minimum of 4 by 3 inches. (343)

stitching. *See:* SADDLE STITCHING; SIDE STITCHING.

stock. 1. The hides or skins in a tannery awaiting processing, or in some stage of processing into leather. 2. Paper pulp which has been beaten and refined, treated with sizing, color, filler, etc., and which after dilution is ready for sheet or web formation. 3. Paper, cloth, leather, etc., on hand in inventory. 4. Paper or other materials to be printed, especially paper for a particular printing job. 5. All of the books, manuscripts, etc., in a library. (17, 42, 74, 363)

stocking. The process of forcing oil into a skin mechanically during OIL TANNING. (291)

stone marble. Perhaps one of the earliest of the cover marbles. The cover was first sprinkled with black, followed by brown, in large drops in three or four places, which ran down the sides in streams. This was followed by an application of dilute sulfuric acid on the areas not covered by the brown. (97, 152)

stone papers. Plain, dull-coated brown, green, and slate-gray papers, which were used for Bibles beginning in about 1821, and a short time later appeared in the early cloth bindings. Their smooth-coated finish, usually in very somber shades, were very respectably Victorian, and although perhaps practical, were unattractive; however, their use continued until the end of the century. *See also:* SURFACE PAPERS. (217, 236)

stops. Small, circular finishing tools, designed to "stop" a fillet when it intersects another line at an angle. It is used to avoid the time required for mitering. The same tools are also used in stopping up a full gilt spine. (94, 241)

storage life. The length of time an unopened package of adhesive can be expected to remain in usable condition under specified conditions of temperature and humidity. (309)

stormont marble. A marble pattern developed in the late 18th century and one especially identified with English bookbinding (sometimes being called the "English stormont"). Its distinctive feature is the red vein running through a network of slaty blue. Indigo is especially suitable for this pattern because of the absence of any pasty or sticky quality to it. Instead of the usual oxgall, a small amount of turpentine is added to the blue, which causes the color to break up into a fine network of lacy spots. Because the turpentine evaporates rapidly, the marbler must handle the colors quickly, keeping them stirred constantly. The name "stormont" applies to all colors mixed with turpentine, which may be used in combination with a French or shell color. The pattern is usually produced on a size of gum tragacanth and flea seed. (217, 368)

straight. A term prefixed to a tanning or coloring process to indicate that only the process thus specified has been employed in the manufacture of a leather, e.g., "straight vegetable," indicating tannage solely by the use of vegetable tannins, or "straight dyed," indicating coloring solely by immersion of the leather in a dye bath without subsequent application of pigmented finishes. (61)

straight-grain (morocco). Ostensibly, a goatskin having creases in one direction on the grain surface. The term is generally applied to leathers other than goatskin, which makes the expression "morocco" virtually meaningless. Originally, the creasing was done by BOARDING (1) the skin in the wet condition; however, a similar effect is now obtained by plating the skin with a (heated) engraved steel plate, which renders the term completely meaningless, as well as inaccurate, because the grain of a true morocco is *always* produced by boarding in the wet condition. The technique dates from the second half of the 18th century. (61, 97, 154)

straight-grained roan (long-grained roan). A sheepskin that is split, dyed, seasoned, machine finished, and grained horizontally on the grain surface with a straight-grain. When the flesh split is so treated, it is called a "straight-grained split."

strappings. *See:* CLOTHINGS.

strapwork. A form of decoration consisting of interlaced double lines, usually forming a geometrical pattern. (264, 347)

straw. A fibrous material used in the production of two distinctly different paper products: 1) a coarse, yellowish fiber used for STRAWBOARD and cheap wrapping papers; and 2) a bleached fiber that has some of the properties of ESPARTO PAPER, as well as the shorter-fibered wood pulps, and which is used in the manufacture of relatively high grades of paper.

Any of the cereal straws may be used to make paper pulp, and although wheat is the one most often employed, barley, rye, oat and rice straws are also used. There is probably no significant difference in the grade of pulp obtained from them. Even though the supply of straw runs into the millions of tons, it has not found very wide application in the manufacture of paper and board, except for its widespread use during the Second World War. The cereals are all annual crops and the bulk of the supply for a year's production of a paper mill would have to be gathered within a very brief period, which means that the mill would have to have a very large capacity for baled straw. In addition, unless the mill has means to protect the straw from the weather, deterioration might take place. In most cases the pulp mills are not located near the areas where the straw is produced; therefore, transportation costs would have to be considered. This is particularly significant since the bulk of straw is so much greater than that of wood, which means that the amount of paper pulp obtainable from a given digester capacity is relatively low.

Chemical tests for determining the presence of straw in paper include the aniline sulfate test, which gives a pink stain. (143, 198)

strawboard. A coarse, yellowish board produced largely from straw pulp. Strawboard lacks the mechanical strength to be used as the boards of a book; however, as the bending of a material results in the maximum stretching and compression at the outer surfaces, if the surface of the board could

be stiffened the entire board would then become more rigid. The additional rigidity may be obtained by pasting a hard, tough paper on both sides of the board, thus producing a board that is lightweight and stiff, free from excessive lamination, and relatively easy to produce. Vellum tips could also be used to strengthen the board at the corners in some instances.

While not as strong mechanically as millboard, strawboard is much less laminated and is therefore less likely to split or open out when handled. If its weakness to bending stresses could be improved, as described above, it would actually be preferable to millboard for use in bookbinding. In addition, it has been demonstrated that strawboard is less likely to form sulfuric acid because it contains a lower percentage of iron impurities than does millboard, and it is alkaline, which in itself promotes greater permanence.

The use of strawboard in bookbinding was unknown until about the middle of the 18th century, and its use has never been extensive. (58, 198, 236)

stretch. An extension of the length of a material to the point of rupture to determine its tensile strength. Stretch is generally measured as a percentage of the original length. (17)

strike. 1. The impression created by a finishing tool. 2. In paper ruling, strike is the point at which the pens drop and come into contact with the paper; at this point ruling commences. (82, 274)

strike in. The relative penetration of a liquid into a material. The term is generally used with reference to printing, where it refers to the absorption of the ink vehicle into the paper. Newspaper ink "dries" by means of strike in (absorption). Strike in, however, may not be desirable as the absorbed ink may result in SHOW THROUGH. (17)

strike through. A severe case of STRIKE IN, where the ink used in printing actually penetrates the sheet and is visible on the opposite side. *See also:* SHOW THROUGH. (17)

striking out. *See:* SETTING OUT; SLICKING (1).

stringiness. The property of an adhesive which causes it to form filaments, threads, etc., when the applicator is removed from the adherend, or when transfer surfaces are separated. Transfer surfaces include rolls, picker plates, stencils, and the like. (309)

string prints. Decorative end- and cover papers produced by using string as a medium for printing. This technique, in which a line pattern is emphasized, involves tying string around a block, inking it with a brayer and then pressing the block against the paper. The paper may also be pressed against the block. The string may also be tied around the brayer, which is then rolled over the printers' ink and then onto the paper. As the brayer rolls across the sheet the pattern repeats itself. Rolling in different directions and using more than one color results in a variation of design. For more control in shaping the design in a formal arrangement, the string can be glued to the block in the pattern desired and then inked and printed. String prints may also be combined wtih other media, the paper being rolled first with one color and the string print applied over it in a different color. The technique is also used in the production of paste papers. (183)

strip covers (strip advertisements). An instruction to a library binder to remove and discard the covers of periodical issues before binding. "Strip advertisements" is an instruction to remove all full-page advertisements (on both recto and verso of the leaf) before binding. Their removal makes for a thinner volume, and thus reduces shelf space required; but the space actually saved compared with the cost to the library of having covers and advertisements removed, plus the loss of potentially valuable historical material, make the practice of debatable value. *Cf:* BIND ALL. (259)

strip gumming. The application of a line of adhesive along the edge of a sheet, either by hand or by means of a gumming machine. (58, 82)

stripping. 1. The process of removing dirt, grease, or uneven tan deposition from the grain of a newly tanned leather by drumming the skins in a solution of warm water (40° C.) and a small amount of milk alkali, e.g., 1% by weight of the stock of soda ash, borax, or sodium bicarbonate. Too vigorous or prolonged stripping is to be avoided as it can seriously de-tan the leather. If heavy stripping is carried out, or if the original tannage was not satisfactory for the leather required, it is possible to retan the skins at this stage. 2 A term used mainly in library binding to indicate GUARDING. (306)

stripping machine. A device used to apply a strip of cloth or paper to endpapers, reinforce side stitched or sewn books between the cover and outer sections, reinforce the folds of sections, hinge or guard folded maps, and apply strips of cloth or paper to pads, check books, composition books, and the like. The machine can accommodate books up to 2 inches thick and apply strips ½ to 3 inches wide. It can be used with hot melt or cold adhesives, or water if the material used is pre-glued. (264)

stub (stubbed). 1. That part of an original leaf which is left after most of it has been cut away from its conjugate leaf. *See also:* CANCEL (1). 2. A narrow strip of paper or linen sewn between sections of a book for the purpose of attaching plates, maps, etc. A book which has had stubs bound in is said to be "stubbed." *See also:* COMPENSATION GUARD; GUARD (2). (12, 102, 335)

stub book. *See:* GUARD BOOK.

stuck-on headband. *See:* HEADBAND.

stuffing. 1. The operation of inserting layers of chipboard into a book having excessive sewing swell before nipping, so as to prevent the book from starting. Also called "packing." *See:* START. 2. The process of incorporating grease into a tanned hide, either by hand or by drumming, so as to improve its quality or to impart special properties. DUBBIN is frequently employed in this process, although other materials are also used. The mixture spreads over the damp fibers, and penetrates into them as the leather dries. The oil enters the hide easily, while the harder fat remains on the surface or in the surface layers. Stuffing is generally used on heavy hides in lieu of FATLIQUORING. (305, 339, 363)

stumpwork embroidery. An elaborate colored embroidery with intricate padded designs and scenes in high relief. Stumpwork embroidery was especially popular in English embroidered bindings of the 17th century. (347)

stylus. An implement for writing, used in ancient and medieval times for writing on wax or clay. The stylus is pointed at one end and is sometimes flattened on the other end for flattening out previous writing.

substance. 1. The weight of a paper expressed in terms of weight per ream of sheets of a given size. It is usually based on a ream of 500 sheets. The weight of a ream of a given size and number of sheets is called the substance number, the "substance" being the product of the density, i.e., the degree of dilution of the pulp suspension flowing onto the papermaking machine wire, the rate at which it flows, and the speed of the wire. *See also:* BASIS WEIGHT. 2. The total weight of a hide or skin suitable for conversion into leather. While "substance" in this context will vary greatly, depending on the type of hide or skin, age and sex of the animal, etc., as an example of substance, 100 pounds of green salted calfskin will average:

    43.8 pounds water
    5.9 pounds (dry) hair
    3.8 pounds (dry) fleshings
    .8 pounds pate or cheekings
    2.0 pounds (physiologic) fat
    .5 pounds minerals
    12.0 pounds salt (NaC1)
    31.2 pounds hide substance
                     (17, 248, 306)

substantive dyes. *See:* DIRECT DYES.

substrate. A broader term than ADHEREND, used with reference to the surface upon which an adhesive, e.g., acrylic resin, is spread for bonding, coating, etc. (309)

subway test. A test designed to simulate the distortion imparted to a paperbound book by a reader holding it in one hand with covers touching. The volume is bent through 360° to bring its covers back to back. If a leaf becomes detached, the volume fails the test. In flattening a book in preparation for use in most copying machines, a book also undergoes a partial distortion, so that the subway test, with its resultant stresses on the binding, is valid, at least to a limited extent, in determining the durability of the binding. The test, nevertheless, is subjective and care must be taken that it is conducted by the same trained individual every time in order to avoid operators' variables as much as possible. The name of the test derives from the habit some (standing) public transit riders have of holding the overhead strap or bar with one hand while holding a book (usually a paperback) in the other. *See also:* PAGE FLEX TEST.

sudoriferous glands. The sweat glands of a hide or skin, usually more or less completely removed during the beamhouse operations of liming, unhairing, bating, and scudding. (363)

suede (suede calf; suede kid; suede splits) leather. A term taken from the French, "gants de Suède" (Swedish gloves), and applied to a leather finished on the flesh side by buffering so as to raise a velvet-like nap. The typical suede leather is produced from the smaller skins, such as calfskin, kidskin, lambskin and goatskin, although cowhide has also been used.

    The nap is produced by buffing or wheeling the surface on the flesh side, or the split side of flesh splits; velvet suedes, however, are buffed on the grain side. A common criterion of good suede leather is that the fibers of the nap should be of uniform length and tightly packed together, in order to give a resilience to the nap so that it does not readily shown fingermarks. The firmness of the nap depends upon the density and compactness of the fiber structure. Velvet suedes are finer than flesh suedes and a younger animal, such as a SLUNK, produces an even finer suede.

A principal concern in making suede leather is to retain the fine nap and still produce a soft leather; however, the leather must not be made soft by means of improper FATLIQUORING, because even a small excess of oil will produce a greasy suede nap.

Suede leather, often tooled in blind, was used in England as early as the 17th century, and in the 18th and early 19th centuries in blankbook binding. (61, 173, 291, 306, 325)

sulfate paper. *See:* KRAFT PAPER.

sulfate process (sulfate pulp). One of the two principal chemical methods of converting wood into pulp for papermaking, the other being the SULFITE PROCESS. Today, the terms "sulfate" and kraft, when applied to paper pulp, are generally used interchangeably, although there are slight differences between them. The term "kraft" was first applied to the strong brown paper produced from pulp made by the sulfate process, and later to indicate the pulp itself. Originally, the term "sulfate" designated all paper pulps made by the sulfate process; later, it was used strictly with reference to special grades of pulp, such as bleachable sulfate pulp, bleached sulfate, etc., while "kraft" became restricted to that particular quality of unbleached sulfate pulp which had been cooked so as to produce a high yield or pulp of exceptional strength. Today, however, the term "sulfate" is generally used in the paper industry to indicate all grades of pulp produced by a process which utilizes sodium sulfate as its principal chemical constituent. The only exceptions to this common practice are certain speciality grades of pulp, such as easy-bleaching sulfates made from both softwood and hardwood trees.

Sulfate pulps were first used primarily for the production of various grades of paper and board where physical strength was of greatest importance. Although the stronger grades are produced from the softwoods, very large quantities of hardwood sulfate pulps are also produced. Mixtures of hardwoods, with their longer fiber improve the formation and surface features of the paper or board. (17, 72, 143, 198, 320)

sulfite process (sulfite pulp). One of the two principal chemical methods of converting wood into pulp for papermaking, the other being the SULFATE PROCESS. Bleached or unbleached sulfite pulp is used in the manufacture of nearly all classes of paper, and bleached sulfite pulp is also used in the manufacture of rayon, cellophane, and other cellulose esters and ethers. Although it is possible to produce bleached sulfite pulp from the hardwoods, the pulp is usually made from softwoods of low resin content, e.g., spruce, balsam, fir, and hemlock. Traditionally, sulfite pulping has involved the digestion of the wood with a calcium acid sulfite cooking liquor, generally a mixture of calcium bisulfite and excess sulfurous acid; however, since processing for waste liquor recovery is both difficult and impractical with calcium-base liquors, more soluble bases, such as sodium, ammonium, and magnesium are now being substituted for calcium.

The sulfite cooking process may be modified to produce pulps that can be roughly classified as soft, medium, or strong, which are classifications that depend to a great extent on the degree to which lignin is removed and the cellulose of the fiber is depolymerized. Sulfite pulping is superior in the amount of lignin removed, and produces papermaking fibers that are white in color and can be bleached to higher whiteness with less chemicals than required for the sulfate process. Sulfite fibers also give fewer problems in maintaining desired formation characteristics of the finished paper; however, paper made from sulfite fibers is not as strong as that made from sulfate pulp. (17, 72, 98, 143)

sulfonated oils. Oils rendered soluble in water by chemical treatment with sulfuric acid. Most sulfonated oils are actually soaps, but the fatty acid has a soluble sulfonic group combined with it, which tends to give it a limited water solubility even when the soap is decomposed by the addition of the acid. Sulfonated oils are used in FATLIQUORING leather, in the preparation of cotton fiber, as mordants for certain dyes, as finishing oils in silk, linen, and leather manufacture, and in paint and varnish making. (305, 363)

sulfur dioxide. One of the oxides of sulfur. Sulfur dioxide (SO_2), which is probably the most common cause of the deterioration of paper, is produced when sulfur, or materials containing sulfur—e.g., coal, oil—is burned in air. It is present in varying amounts in the atmosphere of almost all industrialized nations. Sulfur dioxide, even at higher concentrations than are normally found in the atmosphere, is not in itself harmful to paper or bookbinding materials, but it can be converted into highly destructive sulfuric acid, either by being oxidized to sulfur trioxide (SO_3), and then into sulfuric acid ($SO_3 + H_2O = H_2SO_4$), or by reaction of SO_2 with water to form sulfurous acid, which in turn oxidizes to form sulfuric acid ($H_2SO_3 + H_2O = H_2SO_4 + 2H$). Some authorities maintain that this conversion of sulfur dioxide to sulfuric acid requires the presence of small amounts of copper or iron, i.e., minute particles of metal broken from the refining apparatus and entering the pulp, as is almost always the case with papers produced during the past 150 to 200 years; whereas others maintain that the process will take place regardless of metallic content and that the copper and/or iron impurities simply function as catalysts and thus quicken the rate of deterioration.

Archival papers should be protected against atmospheric sulfur dioxide, insofar as possible, by: 1) removing dangerous or potentially dangerous impurities, e.g., catalytic materials, from the paper, or, alternatively, manufacturing paper free from them; 2) the addition of alkaline and buffering agents to neutralize any sulfuric acid that does form; 3) destroying the chemical (catalytic) activity of the metallic impurities by the use of inhibitors, such as magnesium salts; and 4) storing paper in an atmosphere as free as possible from sulfur dioxide.

Sulfur dioxide is also used as a reducing agent in the preparation of basic chrome tanning liquor from sodium dichromate in acid solution: $Na_2Cr_2O_7 + H_2O + 3SO_2 = 2Cr(OH)SO_4 + Na_2SO_4$. (193, 198, 248)

sulfuric acid. A heavy, viscous, colorless, odorless, and relatively non-volatile acid (H_2SO_4). It is miscible in all proportions with water and can be formed in book materials, especially in paper. *See:* SULFUR DIOXIDE. It is a very powerful acid and is highly destructive to cellulosic and proteinaceous materials, such as paper and leather. Sulfuric acid was also used, particularly in the 19th century, in the execution of many so-called cover marbles, and is still used in leather manufacture for bleaching, deliming, pickling, pH control, and the like. (207, 235, 363)

sulfurous acid. An unstable, relatively weak acid (H_2SO_3), formed by dissolving SULFUR DIOXIDE in water. It is used as a reducing and bleaching agent, and forms SULFURIC ACID when oxidized.

sulfurous anhydride (sulfurous acid anhydride. See: SULFUR DIOXIDE.

sulfur oxide. Any of the several oxides of sulfur. See: SULFUR DIOXIDE; SULFUR TRIOXIDE.

sulfur trioixde. A compound (SO_3) that reacts violently with water to form SULFURIC ACID. It is formed by the oxidation of SULFUR DIOXIDE.

sumac. A vegetable tanning material obtained from the dried leaves of certain species of *Rhus*, especially *R. coriaria* (from the Mediterranean region—Sicilian sumac) and more recently from various American sumacs, including the dwarf sumac (*R. copallina*), the white sumac (*R. glabra*), and the staghorn sumac, (*R. typhina*). Sumac provides a very desirable tannin where white or light-colored, soft and supple leathers are required. Because it produces such desirable qualities of drape, feel, flexibility, etc., it is used in the tannage of goatskins (morocco leather), skivers, roans, etc. Another important advantage of sumac is that the leather produced with it does not darken upon exposure to light and is less likely to decay than leather produced by use of some other tannins.

In spite of its special value for certain classes of leather, the use of sumac as a tanning agent has declined in recent decades. This decline has been due in part to the development of less expensive tannins, such as wattle, quebracho, and myrabolans for general tanning, and also perhaps to the adulteration of the product by commercial harvesters of sumac in the Mediterranean region.

Good quality sumac is sold in the form of a light, yellowish-green powder, which has a tannin content of about 26 to 27%; however, the tannin content may vary from 25 to 30%. Sumac generally has a higher pH value than other tannin materials in its class, i.e., about 4.0, and also a very high acids and salts content. A large proportion of the salts are weak acids. Sumac, which is one of the pyrogallol class of tannins, is very mild in its action and penetrates the hide substance very

slowly. Unlike most of the pyrogallol tannins, sumac does not form BLOOM (1). Its first recorded use as a tanning agent was in England in 1565. See also: VEGETABLE TANNINS. (175, 207, 363)

sun damage. Damage that occurs to a hide or skin when it becomes heated above a certain critical temperature while it is still moist and is laid out in the sun to dry (cure). A completely dry skin can become very hot and still not be affected under normal conditions of cure, but prior to this a skin is very susceptible to damage. Also, the drying of a salted skin proceeds so uniformly throughout its entire thickness that the cooling effect produced by evaporation off its surfaces maintains the temperature of the entire skin below the danger point until it is uniformly dry. Without salt, however, a skin tends to dry unevenly when laid out in the usual manner, which is flesh side up. This can happen because the flesh side can dry out completely and begin generating heat, while the underside remains moist, and, being shielded from evaporation, also begins to generate heat. This is especially the case when pieces of flesh, generally of a fatty nature, are present on the flesh side, and further retard the drying of areas beneath them. The result of overheating moist skins is to "cook," and therefore gelantinize, the skin fibers, so that they are no longer leather-forming collagen. The damage, however, is not visible in the dried skin, nor can it be detected even after the skin is soaked to return it to the pre-cured condition. It is only after liming that the damaged areas tend to disintegrate, leaving holes in the skin, that the damage becomes apparent. In many cases the damage is largely limited to the grain surface, which becomes deeply corroded, giving rise to the trade term "blister" for this particular type of damage. See also: PUTREFACTIVE DAMAGE. (248)

sundex process. A British process of laminating a paper document. The process utilizes semi-transparent glassine paper in lieu of cellulose acetate foil, with the three components of the "sandwich," i.e., the document and the two sheets of glassine being sealed together with an aqueous adhesive, such as carboxymethylcellulose (C. M. C.) or starch paste. The sandwich is then consolidated by pressing it between heated surfaces. The Sundex process is safer than conventional LAMINATION in that an operating temperature below 100° C. is needed in place of the much higher temperature required in con-

ventional laminating. In addition, the treated document need only be soaked in water (assuming the document itself is not sensitive to aqueous solutions) for delamination to take place. Another important advantage claimed for the process is that the components of the sandwich are closely related materials, and the adhesive is compatible with both. The final sandwich is therefore more mechanically and chemically homogeneous than the usual laminated sandwich, and consequently less liable to unbalanced stresses due to changes in moisture content and temperature of the surrounding atmosphere. (198)

sunfast. See: FAST COLORS.

sun spots. A variation of the Turkish, snail, or wave marbles, consisting of a color or colors which are made to spread out in a raylike effect somewhat like the rays of the sun. The effect is produced by adding a small amount of kaolin (in water) and boiled potash to the colors. The colors are then dropped on the size, a drop of potash water is dropped on, causing the color to contract, followed by another drop of the color directly over the first, which causes the color to radiate outward. (264)

super. See: MULL.

"super" binding. An obsolete term once used in the United States to describe a binding having the spine lined with both cloth and paper. See: SECOND LINING; SPINE LINING (1). (169)

supercalender. An off-machine calender stack used to impart density, gloss, and smoothness to paper. It is similar to the calender except that alternate chilled cast iron and softer rolls are used. The rolls used to supercalender uncoated paper usually consist of cast iron and highly compressed paper, while the rolls used for coated paper are usually cast iron and highly compressed cotton. The finish produced varies according to the raw material used to make the paper and the pressure exerted on it, and ranges from the highest English finish to a highly glazed surface. Supercalendered papers are sometimes used for books containing fine line blocks or halftones because they print well from type and halftones, although for the latter they are not as good as coated paper. (17, 52, 182, 287)

superficial fascia. The relatively thin layer of flesh on a hide or skin, known in the leather trade simply as "flesh" and containing adipose (fatty) and areolar (loose connective) tissues and sometimes muscle tissues. (363)

superfinish. A polishing process applied to some book cloths, especially those with a hard surface. Finishing is done by die-embossing the cloth, and air-brush coloring. (164)

supported French joint. A modification of the FRENCH JOINT. It is used to impart additional support to the shoulders of large books. A thin board is glued to the book board; however, instead of

SUPPORTED FRENCH JOINT

stopping at the inside edge of the thicker board, it extends the exact distance of the intended gap between the board and the shoulder, i.e., the distance of the French joint. When the boards are attached, these thin boards press against the shoulders and help support them.

surface-active agent (surfactant). A substance that, when used in small quantities, modifies the surface properties of liquids or solids. A surface-active agent reduces surface tension in a fluid or the interfacial tension between two immiscible fluids, such as oil and water. Surfactants are particularly useful in accomplishing the wetting or penetration of solids by aqueous liquids and serve in the manner of detergent, emulsifying, or dispersing agents. They are more effective than soap in certain situations and are used by conservators for such purposes as cleaning, wetting, and dispersing. *See also:* WETTING AGENT.

surface color. 1. The color of a coating or top layer as opposed to a substance that is colored throughout its mass. 2. The color effect presented by a surface when viewed by reflected light, especially when associated with metals, e.g., the yellow of gold, the white of platinum, etc. (233)

surface papers. Decorative endpapers, colored on one side only subsequent to the manufacture of the paper. They were produced in several (usually drab) colors and some were glazed. Endpapers of this type were in common use by the 1820s, generally with the drab colors predominating, although clear yellow papers of varying shades were also produced later on in the century. The endpapers were used

in publishers' cloth and leather bindings, as well as in miscellaneous bindings of cloth and leather. The color was applied to the paper in pigment form, which imparted a somewhat artificial effect, unlike the vegetable-stained, surface-colored papers which preceded them. Crudely pigmented surface papers were used in the later 18th century, but only rarely. This type of paper is never found on the sides of half-bindings because it was too easily stained by grease; however, it was used for the covers of inexpensive "yellow-back" books of the 19th century. The darker colors, especially brown, mauve, and black, were often used for devotional books. Also called "coated papers." (236)

surface sized. Paper or board sized when the web or sheet is dry or partially dry, usually on the papermaking machine but also as a separate operation. (316)

surface-size press. A part of the papermaking machine, usually located between two drier sections, and used to apply relatively light coatings of a surface size or other material to the surface of the paper web. The unit may be vertically or horizontally oriented and is equipped to spray or otherwise apply material to one or both sides of the paper web as it moves through the papermaking machine. (17)

surface tension. A force which tends to bring the contained volume of a body, e.g., a liquid, into the form having the least surface area, as in the tendency of a drop of water to assume a spherical shape, i.e., the smallest surface area for the given volume of liquid. (17)

surfactant. *See:* SURFACE-ACTIVE AGENT.

Sutcliffe, George (1878-1943). An English bookbinder apprenticed to Maudie's Library and then employed in the shop of Douglas Cockerell in 1899. In 1901, Sutcliffe and FRANCIS SANGORSKI opened their own bindery and began producing the jewelled bindings on which their great reputation was largely built. Of the hundreds of such bindings, the finest and their most outstanding achievement was a binding known as the GREAT OMAR. (94, 236)

"Sutherland" decoration. A manner of tooling in colors, usually carried out on vellum and analogous materials, and called "Sutherland" because of the patronage of the Duchess of Sutherland. The process involved the use of a resin, which was applied to the vellum, followed by colors which were sprinkled on and then tooled. Until this technique was introduced by the Eng-

lish binder George Bagguley, in 1896, tooling in color had never been successful and foils, of course, did not exist.

Solid tooling was not possible, but very beautiful and delicate tooling on bright colors with highlights in gold was done by means of fine gouges and pallets. Because the decoration was much too delicate for normal handling, Bagguley usually restricted his technique to doublures, and even then generally vellum doublures. (94, 236)

sweat glands. *See:* SUDORIFEROUS GLANDS.

sweating. 1. A pressing operation employed in handmade papermaking following the initial pressing of the WATERLEAF sheets between felts. Each sheet is removed from the felt, pressed, laid one on top of another, with the other of the sheets being rotated after each pressing, until the desired pressure has been reached. This process of repeated pressing was not a common practice until the 16th century, as evidenced by the roughness and absence of finish of paper made before that time.

2. An old and virtually obsolete method of loosening the hair of skins, by allowing controlled putrefaction to take place in a confined, warm area. It is probably the oldest method of unhairing and possibly is still being used in some countries, particularly for sheepskins (where the hair is often more valuable than the skin). Sweating consists of little more than putrefaction of the Malpighian layer. Because of the danger of damage to the skins in the sweat chambers, unless the process is very carefully controlled (*see:* RUN PELTS), its use was discontinued for the best grades of skins following the introduction of safer methods of unhairing (*see:* LIMING).

The skins are generally hung from beams in a closed room in which the air is kept warm and humid. During the process a considerable amount of ammonia and amines are generated, which assist in the unhairing action. As soon as the hair slips away easily, the skins are taken from the sweat chamber and placed in saturated lime water, which retards further bacterial actions and causes some swelling of the skins. (79, 291, 363)

sweet oil. A mild oil, e.g., olive oil, mixed with paste, colors, and water to make the coloring matter used for sprinkling the edges of books, largely in the 19th century. The oil apparently was used to promote the penetration of the color and paste into the paper. (371)

swell. The additional thickness in the spine of a book caused by the sewing thread and/or extensive guarding. If the sections are thin and large in number, the sewing swell may become so great as to cause problems in subsequent operations. This is particularly true with hard-finished papers, because, when a book is made up of soft paper, the sewing threads will become embedded in the paper to some degree when the book is smashed or nipped and the swell reduced; however, since the threads will not be forced into hard paper by smashing without cutting it, the book retains the swell. Excessive swell can cause the spine of the book to buckle and run in, uneven trimming, and poor rounding and backing. While excesive swell is undesirable, some swell is required for proper rounding and backing. In hand binding, the danger of excessive swell can sometimes be avoided by sewing the book TWO ON. (256, 339)

swelling. An increase in the volume of the protein fibers and jellies of a hide or skin caused by the absorption of water, and seen as an increase in the thickness of the skin. Swelling is an important aspect in liming, unhairing, and splitting.

symmetrical design. A decorative design for a book built up by means of repeating tools at regular intervals—as in a diaper design, for example—or by drawing some symmetrical form and repeating small tools in conjunction with this form, in order to carry out a decorative scheme. (115)

syneresis. The separation of a liquid from a gel, as, for example, water from paste, upon standing. (309)

syntans. A contraction of "synthetic tannins," which are chemicals that combine with, or affect, the protein constituents of hides and skins and produce a product that is flexible, porous, and has the desirable qualities of leather. The most widely known syntans are made by treating aromatic substances, e.g., cresols, phenols, naphthalenes, etc., with formaldehyde and sulfuric acid. There are many variations in the ingredients of syntans, relative quantities used, and methods of manufacture. Syntans produce white or buff-colored leather, depending on the ingredients, which darken upon exposure to light, and generally behave much like vegetable-tanned leathers. Although syntans do exist which can be used alone to produce leather (so-called exchange or replacement syntans), many syntans lack the filling power of vegetable tannins and produce an undesirably thin, "papery" leather. They are also more expensive than the natural tannins. Syntans do have desirable properties, however, and are widely used in both chrome and vegetable tannages. When used in conjunction with other tanning agents, where they are known as "auxiliary syntans," they perform the following functions: 1) the presence of 5% syntan helps dissolve solid vegetable tannin extracts and reduces any tendency to form REDS (condensed tannins) or BLOOM (pyrogallol tannins); 2) a pretannage with 5 to 10% syntan improves the shade, i.e., makes it paler, and the levelness of color of a subsequent vegetable tannage; 3) a pretannage with a syntan or admixture with a vegetable tannage improves penetration of tannin into the skin; 4) when syntan is used with a vegetable tannin the leather develops a more uniform but paler color upon being dyed, but the syntan generally prevents the development of deep, full shades; 5) some types of syntan may be adjusted with an alkali to a pH of 6.0 to become "neutral syntans," often called synthetic mordants (but should be called "synthetic leveling agents") which have value in dyeing leather;

and 6) some syntans retard mold growth and/or remove iron stains. (248, 291, 306, 363)

synthetic glues. *See:* RESINOUS ADHESIVES.
synthetic leveling agents. *See:* NEUTRAL SYNTANS; SYNTANS.

synthetic resins. A group of complex, partially amorphous, organic semi-solid or solid substances that are produced by chemical reaction or by polymerization of relatively simple compounds. Synthetic resins are comparable to natural resins in various physical properties but are considered to be superior to them in that they are more uniform, possess greater clarity, durability, flexibility and resistance to chemical change. The synthetic resins include: 1) formaldehyde condensation products of phenol, urea, and melamine; 2) reaction products of polyhydric alcohols and polybasic acids (alkyd and polyester resins); 3) polymerization products of acrylic acid and its derivatives (acrylic resins) or styrene (polystyrene); and 4) polymers of butadiene and its derivatives, or copolymers, with other materials (synthetic elastomers, etc.).

According to the manner in which they react to heat and pressure, synthetic resins are classified broadly as being either *thermoplastic* or *thermosetting.* Although the cellulose polymers, cellulose acetate, cellulose nitrate, and ethyl cellulose, are prepared from natural materials and, therefore, do not conform to the definition of a synthetic resin, they are nonetheless classed along with them. These resins also find use in papermaking as adhesives in coating and laminating, as barrier materials, and as agents to impart special properties to paper, e.g., improved wet and dry strength. Synthetic resins are also used extensively in the application of finishes to the grain surface of leather. (17, 306)

tab 258 tag board

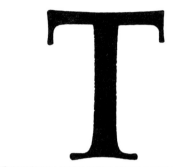

tab. 1. The crescent-shaped tongue of leather extending above and below the spine of some 12th century bindings and probably intended to facilitate the removal of the book from a chest where it was stored spine uppermost. 2. A small square or rectangular piece of paper, card, plastic, leather, or fabric attached to the fore edge of a leaf, and bearing one or more characters to serve as a guide or INDEX. *See also:* TAB INDEX. (12, 156, 236)

tab index. A form of the index used when the ordinary cut INDEX is not feasible, such as with loose-leaf bindings. The set of 24 tabs (I and J are generally combined and X is omitted) are prepared in one strip of material, which is glued along half its length, leaving splits for attachment to the leaves. The letters are printed or blocked on the strip and the individual letters are then separated. The tabs are attached to the leaves in a complete series along the fore edge from head to tail (and usually from front to back) with the letters projecting. (276)

table book. 1. An elaborately decorated edition of a book, often covered in velvet or silk, and intended for display on a drawing room table. This type of binding was popular in the 19th century. Its 20th century equivalent is the "coffee table" book, usually a large illustrated art book. 2. An ancient writing book consisting of wax-covered tablets of metal, ivory or wood fastened together at the back by rings or leather thongs. The writing was done with a stylus. *See also:* DIPTYCH. 3. An obsolete name for a notebook. (156, 203, 310)

tablet. 1. An early writing material made of clay (which was inscribed while soft and then fired to make the writing permanent), stone, wood, or ivory (covered with wax, which was then inscribed with a pointed instrument). 2. *See:* PAD. (156, 264)

tablet-back board. A board used as a (more or less) stiff backing for a PAD. It is generally produced from ordinary chipboard, or newsboard, and ranges in thickness from 0.020 inch and upward. (17)

tack (tackiness). 1. A general term applied to the state or property of tending to adhere, the relative stickiness of

an adhesive film, the resistance offered by an adhesive film to division of the adhesive surface, or the resistance offered by the adhesive (while in the plastic state) to removal of the adherends. Some printing inks, varnishes, and similar viscous liquids also display tack. *See also:* BLOCKING (2, 3). 2. That property of an adhesive which results in a bond of considerable strength immediately after application and contact under low pressure. 3. The resistance of an ink film to being split between two surfaces, such as between rollers, between plate and blanket, or between blanket and paper. (164, 309)

tacketing. A method originally employed in non-adhesive binding to secure the section (or sections) and covers of limp vellum bindings. The technique was later used to secure the loose, jacketlike cover to the text block of some bindings, and, from late medieval times, as a method of decorating the covers of stationery bindings. Tacketing in one form or another dates back to at least the early 12th century. In the past 100 years or so, tacketing has been used to reinforce the sewing of large blankbooks. The tackets are secured around the folio, webbing, and clothings of the spine. In this latter use, it was restricted to the better grades of stationery bindings. Over a period of some 800 years, therefore, tacketing has evolved from a method of constructing a bookbinding to a method of reinforcing and decorating the spine and covers of a book.

Early tacketing involved punching two holes through the center fold of each section, as well as the vellum cover, about ½ to ¾ inch apart. The ends of a strip of vellum, gut, or

leather lacing were passed through the holes from the inside, wound around each other and knotted at each end. When tacketing stationery bindings, the holes were punched through the sections, the cover, and the bands, and then wound around each other. Those stationery bindings having spring-backs were tacketed to help secure the folios to the clothings on the spine, or, if webbing were used, the folios, webbings and clothings.

When tacketing is employed in modern-day stationery binding, the tackets, which are usually made of catgut, are used at each webbing, but only on the first and last three folios. (99, 236, 343)

tacking. The operation of attaching a tanned, damp hide or skin to a wooden frame so as to allow it to dry in a smooth and somewhat stretched condition. As this method of drying is slower than tunnel drying, it is more expensive. The stretching action, which is accomplished by "enlarging" the frame must be carefully controlled because excessive stretching may weaken the leather, resulting in a loose and PIPEY LEATHER. It is an operation requiring considerable skill on the part of the workman tacking the skins to the frame, especially since many leathers are sold by the square foot; consequently, judicious tacking (and stretching) can add to the area of the leather. (363)

tack range. The length of time an adhesive will stay tacky-dry after application, under specified conditions of temperature and humidity. (309)

tack stage. The length of time during which an adhesive is sticky, or resists removal or deformation of the cast adhesive. (309)

tacky-dry. The state of an adhesive when the solvent and other volatile ingredients have evaporated sufficiently, or have been absorbed enough, so that the adhesive is in the proper tacky state. (309)

tag(s). 1. A grade of manila board used for the boards of semi-flexible bindings. 2. The band to which a seal is attached in old manuscripts. 3. *See:* CATCHWORD. 4. The straight or crossed tips of a lace. (94, 154, 261)

tag board. A lightweight board used for

envelopes, file folders, temporary wrapping, and the like. It is manufactured from jute, rope, chemical and mechanical wood pulps, or combinations thereof, usually on a cylinder machine but sometimes on a FOURDRINIER MACHINE. The board has a smooth surface and

is available in a wide range of colors. Basis weights range from 80 to 300 pounds (22½ × 28½ — 500), the most common weights being 80, 100, 125, 150, 175, 200, and 275 pounds. Tag board should have good bending and folding strength, high bursting and

tensile strength, good resistance to tearing, and a finish suitable for writing or printing. (17, 142, 264)

tail. 1. The lower or bottom edge of a book, usually implying the very edge of the covers and spine. 2. The lower portion of a letter, e.g., "g" and the projection of an upper case letter, e.g., "Q." (287)

tailband; tailcap. *See:* HEADBAND; HEADCAP.

tail edge. *See:* TAIL (1).

tail margin. The area between the bottom line of letterpress or writing and the bottom edge of the leaf. *See also:* MARGIN (1).

take off. A term applied to the flaying (removal of the skin) of an animal.

talc. A hydrous mineral consisting of magnesium-silicate$(3MgO\cdot4SiO_2\cdot H_2O)$. Commercial talc is seldom if ever a pure mineral and therefore its physical and chemical properties usually vary over a relatively wide range. A commercial talc, such as soapstone, when ground into a very fine powder generally has a soft and greasy feel and is usually creamy to greenish-white in color. Talc is used as a filler in cultural papers, to which it imparts a raglike feel. (17)

talipot palm. A fan palm, *Corypha umbraculifera,* found in Ceylon and the Philippines, and other areas of the Far East. It has very large, fan-shaped leaves which are cut into strips and processed for use as a substitute for paper. *See also:* PALM LEAF BOOK.

tall copy. 1. A book which has had its head and tail edges trimmed very slightly. 2. A comparison of several copies of the same book in the same edition and on the same paper, one of which may be taller than the others. 3. *See:* LARGE PAPER COPY. (69)

tambour. 1. A form of embroidery consisting of looped stitches similar to a chain stitch and worked with a fine hook. Tambour was used on embroidered bindings. 2. A metallic embroidery thread either worked through the material or sewn to it with silk of the same color. It was sometimes sewn flat and sometimes raised over thread or cord if the relief was to be high; however, this technique was never employed on silk, only on satin and velvet. It was usually double, the lines being laid down side by side with only the ends being taken through the back. Occasionally, it was sewn down with a bright lustrous red silk. *See also:* COUCHING (2). (280)

tan (tannage; tanned). 1. To convert a

TACKETING

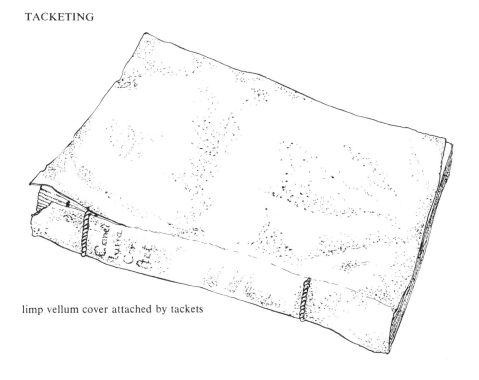

limp vellum cover attached by tackets

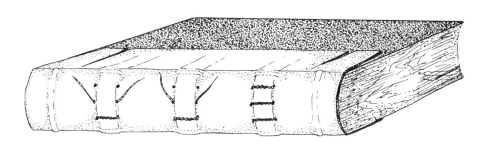

blankbook spine reinforced by tackets

hide or skin into leather. 2. Tannage, which is the act, process, or result of tanning a hide or skin. 3. A tanned hide or skin, i.e., one which has been converted into leather.

tannery. The establishment or place in which the processes involved in converting raw hide or skin into leather take place.

tannic acid. A tannin, usually in the form of a yellowish-white or pale brown powder, obtained from fermented oak galls by extraction with water-saturated ether. Tannic acid is soluble in water, alcohol, and acetone, and gives precipitates with most metallic salts, proteins, and alkaloids. Chemically, it is a penta-m-digalloyl-glucose having a high molecular weight. Upon hydrolysis with sulfuric acid, it gives gallic acid and glucose. *See also:* VEGETABLE TANNINS.

tanning. *See:* CHROME TANNING; VEGETABLE TANNING.

tapa cloth. A coarse type of "cloth" produced in the Far East from the mashed bark of the paper mulberry and breadfruit trees and used as a covering material for books. It is usually decorated with geometric patterns. (332)

tapes. The strips of cloth (usually linen), vellum, nylon, etc., to which the sections of a book are sewn, and whose free ends, or SLIPS (1), are attached to the boards, or are glued between SPLIT BOARDS to impart additional strength to the binding structure. *Cf:* BANDS (1); CORDS; WEBBING(S) (1). (183, 198)

tape sewing. 1. A method of fold sewing which utilizes strips of cloth, vellum, etc., in lieu of raised or recessed cords. In this method of sewing, the tapes rest against the backs of the gathered sections and the thread passes across but does not loop around them. The width of the tapes, which should be in proportion to the size of the book, generally ranges from ⅜ to ¾ inch. In general, a larger number of narrow tapes is probably superior to a smaller number of wide tapes, as the former reduces the possibility of the thread loosening between tapes. It is recognized, however, that the problem of looseness of sewing thread can be overcome by the use of the CATCH STITCH.

The use of ¾ inch tapes has long been the standard method employed in sewing blankbooks (stationery binding), and was also the accepted method of sewing library books (on ½ inch tapes) in the United States until superseded by OVERSEWING. Tape sewing library books is still done in

Great Britain and on the Continent of Europe.

2. A method of machine sewing in which the sections of a book are sewn by the conventional edition sewing method, on a machine adapted for the use of tapes. The sewing proceeds from section to section in the usual manner of machine sewing but through tapes rather than simply through the folds of the sections. This results in sewing that is considerably stronger than the ordinary edition sewing, although, because the threads are secured to the tapes (and not around them, as in hand sewing), flexibility in the spine of the book is somewhat reduced.

3. A method of sewing single leaves in lieu of conventional oversewing or side sewing. Groups of leaves are overcast (or oversewn) to form "sections," which are then sewn to tapes in the usual manner. While this method does not enable the book to be opened any better than does oversewing, it does provide slips to help secure the boards to the text block. (161, 264)

tape slotting. A form of stabbing performed by hand or machine, invented by the Englishmen F. C. Gould and Thomas Harrison, in whose names a patent was granted in 1934 for a tape-slotting machine. The purpose of tape slotting is to enable tapes to be passed through slots near the spine of the leaves, thus securing them as one unit. The advantage of this method over stabbing (with cords) is that the width of the tapes not only provides support to the leaves of the book, but also imparts strength without the bulk that would result from the use of cords.

Grooves are first cut across the spine, and then parallel to the spine, producing a shape something like that of an inverted T with a long bar and a very short stem. When done by machine, the slots may be punched through the leaves, thus eliminating the grooves. The latter method, however, makes it more difficult to insert the tapes through the slots. In the hand method, the grooves can be filled in with cord or other material after the tapes have been inserted.

Tape slotting is particularly suitable for large books printed on thin paper, e.g., unabridged dictionaries, encyclopedias, etc., which lack the margin required for side sewing. At times, two tapes are put through each slot for additional strength. (236)

tapestry stitch. An embroidery stitch on canvas that somewhat resembles tapestry. (111)

taping. A technique used to impart additional strength to blankbooks; it involves pasting strips of linen to the folds of certain folios within a section. Each section is taped *inside* the fold of the outside folio and *outside* the fold of the inside folio. The number of sections to be taped depends on the size of the book, but generally the first and last six sections are so treated. Strips of linen are also attached between the first and last three or four sections so as to fill in any gaps that may appear when the book is rounded, especially when the sections are very thick. (82, 343)

tara. A vegetable tanning material obtained from the dried pods of a tree or shrub, *Caesalpinia spinosa*, which is found in widespread areas of north western South America. The tannin content of the pods is said to range from 35 to 55%. The principal value of tara is in the tanning of light leathers, and, under certain circumstances, it may also be used as a substitute for sumac or gambier to produce light-colored leathers. Tara is of the pyrogallol class of tannins, somewhat similar to, but more astringent than, sumac. Its major shortcoming seems to be the presence in it of diffusion-inhibiting mucilaginous material. It is also used to some extent in dyeing and the manufacture of ink. *See also:* VEGETABLE TANNINS. (175)

tar board. A tough, strong, heavy MILLBOARD (1), manufactured from old tarred rope, sail cloth, sacking, etc. It is virtually impossible to obtain today, except as discarded boards from old books. (256)

tarnish. To dull or discolor the surface of a mineral or metal, either by chemical reaction, such as the tarnishing of silver by oxidation, or by the deposition of a thin film of grime. (233)

tawing (tawed "leather"). An ancient process of treating prepared hide or skin (usually pigskin or goatskin) with aluminum salts and (usually) other materials, such as egg yolk, flour, salt, etc. A skin may actually be tawed simply by immersing it in an aqueous solution of potash alum at a temperature between 20 and 30° C; however, salt is usually included in the alum solution because it improves the substance (thickness) of the final product. After treatment the skin is dried in air (crusted) and held in this condition for several weeks to allow the development of stabilization or "aging" effects. Tawed skins also undergo STAKING to impart of soft, flexible handle. Apart from this soft, warm handle, the tawed skins have a high degree of stretch. Handle and stretch may also be improved by the addition of egg yolk and flour to the basic alum and salt solution. A tawed skin is usually white in color but may yellow slightly with age.

Tawing does not actually produce a skin that is stable in the wet condition, i.e., imputrescible in the wet state, and therefore cannot accurately be described as having been tanned; consequently, in a strict sense, a tawed skin is not leather. (61, 237, 291)

tearing resistance (tearing strength). 1. The force required to tear a specimen of paper under specified controlled conditions. In archival work, the two most important measures of tearing resistance are: 1) internal (or continuing) tearing resistance, where the edge of the sheet is cut before the actual tear is made; and 2) edge tearing resistance, i.e., the resistance offered by the sheet to the onset of tearing at the edge, and which appears to be dependent on both the extensibility and the tensile strength of the paper.

The Library Binding Institute specifications for library binding call for endpapers (60 pound basis weight, 24 × 36 − 500) to have a tearing resistance with the machine direction of the paper of 140 pounds per one-inch strip and 160 pounds in the cross direction; the test being conducted on the Elmendorf tester. 2. The force in pounds required to tear a specimen of leather at a place where the specimen is cut before the actual tear. (17, 62, 209, 363)

tear ratio. The relationship between the machine direction and cross direction tearing resistance of paper, or the warp and filling direction of a fabric.

T. E. G. (t. e. g.). Abbreviation for TOP EDGE GILT.

tellers. The small right angle marks printed on a page to indicate to the binder the proper position for tipping plates or mounts. (307)

temper. The resistance offered by a light leather to bending, and the extent to which it recovers its shape after release of the bending force. Quickness of rebound to its original shape is an indication of good temper in a leather, which is a property closely associated with resilience and elasticity. (248, 363)

temperature conversion. Centigrade is converted to Fahrenheit by multiplying the Centigrade figure by 9, dividing by 5, and adding 32, or by multiplying the Centigrade figure by 1.8 and adding 32. Fahrenheit is converted to Centigrade by subtracting 32 from the Fahrenheit figure, multiplying by 5 and dividing by 9. In the chart below, the center figure represents the temperature one has read; the figure to the left is the conversion of that figure into Centigrade if read in Fahrenheit, while that to the right represents the conversion to Fahrenheit if read in Centigrade, e.g., the temperature 88 (Fahrenheit) converts to 31.1 C., while the temperature 88 (Centigrade) converts to 190.4 F.

C.		F.
−17.8	0	32.0
−17.2	1	33.8
−16.7	2	35.6
−16.1	3	37.4
−15.6	4	39.2
−15.0	5	41.0
−14.4	6	42.8
−13.9	7	44.6
−13.3	8	46.4
−12.8	9	48.2
−12.2	10	50.0
−11.7	11	51.8
−11.1	12	53.6
−10.6	13	55.4
−10.0	14	57.2
− 9.4	15	59.0
− 8.9	16	60.8
− 8.3	17	62.6
− 7.8	18	64.4
− 7.2	19	66.2
− 6.7	20	68.0
− 6.1	21	69.8
− 5.6	22	71.6
− 5.0	23	73.4
− 4.4	24	75.2
− 3.9	25	77.0
− 3.3	26	78.8
− 2.8	27	80.6
− 2.2	28	82.4
− 1.7	29	84.2
− 1.1	30	86.0
− 0.6	31	87.8
0.0	32	89.6
0.6	33	91.4
1.1	34	93.2
1.7	35	95.0
2.2	36	96.8
2.8	37	98.6
3.3	38	100.4
3.9	39	102.2
4.4	40	104.0
5.0	41	105.8
5.6	42	107.6
6.1	43	109.4
6.7	44	111.2
7.2	45	113.0
7.8	46	114.8
8.3	47	116.6
8.9	48	118.4
9.4	49	120.2
10.0	50	122.0
10.6	51	123.8
11.1	52	125.6
11.7	53	127.4
12.2	54	129.2
12.8	55	131.0
13.3	56	132.8
13.9	57	134.6
14.4	58	136.4
15.0	59	138.2
15.6	60	140.0
16.1	61	141.8
16.7	62	143.6
17.2	63	145.4
17.8	64	147.2
18.3	65	149.0
18.9	66	150.8
19.4	67	152.6
20.0	68	154.4
20.6	69	156.2
21.1	70	158.0
21.7	71	159.8
22.2	72	161.6
22.8	73	163.4
23.3	74	165.2
23.9	75	167.0
24.4	76	168.8
25.0	77	170.6
25.6	78	172.4
26.1	79	174.2
26.7	80	176.0
27.2	81	177.8
27.8	82	179.6
28.3	83	181.4
28.9	84	183.2
29.4	85	185.0
30.0	86	186.8
30.6	87	188.6
31.1	88	190.4
31.7	89	192.2
32.2	90	194.0
32.8	91	195.8
33.3	92	197.6
33.9	93	199.4
34.4	94	201.2
35.0	95	203.0
35.6	96	204.8
36.1	97	206.8
36.7	98	208.4
37.2	99	210.2
37.8	100	212.0

template. A pattern made of board, metal, or plastic and used as a guide in cutting leather for covers or spines and corners, or cases for library or hand edition bindings. Before the days of machine edition binding, a template made to the proper size for the edition being bound, when positioned on the sides, level with the outer edge of the cover, could be marked to give the trimming positions, which not only saved time by eliminating the necessity of making hundreds of marks with dividers, but also made it possible to cut all siding papers together to one size. (236, 256)

tender. Sometimes said of a paper which is lacking or has lost a certain amount of its strength, ether because of some aspect of its manufacture, or as a result of deterioration. (17)

tenon saw. *See:* BACK SAW.

tensile energy absorption. The ability of a material, such as paper, to absorb energy in tension. The property is proportional to the area between the load-elongation curve and the elongation axis, and is expressed in energy units per unit area of material, e.g., foot-pounds/square foot, kilograms-centimeter/square centimeter, etc. Measurement of tensile energy absorption has been recommended as an effective means of determining the deterioration of paper; to date, however, it has not received widespread acceptance. (17)

tensile strength. 1. That property of a material, such as paper, which enables it to resist rupture under tension. The force used to cause rupture is applied parallel to the plane of a paper specimen of specified width and length and under specified conditions of loading. Tensile strength of paper is expressed as load per unit width, or as BREAKING LENGTH, and of cloth as the breaking load or force in pounds per inch, or BURSTING STRENGTH.

The Library Binding Institute specifications for endpapers used in library binding call for a paper having a tensile strength in the machine direction of not less than 44 pounds (1 inch strip and in the cross direction of not less than 25 pounds (1 inch strip) for 60 pound basis weight paper (24 × 36 − 500).

2. In leather, tensile strength is defined as the force per unit area of cross section required to produce failure. Numerous factors affect the tensile strength of any given leather, including the kind of tannage, the length of the tannage, the species and age of the animal, the degree of splitting, and so on. Most leathers will show a tensile strength of between 2,000 and 6,000 pounds per square inch. (17, 209, 363)

tension. The degree of firmness with which the thread used in sewing a book is drawn from section to section. The tenson of all stitches should be equal. (172, 306)

ternion. A gathering consisting of three sheets folded once and insetted. This was the form in which some manu-scripts and early printed books, especially those of vellum, were assembled, with the first and sixth, second and fifth, etc., leaves being conjugate. *See also:* QUARTERNION; QUINTERNION; SEX-TERNION. (156)

terra alba. *See:* GYPSUM.

tertiary colors. Any hue produced by a mixture of secondary colors. In pigment mixtures, such colors tend to be subtle and blackish, and are usually chromatic variations of grays and browns. *See also:* COLOR (1). (233)

terylene. A generic name for a synthetic thread which has the advantages of nylon thread, but does not have the undesirable high degree of elasticity. Because of its lower elasticity, it does not present the problem of thread retraction after cutting. As with nylon thread, it is highly resistant to moisture and retains a large part of its dry strength when wet. Terylene is also almost entirely free from contaminating metals which might tend to cause degradation. It is also used in sheet form in the repair of documents and the leaves of books. (81)

texodern. One of the earliest of the imitation leathers. It was said to be strong, durable, as well as resistant to water, stains, and insects. (264)

text block. The body of a book, consisting of the leaves, or sections, making up the unit to be bound, rebound, or restored. It excludes all papers added by the bookbinder, including board papers, endpapers, doublures, etc.

textile bindings. A very ornate style of fabric binding, popular in England and France during the Renaissance, and in England into the 18th century. The books were sumptuously bound in satin and velvet of various colors, and were often embellished with needlework in multi-colored silks, as well as gold and silver threads. (156, 254, 347)

texture. A term applied to the general identifying characteristics of paper, cloth, leather, etc., pertaining to the feel and appearance of the material. *See also:* FEEL; FINISH (1, 3); FORMATION; GRAIN; HANDLE; LOOK-THROUGH; WILD (1). (17)

t4s. Abbreviation for TRIMMED FOUR SIDES.

Thames board. A binder's board made in England and used to a considerable extent in edition binding. It is a soft gray board and is sometimes lined with kraft paper to impart stiffness, provide equal surface tension, and a firm, smooth surface. (156, 237)

thermoplastic binding (thermoplastic binding machine.) *See:* ADHESIVE BINDING; ADHESIVE BINDING MACHINE.

thermoplastc resins. Resins composed of separate linear non-reactive macro-molecules which, upon being heated, become plastic due to the reduction of intermolecular forces. Such resins can be made to flow under pressure in this state; upon cooling they regain their original physical properties. The heating-cooling cycle can be repeated as long as there is no thermal degradation of the polymer. Most thermoplastic resins are produced by forcing the heated material into a mold or through a die under pressure, followed by cooling. The important thermoplastic processing techniques include injection molding, extrusion, and calendering. Many such resins are also soluble in various organic solvents, with the same intermolecular cohesive forces being overcome in the process of solution. The more important thermoplastic resins include polyvinyl chloride, polyethylene, polystyrene, and cellulose acetate. (233)

thermosetting. That property which enables a material to be hardened, or fused and hardened, by means of heat. Materials having this property are called "thermosets." Once hardened they cannot subsequently be softened by reheating. The synthetic resins, according to the manner in which they react to heat, are classified as either thermosetting or thermoplastic. (179, 233)

thickness. The smallest of the three dimensions of a material, such as leather or paper, usually expressed in thousandths of an inch, or, in the metric system, in millimeters. The thickness of leather is measured in millimeters, or in fractions of an inch, e.g., OUNCE or IRON (2). In the measurement of paper, it is also called CALIPER (1).

thinner. A volatile liquid added to an adhesive, ink, or other substrate, to modify the consistency or other properties. *See also:* DILUENT. (309)

thirty-sixmo. A rarely encountered gathering consisting of 36 leaves or 72 pages. The 36mo can be obtained by folding three sheets, each with two parallel folds followed by two right angle folds, resulting in three 24-page sections which are then insetted. The 36mo is used when an OBLONG format is required. Written as 36mo or 36°.

thirty-twomo. An uncommon gathering consisting of 32 leaves or 64 pages. Although such a section may be formed by making five consecutive right angle folds, in practice it is unusual to fold a sheet with more than three consecutive right angle folds, because of buckling, trapped air, etc.; therefore the 32mo is generally formed by folding a full sheet with two parallel folds, followed by three right angle folds, and a half sheet with two parallel and two right angle folds, and insetting the latter. Written as 32mo or 32°.

thixotropy. 1. A phenomenon exhibited by various gels, in which the system displays the mechanical properties of a gel when undisturbed, but becomes a liquid when mechanically agitated and again becomes a gel when allowed to stand. This "reduction in viscosity" is due to a temporary breaking down of an internal structure of a system under shear. The viscosity of thixotropic systems depends on the "shear history," i.e., the extent of previous mechanical agitation to which the material has been subjected. The property is important in paper coating colors because it allows the mixing of color formulation to a viscosity which permits the color to be applied and allows surface leveling due to after flow of the color on the material. 2. A property of adhesive systems which causes them to thin upon isothermal agitation and thicken when allowed to stand. (17, 309)

thong binder. A binding consisting of two specially constructed wooden boards joined together by woven cotton or nylon thongs. One end of each thong is fastened to a clamping bar which is hinged to the back edge of the upper board, while the other end is fastened to a movable bar enclosed in the lower board. A key allows the thongs to be slackened between the clamping bars, enabling the punched leaves to be added or removed from the binder. The clamping bar, together with the oval T-shaped punching, secures the leaves firmly. A relatively extensive binding margin is required for this type of binder, which is equally as strong and usually lighter in weight than the POST BINDER, and is reasonably durable. (276)

thongs. 1. Narrow strips of leather, alumtawed skin, etc., used to attach vellum covers in limp bindings, as well as to hold the covers of books closed. Thongs were used before the invention of CLASPS and were, in fact, used on COPTIC BINDINGS. 2. The narrow strips of vellum, leather, or alumtawed skin used in the early days of FLEXIBLE SEWING. Thongs had begun to be replaced by cords in this use by

the latter part of the 16th century. (236)

Thou, Jacques Auguste de (1553-1617). The French historian, statesman, royal librarian, and perhaps the most famous bibliophile since JEAN GROLIER. Thou inherited his father's library of (rare) books in 1583. Many of his books were simply bound in red, olive, or citron colored morocco, with plain boards, a few border lines in gilt, and his coat of arms in the center of the upper cover, surrounded by laurel branches, but with only the title and his cipher on the spine. Other volumes were bound in the celebrated FANFARE STYLE. Thou had books printed on paper made especially for him, and by the time of his death had accumulated a library of some 1,000 manuscripts and 8,000 books. His library was sold in a series of sales by several owners from 1680 to 1789. Because of the high quality of his books and the ease with which they can be recognized, their survival rate is very high.

Thou is generally called de Thou and is often indexed under D, although his Latin name, and the one under which he wrote, was and is Thuanus. (50, 94, 286)

Thouvenin, Joseph (1790-1834). A 19th century French bookbinder (gilder), Thouvenin (l'aine), as he was often called, was the oldest of three brothers, all bookbinders active during the French Restoration, or thereafter. Joseph Thouvenin actually did most of his work during the period of the Empire, starting his apprenticeship with the younger Bozerian in 1802. Although he is generally credited with raising the standards of French bookbinding from the depths to which it had declined during the Revolution and thereafter, he is probably best remembered for his revival of a style of binding, which, because of him, came to be known as the FANFARE STYLE, taking that name from his binding of *Fanfares et Corvées abbadesques.* He is also credited with the introduction of the FLY EMBOSSING PRESS. (288, 347)

thread count. The number of warp and filling yarns per inch in a woven fabric. The Library Binding Institute standards for library binding call for 110 threads in the warp (grade F buckram) for pyroxylin impregnated covering fabric, 45 in the warp and 38 in the filling for spine lining cloth for books more than ½ inch thick, and 33 in the warp and 25 in the filling for books ½ inch thick or less. (209, 341)

threadless binding. *See:* ADHESIVE BINDING; SADDLE STITCHING; SIDE STITCHING.

three and one half times the width method. A technique used in applying a second (paper) lining to the spine of a book. A heavy piece of paper three and one-half times the width of the rounded spine is cut and glued across the spine from a line approximately 3/16 inch in from the edge of the spine. The paper is then folded back on itself and glued to the remaining 3/16 inch of the cloth spine lining. Finally, the paper is folded back and glued to itself. It is a somewhat poor technique as it does not provide for a HOLLOW at the 3/16 inch area. (259)

three-dimensional appliques. A form of book decoration consisting of textured and raised-surface designs on the covers. They are in the form of collages, appliques, mosaics, sculptured forms, onlays, etc. Common materials, such as string, yarn, cloth, and the like, are used in the execution of such bindings today, along with fired enamel, glazed clay, metals, and glass. (183)

three-knife trimmer. A cutting machine designed to trim all three edges of a book in two cuts but with only one handling of the book. The stack of books to be cut is placed in the machine and secured by the clamp. The fore edge knife makes the first cut, returns to its raised position, and the other two knives simultaneously cut the head and tail. If a book has too much sewing swell, a shaped piece of chipboard must be glued to the clamp to compensate for it, so that the same pressure is applied to both the fore edge and spine of the pile, otherwise the pull of the knives may cause the pile to shift due to the shearing action of the knives exerting a diagonal pressure. The three-knife trimmer is designed for relatively large numbers of books of the same dimensions, as in edition binding. *See also:* GUILLOTINE. (320)

three on. A method of sewing a book by hand in which three sections are sewn on one length of thread from kettle stitch to kettle stitch. The technique is designed to reduce sewing swell in the spine and is generally used only when sewing books made up of a relatively large number of thin sections. *See also:* ALL ALONG; TWO ON. (236)

three-plane watermark. A WATERMARK showing three thicknesses in the same sheet of paper.

three-quarter binding. 1. A binding having one type of material, e.g., vellum or cloth, covering the spine and part of the sides, as well as enlarged corners, and a different material, e.g., paper, covering the remainder of the sides. The material extends almost to the corners on the sides, i.e., much more than in the case of a HALF BINDING. Since it is difficult to imagine that the three-quarter binding was originated to economize on the more expensive covering material (cloth, or even vellum or leather), the three-quarter binding may have been developed simply as a new style. In the eyes of many, it is a style that appears badly proportioned on the sides. 2. In stationery (blankbook) binding, a three-quarter binding is one having a spine of Russia leather, with leather corners extending over the edges, a spring-back and raised bands, tar board sides covered with cloth, and gold lettering on the spine. *See also:* QUARTER BINDING. (256)

three-quarter leather. A term applied specifically to a book having the spine and part of the sides, as well as enlarged corners, covered with leather, and the remainder of the sides covered with cloth or paper. The leather on the sides extends almost to the corners, i.e., much more than in the case of a HALF LEATHER BINDING. *See also:* QUARTER LEATHER; THREE-QUARTER BINDING.

three times the width method. A form of the HOLLOW consisting of a length of

THROW OUT

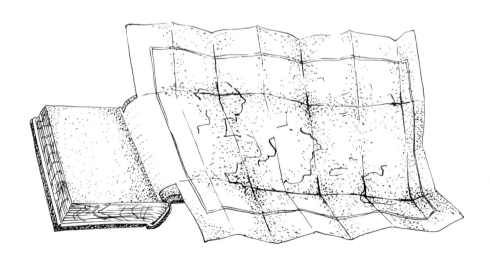

paper cut three times the width of the rounded spine of the book. The paper is folded into thirds, the center third is glued to the spine, and the two wings are glued to each other. It is a superior form of the hollow to the THREE AND ONE HALF TIMES THE WIDTH METHOD. (259)

three up. A method of imposing periodical issues which results in three issues (in a line) folded and saddle stitched together and then cut apart in the trimming operation. (320)

throwing colors. *See:* DROPPING COLORS.

throw out. A map, table, diagram, etc., designed to be consulted regardless of the page of the text the reader is consulting. It is done by means of an extended guard (the size of the leaf of the book), to which the map, etc., is attached at the outer edge. If the map is to be folded, a compensation guard may be required to compensate for the thickness of the map. The map and its guard are usually printed on paper that differs from that of the text. (156, 339)

throw up. The rising up or buckling of the spine of a book when it is opened. It is a characteristic of the HOLLOW BACK, and because of it the leaves lie flatter than they ordinarily would. "Throw up" is especially important in library binding, where the sewing, which is usually oversewing, is relatively tight and inflexible. *See also:* SPRING-BACK (1).

thumbhole. A semi-circular or triangular cut in the sides of a slipcase designed

to facilitate removal of the enclosed book. The semi-circular cut is used in the best work, while the triangular cut, which is used principally by library and edition binders in the United States, is much more economical, especially since it is usually made after the case has been covered.

thumb index (thumb cuts). A type of INDEX which utilizes a series of rounded notches cut into the fore edge of the book. Each generally has a label bearing a letter or letters indicating the arrangement. The index proceeds from head to tail and front to back of the volume. The maximum number of thumb cuts, and therefore the number of letters represented by each, depends on the height and thickness of the book. The thumb index is used principally for Bibles and dictionaries. The cuts are usually made by a machine designed for the purpose. Also called "cut-in index." (264)

thymol. A colorless, crystalline compound $(C_{10}H_{13} \cdot OH)$, obtained from origanum and other oils, or prepared synthetically by the hydrogenation of piperidine, obtained from *Eucalyptus dives* and *E. piperita*. Thymol is very slightly soluble in water, and is soluble in alcohol and chloroform. It is used as a preservative in paste and also as a fungicide. It can be applied as a solution in alcohol or vaporized for use as a fungicide. (237)

tide marks. Markings on the grain surface of a leather caused by paste soaking through from the flesh side in areas which happen to be thinner or more porous than others. Tide marks generally occur only when the grain side has not been moistened or has been inadequately moistened. (204)

tidying. A 19th century practice of issuing paper-boarded and cloth-cased books untrimmed, but with the longest leaves trimmed or "tidied" to the general level of the other leaves. Early in the 19th century, this was done with trimming shears which were fixed to the press; however, by about 1830 the shears had been superseded by trimming knives. This type of trimming was also done in the better binderies, usually in combination with a gilt top. (236)

tied down (tied bands). A simple binding ornamentation consisting of lines impressed along either side of each raised band, which continued onto, and were joined part way across, the sides. A small floral or leaf design was used to terminate the lines. The lines were either in gilt or blind and were executed with a pallet. The decoration is derived from the early technique of TYING DOWN the bands. Also called "ties." (156)

tie down. The stitch which is carried under the kettle stitch when working headbands. Its purpose is to secure the band solidly to the text block. (83, 335)

ties. 1. Tapes or ribbons, sometimes made of leather, and usually in pairs, attached to the sides of a book close to the fore edge, and occasionally at head, tail, and fore edge, and designed to prevent the covers from warping or gaping. They often consisted of linen, about ¾ inch wide, and were generally of a drab green color, although brown and blue were also used at times. Ties were usually threaded through a hole (not a slot) in the board and, on the inside of the cover, the end was frayed out and attached to the leather turn-in. They were frequently used on fine bindings from about 1530 to 1640, and elaborate silk ties were used on Bibles and devotional books well into the 18th century. Their use today is largely restricted to portfolios. *See also:* CLASPS. 2. *See:* TIED DOWN. (94, 236)

tight back. A book which has the covering material, usually leather, glued directly to the spine or to the (leather) lining on the spine.

In the early days of the English codex, the leather cover was not attached directly to the spine, nor, for that matter, was the spine glued up at all. Aside from these early bindings, however, as well as limp (vellum) bindings and some vellum-covered stationery bindings, the use of the tight back was virtually universal until the times of the Derômes in France (*see:* DEROME STYLE). It was at this time that the HOLLOW BACK began to be used in France.

Until about the last quarter of the 18th century, it was not unusual to line the spines before covering, and bindings that did not have raised bands were often lined with three or more layers of paper, or, at times, canvas. Craft bookbinders in 17th and 18th century France generally lined the spines of books with strips of parchment manuscripts which overlapped the joints and were pasted down under the endpapers. *See:* SPINE LINING (1).

The use of the tight back declined dramatically after about 1820, except by fine binders who often used it along with false raised bands. *See:* MOCK FLEXIBLE. Similarly, all so-called

boarded books had tight backs and boards that were laced in this practice continued from the 1770s, when the style was first used, until the 1820s, when casing-in was introduced. Others had tight backs until the late 1830s, when "boards" more or less passed out of existence.

The tight back was revived in craft bookbinding, at least to a certain extent, by T. J. Cobden-Sanderson and Douglas Cockerell, who influenced a host of amateur fine binders for several decades.

The objection to the tight back, other than the fact that it is a more expensive technique, is that if the leaves of the book are relatively thick in relation to their area, they will not lie flat by themselves, but, because of the inflexibility of the spine, will tend to open like a fan. This tendency may be lessened by having the grain direction of the paper run parallel to the spine. In addition, some bookbinders object to the tight back because it causes the leather on the spine to flex every time the book is opened, which can cause cracking of the gold tooling on the spine.

Also called "fast back." (83, 236)

tight fit. The case of a book which is too small for the text block, resulting in a tendency for the covers to gape. It is caused by an error in the measurement of the boards resulting in an INLAY (1) that is too narrow, with the consequence that the covering material on the spine is not the full width of the spine.

tight joint. *See:* CLOSED JOINT.

tinny. An expression used to describe a leather that is "empty," i.e., lacking in substance, and weak. The defect is caused when BATING is carried too far, resulting in excessive "digestion" of the collagen of the leather. (291)

tip. 1. The thinnest available MILLBOARD (1). It is used in some instances for making the SPRING-BACK (1) of a blankbook, as the inner boards of SPLIT BOARDS, and to a considerable extent as a lining board. 2. A thin, flat brush consisting of a relatively small number of camel or squirrel hairs fixed between two pieces of card. It is used by some gilders for picking up gold leaf and placing it on the surface to be gilded. 3. *See:* TIP-ON. (97, 159, 233)

tip-on. A leaf that has been pasted onto the stub of another leaf, e.g., a CANCEL (1).

tipped endpapers. Endpapers tipped onto the first and last sections (leaves) of a

book. The technique is used frequently in edition binding. *See also:* SELF-ENDPAPERS. (365)

tipped in. A separately printed illustration, etc., cut to the size of the leaf of a book and pasted along the inner margin of the appropriate text page prior to gathering. Such an illustration is said to be a "paste in." Tipping is a time-consuming, and therefore costly, aspect of book production. (140)

tipping (tipping in). 1. The process of pasting the edges of a section to adjacent sections. 2. The operation of tipping on an INSET (2) around or in a larger section. (58, 320)

tipping front and back. The process of placing a narrow line of adhesive on the sides of a sewn pamphlet near the spine, for the purpose of securing the cover of the publication along the sides instead of simply at the spine, which may have insufficient surface area to hold the cover securely. However, it is usually necessary to score the covers at the edge of the line of adhesive, otherwise there is the risk that the cover paper will break at the adhesive line. 2. The process of attaching endpapers in edition binding. (142)

tipping machine. A machine used for gluing plates or endpapers to sections of a book. In the usual case, the sections and endpapers are fed into the machine, edged with adhesive along the binding edge, and pressed together. A plate is generally tipped along the left or right edge and pressed onto the leaf. (156, 343)

tips. Tiny corners, usually of vellum when leather is used on the spine, and employed mainly by French bookbinders.

tissued plate. *See:* BARRIER SHEET.

tissue papers. A class of papers, made in basis weights lighter than 18 pounds (24 × 36 — 500). These papers are made on any type of papermaking machine, from any type of pulp, including reclaimed paper stock, and may be glazed or unglazed. Some tissues are relatively transparent. *See also:* BARRIER SHEET.

titanium dioxide. A white compound, the oxide of titanium (TiO_2). It occurs naturally in the rutile, anatase, and brookite crystalline forms. The rutile form is used in the manufacture of pigmented paper coatings, while the anatase form is used as a filler pigment in paper manufacture. Both types (as used in papermaking) are important because of their whiteness, high brightness, and high refractive index (2.52 to 2.76), all of which results in a paper of improved brightness and opacity. (17, 235)

titanium potassium oxalate. A white, crystalline substance ($K_2TiC_2O_5 \cdot 2H_2O$), that is soluble in water. It precipitates vegetable tannin materials and acts as a mordant with the dyes and dyewoods used in coloring leather. (306)

title. 1. The inscription printed on the title page of a book or other publication, and usually intended to describe the contents of the publication. In its broadest use, it includes the sub-title, alternative title, or associated descriptive matter, but not the author and/or editor, translator, etc., unless the name forms a gramatically inseparable part of the title. *See also:* BINDER'S TITLE; COVER TITLE (1). 2. In hand binding, usually the space or panel between the first two raised bands (from the head) on the spine of a book, on which the title is lettered. (156, 183, 241)

titled. *See:* PIECED (1).

title leather. A highly polished, very thin SKIVER attached to the title panel of a book, and lettered with the title of the book. *See also:* LABEL. (264)

title mounted. A title page that has become frayed or otherwise damaged, and has been mounted on another leaf to preserve it. (169)

title page. In the usual case the recto of the second leaf of a book, displaying the full title, the sub-title (if any), and usually the name of the author, the edition, the publisher and date of publication (sometimes the date is printed on the verso of the same leaf). The verso may also give particulars of the edition, i.e., the printer (and perhaps his address), the binder, specifications of type and paper, registration of copyright, as well as (in the United States) the Library of Congress card number, ISBN number, and CIP information. In cases where more than one page giving particulars of the title are present, that giving the fullest information is the title page. (156)

title roll. *See:* ROLL (1).

tizra. A vegetable tanning material obtained from the roots and heartwood of a shrub or small tree, *Rhus pentaphylla*, occurring throughout the western part of North Africa. The heartwood may be expected to produce 20 to 23% tannin, while the roots may have a tannin content as high as 28 to 29%. Tizra, which is of the condensed class of tannins, closely resembles QUEBRACHO both in chemical properties and tanning qualities. It has long been used in Morocco in the tanning of

MOROCCO leathers. *See also:* VEGETABLE TANNINS. (175)

toggling. The operation of stretching damp leather and securing it in place for drying in a smooth and stretched condition by means of toggles, which are metal clamps equipped with jaws to grip the leather and prongs to hold it in place in a slotted metal frame. *See also:* TACKING. (363)

toluene. A colorless, refractive, aromatic liquid hydrocarbon (C_7H_8), obtained from coal-tar light oil by cracking, by heating toluic acid with lime, and by other processes. It is used as a solvent to remove pressure sensitive tape from paper, in finishing leather, and in removing grease from leather. (173, 235)

tongue and slot. One of the techniques used to attach the covers to a book. The tongue is formed by covering the spine of the book and carrying the leather onto the waste sheet of the endpapers, together with the spine lining and slips. The leather or cloth hinges are also glued to the same sheet. The laminated flange (tongue) thus formed is cut to shape to fit a slot (not unlike an enclosed split board) cut into the back edge of the board. The board is then covered and finished in whatever manner is required, separate from the book, and is attached to it by gluing the tongue into the slot. The entire assembly is then pressed to insure proper adhesion.

The tongue and slot technique is said to offer the following advantages: 1) the boards can be finished, e.g., doublures attached, more easily off the book; 2) large and/or very heavy books can be handled more easily; 3) more than one skin can be used in covering; 4) a design which calls for blocking the covers can be handled with greater facility; 5) attachment of the covers in this manner facilitates removal by a future restorer for work on the text block; and 6) at least part of the original bookbinder's design can be preserved if and when a more or less complete restoration of the book is required. (311)

toning. The process of reducing the shade (whiteness) of a document or leaf as nearly as possible to its original color following washing and/or deacidification. The "toner" may be the gelatin size itself, which will reduce whiteness to a slight extent, or, if a greater toning effect is required, a surface active (cationic) vegetable dye in very dilute solution may be used. (154, 235)

tooling. *See:* BLIND TOOLING; FINISHING (1); GOLD TOOLING.

tooling leaf. *See:* ALUMINUM LEAF; DUTCH GOLD; GOLD LEAF; PLATINUM LEAF; SILVER LEAF.

tooth. A characteristic of the grain surface of various papers. Tooth is often a result of the wove marks impressed on the underside of the web of paper by the Fourdrinier wire of the papermaking machine, but it may also be caused by very small depressions between fibers or groups of fibers in the surface of the paper, or by the impression of the mesh of the felt fabric on the web of paper as it travels through the press rolls. Tooth is a characteristic of low finish in drawing papers, and is characteristic of virtually all handmade papers. The "tooth," meaning the roughness of a paper, expresses its ability to take pencil and crayon writing or drawing. Also called BITE (2). (17, 316)

top. 1. *See:* HEAD (1-4). 2. The felt side of a machine-made paper. 3. The side of superior quality of boards composed of different grades of stock. *See also:* TOP OF THE HIDE.

top combs. *See:* MARBLING COMBS.

top cover. *See:* UPPER COVER.

top edge gilt. The head edge of a book which has been cut smooth and gilded. The other two edges, which are not gilded, may be cut smooth, trimmed slightly, or left uncut. Abbreviated "g.t." or "g.t.e." Also called "gilt top." *See also:* TRIMMED BEFORE SEWING. (69)

top finished. A leather which has been given a final coating of a finish for the purpose of imparting special properties, such as gloss, level color, fastness to wet rubbing, water resistance, etc. (61)

top margin. The area between the top line of print and the upper edge of the leaf. *See also:* MARGIN (1). (156)

top of the hide. The finest grade of leather used for the covering of a book. Literally, it means the area of the skin on the top, i.e., the back of the animal. This seldom used expression is somewhat inaccurate in that, although the best part of a hide or skin is located on the back, the very best is found in the butt area of the back. (164)

torn paper designs. A collage technique of decorating a binding, using designs produced by tearing paper into shapes and pasting them to the covers of the book. (183)

tortoise shell. A cover sprinkle executed by washing the leather with yellow dye and, when dry, sprinkling heavily with black. When this is dry the cover is then spotted with blue, red and black. (154, 280)

tortoise shell covers. A 17th century technique which used tortoise shell to decorate the covers of a book. Additional decoration sometimes consisted simply of a border of silver corners and clasps, but more often included inlays of silver and mother of pearl. (154, 280)

Tory, Geoffrey (1480-1533). A French printer, wood engraver, designer, and royal printer to Francis I. For the embellishment of bindings, he designed two panels in the form of arabesques in the contemporary Italian style, of which the famous *pot cassé* device forms a part. In his smaller stamps, only the broken pitcher appears, but in his larger panel the vase is pierced by a wimble (gimlet, drill, auger, or *"toret"*). The device apparently was employed in allusion to the death of his daughter; however, it may have been a pun on the name Tory, although he used the device on his own publications. (94, 347)

total transmittance. A special form of TRANSMITTANCE of a material. It is measured by means of a special instrument designed for the purpose. Total transmittance, in conjunction with PARALLEL TRANSMITTANCE, is useful in determining the degree of transparency of a transparent paper. (17)

t pattern. A pattern on a book cloth consisting of longitudinal regular ridges and valleys. (256)

tracing paper. A paper used for duplicating drawings, figures, etc. It may be either a translucent, greaseproof paper, or a bond or manifold paper treated chemically, or oiled, so as to increase its transparency. It is produced from cotton fiber, chemical wood pulps, or combinations thereof, in basis weights ranging from 7¼ to 16 pounds (17 × 22 − 500). Important properties include proper receptivity to drawing ink and transparency, so that prints from the tracings can be made. (17, 316)

trade binding. Plain calfskin or sheepskin bindings issued by publishers in England from the 15th to the 18th centuries. They were rarely lettered. (236)

traditional format. A term used occasionally to indicate the format of some Oriental books, consisting of double leaves with the folds at the fore edge and with the free edges serving as the binding edge. (156)

tragacanth. *See:* GUM TRAGACANTH.

tranchfille chapiteau. A type of double HEADBAND of French origin. (115)

transfer binder. *See:* POST BINDER.

transfer box (transfer file). A box similar to a PAMPHLET BOX but not of as sturdy construction. It is used for storage of lesser used pamphlet or sheet material. (156)

transfer marble (transfer edge). *See:* MARBLE TRANSFER.

transitory materials. Library materials designated by the Library Binding Institute as being: 1) materials subject to "normal library usage" that are complete but which may at some later date be discarded and thus are not considered to be a permanent part of the library's collection; and 2) materials not subject to normal library usage, so little used that completeness is not a factor of importance, and not considered to be part of the permanent collection. For the former category, the L. B. I. recommends that such materials be considered permanent insofar as binding is concerned and therefore bound according to the L. B. I. standards; for the latter, treatment would depend on the purpose of the library, the physical condition of the materials, and reader requirements. Such materials do not require library binding in accordance with L. B. I. standards; however, Certified Library Binders (L. B. I. members), will either develop a type of binding meeting the library's particular requirements, or bind according to the specifications for lesser used materials. *See:* LUMSPECS. (208)

translucency. The property of partial transparency that indicates the ability of a material to transmit strongly scattered light waves. A translucent material admits light but does not transmit sharp images. (17)

transmittance. The fraction of incident light that can be seen through a material. The fraction actually has meaning only when the nature of the incident light and the design of the measuring instrument are specified. *See also:* PARALLEL TRANSMITTANCE; TOTAL TRANSMITTANCE. (17)

transparency. That property of a material which permits the passage of light. The more transparent the material, the more clearly objects can be seen on the other side. (17)

transparency ratio. One of the measures of TRANSPARENCY (1), being the ratio of parallel transmittance to total transmittance, and generally expressed as a percentage. (17)

transparent marble. A cover marble pre-

pared by first executing the usual TREE CALF, placing an oval of paper on each cover, and blackening the covers around the ovals. When this color is dry, the areas are sponged with basil water, and then red is thrown on in spots. When the red is dry, the ovals are removed and the red spots are washed with water. As a further embellishment, the ovals are sometimes colored with a mixture of wine and powdered tumeric. Also called "variegated." (95)

transparent vellum. VELLUM rendered transparent by any of several processes, some of which date back to medieval times (when vellum was sometimes used in lieu of window glass). The most common method of making vellum transparent seems to have involved treating a wet (thin) skin with fluid substances of high water-binding capacity, such as egg white, gum arabic, animal glue or size, before drying the skin on the stretching frame. Other methods included smearing olive oil or cedar wood oil over both sides of the skin, or steeping the skin in very hot water for a brief period of time. In the 18th century EDWARDS OF HALIFAX patented a method (1785) which proved to be the simplest of all the methods. He soaked ordinary vellum in a weak solution of potassium carbonate (pearl ash) and, stretching it tightly, placed the skin under considerable pressure. (236, 291)

transverse porosity. *See:* LATERAL POROSITY.

Trautz, Georges (1808-1879). A German bookbinder who emigrated to Paris in 1830 and entered the employ of Antoine Bauzonnet. Bindings produced in Bauzonnet's workshop before 1848 were signed Bauzonnet-Trautz. It was possibly in this year that Trautz assumed control of the bindery, changed the name to Trautz-Bauzonnet, and rapidly became one of the leading bookbinders of 19th century France. Many of the books, which are exceptionally well bound, are in the style of JOSEPH THOUVENIN. The forwarding is good, the tooling delicate, and the materials excellent. Many of Trautz's tools were modelled on the work of previous binders, and he was highly successful in incorporating the styles of such bookbinders (or gilders) as Le Gascon, Padeloup, and Derome. In fact, he was one of the most important of the RETROSPECTIVE BINDERS. Trautz always varied his designs, so that no two bindings were alike. In addition, aside from being an excellent craftsman in gold tooling, he was an expert in the art of inlaying. *See:* PLATES VI, VII, VIII. (94, 140)

tree calf (tree marble). A form of cover decoration consisting of a smooth, light-colored calfskin treated with chemicals in such a manner as to represent a tree trunk with branches. In the usual manner, a dual design appears on upper and lower covers. The leather is first paste-washed, and the book is then hung between two rods which keep the covers flat. The book is tilted so that it inclines upward towards its head. In order to bend the boards outwards, i.e., warp slightly to a concave shape, so that the solutions will run properly, the insides of the boards are not filled in until the decoration is done. A small amount of water is applied to the center of both covers to form the trunk, then more water is thrown on the covers so that it runs down to the trunk and to a central point at the lower edge of the boards. Copperas (a green hydrated ferrous sulfate) is then sprinkled in fine drops on the covers, followed by potassium carbonate (salts of tartar), which causes the chemical reaction that etches the leather to form a permanent pattern in shades of gray, ranging from faint to very dark. Calfskin was used for this decoration in preference to sheepskin (although 19th century examples of sheepskin tree do exist) because in addition to being a much superior leather, it takes a better polish, which suits this style of decoration admirably.

The spine of the book is protected during the marbling so that it will not be touched by the water or chemicals. The entire process calls for considerable experience and dexterity of execution, because if the result is to be effective the copperas and potassium carbonate must be applied in the correct amounts, as well as in the proper manner, while the initial water is still running down the covers; otherwise the effect will be little more than sprinkling.

Late in the 19th century attempts were made to produce the tree calf effect with the use of an engraved block, which was used to print a design on the covers in black, but the results were ineffective because the block did not provide the shading which the genuine method achieved. The popularity of tree calf began to decline before the First World War, and by the late 1920s this once very popular form of decoration had vir-

tually passed from existence. The first known tree calf decoration dates from about 1775. *See:* PLATE V. (83, 94, 236, 264)

trial binding. A term descriptive of a tentative cover design for a book submitted to the publisher by the publisher's (edition) binder. Such bindings have been produced regularly since the early days of edition cloth bindings. Today, the bindings are generally dummies made up of blank leaves. *See:* DUMMY (1). In the 19th century, however, finished copies were often used, as there are examples of books with identical contents but different bindings from that of the version offered for sale. Some publishers used trial bindings to fulfill copyright obligations or gave them as free copies to the author. (69)

triethanolamine. One of the ethanolamines ($(HOCH_2CH_2)_3N$), used in conjunction with fatty acids to produce fine, stable emulsions of oils and waxes in water. It is used in the manufacture of leather. (262)

trim. 1. A term applied to the widest sheet of machine-made paper, trimmed of its deckle edges, that can be produced on a given papermaking machine. 2. To cut a sheet of paper to an exact size. 3. The paper that is trimmed off of the edges of a leaf, or group of leaves of a book. 4. To cut the edges of a leaf, or group of leaves of a book. 5. The operation of cutting off the bleeds or bolts of a book. 6. The excess of paper allowed around a printed sheet for bleeds. (12, 17)

trimmed. 1. Paper which has been trimmed on one or more sides to insure exactness of corner angles and to reduce the sheet to the size required. 2. A book which has had one or more of its edges cut in the guillotine, three-knife trimmer, or with the plow, so that they are smooth, even and solid. Usually all three edges are so cut, but sometimes only the head edge. (156, 343)

trimmed before sewing. A book that has had its edges cut before it is sewn. Trimming before sewing is a technique employed when the book is to be rough gilt. Trimming is usually done section by section in a paper cutter, so as to provide a degree of roughness if only the head is to be gilt. (83)

trimmed four sides. Lifts of paper, usually printing paper, that have been trimmed in the guillotine on all four sides. This is done because paper as it comes from the papermaking mill is not uniform in size as required for

the proper registration in two-side printing, as well as folding. Abbreviated T4S. (269)

trimmed in the round. A book that is trimmed after rounding. Books that are to be gilded on all three edges are sometimes trimmed in this manner to facilitate the work of the gilder. In order to trim the fore edge in the round, the round must first be removed temporarily by forcing the spine against the guide of the cutting machine, or by the use of TRINDLES, if the book has laced-on boards and is to be trimmed with the plow. It is very difficult and frequently impossible to remove all of the round by either method. If the book is to be trimmed in the guillotine, the concave fore edge is filled in with CHIPBOARD to keep the paper from breaking away when the head and tail are trimmed. *Cf:* TRIMMED IN THE SQUARE. (339)

trimmed in the square. The most common method of cutting a sewn book, in which the edges are trimmed before the book is rounded. In cutting the head and tail, the spine of the book is placed in the cutter against the guide so as to avoid breaking pieces out of the folds. If there is much sewing swell in the spine, it may be necessary to build under the clamp of the cutter to compensate for the swell, otherwise the book may slip under the clamp because of the shearing action of the guillotine knife. *Cf:* TRIMMED IN THE ROUND. (339)

trimmed size. The final dimensions of a sheet of paper or the text block of a book. (156)

trimming. 1. The operation in which bound books and other printed materials are reduced to their final size before casing or attachment of the boards. Trimming a book removes the folds at head and fore edge (bolts), thus freeing the leaves for turning; it also smooths the edges, and divides two-up or three-up books or periodical issues into individual units, the latter operation usually being referred to as "splitting" or "cutting apart," even though it may be done as part of trimming. In edition- and library-binding, trimming is done after smashing or nipping, while in hand binding it may come either before or after rounding. *See:* TRIMMED IN THE ROUND; TRIMMED IN THE SQUARE. In the manufacture of cut flush books, the book and covers are trimmed together, and, as most paperback books and periodical issues are within this category, trimming is, in such cases, the final step in binding.

Many devices are used for trimming books, including the GUILLOTINE, PLOW, THREE-KNIFE TRIMMER, knife, shears, or even a chisel. One of the earliest methods was to cut each leaf separately (in all likelihood before sewing) and probably with shears instead of a knife and straight edge.

The Library Binding Institute specifies that when volumes are trimmed, the trimming shall be as slight as possible, and that periodicals shall be trimmed to sample, or recorded size, where possible—otherwise, as slightly as possible. In practice, the standard trim in library binding is ⅛ inch at head, tail, and fore edge.

2. In leather manufacture, the process of cutting away unwanted or unsightly parts of hides, skins, or the leather itself. (106, 161, 209, 236, 320, 335)

trimming out. The operation of cleaning surplus leather, cloth, etc., from the inside of the boards of a book bound by hand before filling-in or pasting down. Trimming out the sides of half leather bindings before attaching the paper sides was virtually unknown until approximately the middle of the 19th century, consequently the edges of the leather spine and corners are ragged, and the raggedness is usually emphasized by the abrasion and darkening of the paper over the bumps. Not until about the 1870s, when superior craftsmanship was applied to some half leather bindings, did trimming out become customary, except in economy bindings. The outside finish of half bindings was also improved by "filling-in" with a layer or layers of paper under the marbled paper or cloth sides, making them level with the leather. (236, 335)

trimming to recorded size. A volume, usually a periodical, that has been trimmed to the extent that the bound volume is of the same height as that of previously bound volumes of the run. *See:* MATCHING SETS.

trindles. The U-shaped pieces of metal or wood placed between the cords and the boards at the spine of a book to remove the round, and thus flatten the spine when the book is to be TRIMMED IN THE ROUND. (161)

triple lining. A procedure for lining the spine of a book, generally used for higher quality edition bindings. The triple lining consists of the customary cloth lining, a crepe manila lining, and the headbands, which represent the

"third" lining. In some cases the headbands are glued to the crepe manila lining and a second cloth lining is glued over the first, the crepe manila then becoming the third lining. This is unusual, however, as two consecutive cloth linings are seldom encountered in bookbinding. (140)

triple liner and headbanding machine. An edition binding machine used for applying the spine linings and headbands to a book. The machine receives the books from the rounding and backing machine and inserts them spine down into spring-loaded pockets by means of a formed lifting bar corresponding to the shape of the spines of the book being processed. When the book is properly oriented in the pocket, the machine then applies one cloth and one or two paper linings, with or without headbands. It operates at speeds up to 40 books per minute. (320)

tripoli. An inferior grade of ESPARTO (GRASS), grown in North Africa. *See also:* SPANISH. (156)

triptych. An ancient hinged writing tablet consisting of three tablets of wood, metal, or ivory, covered with wax on the inside surfaces, on which writing was done with a stylus. (156, 373)

true skin. A term used in the leather trade to denote the derma or corium of a hide or skin.

trypsin. A crystalline proteinase produced in the pancreas of an animal and used in BATING hides and skins. It is usually obtained from the pancreas of the sheep or pig. (306)

t. s. Abbreviation for TUB SIZED, tub sizing, or TYPESCRIPT.

tub. The stand which supports the LYING PRESS, and also catches the shavings from the PLOW.

tub sized. Paper that has been sized by passing the web through a size press, or by dipping the waterleaf sheet into a tub of size by hand, or by carrying it through the size bath between two felts, which are either perforated or have an open weave so as to allow the excess size to run off during passing through the squeeze rolls. Most papers of high rag content are tub sized and the sizing is sometimes done with the use of 100% animal gelatin, followed by air drying. If done properly, a tub-sized paper is stronger than a similar paper that is internally sized. (17, 156, 198)

tub-size press. A sizing device that is usually part of the papermaking machine. It is essentially a vat (tub) which contains the size, and a set of vertically oriented rolls, the lower part of the unit being immersed in the size. The

paper is sized as it travels through the papermaking machine. Sometimes a set of horizontally oriented rolls is used and the size solution is then pumped into the "valley" created on both sides of the paper. The tub-size press is designed for relatively heavy applications of size to paper. *See also:* SURFACE-SIZE PRESS. (17)

tuck. A flap on the edge of a book cover designed to be inserted into the edge of the other cover. Its purpose is to keep the covers of the book closed. The extension is usually on the lower cover, and tucks into a slit in the upper. The tuck was a common feature of the bindings of mid-19th century Bibles and prayer books, although it was rarely used for the larger sizes. *See also:* CLASPS; WALLET EDGE. (274)

tumbling drum. A device designed to test aspects of a binding. It consists of a revolving octagon-shaped drum equipped with a pocket that lifts the book to the top of the drum and lets it free-fall (about 2 feet) to strike the lower sides. The number of impacts required to produce failure of the joints is recorded. The tumbling drum was developed by the United States Testing Company. *See also:* UNIVERSAL BOOK TESTER.

tumeric. A yellow or saffron coloring material prepared form the roots of the East Indian perennial herb, *Curcuma longa,* and used in dyeing and as a coloring material for certain marbles. *See also:* TRANSPARENT MARBLE.

Turkey leather. A vague and obsolete expression used variously at times to indicate a leather—perhaps an early morocco—or for the color of leather, for instance, Turkey red, a brilliant madder red used in the dyeing of cotton. (69)

Turkey marble. A vein marble featuring white streaks, and executed by dropping blue color on a weak size of sprinkling water (which allows the blue to expand), followed by green sprinkled on the blue. The ox-gall used to produce the white veins is then sprinkled on the blue and green, followed by the ground color in large drops. Also called "stone marble." (161)

Turkey morocco. 1. Reputedly, a strong, durable leather produced in the 18th century in Turkey from goatskin, with the characteristic MOROCCO grain. 2. A term applied to a leather, frequently produced from calfskin, embossed with a hard grain or bold cross grain in imitation of a Turkey morocco. (129, 264)

Turkey papers. An early name for marbled

papers, so called because at one time it was thought that the art of marbling was introduced into Europe by way of Turkey. (236)

turnaround time. The time interval (or time required) between the pick-up of unbound books from the library, including loading and unloading, and their return to the library. The commonly stated turnaround time for library binding is anywhere from four to six weeks.

turn-ins. 1. The extra length and width of the covering material of a book overlapping the head, tail, and fore edge of the cover, and turned over the edges of the board and glued to the inside surface. In leather binding, the leather is usually pared around these edges so as to make it thinner on the inside of the boards. The extent of the turn-in varies according to the SQUARES of the book, the taste of the times, or the judgment of the binder. 2. The extensions of a book jacket which fold over the fore edges of covers of a book and in over the inside of the covers. (82, 156)

turning-in steel. A thin length of steel about 8 inches long and 2½ inches wide, rounded at the ends, and used to turn in and rub down the cloth when making cases by hand. (264)

turpentine. A light, volatile essential oil obtained as an exudate from coniferous trees. Turpentine is a mixture of cyclic terpene hydrocarbons. It is used in place of ox-gall in the execution of stormont marbles. (335, 368)

twelvemo. A sheet folded to form 12 leaves or 24 pages. Although two parallel folds followed by two right angle folds will produce this gathering, the more common method is to print the sheet 12 up on each side, and then cut the sheet into 2 sheets of 8 and 4 leaves. The larger sheet if folded three times, and the smaller twice, the latter being insetted. The insetted section may be given a sub-signature, e.g., B1 or B*, which the binder notes when binding the book. If the printer imposes 2 rows of 6 pages (on each side), the result is known as "long twelves," but if 3 by 4, "short" or "square" twelves. Where the width of the leaf is greater than the height, the term "broad twelves" is used. Also written 12mo or 12°. *See also:* OBLONG.

twenty-fourmo. A sheet folded to form 24 leaves or 48 pages. There are several methods of producing a 24mo, one of the most common being to fold two sheets (separately) with two parallel folds in thirds, followed by a

right angle fold, another parallel fold and insetting the second within the first. Also written 24mo or 24°.

twin-wire paper. A type of duplex paper produced by forming two webs of paper and then uniting them wire side inward so that the resulting sheet has two felt (top) sides. This type of paper is said to give superior results in offset printing. (17, 140, 156)

twisted pineapple. A decorative ornament found on several English and French rolls, and consisting of twisted stems interrupted at intervals by conventional pineapples. (250)

two-letter index. An INDEX consisting of thirteen divisions of two letters each. If Mac is used, two other letters, usually I and X are omitted, or I, J, and K are combined and X is omitted. (82)

two-line tool. A roll or fillet with two lines of designs, or two plain lines (in the case of the fillet), on the circumference. (335)

two-on. A method of sewing a book by hand in which two sections are sewn on a single length of thread from kettle stitch to kettle stitch. After the first (or first two or three) section is sewn ALL ALONG, two sections at a time are placed in the sewing frame, and the sewing alternates from section to section. There are several techniques of sewing two on, a common method being to alternate from one section to the next at each cord. Whatever the method used, two sections receive as many stitches as does one in the all along method, and when sewing on five cords, alternating sections received two and three stitches, respectively.

Sewing two-on was quite common until the last quarter of the 19th century, at which time sewing machines began to be used in trade (edition) binding. Even the thinnest books were sewn two-on, not so much to reduce sewing swell as to reduce costs. Sewing two-on today is used in fine binding only to reduce swell. Also called "two sheets on" and "off and on." *See also:* THREE ON. (94, 236, 335)

two on and one off. A form of the HOLLOW, consisting of the basic cloth lining applied directly to the spine of the book followed by a strip of heavy kraft paper three times the width of the rounded spine glued to this lining, overlapping the spine on one side only. The overlapping part is folded back on itself even with the joint, slid off the spine, and then folded over to make a tube. This is replaced on the spine and the superfluous paper is trimmed off. Depending on the way the hollow

is glued on, this method gives "two on and one off" or "one on and two off." Variations of this technique may be achieved by increasing the width of the kraft paper to give "two on and two off," "two on and three off," etc. *See also:* SPINE LINING (1). (236)

two page spread. *See:* DOUBLE SPREAD (1).

two sheets on. *See:* TWO ON.

two-shot method. A method of applying adhesive in high speed paperback (adhesive) binding. The adhesive binding machine applies a polyvinyl (cold) adhesive as a primer followed by a hot-melt adhesive. It is not as fast a method as the ONE-SHOT METHOD (1), but it results in a stronger hinge and good cover adhesion. *See also:* ADHESIVE BINDING. (179, 294)

two-sided sheet. A term used with reference to the difference in shade and/or texture between the felt and wire sides of a sheet of paper. The term is generally applied to dyed papers, and usually refers to a difference in the depth of color, with the felt side being darker and the wire side lighter. Two-sidedness in paper may also be produced by using a mixed furnish, e.g., long- and short-fibered stock, the short fibers (as they are lighter) being on the top or felt side and the long fibers on the bottom or wire side. Another form of the two-sided sheet is the filled paper, in which more pigment is retained on the top side of the sheet. (17, 98)

two up. 1. A method of imposing and processing two books (or periodical issues) as a single unit, all the way from printing form through all of the binding processes. The two books or issues are separated at the trimming station during binding. *See also:* THREE UP. 2. The process of printing two texts, or duplicate stereos made from the same form, side by side on the same sheet of paper. It is an economical way of printing short runs. (156, 320)

tying down. One of the steps employed in working headbands. The thread used in forming the headband is taken down the spine to a point beneath the kettle stitch and then back up to be wound around the core of the headband once again. The purpose is to anchor the headband solidly to the spine. In the early days of headbanding, tying down was done in the center of each section; today, however, it is usually done at every three or four sections and even then not always in the center. (236)

tying up. The technique of wrapping cord tightly around a book from spine to fore edge, one cord on either side of each raised band. Tying up is done subsequent to covering, its purpose being to make the leather adhere securely to the sides of the bands. The term is also applied to the process of tying cord from head to tail at the spine so as to pinch the headcaps.

TYING DOWN

Tying up, which represented the first effort to mold the leather around the raised bands, was first used in the early 13th century. The technique seems to coincide more or less with the first use of the groove method of attaching boards. Virtually all books sewn on raised cords were "tied up" until early in the 19th century. Although BAND NIPPERS are now used in lieu of tying up, the practice is still employed in the restoration of pre-19th century rare books, primarily to give the appearance of the binding technique of the times.

That tying up declined after the early 19th century was probably due to several factors, including: 1) leather in trade binding was replaced by cloth; 2) sewing on raised cords itself declined; and 3) standards of finishing in fine binding were improving and neater work could be done without the use of cords, and, in any event, tying up was unnecessary if the leather was properly prepared and drawn on. Large books were (and still are) tied up, especially when the covering leather is intractable, e.g., pigskin.

Indenting of the leather on the fore edge of the boards is prevented by the use of specially shaped wooden boards. *See* TYING-UP BOARDS. As an alternative method, millboard can be bent to shape. The leather of old bindings is sometimes marked by the pressure of the tying-up boards, because the cords used for large books were tied very tightly. (173, 236, 335)

tying-up boards. Thin, sturdy boards with right-angle projections, used to protect

the sides and fore edges of the leather of a book during TYING UP. (237)

type. 1. A small rectangular block of metal or wood, usually the former, cut on its top with a raised letter, figure, or other character, for use in letterpress printing, or in a lettering pallet for lettering the spine of a book. The nomenclature of a single piece of type for letterpress work has always been compared to a headless human being standing erect: a body, a face, beard, neck, shoulder, back, belly and feet. Type letters are formed with three imaginary lines: the "base line" on which the bases of capitals rest, the "mean line" along the top of lower-case letters which do not have ascenders, and the "cap line" across the top of the capital letters. 2. A number of such characters. (156, 189)

type area. The area, usually a vertical rectangle, or a page of a book, or other publication, which is, or will be, filled with printed matter. (156)

type face. 1. The printing surface of the upper end of a piece of type which bears the character to be printed or impressed. 2. The style, or design, of characters on a set type—e.g., Times Roman—and comprising all the sizes

—e.g., 10pt., 12pt.—in which the particular design is made. Type faces are available in hundreds of designs, sizes, and weights. (157, 234)

type font. *See:* FONT.

type metal. An alloy of tin, lead, antimony, and sometimes copper, used for casting type. 2. The handle or pallet letters used by bookbinders, which are usually made of brass. (156, 278)

type pallet. *See:* LETTERING PALLET (1).

typescript. A copy of a work in typewritten form, as distinguished from one that is printed or handwritten. Abbreviated t. s.

type size. The measure of the dimensions of type, taken from the body of the individual type rather than from the actual printing area. (179, 365)

typewriter paper. Often a good quality paper, usually a bond cut to 8½ by 11 inches. It receives the usual bond finish and has no special surface other than the customary bond paper texture. The quality of typewriter paper varies considerably, with higher grades containing up to 25% cotton fiber content. (17)

typography. The art or process of printing from movable type, as in LETTERPRESS PRINTING.

TYING UP

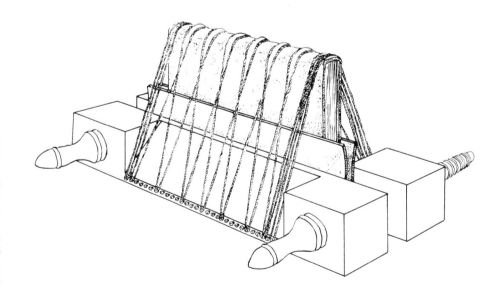

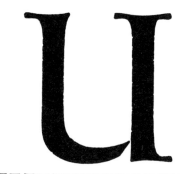

ultramarine. A blue pigment occurring naturally in small amounts as the mineral lapiz lazuli, and manufactured in very large amounts. It is a complex silicate of sodium and aluminum. Ultramarine is used as a mineral coloring agent in the manufacture of paper and leather. (60, 235)

ultrasonics. Vibrations with frequencies in the range of 2.0×10^5 cycles per second. Ultrasonic vibrations may be generated by applying alternating electric current to quartz, tourmaline, or Rochelle salt, or by the effect of oscillating magnetism on a rod of magnetic material immersed in a liquid. Ultrasonics are used to seal documents within polyester foils by fusing. (195)

ultraviolet light. Electromagnetic radiation of shorter wavelengths than visible light. *See:* WAVELENGTHS. It has much greater energy than visible radiation, but also much less power of penetration. Ultraviolet light is capable of initiating photochemical reactions, including fading of pigments, dyes, etc., and, being destructive to all organic matter, it can have a deleterious effect on such materials as paper and leather. Fortunately, its poor power of penetration (probably) reduces its likelihood of causing much damage, except on the surface of a material. Glass is opaque to ultraviolet light below 3300 A, and most other substances (quartz being a notable exception) below 2000 A. Exposure over a period of years, however, conceivably could be damaging; therefore, fluorescent lighting, which emits more ultraviolet radiation than does incandescent lighting, should be properly filtered with ultraviolet absorbing plastic panels. (143, 198, 235)

umber. A natural product composed of magnesium silicate and iron compounds, and used as a coloring pigment. The "false" umbers are brown ochers produced artificially by burning the hydrated iron earths. Burnt umber is the calcined raw umber. (60, 235)

unbleached groundwood paper. A paper manufactured from pulp produced by grinding wood to a relatively fine fiber length. The pulp is well screened to eliminate shives and dirt, and possesses relatively good brightness. The paper produced from it is relatively opaque, well closed up, and has a uniform printing surface. (17, 98)

unbleached sulfate pulp. A paper pulp produced mainly from softwood trees containing a relatively high proportion of resin, e.g., the pines, which are cooked for relatively short cycles. The pulp has a very low color, is relatively shivey, and is unsuitable for bleaching because of its high chlorine requirement. It is characterized by exceptional strength. (17, 98)

unbleached sulfite pulp. A tan or brown paper pulp that requires 2.5 to 4.5% chlorine to bleach it to a suitable white color. Characteristics expected of this type of pulp include softness, absorbency, cleanliness, and brightness. Peroxide is sometimes used in a single stage or final stage of bleaching to gain brightness and improve brightness stability. (17, 98)

unbound. A book that has never been bound, i.e., a "book" in sheets, signatures, or gatherings. The term is sometimes used improperly to describe a book which has been PULLED for rebinding. (69)

unctuous. Leather which has a soft, full, oily feel.

uncut (uncut edges). The edges of a newly printed book which have not been cut or trimmed, thus leaving the "bolts," which must be cut before the book can be read. Until this is done the book is said to be "unopened." In rebinding a book, the term signifies that the edges are left in the original uncut state, with or without bolts as received. (93, 196)

un-dehaired leather. A rarely encountered bookbinding leather, one that has been tanned in the natural state (with the hair left on). Although calfskin, usually a SLUNK, has been tanned in this manner for bookbinding purposes, most of the examples of this type of leather in bookbinding are the skins of wild animals. (332)

underbands. *See:* BANDS (2).

unfinished. 1. A book of which only part was published, the remainder never having been completed or published. 2. A completely forwarded volume that has not been tooled, blocked, or lettered. 3. A binding that has not been completed. (256)

ungathered. The printed sheets of a book which may have been folded but whose sections, if folded, have not been gathered into correct order.

unhairing. The beamhouse process in leather manufacture of removing the hair (or wool) and other epidermal structures from hides and skins, following liming (or any other preliminary unhairing process), but before tannage. Unhairing is generally considered to be the second of the three major beamhouse operations, the others being LIMING and BATING. The term "unhairing" is perhaps limiting in scope, because not only does the liming-unhairing process loosen the hair and other epidermal structures, it also cleans, loosens, and expands the dermal fiber network and alters the swelling characteristics of the skin.

Unhairing may be accomplished by: 1) treatment with lime (calcium hydroxide), caustic soda (sodium hydroxide), barium hydroxide, sodium carbonate, or ammonium hydroxide, etc.; 2) treatment with lime, as in treatment 1, sharpened by the addition of sodium sulfide, sodium bisulfide, antimony sulfides, or other appropriate chemicals; 3) treatment with lime, as in treatment 1, sharpened by the addition of amines, such as methylamine, or degradation products themselves from the skins being processed; 4) treatment with aqueous buffer systems containing inorganic salts, e.g., ammonium sulfate, sodium chloride plus enzymes with proteolytic and/or carbohydrase activity, usually derived from molds, bacteria, fermenting plant materials or animal tissues; 5) treatment with aqueous solutions of inorganic salts, such as potassium perchlorate, potassium thiocyanate, sodium chloride or sodium silicofluoride; 6) treatment with hot water, i.e., scalding;

7) treatment with strong aqueous solutions of sodium hydroxide, sodium sulfide, etc., i.e., pulping; 8) action of bacteria, or SWEATING (1); 9) treatment with ammonia; and 10) alternating cycles of freezing and thawing in water. The last two methods are not in commercial use; scalding is used only for certain skins, such as peccary and pigskin; and treatment with strong aqueous solutions of strong alkalis, e.g., sodium hydroxide, is useful only when the tanner has no market for the hair. Treatment by sweating is virtually obsolete.

Conventional unhairing involves loosening the hair by means of one of the lime solutions given above, followed by mechanical unhairing by machine. The unhairing machine is similar to the fleshing machine, except that the blades of the cylinder are smooth instead of sharpened, and the machine runs at a slower speed so that the spiral blades scrape or rub the hair off without damage to the grain surface of the hide or skin. The hair is generally gathered, washed, dried, baled, and weighed for shipment. (248, 291, 306, 363)

uniformity. A term applied to the formation of a sheet of paper, i.e., the regularity of fiber distribution throughout the sheet structure, as well as other properties of the paper, including color and finish. (17)

unit tools. The various finishing tools which have some device or design cut on the end of a brass shank. They are used separately or in conjunction with each other, as well as with line tools to form patterns. They may be "solid" or "line" in form, and when meant to be used by hand, generally do not exceed ¾ by ¾ inch in size; otherwise they become very difficult to use. A larger tool meant to be used in a press or blocking device, is more appropriately called a STAMP (2). Unit tools range in complexity from a simple dot to very intricate lacelike designs. The use of unit tools has declined in recent years, primarily because of the different conception of design prevailing today, but the same principle of building patterns from separate tools in still valid. (66, 161)

universal book tester. A device designed to test the durability of several aspects of a binding, including the durability of the covering material, the strength of the hinges, the stiffness and resistance to delamination of the boards, and, to a limited degree, the durability of the sewing. The device consists essentially of a rectangular test chamber constructed of aluminum, lined with 50 by 50 mesh of No. 304 stainless steel wire 0.009 inch in diameter. The chamber is supported and rotated by a drive shaft attached perpendicular to the center of its base. Viewed from the front, the drive is inclined at an angle of 20° from the horizontal, and rotates in a clockwise direction (at a speed of 20 r.p.m.). The dimensions of the test chamber vary with the size of the volume being tested, according to the following table:

Test Chamber Type	Internal Dimensions of Chamber (in Inches)			Overall Dimensions of Volume to be Tested (in Inches)	
	Width	Height	Depth	Width	Height
A	13	16	4	5 to 7	7 to 10
B	15	19	4	8 to 10	10 to 13
C	15	15	4	8 to 10	6 to 9
D	11½	13	4	4 to 7	5 to 6
E	18	23	4	11 to 13	14 to 17

Each chamber is rounded to a 1½ inch radius along the sides of the bottom to concentrate the abrasive stresses along the edge of the spine of the book. The chamber was designed in this manner to stimulate observed patterns of wear.

The Universal Book Tester is said to produce the following results: 1) abrasion of the shoulder of the spine; 2) impact and abrasion of the headcaps (if any), otherwise the edges of the head and tail of the spine; 3) light abrasion of the covers (sides); 4) limited flexing of the joints; 5) breaking and tearing on the internal hinge; and 6) occasional failure of the sewing, i.e., loosening of the sections and splitting of the spine. (16)

unlettered. A book which has not been blocked or otherwise marked with identifying information on the spine or cover. Before about 1600, books that were lettered at all generally had the title inked or painted on the fore edge, as books were shelved fore edge outward, and binders did not bother to letter the spines of books. Nor did they bother to letter them long after the practice of shelving fore edge outward was discontinued. Possibly it was a matter of economy and perhaps the PRESS MARK (2) sufficed. Labels on spines were unusual in England before about 1660, so that few books were lettered before the middle of the 17th century. Many owners wrote the titles on paper labels or directly on the covering material of the books. Gilt lettering on labels for those particular books was usually stuck on at a later date. (69)

unopened. A book whose "bolts," i.e., the folded edges of the sections, have not been trimmed off or opened with a knife. The term is not to be confused with UNCUT. (83, 156)

unsewn binding. See: ADHESIVE BINDING.

unsized paper. A paper having no sizing material added either during or subsequent to manufacture, i.e., a WATERLEAF (1) sheet. (17)

unsplit. A hide or skin in its entire original thickness. See also: FULL WEIGHT.

untouched (untouched edges). 1. A book whose pages have not been rubricated or illuminated. 2. The edges of a book that have not been trimmed, cut, marbled, sprinkled, or decorated in any manner. (140)

untrimmed. A book that has not had its edges cut smooth in the guillotine, plow, or three-knife trimmer, and which may have unevenly projecting leaves, generally at the head and fore edge, or flat paper which has not been trimmed in the guillotine or other cutting machine. (17)

upper cover. The top or first cover of a book, or the portion of the covering of a book over the front or first part.

upright. A book which is taller than it is wide. Cf: OBLONG.

urea. A nitrogenous substance ((NH_4)$_2$ CO_3), abundant in perspiration and urine. It is readily attacked by microorganisms which may result in the formation of ammonia compounds detrimental to the permanence of leather. It is also used in the manufacture of paper. (363)

usability. The durability of a binding in terms of the circulation it is likely to be capable of withstanding before rebinding or replacement becomes necessary. (16)

uterine vellum. See: SLUNK; VELLUM. See also: PARCHMENT.

utilitarian protective binding. See: GIRDLE BOOK.

V. The Roman equivalent of 5. *See:* ROMAN NUMERALS.

vacuum deposition. A process used for coating a film or other base material. The coating material is heated and evaporated in a high vacuum and condenses on the chilled surface of the material to be coated. Blocking foils are an example of vacuum deposition.

valence. The power of combining with another element or radical, i.e., the number of atoms of other elements with which the atoms of any one element can combine directly. Hydrogen, for example, is univalent and therefore can only become attached to one atom of another element, e.g., it combines with chlorine, another univalent element, atom for atom, forming H-Cl (hydrochloric acid). Bivalent elements, e.g., oxygen, can combine with two, such as with two hydrogens, forming H_2O. Valencies up to eight are possible.

valonea (vallonea; valonia). A vegetable tanning material obtained from the dried acorn cups and beards of the Mediterranean (valonea) oak, *Quercus aegilops,* and allied species. The cups contain tannin in the amount of 25 to 31%, while the beards usually contain 40% or more. Valonea is of the pyrogallol class of tannins and produces a leather of firm texture and light color. It also deposits considerable bloom because of its relatively high content of ellagitannic acid. It has a fairly high natural pH (3.6) for a pyrogallol tannin, as well as a moderately high acid and salts contents. *See also:* VEGETABLE TANNINS. (175, 306)

Van der Waals forces. The physical forces of attraction and repulsion existing between molecules and which are responsible for the cohesion of molecular crystals and liquids. The forces stem partly from dipole-dipole, or dipole-induced-dipole interactions; however, even nonpolar molecules and atoms exert a certain attraction on one another. Van der Waals forces act only over relatively short distances, and are proportional to the inverse of the seventh power of the intermolecular distances. The forces are important in the mechanics of ADHESION. (235)

vapor density. The ratio between the weight of a given volume of a gaseous substance and that of the same volume

of another gas (usually hydrogen) measured under the same conditions of pressure and temperature. Vapor density is not an integer but may be compared with a value based on whole mass units. (235)

vapor permeability. That characteristic of a material which permits the passage of a vapor or gas. The PERMEABILITY is measured under carefully specified conditions, such as total pressure, partial pressure on the two sides of the specimen, temperature and relative humidity. As the fibers of a material such as paper have such a high affinity for water (vapor), vapor permeability should not be confused with air permeability or porosity. *See also:* WATER-VAPOR PERMEABILITY. (17, 42)

vapor-phase deacidification. A method of deacidifying paper which involves the use of a material that is capable of supplying the deacidification agent in the form of a vapor. Ammonia, diethyl zinc, morpholine, or other volatile alkaline substances can be used, but most are not permanent in the presence of high relative humidity. Another method, and one which has received considerable notice, involves the use of cyclohexylamine carbonate. The books are interleaved with tissue paper impregnated with the compound, while loose documents may be treated by placing sacks containing the compound with the documents in box files. The deacidification agent is the free amine given off as a vapor. No alkaline reserve is left in the paper by this method, and this, along with its disagreeable (fishy) odor, represent its chief shortcomings. Some authorities also contend that the vapor is potentially toxic. *See also:* BARROW, WILLIAM J.; DEACIDIFICATION; DIETHYL ZINC; MORPHOLINE;

NON-AQUEOUS DEACIDIFICATION. (198)

vapor pressure. The pressure which exists over every liquid (or solid). In a closed vessel, given sufficient time, equilibrium is attained, in which as many molecules leave the liquid surface to form vapor as return to it from the vapor phase to form liquid. The pressure of vapor above any liquid or solid at any temperature, when equilibrium exists, is called the vapor pressure of the liquid or solid at that temperature. (235)

variegated marble. *See:* TRANSPARENT MARBLE.

varnish. A solution of a RESIN in a solvent, such as turpentine, boiled linseed oil, etc., containing a drier, which, after evaporation of the volatile constituents of the vehicle and oxidization of the nonvolatile vehicle, leaves a thin, glossy, more-or-less uniform layer of the dissolved materials. At one time varnish was used to impart additional gloss to leather and cloth. Book jackets, showcards, and the like, are also varnished to enhance their appearance and improve wear resistance. Small sheets are usually varnished by hand with a brush, but large sheets are generally varnished in a varnishing machine. In the latter case drying in a dust free atmosphere is made possible by the use of a drying apparatus usually attached to the varnishing machine. Varnishing can also be done on letterpress and lithographic printing presses but the finish is usually not equal to that obtained by hand or in a varnishing machine. Paper to be varnished must be hard sized, otherwise the varnish will be absorbed rather than remain on the surface. Varnish is also used to dilute ink, or as an ingredient in its manufacture. The correct selection of printing inks for work which is to be varnished is important because some inks are affected by varnish. (320)

varnishing machine. A machine resembling a printing press in many respects and used to varnish printed sheets, usually for the purpose of brightening and preserving colors, as well as to impart additional wear resistance. The varnish is applied from a fountain by means of rollers, as in printing, and the sheets are then conveyed on a canvas web into a drying oven for drying in a dust free atmosphere. (320)

vaseline. A trade name for soft paraffin. Yellow and white varieties are produced, consisting of semi-solid, partly translucent mixtures of hydrocarbons of the paraffin series ranging from $C_{15}H_{32}$ to $C_{20}H_{42}$. White vaseline is sometimes used to make gold leaf adhere to the surface of leather before application of the tool. Under no circumstances should it be applied to leather as a dressing. (235, 335)

vat dyes. Dyestuffs that are insoluble in water, but the "leuco" compounds of which, subsequent to reduction, are soluble in dilute alkalies. In this state vat dyes have a great affinity for cellulosic fibers, e.g., cloth, paper, etc. After being impregnated with the reduced dye, the material is then exposed to the oxygen of the air, which causes re-oxidation of the leuco compound back to the insoluble state. Vat dyes are among the fastest dyes known, and, despite the development of new classes of fast dyestuffs, they continue to be used where high standards of color stability are required. (17, 235)

vat machine. *See:* CYLINDER MACHINE.

vat papers. 1. A term sometimes applied to papers that are made by hand. 2. An English term for papers produced on a CYLINDER MACHINE. (156)

veal. A leather produced with a grain pattern similar to, but somewhat coarser than, calfskin, and made from the skins of immature bovine animals which have not been fed on grass subsequent to weaning. The animals are allowed to grow to a comparatively large size, yielding skins larger and heavier than calfskins but smaller than cowhides. *See also:* KIP (2). (61)

vegetable glue. An adhesive made from vegetable materials, as, for example, by treating starch with an alkali. Vegetable glue is soluble in water and gives a high "solids to water" ratio, which justifies its use as a substitute for animal glue in certain applications. The glue lack the rapid initial set characteristic of animal glue but it can be made to give reasonably satisfactory results with careful use. Because it does not have to be heated, it offers the important advantage of always being ready for immediate use. *See also:* DEXTRIN. (198, 355)

vegetable parchment paper. A paper made by passing a WATERLEAF sheet through a bath of sulfuric acid, or (at times) zinc chloride, under established conditions of time, temperature, and the like. The treated paper is then washed thoroughly so as to remove the acid or zinc salt, after which it is dried. The chemical partially dissolves or gelatinizes the paper, which is then regenerated when the chemical is diluted by the washing. This forms a very tough, stiff, smooth paper with an appearance somewhat like that of a genuine parchment. Because paper treated in this manner has a tendency to become brittle and to wrinkle upon drying, it is frequently treated with a plasticizing agent, usually glycerine or glucose. The waterleaf sheet is made from rag or (more usually) chemical wood pulp. (17, 82, 143)

vegetable tanned. Leathers that have been tanned *exclusively* with vegetable tanning agents, or with vegetable tannins plus small amounts of other agents, the latter being used solely to assist in the tanning process or to improve or modify the leather, but which are not present in sufficient quantities to noticeably alter the essential vegetable-tanned characteristics of the leather. *Cf:* CHROME RETAN. *See also:* VEGETABLE TANNING. (61)

vegetable tanning. The process of converting the protein (collagen and its related proteins) of a raw hide or skin into LEATHER by means of vegetable materials. Vegetable tanning produces a relatively dense leather, one that is firm and solid and yields a high weight of leather per unit of raw stock. It also produces a leather that is pale brown in color, and which tends to darken upon exposure to natural light. Depending upon the finishing treatment employed, the tanning material washes out of the leather very slowly.

Vegetable tannages are used to produce bookbinding leather, not only because of tradition, but because they produce leathers having a soft drape and handle (in addition to their firmness), which retain applied grain patterns particularly well. Unless specifically treated, however, vegetable tanned leathers have but little water resistance.

The classical method of vegetable tanning, especially where flatness of the leather (and particularly of the grain surface) is of great importance, as with bookbinding leather, is pit tannage—usually accomplished by means of suspension in a rocker vat. Traditionally, the skins are limed and unhaired, and delimed to a pH of 4.0 to 5.0, bated (and sometimes drenched with bran or acetic acid). The stock is then suspended as smoothly and flatly as possible in rocker vats containing used or new tanning liquor of a relatively low BARKOMETER reading. The strength of the tan liquor is gradually increased (the stock being transferred into pits containing progressively stronger liquor) until the tanning has just penetrated through the entire thickness of the skin, i.e., it has *struck through*. Splitting, if required and if not done previously, finishing, etc., are then carried out after drying.

The traditional method of vegetable tanning was slow and expensive and, furthermore, did not always give the characteristics desired in the leather. Not only was there sometimes too much firmness to the leather, but frequently the color of the leather was not as pale or as uniform as it can be made by the use of more modern methods of tanning.

The use of stronger liquors, mechanical action, pH control, and control of the contents of acids and salts have enabled the tanner to produce satisfactory leather in a much shorter time, and efforts are constantly being made to reduce the time of tannage even further. Increased mechanical action, such as drumming, accelerates the speed of tannin penetration but also results in pebbling of the grain, unless some form of pre-tannage is employed. Some tanners in both Europe and the United States employ such systems, in which a comparatively short rocker pit tannage is used to assure sufficient tannage to protect at least the outer quarter or third of the stock, with the stock then being drummed with strong liquors so as to rapidly tan the interior of the corium. There are many variations of this method, ranging from stock struck through in the rocker pits, and then being tumbled in liquors of 100° Bk. or more for as long as 48 hours, to stock only partially penetrated and then being hung on sticks in slowly rotating rotors, being drawn through a comparatively small volume of tanning liquor of gradually increasing strength.

Leather to be used for bookbinding should be tanned to give a pale, uniform, biscuit shade—one which can be readily dyed and finished in a variety of colors. The tannins in the leather should be well fixed and not easily removed by wetting the leather, otherwise they may cause stains when the leather is paste-washed or otherwise moistened.

Light leathers, e.g., goatskins, calfskins, etc., in the finished state, are usually sold on the basis of area (price per square foot); therefore, there is not the temptation to fix an unduly high proportion of tan on the fibers, as is sometimes done in the case of leathers sold by weight. Overly prolonged vegetable tannage is to be avoided as it may cause difficulties in dyeing and finishing. *See also:* BATING; DRENCHING; FATLIQUORING; LIMING; SOAKING (1); SPLITTING (1); UNHAIRING. *Cf:* CHROME TANNING. (248, 291, 306, 351, 363)

vegetable tannins. A group of complex hydrocarbon substances common throughout most of the vegetable kingdom, and having the capability, to a greater or lesser degree, of converting hide and skin, i.e., protein, into leather. Tannins are complex organic materials, and frequently have very large molecules and high molecular weights, on the order of 2,000 or greater, although it is still not certain whether they might better be considered macro-molecular substances, i.e., those with very large molecules and high molecular weights which break down into smaller fragments. Tannins were at one time classed with the glucosides because of the sugar groups that most of them contain, but they are now more often regarded as constituting a class by themselves, as some, e.g., the hemlock tannins, do not have the sugar group in the molecule. In addition to carbon, hydrogen, and oxygen, some nitrogen, phosphorus, as well as traces of inorganic ions, may be present.

Vegetable tannins for the most part are uncrystallizable colloidal substances with pronounced astringent properties. They have the ability to precipitate gelatin from solution and to form insoluble compounds with gelatin-yielding tissues, which is the property which enables them to convert raw hide and skin into leather, consolidating the dermal network of the hide into firmer and drier structures of improved thermal stability, durability, and water resistance.

Because they are extremely complex substances, vegetable tannins are difficult to classify; however, they are usually considered to consist of polyphenolic systems of two types: the hydrolized tannins (the pyrogallol class), the main constituents of which are esters of glucose with acids such as chebulic, ellagic, gallic and m-digallic; and the condensed (catechol) tannins, which are based on leuco-anthocyanidins and like substances joined together in a manner not clearly understood. The pyrogallol tannins may be hydrolyzed by acids or enzymes and include the gallotannins (from plant galls) and the ellagitannins, which produce BLOOM (1) on leather, and which are

characteristic of divi divi, myrabolans, sumac, tara, valonea, and other well-known tannins. The condensed tannins are not hydrolyzable and are characteristic of hemlock, mangrove, quebracho, wattle, and the like. The condensed tannins are more astringent, i.e., they tan more rapidly, than the pyrogallols, have larger molecules and are less well buffered. They yield less sediment, or lose less upon standing, but the leather they produce often tends to turn a reddish color upon exposure to natural light. They also yield phlobaphenes or REDS.

The terms "condensed" and "pyrogallol," as such do not mean that the tannins contain these substances but simply indicate that dihydric and trihydric phenols are produced respectively when the materials are heated (dry distillation). Quite often the "tannin" derived from a plant material, e.g., oak bark, has characteristics of both groups and consequently is generally considered to be a mixture or compound of the two principal types.

The two classes of tannin also display different reactions towards aqueous solution of iron salts. The condensed tannins produce green-black colors, while the pyrogallol class gives blue-blacks (a reaction important in the manufacture of some inks). Furthermore, they differ in their tanning properties. Pyrogallol tannins, for example, being less astringent than the condensed class, tan more slowly and produce leather of less solidity. In addition, when extracted from the plant, they generally contain smaller molecules of tannin, and, being better buffered, i.e., containing weak organic acids and their salts, they resist changes in pH value when acid or alkali is added.

For a complete and even reaction with the skin or hide to take place during tannage, it is necessary to use the tanning material in the form of a liquor, i.e., an aqueous infusion of the plant material. Modern tanneries use extracts that are concentrates of aqueous liquors, the latter usually being concentrated under reduced pressure to provide highly viscous or even solid products. Other materials extracted are known as non-tannins (abbreviated non-tans) and may include: hydrolysis products of the tannins, starches, gums, hemicelluloses, poly-saccharides, hexoses, pentoses, uronic acid, organic acids (lactic and acetic), together with their salts, inorganic salts, proteins and zymoproteins (enzymes), if the tem-

perature is not too high, as well as coloring matters such as brasilin, fisetin, and quercetin.

Vegetable tanning liquors are extremely complicated in their chemical composition, and the tannin/non-tannin ratio, the color, and the particular substances involved have a considerable (and far from completely understood) bearing on their tanning properties and, therefore, on the quality of the leather produced.

Although tannins occur throughout the greater part of the vegetable kingdom, they are more prevalent among the Angiosperms, or higher plants, especially in certain Dicotyledon families, than they are among the lower types, such as fungi, algae, etc. The Gymnosperms also have classes in which tanning is well developed, e.g., the pines, spruces and hemlocks.

The Dicotyledons include many families in which tannin occurs quite freely, among which the most noteworthy are the *Leguminosae*, e.g., the black wattle; the *Anacardiaceae*, e.g., quebracho and sumac; the *Combretaceae*, e.g., myrabolans; *Rhisophoraceae*, e.g., mangroves; *Myrtaceae*, e.g., eucalyptus; and *Polygonaceae*, e.g., canaigre.

Tannin may occur in almost any part of a plant, including roots, stems or trunk, bark, leaves, fruit, and even hairs. It may occur either in isolated individual cells, in groups or chains of cells (the more common occurrence), or in special cavities or sacs. It may also be present in latex vessels and lactiferous tissue accompanied by other substances.

In the living plant, tannin is present chiefly in solution in the vacuoles. As the cell ages and loses its protoplasmic contents, the tannin usually becomes absorbed in the cell wall; in dead plant tissue tannin often accumulates in considerable quantities. Tannins often occur in green or immature fruits, the quantity decreasing as the fruit ripens, and they may also occur in seeds, often becoming more abundant following germination. Tannin is also quite prevalent in tissues as a result of pathological conditions, such as plant galls. Certain of these galls constitute the richest sources of tannin in plants, e.g., Chinese galls, which have a tannin content ranging from 50 to 80%.

The use of vegetable tannins in the manufacture of leather probably predates recorded history, and there is creditable evidence that they were in use in Egypt as far back as 5000 B.C.

The ancient Greeks and Romans were well versed in the art of vegetable tanning, and evidence indicates that vegetable tannins were used in China many thousands of years ago. (175, 248, 291, 306, 363)

vegetable vellum. A term at one time applied to a Japanese vellum paper specially prepared in imitation of genuine VELLUM. (197)

vehicle. The liquid portion of a material such as ink, paint, varnish, or a coating composition, including the binders, adhesives, modifiers, and the like.

vein colors. The colors employed in marbling to produce the veins of the pattern. They are applied to the marbling size prior to the dropping on of the FRENCH (or body) COLOR. (217)

veining liquid. A special marbling size designed to promote the formation of veins in the colors after they are dropped. The size is produced by mixing soft water, e.g., rain water, and soap, in the proportions of 1⅛ pints of water to 2 ounces of soap. *See also:* SPRINKLING WATER. (161)

veiny leather (veined). The colored pattern of arteries, veins, and other blood vessels sometimes seen in parchment and vellum, or even leather, where the pattern of the larger vessels appears on the grain surface in the form of indentations. In parchment and vellum it is caused by insufficient removal of blood from the vascular system of the skin, while in the case of leather it is due to bacterial degradation of collagen fibers in the vicinities of the blood vessels. Veininess usually results from the use of skins of animals found dead of natural causes, from improper or delayed curing after flaying, or for some reason wherein the blood is not drained from the animal immediately after slaughter. In some cases, veininess can actually enhance the beauty of vellum, especially if the blood vessels form geometrical and/or attractive patterns. (291, 363)

vellucent binding. A method of decorating (and protecting) a bookbinding utilizing TRANSPARENT VELLUM. The technique was developed by CEDRIC CHIVERS sometime around 1903, and is designed not only for the protection of leather bindings, but also to protect covers bearing colored designs (usually pictorial in nature) painted on paper, attached to the boards, and then covered with the vellum. The vellucent covering is also suitable for highly decorative designs because it is possible to further embellish the design by means of mother-of-pearl, irridescent

shell, and the like, all of which may be covered and permanently protected by the vellum. The surface of the vellum itself can be tooled in gold, thus further enhancing the entire effect. *See also:* EDWARDS OF HALIFAX. (94, 236)

vellum. Originally, a translucent or opaque material produced from calfskin that had been soaked, limed and unhaired, and then dried at normal temperature under tension, usually on a wooden device called a stretching frame. Today, however, vellum is generaly defined as a material made from calfskin, sheepskin, or virtually any other skin obtained from a relatively small animal, e.g., antelope. Some authorities do not even distinguish between vellum and parchment, although traditionally the former was made from an unsplit calfskin, and consequently had a grain pattern on one side (unless removed by scraping), while the latter was produced from the *flesh* split of a sheepskin, and consequently had no grain pattern. The important distinction between vellum (or parchment) and leather is that the former is not tanned but is prepared essentially by soaking the skin in lime and drying it under *tension*. For a description of its manufacture, see PARCHMENT.

Most medieval manuscripts, whether illuminated or not, were written on vellum. Uterine vellum was made in the 13th and 14th centuries from the skins of unborn or still-born animals. *See:* SLUNK. Limp vellum or limp-parchment bindings were used frequently in the 16th and 17th centuries, and were sometimes gilt but were also often not embellished. In later centuries vellum has been more commonly used like leather, that is, as the covering for stiff board bindings.

Vellum can be stained virtually any color but seldom is, as a great part of its beauty and appeal rests in its faint grain and hair markings, as well as its warmth and simplicity. *See also:* VEINY LEATHER. (192, 218, 236, 291)

vellum binder. A term sometimes used in Great Britain to indicate one who binds account books (blankbooks), as well as other stationery bindings. It derives from the time when stationery binding was referred to as "vellum binding."

vellum binding. *See:* STATIONERY BINDING.

vellum painting. A painting executed on the under surface of TRANSPARENT VELLUM, or on white paper, prior to covering. Many vellum paintings were also executed on the outer surface of vellum, although by strict definition

these were not actually "vellum paintings." *See also:* EDWARDS OF HALIFAX. (347)

vellum parchment. A very tough handmade vellum paper, produced in England, somewhat similar in appearance to genuine vellum. It is said to be extremely durable and not easily affected by heat, mildew, and insects. Its equivalent in the United States is ART PARCHMENT.

velvet. 1. A fabric produced in a wide range of construction and weights from silk, rayon, cotton, nylon, or wool. Velvet is characterized by a short, soft, dense pile produced either by weaving an extra warp into a single cloth, which is looped over wires and later cut, or by weaving a double cloth with an extra warp connecting the two fabrics which are later separated by cutting. Uncut velvet, or terry, is sometimes woven simultaneously with the cut to create figures on the cloth. Velvet brocades, which are the most luxurious of all velvets, are made with gold and silver threads as an extra weft, or filling, the figures being wrought by hand, as with embroidery. Velveteen and plush are cotton or wool fabrics woven in much the same manner as true velvet.

Book covers of velvet, often studded with jewels, were produced, (for royalty) as early as the middle ages; however, velvet attained to its greatest use in bookbinding in EMBROIDERED BINDINGS. As velvet is difficult to work, embroidered velvet bindings usually included a large area of applique, laid, or couched work in colored silk or satin, always with large spaces that were unworked. Such work as actually was done on the velvet was always in thick gimp or gold cord.

2. A leather finished with a fine nap on the grain side, in contrast to SUEDE, which has a (usually coarser) nap on the flesh side. (111, 280)

velvet calf. A calfskin leather finished with a fine nap on the grain side. *See:* VELVET (2).

velvet Persian. A term sometimes applied to a sheepskin. The origin of the term is obscure. (133)

velvet wrapper binding. A form of protective covering for book covers, designed to be wrapped over the edges of the book. Used in medieval times, the velvet wrapper binding is frequently represented in Flemish paintings of the 15th century. The wooden boards, with no preliminary covering, are covered in velvet cut so as to extend above and below head and tail, and beyond the fore edge of the upper cover. The edges of the velvet were sometimes finished with embroidery of red floss and silver. (347)

"v" endpaper. *See:* ZIG-ZAG ENDPAPER.

Venetian binding. A style of binding, obtained directly from the Near East, probably in the 1480s, the boards of which were composed of, or coated with, some form of paper composition that permitted the corners and centers to be stamped in sunken panels or shaded compartments. The entire board was generaly covered with thinly pared leather, which was then coated with a colored laquer and painted with arabesques in gold. This style of binding often incorporated the lion of St. Mark painted on the center panel, and was perhaps used as the official binding of the Statutes and Commissions of the Venetian Senate. (124, 280, 371)

Venetian red. A coloring earth of a deep, reddish brown, which, in its natural form, may consist of nearly pure ferric oxide (Fe_2O_3) of the hematite type. It is prepared synthetically by calcining ferrous sulfate in the presence of lime, and is then known as "caput mortuum." It is used in coloring paper. Also called "India red" or "Indian red." (72)

ventilating power. The capability of a leather to transfer water vapor from an atmophere of higher to one of lower relative humidity. (363)

verdigris. A green or greenish-blue pigment prepared by the action of acetic acid on copper. Verdigris, which is toxic, was at one time used to make a green marbling color. It is also very destructive to paper because it acts as an oxidation catalyst. (97, 152)

vermicular. Inlays which resemble somewhat the track of a wriggling worm. (261)

verso. 1. The back or reverse side of a leaf of an open book or manuscript, and one which usually bears an even page number. 2. The reverse, or second, side of a sheet to be printed. 3. The back of a separately printed sheet, which in former times was called the "folio verso." 4. A term sometimes applied to the outer side of the lower cover of a book. (209)

vertical stroke. A device that can be attached to a shear or double-shear stroke GUILLOTINE so as to bring the knife down vertically, instead of in a shearing motion. It is used with knives of a special shape designed to cut irregular or fancy edges. (145)

vinegar. A dilute solution of ACETIC ACID.

It is used as an astringent to help close the pores of a porous leather before tooling. This operation is essential, as close tooling may ruin adjacent lines unless the surface of the leather is compact and solid. Vinegar also helps to raise the grain of leather and thus accentuate the pattern. (130, 335)

vinyl coating. A relatively heavy coating of a plastic material applied to a substrate, such as a fabric. Impregnated buckram is an example of a cloth having a vinyl coating. The finished glossy, soft, pliable surface is obtained by heat curing. (309)

vinyl resin. Any of the thermoplastic synthetic resins prepared by the polymerization or copolmerization of various vinyl compounds, principally vinyl acetate, vinyl chloride, and vinylidine chloride. Vinyl resins are clear water-white, non-yellowing materials, some of which are used in the preparation of coating materials, foils, and the like. *See also:* POLYVINYL ACETATE; POLYVINYL CHLORIDE. (233)

viscosity. 1. That property of a fluid manifest as a resistance to flow and measured by the tangential force per unit area of either of two horizontal planes at unit distance apart, one of the planes moving with unit velocity relative to the other, the space between being occupied by the flowing liquid. If the velocity of flow is proportional to the force applied, the fluid is said to exhibit Newtonian behavior; however, many colloidal dispersions and suspensions display anomalous non-Newtonian flow, i.e., the velocity of flow is not proportional to the force applied.

Viscosity diminishes as temperature rises, often by about 2% per degree C; it also increases with an increase in pressure.

2. That property of a cellulose paper pulp, or other polymer, expressed by the viscosity of a solution of the material in a suitable solvent and under specified conditions. Viscosity in this respect is related to the strength, as well as other properties of the paper pulp fibers. (17, 72, 195, 309)

viscosity coefficient. The tangentially applied shearing stress capable of inducing a velocity gradient. When a shearing stress of 1 dyne per square centimeter produces a velocity gradient of 1 centimeter per second/second, a material is said to have a viscosity of 1 poise. (309)

visible cloth joint. An inner hinge made of cloth (usually cambric), constructed

by joining the first flyleaf and the board paper. It is sometimes reinforced to the text block by mounting or sewing. *See also:* HINGE (1). (256)

void fraction. The ratio of the volume taken up by air spaces (the voids) to the total volume of a material. (17)

volant. A term at one time applied to a print or illustration hinged at one edge only so that it could be turned over for viewing of the reverse side.

volumen. The papyrus roll used in ancient Egypt, Greece, and Rome, written on one side only with a reed pen. The text was in columns, the lines of which ran parallel the length of the roll. The final papyrus sheet of the volumen was rolled around a knobbed rod which served as a handle. The rolls were stored in boxes or on shelves, and, in the latter case, had an identifying label of vellum attached to the end of the roll. The label, which was sometimes colored, bore the title of the work. A wooden case (manuale) was sometimes used to protect the edges of the roll. "Volumen" is Latin for "a thing rolled up." (156)

volume signature (part signature). The number of the volume or part, or a letter indicating its sequence, placed on the same line as the signature, in order to prevent the binder from mixing the sections of various volumes of a work. (156)

volute. A decorative ornament, often found on heads-in-medallions rolls, which consists of a large curl (spiral) in roughly volute form at one end, the other end having a small curl turning in the opposite direction. The volute was always used in pairs. Its use as a single tool, with a reverse partner, was common in English restoration bindings, often pointillé. (250)

V through. A V-shaped device, usually constructed of wood or sheet metal, and used for punching holes by hand in single-section publications in preparation for saddle sewing by hand. (259)

vulcanization. 1. The process of reacting rubber with sulfur or other suitable agent so as to change its physical properties in the direction of decreased plastic flow, diminished surface tackiness, and increased tensile strength. *See also:* SELF-VULCANIZING. 2. The cross linkage of an adhesive substance obtained by the application of heat and catalysts. (309)

wagon. A hand instrument somewhat resembling a sled (with its runners) and used in the manufacture of gold leaf to trim the edges of the leaves to proper size. A finely sharpened knife made of the bark of a reed is used in conjunction with the wagon. This knife is said to be so sharp that not even the finest steel can be honed to an edge equally suitable for trimming the leaves. (29)

wainscot. A cover marble executed by first painting the covers with a brown coloring and then water, followed by splashes of copperas (ferrous sulfate). A solution of alum is then thrown on, followed by a bold sprinkle of dilute sulfuric acid. An alternative "wainscot" consists of brown, a coating of glair, black in large spots, brown again, this time in large spots, and finally the dilute sulfuric acid. (95, 97, 152)

wallet edge. A type of limp binding which has the covering of the lower cover, along the entire length of the book, overlapping the fore edge of the book, terminating in a tongue which is inserted through a slot in the upper cover. *See also:* YAPP STYLE. (140)

walnut marble. A type of TREE CALF executed by sprinkling the covers with black and brown coloring only. (97, 152)

walrus hide. A leather produced from the hide of a walrus, or the skin of a seal or sea lion, split, and used occasionally for covering books. Subsequent to tanning and splitting, it is difficult to distinguish between leather made from sealskin and walrus hide, and the names are often used interchangeably. "Walrus grain" is a term used to indicate a cowhide, sheepskin, or goatskin, as well as splits of various hides, embossed in imitation of walrus hide. In such cases, the proper description is "walrus-grained cowhide," etc. (261, 351)

warbles. A defect in leather seen as small pinholes or as tiny scars. Warbles are caused by the larvae of the grub or warble fly (family *Oestridae*), which develop under the skin of the animal and emerge in the area of the backbone. If the animal is slaughtered before the wounds heal, the defect is known as "open warbles," while if sufficient time elapses for the animal to develop scar tissue, they are then called closed or "blind warbles." In either

case leather produced from a warbled hide is unsatisfactory in both strength and appearance. (363)

warehouse work. An expression sometimes applied to the bookbinding work consisting of simple forms of binding, such as pamphlets, periodicals and booklets, as well as miscellaneous operations, such as cutting, folding, and stitching. (58)

warm colors. Colors having red and yellow as the dominant hue. Yellowish or brownish grays are called the "warm grays." All warm colors lie in the red-yellow half of the color circle. *Cf:* COOL COLORS. (233)

warp. A series of parallel yarns extended lengthwise in a loom, thereby forming the lengthwise threads of a fabric. They are usually twisted tighter than the filling yarns and are sized so as to protect them during the weaving of the filling threads.

The warp direction of a cloth is the stronger of the two directions. There is some disagreement as to which direction the warp of a book cloth should run with relation to the spine of the book. Some contend that the warp should run across the joint of a case-bound book, as this will give more strength in the joint; others maintain that the warp should run parallel to the spine because: 1) it makes a neater joint; 2) in the event the cloth becomes damp or wet there is less likelihood of the covers warping in such a manner that the head and tail pull outward thus damaging the inner hinge; and 3) the cloth will adhere better in the joint. (152, 209)

warping. The distortion of the covers of a book subsequent to binding, to the extent that the covers do not lie flat against the text block. This distortion is caused by the difference in expansion and contraction of the various com-

ponents of the cover—cloth, boards, board paper, and, to a lesser extent, the films of adhesive which secure these components together. Warping is found to occur in the direction of: 1) the side of the material which has the greater stretch; 2) the side of the material with the least moisture content; and 3) the side which is lined or has the greater number of layers. On newly bound books these factors are at work because of the setting and drying of the adhesives; subsequent to binding, stresses may occur because of atmospheric changes. The practical means of minimizing warping include the use of well-matured boards, cutting the boards and board papers so that the grain (machine direction) runs parallel to the spine of the book, the use of adhesives containing a minimum amount of water (and no more than the minimum amount required of plasticizer), and adequate pressing of the books after casing-in or covering. In addition, maintenance of a stable atmospheric environment is important.

waste sheet. 1. A sheet of paper tipped to the outside over the permanent endpaper to prevent it from becoming damaged or soiled during the binding of the book. Special instructions on binding the book may also be written on this sheet. Originally, the waste sheet was printed with an abbreviated title so that the publication could be identified. The so-called printed waste sheet is known as the half-title paper and is always found in books of any pretension to high quality. 2. An old term for the advertisements, blurbs, etc., at the front and back of some publications. 3. Sheets of paper used in press makeready and register, or the spoiled sheets resulting from errors in printing and binding. (69, 94)

water. A colorless or faintly blue-green liquid (H_2O). Molecules of water enter into the constitution of many crystalline salts, e.g., alum—$K_2SO_4 \cdot Al_2(SO_4)_3 \cdot 24H_2O$, in which they may be reversibly held. The outstanding chemical reactions of water are: 1) its reaction with certain metals, e.g., Na, Ca, Fe, more or less easily, with the liberation of hydrogen, such as, $Na + H_2O \rightarrow NaOH + H$; 2) its reaction with oxides of non-metals, e.g., with SO_3 to form acids, such as, $SO_3 + H_2O \rightarrow$

H_2SO_4; 3) with halides of nonmetals, to form hydrogen halides and an oxyacid, such as $PCl_3 + 3H_2O \rightarrow H_3PO_3 + 3HCl$; 4) with dissolved salts of weak acids or weak bases, forming solutions with an alkaline or acid reaction (hydrolysis), such as $Na_2CO_3 + H_2O \rightleftharpoons NaOH + NaHCO_3$; and 5) with coke at high temperature to form water gas, $C + H_2O \rightarrow CO + H_2$. (235)

watercolor inks. Thin, semi-transparent inks that contain no oils, and which are used when printing in colors from a rubber surface. As they remain water soluble, even after printing, they cannot be used where inadvertent wetting may occur, nor can papers printed with them be washed or deacidified by means of aqueous systems. (140)

watercolor paper. A paper designed to be used with watercolors. It is a typical drawing paper, either made by hand or machine; tub sized, and machine, air, or loft dried. The paper has a hard-sized surface, and a texture designed to enhance the absorption of watercolors so that they will not run or penetrate too deeply into the paper. When intended for use with oil paints, the paper is made to simulate the surface of canvas. (17)

watered silk. A silk cloth having a wavy or damasklike pattern, i.e., a MOIRÉ EFFECT. While seldom used as a covering material, it is sometimes used for doublures and fly leaves. *See also:* MOIRÉ BOOK CLOTH. (140)

water glass. *See:* SODIUM SILICATE.

waterleaf. 1. A completely unsized sheet of paper, and one having low water resistance. *See also:* ABSORBENT PAPERS. 2. Handmade paper in its initial stage of manufacture, consisting of paper fibers spread evenly over the surface of the hand mold; they are then removed and pressed between felts. As it is unsized, it is very absorbent and has low water resistance. It is generally surface sized to make it suitable for writing or printing. *See also:* SIZING (1). (17, 156)

watermark. A distinguishing letter, design, symbol, etc., incorporated into a paper *during manufacture. True* watermarks are a localized modification of the formation and opacity of the paper while it is still wet, so that the marks can be seen in the finished sheet of paper when viewed by transmitted light. This type of sheet modification may be accomplished by means of a bronze letterpress-type dandy roll that impresses a design in the wet web, or by means of a design wired to the grid of the mold in paper that is made by

hand. The place where the dandy roll impresses, or the location of the wired design, will contain less fibrous material and, therefore, will have greater translucency. Another method is to use a bronze, intaglio-type device on the dandy roll, the resulting modification being that *more* fibrous material is located at the point of impress. *See:* SHADE-CRAFT WATERMARK. A variation of the letterpress method incorporates the use of a soft rubber, letterpress-type device that impresses a design in the web of paper on the *underside* of the web, i.e., the wire side (where the watermark is found in handmade paper), so that it is seen through the sheet from the top. This type of watermark, which is produced at a point on the papermaking machine where the web is no longer sufficiently wet to modify the formation and opacity of the paper, is actually, therefore, a form of embossing and cannot be called a true watermark.

Forms of the watermark are generally divided into four very broad classes: 1) the very earliest, generally consisting of simple circles, crosses, knots, ovals, three-hill symbols, triangles, and the like, which were easy to construct simply by twisting and bending soft wires. (These early marks also included many pomme crosses, based on the Greek cross with balls or circles at the ends of the cross bars. A similar watermark, found on Italian paper of the 14th century, consists of a circle above which is a patriarchal or papal cross. These earliest marks were prevalent from about 1282 to 1425); 2) watermarks emphasizing man and his works. (Thousands of designs of this nature have been noted, a large number of them featuring human hands in various forms); 3) watermarks consisting of flowers, fruit, grains, trees and other plants, etc.; and 4) watermarks consisting of wild, domesticated, and legendary animals.

More recent developments of the watermark have resulted in some complicated and occasionally artistic forms, reflecting an increasing skill in design and manufacture. "Light and shade" watermarks have been used from time to time in the 20th century, but they are relatively uncommon because of the difficulty and expense of producing them.

The papermaker's initials or name, the place or date of manufacture of the paper (if included) were more likely to be found in the COUNTERMARK, which was a subsidiary and smaller mark in-

troduced in the 17th century, and was generally located in the opposite half of the sheet to the watermark itself.

Watermarks in paper, particularly in endpapers, can provide valuable information about the history of bookbinding. (17, 69, 143, 177, 198)

waterproof. A relative term indicating that a material has been treated, i.e., sized, coated, impregnated, etc., in such a manner as to increase its resistance to the penetration of water. The basic principle of waterproofing is that the presence of the waterproofing chemical or other material in or on a fibrous substance modifies the surface tension between water and the substances of the fiber. WATER RESISTANCE is probably a better term to use with respect to any of the materials used in book and paper conservation. (17)

water resistance. That property of a material which enables it to resist, but not completely prevent, the action or penetration of water. A material may be made water resistant to a greater or lesser degree by the application of sizing, coating, impregnating, or other materials.

Waters, Peter (1930–). An English bookbinder and conservator who studied bookbinding under William Matthews at the Guilford College of Art, Surrey, after which he attended the Royal College of Art, London. He then worked for three years with Roger Powell before entering as a partner in the firm of Powell and Waters in 1956. In this same year, Waters succeeded Powell as lecturer in bookbinding at the Royal College of Art. From 1956 to 1971, he executed a number of bindings for private collectors, museums, and presentation, and worked with Powell in the repair and restoration of a number of valuable books in the libraries of Trinity College, Dublin, Aberdeen and Winchester Universities, and others. In 1966 Waters served as consultant to the Biblioteca Nazionale, Florence, Italy, as Technical Director for the restoration of flood-damaged collections and was principally responsible for the design and incorporation of the restoration system employed. From 1968 to 1971 he was codirector with James Lewis of a research project at the Imperial College of Science and Technology, London, relating to the conservation of library materials. In 1971 Waters was appointed Restoration Officer in the Preservation Office of the Library of Congress. There he inaugurated new concepts and programs relating to the conservation of the Library's extensive collection of books, manuscripts, maps, and other archival materials.

Waters' philosophy has been rooted in the Bauhaus tradition of "fitness for purpose" in design, which through his extensive knowledge of book structure has found expression ranging from the binding of individual books to the planning of comprehensive conservation measures, culminating in his now widely followed concept of "phased preservation."

water stain. A blemish on book papers, documents, etc., caused by the movement of materials within the paper, such as coloring matter, dust, acids, and the like, resulting from the paper being wetted with water, either accidentally or during washing. The water itself does not stain the paper, unless it contains impurities which leave it and enter the paper fibers. Water stains can frequently be removed or reduced by hot water or a size bath.

water-vapor permeability. A form of PERMEABILITY applied specifically to water vapor. Because the cellulosic fibers of paper have a very high affinity for water, water vapor permeability does not generally correlate with the permeability of other vapors and gases. *See also:* VAPOR PERMEABILITY. (17, 72)

wattle (bark). A vegetable tanning material obtained from the bark of the black wattle (*Acacia mollissima*), indigenous to Australia but cultivated extensively in South Africa and other areas. Large quantities of wattle are exported, much of it to England, in the form either of the bark itself, or as the extract. The tannin content of the bark ranges from 30 to 45%, with the average being about 35 to 39%. Wattle is essentially a tannin of the condensed class; it has a high pH value, a low salts and acids content, and a relatively low viscosity, especially in warm solutions. It is very astringent, penetrates the hide substance rapidly, and has a high degree of tan fixation. Like most other vegetable tannins, it is seldom used alone, but generally in mixtures with myrabolans, sumac, valonea, etc. Also known as "mimosa." *See also:* VEGETABLE TANNINS. (175)

waved. A term used occasionally to indicate a book cover that has warped or curled.

wavelengths. The electromagnetic spectrum consisting of a continuous range of electromagnetic waves travelling at the speed of light, or approximately 186,300 miles per second. The length of these waves ranges from several miles (low frequency radio transmissions) to as short as 10^{-12} cm (γ-rays). Wavelengths may be expressed in centimeters; however, the shorter wavelengths are more commonly expressed in Ångstrom (Å) units, defined as 1 Å $= 1 \times 10^{-8}$ cm. Approximate wavelengths for various types are:

Type	Wavelength in Centimeters		In Å
γ-rays	10^{-12}	to 10^{-10}	0.01
X-rays	10^{-9}	to 10^{-7}	0.1 to 10
Ultraviolet light	10^{-6}	to 4×10^{-5}	100 to 4,000
Visible light	4×10^{-5}	to 8×10^{-5}	4,000 to 8,000
Infrared light	8×10^{-5}	to 0.1	8,000
Radio waves	1	to 10^5	

(195)

wave marble (wave nonpareil marble). A marble pattern consisting of colors drawn into an undulating form, with the points of each row meeting each other. The colors—red, yellow, blue, and green—are dropped on the size, over which the marbler beats a small quantity of white. The colors are then raked with a double rake (one having teeth 3 or 4 inches apart, those of the rear rake being adjusted so as to be exactly in the center of the spaces of the forward rake, and about 1½ inches behind it). The rake is then drawn through the colors in a manner similar to that used in executing the NONPAREIL MARBLE, i.e., from left to right. The raking is done with an undulating or see-saw motion, but only enough to make the top of the last wave touch the bottom of the first, thus producing a uniformity over the entire sheet and giving the pattern the appearance of squares. (241)

wavy edges. An effect in book and other printing papers similar to the warping of book covers. It is usually caused by a more rapid rate of change in the moisture content of the edges of sheets in a pile as compared with the center. (17)

wax. An animal or plant substance, such as BEESWAX or CARNAUBA WAX, that differs from fat in that it is less greasy, harder, and more brittle. Wax is essentially an ester of monohydric alcohols and fatty acids of high molecular weight, in association with some free acids and alcohols. *See also:* CANDELILLA WAX; CHINESE WAX; INSECT WAX; JAPAN WAX; LANOLIN; MICROCRYSTALLINE WAX; PLANT WAX; SPERMACETI WAX. (291)

wax emulsion. A stable aqueous emulsion usually made of paraffin or microcrystalline wax; it sometimes contains rosin. It is prepared by means of emulsifying agents and mechanical agitation. The emulsion may be either acid- or alkali-stable, depending on the emulsifying agent employed. Wax emulsions are used for sizing and waxing paper, and in the maufacture of leather. (17)

wax resist. A method of producing decorative end- and cover papers, similar to the process used in BATIK. The wax acts to resist the paint in the CRAYON-RESIST process. Approximately equal parts of beeswax and paraffin are used. The mixture is heated, and, if a crackled effect is desired, additional brittleness may be imparted by the addition of more paraffin. The melted wax is applied to the paper in lines, spots and/or various shapes. A water color wash is applied over the entire surface of the paper, and adheres only to the unwaxed areas. The wax is removed by placing the paper between protective sheets and pressing with a warm iron. The wax-resist process is also used at times in decorating the leather covers of books. (183, 311)

wax size. A sizing agent containing paraffin or as similar type of wax.

wear resistance. A term used in the leather trade to indicate the reciprocal of the loss in thickness of a specimen of leather after a specified degree of abrasive action upon it.

web. Paper on, or as it comes from, the papermaking machine in its full width, or from a roll of paper in any converting operation. The expression "in the direction of the web" means in the direction of the run of the papermaking machine when the paper is being made. It also means the direction in which the greater proportion of the paper fibers are oriented, i.e., the grain (machine direction) of the paper. The direction of the web is important in work printed to register, as paper stretches more across the web than in the direction of it.

webbing(s). 1. The strong, narrow fabric, closely woven of plied yarns, on which heavy blankbooks are sewn. 2. Filaments or threads that sometimes form when adhesive surfaces are separated. *See also:* STRINGINESS. (83, 309)

wedge shaped. A bound book that is thicker at the spine than at the fore edge. The condition is caused by excessive, uncompensated sewing swell, compensation guards that are too thick for the inserted material, excessive guarding of damaged folds, or by guards made of paper that is too thick. Such a condition may at times also be the reverse, where the fore edge is thicker than the spine, because of swelling of the paper, or an improperly folded map, etc. In the latter case, the fore edge swells but the spine, being fixed in position, does not. (236, 256)

weft. The threads or yarns in a fabric that cross the WARP and extend from selvage to selvage, i.e., the threads carried by the shuttle. The typical cloth is stronger, i.e., has a greater breaking strength, in the warp direction than in the weft. Also called "filling." (341)

well-closed formation. A paper is said to have a well-closed formation when the paper fibers are arrayed in an even, regular manner so that the paper has a uniform appearance. It is the opposite of a WILD (1) formation. (17)

"w" endpaper. *See:* ZIG-ZAG ENDPAPER.

west end marble. A marble pattern executed in much the same manner as the SPANISH MARBLE, the major difference being that the paper is laid down without shading. Aside from the veins, it consists of two hues of the same color, one of which is dark and dotted all over with small white spots, while the other, or top color, is lighter in shade. The vein colors are mixed with gall and water, as in the case of the Spanish marble. The dark color is sprinkled on full so as to drive the veins up well, and the white is then beaten on finely and evenly all over. The light or top color is sprinkled on lightly and evenly, and the paper is then laid on. (159, 241)

wet press. A dewatering unit on the Fourdrinier papermaking machine, situated between the sheet-forming equipment and the driers. It uses pressure, or a combination of pressure and suction to remove water from the wet web before it reaches the driers. The press consists of pressure nips, each formed by a pair of heavy rollers. One of each pair is usually covered with rubber and may be perforated and fitted with an internal suction device which further reduces the amount of water in the web. The paper web is carried through the nip of each wet press on a FELT (2), which itself, being both bulky and porous, absorbs and thus removes water from the paper. (17)

wet-rub resistance. The ability of the coating of a material to resist softening and abrading due to rubbing, or, in the case of a printing paper, from the combined action of fountain solution and blanket.

wet-salting. A method of curing hides and skins for storage and/or transportation subsequent to flaying. The hide is spread out, flesh side up, and well sprinkled with salt (sodium chloride). Coarse, or round salt is preferred to fine salt, as the former spreads evenly, while the latter tends to form patchy, wet cakes. A second hide is laid over the first and sprinkled with salt, a process which is repeated until a stack 5 to 8 feet high is formed, the top hide being well overlaid with salt. The pack is left for approximately 30 days, during which time the salt dissolves in the moisture of the hides and the brine thus created permeates throughout the pile. The amount of salt used is generally 1 pound of salt for each pound of hide. When the hides are ready for shipment, they are "taken up," the salt is knocked off and the hides are then bundled and tied. Also called "green salting." *See also:* BRINING; DRYING (1); DRY-SALTING. (248, 306, 363)

wet strength. The resistance to breakage of an applied adhesive as measured immediately after removal from immersion under specified conditions of time, temperature, and pressure. (72, 309)

wet-strength paper. A paper which, even when saturated with water, has an unusually high resistance to rupture or disingtegration. This property is produced by subjecting the paper or the fibers from which the paper is made to chemical treatment. Wet strength, which is most evident and significant when it occurs in absorbent papers, should not be confused with water repellency or the resistance of paper to wetting when exposed to water. Normally, a paper loses most of its strength when saturated with water, and one which retains more than 15% of its dry strength when completely saturated with water may correctly be referred to as a "wet-strength paper." A very superior wet-strength paper may retain as much as 60% of its dry strength when wet. (17, 42)

wettability. The state or condition of being wettable, or the relative affinity of liquid for the surface of a solid, such as the affinity of water for paper or leather. Wettability increases directly with increasing affinity, as measured by the contact angle formed between the liquid and the solid. This increases from non-wettability at an angle greater than 90° to complete wettability when the contact angle is 0°. (17)

wetting. The relative capability of a liquid adhesive to display affinity for an adherend, i.e., to flow uniformly over the adherend surface.

wetting agent. A substance, usually a SURFACE-ACTIVE AGENT, which reduces the surface tension of a liquid and therefore increases its adhesion to a solid surface. Improved wettability is observed as a lower (often zero) contact angle between the solid and liquid. A wetting agent usually consists of a molecule with a hydrophilic (water attracting) group at one end and a hydrophobic (water repelling, and therefore oil attracting) group at the other. Wetting agents are used to improve obsorbency of blotting papers, and for improving dispersibility of pigments, such as calcium carbonate and titanium oxide. (98, 222)

wetting down. The process of dampening paper before printing. Wetting down was necessary in the early days of printing because of the non-uniformity of the height of the type used, and because type was used longer and, therefore, wore down more. In addition, the early hand-operated presses were not as powerful as later presses. Slightly dampened paper takes ink more readily than dry paper, and does not require as much pressure to make the impression on the softened surface of the paper. The impression, however, makes a thicker line and may also show on the other side of the sheet. Wetting down also often resulted in uneven stretching of the paper fibers during impression, causing the book to be thicker in the printed area than in the margins. *See also:* CONVEX COVERS.

wetting out. The process of dipping large sheets of handmade paper into cold water so as to remove wrinkles and cockles. The paper is then again made up into packs and pressed. (197)

Whatman, James (1741-1798). An 18th century English papermaker. His father, James Whatman (1702-1759), acquired a part ownership in the Turkey Mill papermaking establishment near Maidstone in 1740 and developed it until it became one of England's leading papermaking firms. The Whatmans are credited with the first manufacture of WOVE PAPER in Europe, in about 1755, and they may also have invented the wove-wire mold (about 1756). Whatman paper is still being made, and is used for special editions and privately printed books. (140)

wheeling. The process of tumbling hides and skins, or leather, in a revolving drum. Newly tanned leather is wheeled after pressing in order to remove wrinkles and creases. (363)

whipping. The process of overseaming or overcasting an insert in a book. *See also:* WHIP STITCHING.

whip stitching. The process of sewing single sheets into "sections," the number of sheets so sewn depending on the thickness of the paper. The "sections" are then sewn on tapes or cords in the usual manner of hand sewing. (82)

whistling joint. A wrinkled joint (inner hinge) caused by the board paper not adhering securely in the joint and inside edge of the board. (65)

white dressing. A 19th century and earlier process of treating skins with weak organic acids during the manufacture of vellum and parchment. Subsequent to soaking, washing, and fleshing, the skins were immersed in a series of acid vats, much in the same manner skins are limed today. There were generally five such baths; the first was usually intended to cleanse the skins, the second to soften the hair and epidermis for unhairing, and the final three to swell and plump the skins and give them body. The entire process generally took 5 to 6 weeks. (291)

white edges. The edges of a book which have been trimmed smooth but not colored, marbled, gilt, sprinkled, or otherwise decorated or treated in any manner. Also called "plain edges." (156)

white gold. A pale gold alloy which somewhat resembles silver or platinum and usually contains nickel with or without other metals, such as copper, tin, or zinc. It is used to a limited extent for embellishing books. It is considerably thicker than regular ($23\frac{1}{2}$ karat) gold leaf. (130)

whiteness. The condition of being white, i.e., the degree to which the color of a material, such as paper, approaches that of "ideal white." Whiteness in paper in associated with low colorimetric purity and high luminous reflectively. (17)

white size. *See:* ACID SIZE.

white spot. A technique used in coloring the edges of a book. Drops of melted wax are spattered on the edges, which

are then colored in the usual manner. When the wax is removed, the edges appear to be colored with white spots. The pattern may be varied by using two or three colors, or by sprinkling the edges before the wax is applied and then again after it is removed. (241)

whittawed leather. *See:* TAWING.

wholesale trade binding. 1. A term synonymous with TRADE BINDING (1) in the 18th and 19th centuries. 2. A term sometimes associated in England in the first half of the 19th century with bindings of wholesale booksellers, especially those who catered to the provincial and foreign book trade. The booksellers brought new books in sheets and had them bound independently of the publishers. This type of binding was prevalent before the introduction of modern EDITION BINDING (1825-30). It was most prevalent in the field of fiction, and because it continued to satisfy the demand of distributors of the novel, such publications were the last type of book, at least those published in large editions, to be bound in publisher's cloth. This was essentially the reason why equal numbers of boarded and half-cloth books of fiction were issued in wholesalers' as well as in publishers' bindings between 1820 and at least 1845. Similar (printed) labels were applied to each and it was usually very difficult to distinguish between them. (69)

wide lines. *See:* CHAIN LINES.

wild. 1. An irregular formation of the fibers in a sheet of paper, resulting in a mottled appearance in the LOOK-THROUGH of the sheet, as opposed to a CLOSE FORMATION. It is caused by: 1) partial clotting or lumping of the fibers; and 2) high freeness or excessive vacuum at the first suction box of the papermaking machine. It is especially noticeable in long-fibered papers, although it is possible to imitate a wild formation in paper made up of short fibers by manipulating the sheet forming equipment. Also called "cloudy." 2. *See:* MARBLED GRAIN. (17, 42)

willow. 1. A machine consisting essentially of two rotating drums having spikes attached to their interior surfaces. The willow is used to tear raw material, e.g., rags, waste paper, etc., for use in making paper. The willow frequently utilizes air currents to remove dust from the usable papermaking material. Also called a "devil." 2. A long grain in leather. The willow grain is produced by drawing the

leather from head to butt over a dull blade. (130, 156, 172)

willow calf. A leather produced from calfskin, usually brown in color, and generally with a typical box grain pattern. It is a full chrome-tanned leather boarded either in one direction—head to butt—or in two directions, as with box calf. (61)

willow side. A side of a cattle hide, i.e., cut down the backbone, full chrome, semi-chrome, or vegetable tanned, and usually colored brown but also produced in other colors, but never black. It has a grain pattern formed by BOARDING (1) in one direction (head to butt). There is some confusion concerning this leather because at times it is boarded in two directions, producing a grain pattern similar to that of BOX SIDE. (351)

windows. The uncolored areas of marbled papers.

"window" copy. A leaf with an illustration, or other printed matter, on both sides, attached along its edges to a larger leaf provided with an opening or "window" so that the image area on both sides of the smaller leaf is visible. (156)

wire binding. Any form of binding in which the leaves are secured by wire. The term formerly restricted to wire-stitched pamphlets but is now applied to various forms of spiral, coil, or comb bindings. (339)

wire lines (wire marks). *See:* CHAIN LINES (1); LAID LINES.

wire sewing. A 19th century method of "sewing" the sections of a book through the folds and onto tapes, webbings, or muslin, by means of wire staples. This method of "sewing," which originated in Germany in about 1880, while strong, fell into disuse because of the development of edition (thread) sewing machines, and also because the staples rusted and disintegrated and the books came apart. *See also:* SADDLE STITCHING. (25)

wire side. That side of a sheet of paper formed in contact with the wire of the mold in handmade paper, or the wire of the papermaking machine. *See also:* FELT SIDE. (17, 52)

wire stabbing (wire stitching). *See:* SADDLE STITCHING; SIDE STITCHING; WIRE SEWING.

wire thread. A very small gauge steel or brass wire in reels, which is drawn and formed into staples for use in saddle- or side-stitching pamphlets and booklets. (199, 339)

witherite. A naturally occurring barium carbonate ($BaCO_3$), used as a coating material in the manufacture of paper. (17)

without spring-back or hubs. An economical form of blankbook binding used in the United States. The book is bound without a SPRING-BACK (1) or HUBS and is usually covered in half leather with canvas or a lighter cloth on the sides. Although the book sometimes has a hollow back, it more often has a tight back, as the latter imparts additional strength to what is essentially a weak form of blankbook binding. (339)

with the grain. Paper that has been folded in the direction in which the majority of the fibers of a machine-made paper are oriented. *See also:* MACHINE DIRECTION.

witness. The leaves of a book which are untrimmed and therefore show the original size of the sheet of paper. Even if the other leaves are trimmed, this leaf (or leaves) functions as a "witness" that the book has not been excessively cut. *See also:* UNCUT. (25, 140, 371)

wood. A heterogeneous material consisting essentially of cellulose (the principal constituent of the cell wall of all plants), hemicelluloses, lignin, organic extratives (essential oils, resins, and the like), water, and soluble salts. It is the raw material for making mechanical and chemical pulps used in the manufacture of paper, as well as numerous other products. Wood, usually in the form of sawdust and shavings, is also used extensively as an inexpensive source of cellulose in a wide variety of chemical processes. Wood bark, and wood itself to a lesser extent, is an important source of vegetable tanning materials.

Green wood contains approximately 40 to 60% water, while dry wood consists of approximately 50% carbon, 6% hydrogen, 40 to 42.5% oxygen, 1% nitrogen, and yields 0.81 to 3.3% ash.

wood ashes. The residue of burned wood, which contains potash—a very strong alkali. The alkali is recovered by leeching the ashes with water, and either it or the ashes themselves are used in some areas of the world, in a mixture with indigo, to render the hair of a hide brittle and easily removed by scraping. (130)

woodcut book covers. Pasteboard, or similar binder's board, covered with paper and printed from a woodblock. They were produced in Ferrara, Italy, at the end of the 15th century, and at Augsburg at about the same time. (347)

wood flour. *See:* FINES.

wood paste. A paste made from finely ground wood meal mixed with wheat paste, or other adhesive, and used to fill in cracks or holes in book boards, or for rebuilding damaged corners. (237)

woof. *See:* WEFT.

wool wax. *See:* LANOLIN.

wooze. *See:* OOZE. *See also:* VEGETABLE TANNINS.

worked headband. *See:* HEADBAND.

working life. The length of time during which an adhesive, after being mixed with catalyst, solvent, etc., remains suitable for use. *See also:* STORAGE LIFE. (309)

wormhole (worm bore). A hole or series of holes bored into, or through, a book or board by one or more BOOKWORMS. A book containing such holes is said to be "wormed." (83, 261)

Wotton, Thomas (1521-1587). An English bibliophile sometimes referred to as the English Grolier, not only because he adopted Grolier's motto for use on his own books, but because he also used decorative designs similar to those found on Grolier's books. *See:* JEAN GROLIER. The more elaborate of Wotton's bindings, which are distinguished by their painted strapwork, were collected during his youth, probably before 1553, while his later bindings are decorated only with armorial stamps. All of his elaborate bindings were probably executed in Paris for him during visits there in the period from 1545 to 1552. The Parisian bindings seem to be the work of four or five different ateliers. Some of these bindings have the motto: *Thomae Wottoni et Amicorvm,* while another group has the date 1552 stamped on the cover. Most of his bindings are of brown calfskin.

Most of Wotton's books, of which some 130 to 140 are extant, descended through one female line to the Earls of Chesterfield, who moved them from Kent to Derbyshire in 1747, and eventually to the 5th Earl of Carnarvon, who sold the collection in 1919. (132, 253)

wove. The type of wire mark on a sheet of machine-made paper. Wove papers do not have the wire marks known as LAID LINES. (17)

wove paper. A paper having something of a clothlike appearance when viewed by transmitted light. The effect is produced in machine-made papers by the weave of the dandy roll, and in handmade papers by the wires of the mold. James Whatman was probably the first

to produce wove paper, and it was first used by John Baskerville in 1757, for Baskerville's type, which was considered to give a superior appearance on paper that did not have chain lines. Wove paper, in addition, does not have laid lines. (69, 156, 287)

wraparound cover. A soft cover used for pamphlets, etc. It consists of one folio that forms the spine as well as the two covers. *See also:* SELF COVER. (316)

wrap arounds. Units of 4 pages (2 leaves), or multiples of 4, generally consisting of illustrative matter, wrapped around a section and sewn with it. (156)

wrapper binding. *See:* GIRDLE BOOK.

wrappers (wrappered). 1. Originally, a temporary paper covering for books designed to protect them until they are bound in a permanent binding. They were plain, marbled, printed, or otherwise decorated. 2. The paper cover of a book, such as the modern paperback. 3. *See:* BOOK JACKET. (69, 82)

wrapping. The process of attaching a paper or board cover by means of a line of glue at the spine of a side-stitched or sewn book. The book usually has a flat spine.

wrapping bands. An early form of the clasp. In its earliest form, which was on Coptic bindings, it consisted of a strap attached to the fore edge of the upper cover and wound around the book over the fore edge several times, with the end, which was fitted with an ornamental piece of bone, being tucked between the strap and the lower cover. Another strap was similarly wrapped around the head and tail. *See also:* CLASPS. (236)

wringer. A power-driven device, consisting of two rubber rollers, through which handmade cases are passed to smooth the covering material and secure it on the outside and to the boards at the turn-ins. The wringer is used principally in library binding. (256)

wringing. The process of removing the bulk of water from wet leather by passing it through a wringing machine, which consists essentially of two large, felt-covered rollers. Wringing generally follows tannage and precedes fatliquoring. *Cf:* PRESSING; SETTING OUT. (363)

wringing down. The process of bringing the platen of a press closer to the bed plate, i.e . screwing a press shut. (115)

writing foil. A BLOCKING FOIL backed with a pressure-sensitive adhesive, and used for writing titles or classification numbers on books with an electric pen or stylus. (92)

wrong side. *See:* RIGHT SIDE.

X. The Roman equivalent of 10. *See:* ROMAN NUMERALS.

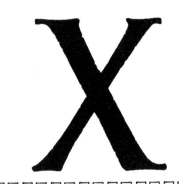

xylographic book. *See:* BLOCK BOOK.

XX. A symbol indicating 23 karat, or "deep" GOLD LEAF. (82)

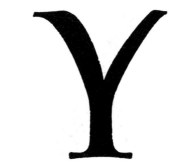

Yankee machine. A type of papermaking machine that utilizes one large steam-heated cylinder for drying the newly formed sheet of paper instead of numerous smaller cylinders. The wet paper web is pressed against the surface of the cylinder and is usually held in place by a canvas drier felt as the cylinder revolves. The Yankee drier produces a machine-glazed finish on the side next to the cylinder. The wet end of the machine may be either a cylinder or Fourdrinier machine and may have any number of presses or auxiliary driers of the conventional type. The characteristic features of the Yankee machine are its large cylinder (ranging from 9 to 15 feet in diameter) and its very smooth surface. (17, 67)

Yapp style (Yapp edges). A style of binding featuring a cover (leather, or other material, but customarily leather) that overlaps the three edges of both upper and lower covers continuously. The covers are always limp or semi-flexible, and are sometimes fitted with a zipper, which was a later refinement. Yapp books, named after the English bookseller of the second half of the 19th century, William Yapp, always have round corners, and the endpapers are frequently made from a "surface" paper, usually black. The edges are sometimes gilt, frequently over red, or are stained or otherwise colored. The Yapp style is especially associated with books of devotion (almost exclusively today), although a half century ago books of verse were sometimes bound in somewhat similar covers. *See also:* CIRCUIT EDGES. (81, 82, 236)

yarn. A continuous strand, often of two or more plies, composed of carded or combed fibers twisted together by spinning filaments laid parallel or twisted together, or a single filament. It is made from natural or synthetic fibers and filaments, or blends of these, and is used for the warp and filling in weaving cloth.

yawning boards. Book cover boards that curl away from the text block of the book. *See also:* WARPING. (115)

yellowback. A cheap popular novel, usually of an inferior quality (although not without a certain glittering appeal), and usually sensational in nature. The name derives from the fact that such books were published in yellow enameled paper covers with an illustration is blue or green and black ink on the upper cover. Yellowbacks, which were originated by the Englishman Edmund Evans, flourished between 1855 and 1870, but their production continued until the 1890s. They sold for 1 or 2 shillings and measured 4⅛ by 6⅝ inches. Their yellow covers earned them the nickname of "mustard plasters." (69, 89, 236)

yellow edge. *See:* HYMNAL STYLE.

yellowing. A process or result of a gradual change from the original appearance of a material, such as paper, due to aging or environmental changes, or both. While yellowing in paper is especially pronounced in papers produced from mechanical wood pulps, it occurs to a greater or lesser degree in virtually all types of vegetable fibers. It is frequently associated with brittleness in paper (although not necessarily), and is sometimes referred to as "color reversion." (17, 72)

yellow prussiate of potash. *See:* POTASSIUM FERROCYANIDE.

yield. The amount of a substance, usually expressed as a percentage of the starting material, which remains after manufacturing or processing action or actions. In papermaking, yield is the pulp obtained from pulpwood, the amount of paper produced from the pulp, etc. In leather manufacture, it is defined as the number of pounds or square feet of finished leather obtained from 100 pounds purchased weight of raw stock. (17, 363)

yield value. The stress (either normal or shear) at which a significant increase in deformation occurs with no increase in load. (17, 309)

Yoshino. A Japanese tissue paper produced from the fibers of the paper mulberry, and named after the town of Yoshino in central Honshu, Japan. (17)

YAPP STYLE

Zaehnsdorf, Joseph (1816-1886). An Austro-Hungarian bookbinder, born in Budapest and apprenticed at the age of 15 to a Herr Knipe, a bookbinder of Stuttgart, with whom he worked for 5 years. Thereafter, he travelled to Vienna, where he worked in the shop of a Herr Stephan. Zaehnsdorf left Vienna in about 1836, travelled in Europe, and finally arrived in London in 1837. There he went to work for Messrs. Westley & Co., stayed for 3 years, and then went to work for John Mackenzie for another 3 years, 1840 to 1842. He then established his own bookbinding firm, which flourished until his death, and was then taken over by his only son, Joseph William Zaehnsdorf (1853-1930).

One of the most influential bookbinders of his time, Zaehnsdorf was considered to be an excellent craftsman, with his forwarding and finishing being of equal merit, although in the latter he copied more than he innovated, although invariably in good taste. During his lifetime, fine examples of his workmanship were to be found in libraries of all of the great English book collectors. (94, 347, 371)

zebra marble. A marble pattern consisting of red, black, blue and orange raked from front to back on the size, followed by application of buff or yellow top colors in spots. The paper is either laid flat or shaded. The lines of red, blue, black, and orange are formed into irregular wavy lines by the spots of top color. (369)

zero angle. A completely flattened configuration of the fiber bundles of a skin, in which the fibers are not distributed in the customary complex three-dimensional network, as in leather, but are aligned into layers parallel to the grain and flesh surfaces of the skin. A true zero angle is probably not attainable, although PARCHMENT and vellum generally have a very low angle. This type of configuration results from drying a skin under high tension. (291)

zig-zag endpaper. A type of ENDPAPER devised by either Douglas Cockerell or T. J. Cobden-Sanderson toward the end of the 19th century. The zig-zag endpaper is designed to eliminate drag on the fly leaves and text block, some-

thing usually accomplished by sewing the endpaper below the gusset so that it can expand with the movement of the board as the book is opened. Unfortunately, sewing the endpaper at only one point is structurally unsound, as it leaves the fly leaves, as well as the leather joint (if used), secured only by tipping. If the endpaper is sewn through both the fly leaves and the made endpaper, which is the usual practice, the advantage of flexibility is negated and drag results, which the endpaper was intended to eliminate. Also called "v" endpaper, "w" endpaper. (81, 161, 343)

zig-zag fold. *See:* CONCERTINA FOLD.

zig-zag guard. A continuous one-piece guard prepared by folding a sheet of heavy paper, linen, or Japanese copying paper concertina-wise. It is used in the construction of photograph albums and similar guard books, as well as for sewing the folios of large blankbooks and for resewing the sections of books in conservation binding. For conservation sewing, the thin Japanese copying paper is used, its purpose being to prevent the adhesive used in gluing up from reaching the sections and the inside of the book. (367)

zinc hydrosulfite. A crystalline salt (ZnS_2O_3), prepared by the reaction of sulfur dioxide with an aqueous suspension of powdered zinc, and used for bleaching mechanical wood pulp. (17)

zinco. A economical metallic substitute for BINDER'S BRASS, produced by a photomechanical process. Zinco is much less durable than brass, and impressions made with it tend to be lacking in sharpness. (140)

zincs. 1. Metal plates used for interleaving or for fences in casing or covering books. 2. Large sheets of metal inter-

posed between lifts of flat printed India or other thin papers on automatic feeders of folding machines. They are used to prevent sagging of the lifts. 3. Polished sheets of zinc used in plating paper.

zinc sulfide. A compound (ZnS), which occurs naturally as "blende," and is prepared directly from the elements and by precipitation of a zinc salt solution with ammonium sulfide. It is used as a pigment, or as a component of LITHOPONE as a loading material or coating pigment in the manufacture of paper. (17)

zinc white. Zinc oxide (ZnO), a permanent white pigment produced by a flame process in high temperature furnaces. It is used as a white pigment in making water colors and imparting opacity and color to paper. Because of its ability to pick up, retain, and release electrostatic charges, it is also used in the manufacture of certain copying papers. While zinc white is the whitest of all pigments, it lacks the opacity of a pigment such as titanium dioxide; however, it is also less expensive. (17)

zirconium tanning. A method of producing leather utilizing salts of zirconium, usually under very acid conditions. The high acidity permits the zirconium salts to precipitate basic salts at lower pH values (on the order of 2.0) than either aluminum or chromium, which are also used in the production of leather. Zirconium salts tend to be very astringent, and normally produce a tight, firm leather; they also cause rapid tannage of the grain of a leather and produce a fine, short nap on suede leathers. By the use of masking salts, such as acetates, their astringency can be reduced, resulting in a softer, smooth-grained leather. Zirconium-tanned leather is usually fuller and firmer than that produced by chrome tanning and actually feels more like a vegetable-tanned leather. The leather so produced is of a pleasing white color, has good light fastness, and is superior to alum-tawed skin in that it does not wash out and has a higher (90°C) shrinkage temperature. (248, 306, 363)

zirconium tetrachloride. A white, crystalline solid $(ZrCl_4)$, that reacts vigorously with water, and is prepared by the action of chlorine on a mixture of zircon or zirconium oxide and charcoal, or by the action of chlorine and carbon tetrachloride on the oxide at 800°C. The basic salt has tanning properties and is used in producing white leathers. (309)

SOURCES AND BIBLIOGRAPHY

1. Abbey, John Roland. *English bindings, 1490-1940, in the library of J. R. Abbey.* Edited by G. D. Hobson. London. Privately printed at the Chiswick Press. 1940.

2. —— *An exhibition of modern English and French bindings from the collection of Major J. R. Abbey.* London. Arts Council. 1949.

3. —— *French and Italian collectors and their bindings, illustrated from examples in the library of J. R. Abbey.* Edited by A. R. A. Hobson. Oxford. Printed for presentation to the members of the Roxburghe Club. 1953.

4. Adrosko, Rita J. *Natural dyes in the United States.* Washington, D.C. Smithsonian Institution Press. (United States National Museum Bulletin 281). 1968.

5. Ainsworth, John H. *Paper; the fifth wonder.* 2nd ed. Kaukauna, Wisc. Thomas. 1959.

6. Alexander, Jerome. *Glue and gelatin.* New York. Chemical Catalog Co. (American Chemical Society, monograph series). 1923.

7. *American archivist.* Society of American Archivists. Washington, D.C.

8. *American dictionary of printing and bookmaking . . .* Ed. by W. W. Pasco. Detroit. Gale Research Co. 1967.

9. American Institute of Graphic Arts. *Book production; How? Why? When?,* by C. E. Nicholson, and others. New York. American Institute of Graphic Arts. 194–.

10. *American leather chemists association.* Easton, Pa. American Leather Chemists Association.

11. American Library Association. *American libraries.* Chicago. American Library Association.

12. —— Editorial Committee. Subcommittee on library terminology. *A. L. A. glossary of library terms, with a selection of terms in related fields.* Compiled by Elizabeth H. Thompson. Chicago. American Library Association. 1943.

13. —— Committee on bookbinding. *Binding for libraries.* 2nd ed. Chicago. American Library Association. (A. L. A. library handbook no. 5). 1915.

14. —— Committee on bookbinding. *Care and binding of books and magazines.* Chicago. American Library Association. 1928.

15. —— Library Technology Program. *Development of performance standards for library binding, phase I.* Chicago. American Library Association. (L. T. P. publications no. 2). 1961.

16. —— Library Technology Program. *Development of performance standards for binding used in libraries, phase II.* Chicago. American Library Association. (L. T. P. publications no. 10). 1966.

17. American Paper and Pulp Association. *The dictionary of paper, including pulp, paperboard, paper properties and related papermaking terms.* 3rd ed. New York. American Paper and Pulp Association. 1965.

18. American Society for Testing and Materials. Committee D-6 on paper and paper products. *Paper and paperboard; characteristics, nomenclature, and significance of tests.* 3rd ed. Philadelphia. American Society for Testing and Materials. (Special technical publication 60-B). 1963.

19. American Society for Testing Materials. *Symposium on testing adhesives for durability and permanence.* Philadelphia. American Society for Testing Materials. (ASTM special technical publication no. 138). 1952.

20. Apps, E. A. *Ink technology for printers and students.* New York. Chemical Publishing Co. 1963. 3 vol.

21. —— *Printing ink technology.* London. Hill. 1958.

22. Atkins, J. Howard. *Tying the future to a thread.* Medford, Mass. Oversewing Machine Co. of America. 1968.

23. Baarlaer, Joseph L., comp. and ed. *Graphic arts encyclopedia . . .* Cincinnati. Cincinnati Typesetting Co. 1966.

24. Bailey, Arthur Low. *Bookbinding.* Chicago. American Library Association. 1911.

25. —— *Library bookbinding.* New York. Wilson. 1916.

26. Bailey, Frederick T. *Textbook on histology.* 16th ed. Ed. by Wilfred M. Copenhaver, and others. Baltimore. Williams & Wilkins. 1971.

27. Banister, Manley Miles. *Pictorial manual of bookbinding.* New York. Ronald. 1958.

28. Barber, Giles. *Textile and embroidered bindings.* Oxford. Bodleian Library. 1971.

29. Barnes, Richard H. *Gilding & the making of gold leaf.* n.p. 1962.

30. Barrett. Firm. Bookbindery. *Barrett reading room supplies.* Chicago. Barrett. 1914.

31. Barrow, William J. *The Barrow method of preserving deteriorated documents.* Richmond, Va. The author. 1965.

32. —— *Deterioration of book stock, causes and remedies . . .* Ed. by Randolph W. Church. Richmond, Va. Virginia State Library Publications, No. 10. 1959.

33. —— *Instructions for the deacidification and lamination of documents.* c. 1954.

34. —— *Manuscripts and documents, their deterioration and restoration.* 2nd ed. Charlottesville, Va. University of Virginia Press. 1972.

35. —— *Procedures and equipment used in the Barrow method of resorting manuscripts and documents.* Richmond, Va. W. J. Barrow. 1952.

36. Barrow (W. J.) Research Laboratory. *Physical and chemical properties of book papers, 1507-1949.* Richmond, Va. Barrow (W. J.) Research Laboratory. Permanence/durability of the book, no. 7. 1974.

37. —— *Polyvinyl acetate (PVA) adhesives for use in library bookbinding.* Richmond, Va. Barrow (W. J.) Research Laboratory. Permanence/durability of the book, no. 4. 1965.

38. —— *Spot testing for unstable book and record papers.* Richmond, Va. Barrow (W. J.) Research Laboratory. Permanence/durability of the book, no. 6. 1969.

39. —— *Spray deacidification.* Richmond, Va. Barrow (W. J.) Research Laboratory. Permanence/durability of the book, no. 3. 1964.

40. —— *Strength and other characteristics of book papers 1800-1899.* Richmond, Va. Barrow (W. J.) Re-

search Laboratory. Permanence/durability of the book, no. 5. 1967.

41. —— *Test data of naturally aged papers*. Richmond, Va. Barrow (W. J.) Research Laboratory. Permanence/durability of the book, no. 2. 1964.

42. Battista, Orlando A. *Synthetic fibers in papermaking*. New York. Interscience. 1964.

43. Beckwith, Theodore Day, and others. *Deterioration of paper; the cause and effects of foxing*. Berkeley, Calif. University of California Press. 1940.

44. *Bibliographica*. Westport, Conn. Greenwood Reprint Corp. 1970.

45. Bibliographical Society of America. *Papers*. New York. The Society.

46. Blades, William. *Books in chains and other bibliographical papers*. Detroit. Gale Research Co. 1968.

47. —— *The enemies of books*. London. Stock. 1896.

48. Blomquist, Richard Frederick. *Adhesives; past, present and future*. Philadelphia. American Society for Testing and Materials. Edgar Marburg Lecture 1963. 1963.

49. Bookbinding Leather Committee. *The causes and prevention of the decay of bookbinding leather*. Memorandum no. 6. London. Printing Industry Research Association and British Leather Manufacturers Research Association. 1933.

50. *Book collector*. London. Queen Anne Press.

51. *The Bookman's glossary*. 3rd ed. New York. Bowker. 1951.

52. Book Manufacturers' Institute. *Helpful aids in book production*. New York. Book Manufacturers' Institute. 1953.

53. *Book manufacturers' monthly*. New York. Book Manufacturers' Institute.

54. *Book Production. Tricks of the trade*. New York. Bookbinding and Book Production. 1944.

55. *Book production industry*. Cleveland. Penton. Market Publications, Inc.

56. Bouchot, Henry Francois X. M. *The book; its printers, illustrators, and binders, from Gutenberg to the present time*. London. Grevel. 1890.

57. Brassington, William Salt, ed. *A history of the art of bookbinding, with some account of the books of the ancients*. London. Elliot Stock. 1894.

58. British Federation of Master Printers. *Preliminary technical course in printing*. London. British Federation of Master Printers. 1967. 7 vol.

59. British Museum. *Bookbindings from the library of Jean Grolier*. London. British Museum. 1965.

60. British Paper and Board Makers' Association. *Paper making; a general account of its history, processes and applications*. Rev. ed. London. British Paper and Board Makers' Association. 1965.

61. British Standards Institution. *British standard glossary of leather terms*. B. S. 2780: 1956. London. British Standards Institution.

62. Britt, Kenneth W., ed. *Handbook of pulp and paper technology*. 2nd ed. New York. Van Nostrand Reinhold. 1970.

63. Browning, Bertie Lee. *Analysis of paper*. New York. Dekker. 1969.

64. Buck, Mitchell Starrett. *Book repair and restoration; a manual of practical suggestions*. Philadelphia. Brown. 1918.

65. Buffum, Clara. *Hand-bound books . . .* Providence, R.I. 1935.

66. Burdett, Eric. *The craft of bookbinding; a practical handbook*. London. Davis & Charles. 1975.

67. Calkin, John Burgess. *Modern pulp and paper making*. 3rd ed. New York. Reinhold. 1957.

68. Carlsen, Darvey E. *Graphic arts*. 4th ed. Peoria, Ill. Bennett. 1970.

69. Carter, John. *A B C for book collectors*. 5th ed. London. Hart-Davis. 1972.

70. —— *Binding variants in English publishing, 1820-1900*. London. Constable. 1932.

71. —— *Publisher's cloth; an outline history of publisher's binding in England, 1820-1900*. New York. Bowker. 1935.

72. Casey, James P. *Pulp and paper: chemistry and chemical technology*. 2nd ed. New York. Interscience. 1960-61. 3 vol.

73. *Chamber's encyclopedia*. New York and London. W. & R. Chambers.

74. Chidester, Otis Holden. *First year graphic arts*. Tucson, Ariz. Graphic Arts Press. 1949.

75. Chivers, Cedric. *The paper of lending library books, with some remarks on their bindings*. London. Truslove & Hanson. 1909.

76. Clapp, Anne F. *Curatorial care of works of art on paper*. Rev. ed. Oberlin, Ohio. Intermuseum Conservation Association. 1973.

77. Clapperton, Robert Henderson. *Modern paper-making*. 3rd ed. Oxford. Blackwell. 1952.

78. —— *Paper and its relationship to books*. London. Dent. 1934.

79. —— *Paper; an historical account of its making by hand from the earliest times down to the present day*. Oxford. Shakespeare Head Press. 1934.

80. —— *The paper-making machine; its invention, evolution and development*. New York. Pergamon Press. 1967.

81. Clough, Eric A. *Bookbinding for librarians*. London. Association of Assistant Librarians. 1957.

82. Clowes, William Beaufoy. *A guide to printing*. London. Heineman. 1963.

83. Cockerell, Douglas. *Bookbinding, and the care of books; a textbook for bookbinders and librarians*. 5th ed. London. Pitman. 1971.

84. —— *Some notes on bookbinding*. Oxford. Oxford University Press. 1929.

85. *College & research libraries*. Chicago. Association of College & Research Libraries.

86. Collins, Arthur Frederick. *Book crafts for senior pupils; a handbook for teachers and students*. Leicester. Dryad Press. 1938.

87. *The Colophon; a quarterly for book lovers*. New York. Pynson.

88. *Columbia University Quarterly*. New York. Columbia University Press.

89. Comparato, Frank E. *Books for the millions; a history of the men whose methods and machines packaged the printed word*. Harrisburg, Pa. Stackpole. 1971.

90. Conference on a Permanent/Durable Book Paper. Washington, D.C. 1960. *Permanent/durable book paper; summary*. Richmond, Va. Virginia State Library. (Virginia State Library publication, no. 16). 1960.

91. Conkey, W. B. Company. *What a businessman should know about printing and bookmaking*. Rev. ed. Hammond, Inc. W. B. Conkey. 1928.

92. Corderoy, John. *Bookbinding for beginners*. New York. Watson-Guptill. 1967.

93. Coupe, Raymond Richard. *Science of printing technology*. London. Cassell. 1966.

94. Coutts, Henry T., and George A. Stephen. *Manual of library bookbinding; practical and historical*. London. Libraco. 1911.

95. *Cowie's bookbinder's manual; containing a full description of leather and vellum binding . . .* 7th ed. London. Strange. (186–).

96. Craig, Maurice James. *Irish bookbindings, 1600-1800.* London. Cassell. 1954.

97. Crane, W. J. E. *Bookbinding for amateurs . . .* New York. Scribner. 1903.

98. Crown Zellerbach Corp. *Making pulp and paper.* San Francisco. Crown Zellerbach Corp. 1958. 1 vol.

99. Cummins, John Francis. *The printer's guide.* 2nd ed. Dublin. n.p. 1952.

100. Cundall, Joseph, ed. *On bookbinding, ancient and modern.* London. Bell. 1881.

101. Cuneo (John F.) Co. *Plan for a good book . . .* Chicago. John F. Cuneo Co. 1951.

102. Cunha, George Daniel Martin. *Conservation of library materials.* Metuchen, N.J. Scarecrow. 1967.

103. *Curator.* New York. American Museum of Natural History.

104. Dahl, Svend. *History of the book.* 2nd English ed. Metuchen, N.J. Scarecrow. 1968.

105. Dana, John Cotton. *Notes on bookbinding for libraries.* Rev. ed. Chicago. Library Bureau. 1910.

106. Darley, Lionel S. *Bookbinding, then and now . . .* London. Faber and Faber. 1959.

107. —— *Introduction to book binding.* London. Faber and Faber. 1965.

108. Davenport, Cyril James Humphries. *Beautiful books.* London. Methuen. 1929.

109. ——*The book; its history and development.* New York. Smith. 1930.

110. —— *Cameo book stamps, figured and described.* London. Arnold. 1911.

111. ——*English embroidered bookbindings.* London. Kegan Paul, Trench, Trübner. 1899.

112. —— *Roger Payne, English bookbinder of the eighteenth century.* Chicago. Printed for the Caxton Club. 1929.

113. —— *Royal English book bindings.* New York. Macmillan. 1896.

114. —— *Thomas Berthelet, royal printer and bookbinder to Henry VIII . . .* Chicago. Caxton Club. 1901.

115. Diehl, Edith. *Bookbinding; its background and technique.* New York. Rinehart. 1946. 2 vol.

116. Direnger, David. *The hand-produced book.* New York. Hutchinson's Scientific and Technical Publications. 1953.

117. —— *The illuminated book; its history and production.* Rev. ed. New York. Praeger. 1967.

118. Donnelley (R. R.) & Sons Co. *Extra binding at the Lakeside Press.* Chicago. Donnelley. 1925.

119. —— *A rod for the back of the binder . . .* Chicago. Donnelley. 1929.

120. Douglas, Clara, and Constance Lehde. *Book repairing . . .* Seattle. University of Washington Press. (University of Washington extension series no. 7; University of Washington bulletin 624). 1940.

121. Drewery, R. F. *Library binderies.* London. Library Association. (Library Association pamphlet no. 3). 1950.

122. Duff, Edward Gordon. *Early printed books.* London. Kegan Paul, Trench, Trübner. 1893.

123. Dunn and Wilson Group. *The art and craft of bookbinding.* Falkirk. Dunn & Wilson. 1968.

124. Dutton, Meiric Keeler. *Historical sketch of bookbinding as an art.* Norwood. Holliston Mills. 1968.

125. Eddy (E. B.) Co. *The Eddy handbook of production.* Hull, Canada. Eddy Co. 1944.

126. Ede, Charles. *The art of the book . . .* New York. Studio. 1951.

127. Eggeling, Arthur, and associates. *Bookbinding by hand.* New York. Eggeling Bookbindery. 1925.

128. Ellis. Firm. Booksellers. London. *A collection of armorial bookbindings of the Tudor, Stuart and Hanoverian periods, described by George Smith and Frank Benger.* London. Ellis. 1927.

129. Emerson, Gilbert D. *Bookbinding for libraries.* Philadelphia. n.p. 1909.

130. Fahey, Herbert, and Peter Fahey. *Finishing in hand bookbinding . . .* San Francisco. The authors. 1951.

131. Feipel, Louis Nicholas, and Earl W. Browning. *Library bookbinding manual . . .* Chicago. American Library Association. 1951.

132. Fletcher, William Younger. *Bookbinding in England and France.* London. Seeley. 1897.

133. Forsyth, K. Marjorie. *Bookbinding for teachers, students and amateurs.* London, Black. 1932.

134. Frey, Ralph Wylie, and F. P. Veitch. *Preservation of leather bookbindings.* Washington, D.C. U.S. Government Printing Office. (U.S. Department of Agriculture, leaflet no. 69). 1930.

135. Garnett, Porter, ed. *The fine book; a symposium . . .* Pittsburgh. The Laboratory Press. 1934.

136. Gaskell, Philip. *New introduction to bibliography.* New York. Oxford University Press. 1972.

137. Gaskill & Cooper. Firm. *Bookbinders tool engraving and furnishing establishment. Philadelphia.* n.p.

138. Gaylord Brothers. Firm. *Bookcraft . . .*, by Donald M. Kidd, Syracuse. Gaylord Bros. 1941.

139. Gazurian, Johnny A. *The advertising & graphic arts glossary.* Los Angeles. Los Angeles Trade-Technical College. 1966.

140. Glaister, Geoffrey Ashall. *An encyclopedia of the book.* Cleveland. World. 1960.

141. Goldschmidt, Ernst Philip. *Gothic and Renaissance bookbindings.* 2nd ed. Amsterdam. Israel. 1967. 2 vol.

142. Goodwin, Bancroft L. *Pamphlet binding . . .* Chicago. United Typothetae of America. (Typographic technical series for apprentices, pt. 5, no. 30). 1925.

143. Grant, Julius. *Books & documents; dating, permanence and preservation.* London. Grafton. 1937.

144. —— *A laboratory handbook of pulp and paper manufacture.* 2nd ed. London. Arnold. 1961.

145. Gray, Niel. *Paper-cutting machines . . .* Chicago. United Typothetae of America. (Typographical technical series for apprentices, pt. 1, no. 10). c. 1918.

146. Grimm, Francis W. *A primer to bookbinding.* Boston. Houghton Mifflin. 1939.

147. Groome, George C. *Bookbinding materials.* Washington, D.C. U.S. Government Printing Office. 1938.

148. Guldbeck, Per Ernst. *The care of historical collections; a conservation handbook for the nonspecialist.* Nashville. American Association for State and Local History. 1972.

149. Guttman, Werner H. *Concise guide to structural adhesives.* New York. Reinhold. 1961.

150. Hague, Clifford Wilson. *Printing and allied graphic arts.* Milwaukee. Bruce. 1957.

151. Halfer, Josef. *The progress of the marbling art . . .* Translated by Herman Dieck, Buffalo. Kinder. 1893.

152. Hannett, John. *Bibliopegia; or, the art of bookbinding . . .* London. Simkim, Marshall. 1848.

153. —— *An inquiry into the nature and form of the books of the ancients . . .* London. Groombridge. 1837.

154. Harrison, T. *The bookbinding craft and industry; an outline of its history, development, and technique.* London. Pitman. 1926.

155. —— *Fragments of bookbinding technique.*

156. Harrod, Leonard Montague. *The librarians' glossary of terms used in librarianship and the book crafts, and reference book.* 3rd ed. London. Deutsch. 1971.

157. Harrop, Dorothy. *Modern book production.* London. Bingley. 1968.

158. Harthan, John P. *Bookbindings.* 2nd ed. London. H. M. Stationery Office. (Victoria & Albert Museum illustrated booklet no. 2). 1961.

159. Hasluck, Paul Nooncree, ed. *Bookbinding.* Philadelphia. McKay. 1903.

160. Heckman Bindery, Inc. *For the lack of a stitch.* North Manchester, Ind. Heckman Bindery, Inc. 195–.

161. Hewitt-Bates, James Samuel. *Bookbinding.* 8th ed. Leicester. Dryad. 1967.

162. Higham, Robert R. A. *A handbook of paper board and board; its manufacturing technology, conversion and usage.* London. Business Books. 1970-71. 2 vol.

163. —— *A handbook of papermaking.* London. Oxford University Press. 1963.

164. Hitchcock, Frederick H. *The building of a book . . .* 2nd ed. New York. Bowker. 1929.

165. Hobson, Geoffrey Dudley. *Bindings in Cambridge libraries . . .* Cambridge. Cambridge University Press. 1929.

166. —— *Blind-stamped panels in the English book-trade, c. 1485-1555.* London. The Bibliographical Society. 1944.

167. —— *English bindings before 1500.* Cambridge. Cambridge University Press. 1929.

168. —— *Maioli, Canevari and others.* Boston. Little, Brown. (Monographs on bookbindings, no. 1). 1926.

169. Holden, John Allen. *The bookman's glossary . . .* 3rd ed. New York. Bowker. 1951.

170. Holme, Charles, ed. *The art of the book . . .* New York. The Studio. 1914.

171. Holmes, Thomas James. *The bookbindings of John Ratcliffe and Ed-*mund Ranger . . . Worcester, Mass. The Society. 1929.

172. Horne, Herbert Percy. *The binding of books; an essay in the history of gold-tooled bindings.* 2nd ed. New York. Haskell House. 1970.

173. Horton, Carolyn. *Cleaning and preserving bindings and related materials.* Chicago. American Library Association. (Conservation of library materials pamphlet no. 1; Library Technology Project publications, no. 16). 1969.

174. Howes, Frank Norman. *Vegetable gums and resins.* Waltham, Mass. Chronica Botanica. 1949.

175. —— *Vegetable tanning materials.* London. Butterworth. 1953.

176. Hunter, Dard. *Paper-making; the history and technique of an ancient craft.* 2nd ed. New York. Knopf. 1947.

177. —— *Papermaking through eighteen centuries.* New York. Franklin. (Burt Franklin research and source series, 735). 1971.

178. Husayn, Muhammad Admad. *Origins of the book; Egypt's contribution to the development of the book from papyrus to codex,* by Mohamed A. Hussein. Translated by Dorothy Jaeschke and Douglas Sharp. New York. Graphic Society. 1970.

179. Hutchings, Ernest A. D. *A survey of printing processes.* London. Heinemann. 1970.

180. Ireland, Graham H. *Paperboard on the multi-vat cylinder machine.* New York. Chemical Publications. 1968.

181. Jamieson, Eleanore. *English embossed bindings, 1825-1850.* Cambridge. Cambridge University Press. 1972.

182. Jennett, Sean. *The making of books.* 4th ed. New York. Praeger. 1967.

183. Johnson, Pauline. *Creative bookbinding.* Seattle. University of Washington Press. 1963.

184. Kantrowitz, Morris S., and others. *Bindery glues.* Washington, D.C. U.S. Government Printing Office. (GPO-PIA joint research bulletin, B-3). 1948.

185. —— *Flexible glues for bookbinding.* Washington, D.C. U.S. Government Printing Office. (Technical bulletin, no. 24). 1941.

186. —— *Miscellaneous bookbinding adhesives.* Washington, D.C. U.S. Government Printing Office. (GPO-PIA joint research bulletin, B-4). 19—.

187. —— *Pyroxylin-treated book cloths.* Washington, D.C. U.S. Government Printing Office. (GPO-PIA joint research bulletin, B-7). 1948.

188. —— *Starch-filled book cloth.* Washington, D.C. U.S. Government Printing Office. (Technical bulletin, no. 21). 1934.

189. Karch, Robert Randolph. *Graphic arts procedures.* 4th ed. Chicago. American Technical Society. 1970.

190. —— *Printing and allied trades.* 5th ed. New York. Pitman. 1962.

191. Katz, Irving. *Adhesive materials, their properties and usage.* Long Beach, Calif. Foster. 1971.

192. Kenyon, Frederick George. *Books and their readers in ancient Greece and Rome.* 2nd ed. Folcroft, Pa. Folcroft Library Editions. 1971.

193. Kimberly, Arthur Evarts, and B. W. Scribner. *Summary report of National Bureau of Standards research on preservation of records.* Washington, D.C. U.S. Government Printing Office. (National Bureau of Standards miscellaneous publications, M 154). 1937.

194. Kinder, Louis Herman. *Formulas for bookbinders . . .* London. Putnam. 1905.

195. Kingzett, Charles Thomas. *Kingzett's chemical encyclopedia; a digest of chemistry & its industrial applications.* Ed. by D. H. Hey, and others. 9th ed. London. Baillière, Tindell and Cassell. 1966.

196. Klinefelter, Lee Miller. *Bookbinding made easy.* Rev. ed. Milwaukee. Bruce. 1960.

197. Labarre, E. J. *Dictionary and encyclopaedia of paper and papermaking.* 2nd ed. London. Oxford University Press. 1952.

198. Langwell, William Herbert. *The conservation of books and documents.* London. Pitman. 1957.

199. Latham. Firm. *Monitor book wire stitchers.* Chicago. Latham Machinery Co. n.d.

200. Lehmann-Haupt, Hellmut Emile. *Bookbinding in America; three essays.* Portland, Maine. Southworth-Anthoensen. 1941.

201. —— *The book in America . . .* 2nd ed. New York. Bowker. 1951.

202. —— *The life of the book . . .* New York. Abelard-Schuman. 1957.

203. Leighton, Douglas. *Modern bookbinding: a survey and a prospect.* New York. Oxford University Press. 1935.

204. Lewis, Arthur William. *Basic*

bookbinding. New York. Dover, 1957.

205. *The library; a quarterly review of bibliography.* London. Milford.

206. Library Association. *Book construction.* London. Library Association. 1931.

207. —— *Leather for libraries,* by Edward Wyndham Hulme, and others. London. Library Supply Co. 1905.

208. Library Binding Institute. *Library binding handbook.* Rev. ed. Boston. Library Binding Institute. 1971.

209. —— *Library Binding Institute standard for library binding.* 5th ed. Boston. Library Binding Institute. 1971.

210. —— *Library Binding Institute standard for pre-library bound new books.* 3rd ed. Boston. Library Binding Institute. 1960.

211. *Library journal.* New York. R. R. Bowker.

212. *Library quarterly.* Chicago. University of Chicago Press.

213. *Library resources & technical services.* Richmond, Va. Library Resources & Technical Services. (American Library Association).

214. *Library trends.* Urbana, Ill. University of Illinois Library School. University of Illinois.

215. Linton, C. Burton. *Hints on forwarding, finishing and ruling.* Williamsport, Pa. Burt. 1910.

216. London. University. *Historical armorial bookbindings in the university library* . . . London. University of London. 1937.

217. Loring, Rosamond Bowditch. *Decorated book papers* . . . 1st ed. 1942; 2nd ed. 1952. Cambridge, Mass. Harvard University Press.

218. Lydenberg, Harry Miller, and John Archer. *The care and repair of books.* 4th ed. New York. Bowker. 1960.

219. McDonald, Margaret. *Hot-melt adhesives.* Park Ridge, N. J. Noyes Data Corp. 1971.

220. —— *Nonwoven fabric technology.* Park Ridge, N. J. Noyes Data Corp. 1971.

221. McGuire, Edward Patrick. *Adhesive raw materials handbook.* Mountainside, N. J. Padric. 1964.

222. —— *American adhesive index.* Mountainside, N. J. Padric. 1962.

223. McLean, Ruari. *Modern book design, from William Morris to the present day.* Fair Lawn, N. J. Essential books. 1959.

224. —— *Victorian publishers' book-*

bindings in cloth and leather. London. Fraser. 1974.

225. McMurtrie, Douglas Crawford. *The book; the story of printing & bookmaking.* 3rd ed. New York. Oxford University Press. 1943.

226. —— *The golden book; the story of fine books and bookmaking—past & present.* 3rd ed. New York. Covici-Friede. 1934.

227. Madagan, John R. *Bookbinding methods and aids for the printing trade.* Charlotte, N. C. Washburn Printing Co. 1952.

228. Mansfield, Edgar. *Modern design in bookbinding; the work of Edgar Mansfield.* London. Peter Owen. 1966.

229. Martin, A. G. *Finishing processes in printing.* New York. Focal Press. 1972.

230. Mason, John. *Paper making as an artistic craft, with a note on nylon paper.* London. Faber and Faber. 1959.

231. —— *A practical course in book-crafts and bookbinding.* Leicester. C. H. Gee. 1935.

232. Matthews, William F. *Bookbinding, a manual for those interested in the craft of bookbinding.* London. Gollancz. 1929.

233. Mayer, Ralph. *A dictionary of art terms and techniques.* New York. Crowell. 1969.

234. Melcher, Daniel, and Nancy Larrick. *Printing and promotion handbook* . . . 3rd ed. New York. McGraw-Hill. 1966.

235. Miall, Laurence Mackenzie, and D. W. A. Sharp, eds. *A new dictionary of chemistry.* 4th ed. New York. Wiley. 1968.

236. Middleton, Bernard C. *A history of English craft bookbinding technique.* New York. Hafner. 1963.

237. —— *The restoration of leather bindings.* Chicago. American Library Association. (A. L. A. Library Technology Project, LTP publication no. 18). 1972.

238. Mitchell, William Smith. *A history of Scottish bookbindings, 1432-1650.* London. Oliver and Boyd. 1955.

239. *New colophon; a book-collector's miscellany.* New York. Duschnes, Crawley.

240. *New York public library. Bulletin.* New York. New York Public Library.

241. Nicholson, James B. *A manual of the art of bookbinding* . . . Philadelphia. Baird. 1856.

242. Nixon, Howard M. *Broxbourne*

library; style and designs of bookbindings, from the twelfth to the twentieth century. London. Maggs. 1956.

243. —— *The development of certain styles of bookbinding.* London. Private Libraries Association. 1963.

244. —— *Five centuries of English bookbinding.* London. Scolar. 1978.

245. —— *Sixteenth-century gold-tooled bookbindings in the Pierpont Morgan Library.* New York. Pierpont Morgan Library. 1971.

246. —— *Studies in the book trade in honour of Graham Pollard.* Oxford. Oxford University Press. 1975.

247. O'Conor, John Francis Xavier. *Facts about bookworms; their history in literature and work in libraries.* New York. Harper. 1878.

248. O'Flaherty, Fred, and others, eds. *The chemistry and technology of leather.* New York. Reinhold. (American Chemical Society monograph series, no. 134). 1956-65. 4 vol.

249. Oldham, James Basil. *Blind Panels of English binders.* Cambridge. Cambridge University Press. 1958.

250. —— *English blind-stamped bindings.* Cambridge. Cambridge University Press. 1952.

251. Organ, Robert M. *Design for scientific conservation of antiquities.* Washington, D.C. Smithsonian Institution Press. 1968.

252. Oswald, John Clyde. *A history of printing; its development through five hundred years.* New York. Appleton. 1928.

253. Oxford University. Bodleian Library. *Fine bindings 1500-1700 from Oxford libraries: catalogue of an exhibition.* Oxford. Bodleian Library. 1968.

254. —— *Textile and embroidered bindings.* Oxford. Bodleian library. (Bodleian picture books, special series, no. 2). 1971.

255. *Pacific bindery talk.* Los Angeles. Pacific Library Binding Co.

256. Palmer, Elbridge Woodman. *A course in bookbinding for vocational training.* New York. Employing bookbinders of America. 1927.

257. *The paper maker.* Kalamazoo, Mich. Paper Makers Chemical Department. Hercules Powder Co.

258. Percival, George Stanley, and Rigby Graham. *Unsewn binding.* 2nd ed. Leicester. Dryad. 1966.

259. Perry, Kenneth Frederick, and Clarence T. Babb. *The binding of books.* Rev. ed. Bloomington, Ill. McKnight & McKnight. 1967.

260. —— *Instruction units in bookbinding; Pt. I: fabrikoid and buckram books.* Greeley, Colo. Colorado State College of Education. 1935.

261. Philip, Alexander John. *The business of bookbinding for librarians* . . . Gravesend. A. J. Philip. 1935.

262. Pierpont Morgan Library. *A guide to an exhibition of armorial and related bookbindings, 1500-1800.* New York. Pierpont Morgan Library. 1935.

263. Pinner, H. L. *The world of books in classical antiquity.* Leiden. Sijthoff. 1948.

264. Pleger, John J. *Bookbinding.* Rev. ed. Chicago. Inland Printer. 1924.

265. Plenderleith, Harold James, and A. E. A. Werner. *The conservation of antiquities and works of art; treatment, repair and restoration.* 2nd ed. London. Oxford University Press. 1971.

266. —— *The conservation of prints, drawings, and manuscripts.* Oxford. Oxford University Press. 1937.

267. —— *The preservation of leather bookbindings.* London. British Museum. 1967.

268. Plungerian, Mark. *Cellulose chemistry.* Brooklyn. Chemical Publishing Co. 1943.

269. *Pocket encyclopedia of paper & graphic art terms.* 2nd ed. Kaukauna, Wisc. Thomas. 1965.

270. Pollard, Alfred William. *Early illustrated books; a history of the decoration and illustration of books in the 15th and 16th centuries.* 2nd ed. New York. Haskell House. 1968.

271. —— *Fine books.* New York. Cooper Square. 1964.

272. —— *A short-title catalogue of books printed in England, Scotland, & Ireland 1475-1640.* London. The Bibliographical Society. 1926.

273. Portalis, Roger, Ed. *Researches concerning Jean Grolier, his life and his library.* Translated by Carolyn Shipman. New York. Grolier Club. 1907.

274. Porte, Roy Trewin. *Dictionary of printing terms.* 4th ed. Salt Lake City. Porte. 1941.

275. Post, Daniel. *Chemical treatment of hides and leather,* by John Partridge. Park Ridge, N. J. Noyes Data Corp. 1972.

276. *Practical printing and binding; Odhams complete guide to the printer's craft,* edited by Harry Whetton. 3rd ed. London. Odhams Books. 1965.

277. Pratt, Guy A. *Instruction sheets in bookbinding.* East Chicago, Ind. The author. 1937.

278. —— *Let's bind a book.* Rev. ed. Milwaukee. Bruce. 1944.

279. Prideaux, Sarah Treverbian. *Bookbinders and their craft.* New York. Scribner. 1903.

280. —— *An historical sketch of bookbinding.* London. Lawrence & Bullen. 1893.

281. —— *Modern bookbindings, their design and decoration.* London. Constable. 1906.

282. Procter, Henry Richardson. *Leather industries laboratory book of analytical and experimental methods.* 2nd ed. New York. Spon and Chamberlain. 1908.

283. —— *The making of leather.* New York. Putnam. 1914.

284. Putnam, George Haven. *Books and their makers during the middle ages* . . . New York. Putnam. 1897. 2 vol.

285. Quaritch, Bernard. *Examples of the art of bookbinding* . . . London. Quaritch. 1897.

286. Quayle, Eric. *The collector's book of books.* New York. Potter. 1971.

287. Radford, Richard George. *Letterpress machine work.* New York. Staples Press. 1951. 2 vol.

288. Ramsden, Charles. *French bookbinders, 1789-1848.* London. Humphries. 1950.

289. Reed, John Henry. *The science of imposition* . . . Chicago. Inland Printer. 1928.

290. Reed, Robert Findlay. *What the printer should know about paper.* Pittsburgh. Graphic Arts Technical Foundation. 1970.

291. Reed, Ronald. *Ancient skin, parchments and leathers.* London. Seminar Press. 1972.

292. —— *Science for students of leather technology,* edited by Ronald Reed. New York. Pergamon Press. 1966.

293. Remploy Limited. *An introduction to library binding.* Newcastle-under-Lyme. Remploy. 1967.

294. Research and Engineering Council of the Graphic Arts Industry. Committee on Binding and Finishing. *Proceedings of seminar on perfect binding* . . . Washington, D.C. Research and Engineering Council of the Graphic Arts Industry. 1963.

295. Richardson, Edward, and James Richardson. *Leather for bookbinding and upholstery* . . . 3rd ed. Newcastle-on-Tyne. 1910.

296. Robinson, Ivor. *Introducing bookbinding.* New York. Watson-Guptill. 1968.

297. *The Rothschild library; a catalog of eighteenth century printed books and manuscripts formed by Lord Rothschild.* Cambridge. Cambridge University Press. Privately printed. 1954. 2 vol.

298. Royal Society of Arts. London. Committee on Leather for Bookbinding. *Report of the committee on leather for bookbinding* . . . London. Bell. 1905.

299. Sadlier, Michael. *The evolution of publishers' binding styles, 1770-1900.* New York. Smith. 1930.

300. Salade, Robert Francis. *Finishing the printed job* . . . New York. American Printer. 1926.

301. Samford, C. Clement, and John M. Hemphill II. *Bookbinding in Colonial Virginia.* Williamsburg, Va. Colonial Williamsburg. 1966.

302. Sawyer, Harriet Price. *How to care for books in a library.* 2nd ed. Madison, Wisc. Wisconsin Free Library Commission. (Wisconsin Free Library Commission. Instructional Dept. Pamphlet no. 7). 1912.

303. Scribner, Bourdon Walter. *Protection of documents with cellulose acetate sheeting.* Washington, D.C. U.S. Government Printing Office. (U.S. National Bureau of Standards, Miscellaneous publication, M 168). 1941.

304. Schoen, Harriet Hetta. *Let's bind a book.* New York. Macmillan. 1934.

305. Sharphouse, John Henry. *Leather technicians handbook.* New ed. London. Leather Producers' Association. 1971.

306. —— *The leatherworker's handbook.* London. Leather Producers' Association. 1963.

307. Simon, Oliver. *Introduction to typography.* 2nd ed. London. Faber and Faber. 1963.

308. Skeel, Emily Ellsworth (Ford). *Mason Locke Weems, his works and ways.* New York. 1929. 3 vol.

309. Skeist, Irving. *Handbook of adhesives.* New York. Reinhold. 1962.

310. Smith, Frederick Richard. *Bookbinding.* London. Pitman. 1929.

311. Smith, Philip. *New directions in bookbinding.* New York. Van Nostrand Reinhold. 1974.

312. Somerlad, Michael John. *Scottish "Wheel" and "Herringbone" bindings in the Bodleian library . . .* Oxford. Oxford Bibliographical Society. 1967.

313. Steinberg, Sigfrid Henry. *Five hundred years of printing.* 2nd ed. Baltimore. Penguin. 1962.

314. Stephen, George Arthur. *Commercial bookbindings . . .* London. Stonhill. 1910.

315. —— *Machine book-sewing with remarks on publishers' binding.* Aberdeen. Aberdeen University Press. (Reprinted from the Library Association Record. June 1908). 1908.

316. Stevenson, George A. *Graphic arts encyclopedia.* New York. McGraw-Hill. 1968.

317. —— *Graphic arts handbook and products manual.* Torrance, Calif. Pen and Press Publications. 1960.

318. Stewart, Alexander A. *The printer's dictionary of technical terms . . .* Boston. School of Printing, North End Union. 1912.

319. Stonehouse, John Harrison. *The story of the Great Omar bound by Francis Longinus Sangorski and its romantic loss.* London. Piccadilly Fountain Press. 1933.

320. Strauss, Victor. *The printing industry . . .* Washington, D.C. Printing Industries in America. 1967.

321. *Studies in conservation. Etudes de conservation.* Journal of the International Institute for the Conservation of Historic and Artistic Works. London.

322. Summerfield, Melvin B. *Bound-to-stay-bound: the story of a book . . .* Jacksonville, Ill. New Method Book Bindery. 1956.

323. Sutermeister, Edwin. *Chemistry of pulp and paper making.* 3rd ed. New York. Wiley. 1941.

324. —— *The story of papermaking.* Boston. Warren. 1954.

325. Tanners' Council of America, Inc. *Dictionary of leather terminology.* 6th ed. New York. Tanners' Council of America. 1969.

326. Tauber, Maurice Falcolm. *Library binding manual . . .* Boston. Library Binding Institute. 1972.

327. Tavik, Anton. *The art and practice of edge marbling.* Baltimore. The author. 1908.

328. Technical Association of the Pulp and Paper Industry. Adhesives Testing Committee. *Testing of adhesives.* William H. Neuss, ed. New York. Technical Association of the Pulp and Paper Industry. (TAPPI Monographs Series, no. 26). 1963.

329. Teigen, Kit. *Graphic arts, an introduction . . .* Wayne, Pa. Management Development Institute. 1968.

330. Thomas, Henry. *Early Spanish bookbindings, XI-XV centuries.* London. Oxford University Press. 1939.

331. Thompson, Elbert A., and Lawrence S. Thompson. *Fine Binding in America; the story of the Club Bindery.* Urbana, Ill. Beta Phi Mu. (Beta Phi Mu. Chapbook no. 2). 1956.

332. Thompson, Lawrence Sidney. *Bibliopegia fantastica.* New York. New York Public Library. 1947.

333. Thrift, Timothy Burr. *Modern methods in marbling paper.* Winchester, Mass. Lucky Dog Press. 1945.

334. Toldo, Vittorio de. *The Italian art of bookbinding.* London. Batsford. (Monographs of decorative arts, 3). 1925.

335. Town, Laurence. *Bookbinding by hand, for students and craftsmen.* New York. Pitman. 1950 (1951).

336. Tsuen-Hsuin, Tsien. *Written on bamboo and silk; the beginnings of Chinese book inscriptions.* Chicago. University of Chicago Press. 1962.

337. Turnbull, Arthur T., and Russell N. Baird. *The graphics of communication; typography—layout—design.* 2nd ed. New York. Holt, Rinehart, and Winston. 1968.

338. U.S. Bureau of Naval Personnel. *Printer 3 & 2.* Washington, D.C. U.S. Government Printing Office. 1952.

339. U.S. Government Printing Office. *Theory and practice of bookbinding.* Rev. ed. Washington, D.C. U.S. Government Printing Office. 1962.

340. U.S. Library of Congress. *Papermaking, art and craft . . .* Washington, D.C. Library of Congress. 1968.

341. U.S. National Bureau of Standards. *Fabrics for book covers.* Washington, D.C. U.S. Government Printing Office. (Product Standard PS 9-68). 1968.

342. Uzanne, Louis Octave. *The French bookbinders of the eighteenth century.* Translated by Mabel McIlvaine. Chicago. Caxton Club. 1904.

343. Vaughan, Alexander J. *Modern bookbinding; a treatise covering both letterpress and stationery branches of the trade . . .* New ed. London. Skilton. 1960.

344. Veitch, Fletcher Pearre, and others.

Polluted atmosphere a factor in the deterioration of bookbinding leather. Easton, Pa. American Leather Chemists Association. (Reprinted from the Journal of the American Leather Chemists Association, Mar. 1926). 1926.

345. Vervliet, Hendrik D. L., ed. *The book through five thousand years; a survey.* New York. Phaidon. 1972.

346. Virginia. State Library. Richmond. *The manufacture and testing of durable book papers.* Based on the investigations of W. J. Barrow. Edited by Randolph W. Church. Richmond, Va. (Virginia State Library publications, no. 13). 1960.

347. Walters Art Gallery, Baltimore. *The history of bookbinding 525-1950 A.D.* Compiled by Dorothy Miner. Baltimore. Trustees of the Walters Art Gallery. 1957.

348. Walton, Robert Petrie. *Causes and prevention of deterioration in book materials.* New York. New York Public Library. (Reprinted from the New York Public Library. Bulletin. April 1929). 1929.

349. Wardle, David Bernard. *Document repair.* London. Society of Archivists. 1971.

350. Warren (S. D.) Co. Boston. *Facts and views of papermaking at S. D. Warren Company.* Boston. S. D. Warren Co. 1965.

351. Waterer, John William. *A guide to the conservation and restoration of objects made wholly or in part of leather.* 2nd ed. London. Bell. 1973.

352. —— *Leather and craftsmanship.* London. Faber and Faber. 1950.

353. —— *Leather craftsmanship.* London. Bell. 1968.

354. —— *Leather in life, art and industry . . .* London. Faber and Faber. 1946.

355. Watson, Aldred Auld. *Hand bookbinding, a manual of instruction.* New York. Reinhold. 1963.

356. Wehmhoff, Byron Louis, and F. R. Baylock. *The evaluation of bronze stamping leaf.* Washington, D.C. U.S. Government Printing Office. (Technical bulletin, no. 17). 1933.

357. Wheatley, Henry Benjamin. *Remarkable bindings in the British Museum . . .* London. Low, Marston, Searle, and Rivington. 1889.

358. Wheelock, Mary E. *New books for old.* St. Louis. St. Louis Public Library. 1916.

359. Williams, Alec. *Printing inks.* Park

Ridge, N. J. Noyes Data Corp. 1972.

360. Williamson, Hugh Albert Fordyce. *Methods of book design; the practice of an industrial craft.* 2nd ed. London. Oxford University Press. 1966.

361. Wilson, John Arthur. *Analysis of leather and materials used in making it.* New York. McGraw-Hill. 1931.

362. —— *The chemistry of leather manufacture.* New York. Chemical Catalog Co. 1923.

363. —— *Modern practice in leather manufacture.* New York. Reinhold. 1941.

364. Wilson, William Kester, and B. W. Forshee. *Preservation of documents by lamination.* Washington, D.C. U.S. Department of Commerce. (National Bureau of Standards, monograph 5). 1959.

365. Winans, Leonard G. *The book from manuscript to market.* New York. Grosset & Dunlap. 1941.

366. Winger, Howard W., and Richard D. Smith, eds. *Deterioration and preservation of library materials* . . . Chicago. University of Chicago Press. (34th Annual Conference of the Graduate Library School). 1970.

367. Woodcock, John. *Binding your own books.* Harmondsworth, Middlesex. Penquin. 1955.

368. Woolnough, Charles W. *The art of marbling as applied to book edges and paper.* 2nd ed. London. Heylin. 1854.

369. —— *The whole art of marbling as applied to paper, book edges* . . . Rev. ed. London. Bell. 1881.

370. Young, John Lockwood. *Books; from ms. to the bookseller.* 3rd ed. London. Pitman. 1947.

371. Zaehnsdorf, Joseph William. *The art of bookbinding* . . . London. Bell. 1890.

372. Zaehnsdorf. Firm. Bookbinders. London. *A short history of bookbinding* . . . London. Chiswick. 1895.

373. Zahn, Otto. *On art binding, a monograph.* Memphis. Toof. 1904.

Type	Times Roman (Linotype) 9 point, leaded 1 point				

Paper	pH	Alkalinity (CaCO$_3$)	Basis Weight (pounds per ream)	Folding Endurance (1 kg. tension)	
				Machine Direction	Cross Direction
Text	9.7	4.2%	70	50	36
Plates	8.7	8.3%	80	131	99
Endpapers	9.4	3.5%	100	45	35

Binding   Smyth sewn on tapes; 19 signatures. Case binding. Cloth. Stuck-on headbands. Gold (22 karat) stamping.

Books, Information,
Answers
@your library™

Tampa-Hillsborough County Public Libraries
813-273-3652